THE BLUE GUIDES

Countries	**Austria**
	Belgium and Luxembourg
	Channel Islands
	Corsica
	Crete
	Cyprus
	Egypt
	England
	France
	Germany
	Greece
	Holland
	Hungary
	Ireland
	Northern Italy
	Southern Italy
	Malta and Gozo
	Morocco
	Portugal
	Scotland
	Sicily
	Spain
	Switzerland
	Turkey: Bursa to Antakya
	Wales
	Yugoslavia
Cities	**Boston and Cambridge**
	Florence
	Istanbul
	Jerusalem
	London
	Moscow and Leningrad
	New York
	Oxford and Cambridge
	Paris and Versailles
	Rome and Environs
	Venice
Themes	**Churches and Chapels of Northern England**
	Churches and Chapels of Southern England
	Literary Britain and Ireland
	Museums and Galleries of London
	Victorian Architecture in Britain

Front gate, Kolomenskoye, near Moscow

BLUE GUIDE

MOSCOW
AND
LENINGRAD

Evan Mawdsley

*Street atlas and ground plans
by Doug London*

A & C Black
London

W W Norton
New York

Second edition 1991

Published by A & C Black (Publishers) Limited
35 Bedford Row, London WC1R 4JH

ISBN 0–7136–3387–5

A CIP catalogue record for this book
is available from the British Library.

Published in the United States of America by
W W Norton & Company, Inc.
500 Fifth Avenue, New York, NY 10110

Published simultaneously in Canada by
Penguin Books Canada Limited
2801 John Street, Markham, Ontario L3R 1B4

ISBN 0–393–30773–5   USA

Evan Mawdsley is a Senior Lecturer at the University of Glasgow,
specialising in Modern European History. He was educated in
America at Haverford College and later received a PhD. from
the University of London's School of Slavonic and East European
Studies. He is the author of *The Russian Revolution and the Baltic
Fleet* and *The Russian Civil War*.

Typeset by CRB Typesetting Services, Ely, Cambs.
Printed and bound in Great Britain by
BPCC Hazell Books
Aylesbury, Bucks, England
Member of BPCC Ltd.

PREFACE

This is intended to be the most comprehensive general guide-book to Moscow and Leningrad which is available in the English language. It is hoped that the book will be of use not only to the increasing numbers of visitors to the Soviet Union, but also to anyone with an interest in Russian history and culture.

The editors of the first edition originally saw the need for such a guide-book in the early 1970s, when they realised that the best available work was still the 1914 *Baedeker's Russia* (reprinted in 1971). The intention was not to supersede that excellent, accurate, and still useful book (which covered not only St. Petersburg and Moscow, but the whole of the Russian Empire), but it was felt that a guide-book suitable for the modern reader would have to take into account the extraordinary changes of the Soviet period. Nevertheless, the basic aim of the Moscow and Leningrad Blue Guide is the same as that given by the editor of Baedeker: 'to supply the traveller with such information as will render him as nearly as possible independent of hotel-keepers, commissionaires and guides, and thus enable him the more thoroughly to enjoy and appreciate the objects of interest he meets with on his tour'. The guided tour has many advantages for someone completely unfamiliar with the place being visited, and the guides provided by Intourist, the Soviet tourist bureau, are generally conscientious and well-informed. Many visitors, however, will want to be more independent and follow their own interests; this guide is intended to help them and other travellers get the most out of their stay in Moscow and Leningrad.

Like other Blue Guides, this book is divided into routes, most of which can be followed on foot in a day or less; there are 17 routes for Moscow and 14 for Leningrad. The State Hermitage is treated as a separate route, and there is extensive coverage of the other major museums within various routes. Two further routes take in the immediate outskirts of the two cities, i.e. the districts open to foreign visitors. In addition there is a summary of major places of interest in Moscow Region (Oblast').

The routes contain considerable material on the most recent developments in Moscow and Leningrad, but the main stress is on the historic town centres rather than on the new industrial and residential areas. Moscow is the largest city in Europe, and Leningrad the sixth largest. To discuss all aspects of them in a work of this length would be impossible.

The 'Notes on History and Culture' in the introductory section are not intended to be a mini-encyclopaedia of Russia, but rather an outline of some developments in areas most likely to be useful to the visitor; particular attention is paid to history, architecture, and art. The 'Practical Information' contains up-to-date material on means of transport, hotels, restaurants, theatres, museums, embassies, etc. Little is said about the standards of hotels and restaurants; this is partly because of the difficulty of getting information, partly because of the general Blue Guide format, and partly because—in the case of hotels at least—the element of choice is slight. There is also little point in providing information on travel to and from the Soviet Union; travel arrangements vary with the country of origin, are liable to change, and are normally made through an accredited agency.

The 'Practical Notes' also include a brief introduction to the Russian language. The importance of mastering at least the Cyrillic alphabet cannot be over-stressed; without it the tourist can have little freedom of movement. Some Cyrillic text is used in the introduction; note that capital letters are used where these would be found on signs, etc. In the main text a fairly strict transliteration system is used so that the Cyrillic original can be worked out from it, or checked against it. For the transliteration scheme see p 75.

Mr Douglas London and **Mr John Callow** undertook the main work on the 16-page four-colour atlas section at the end of the book, as well as the black and white plans in the text. A new policy of geographic openness was announced by the Soviet authorities in the summer of 1989 and some of the first fruits of this have been incorporated here. In any event the street atlas is still the most comprehensive to be included in any recent Western guide to Moscow and Leningrad and is perhaps the most accurate available commercially; the collection of plans to museums, palaces, monasteries, and churches is extensive.

Margaret Mawdsley was the co-editor of the first edition of this book. She shared in the research and writing, contributing especially a wide knowledge of Russian language, literature, theatre, art and ballet. Above all she brought to the project a love of Russia, its culture, and its people. She died in 1984, at the age of 36. Although the second edition has been brought up to date her contribution can still be found throughout it.

The difficulty of avoiding mistakes in a guide-book of this sort is great. This is especially the case for a Russian subject—in view of the special problems of language and transliteration, the relative lack of sources, and the fact that both Moscow and Leningrad are developing rapidly. The Soviet system itself is undergoing profound changes. Non-Communist reform groups won control of both the Moscow and Leningrad municipal councils in the spring of 1990. Government plans for large-scale privatisation and encouragement of foreign investment will have unpredictable effects.

Information sent by users of the first edition has already been incorporated, and further suggestions for corrections, improvements, and additions would be gratefully welcomed.

A NOTE ON BLUE GUIDES

The Blue Guides series began in 1918 when Muirhead Guide-Books Limited published 'Blue Guide London and its Environs'. Finlay and James Muirhead already had extensive experience of guide-book publishing: before the First World War they had been the editors of the English editions of the German Baedekers, and by 1915 they had acquired the copyright of most of the famous 'Red' handbooks from John Murray.

An agreement made with the French publishing house Hachette et Cie in 1917 led to the translation of Muirhead's London Guide, which became the first 'Guide Bleu'—Hachette had previously published the blue-covered 'Guides Joanne'. Subsequently, Hachette's 'Guide Bleu Paris et ses Environs' was adapted and published in London by Muirhead. The collaboration between the two publishing houses continued until 1933.

In 1931 Ernest Benn took over the Blue Guides, appointing Russell Muirhead, Finlay Muirhead's son, editor in 1934. The Muirheads' connection with Blue Guides ended in 1963 when Stuart Rossiter, who had been working on the Guides since 1954, became house editor, revising and compiling several of the books himself.

The Blue Guides are now published by A & C Black, who acquired Ernest Benn in 1984, so continuing the tradition of guide-book publishing which began in 1826 with 'Black's Economical Tourist of Scotland'. The Blue Guide series continues to grow: there are now more than 40 titles in print with revised editions appearing regularly and many new Blue Guides in preparation.

'Blue Guides' is a registered trade mark.

CONTENTS

Maps and Plans

EXPLANATIONS

Type. Large type is used for the main routes. Smaller type is used for branch-routes, for historical and preliminary material, and—in general—for detailed description or minor items.

  Asterisks indicate special interest.

  Abbreviations. The following occur in the text:

Bol. (Бол.) = Bol'shoy (-aya) (Большой, -ая) (Great or Large)
Bul'v (Бульв.) = Bul'var (Бульвар) (Boulevard)
C = century
c = circa
Gos. (Гос.) = Gosudarstvennyy (Государственный) (State…)
im. (им.) = imeni (имени) ('…named after…')
km = kilometres
m = metre
Mal. (Мал.) = Malyy (-aya) (Малый, -ая) (Small)
min. = minute
Nab. (Наб.) = Naberezhnaya (Набережная) (Embankment)
o.s. = old style Russian date
Per. (Пер.) = Pereulok (Переулок) (Lane)
Pl. = atlas plan
Pl. (Пл.) = Ploshchad' (Площадь) (Square)
Pr. (Пр.) = Prospekt (Проспект) (Avenue)
Rte = route
SS. = Saints
Ts. (Ц.) = Tserkov' (Церковь) (Church)
Ul. (Ул.) = Ulitsa (Улица) (Street)

Russian terms. In addition to those given above, the following are important:

Dom (Дом) = House, Building
Dvorets (Дворец) = Palace
Gostinitsa (Гостиница) = Hotel
Kanal (Канал) = Canal
Kol'tso (Кольцо) = Ring Road
Liniya (Линия) = 'Line', name given to some streets in Leningrad
Monastyr' (Монастырь) = Monastery, Convent
Most (Мост) = Bridge
Muzey (Музей) = Museum
Ostrov (Остров) = Island
Park (Парк) = Park
Proyezd (Проезд) = Lane
Reka (Река) = River
Restoran (Ресторан) = Restaurant
Sad (Сад) = Gardens
Shosse (Шоссе) = Highway or major road (from *chaussée*)
Sobor (Собор) = Cathedral
Stadion (Стадион) = Stadium
Teatr (Театр) = Theatre
Vokzal (Вокзал) = (Railway) Station
Vystavka (Выставка) = Exhibition

NOTES ON HISTORY AND CULTURE

A. History

Major Russian Rulers
Vladimir (980–1015)
Yuri Dolgorukiy (1149–57)
Alexander Nevskiy (1252–63)
Daniil (Prince of Moscow, 1276–1303)
Ivan (I) Kalita (1328–40)
Dmitry Donskoy (1359–89)
Ivan III (1462–1505)
Ivan (IV) the Terrible (1533–84)
Boris Godunov (1598–1605)
Mikhail Romanov (1613–45)
Aleksey (1645–76)
Peter (I) the Great (1682–1725)
Anna (1730–40)
Elizabeth (1741–61)
Catherine (II) the Great (1762–96)
Paul (1796–1801)
Alexander I (1801–25)
Nicholas I (1825–55)
Alexander II (1855–81)
Alexander III (1881–94)
Nicholas II (1894–1917)
V.I. Lenin (1917–24)
I.V. Stalin (1929–53)
N.S. Khrushchev (1955–64)
L.I. Brezhnev (1964–82)
M.S. Gorbachev (1985–)

The Rise of Muscovite Russia: 9C–17C. The first Russian state, founded in the 9C, was centred on the city of Kiev. At the end of the first millennium this state reached its peak, and in 988 Grand Prince Vladimir made Christianity, in its Greek Orthodox form, the official religion. Kievan Russia, however, was short-lived because of conflict within the ruling family and invasion by nomads from the East. In little more than a century after Prince Vladimir, Russia had broken up into a number of principalities. Then in 1237 came the conquest of Russia by the Mongols and their Tatar allies, who dominated the country for more than two centuries—until 1480.

Even before the 'Mongol Yoke' the centre of power had shifted to the forest lands of the North-East, and under Andrey Bogolyubskiy (1157–74) the seat of the Grand Princes was moved from Kiev to the town of Vladimir. The first reference in the Chronicles to Moscow—168km SW of Vladimir—concerns the year 1147, during the reign of Prince Yury Dolgorukiy of Suzdal (the father of Andrey Bogolyubskiy); on the 800th anniversary of this event (1947) the government decided to erect the statue of Prince Yury which now stands opposite the Moscow Soviet. In reality, however, the area around the modern Moscow Kremlin had been settled for some time before the 12C.

Despite the sack of Moscow by the Mongols in 1237–38 the town grew in importance. The first real Prince of Moscow was Daniil (1276–1303), son of Alexander Nevskiy (Grand Prince, 1252–63). Prince Daniil and his sons fought to make their city the strongest in the North-East and several factors aided Moscow's rise to primacy. The city occupied a central geographical position and was close to the major river trade routes. The energetic Moscow princes were able to win the support of the 'Golden Horde', the Mongol-Tatar state; indeed Ivan Daniilovich (1325–40) was such a good tax-collector for the Golden Horde that he was made Grand Prince—and earned the nickname 'Kalita' (Money-Bags). It was also fortunate for Moscow that Metropolitan Peter (1308–26), the head of the Russian church, died in the town and made it a holy place. Peter's successors settled in Moscow rather than remaining in Vladimir. The first stone Cathedral of the Assumption in the Moscow Kremlin was built about this time by Ivan Kalita.

As time went by the Moscow princes became identified with the struggle against the Tatars. Grand Prince Dmitry (1359–89), the grandson of Ivan Kalita, inflicted the first major defeat on the Tatars, at Kulikovo on the Don (1380)—hence his name 'Donskoy'. Nevertheless, two years after Kulikovo the Tatars were able to burn Moscow to the ground, and Tatar influence was to survive for another century. Moscow's defences were improved in the 14C with the completion of the 'White Stone' Kremlin (1367). The outer defences included a wooden outer wall (on the line of the modern Bul'varnoye Kol'tso) incorporating the fortified St. Peter, Nativity, and Sretenskiy monasteries. To the S and E were outposts—the Andronikov and Simonov monasteries. The similar New Monastery of the Saviour was founded later, in the 15C, and the New Convent of the Virgin and the Don Monastery in the 16C.

The reign of Grand Prince Ivan III (1462–1505), following decades of political uncertainty, was among the most important in the history of Muscovy. In 1480 the control of the Tatars was effectively ended, and as many of the neighbouring principalities were annexed Ivan began to style himself ruler 'of all Russia'. Moreover, in 1472 he married a niece of the last Byzantine Emperor, and claimed for Moscow the status of the 'Third Rome'; it was from this time that Muscovy took the double-headed eagle of the Byzantine Empire as its symbol. Ivan was also a great builder, and the fortifications and magnificent cathedrals of the modern Kremlin date from his reign.

In the 16C came the dramatic reign of Ivan (IV) the Terrible (1533–84), grandson of Ivan III and the first ruler to be crowned 'Tsar'. Ivan raised further the international status of Muscovy; he fought a successful war against the Volga Tatars (St. Basil's Cathedral commemorates the capture of Kazan), and in these years the Russian conquest of Siberia was begun. Russia became more open to the West with the arrival of the first English merchants in the 1550s; the house where they lived (in Ul. Razina) has been partly restored. Printing in Moscow was traditionally believed to have started with the publication of the 'Apostol' in 1563, and there is a statue of Ivan Fyodorov, the first known printer, on Pr. Marksa. Despite these changes, the later part of Ivan's reign was a sombre period, especially during the so-called 'Oprichnina' (1565–72), a reign of terror against the boyars (great nobles).

Moscow continued to grow, and by the middle of the 16C its population of 100,000 made it one of the largest cities in Europe. The main part of the town E of the Kremlin was enclosed by a brick wall

*The Kremlin in the reign of Ivan III (1462–1505)
(A.M. Vasnetsov). Looking from the site of modern
Moskvoretskii Bridge*

in the 1530s and became known as the Kitay-Gorod. The wooden
fortified line beyond the Kremlin and the Kitay-Gorod walls was
replaced by a white stone wall some 9km long (now the Bul'varnoye
Kol'tso). At about the same time a 16km wooden outer wall was
erected on what is now the second ring road, the Sadovoye Kol'tso;
this was to remain the boundary of the town until the 17C.

Tsar Fyodor (1584–98), the feeble son of Ivan IV, ruled only with
the help of his advisers, the most important of whom was his brother-
in-law Boris Godunov. Fyodor's reign saw the last Tatar raid on
Moscow and, more important, the establishment in 1589 of a Russian
Patriarchate. But the dynasty died out with Fyodor, and the tragic
reign of Boris, who was chosen to replace him, is familiar to Western
readers from Mussorgsky's opera of 1874. The accession of Boris
coincided with a great famine, and then the forces of a pretender
claiming to be Dmitry, the murdered son of Ivan IV, invaded Russia
from Poland. After the sudden death of Boris Godunov in 1605 the
'False Dmitry' entered Moscow and proclaimed himself Tsar. The
seven years that followed are known as the 'Time of Troubles'. The
'False Dmitry' was murdered by his former boyar supporters, but a
second 'False Dmitry' emerged. Russia was ravaged by civil war,
peasant and cossack rebellions, and Polish and Swedish invasions.
The saviours of Russia were Kuz'ma Minin, a butcher from the Volga
town of Nizhniy Novgorod, and Prince Dmitry Pozharsky; in November 1612 Minin and Pozharsky led a Russian 'national' army which
recaptured the Kremlin from the Poles. A statue of Minin and
Pozharsky, erected in 1818, still stands in Red Square.

A Zemskiy Sobor or Council of the Land met in 1613 and elected as Tsar Mikhail Romanov (1613–45), a sixteen-year-old from the Romanov family of boyars; the Romanov dynasty was to rule Russia for more than 300 years. The first seventy years—under Mikhail, his son Aleksey (1645–76), and Fyodor Alekseyevich (1676–82)—were relatively calm, at least compared to the reign of Ivan the Terrible and the Time of Troubles. Russia made territorial gains, of which the most important was the annexation of the Ukraine; the contact with the more Westernised city of Kiev was to have an important cultural impact. In 1687 the first Russian institution of higher education, the Slavo-Graeco-Latin Academy was founded in Moscow. On the negative side, the liturgical reforms introduced by Patriarch Nikon in the 1650s had the effect of splitting the Russian Church, for the Schism (Raskol) resulted in many traditionalists or 'Old Believers' breaking away from the Orthodox Church. (Later, in the 18C and 19C, the Old Believers took an important part in Russia's trade; their centre in Moscow, the Rogozhskaya Commune, survives.) The 17C was also a time of some social unrest, with the Moscow riots of 1648 and 1662 and the revolt led by Stepan Razin (1670–71). This tension was still evident in 1682 when Tsar Fyodor died; the unruly garrison of strel'tsy (musketeers) intervened violently to ensure the dual reign of Fyodor's younger brothers Ivan and Peter.

Ivan and Peter were little more than children and effective power was held by the Regent, their sister Sof'ya Alekseyevna. Under Sof'ya and her favourite, V.V. Golitsyn, there was tentative Westernisation, but the Regency ended in 1689. Sof'ya was forced to retire to the New Convent of the Virgin and a new era began under Peter I (1682–1725), known to history as Peter the Great. (The sickly Ivan died in 1696.)

Imperial Russia: 18C–early 19C. Young Tsar Peter had been exposed to Western influence in the Nemetskaya Sloboda, the foreign quarter located in the NE part of Moscow, on the Yauza River. Nearby, at Izmaylovo, he began experimenting with boats, and at the villages of Preobrazhenskoye and Semyonovskoye he quartered his 'Toy' regiments. In 1697–98 Peter made his historic tour of Western Europe, but the most important element in his reign was the' Great Northern War with Sweden of 1700–1721, which forced the pace of modernisation and led to the foundation of a new capital—St. Petersburg.

St. Petersburg was founded on the delta of the Neva River, which flows from Lake Ladoga to the Gulf of Finland. The Neva had been part of the Russian principality of Novgorod, and Prince Alexander Nevskiy ('of the Neva') fought a battle here in 1240. When Ivan III annexed the Novgorod lands in the 1470s this region became part of Muscovy, but it was later captured by the Swedes and in 1617 was ceded to them.

At the start of the Great Northern War Peter's army was routed at the Battle of Narva, but the Swedish King Karl XII then turned on Poland, and the Russians were able to rebuild their forces and capture the enemy outposts on the Neva. Fort Nyenschanz (sited opposite the present Smolny) was captured after a day's bombardment, and two weeks later, on 16 May 1703, Peter began the construction of a new fortress 6km downstream; this Peter-Paul Fortress was to be the kernel of the modern city of Leningrad. At first 'Sanktpeterburg' was primarily a forward military base, exposed to Swedish attack. The Swedish fleet was kept away by a fort built out in the Gulf at Kronstadt, but the last enemy attack by land was driven off only in 1708. The next year, however, Karl XII was decisively defeated by Peter at the Battle of Poltava, and the development of St. Petersburg began in earnest. As early as 1704 Peter had called the new town his 'stolitsa' or capital, although government offices had remained for some time in Moscow. After Poltava, in 1712, the Court moved north, followed by the diplomatic corps and, under some compulsion, by nobles and merchants. Many of the Tsar's humbler subjects were drafted in as forced labour, and by 1725 the population had reached 40,000.

Panorama of St. Petersburg (A. Tozelli, 1817–20). Looking at the Peter-Paul Fortress from Vasil'yevskii Island

Most of the new buildings appeared on the left (S) bank of the Neva—on the Russian 'mainland'—and the Admiralty became the real centre of the town. This was contrary to the town plan prepared in 1716–17 by Alexander Le Blond (1679–1719), which would have made the town centre on the right bank, on Vasil'yevskiy Island. Several buildings survive from the Petrine era; there is the Cabin of Peter I, where the Tsar lived in 1703–09, and the Summer Palace (1710–12), and at suburban Petrodvorets (formerly Peterhof) the little Monplaisir Palace and the nearby pavilions; the Great Palace at Petrodvorets was begun in Peter's time but much enlarged later. The surviving homes of the great nobles include the Menshikov Palace (1710–16) and the Kikin Palace (1714). Peter founded the Alexander Nevskiy Monastery, and a number of the buildings there date from his reign. Other major buildings which were begun by Peter but completed after his death were the Cathedral of SS. Peter and Paul, the Kunstkamera, and the Twelve Colleges; the last was intended to be the administrative centre of the Russian state.

The period after Peter I was one of political uncertainty, and between 1725 and 1762 there were no fewer than seven rulers. This was partly Peter's fault as he had introduced the right of the monarch, now known as the Emperor or Empress (Imperator/ Imperatritsa), to name a successor. Peter had fallen out with his own son Aleksey, whom he imprisoned in the Peter-Paul Fortress and finally had killed. There was relative stability under Peter's niece Anna (1730–40) and daughter Elizabeth (1741–61), but Peter III (1761–62) was killed after a palace coup which put his wife, Catherine II (1762–96), on the throne. In general, the variety of royal candidates made it possible for the palace guards and even foreign ambassadors to affect the choice of ruler, and the predominance of women and children led to the influence of favourites.

Nevertheless, the Westernisation begun by Peter I continued, despite the temporary return of the capital to Moscow at the end of the 1720s. Empress Anna moved back to St. Petersburg, and the northern capital resumed its development. In the aftermath of the great fire of 1737 a 'Committee for St. Petersburg Building' drew up a new general plan for the town. By the 1750s the basic layout of the centre of modern Leningrad had become apparent, with three long straight avenues radiating from the Admiralty: Nevskiy Pr., Gorokhovaya Ul. (Ul. Dzerzhinskovo), and Voznesenskiy Pr. (Pr. Mayorova). In 1762 a 'Commission for Masonry Construction in St. Petersburg and Moscow' was set up to oversee further development, and among its great achievements in St. Petersburg were the beautiful granite embankments and bridges. The 18C also saw the creation of many of the finest buildings in the city and its outskirts; the reign of Elizabeth was perhaps the most important as it was for her that Rastrelli created the Winter Palace and the suburban palaces at Peterhof and Tsarskoye Selo (Pushkin). Catherine II built the Great Palace at Pavlovsk for her son Paul (Pavel) and the Alexander Palace at Tsarskoye Selo for her grandson Alexander Pavlovich. Catherine also commissioned the Marble and Tauride Palaces for her favourites Grigory Orlov and Grigory Potyomkin. Catherine II earned the title 'the Great' from her successful expansionist foreign policy. In the park at Tsarskoye Selo are monuments commemorating Russian victories over the Turks, including the Chesma Column; the Rumyantsev Obelisk on Vasil'yevskiy Island honours one of Catherine's leading commanders.

Russia became involved in more wars under Paul I (1796–1801). The Maltese Chapel of the former Corps of Pages is a relic of Paul's infatuation with the Knights of Malta, while the Statue of Suvorov N of Marsovo Pole commemorates the brilliant Italian campaign of Generalissimo Suvorov. Nevertheless, Paul's reign is best remembered for its violent end; he was murdered a month after moving into a fortress-like palace, the Michael Castle (Engineers Castle), which he had built to protect himself.

The reign of Alexander I (1801–25) was dominated by the Napoleonic Wars. Russia joined the 2nd Coalition but her armies were defeated at Austerlitz and Friedland, and in 1807 she had to make peace. Then, in June 1812, came the invasion of Russia by France and her allies.

Moscow, the main objective of Napoleon's campaign, emerged once again as a national symbol. At Borodino, 110km W of the city, was fought on 26 August a terrible but indecisive battle in which tens of thousands of men were lost on either side. (A huge circular panoramic painting of the battle may be seen in Moscow.) While the Russians under Field Marshal Kutuzov were finally forced to withdraw, their army was not destroyed. At a meeting on the outskirts of Moscow, at Fili, Kutuzov decided not to fight again before the city. The hut where this meeting took place is now part of the memorial complex on Kutuzovskiy Pr. in Fili.

Napoleon reached the hills overlooking Moscow on 2 September and was surprised when no one appeared to surrender the town. The next day he rode in and established his headquarters in the Kremlin, but his triumph was short lived. That night a terrible fire began which virtually razed the city; it is estimated that of 9200 houses some 7600 were destroyed. Having taken Moscow and savaged Kutuzov's army, Bonaparte tried to make peace with the Russian Emperor. He failed, and on 7 October the French withdrew the bulk of their army from the ruined town. A rear guard blew up some of the remaining buildings, but the arrival of the Russian Army saved such national treasures as the Kremlin and the New Convent of the Virgin. As it withdrew through Russia the Grande Armée was cut to pieces and the French Emperor narrowly escaped capture. Russian troops pursued the enemy over the border and two years later were in Paris.

The 'Fatherland War' was one of the great episodes of Russian history. Among the memorials to this struggle are the arch of the Main Staff in St. Petersburg; the huge column in front is dedicated to Alexander I. Kutuzov was buried in the Kazan Cathedral and his statue stands nearby. Triumphal arches were erected in St. Petersburg and Moscow (now on Pr. Stachek and Kutuzovskiy Pr.). The enormous Cathedral of Christ the Saviour, which dominated Moscow until its demolition in the 1930s, was another monument to this war.

The later years of Alexander I were a time of reaction culminating in the first stirring of political action. Aristocratic young officers who had been inspired by liberal ideas during the campaigns in the West formed secret societies, and in December 1825 after Alexander's death they assembled troops in Senatskaya Pl. (now Pl. Dekabristov) in the hope of preventing the accession of Grand Duke Nicholas Pavlovich. They won over only part of the St. Petersburg garrison, and troops loyal to the new Emperor Nicholas were able to disperse the demonstration. The Decembrists (Dekabristy), as they came to be called, were arrested; five were hanged near the Peter-Paul Fortress, and many were exiled to Siberia. The room in the fortress where the trials took place is now part of a museum.

Under Nicholas I (1825–55) the Russian state seemed to be very strong, and this was partly expressed in an ambitious building programme in the capital. Although the Russian economy was falling behind that of Western Europe, the first railways were built in this period; the line to Tsarskoye Selo was opened in 1837, while the 'Nicholas Railway' between St. Petersburg and Moscow entered service in 1851.

Internal reaction was a characteristic of the reign. The Decembrists remained in Siberia and opposition to autocracy was crushed by the newly-organised Corps of Gendarmes. In the aftermath of the European Revolutions of 1848 the political 'circle' of Petrashevsky was broken up and its members, including the young Dostoyevsky, were forced to undergo mock executions.

In the years after the Napoleonic Wars Russia enjoyed great international prestige. The Moscow Triumphal Arch in St. Petersburg was a monument to Russian victories in the Near East and to the suppression of the Polish rebellion of 1830. Nevertheless, the era of Nicholas I ended with the humiliation of the Crimean War (1853–56). Most of the fighting took place around Sevastopol on the Black Sea, but the British Royal Navy blockaded St. Petersburg and many of the capital's treasures were sent to Moscow for safe keeping. Nicholas died in the middle of the war, and it was left to his son Alexander II (1855–81) to attempt the reform of Imperial Russia.

From Reform to Revolution: 1855–1917. The 'Great Reforms', the abolition of serfdom and the creation of the zemstvos (rural councils) and a modern legal system, represented a remarkable body of legislation, but Alexander, the 'Tsar Liberator', knew little peace in the last years of his reign. From the growing Russian intelligentsia, a radical movement known as Populism emerged as a challenge to the existing political and social order. A student named Karakazov fired a shot at Alexander outside the Summer Gardens in 1866, and at the end of the 1870s the 'People's Will' terrorist organisation began a systematic campaign to kill the Emperor. Several attempts failed, most notably a bomb explosion in the Winter Palace, but in March 1881 Alexander was ambushed and mortally wounded on the embankment of the Catherine (now Griboyedov) Canal. The Pseudo-Russian Church of the Resurrection now stands on the site of the attack; another lavish monument was erected in the Kremlin, but this was demolished by the Communists. Meanwhile the government also struck at the revolutionaries, and even in the reign of Alexander II the political prison in the Peter-Paul Fortress became a symbol of Tsarist oppression; it has been preserved as a museum.

Alexander III (1881–94) and Nicholas II (1894–1917), the son and grandson of Alexander II, attempted to maintain the position of the autocracy in the face of growing opposition. Alexander III was able to suppress the revolutionary movement for a decade or more, but in the 1890s and 1900s new Populist, Marxist, and liberal groups appeared. Nicholas II seemed dogged by misfortune from the time of the Khodynka Field disaster in 1896 when 1500 people were killed during his coronation celebrations in Moscow. The disastrous war with Japan began in 1904 and was followed by the Revolution of 1905.

This political and social ferment was due in part to the remarkable changes in the Russian economy brought about by the Emancipation of the serfs in 1861 and by the government-sponsored industrialisation of the 1890s. Both St. Petersburg and Moscow developed from largely administrative centres into great industrial cities. The population of the capital rose from 470,000 in the 1840s to 2,200,000 in 1914, as large factories appeared in the suburbs, especially on Vasil'yevsky Island and the Vyborg Side, and S of the Obvodnyy Canal. A similar phenomenon occurred in Moscow, where there was a great expansion of the industrial suburbs beyond the Sadovoye Kol'tso and in Zamoskvorech'ye, and the population increased from 350,000 in the 1840s to 1,400,000 in 1914. Much of Russian industry was controlled by foreigners, as some of the factory names indicated—LaFerme, Siemens-Schuckert, and Thornton in St. Petersburg or Bromley and Goujon in Moscow, but the turn of the century also saw the growth of an indigenous Russian bourgeoisie, especially in Moscow.

Little attempt was made by the municipal authorities to deal with problems of overcrowded housing, poor sanitation, and lack of public transport. Given the difficult living conditions of the working class and the alienation of the intelligentsia, the appearance of revolutionary groups was not surprising. The young Vladimir Lenin was active during the 1890s in a St. Petersburg Marxist group—for which he was exiled to Siberia. Another important workers' movement was led by a priest named Georgy Gapon, who on 9 January 1905 organised a series of marches to present a petition to the Emperor. The violent dispersal of the marches by the army and police were known as 'Bloody Sunday' and it triggered off the Revolution of 1905. The high point of the revolt came in October of that year, when the Emperor was forced to grant major concessions, but thereafter the government was able to crush the extreme left of the movement. The St. Petersburg Soviet (Council) of Workers' Deputies—latterly led by Leon Trotsky—was closed, and the ill-timed December Uprising in Moscow was crushed by troops loyal to the Tsar.

The Imperial Government had saved itself by granting a parliament; the State Duma met in the Tauride Palace, while the upper house, the State Council, met in the Mariya Palace. Whether the parliamentary system could have developed is an open question, given that the experiment had only eight years to run before the start of the Great War. Certainly Nicholas II was reluctant to concede any of his power, and he was encouraged in this attitude by Empress Alexandra Fyodorovna. There were, however, to be two final moments of grandeur for the Tsarist regime. The first came in 1913 with the celebration of the 300th anniversary of the Romanov Dynasty. An obelisk unveiled next to the Kremlin later became a monument to revolutionary thinkers, but a Pseudo-Russian church built behind the Moscow Station in Leningrad survives. The second moment was the wave of patriotic feeling that accompanied the outbreak of the First World War. There were popular demonstrations in St. Petersburg—including an attack on the German embassy—and a great Te Deum in the Kremlin. Another result of the anti-German mood was the decision to change the name of St. Petersburg to Petrograd (or Peter's Town).

The Russian Revolution. A new era began in February 1917 as mass demonstrations in Petrograd were followed by the mutiny of local regiments. A Soviet of Workers' and Soldiers' Deputies and a Provisional Government were formed simultaneously in the Tauride Palace. The Emperor, who was en route from the army headquarters at Mogilyov to Tsarskoye Selo (Pushkin), was isolated. On 2 March he abdicated, followed the next day by his brother, and with this ended the Romanov dynasty. The February Revolution had involved considerable bloodshed, and many victims were buried in Marsovo Pole—where a monument stands today.

The Provisional Government and the Soviet co-existed for eight troubled months. The former, headed from July by Alexander Kerensky and based in the Winter Palace, failed to deal with the outstanding problems of the day—the war, land reform, and industrial disorder. Lenin arrived at the Finland Station in April and moulded the Bolshevik Party into the main opposition group. The Bolsheviks survived the chaotic demonstrations of the 'July Days' (after which Lenin was forced to go into hiding). The abortive attempt by the supreme commander, General Kornilov, to march on Petrograd in late August restored their position; within days the Bolsheviks had gained control of both the Petrograd and Moscow Soviets.

In October 1917 the Bolshevik Central Committee decided to seize power. A crisis was provoked with the Kerensky government on the eve of the 2nd All-Russian Congress of Soviets, and on the night of 24–25 October Bolshevik-led forces occupied many key points in the capital in the name of Soviet power. On the following night the

'An October Night; the Storming of the Winter Palace,
1917' (R.R. Frents, 1929). Looking from Palace Square
back through the arch of the Main Staff building

insurgents closed in on the final government stronghold, the Winter
Palace. The cruiser 'Avrora' fired a blank shell, the rebels entered the
palace, and early on the morning of the 26th the ministers were
arrested. At the same time the Congress of Soviets, which was
meeting in the Smolny Institute, supported the uprising. An attempt
by military cadets to lead a counter-revolution was crushed with
considerable bloodshed a few days later, and pro-Kerensky troops
were stopped on the southern approaches to Petrograd, the Pulkovo
Heights.

The Revolution was more violent in Moscow than in the capital.
The Kremlin was occupied by pro-Bolshevik soldiers on 26 October,
but two days later loyalist troops regained control of the fortress and
most of the town centre; meanwhile, the first outbreak of shooting

had occurred in Red Square on the 27th. In the days that followed there were armed battles in the streets, but the consolidation of Soviet power in Petrograd disheartened the loyalists and encouraged the rebels. On the morning of 3 November the Red forces took the Kremlin by storm.

The October Revolution was followed by three years of Civil War. In March 1918 the Soviet government moved from Petrograd to Moscow, as the great city on the Baltic had seemed at the mercy of a German attack from Estonia and Finland. Petrograd was in fact twice threatened by counter-revolutionary armies during the Civil War, and in October 1919 the 'Whites' even briefly occupied Detskoye Selo (formerly Tsarskoye Selo, later Pushkin). The British Royal Navy blockaded the Baltic Sea and raided Kronstadt. There was fighting in Moscow in July 1918 when the Left Socialist-Revolutionaries attempted a coup d'état, but the White armies threatened the Soviet capital only once, in September 1919, during General Denikin's offensive; they were finally turned back at Oryol, 340km S of Moscow.

The Civil War caused terrible hardship. Many townspeople moved to the countryside; between 1917 and 1920 the population of Petrograd dropped from 2,500,000 to 720,000 and that of Moscow from 1,900,000 to 1,000,000. The peasants had been alienated by grain requisitioning, and in the early spring of 1921 there were strikes in Petrograd and an anti-Communist revolt at Kronstadt. In response the government tried to regain popular support by granting concessions to the peasants and adopting the less rigorous 'New Economic Policy'.

Soviet Russia. Political debate and economic reconstruction marked the 1920s, the decade of NEP. Lenin, the undisputed leader, suffered a series of strokes and from the spring of 1923 was effectively removed from political life. He died at Gorki (now Gorki Leninskiye) near Moscow in January 1924; as a tribute Petrograd, 'the cradle of the Revolution', was renamed Leningrad. It took several years to resolve the question of succession, but in 1929–30 Joseph Stalin emerged as the dominant figure in Soviet politics.

The Stalin era was characterised by rapid economic change and by intense political terror. The First Five-Year Plan (1928–32) began the development of heavy industry, and this system continues to the present day; the Twelfth Five-Year Plan ended in 1990. The collectivisation of agriculture began in 1929, as millions of peasants were brought together in collective farms. Stalin's personal dictatorship was developed by propaganda and by the liquidation of his opponents. In 1934 Sergey Kirov, the leader of the Communist Party in Leningrad, was assassinated at the Smolny Institute and this signalled the beginning of the purge of the Party, the 'show trials' in the House of Unions in Moscow, and the execution or deportation to the camps of great numbers of people. (There are now plans to erect a memorial in Moscow to the victims of Stalin's repression.)

One aspect of the economic transformation of Stalin's Russia was the steady growth of the cities. By 1939 the population of Leningrad had reached 3,100,000, but it had been replaced as the largest city by Moscow, with 4,200,000 inhabitants. The 'Stalin Plan for the Reconstruction of Moscow', dating from 1935, was one of the world's first comprehensive urban plans, and in the 1930s, great avenues were laid out—including Pr. Marksa, Tverskaya Ul., Leninskiy Pr., Leningradskiy Pr., and Pr. Mira. The first line of the Moscow Metro

'Stalin and Voroshilov in the Kremlin' (A. Gerasimov, 1938). In the background is the Vodovzvodnaya Tower of the Kremlin Wall. Voroshilov was Stalin's Minister of War

was completed in 1935, and the system was soon extended. Another important development was the completion in 1937 of the Moscow–Volga Canal. Leningrad also had a General Plan, worked out in 1935–36, and this was in some ways even more remarkable than that of Moscow, as it envisaged the creation of a complete new town centre with Mezhdunarodnyy (now Moskovskiy) Pr. as the main axis. In the 1920s and 1930s new building in Leningrad was concentrated in the south, along Mezhdunarodnyy Pr., Pr. Stachek, and farther E at Shchemilovka.

The Second World War was perhaps the central event in Russian history after the Revolution. For the Soviet Union the 'Great Fatherland War' (Velikaya Otechestvennaya Voyna) began suddenly on 22 June 1941 with Hitler's 'Operation Barbarossa'. The two great Russian cities were to have a key role in this devastating war, but the initial German plans concentrated on the destruction of the Red Army, and the offensive against Moscow, 'Operation Typhoon', was launched only on 2 October. There was some panic in the capital as government offices were evacuated to the East, but the defenders were rallied and there was even a parade in Red Square on the anniversary of the Revolution, 7 November. By the beginning of December some German troops were only about 40km NW of the Kremlin. Then came the Soviet counter-offensive under General Zhukov when the German Army was driven back several hundred kilometres. The Battle of Moscow was the first major Nazi defeat and, arguably, the turning point of the whole Second World War. One Soviet soldier who fell in this battle was reburied in 1965 in the impressive war memorial next to the Kremlin, and in 1977 a monument to the defenders of Moscow was erected on Kutuzovskiy Pr. After the battle Moscow was relatively safe from direct German attack, although there were occasional air raids. The great battles of 1942–45 that finally broke the German Army were directed from the Stavka (GHQ) in the Kremlin, and as one by one Soviet cities were recaptured victory salutes were fired by the guns of the Kremlin garrison.

If the Battle of Moscow was the first Soviet triumph, the Blockade, the Siege of Leningrad, was the great tragedy of the war. German tanks made rapid progress through the Baltic republics and by early September 1941 Leningrad was sealed off from the Soviet 'mainland'. Hitler decided not to take the city by storm but to starve it into submission, and the result of the '900 Days' was the death of nearly 600,000 Leningraders. Two-thirds of those who perished were buried at what is now the Piskaryovskoye Cemetery, with its impressive memorial. That Leningrad survived the terrible winter of 1941–42 at all was due to the 'Road of Life' across frozen Lake Ladoga to the NE. In the spring the situation improved as non-combatants were evacuated, but the city continued to suffer from shelling and air raids and was encircled by enemy troops. In the 1960s a 'Green Belt of Glory' was begun to mark the front-lines of the besieged city and a monument to the defenders of Leningrad was created at the S end of Moskovskiy Pr. in 1975. A narrow access corridor was broken through the German ring in January 1943, but the real end of the siege came twelve months later when the Red Army forced the Germans to withdraw from the Leningrad area. Among the first towns recaptured were Peterhof (Petrodvorets), Pushkin, and Pavlovsk, their palaces now in ruins.

The years of reconstruction after 1945 were also the last years of Stalin. One grim episode of the period was the so-called 'Leningrad Case' of 1949–50, the arrest and execution of a number of senior Leningrad Party officials. Stalin died in 1953 at his dacha in Kuntsevo (in the western suburbs of Moscow) and his body was placed alongside that of Lenin in the Red Square mausoleum.

Stalin's death began a new era in the Soviet history; at home there was a cultural 'thaw', and in foreign relations the principle of 'peaceful co-existence' was stressed. One symbolic change was the re-opening of the Kremlin to visitors in 1955, and at the same time it became easier for foreigners to visit the USSR. The 20th Congress of the CPSU in 1956 began the denunciation of Stalin; five years later his remains were removed from the Lenin Mausoleum. In 1957 the figure behind these changes, Nikita Khrushchev, emerged as the principle leader of the country; he was, however, overthrown by his Politburo colleagues in 1964.

Khrushchev was followed by a collective leadership, but as time passed Leonid Brezhnev became the principal leader. By the time Brezhnev died in 1982 there was a strong sense of economic and political malaise in the country; another problem was high-level corruption. The emergence of Mikhail Gorbachev in 1985 as General Secretary of the Communist Party began a period of *glasnost'* (openness) and *perestroyka* (reconstruction). The two decades of the Brezhnev era were now openly condemned as an era of 'stagnation'. Ambitious political, economic, cultural, and foreign policy initiatives were undertaken. In the long term one effect of these changes may be to open the USSR further to visitors; Western firms have already become involved to an unprecedented extent in the Soviet economy, not least in joint ventures in tourism. The kiosks and

private restaurants of the growing 'co-operative' sector are also
highly visible. Liberalisation, however, has also brought political,
economic, and nationalist dissatisfaction into the open within the
USSR; it has also brought revolution to Soviet allies. At the time of
writing the outcome of the Gorbachev initiatives remains in doubt,
but the USSR of the 1990s will probably be very different from that of
the 1970s.

Both Moscow and Leningrad changed dramatically in the post-war
period, especially after the mid-1950s when stress was placed on the
construction of new flats. Vast new housing estates like Novyye
Cheryomushki and Khoroshovo–Mnevniki were created around
Moscow. These originally consisted of simple and monotonous five-
storey blocks, but later there was more variety in both height and
decoration, with tall flats predominating. The mikro-rayon (micro-
district), a group of flats combined with shops and social limits,
became the main unit of residential organisation. The city limits of
Moscow were extended to the Ring Motorway in 1961, and are now
spilling over it. Moscow also benefited from holding of the XXII
Olympic Games in 1980; a large number of new sporting facilities
were erected, and the Olympic Village is now a model housing
estate. The present area of the city is 994 sq. km (compared to 356 sq.
km in 1961 and 228 sq. km in 1917; the area of modern Greater
London is 1580 sq. km). The population is more than 8,400,000. In
1971 a new General Plan for Moscow envisaged the development by
the year 2000 of a polycentric city divided into eight planning zones;
the slogan has been devised of making Moscow a 'Model Communist
City'.

In Leningrad much rebuilding was required, as some 3000 buildings had been destroyed in the war and another 10,000 damaged. A
new General Plan was drafted in 1948 which abandoned the new
centre in the S; instead the 'historic' heart of Leningrad was maintained with balanced development to N and S. One important
development was the Leningrad Metro, which went into operation in
1955 and now has lines running far into the suburbs. The General
Plan approved in 1966 included the creation of vast housing estates
to the N and S, and along the shore of Vasil'yevskiy Island. The new
residential districts are virtually indistinguishable from those in
Moscow, but in the centre of Leningrad the construction of high-rise
buildings has been avoided. With the exception of a few structures
like the Television Tower and the Leningrad Hotel, the skyline
around the Neva has hardly altered since the beginning of the 20C.
In recent years the emphasis in the historic centre has been on
preservation and reconstruction; the aim is to internally modernise
old blocks of flats while retaining their façades.

The area of Leningrad increased from 389 sq. km in 1959 to 1400
sq. km in 1988 (compared to 104 sq. km in 1897); the population is
now more than 4,900,000. In 1987 an integrated General Plan for the
town and its surrounding Region up to the year 2005 was approved.
This divided the city into three zones. The historic centre was to
continue to be renovated. In the mixed industrial-residential zone,
major modernisation and amelioration would be undertaken—
including the relocation of factories. The outlying new residential
zone would be further improved, and with the completion of a flood
defence barrage the coastline of the Gulf of Finland would be
extensively developed. In 2003 Leningrad will celebrate its 300th
anniversary.

B.   Literature

Russian written literature dates back to medieval times, but the foundation of the modern literary language was laid by Mikhail Lomonosov (1711–65), the 'Peter the Great' of Russian letters. The novelist and historian Nikolay Karamzin (1766–1826), the fable writer Ivan Krylov (1768–1844), and the Romantic poet Vasily Zhukovsky (1783–1852) continued the development of Russian literature, but it was only with Alexander Pushkin (1799–1837) that a writer of international stature emerged. Pushkin is revered in the Soviet Union as both a great writer and the liberator of the Russian literary language. His brilliant 'novel in verse' 'Yevgeny Onegin' (1831), with its vivid description of St. Petersburg life, was the precursor of the outstanding Russian novels of the late 19C. Other important writers active in the first half of the 19C were the dramatist Aleksandr Griboyedov (1795–1829), the poet and novelist Mikhail Lermontov (1814–41), and Nikolay Gogol (1809–52). Griboyedov's 'Woe from Wit' (1823), a satire of Moscow society of the 1820s, was the first major Russian play, while in 'A Hero of Our Time' (1840), Lermontov created Russia's first psychological novel. Gogol, a master of satire, wrote the play 'The Government Inspector' (1836) and the novel 'Dead Souls' (1842). An important influence at this time was the critic Vissarion Belinsky (1811–48), who emphasised the social significance of literature.

The great literary tradition was continued in the second half of the 19C. Ivan Turgenev (1818–83) produced half a dozen outstanding novels, including 'Fathers and Sons' (1862), as well as the play 'A Month in the Country'. Fyodor Dostoyevsky (1821–81) wrote 'Crime and Punishment' (1866), set in the sinister gloom of the St. Petersburg slums, and 'The Brothers Karamazov' (1880). Leo Tolstoy (1828–1910), the creator of 'War and Peace' (1869) and 'Anna Karenina' (1876), was equally celebrated, both in Russia and abroad. In both his great novels Tolstoy contrasts the spontaneous simplicity of the 'Russian' city of Moscow with the false and corrupting civilisation of the artificial Imperial capital of St. Petersburg. These three men were far from isolated: there were also the poet Fyodor Tyutchev (1803–73); Ivan Goncharov (1812–91), the author of 'Oblomov' (1859); the 'civic' poet Nikolay Nekrasov (1821–77); the prolific dramatist Aleksandr Ostrovsky (1823–86), who portrayed the Moscow merchant class; and the satirist Mikhail Saltykov-Shchedrin (1826–89).

The last decades of the Russian Empire were also a time of remarkable cultural activity, the 'Silver Age'. Anton Chekhov (1860–1904), a doctor by profession, was both a master of the short story and the creator of some of the classics of world drama, including 'The Seagull' (1896), 'Three Sisters' (1901), and 'The Cherry Orchard' (1904). The Moscow Arts Theatre (MKhAT), founded in 1898 by Konstantin Stanislavsky (1863–1938) and Vladimir Nemirovich-Danchenko (1858–1943), staged Chekhov's plays using a new realist style of acting and production. Also revered in the USSR is Maxim Gorky (1869–1936), who wrote realist novels and plays, including 'The Lower Depths'. The 'Silver Age' included the Symbolist poets Aleksandr Blok (1880–1921), Andrey Bely (1880–1934), and Valery Bryusov (1873–1924), and among the other writers of the day were Ivan Bunin (1870–1953) and Leonid Andreyev (1871–1919).

The turbulent period from 1918 to 1929 was a time of bold experimentation in literature. Among the most notable writers were

Group of writers in the Summer Garden (I.A. Krylov, A.S. Pushkin, V.A. Zhukovskii, N.I. Gnedin) by G.G. Chernetsov, 1832

the poets Vladimir Mayakovsky (1893–1930) and Sergey Yesenin (1895–1925), both of whom were to commit suicide. Also outstanding were the Jewish short-story writer Isaac Babel (1894–1941) and the novelist Yevgeny Zamyatin (1884–1937). These and many other creative artists fell foul of the authorities for their failure to conform to the canon of Socialist Realism, which became the central ideology of Soviet culture in 1932. This doctrine held that literature and art must serve as tools in the construction of socialism. Among the major writers who suffered in the 1930s and 1940s were the poetess Anna Akhmatova (1889–1966) and the satirist Mikhail Bulgakov (1891–1940) (author of 'The Master and Margarita').

Other writers were more acceptable to the authorities, including Maxim Gorky, who returned from self-imposed exile in 1928 to become the doyen of Socialist Realism, and the Nobel Prize winner Mikhail Sholokhov (1905–84), the author of 'Quiet flows the Don'. Although the Khrushchev period saw the persecution of Boris Pasternak (1890–1960), one of the finest poets of the 1920s and the author of 'Dr Zhivago', the post-Stalin liberalisation, the 'Thaw', also produced a new generation of writers who enjoyed both Soviet and international recognition; among the most important were the poets Yevgeny Yevtushenko (born 1933) and Andrey Voznesensky (born 1933). In the 1960s many of the writers who had suffered during the 1930s and 1940s were rehabilitated—often posthumously—and their works put back in print. Nevertheless, the uncompromising epic narratives of Alexander Solzhenitsyn (born 1918) were not published in the Soviet Union, and he was exiled in 1974; other writers also went abroad in the Brezhnev years. In contrast, one of the most remarkable features of the later 1980s was literary *glasnost*'; 'Dr Zhivago' and even the works of Solzhenitsyn were published in the USSR, and writers like Anatoliy Rybakov (born 1911) were prominent spokesmen of the new era.

In the field of drama, the first years of Soviet rule witnessed experiments in mass theatre, most notably the production of 'The Storming of the Winter Palace' by Nikolay Yevreynov (1879–1953); the cast included 8000 actors and the performance was staged in Petrograd's Palace Square. In the 1920s three leading directors, Vsevolod Meyerhold (1874–1940), Yevgeny Vakhtangov (1883–1922), and Aleksandr Tairov (1885–1950), were inspired by German Expressionism, and opposed this to the theories of Stanislavsky. Often working with Constructivist artists and designers they created (each in his own way) exciting and dynamic productions of plays by Mayakovsky and Western dramatists. However, by the 1930s official policy had rejected experimentation and a devitalised version of the Stanislavsky 'system' took over. The period after Stalin's death saw a liberalisation in the theatre, with interesting new productions at a number of Moscow and Leningrad theatres under directors like Yury Lyubimov (born 1917) and Oleg Yefremov (born 1927). In the 1980s the work of the dramatist Mikhail Shatrov (born 1932) was in the vanguard of perestroyka.

C.   Music

Until the 19C Russian music existed only in the forms of folk or religious music. The various cultures of the Russian Empire combined to make a rich heritage of folk art with sources as disparate as the Nordic epic, Byzantine liturgy, and the native Slav tradition. The music of religious ceremonies was itself tinged with elements of peasant culture, and Orthodox Christianity was here imbued with survivals of old pagan customs.

After a long period of Church domination of the arts, the Tsars began in the 16C to employ musicians from the West and, from the 1730s onwards, music at the Court was largely Italian in origin. However, a reaction against foreign music occurred later, and a nationalist movement developed. The first really important composer to emerge from this movement was Mikhail Glinka (1804–57), known as the 'father of the Russian opera'. In his works, notably 'A Life for the Tsar' ('Ivan Susanin') and 'Ruslan and Lyudmila', he fused elements of Russian folk music with forms favoured by Western composers.

By the mid-19C St. Petersburg had become a leading musical centre. Berlioz, Verdi, Johann Strauss, and Wagner all conducted their works there. In 1862 the St. Petersburg Conservatory was established under the directorship of Anton Rubinstein (1829–94), and four years later his brother Nikolay (1835–81) became director of the newly-founded Moscow Conservatory. It was, however, the example of Glinka that influenced the group of nationalist compos-ers, largely self-taught, known as the 'Mighty Handful' (Moguchaya Kuchka): Aleksandr Borodin, César Cui, Mily Balakirev, Modest Mussorgsky, and Nikolay Rimsky-Korsakov. Borodin (1834–87), a professional chemist, wrote symphonies, chamber music, and songs, but is best known for the opera 'Prince Igor' with its exotic 'Polovtsian Dances'. The most famous work of Mussorgsky (1839–81) is perhaps 'Pictures from an Exhibition', but his masterpiece is undoubtedly the opera 'Boris Godunov', based on Pushkin's tragedy. 'Boris Godunov' is remarkable for its dramatic intensity and for the important role played by the chorus—a feature of Russian operas. Rimsky-Korsakov (1844–1908) wrote many colourful orchestral works, such as 'Sche-herezade', as well as a number of operas. He became a professor at the St. Petersburg Conservatory.

Pyotr Tchaikovsky (1840–93) used Russian folk tunes in his works, but the forms he chose were of the more classical Western type. The last three of his six symphonies are among the most popular ever written, and his three great ballets—'Swan Lake', 'The Sleeping Beauty', and 'The Nutcracker'—form the backbone of the Classical ballet repertoire. In addition Tchaikovsky wrote several concertos, a number of operas (notably 'Yevgeny Onegin' and 'The Queen of Spades'—both based on Pushkin), chamber music, and songs. Also popular are his orchestral overtures 'Romeo and Juliet' and '1812'; the latter recalled the defeat of Napoleon's invasion of Russia. Tchaikovsky was a professor at the Moscow Conservatory.

Aleksandr Scriabin (1872–1915) was a pianist who wrote many works for his instrument and also for orchestra; he evolved eccentric philosophical theories, and even his own musical language. Another pianist-composer was Sergey Rachmaninov (1873–1943), whose highly Romantic works include much piano music, as well as con-certos, symphonies, operas, and songs. Rachmaninov left Russia in 1917 and died in California. A contemporary of Rachmaninov's was Aleksandr Glazunov (1865–1936), also a symphonist but now remembered for his ballets 'Raymonda' and the 'The Seasons'.

Igor Stravinsky (1882–1971), a pupil of Rimsky-Korsakov, left Russia to work in the West, and there he developed into a truly cosmopolitan artist and one of the most important composers of the 20C. Some of the works he wrote in Paris, notably the ballets 'The Firebird', 'Petrushka', and 'The Rite of Spring' were inspired by Russian themes. Sergey Prokofiev (1891–1953) also spent a consider-able time abroad but he returned permanently to his native land in 1934. He wrote seven symphonies, the best known being No. 1 (the 'Classical' Symphony), as well as concertos, operas, ballets, and film music. Especially well known are his scores for Eisenstein's films 'Alexander Nevskiy' and 'Ivan the Terrible'. His ballets include the famous 'Romeo and Juliet', and he also created the ever-popular piece for children, 'Peter and the Wolf'. In response to official criticism of his music Prokofiev developed a deliberately 'under-standable' style in his last works.

Dmitry Shostakovich (1906–75) was a composer of exceptional gifts, whose music, like that of Prokofiev, at times provoked criticism from the authorities. His main works were his symphonies and string quartets, the Symphonies Nos 1, 5 and 10 being particularly important. Symphony No. 7 was composed in Leningrad during the Blockade. Shostakovich also wrote concertos, operas, and film music. Finally, the Armenian Aram Khachaturian (1903–78) became well known as the composer of the ballets 'Gayaneh' and 'Spartacus'.

These and a host of lesser composers have contributed to making the Russian classical music repertoire an exceptionally fine one, but many performing artists have also helped foster the idea of the Russians as a particularly musical people. The pianist Svyatoslav Richter (born 1914), the violinist David Oistrakh (1908–74), and the cellist and conductor Mstislav Rostropovich (born 1927) must be mentioned here, as well as the legendary bass Fyodor Chaliapin (1873–1938). A number of world-class orchestras are based in Moscow and Leningrad, while the opera companies of the Bolshoy and Kirov Theatres are renowned for their choruses and lavish productions.

D.   Ballet

The foundations of Russian ballet were laid in the reign of Empress Anna Ivanovna. In 1738 the Empress granted the Frenchman Jean-Baptiste Landé (died 1748) permission to open a small school in St. Petersburg to train twelve of the children of palace employees to dance 'theatrically'; at first the dancers performed for the Court, but later performances were also given in the Summer Gardens theatre. In 1733 a ballet school was set up in Moscow, with pupils drawn from the Moscow orphanage.

A succession of foreign ballet masters and dancers were brought to St. Petersburg, of whom the most important was Charles Didelot (1767–1837). Didelot, who arrived in 1801, not only reorganised the training at the Imperial Ballet School according to the best traditions of the French classical school; in addition he introduced the elaborate narrative ballet to Russia. Also important were the visits of the Italian ballerina Marie Taglioni in the 1830s, which were responsible for an upsurge in interest among the ballet-going public.

One of the reasons for the rise of Russian ballet is that the art was always held in higher esteem there than elsewhere. Whereas in Western Europe ballet was often seen as a second-class entertainment given before or after an opera or even interpolated as light relief, in Russia it enjoyed royal patronage and was considered as prestigious as opera. When ballet went into a decline in the West in the 1860s, Russian ballet, encouraged by its enthusiastic audience and guided by such masters as Jules Perrot (1810–92) and Arthur Saint Léon (1821–70), maintained its high standard of technique.

In 1847 Marius Petipa (1818–1910), a young Frenchman, joined the St. Petersburg company as a principal dancer, and in 1869 he was appointed principal ballet master. From this time and almost until his retirement in 1903 Petipa virtually ruled the Imperial Ballet. He choreographed over 60 ballets, outstanding among which are Tchaikovsky's 'The Sleeping Beauty', 'The Nutcracker', and 'Swan Lake'. Petipa was the master of the large scale spectacle that became synonymous with the Russian Imperial Ballet, and it was also under Petipa's regime that the Russian style of dance evolved. The French training had produced many fine Russian dancers, and yet leading roles were usually allocated to Italian guest stars noted for their virtuosity. In time the Russian dancers helped by the teaching of Enrico Cecchetti (1850–1928) equalled the technical brilliance of the Italians, and henceforth it was Russians who reigned supreme at St. Petersburg's Mariya Theatre. The principal dancers at the turn of the century were Mathilde Kschessinska (1872–1971), Olga Pre-obrazhenska (1870–1962), and the Legat Brothers Nikolay (1869–1937) and Sergey (1875–1905), while among the young dancers recently graduated from the Imperial Ballet School were Anna Pavlova (1881–1931), Mikhail Fokine (1880–1942), Tamara Kar-savina (1885–1978), and Vaslav Nijinsky (1889–1950).

By the time of his retirement Petipa's inspiration had been exhausted, but soon Fokine emerged as a very promising choreographer. Fokine believed that ballet should be a dramatic whole involving a synthesis of the arts—not merely a series of spectacular dances designed to show off a particular ballerina. He was influenced by Serge Diaghilev (1872–1929) and other members of the 'World of Art' group, as well as by the American dancer Isadora Duncan (who performed in Russia in 1905). It was the ballets of Fokine, including 'Les Sylphides', 'The Firebird', and 'Petrushka', that formed the basis of the repertoire that Diaghilev took to Paris in 1909–11 for the first spectacular Ballets Russes seasons; these in turn heralded the rebirth of ballet in the West. Curiously, some of these productions have never been seen in Russia, and the influence of Fokine and the Ballets Russes on Russian ballet was negligible.

After the 1917 Revolution the fate of ballet was at first uncertain, because of its close association with the old order and because of the emigration of leading dancers (some had left before the Revolution, with Diaghilev). It survived and flourished, however, and after a brief period of experimentation official policy approved a return to the full-length narrative ballet—with a stress on the need for accessibility to the mass audience. New ballets of the Soviet period have fallen into a number of narrow categories: 'The Red Poppy' (1927) and 'Spartacus' (1956/68) have revolutionary themes, while 'Romeo and Juliet' (1946) and 'Anna Karenina' (1972) are based on literature, and 'Ivan the Terrible' (1975) takes its theme from history. The high technical standard of Soviet ballet has been maintained thanks to teachers such as Agrippina Vaganova (1879–1951); Vaganova, a ballerina of the Imperial Ballet, remained in Petrograd after the Revolution, and her system of training was adopted throughout the country.

The outstanding ballet companies are those of the Bolshoy Theatre in Moscow and the Kirov (formerly Mariya) Theatre in Leningrad, although since the Revolution Moscow rather than the old capital has become the centre of Russian dance. Moscow had had its Imperial Ballet company since 1825. The Moscow style has always been more flamboyant, dramatic, and emotional than the elegant classical style of St. Petersburg/Leningrad. The leading figure in Moscow was Aleksandr Gorsky (1871–1924) who, influenced by Stanislavsky, created dance dramas such as 'Don Quixote' (1900) which showed the Moscow dancers to advantage.

The first triumphant tour of the Bolshoy Ballet in the West in 1956 demonstrated the continuing excellence of Russian ballet, and the company has since travelled abroad on a number of occasions; the Kirov Ballet first visited Western Europe in 1961. The outstanding dancers of the Soviet period have included Galina Ulanova (born 1910), as well as Maya Plisetskaya (born 1925), Irina Kolpakova (born 1933), Yekaterina Maksimova (born 1939), and Vladimir Vasiliev (born 1940). Three former Kirov dancers have had great success in the West—Rudolph Nureyev (born 1938), Natalia Makarova (born 1940), and Mikhail Baryshnikov (born 1948); while dissatisfied with the lack of challenge offered by the Soviet repertoire all three acknowledge their indebtedness to the superb Leningrad training. The era of glasnost' has made possible more tours by Soviet companies in the West, and even the return of some of the exiles to the Soviet stage.

E.   Architecture

Early Russian Architecture. The first stone buildings in Moscow followed a line of development which can be traced back through Vladimir, Suzdal, Novgorod, and Pskov to Kiev, and beyond that to the Byzantine architecture of Constantinople. The oldest surviving structure in Moscow is the Cathedral of the Saviour at the Andronikov Monastery. Completed in 1427, its simple external decoration, the tall central section of the walls, and the climbing rows of ogee-shaped gables, are features of the Muscovite style.

Foreign influence made itself felt at an early date. After a locally-designed structure collapsed, Ivan III summoned Italian architects for his Kremlin building programme. Aristotle Fioravanti created the five-domed Cathedral of the Assumption (1475–79), using the 12C Cathedral of the Assumption in Vladimir as a model. The later Cathedral of the Virgin of Smolensk (1524–25) in the New Convent of the Virgin was in turn to be inspired by the Kremlin cathedral, and in the mid-17C Patriarch Nikon held up Fioravanti's building as a model of traditional and pure architecture. Another Italian, Alevisio Novi, built the Kremlin Cathedral of the Archangel Michael in 1505–08; this shows more Western influence in its external decoration than the other Kremlin churches. The nearby Granovitaya Palace (1487–91), the oldest secular building in Moscow, was also created along Italian lines, by Marco Ruffo and Pietro Solario. The first part of the Ivan the Great Bell Tower in the Kremlin was built in 1505–08 by Marco Bono; the tiered octagonal tower became a feature of late Moscow architecture. In addition, the Italians supervised the construction in 1485–95 of the Kremlin walls and towers, with the N Italian swallow-tailed merlons (the 'Russian' tent roofs are 16C additions). Outsiders were also responsible for two other major Kremlin buildings; in the 1480s architects from Pskov built the Cathedral of the Annunciation and the Church of the Deposition of the Robe.

Meanwhile, stone buildings began to appear in the suburbs. Alevisio Novi created in the Kitay-Gorod in 1510 the Church of St. Vladimir (this is now much altered), but the oldest surviving parish church is the Church of St. Trifon in Naprudnoye, a little structure dating from the late 15C. Among the other early churches in Moscow are the Cathedral of the Nativity (in the Convent of the Nativity), the Church of the Conception of St. Anna, and the Church of St. Antipiy, all built in the 16C.

A striking element in some 16C Moscow architecture was the stress on the vertical axis and, in particular, the use of the steep pyramidal or tent roof; the latter was known as the shatyor and derived from native Russian wooden architecture. The Ivan the Great

Bell Tower has already been mentioned, and another striking example was the Church of the Ascension at Kolomenskoye (1532) with its wide base, tiered gables, and octagonal shatyor. The nearby Church of John the Baptist at D'yakovo (1540s/50s) shared several of these characteristics and in turn anticipated St. Basil's Cathedral in Red Square (1555–60). An outstanding example of the shatyor may be found in the Church of the Intercession at Medvedkovo (1627).

The Medvedkovo church was part of the spate of building which followed the end of the Time of Troubles. Many small churches appeared around the city. Some, like the Church of the Intercession at Rubtsevo (1619–26) with its central dome above tiers of gables, differed little from such 16C buildings as the Old Cathedral of the Don Monastery (1593) or the Church of the Trinity at Khoroshovo (1598). Soon, however, a new group of richly decorated churches was built, some sponsored by merchants or the strel'tsy. The earliest and best preserved is the Church of the Trinity in Nikitniki (1635–53), with its picturesquely assembled parts, painted moulding, and shatyor belfry. Among other examples are the exotic Church of the Nativity in Putinki (1649–52), with its three shatyors; the gaily painted Church of St. Nicholas in Khamovniki (1676–82); the Church of the Assumption in Gonchary (1654) and the Church of St. Gregory of Neocaesarea (1667–69) with their rich tile decoration; and the Church of the Trinity in Ostankino (1687–88), which features very elaborate brickwork.

This architectural flowering of the 17C was briefly interrupted in the middle of the century by Patriarch Nikon. In addition to purifying church liturgy, Nikon also condemned 'Russian' architecture and advocated a return to Byzantine forms; the shatyor came in for particular criticism, while the traditional five-domed church was taken as a model. Two examples of Nikon's attempts to return to the authentic roots of Orthodox architecture were the Cathedral of the Saviour at the New Monastery of the Saviour (1645) and the Kremlin Cathedral of the Twelve Apostles (completed in 1655).

Moscow Baroque architecture. Nikon's influence was in the end limited, and the last decades of the 17C were a particularly exciting period for Moscow architecture. The development of the style known as the 'Moscow Baroque' came in part from Western influence transmitted through engravings and via the newly-annexed Ukraine and Belorussia; its main features included ornate decoration, with white stone pilasters and window surrounds set against red brick walls. The Bridge Tower at Izmaylovo (1671) indicated the beginning of new developments, but a more complete example was the Church of SS. Boris and Gleb in suburban Zyuzino (1688). Among the finest surviving Moscow Baroque churches are the Church of the Intercession at Fili (1693), the Church of the Trinity at Troitse-Lykovo (1698–1704), the Church of the Sign 'na Sheremetevom Dvore' (1704), and the Church of the Resurrection in Kadashi (1687–1713). The style was used with great success in the decoration of several monasteries which were reconstructed in the last decades of the 17C. One example is the Cathedral of the Epiphany Monastery (1693–96), another the Gate-Church of the Holy Visage at the Monastery of the Conception (1696), while the Gate-Church of the Virgin of Tikhvin at the Don Monastery (1713–14) was one of the last Moscow Baroque buildings. The finest examples are, however, the ensembles of the New Convent of the Virgin and the Upper Monastery of St. Peter, with their splendid bell towers, churches, and monastery buildings.

The Naryshkin family (the family of the mother of Peter the Great) were the patrons of the Monastery of St. Peter, and Prince Lev Naryshkin was among the leading exponents of what has also been called the 'Naryshkin Baroque'.

Most of the surviving examples of pre-Petrine architecture are churches, but a few secular buildings do exist. Some have been much altered—like the palaces or mansions of Averkiy Kirillov (1656–57), the Boyar Volkov (late 17C), or the Boyar Troyekurov (17C); others are inaccessible—like the splendid Terem Palace (1635–36) and Poteshnyy Palace (mid-17C) in the Kremlin, or the Refectory of the Simonov Monastery (1680s). But open to the public are the Patriarch's Palace in the Kremlin (1645–55) (from Nikon's era) and the Teremok of the Krutitskoye Podvor'ye (1694).

Petrine Baroque architecture. The reign of Peter I (1682–1725) effected an abrupt change in Russian architecture, although this Westernisation had been anticipated by the Moscow Baroque. Peter imported foreign architects and sent young Russians to study abroad; the Baroque, which reached its peak in Counter-Reformation Europe, became the dominant style in Russia for the first two-thirds of the 18C. Many new forms of decoration were evident in the outstanding Church of the Archangel Gabriel (1704–07), by the Ukrainian architect Ivan Zarudny (died 1727), and in the Church of St. John the Warrior (1709–13). These were, however, among the last major buildings in Moscow for a generation. St. Petersburg was founded in 1703, and special attention was devoted to its development; in 1714 Peter prohibited the construction of stone buildings elsewhere in Russia.

Foreigners dominated the architecture of St. Petersburg for over a century. The Italian Domenico Trezzini (1670–1734) designed the simple Summer Palace (1710–12), the towering Cathedral of SS. Peter and Paul (1712–33), the Peter Gate of the Peter-Paul Fortress (1717–18), and the Twelve Colleges (1722–42). Among the other foreign architects were Georg Matarnovi (builder of the Kunstkamera, 1718–34); Giovanni Fontana and Gottfried Schädel (Menshikov Palace, begun 1710); and J.F. Braunstein, A.J.-B. Le Blond, and Niccolò Michetti (Monplaisir Palace at Petrodvorets, 1714–22) (Braunstein also created the Marly and Hermitage Pavilions at Petrodvorets). One important Russian architect was Mikhail Zemtsov (1688–1743), whose main surviving work is the Church of SS. Simeon and Anna (1731–34).

The outstanding St. Petersburg architect of the Baroque era was Bartolomeo Francesco Rastrelli (1700–71), an Italian who spent much of his life in St. Petersburg; his father was a sculptor brought to Russia by Peter I. Rastrelli the Younger was most active during the reign of Empress Elizabeth Petrovna (1741–61), for whom he rebuilt the Great Palace at Petrodvorets (1747–54), the Catherine Palace at Pushkin (1752–56), and the Winter Palace (1754–62). The Vorontsov Palace (1749–57) and the Stroganov Palace (1752–54) were also the work of Rastrelli, but his most interesting project was the Smolny Convent (begun 1748), which combined Baroque and traditional Russian forms.

In St. Petersburg, two other fine Baroque buildings are the Cathedral of St. Nicholas (1753–62) and the Shuvalov Palace (1753–55), both designed by Savva Chevakinsky (1729–c 1780). The Baroque was also used in Moscow once building activity resumed there in the 1730s. One outstanding Baroque structure, the so-called

Beautiful Arch (1757) designed by Prince Dmitry Ukhtomsky (1719–1774/5), was demolished in the 1920s, but the Church of St. Nikita the Martyr (1751), which was probably Ukhtomsky's work, survives. Two of the other rare surviving examples of this style in Moscow are the Church of St. Clement (1754–74) and the Apraksin House (1766).

Gothic architecture. Two trends became prominent in European architecture in the second half of the 18C, Classicism and the Gothic Revival. The latter had some success in Russia, where the style was used by two of the leading Moscow architects, Vasily Bazhenov (1737–99) and his pupil Matvey Kazakov (1738–1812). Both men worked in the 1770s and 1780s on the most ambitious Gothic project, Catherine the Great's unfinished estate at Tsaritsyno, and Kazakov designed the Peter Palace (1775–82) while under Bazhenov's influence. The St. Petersburg Chesma Palace (1774–77), intended like the Peter Palace to serve as a resting place for the Empress while travelling, also contained Gothic elements. Jegor Velten (1730–1801), the architect of the Chesma Palace, created nearby the even more striking Chesma Church (1777–80) and, on the opposite (N) side of St. Petersburg, the Church of John the Baptist (1776–78). The Gothic was popular sixty years later, under Nicholas I, when the British architect Adam Menelaws (died 1831) built the Chapelle (1827) and Arsenal (1830–35) at Pushkin, and Karl Schinkel (1781–1841), the great German architect, built the Gothic Chapel at Petrodvorets (1835). A number of other mid-19C Gothic buildings survive at Petrodvorets, including the Post Office, Railway Station, and Court Stables.

Russian Classicism. Classicism (or Neo-Classicism) was the leading architectural style in Europe from the middle of the 18C, and in Russia it dominated building until the 1840s and 1850s. In Russia, as elsewhere, it was a reaction to the Baroque (or Rococo), and it was a symptom of changing tastes that Rastrelli left St. Petersburg right after the accession of Catherine II (1762–96). One of the first major Classical buildings was the Academy of Arts (1764–88) in St. Petersburg, created by the Frenchman J.-B.M. Vallin de la Mothe (1729–1800) and Aleksandr Kokorinov (1726–72). Vallin de la Mothe built the Classical Small Hermitage (1764–75) as an annex to Rastrelli's Baroque Winter Palace, and he replaced Rastrelli as builder of the Gostinyy Dvor (1757–85) in St. Petersburg. The Roman Catholic Church of St. Catherine (1762–83) (on Nevskiy Pr., opposite the Gostinyy Dvor) was also built by Vallin de la Mothe as one of the first Classical churches. Two other Classical churches were created by Jegor Velten: the Church of St. Catherine (1768–71) and the Church of St. Anne (1775–79). Velten also supervised the construction of the Kamennoostrovskiy Palace (1776–81).

The Italian Antonio Rinaldi (c 1710–94) was another early protagonist of Classicism in St. Petersburg. His most ambitious project was the Marble Palace (1768–85), but he also introduced the monumental column and the Classical triumphal arch with his Chesma Column (1771–78) and Orlov Gate (1778–82, with Quarenghi) at Pushkin. Ivan Starov (1745–1808), the most accomplished of the early native Classicists, was a pupil of Vallin de la Mothe at the Academy of Arts and later studied in Paris and Rome. The Cathedral of the Trinity (1776–90) at the Alexander Nevskiy Lavra and the Tauride Palace (1783–89) were his work. The Scot Charles Cameron (c 1740–1812) arrived in Russia in 1774 where he became one of Catherine's favourite architects. A follower of Robert Adam, he redesigned many of the interiors of Rastrelli's Catherine Palace at Pushkin, and later added a new Classical wing, the Cameron Gallery (1780–95). Cameron's greatest work was the Great Palace at Pavlovsk, built for Grand Duke Paul, Catherine's son.

The most prolific of this generation of St. Petersburg Classicists was the Italian Giacomo Quarenghi (1744–1817), who came to Russia in 1780. His first major commission, the English Palace at Petrodvorets, was destroyed in the Second World War, but many other buildings survive, among them: the Hermitage Theatre (1783–87), the Academy of Sciences (1783–89), the Assignatsionnyy Bank (1783–90), the Alexander Palace (1792–96) at Pushkin, the Horse Guards Riding School (1804–07), and the Smolny Institute (1806–08). (There is a bust of Quarenghi in front of the Assignatsionnyy Bank.) Although Quarenghi worked mainly in the capital, he also designed the Old Gostinyy Dvor (1790–1805) in Moscow and took part in the construction there of the Catherine Palace, the Suburban Palace, and Sheremetev (Sklifosovskiy) Hospital.

A number of other architects reached maturity in the reign of Alexander I (1801–25) and continued the Classical style in St. Petersburg; the later form of Classicism was sometimes called the Russian Empire (Russkiy Ampir). Andrey Voronikhin (1760–1814) was the protégé (and probably the illegitimate son) of the wealthy Count A.S. Stroganov. His best known work is the Kazan Cathedral (1801–11) with its long semicircular colonnade. Other works include the Mining Institute (1806–08), which he gave a fine portico of Doric columns, and Bratsevo, the Stroganovs' estate near Moscow. Andreyan Zakharov (1761–1811) designed one of the most interesting Classical buildings, the Admiralty (1806–23), and its tall spire still dominates the centre of Leningrad. The Exchange (now the Naval Museum) (1805–10) is literally a Greek Doric temple built on the banks of the Neva; it was the work of the Swiss-born architect Thomas de Thomon (1759–1813), who also created the surrounding ensemble with its Rostral Columns.

Vasily Stasov (1769–1848), Carlo Rossi (1775–1849), and Auguste de Montferrand (1786–1858) were the last three great exponents of Classicism in St. Petersburg. Stasov (father of the critic V.V. Stasov) built or reconstructed the Court Stables (1817–23), the Yamskoy Market (1817–19), the Pavlovskiy Barracks (1817–19), the Cathedrals of the Transfiguration (1827–29) and the Trinity (1828–35), and the Narva (1827–33) and Moscow (1834–38) Triumphal Arches; he also took charge of the restoration of the Winter Palace after the great fire of 1837. Carlo Rossi, the most outstanding of the three architects, was born in Naples, the son of an Italian ballerina; the identity of his father is uncertain, but the name of Grand Duke Paul (later Paul I) has even been suggested. Rossi was a pupil of Vincenzo Brenna (1745–1820), who altered Cameron's Pavlovsk and completed Bazhenov's project for the Michael Castle (1797–1800) (now the Engineers Castle). The first major commission given to Rossi in St. Petersburg was the Yelagin Palace (1818–22), and his later work involved the transformation of whole districts of the capital. Rossi created the ensemble of Mikhaylovskaya Pl. (now Pl. Iskusstv), including the Mikhail Palace (Russian Museum) (1818–25), and also built the gigantic Main Staff (1819–29) in Dvortsovaya Pl. The ensemble of Aleksandrinskaya Pl. (Pl. Ostrovskovo) was laid out in the 1820s and 1830s with the Aleksandra (Pushkin) Theatre (1828–32) and the beautiful Teatral'naya Ul. (now Ul. Zodchevo Rossi,

'Street of Rossi the Master Builder'). The Senate and Synod (1829–34) in Senatskaya Pl. (Pl. Dekabristov) was Rossi's last important project, and he died in obscurity. The major work of Montferrand also forms part of the Pl. Dekabristov ensemble. Although he designed the Alexander Column (1830–34) in Dvortsovaya Pl., Montferrand is best known for the huge Cathedral of St. Isaac. His project was approved in 1818 and work continued for forty years. The completion of the cathedral in 1858 marked the end of the Classical era.

Meanwhile, Classicism had been accepted as warmly in Moscow as in St. Petersburg. Catherine II commissioned V.I. Bazhenov (already mentioned in connection with the Gothic Revival) to rebuild completely the Kremlin by creating an enormous Classical palace. This project, fortunately, was never realised, but Bazhenov did build nearby the fine Pashkov House (1784–86) (now part of the Lenin Library), as well as a number of smaller structures. The most important architect was Matvey Kazakov (1738–1812), a contemporary of Quarenghi's, and as prolific in Moscow as the Italian was in St. Petersburg. Kazakov is interesting because of his insularity; unlike his contemporaries he had neither attended the Academy of Arts nor travelled abroad. The Senate, built in the Kremlin in 1776–88, was his first major work and probably his masterpiece, but he also created the Club of the Nobility (House of Unions) (1780s), the 'Old Buildings' of Moscow University (1786–93), the Demidov House (1789–91), and the Golitsyn (1796–1801) and Paul (1802–07) Hospitals. Kazakov's churches include the Church of Metropolitan Filipp (1777–88), the Church of the Ascension (1790–93), and the unique round Church of SS. Cosmas and Damian (1791–93). Regrettably many of Kazakov's buildings perished in 1812 (the year of his death) and were recreated in an altered form. Among the other architects of the time was Rodion Kazakov (1755–1803) (no relation to Matvey), builder of the Church of Martin the Confessor (1782–93) and the Batashov House (Medsantrud Hospital) (1798–1802). The work of serf-architects on the suburban estates of the great magnates is also of interest. Fyodor Argunov (c 1732–c 1768) led the construction of the Sheremetevs' estate at Kuskovo (1769–77), while his nephew Pavel Argunov (c 1768–1806) was involved in the building of Ostankino (1791–98), another Sheremetev estate.

After the great fire of 1812 most of Moscow had to be rebuilt. The chief architect of the Commission for the Reconstruction of Moscow was Osip Bove (1784–1834), who built the Triumphal Arch (1827–34), now located on Pr. Kutuzova, as well as the Church of All Sorrows (1828–33) and the 1st Town Hospital (1828–33). Domenico Gilardi (1788–1845) and Afanasy Grigor'yev (1782–1868) worked together on a number of projects in this period, including the reconstruction of Kazakov's 'Old Buildings' of the university (1817–19), the Opekunskiy Sovet (1823–26) (regarded by some as the finest 'Empire' style structure in Moscow), and the Usachov Estate (1829–31), Gilardi alone rebuilt the Widows Home (1818; originally the work of his father Giovanni Gilardi), the Lunin House (1818–23), and the Gagarin House (Gorky Museum) (1820), while Grigor'yev created the Khrushchov House (Pushkin Museum) (1814), the Church of the Great Ascension (1820s), and the Lopukhin House (Tolstoy Museum) (1822). Other remarkable buildings of this period are the Manezh (Manège) (1817–25) by Augustin Béthencourt (1758–1824) and the Neskuchnoye Estate (Academy of Sciences) (1830s) by Yevgraf Tyurin (1792–1870); Tyurin's Church of the Epiphany (1837–45) has been described as transitional between the era of Classicism and the era which followed it.

Eclecticism in Russian architecture. Following the decline of Classicism in the 1840s, Russian architecture—like European and American architecture—might be divided into two general trends. One trend involved the application of a variety of different historical styles (often to the same building), while the other trend, emerging at the end of the century, attempted to create a new architecture by making use of advances in building technology. Historicism was dominant nearly everywhere until the end of the 19C, but in Russia and the Soviet Union it proved to be particularly enduring and—with the exception of two periods—was the dominant architectural spirit for more than a century.

The most interesting of these 'historical' styles was the attempt to revive Early Russian architecture. In the conservative reign of Nicholas I (1825–55) a 'national' style was especially welcome, and the architect Konstantin Thon (1794–1881), a pupil of Voronikhin, was granted several major commissions: the Great Kremlin Palace (1838–49), the huge Cathedral of Christ the Redeemer (1839–83; demolished in 1931), the Armoury Palace (1844–51), and the twin Nicholas Railway Stations (1843–51) in Moscow and St. Petersburg (now, respectively, the Leningrad and Moscow Stations). Thon's 'Russo-Byzantine' buildings mixed a number of styles, but included many details drawn from the Early Russian tradition. The style, which has also been called 'Pseudo-Russian', continued in Moscow with such ornately decorated buildings as the Historical Museum (1878–83), the Polytechnical Museum (1875–1907), the Upper Trading Rows (GUM) (1889–93), the Town Duma (Lenin Museum) (1890–92), and the Igumnov House (French Embassy) (1892). At the end of the 19C and the beginning of the 20C the spirit of the Russian tradition was evoked more successfully in what has been called the 'Neo-Russian' (as opposed to 'Pseudo-Russian') style. The artist Viktor Vasnetsov (1848–1926) designed his own house (1892) and later the building of the Tret'yakov Gallery (1900–05), while Aleksey Shchusev (1873–1949) built the lovely Church of the Intercession (1908–12) in the Convent of SS. Martha and Mary. Shchusev's Kazan Station, begun in 1913 but completed only in 1926, was the end of the Russian historical style. The 'Pseudo-Russian' found little acceptance in St. Petersburg, where the whole setting was foreign to it. Two exceptions were the Church of the Resurrection (1887–1907) and the Suvorov Museum (1901–04).

The leading St. Petersburg architect of the mid-19C was Andrey Stakenschneider (1802–65), who worked in the spirit of Classical St. Petersburg, even if his style is regarded as Eclectic. His most important commissions were the Mariya Palace (Leningrad Soviet) (1839–44), the Nikolay Palace (Palace of Labour) (1853–61), and the New Mikhail Palace (1857–61); he also redecorated part of the Hermitage. Two other architects might be grouped with Stakenschneider, Leo von Klenze (1784–1864), who in St. Petersburg created the New Hermitage (1839–52), and Albert Cavos (1801–63), who built the Mariya (Kirov) Theatre (1859–60) in St. Petersburg and rebuilt the Mikhail (Malyy) Theatre (1859–60) (St. Petersburg) and the Bolshoy Theatre (1856) (Moscow).

A variety of other historical styles were employed. The Baroque Revival in St. Petersburg included Stakenschneider's Belosel'sky-Belozersky Palace (1846–48), as well as the Yusupov House (1850s) on Liteynyy Pr. and the Peter the Great (Nakhimov) Academy (1912). The Renaissance Revival resulted in such buildings as the former St. Petersburg Commercial Bank (1911–12) and Moscow's Main Post Office. The buildings of late Imperial St. Petersburg included the Mosque (1910–14) and the Gothic Gontskevich House (1913–16), while Moscow saw the completion of such ornate and exotic buildings as the Sandunov Baths (1895), the Morozov House (1894–98), and the Rekk House.

At the beginning of the 20C, however, there was a self-conscious revival of Classicism in Russia. Roman Klein (1858–1924), who worked in Moscow, was among the most influential early adherents of the new Classicism: his work included the Pushkin Fine Art Museum (1898–1912) and the Borodino Bridge (1909–13). The influence of this school survived both the 1917 Revolution and the Constructivist experiments of the 1920s. Ivan Zholtovsky (1867–1959), whose Palladian Tarasov House (1909–10) was an important landmark in the pre-revolutionary Classical Revival, built in 1934 the palazzo on Pr. Marksa (now the Intourist Building), which set the pattern for Soviet Historicism over the next twenty years; his creative career continued to 1949, when he designed the massive block of flats at Leninskiy Pr., 11. Aleksandr Tamanyan (1878–1936) won an award with his monumental Shcherbatov House (1911–13) and later became a leading Soviet architect (although not active in Moscow). The Bryansk (now Kiev) Station was built in 1912–17 by Ivan Rerberg (1869–1932), whose later work included Moscow's Central Telegraph Office (1927) and the Classical building in the Kremlin which now houses the Presidium of the Supreme Soviet (1932–34). In St. Petersburg Ivan Fomin (1872–1936) was one of the leaders of the Classical Revival, not only with his Polovtsov Dacha (1912–16) and Abamelek-Lazarev House (1913–15), but also with his project for a new region of the capital (to be called New Petersburg). After the Revolution Fomin developed a theory of 'Proletarian Classicism' and constructed several important buildings, including the extension to the Moscow Soviet building (1929–30) and the Kropotkinskaya and Lermontovskaya Metro Stations (1935, 1938). Vladimir Shchuko (1878–1939), who created the luxurious Italianate Markov House (1910–11) on Kamennoostrovskiy (Kirovskiy) Pr., continued the Classical tradition with the Propylaea of the Smolny (1923). Vladimir Gel'freykh (1885–1967) collaborated on the later project, and the two architects also worked together on the Lenin Library and, with Boris Iofan (1891–1970), on the proposed Palace of Soviets; the palace, had it been completed, would have been an eight-tiered Classical structure some 400m high.

Soviet architecture in the 1930s, 1940s, and 1950s was Eclectic and attempted to impress with scale and ornamentation. Much of central Moscow is dominated by grandiose buildings, which were erected along the Moskva embankment and the great avenues. Dwarfing the centre of the town are the Council of Ministers Building and the Moskva Hotel, but the outstanding symbols of this era are the 'new' building of Moscow University, and the six other 'skyscrapers' created just after the Second World War: the Foreign Ministry, the Ministry of Transport, the Ukraina and Leningradskaya Hotels, and the apartment houses in Pl. Vosstaniya and on Kotel'nicheskaya Nab. The decoration of these skyscrapers contained a predominantly Gothic element. The growing tendency to over-decoration was also evident in the Moscow Metro; for example the relatively elegant stations of the 1930s (such as Kropotkinskaya, Ploshchad' Sverdlova,

The project for the Palace of Congresses (1930s). The Palace, taller than the Empire State Building and topped by a Lenin statue larger than the Statue of Liberty, was the symbol of the triumph of gargantuan classicism in Soviet architecture. Planned for the site of the demolished Cathedral of the Saviour, it was never completed

and Mayakovskaya) should be contrasted with the stations of the Circle Line, which were completed in the early 1950s. The centre of Leningrad escaped, for the most part, this trend in Russian architecture; minor exceptions are the former Intourist Hotel (1938–44) on the Neva embankment and the spired rotunda of Ploshchad' Vosstaniya Metro Station. To the south of the city, however, in the new districts built in the 1930s–50s along Pr. Stachek, Moskovskiy Pr., and Ivanovskaya Ul., Eclecticism, scale, and decoration reigned supreme. Two examples are the immense House of Soviets on Moskovskiy Pr. and the apartment houses in Komsomol'skaya Pl.

Then, in 1955, Soviet architects were ordered to change their approach. A Party/State decree entitled 'On the Removal of Excesses in Planning and Building' condemned the inefficient internal layout of buildings and the concentration on expensive façades and decoration. This decree marked the end of that trend in Russian architecture which had begun with Thon in the 1840s.

Art Nouveau architecture. If the alternative to Historicism can be taken as the attempt to evolve an entirely new architecture, then the first Russian development in this direction was the Art Nouveau or Style Moderne of the 1890s. In St. Petersburg the most prominent exponent of the trend was Fredrik Lidval (1870–1945), builder of the luxury apartment house at Kirovskiy Pr., 1 (1902–04), as well as of the more conventional Azov-Don Bank (1908–09) and Astoriya Hotel (1910–12). The Kschessinska House (October Revolution Museum), the Bolshevik headquarters in 1917, is another well-known example of Style Moderne, and was designed in 1904 by A.I. Gogen. Other buildings in this style include the Yeliseyev Shop (1903–07), the Singer Building (Dom Knigi) (1902–04), and the Vitebsk Station (1904). But it was in Moscow, with its more daring patrons, that Art Nouveau enjoyed its greatest success. A number of buildings by Franz Schechtel (1859–1926) survive, most notably the Ryabushinsky (1900) and Derozhinsky (1901) Houses (now the Gorky Museum and the Australian Embassy), the Ryabushinsky Bank (1904), the Moscow Arts Theatre (1902), and, most ambitious, the Yaroslavl Station (1902–04). Also of interest are the Metropole Hotel (W.F. Walcott, 1899–1903) and the Pertsov House (S.V. Malyutin and N.K. Zhukov, 1905–07), with their striking mosaics.

Constructivism. Art Nouveau was short-lived in Russia, as elsewhere, and in any event the First World War and the Revolution brought an end to major building work for over ten years. When architects resumed work in the late 1920s the striving for a new architecture took the form of 'Constructivisim'. This was related to the Modern movement which had been pioneered by Sullivan in Chicago in the 1890s, and its spirit had been evident in Russia before the Revolution in a few buildings like the Delovoy Dvor (I.S. Kuznetsov, 1912–13) in Moscow. After 1917, however, the 'revolutionary' link between form and function won the acceptance of a generation of young Russian architects, the Constructivists, who wanted the form and appearance of their projects to reflect the new materials and building methods employed, and who rejected conventional decoration. The result was buildings and projects of a novel geometrical and functional design and making extensive use of reinforced concrete and glass.

The Soviet architectural experiment was first brought before the eyes of the West by the avant-garde Soviet pavilion at an exhibition in Paris in 1925. The young architect responsible, Konstantin Mel'nikov (1890–1974), was among the more successful Constructivists, and his work in Moscow included the Rusakov and Kauchuk Workers Clubs, and also his own private home (all completed in 1928). There was an important connection between the new architecture and revolutionary institutions like workers clubs: two other examples in Moscow are the Zuyev Workers Club (I.A. Golosov, 1926) and the AMO (now Likhachov) Workers Club (Vesnin brothers, 1930–37). In Leningrad there were the Gorky Palace of Culture (A.I. Gegello and D.L. Krichevsky, 1926–27) and the adjacent Kirov Department Store and Factory-Kitchen (1929–31). The idea of communal housing was advanced in Moscow by the Narkomfin House (M.Ya. Ginzburg, 1928–30) and in Leningrad by the 'House of Former Political Prisoners' (1933). Other buildings worthy of mention are the Udarnik Cinema (1928–31) in Moscow and the Lensovet House (1931–35) in Leningrad.

Constructivism seemed dominant at the end of the 1920s. It received official approval with such important commissions as the buildings of the Institute of Marxism-Leninism (S.Ye. Chernyshev, 1927), and the offices of 'Izvestiya' (G.B. Barkhin, 1927) and 'Pravda' (P.A. Golosov, 1929–35). The famous French architect Le Corbusier came to Moscow to build the Tsentrosoyuz Building (1929–36), while Shchusev, the leading figure in the profession, turned to Constructivism for his Narkomzem (Ministry of Agriculture) building (1928–33). Within just a few years, however, Constructivism was dead; it was condemned in the mid-1930s as 'Formalism' and replaced by monumental historicism. The change was conditioned by the technical impractability of some of the Constructivist projects, the internal strife within the architectural profession, and a preference by the political leadership for 'traditional' forms. The turning point came with the competition for the Palace of Soviets in 1933, when the project of Iofan, Shchuko, and Gel'frekh defeated those of Mel'nikov and even Le Corbusier.

Modern architecture. Modern architecture was dormant in the Soviet Union for more than twenty years after the end of the Constructivist movement. Then in 1955 came the decree against architectural 'excesses'. The government was particularly concerned with a rationalisation of housing construction, but there was also a sudden change of architectural taste. Ironically, this was partly signalled by the creation in the International Modern style of the Kremlin Palace of Congresses (1960–61) the successor to the never-completed Palace of Soviets. The main architect, Mikhail Posokhin (born 1910), had won the Stalin prize a dozen years earlier for the Gothic skyscraper in Pl. Vosstaniya, but he went on to lead the Modernist movement with his construction of the new Kalinin Prospekt (1962–67), the Comecon Building (1965–69), and, more recently, the Olympic Sports Complex (1980) on Pr. Mira. Other impressive projects in Moscow which showed the change were the Rossiya Cinema (1961) and the Palace of Pioneers (1958–62). In later decades the International Modern has been used for the many buildings created in the Soviet capital. Among the more notable have been the Rossiya Hotel (1962–69), the Theatre of People's Friendship (formerly MKhAT) (1973), the Ostankino Television Centre (1964–69), the Children's Musical Theatre (1979), the Kosmos Hotel (1980), the RSFSR Soviet Building (1981), and the Taganka Theatre (1974–81). Several of the facilities designed for the 1980 Olympics were quite striking; in addition to Posokhin's Sports Complex there were the Druzhba Multi-Purpose Gymnasium at Luzhniki and the Indoor Cycle Track at Krylatskoye. The greatest impact of the new architectural spirit was in the vast amount of new housing built on the periphery; this has progressed from the narrowly functional to the imaginative.

In Leningrad the International Modern was adopted for the new Finland Station (1960) and the Theatre of Young Spectators (1962). The following decades saw the completion of the Yubileynyy Sports Palace (1967), the Oktyabr'skiy Concert Hall (1967), the Leningrad (1967–70) and Pribaltiyskaya (1976–78) Hotels, the new airport at Pulkovo (1973), and the Lenin Sports-Concert Centre (1980).

F.   Art

Early Russian Art. From the conversion of Russia to Orthodox Christianity (988) until the reign of Peter I (1682–1725), Russian painting was largely confined to icons. More than works of art, icons were designed to assist worship, and they were in themselves regarded as sacred. Many icons were believed to be miracle-working and as such they were carried for protection by armies on campaign. The early icon painters were monks for whom painting was a spiritual exercise accompanied by prayer and fasting. The authorship of many of the most celebrated works is unknown, as they were unsigned. When the colours became dull the icon was repainted and varnished; sometimes they were covered with silver frames encrusted with precious stones, and everything except the faces and hands of the figures was concealed. Icons were displayed publicly on the iconostasis (icon wall) of a church or placed in the corner of a house, lit by an oil lamp. It was only at the 1913 Exhibition of Early Russian Art (held in Moscow to celebrate the third centenary of the Romanov dynasty) that icons, many of them restored to their original colour, began to be generally appreciated as works of art.

Icon painting came to Russia from Byzantium and was bounded by strict conventions. Only certain subjects—Christ, the Virgin, the saints, and events from the scriptures—were deemed appropriate, and the icon painter had to convey the remoteness of the celestial world by eschewing perspective and living models. The first icons brought to Kiev from Byzantium conformed closely to these canons, but the most famous, the Virgin of Vladimir was an exception. Brought to Kiev in the early 12C, and then moved to Vladimir, to the Cathedral of the Assumption in Moscow, and finally to the Tret'yakov Gallery, it conveys a spirit of gentleness and humanity normally absent from Byzantine icons. This spirit was to become a feature of the finest Russian works.

Few Kievan icons survived the Mongol invasion of 1237. Many monks fled north, seeking refuge in the cities of Vladimir, Suzdal, Pskov, and Novgorod. The schools of Vladimir and Suzdal faithfully preserved the Byzantine traditions. The artists of Pskov retained the dark colours of tradition, but were influenced by folk art in their depiction of figures. It was in Novgorod, however, that a Russian national school developed. The earliest Novgorod icons were more narrative in tone and showed the influence of folk art. The sharply-outlined figures became a distinctly Russian type, and in the course of the 13C the palette was lightened by the inclusion of vermilion and yellow, which were far from the sombre colours of Byzantium.

Icon painters had been working in Moscow since the 12C, but it was only towards the end of the 14C that the Moscow school really began to flourish. The first famous painter to work in Moscow was Theophanes the Greek (Feofan Grek) (c 1340–1405). Theophanes came to Russia from Constantinople in 1370 and worked first in Novgorod, where he was influenced by the work of local artists. The icons of Theophanes combine the dignity and sombre colour of the Byzantine tradition with the humanity and grace characteristic of the best Russian icons. In 1390 he moved to Moscow, where the finest examples of his work may be seen on the iconostasis of the Kremlin Cathedral of the Annunciation. The 'miracle-working' icons of the Assumption and of the Virgin of the Don, both in the Tret'yakov Gallery, are also attributed to him.

Theophanes was joined in his work on the Cathedral of the Annunciation by two Russian painters, Prokhor from Gorodets and the greatest Russian master, Andrey Rublyov (c 1360–c 1430). Little is known about Andrey Rublyov except that he was a monk at the Troitse-Sergiyev Monastery (in what is now Zagorsk) and at the Andronikov Monastery in Moscow; the Andronikov Monastery is now the Andrey Rublyov Museum of Early Russian Art. Rublyov painted several of the icons in the Cathedral of the Annunciation, but his most famous work is the Old Testament Trinity (early 15C), which was painted for the Cathedral of the Trinity at the Troitse-Sergiyev Monastery but is now in the Tret'yakov Gallery. The Old Testament Trinity is remarkable for its poetic refinement, delicate use of colour, and the gentle spirituality of the angels.

The outstanding icon painter of the late 15C was a layman named Dionysius (c 1440–1502/08). More sophisticated than his predecessors, he achieved an other-worldly effect by elongating his figures and by the use of subtle colours. His masterpieces, The Crucifixion and the Life of Metropolitan Aleksey, are in the Tret'yakov Gallery, while the Life of Metropolitan Peter is in the Cathedral of the Assumption.

The great fire of 1547 destroyed many icons, and painters were summoned to Moscow from Novgorod and elsewhere to create replacements. These artists worked in the Armoury Palace workshops; the icons they painted were smaller than earlier works, more narrative, and crowded with realistic Russian figures set against elaborate backgrounds. In the late 16C the wealthy Stroganov family established a workshop where a new kind of icon, notable for its decorative rather than spiritual qualities, was created. The small icons of the Stroganov School have been compared to Persian miniatures.

The work of the last renowned master, Simon Ushakov (1626–86), reflects his great interest in Western European art, and indeed some critics have described him as a 'Russian Raphael'. Although Ushakov used Byzantine themes, his works, with their architectural background and use of perspective, are closer to Western religious painting than to icons.

Art of the 18C and early 19C. By the late 16C some of the Moscow icon painters were beginning to move away from the rigid conventions and to experiment with portraiture and perspective. Peter I (1682–1725) continued this trend by urging Russian painters to imitate Western rather than Byzantine models. He established a school of drawing in St. Petersburg, invited a number of W European artists to work in Russia, and sent promising young Russians abroad to complete their studies. Outstanding among the early students of Peter's art school were Ivan Nikitin (1688–1741), Andrey Matveyev (1701–39), Aleksey Antropov (1716–95), and Ivan Argunov (1727–1802), who all produced rather idealised portraits displaying a high level of technical competence. More impressive were the portraits of Fyodor Rokotov (1735–1808) and the fashionable Vladimir Borovikovsky (1757–1825), whose work avoided the tendency to idealise. Anton Losenko (1737–73) painted biblical and mythological subjects. The most distinguished painter of this period was Dmitry Levitsky (1735–1822), whose portraits of contemporaries and especially of the young ladies of the Smolny Institute capture beautifully the spirit of the age of Catherine II.

In the 18C the art of sculpture was flourishing. Fedot Shubin (1740–1805) produced a fine series of portrait busts of Catherine II and her Court. Feodosy Shchedrin (1751–1825) and Ivan Martos (1754–1835) were inspired by the statues of Ancient Greece. Their statues were widely used for decorating buildings and as funerary monuments; there are fine collections of the latter at the Museum of Town Sculpture in Leningrad and the Don Monastery in Moscow. Mikhail Kozlovsky (1753–1802) created the Classical statue of Suvorov in Marsovo Pole (Leningrad) and the statues for the fountains at Petrodvorets. Later sculptors who worked in a similar spirit were Vasily Demut-Malinovsky (1779–1846), Stepan Pimenov (1784–1833), and Giovanni Vitali (1794–1855). Peter Clodt von Jürgensburg (1805–67) is best known for his equestrian groups on the Anichkov Bridge (Leningrad).

In 1757 Catherine II granted Peter's school of art the status of the Academy of Arts. A new building was erected for the Academy in 1764–88 on Universitetskaya Nab. in St. Petersburg. The Academy of Arts offered a sound technical training but denied its students full freedom to develop by an insistence that only historical and classical subjects were worthy of treatment. The Academy's Research Museum still contains a fine collection of work produced by teachers and students. Three outstanding representatives of the academic school were Fidelio Bruni (1800–75), Karl Bryullov (1799–1852), and Aleksandr Ivanov (1806–58). Bryullov won European renown with his melodramatic Last Days of Pompeii (1833), but he also painted some charming portraits. Ivanov devoted twenty years (1837–57) to creating his vast Christ Appearing before the People; he was the first Russian artist to portray Christ in human terms, according to the traditions of Western art. Two other former students of the Academy were Vasily Tropinin (1776–1857) and Orest Kiprensky (1782–1836), who conveyed in many of their portraits the Romantic feeling of the era of the Napoleonic Wars and of the Decembrists; both these artists were from serf families. There is a small Tropinin Museum in Moscow. Kiprensky, known as the 'Russian Van Dyck', produced a famous portrait of Pushkin (1827).

The late 18C saw the birth of a school of Russian landscape painting. Semyon Shchedrin (1745–1804), who like most of the other successful artists of this time spent many years in Italy, became the first professor of landscape painting at the Academy of Arts; Shchedrin painted idealised views of the parks and palaces around the capital. Fyodor Alekseyev (1753–1824) was inspired by the beauty of St. Petersburg itself and produced a fine series of water-colours of the city. Fyodor Matveyev (1758–1826) and Sil'vestr Shchedrin (1791–1830) (a nephew of Semyon Shchedrin) spent much of their lives in Italy and depicted the Italian countryside. Sil'vestr Shchedrin rebelled against the formal academic landscape and began to paint from nature. He also painted the Russian seascapes. The greatest master of the latter genre, however, was Ivan Ayvazovsky (1817–1900), who spent most of his life in the Crimea, where he produced some 6000 canvases depicting the Black Sea in all weathers.

The Realist tradition. Aleksey Venetsianov (1780–1847), one of the earliest genre painters and an opponent of the Academy, painted somewhat idealised portraits and scenes of peasants at work in the fields. Some of his work is not unlike that of J.F. Millet. Among the most influential artists of the first half of the 19C was Pavel Fedotov (1815–52), who was known as 'the father of critical realism'. His satirical scenes from the life of the nobility and bourgeoisie—such as The Aristocrat's Breakfast (1849)—have been compared to the work of Hogarth. One of Fedotov's admirers was Vasily Perov (1833–82), who depicted the misery of the poor and satirised the wealth of the Orthodox Church; his most famous work, however, is probably the portrait of Dostoyevsky (1872). In 1870 Perov became one of the founder-members of the 'Society of Wandering Exhibitions'. The society organised annual exhibitions of their work which toured the main cities of Russia, and its members were known as the Pere-dvizhniki or 'Wanderers'. The Peredvizhniki were a group of socially-conscious artists inspired by the ideas of the writer Nikolay Chernyshevsky. Seeing art as a weapon in the struggle for social reform, they revolted against the 'irrelevant' subject matter pre-scribed by the Academy of Arts; instead, they tried to use their art to reveal social injustice. The Peredvizhniki enjoyed the patronage of P.M. Tret'yakov, and their paintings formed the basis of his great collection. The leader of the movement was Ivan Kramskoy (1837–87), who is, however, better remembered for his portraits of import-ant literary figures than for his more socially-conscious works.

Another member of the Peredvizhniki was Nikolay Gay (1831–94). Influenced by the religious thought of Leo Tolstoy, Gay painted mainly biblical subjects, but he also created such historical works as Peter I Interrogating Tsarevich Aleksey (1871). Vasily Surikov (1848–1916) made a speciality of extraordinarily detailed historical can-vases like Boyarina Morozova (1887) and Suvorov Crossing the Alps (1899). Most of the paintings of Vasily Vereshchagin (1842–1904) reflect his fascination with the peoples and architecture of the East. The Apotheosis of War (1872) expresses the painter's strong anti-war feelings.

Art of the late 19C and early 20C. Amid the mood of greater national awareness in the mid-19C some of the other painters associated with the Peredvizhniki devoted themselves to revealing the beauty of the Russian countryside. Aleksey Savrasov (1830–97) created evocative landscapes, while Ivan Shishkin (1832–98) was known as the 'Poet of the Russian forest'. The great promise of Fyodor Vasil'yev (1850–73) was not realised; his first major painting, The Thaw (1871), conveyed the bleakness of the countryside in winter. Vasily Polenov (1844–1927) painted biblical scenes, but also was notable for landscapes and views of Moscow. Arkhip Kuindzhi (1842–1910) produced some of the most dramatic Russian landscapes with extraordinary lighting effects; an example is his Birch Grove (1879). The greatest of the landscape painters, however, was Isaak Levitan (1860–1900), a friend of Chekhov. An imaginative and enterprising artist, he con-stantly experimented with colour and texture and conveyed better than anyone else the changing moods of the Russian countryside.

Several of the Peredvizhniki worked at the artists' colony which the wealthy industrialist Savva Mamontov established at Abra-mtsevo, his estate NE of Moscow (now preserved as a museum). Among them was the most celebrated painter of the late 19C, Il'ya Repin (1844–1930). Repin's work included the social criticism of The Volga Boatmen (1873). Religious Procession in Kursk Province (1883), and They Did Not Expect Him (showing the return of a political exile) (1884), as well as many historical canvases. He also produced a superb range of portraits of the leading cultural figures of the day; more ambitious was his large painting of the State Council (1903). Penaty, Repin's house NW of modern Leningrad, is open as a museum. Mikhail Nesterov (1862–1942) was another artist associated with Abramtsevo; his early works on religious themes conveyed a tranquil monastic atmosphere.

The artists at Abramtsevo carried out a careful programme of research into Early Russian art and architecture and into folk art. This inspired the Vasnetsov brothers to specialise in depicting themes from Russian history and legend. Apollinary (1856–1933) created a series of paintings of medieval Moscow and Novgorod. Viktor (1848–

1926) illustrated incidents from the bylini, the epic tales of the knightly heroes of medieval Russia; he also designed fairy-tale sets for Mamontov's Private Opera. There are two small museums devoted to the Vasnetsovs in Moscow.

Two other noted artists worked at Abramtsevo but did not belong to the Peredvizhniki. Valentin Serov (1865–1911) was perhaps the finest portraitist of the period and painted many of his contemporaries, including Nicholas II. His most famous paintings, however, were created when he was still a young man: the radiant Girl with Peaches (1887) and Girl in Sunlight (1888). Serov was also a talented landscape artist. The extraordinarily gifted and original Mikhail Vrubel' (1856–1910), a friend of Serov, rejected outright the ideals of the Peredvizhniki, believing rather in art for art's sake. He was inspired by the decorative qualities of Byzantine art and Venetian mosaics; these influences can be seen in his most celebrated works, the exotic and hauntingly mysterious illustrations of Lermontov's poem 'The Demon' and the painting The Swan Princess (1900).

The influence of the Peredvizhniki lasted until almost the turn of the century. In the 1890s, however, there was a growing opposition movement known as the World of Art (Mir Iskusstva) and led by Aleksandr Benois (1870–1960) and Serge Diaghilev (1872–1929). The World of Art was a society, an organiser of exhibitions, and a magazine, all with the slogan 'Art pure and unfettered'. Its members believed in merging the best of the Russian artistic tradition with the finest traditions and innovations of W European art. The first World of Art exhibition (1899) included both foreign and Russian art, but later exhibitions concentrated on the latter. Diaghilev organised a vast retrospective of 18C portraiture in the Tauride Palace (a revelation to many Russians) as well as an exhibition of Russian art in Paris. The magazine 'World of Art' first published in 1898, introduced its readers to the Art Nouveau of W Europe and to the French Impressionists and Post-Impressionists. Perhaps the most celebrated achievement of the movement was the Ballets Russes, for whom Léon Bakst (1866–1924) produced dazzling designs which took Paris by storm in 1909. Other artists particularly noted for their theatre design were the Muscovites Konstantin Korovin (1861–1939) and Aleksandr Golovin (1863–1930); Golovin and Benois created the sets for the production of 'Boris Godunov' which Diaghilev staged in Paris (with Chaliapin).

Benois, and also Konstantin Somov (1869–1939) and Yevgeny Lanceray (1875–1946), painted charming period reconstructions reflecting their fascination with the courtly life of the 18C. Nikolay Roerich (1874–1946) and Ivan Bilibin (1876–1942) shared an interest in medieval Russia; Roerich was an amateur archaeologist who designed the sets for 'The Rite of Spring'.

The work of the Symbolist painter Viktor Borisov-Musatov (1870–1905) evoked a still, dream-like world peopled with elegant and remote figures; delicate blue, green, and purple tones predominate. Pavel Kuznetsov (1878–1968) created landscapes depicting a similarly harmonious world.

20C Russian art. The first three decades of the 20C saw the emergence of a Russian avant-garde which was influenced by developments in the West and in turn influenced Western art. Mikhail Larionov (1881–1964) and Nataliya Goncharova (1881–1962) moved from Symbolism to Cubo-Futurism. Both were to emigrate to the West, as did their better-known contemporary Marc Chagall

(1889–1985). Russian abstract art was developed by Vasily Kandinsky (1866–1944), Kazimir Malevich (1878–1935), Vladimir Tatlin (1885–1953), and El Lissitsky (1890–1941), as well as by the sculptors Anton Pevsner (1886–1962) and Naum Gabo (1890–1977). In the first years of Soviet Russia many of these artists were accepted by the new government, and a number of them held state posts. At the end of the 1920s, however, 'Formalism' (as abstract art was called) fell into disfavour and disappeared.

From the end of the 1920s the emphasis in Soviet art was on accessibility to the masses. Experimentalism was rejected; there was a return to realism with official portraits and the recurring themes of revolution, 'socialist construction', and national defence. Among the best known adherents of this 'Socialist Realism' were the painters Isaak Brodsky (1884–1939), Sergey Gerasimov (1885–1964), Boris Ioganson (1893–1973), Aleksandr Deyneka (1899–1969), and Vladimir Serov (1910–68). Three leading sculptors who worked in a similar spirit were Sergey Konyonkov (1874–1971), Sergey Merkurov (1881–1952), and Vera Mukhina (1889–1953).

Il'ya Glazunov (born 1930) was one painter who broke with previously accepted canons but kept government tolerance. In addition an alternative Soviet avant-garde existed alongside the 'official' artists. One modernist exhibition was ridiculed by Khrushchev in 1962 and another—unofficial and held outdoors—was crushed by bulldozers in 1974. The late 1980s, however, saw greater official toleration for diversity in art, as in other areas of Soviet culture.

PRACTICAL INFORMATION

I Approaches to Moscow and Leningrad

Tourist Information. Intourist: 216 Marsh Wall, Isle of Dogs, London E14 9FJ (Tel: 071-538 8600); 630 Fifth Ave., 868 Fifth Ave., NY 101100; 1801 McGill College Ave., Suite 630, Montreal, Quebec, Canada H3A 2N4; 37 Pitt St., Sydney, NSW 2000, Australia.

Airports. The *Moscow Air Terminal* (Gorodskoy Aerovokzal; Городской аэровокзал) is located in Leningradskiy Pr., 37 (Pl. 2; 2), between Dinamo and Aeroport Metro Stations. Buses from the Air Terminal carry passengers to the main Moscow airports:
Bykovo (Быково) (Pl. 1). Short-distance flights.
Domodedovo (Домодедово). (p 231). Flights to E and SE.
Sheremet'yevo (Шереметьево). (Pl. 1). Sheremet'yevo I handles flights to the Baltic republics, Leningrad, and Minsk. Sheremet'yevo II handles international flights.
Vnukovo (Внуково) (Pl. 1). Flights to S, W, and N.

The *Leningrad Air Terminal* (Gorodskoy Aerovokzal; Городской аэровокзал) is located at Nevskiy Pr., 7–9. Buses carry passengers to the airport at Pulkovo.
Pulkovo (Пулково) (Pl. 8; 8). Pulkovo I handles internal flights into Leningrad. Pulkovo II handles international flights.

Ports. In Leningrad the *Passenger Port* (Morskoy Passazhirskiy Port; Морской пассажирский порт) with its *Sea Terminal* (Morskoy Vokzal; Морской вокзал) (Pl. 12; 3) is located near the end of Bol'shoy Pr. on Vasil'yevskiy Island. The *River Terminal* (Rechnoy Vokzal; Речной вокзал) for long-distance river boats is at Pr. Obukhovskoy Oborony, 195 (Pl. 9; 5) (Metro: Lomonosovskaya).
There are two terminals for long-distance river boats in Moscow. The *Northern River Terminal* (Severnyy Rechnoy Vokzal; Северный речной вокзал) is located at Leningradskoye Shosse, 89 (Pl. 1) (Metro: Rechnoy Vokzal). The *Southern River Terminal* (Yuzhnyy Rechnoy Vokzal; Южный речной вокзал) is on Pr. Yu. V. Andropova (Pl. 3; 5).

Railway Stations. In Moscow the *Central Railway Passenger Service Bureau* (Tsentral'noye Zheleznodorozhnoye Byuro Obsluzhivaniya Passazhirov) is located at Komsomol'skaya Pl., 5 (between the Leningrad and Yaroslavl Stations). Tel. 266-90-00.
Belorussian Station (Belorusskiy Vokzal; Белорусский вокзал). Pl. Belorusskovo Vokzala (Pl. 4; 1). Metro: Belorusskaya. Trains to Belorussia and W Europe.
Kazan Station (Kazanskiy Vokzal; Казанский вокзал). Komsomol'skaya Pl., 2 (Pl. 5; 2). Metro: Komsomol'skaya. Trains to the Urals, W Siberia, and Central Asia.
Kiev Station (Kiyevskiy Vokzal; Киевский вокзал) (Pl. 7; 1). Metro: Kiyevskaya. Trains to the Ukraine and S Central Europe.
Kursk Station (Kurskiy Vokzal; Курский вокзал). Ul. Chkalova, 29

(Pl. 5; 4). Metro: Kurskaya. Trains to the Crimea, the Caucasus, and the E Ukraine.

Leningrad Station (Leningradskiy Vokzal; Ленинградский вокзал). Komsomol'skaya Pl., 3 (Pl. 5; 2). Metro: Komsomol'skaya. Trains to Leningrad, Tallin, and N Russia.

Pavelets Station (Paveletskiy Vokzal; Павелецкий вокзал). Leninskaya Pl., 1 (Pl. 5; 7). Metro: Paveletskaya. Trains to Saratov, Astrakhan, and SE Russia.

Riga Station Rizhskiy Vokzal; Рижский вокзал). Rizhskaya Pl. (Pl. 3; 1). Metro: Rizhskaya. Trains to Riga.

Savelovo Station (Savelovskiy Vokzal; Савеловский вокзал). Pl. Butyrskoy Zastavy (Pl. 2; 2). Trains to the N suburbs and Rybinsk.

Yaroslavl Station (Yaroslavskiy Vokzal; Ярославский вокзал). Komsomol'skaya Pl., 5 (Pl. 5; 2). Metro: Komsomol'skaya. Trains to Gor'kiy, Siberia, and N Russia.

In Leningrad the railway stations are:

Baltic Station (Baltiyskiy Vokzal; Балтийский вокзал). Nab. Obvodnovo Kanala, 120 (Pl. 13; 8). Metro: Baltiyskaya. Trains to the southern outskirts, including Petrodvorets.

Finland Station (Finlyandskiy Vokzal; Финляндский вокзал). Pl. Lenina, 5 (Pl. 10; 4). Metro: Ploshchad' Lenina. Trains to Razliv, Repino, Vyborg, and Finland.

Moscow Station (Moskovskiy Vokzal; Московский вокзал). Pl. Vosstaniya, 2 (Pl. 11; 7). Metro: Ploshchad' Vosstaniya. Trains to Moscow and to N, E, and S Russia.

Vitebsk Station (Vitebskiy Vokzal; Витебский вокзал). Zagorodnyy Pr., 52 (Pl. 10; 7). Metro: Pushkinskaya. Trains to Pushkin and Pavlovsk, to Belorussia (including Vitebsk and Brest), and to the Ukraine.

Warsaw Station (Varshavskiy Vokzal; Варшавский вокзал). Nab. Obvodnovo Kanala, 118 (Pl. 13; 8). Metro: Frunzenskaya. Trains to Tallin and Riga.

Bus Terminals. The main *Bus Station* (Avtostantsiya; Автостанция) in Moscow for long-distance buses is located at Shcholkovskaya Metro Station (Pl. 3; 2). Other services leave from the *Tishinskaya Bus Station* (in Tishinskaya Pl., near Belorusskaya Metro Station) and from the *Izmaylovskiy Park, Kashirskaya, Yugo-Zapadnaya,* and *Vykhino Bus Stations* (located at the Metro stations of those names).

In Leningrad the *Bus Terminal* (Avtovokzal; Автобусный вокзал) is located at Nab. Obvodnovo Kanala, 36.

Useful Vocabulary

паспорт	páspart	passport
билет	bilét	ticket
ТАМОЖНЯ	tamózhnya	customs
чемодан	chimadán	suitcase
багаж	bagásh	luggage
КАМЕРА ХРАНЕНИЯ	kámera khranéniya	left luggage office
носильщик	nasílshchik	porter
КАССА	kássa	booking office, cashier
СПРАВОЧНОЕ БЮРО	správachnaye byuró	enquiry office
пассажир	passazhir	passenger
ПЛАТФОРМА	platfórma	platform
каюта	kayúta	cabin, compartment

БУФЕТ	bufyét	refreshments
самолёт	samalyót	aeroplane
поезд	póyist	train
автобус	aftóbus	bus

II Hotels

One feature of travel to the Soviet Union has been that generally tourists have little choice as to where they stay. All foreign tourists stay at large hotels (usually run by Intourist), and normally cannot choose a particular hotel. In general, however, the standard of accommodation in hotels for foreigners is adequate. The construction of joint-venture hotels in Moscow and Leningrad will lead to a wider range of choice and standards in future.

The following are, at the time of writing, the most important Moscow hotels, or those where foreigners are most likely to stay:

Aeroflot (Аэрофлот). Leningradskiy Pr., 37 (Pl. 2; 2). Metro: Dinamo, Aeroflot. Tel: 155-26-24.

Druzhba (Дружба), Pr. Vernadskovo, 53 (Pl. 2; 6). Metro: Prospekt Vernadskovo. Tel: 432-96-29.

Intourist (Интурист). Tverskaya Ul., 3 (Pl. 4; 4). Metro: Prospekt Marksa. Tel: 203-40-08.

Izmaylovo (Измайлово). Izmaylovskoye Shosse, 69a (Pl. 3; 2). Metro: Izmaylovskiy Park. Tel: 166-01-09.

Kosmos (Космос). Pr. Mira, 150. (Pl. 3; 1). Metro: VDNKh. Tel: 286-21-23.

Leningradskaya (Ленинградская). Kalanchovskaya Ul., 21/40 (Pl. 5; 2). Metro: Komsomol'skaya Ploshchad'. Tel: 225-57-30.

Mezhdunarodnaya (Международная). Krasnopresnenskaya Nab., 12 (Pl. 7; 1). Metro: Ulitsa 1905 Goda. Tel: 253-23-82.

Metropole (Метрополь). Pr. Marksa. 1 (Pl. 4; 4). Metro: Prospekt Marska. Tel: 225-66-77.

Moskva (Москва). Pr. Marska, 7 (Pl. 4; 4). Metro: Ploshchad' Sverdlova, Ploshchad' Revolyutsii, Prospekt Marksa. Tel: 292-10-00.

National (Националь). Pr. Marksa, 14/1 (Pl. 4; 4). Metro: Prospekt Marksa. Tel: 203-65-39.

Rossiya (Россия). Ul. Razina, 6 (Pl. 5; 5). Metro: Ploshchad' Nogina. Tel: 298-54-09.

Savoy (Савойя). Ul. Rozhdestvenka, 3. (Pl. 5; 3). Metro: Dzerzhinskaya. Tel: 225-69-10.

Sevastopol (Севастополь). Bol'shaya Yushun'skaia Ul., 1. Metro: Kakhovskaya. Tel: 119-69-68.

Sovetskaya (Советская). Leningradskiy Pr., 32 (Pl. 2; 2). Metro: Dinamo. Tel: 250-23-42.

Ukraina (Украина). Kutuzovskiy Pr., 2/1 (Pl. 7; 1). Metro: Kiyevskaya. Tel: 243-30-21.

Other hotels in Moscow are:
Akademicheskiy I (Leninskiy Pr.); *Akademicheskiy II* (Donskaya Ul.); *Altay* (Botanicheskaya Ul., 41); *Baikal* (Sel'skokhozyay-stvennaya Ul., 15/1); *Bega* (Begovaya Alleya, 11); *Belgrad I and II* (Smolenskaya Pl., 5 and 8); *Budapesht* (Petrovskiye

Linii, 2/18); *Kiyevskaya* (Kiyevskaya Ul. 2); *Luzhniki*, Lenin Stadium; *Lokomotiv* (Bol. Cherkizovskaya Ul., 125); *Minsk* (Tverskaya Ul., 22); *Mir* (Bol. Devyatinskiy Per., 9); *Molodyozhnaya* (Dmitrovskoye Sh., 27); *Neptun* (Ul. Ibragimova, 30); *Orlenok* (Ul. A. N. Kosygina, 15); *Ostankino* (Botanicheskaya Ul., 29); *Pekin* (Bol. Sadovaya Ul., 1/5); *Salyut* (Leninskiy Pr., 158); *Sayany* (Yaroslavskoye Sh., 116); *Severnaya* (Sushchevskiy Val Ul., 50); *Soyuz I* (Levoberezhnaya Ul., 12); *Soyuz II* (1-ya Krasnogvardeyskiy Pr., 25); *Sport* (Leninskii Pr., 90/12); *Sputnik* (Leninskiy Pr., 38); *Tsaritsyno* (Ul. Bazhenova, 94); *Tsentral'naya I* (Tverskaya Ul., 10); *Tsentral'naya II* (Stoleshnikov Per., 18); *Tsentral'nyy Dom Turista* (Leninskiy Pr., 146); *Turist* (Sel'skokhozyaystvennaya Ul., 17/2); *Ural* (Ul. Chernyshevskovo, 40); *Varshava I* (Leninskiy Pr., 2); *Varshava II* (Kotel'nicheskaya Nab., 1/15); *VDNKh* (Ul. Kibal'chicha, 9); *Volga* (Dokuchaev Per., 10); *Voskhod* (Altuf'yevskoye Sh., 9a); *Vostok* (Gostinichnyy Pr., 9a); *Yaroslavskaya* (Yaroslavskaya Ul., 8); *Yunost'* (Frunzenskiy Val Ul., 34); *Yuzhnaya* (Leninskiy Pr., 87); *Zarya* (Gostinichnaya Ul., 5); *Zvyozdnaya* (Zvyozdnaya Bul'v., 42); *Zolotoy Kolos* (Yaroslavskaya Ul., 15).

Motels are: *Mozhayskiy* (Можайский) at Mozhayskoye Shosse, 165 (Pl. 1) (Tel: 446-36-75) and *Solnechnyy* (Солнечный) at Varshavskoye Shosse, 21-y Km. (Pl. 1).

The **Camping Sites** (Кемпинг) are located at Stantsiya Butovo (Ul. Pushkina 5) (Pl. 1) and at the *Mozhayskaya* (Можайская) hotel/camping area at Mozhayskoye Shosse, 165 (Pl. 1) (Tel: 447-34-34.

The following are the most important hotels in Leningrad, or those where foreigners are likely to stay:

Astoriya (Астория). Ul. Gertsena, 39 (Pl. 10; 5). Tel. 219-11-00.

Leningrad (Ленинград). Vyborgskaya Nab., 5/2 (Pl. 10; 4). Metro: Ploshchad' Lenina. Tel: 542-90-31.

Moskva (Москва). Pl. Aleksandra Nevskovo, 2 (Pl. 11; 7). Metro: Ploshchad' Aleksandra Nevskovo. Tel: 274-95-05.

Pribaltiyskaya (Прибалтийская). Ul. Korablestroiteley, 14. (Pl. 12; 1). Metro: Primorskaya. Tel: 356-51-52.

Pulkovskaya (Пулковская). Pl. Pobedy, 1 (Pl. 8; 8). Metro: Park Pobedy. Tel: 264-51-00.

Sovetskaya (Советская). Lermontovskiy Pr., 43/1 (Pl. 13; 5). Metro: Baltiyskaya. Tel: 259-26-56.

Yevropeyskaya (Европейская). Ul. Brodskovo, 1/7 (Pl. 10; 6). Metro: Nevskiy Prospekt, Gostinyy Dvor. Tel: 210-31-49.

Other hotels in Leningrad are: *Baltiyskaya* (Nevskiy Pr., 57); *Kareliya* (Ul. Tukhachevskovo, 27/2); *Kiyevskaya* (Dnepropetrovskaya Ul., 49); *Ladoga* (Pr. Shaumyana, 26); *Morskaya* (Pl. Morskoy Slavy, 1); *Neva* (Ul. Chaykovskovo, 17); *Oktyabr'skaya* (Logovskiy Pr., 10); *Rechnaya* (Pr. Obukhovskoy Oborony, 195); *Rossiya* (Pl. Chernyshevskovo, 11); *Sportivnaya* (Ul. Khalturina, 34); *Sputnik* (Pr. Toreza, 34); *Turist* (Ul. Sevast'yanova, 3); *Vyborgskaya* (Torzhkovskaya Ul., 3); *Yuzhnaya* (Rasstannaya Ul., 26); *Zarya* (Kurskaya Ul., 40).

The **Camping Site** (Кемпинг) is located at Repino (Klenovaya Ul., 9) (Pl. 1).

Vocabulary and procedure

Guests check in at the reception desk (Administrátsiya. АДМИНИСТРАЦИЯ), where they surrender passport and visa for registration and receive an identity card; the card gives the room number and must be used later to get into the hotel again. The key (klyuch) for each room (nómer or kómnata) is held by a *concierge* (dizhúrnaya) who is on duty on a given floor (itásh, ЭТАЖ). (Note that the Russian 1st floor is the British ground floor, etc.) The key is returned to the dizhúrnaya whenever guests leave the floor. The dizhúrnaya can deal with small problems. Examples of requests are, 'In my room the .... is not working': 'U minyá v nómere lámpa/ lamp (kran/tap; vánna/bath; dush/shower; tualét/toilet; tilifón/ telephone; radiátar/radiator) ne rabótayit'. The dizhúrnaya can often provide simple refreshment: chay/tea; minirálnaya vadá/mineral water; limanát/lemonade.

The hotel will contain a restaurant (ristarán, РЕСТОРАН) and bar (БАР), and there may well be a buffet (Bufyét, БУФЕТ) on several floors.

Many hotels include a service bureau (byuró apslúzhivaniya, БЮРО ОБСЛУЖИВАНИЯ) through which theatre tickets and excursions may be booked and transport or car hire arranged; in Intourist hotels the service bureau will accept 'hard' (non-Soviet) currency. Other facilities in the hotel may include a bank (БАНК), a post office (póchta, ПОЧТА), hairdresser (parikmákhirskaya, ПАРИКМАХЕРСКАЯ), laundry (práchichnaya, ПРАЧЕЧНАЯ), dry cleaning (khimchístka, ХИМЧИСТКА); shoe shine (chístka óbuvi, ЧИСТКА ОБУВИ), etc. In Intourist hotels there is often a Beriozka shop where goods can be bought with foreign currency.

III   Restaurants

There are various kinds of eating establishments, from the restaurant (ristarán, РЕСТОРАН) and the more simple café, (kafé, КАФЕ) to the zakusochnaya (zakúsachnaya, ЗАКУСОЧНАЯ) and buffet (bufét, БУФЕТ), both of which are essentially snack bars, and finally the 'dining room' (stolóvaya, СТОЛОВАЯ) which is self-service and functional. Co-operative (private) restaurants and (less common) international joint-ventures are a feature of the late 1980s and should offer a wider choice and better service; establishments listed below, however, are state-run.

Some of the best restaurants are in hotels. In Moscow these hotels include: Armeniya (the *Ararat* Restaurant specialises in Armenian food); *Belgrad* (Yugoslav food); *Berlin* (German food); *Budapesht* (Hungarian food); Intourist (including the *Inturist, Zvyozdoye Nebo,* and *Valyutnyy Zal* Restaurants); *Metropole*; *Mezhdunarodnaya* (includes the *Continental, Mercury, Russkiy* and *Sakura*; *Minsk* (Belorussian food); *Moskva*; National (includes the *Natsional'* and *Russkiy Zal* Restaurants); *Pekin* (Chinese food); Rossiya (includes the *Rossiya* and *'Top of the Rossiya'*—the latter has a superb view of central Moscow); *Sofiya* (Bulgarian food); Sovetskaya (*Sovetskiy* Restaurant); Ukraina.

Other notable restaurants in Moscow are:
Aragvi (Georgian food) (Tverskaya Ul., 6); *Arbat* (Pr. Kalinina, 29); *Baku* (food from Azerbaydzhan) (Tverskaya Ul., 24); *Delhi* (Indian

food) (Krasnaya Presnya Ul., 23); *Praga* (Arbat Ul., 2); *Sed'moye Nebo* (Ul. Akademika Korolyova, 15—a revolving restaurant at the top of the Ostankino TV Tower); *Slavyanskiy Bazar* (Ul. 25-vo Oktyabrya, 17); *Uzbekistan* (Uzbek food) (Neglinnaya Ul., 29); *Yakor'* (seafood) (Tverskaya Ul., 49).

In Leningrad there are noteworthy restaurants in several hotels; Astoriya; Leningrad (*Petrovskiy Zal Restaurant*); Pribaltiyskaya (*Dubrava*), Sovetskaya (*Sovetskiy*); Yevropeyskaya (*Yevropeyskiy*).
    Other good restaurants in Leningrad are:
Baku (food from Azerbaydzhan) (Sadovaya Ul., 12/23); *Kafe Fregat* (Bol'shoy Pr., 39/14); *Kavkazkiy* (Caucasian food) (Nevskiy Pr., 25); *Kafe Literaturnoye* (Nevskiy Pr., 18); *Metropole* (Sadovaya Ul., 22); *Sadko* (Ul. Brodskovo, 1/7).

Vocabulary and procedure

Russians enjoy eating out, and they like to spend the whole evening in a restaurant. As a result it is not easy to get into the better restaurants. (It is also difficult to make reservations.) Waiter service tends to be slow, and so the combination of an evening meal with a visit to the theatre is not feasible. (In any event, the theatres have buffets—some of them excellent—with open sandwiches, etc.) Many visitors will be on package tours, which minimises the problem of meals; there is little choice of food but the quality, quantity and variety are adequate and the service is generally prompt. One way of getting a better idea of Soviet food is to arrange a 'food tasting' through Intourist. Information should be available at the hotel service bureau.
    If one does wish to eat out but has no reservation, it may well be necessary to join a queue in front of the restaurant and wait for admission by the doorman (shviytsár). Once inside a restaurant or café coats should be deposited at the cloakroom (gardiróp; ГАР-ДЕРОБ); it is considered impolite to eat while wearing outer clothing. The *maître d'hôtel* (administrátar) will normally assign a table (stólik), but if not one can sit down at a likely table. The waiter (afitsiánt) or waitress (afitsiántka) will then bring a menu listing the various dishes the restaurant prepares; only those actually available will have their prices marked. As a result of current government policy it may be difficult to obtain alcohol in restaurants.

Useful phrases

Zdes svabódna?	Is this place unoccupied?
État stol apslúzhivayitsa?	Is this table being served?
Prinisítye, pazhálsta, ...	Please bring ...
Prinisítye, pazhálsta, minyú.	Please bring the menu.
Dáytye, pazhálsta, shchyot.	Please bring the bill.
Yest u vas ...	Do you have ...
Skólka ya dólzhen?	How much do I owe you?

General vocabulary

завтрак	záftrak	breakfast
обед	abét	lunch
ужин	úzhin	dinner, evening meal
блюдо	blyúda	course, dish
вилка	vílka	fork
нож	nosh	knife

ложка	lóshka	spoon
тарелка	tarélka	plate
стакан	stakán	glass
чащка	cháshka	cup
рюмка	ryúmka	wine glass
салфетка	salfétka	table napkin
скатерть	skátert	table cloth
соль	sol	salt
перец	pérets	pepper
горчица	garchítsa	mustard
сахар	sákhar	sugar
масло	másla	butter
хлеб	khlep	bread
чёрный хлеб	chórny khlep	black bread
белый хлеб	bély khlep	white bread

Appetizers
(zakúski, закуски)

салад	salát	salad
селёдка	silyótka	herring
блины ...	bliný ...	pancakes
... с икрой	... s ikróy	... with caviare
... со сметаной	... so smitánoy	... with sour cream
икра	ikrá	caviare
копчёная сёмга	kapchónaya syómga	smoked salmon
заливная рыба	zalivnáya rýba	fish in aspic

Soup
(sup, суп)

борщ	borshch	beetroot soup
Щи	shchi	cabbage soup
солянка	salyánka	fish or meat soup with salted cucumber
окрошка	akróshka	cold vegetable soup
уха	ukhá	fish soup
бульон	bulyón	bouillon
... с пирожками	...s piróshkami	... with meat pasties

Main course
(zharkóye, жаркое; ftaróye blyúda, второе блюдо)

мясо	myása	meat
говядина	gavyádina	beef
бифштекс	bifshtéks	steak
беф-строганов	bef-stróganaf	beef stroganoff
свинина	svinína	pork
баранина	baránina	mutton
плов	plof	pilaff
шашлык	shashlýk	shish-kebab
птица	ptítsa	fowl
курица	kúritsa	chicken
котлеты по-киевски	katléty pa-kíyevski	chicken kieff
котлеты по-пожарски	katléty pa-pazhárski	minced chicken
табака	tabaká	pressed chicken
рыба	rýba	fish
... с рисом	... s rísam	... with rice

Vegetables
(zilyón, зелёнь;óvashchi, овощи)

картофель	kartófel	potato
морковь	markóf	carrot
горох	garókh	peas
грибы	gribý	mushrooms
капуста	kapústa	cabbage
помидор	pamidór	tomato

Desserts
(slátkaye, сладкое)

фрукты	frúkty	fruit
компот	kampót	cold stewed fruit
кисель	kisél	fruit jelly
мороженое	marózhenaye	ice cream, e.g. 'stó/dvésti gramm marózhenava' (100/200 grammes of ice cream).
торт	tort	gâteau
пирожное	pirózhnaye	pastry
конфеты	kanféty	sweets, candy

Beverages
(napítki, напитки)

Alcoholic drinks are sold by the bottle (butýlka, бутылка) or by weight, e.g. 'stó/dvésti gramm vódki' (100/200 grammes of vodka).

вода	vadá	water
лёд	lyot	ice
минеральная вода	minirálnaya vadá	mineral water
лимонад	limanát	lemonade
сок	sok	fruit juice
квас	kvas	simple fermented bread drink
пиво	píva	beer
вино	vinó	wine. Two popular Georgian wines are Tsinandali (white) and Mukuzani (red).
шампанское	shampánskaye	champagne
коньяк	kanyák	brandy
молоко	malakó	milk
кофе	kófe	coffee
чай	chay	tea
...с молоком	...s malakóm	... with milk
...с сахаром	...s sákharam	... with sugar. In simpler establishments sugar may be an extra charge.

Snacks
(in buffets, etc.)

колбаса	kalbasá	salami
сосиски	sasíski	sausages, frankfurters
бутерброд	butirbrót	sandwich
... с мясом	...s myásom	meat sandwich
... с сыром	...s sýrom	cheese sandwich
яйцо	yatsó	egg

пелмеми	pilméni	dumplings
сыр	syr	cheese
ветчина	vitchiná	ham
булочка	búlachka	bun
пирог	pirók	pie
ватрушка	vatrúshka	cheesecake
творог	tvarók	cottage cheese
сметана	smitána	sour cream
кефир	kifír	sour milk

IV Transport

Moscow and Leningrad are both very large cities. Lewis Carroll, who visited St. Petersburg in 1867, reported that 'distances here are tremendous; it is as though one were in a country of giants'. Any visitor wanting to see Moscow or Leningrad independently must make use of the excellent public transport system. It is advisable to purchase the current Public Transport Map (Skhéma Marshrútov Garadskóvo Tránsporta; Схема маршрутов городского транспорта). If available, it is usually displayed on news-stands. For Metro maps see Pl. 14–16.

Metro. The fastest means of public transport in both Moscow and Leningrad is the underground railway or Metro (Метро, Метрополитен). Stations are marked with the symbol **M**.

Metro Stations tend to be crowded, especially in the rush hours, and it is advisable to work out one's route in advance. Service is frequent, with trains at intervals of 1½ to 2½ minutes in the rush hours (06.30–09.30; 16.30–19.00). Trains as a rule run from 06.00 to 01.00.

Any journey, irrespective of distance, costs 5 kopeks. Passengers deposit a 5k coin in a turnstile and pass through when the lights turn from red to green; no ticket is issued. (In the vestibule, before the turnstiles, are machines which change 10k, 15k, and 20k pieces.) In most stations, passengers travel down long and fast-moving escalators to the platforms.

Trains are equipped with loudspeakers, which announce, just before departure: 'Astarózhna, dvéri zakryváyutsya, sléduyushchaya stántsiya…' (Caution, the doors are closing; the next stop will be…). The station which the train is approaching is announced, for example 'Stántsiya Park Kul'tury' ('Park Kul'tury' Station); the names of any other Metro lines at this station are also given, for example 'Pirikhót na Kal'tsivúyu Líniyu' (Transfer to the Circle Line).

Useful signs

ВХОД	Entrance
НЕТ ВХОДА	No entry
КАССА	Cash desk
К ПОЕЗДАМ ДО СТАНЦИЙ …	To trains for stations …
ПЕРЕХОД НА ПОЕЗДА ДО СТАНЦИЙ…	Change for trains for stations …
НЕ ПРИСЛОНЯТЬСЯ	Do not lean (on the doors)
МЕСТА ДЛЯ ПАССАЖИРОВ С ДЕТЬМИ И ИНВАЛИДОВ	Seats for passengers with children and for invalids
СТОП КРАН	Emergency stop (lever)
ВЫХОД В ГОРОД	Exit for town
К ВЫХОДУ	To the exit

The Soviet underground railway systems are deservedly famous, with fast and frequent trains and clean, luxuriously appointed stations.

The Moscow Metro was begun under the supervision of L.M. Kaganovich and N.S. Khrushchev (it was once called the 'Kaganovich Metro'). The first 11.6km line, between Sokol'niki and Park Kul'tury, was opened in 1935 and as the Kirovsko-Frunzenskaya Line (Liniya) has since been extended. The Gor'kovsko-Zamoskvoretskaya Line was completed between Sokol and Ploshchad' Sverdlova in 1938, and extended S to Avtozavodskaya by 1943. These first two lines were the most successful in the architectural sense. Kropotkinskaya (formerly Dvorets Sovetov), Krasnyye Vorota (formerly Lermontovskaya), Mayakovskaya, and Ploshchad' Sverdlova stations are perhaps the finest. The first part of the Arbatsko-Pokrovskaya Line entered service in 1938, while the Circle (Kol'tsevaya) Line was completed in 1954. The stations built in the 1940s and early 1950s are perhaps over-decorated, but the visitor will certainly find them interesting. The Kaluzhsko-Rizhskaya, Filevskaya, and Tagansko-Krasno-presnenskaya Lines were opened in the late 1950s and the 1960s. The stations here, and those on the outlying extensions to the original lines, are well-designed if relatively austere. The Moscow Metro has expanded more or less continually, and there are plans to create a second circle line linking the stations on the outskirts.

Work began on the Leningrad Metro in 1940, but because of the war and its aftermath the trains began running only in 1955. The over-ornate style of the 1940s and 1950s was used for the first 11km stretch of the present Kirovsko-Vyborgskaya Line, between Avtovo and Ploshchad' Vosstaniya. The other stations on this and on the later Moskovsko-Petrogradskaya and Nevsko-Vasileostrovskaya Lines are attractive, but more simple.

Public Road Transport. Moscow and Leningrad have extensive systems of bus, trolleybus, and tram routes. The buses and trolleybuses are similar, although there are more bus routes; both are fast but tend to be very crowded during the rush hours. The trams are slower, but it is easier to find a seat on them, and they are good for sight-seeing. Public road transport is very cheap; for all three forms of transport there is a flat fee of 5 kopeks, irrespective of the distance travelled.

A stop (astanófka, остановка) for the bus (aftóbus) is marked with an A, for the trolleybus (tralléybus, pronounced tralléhbus) with a T or a 𝕋 (a stylised italic 'T'). Signs for the tram (tramváy)—route numbers and the letter T—are sometimes hung from the overhead wires. There is often a notice board at stops indicating 'Frequency of service at rush hours...' (ИНТЕРВАЛ В ЧАСЫ ПИК...). In general, services run from 06.00 to 01.00. The route is normally given on the side of the vehicle.

Entry is usually through the back door. Buses, trolleybuses and trams all employ an 'honesty-box' system; passengers deposit the correct fare and tear off ticket(s). If the vehicle is busy, passengers hand coins to a person nearer the box, with the request 'Piridáyte pazhálsta' (Please pass it on). It may be more convenient to buy a book of ten coupons (knízhka talónaf) from the driver; knock on his or her cabin when the vehicle is stationary and request: 'Dáytye, pazhálsta, knízhku talónaf' (Please give me a book of coupons). Passengers normally punch their own coupons, by using punches fixed to the walls. Although there is no conductor, passengers should make a point of buying a ticket or getting their coupon punched to avoid the attentions of a plainclothes ticket inspector (kantralyór; КОНТРОЛЁР) who has the right to fine passengers on the spot. It is not always easy to get off a vehicle when it is crowded, and passengers should work their way to the door (usually the forward one). The request 'Vy siychás vykhóditye? ('Are you getting off here?') usually serves to clear the way.

Useful signs

ВХОД	Entrance
НЕТ ВХОДА	No entry
ВЫХОД	Exit
НЕТ ВЫХОДА	No exit
МЕСТА ДЛЯ ПАССАЖИРОВ С ДЕТЬМИ И ИНВАЛИДОВ	Seats for passengers with children and for invalids

Route Taxis. The route taxi (marshrútnaye taksí, маршрутное такси) is a mini-bus which follows a fixed route between major squares, terminals, etc. There is a flat fare of 15k.

Taxis. Most of the passenger cars in the streets are still taxis. A taxi rank (stayánka taksí, стоянка такси) is indicated by a T and a checkerboard pattern. It is possible to order a taxi from a hotel. Taxis may be hailed in the street (if one is fortunate); a green light indicates that the vehicle is free. The basic official charge is 20 kopeks, and there is an additional 20k for each kilometre travelled. In 1990 many drivers were reluctant to have foreigners pay them in Soviet currency.

Car hire. Cars may be hired with or without driver from the hotel service bureau. The car hire centre in Moscow is at the Kosmos Hotel (Tel: 215-61-91). It may be difficult to get a self-drive car at short notice. An International Driving Licence is required.

V   Useful Addresses

Post Offices. There is usually a post office (póchta, ПОЧТА) in the major hotels. In Moscow the *Main Post Office* (Главный почтамт) is at Ul. Kirova, 26. There is an *International Post Office* in the Intourist Hotel, Tverskaya Ul., 3–5. This is the poste restante address for Moscow; a passport must be produced when collecting mail. Parcels can be sent from the International Post Office at Varshavskoye Shosse, 37a.

In Leningrad the *Main Post Office* (Главный почтамт) is at Ul. Soyuza Svyazi, 9. The *International Post Office* at Nevskiy Pr., 6 is also the poste restante office; letters can be sent c/o Leningrad C–400. The *Long-Distance Telephone Exchange* (Междугородная телефонная станция) is nearby at Ul. Gertsena, 3/5.

Information Bureaux and Tourist Offices. Most large hotels have a service bureau (byuró apslúzhivaniya, БЮРО ОБСЛУЖИВАНИЯ) and the staff there can get further information by telephone. In the streets are a number of kiosks marked Spravka (СПРАВКА) or 'Information' where, for a small fee, one can find out addresses, locations of streets, telephone numbers, etc. The *Moscow Excursion Bureau* of Intourist is located at Tverskaya Ul., 1, next to the Intourist Hotel. There is an Intourist booking office in Leningrad at Nevskiy Pr., 33-a (rear). The office of *American Express* in Moscow is at Sadovaya-Kudrinskaya Ul., 21a (Tel: 254-44-95).

Embassies in Moscow
Australia (Kropotkinskiy Per., 13). Tel: 246-50-12.
Belgium (Stolovyy Per., 7). Tel: 203-65-66.
Canada (Starokonyushennyy Per., 23). Tel: 241-91-55.
Denmark (Per. Ostrovskovo, 9). Tel: 201-78-60.
Eire (Grokhol'skiy Per., 5). Tel: 288-41-01.
Finland (Kropotkinskiy Per., 15/17). Tel: 246-40-27.
France (Ul. Dimitrova, 43). Tel: 236-00-03.
Germany (Bol. Gruzinskaya Ul., 17). Tel: 252-55-21.
Italy (Ul. Vesnina, 5). Tel: 241-15-33.
Japan (Kalashnyy Per., 12). Tel: 291-85-00.
Netherlands (Kalashnyy Per., 6). Tel: 291-29-99.
New Zealand (Ul. Vorovskovo, 44). Tel: 290-34-85.
Norway (Ul. Vorovskovo, 7). Tel: 290-38-72).
Sweden (Mosfil'movskaya Ul., 60). Tel: 147-90-09.
Switzerland (Stopani Per., 2/5). Tel: 925-53-22.
United Kingdom (Nab. Morisa Toreza 14). Tel: 231-85-11.
United States (Ul. Chaykovskovo, 19/23). Tel: 252-24-51.

Consulates in Leningrad
Finland (Ul. Chaykovskovo, 71). Tel: 273-73-21.
France (Nab. Reki Moyki, 15). Tel: 314-14-43.
Germany (Ul. Petra Lavrova, 39). Tel: 273-55-98.
Japan (Nab. Reki Moyki, 29). Tel: 215-44-24.
Sweden (10-ya Liniya, 11). Tel: 218-35-26.
United States (Ul. Petra Lavrova, 15). Tel: 274-35-26.

Houses of Friendship. The *House of Friendship with Peoples of Foreign Countries* (Dom Druzhby) in Moscow is located at Pr. Kalinina, 16. The similar institution in Leningrad is at Nab. Reki Fontanki, 21. It may be possible to arrange meetings with Soviet people through the Houses of Friendship.

Religious Services. In the functioning Russian Orthodox churches, there are daily services at 10.00 and 18.00, and an additional service at 07.00 on Sundays. The *Yelokhovskiy Cathedral*, formerly the Church of the Epiphany, is in Moscow at Spartakovskaya Ul., 15 (Metro: Baumanskaya). The new seat of the Patriarch is at the Danilov Monastery (Metro: Tul'skaya). One church near the centre of Moscow is the *Church of the Resurrection*, at Ul. Nezhdanovoy, 20. To the SW are the *Church of the Assumption* (in the New Convent of the Virgin), the *Church of St. Nicholas 'in Khamovniki'* (Komsomol'skiy Pr. and Ul. L'va Tolstovo. Metro: Park Kul'tury), and the *Church of the Trinity* (Ul. A. N. Kosygina, near the University). In Zamoskvorech'ye are the *Church of the Resurrection 'in Kadashi' (2-y Kadashovskiy Per., 9), the Church of All Sorrows* (Bol. Ordynka Ul., 20. Metro: Novokuznetskaya), the *Church of St. John the Warrior* (Ul. Dimitrova, 46. Metro: Oktyabr'skaya). The *Church of the Archangel Gabriel* (Telegrafnyy Per., 15a) is a Greek Orthodox church.
   Functioning Russian Orthodox churches in Leningrad include the *Cathedral of the Trinity* in the Alexander Nevskiy Lavra (Metro: Ploshchad' Aleksandra Nevskovo), as well as the *Cathedral of St. Nicholas* (Pl. Kommunarov) and the *Cathedral of the Transfiguration* (Pl. Radishcheva).

In Moscow Roman Catholic services take place at the *Church of St. Louis* (Mal. Lubyanka Ul., 12. Metro: Turgenevskaya) and the chapel of *Our Lady of Hope* (Kutuzovskiy Pr., 7/14). There is a Roman Catholic Church in Leningrad at Kovenskiy Per., 6 (Metro: Ploshchad' Vosstaniya).

English-language Protestant services are held in Moscow at the British and American Embassies, on alternative Sundays. A Baptist church is at Malyy Vuzovskiy Per., 3. In Leningrad there is Baptist church at Bol. Ozernaya Ul., 29a.

The *Synagogue* in Moscow is at Ul. Arkhipova, 8 (Metro: Ploshchad' Nogina) while that in Leningrad is at Lermontovskiy Pr., 2.

In Moscow the *Mosque* is at Vypolzov Per., 7.(Metro: Pr. Mira). In Leningrad the *Mosque* is at Pr. Maksima Gor'kovo, 7. (Metro: Gor'kovskaya).

VI   Entertainment

Theatres, Concert Halls, etc.

In Moscow, the following are particularly important:

Bolshoy Theatre (Гос. академический Большой театр Союза ССР). Pl. Sverdlova. Metro: Ploshchad' Sverdlova.

Central Concert Hall (Гос. центральный концертный зал). Moskvoretskaya Nab., 1 (in the Rossiya Hotel). Metro: Ploshchad' Nogina.

Central Puppet Theatre (Гос. центральный театр Кукол). Sadovaya-Samotyochnaya Ul., 3.

Maly Theatre (Гос. академический Малый театр). Pl. Sverdlova, 1/6. Metro: Ploshchad' Sverdlova.

Moscow Arts Theatre (MKhAT) (Московский Художественный академический театр Союза ССР им М. Горького). Proyezd Khudozhestvennovo Teatra, 3. Metro: Pr. Marksa.

Palace of Congresses (Кремлёвский Дворец съездов). Kremlin. Metro; Kalininskaya.

Stanislavsky and Nemirovich-Danchenko Musical Theatre (Московский академический музыкальный театр им. К.С. Станиславского и В. И. Немировича-Данченко). Pushkinskaya Ul., 17. Metro: Ploshchad' Sverdlova.

State Circus (Государственный цирк). Pr. Vernadskovo, 7. Metro: Universitet.

Taganka Theatre (Театр драмы и комедии на Таганке). Ul. Chkalova, 76. Metro: Taganskaya.

Tchaikovsky Concert Hall (Концертный зал им П. И. Чайковского). Bol. Sadovaya Ul., 20. Metro: Mayakovskaya.

Tchaikovsky Conservatory (Московская гос. консерватория им. П. И. Чайковского). Ul. Gertsena, 13.

Other centres of the performing arts in Moscow include: *Central Childrens Theatre* (Pl. Sverdlova, 2/7);*Chamber Music Theatre* (Leningradskiy Pr., 31); *Childrens Musical Theatre* (Pr. Vernadskovo, 5); *Durov Animal Theatre* (Ul. Durova, 4); *Film Actors Theatre Studio* (Ul. Vorovskovo, 33); *Gogol Theatre* (Ul. Kazakova, 8a); *Gypsy Theatre* (Leningradskiy Pr., 32); *Izmaylovo Concert Hall*

(Izmaylovskoye Shosse, 71); *Leninskiy Komsomol Theatre* (Ul. Chekhova, 6); *Malaya Bronnaya Theatre* (Mal. Bronnaya Ul., 4); *Maly Theatre* (Branch) (Bol. Ordynka Ul., 69); *Mayakovsky Theatre* (Ul. Gertsena, 19); *Mayakovsky Theatre* (Branch) (Ul. Khmeleva, 21); *Mime Theatre* (Izmaylovskiy Bul'v., 39/41); *Theatre of Miniatures* (Ul. Karetnyy Ryad, 3); *New Dramatic Theatre* (Ul. Prokhodchikov, 2); *Moscow Arts Theatre* (MKhAT) (Branch) (Ul. Moskvina, 3); *Mossovet Theatre* (Bol. Sadovaya Ul., 16); *Mossovet Theatre* (Studio Theatre) (Ul. Khamovnicheskiy Val, 2); *Operetta Theatre* (Push-kinskaya Ul., 6); *Theatre of Peoples Friendship* (Tverskoy Bul'v., 22); *Puppet Theatre* (Spartakovskaya Ul., 26); *Pushkin Theatre* (Tverskoy Bul'v., 23); *Theatre of Satire* (Bol. Sadovaya Ul., 2); *Satirikon Theatre* (Sheremet'yevskaya Ul., 8); *Soviet Army Theatre* (Pl. Kommuny, 2); *Sovremennik Theatre* (Chistoprudnyy Bul'v., 19); *Stanislavsky Theatre* (Tverskaya Ul., 23); *Vakhtangov Theatre* (Ul. Arbat, 26); *Variety Theatre* (Bersenevskaya Nab., 20/2); *Yermolova Theatre* (Tverskaya Ul., 5); *Theatre of Young Spectators* (Per. Sadovskikh, 10); *Znamenskiy Cathedral Concert Hall* (Ul. Razina, 8a).

Major theatres, etc., in Leningrad include:
Circus (Цирк). (Nab. Reki Fontanki, 3).
Glinka Hall (Small Hall of the Philharmonia) (Малый зал им. М. И. Глинки). (Nevskiy Pr., 30). Metro: Nevskiy Prospekt.
Gorky Theatre (Гос. академический Большой драматический театр им. М. Горького). (Nab. Reki Fontanki, 65).
Kirov Theatre (Гос. академический театр оперы и балета им. С.М. Кирова). (Teatral'naya Pl., 1).
Leningrad Concert Hall (Ленинградский концертный зал) (Pl. Lenina, 1). Metro: Ploshchad' Lenina.
Lenin Sports-Concert Centre (Спортивно-Концертный комплекс им. В. И. Ленина). Pr. Yu. Gagarina, 8. Metro: Park Pobedy.
Maly Theatre (Гос. академический Малый театр оперы и балета). (Pl. Iskusstv, 1). Metro: Nevskiy Prospekt.
Oktyabr'skiy Concert Hall (Большой концертый зал 'Октябрьский'). (Ligovskiy Pr., 6). Metro: Ploshchad' Vosstaniya.
Pushkin Theatre (Гос. академический театр драмы им. А. С. Пушкина). (Pl. Ostrovskovo, 2). Metro: Gostinyy Dvor.
Shostakovich Philharmonia (Large Hall) (Гос. филармония им. Д. Д. Шостаковича; Большой зал). (Ul. Brodskovo, 2). Metro: Nevskiy Prospekt.

Other centres of the performing arts in Leningrad include:
Academic Comedy Theatre (Nevskiy Pr., 56); *Bolshoy Puppet Theatre* (Ul. Nekrasova, 10); *Briantsev Theatre of Young Spectators* (Pionerskaya Pl., 1); *Theatre Buffo* (Narodnaya Ul., 1); *Comedy Theatre* (Nevskiy Pr., 56); *Theatre of Drama and Comedy* (Liteynyy Pr., 51); *Eksperiment Studio Theatre* (Kirovskiy Pr., 35/75); *Glinka Choir* (Nab. Reki Moyki, 20); *Komissarzhevskaya Theatre* (Ul. Rakova, 19); *Leninskiy Komsomol Theatre* (Park im. Lenina, 4); *Lensovet Theatre* (Vladimirskiy Pr., 12); *Maly Dramatic Theatre* (Ul. Rubinshteyna, 18); *Theatre of Musical Comedy* (Ul. Rakova, 13); *Puppet Theatre* (Nevskiy Pr., 52); *Puppet Fairy-Tale Theatre* (Moskovskiy Pr., 121); *Rimsky-Korsakov Conservatory* (Opera Studio) (Teatral'naya Pl., 3); *Variety Theatre* (Ul. Zhelyabova, 27); *Vremya Theatre-Concert Hall* (Pr. Stachek, 105); *Youth Theatre* (Nab. Reki Fontanki, 114).

Vocabulary and Procedure

Tickets can often be booked through the service bureau (byuró apslúzhivaniya, БЮРО ОБСЛУЖИВАНИЯ) of a hotel. In Intourist hotels one can pay in foreign currency (valyuta). It is possible to book tickets through the *Moscow Excursion Bureau* of Intourist (Tverskaya Ul., 1), or their ticket office at Pl. Sverdlova, 2. There is an Intourist office in Leningrad at Nevskiy Pr., 33-a (rear). Intourist may be able to provide an English-language synopsis for ballets, operas, etc. The *Central Booking Office* in Leningrad is at Nevskiy Pr., 42. The request, 'Do you have tickets for...', is 'U vas yést bilйty na...'. It is common practice to try to get tickets in front of the theatre. The request is: 'U vas net líshniva biléta?' (Do you have an extra ticket?)

Useful vocabulary

КАССА	kássa	box office
ГАРДЕРОБ	gardiróp	cloakroom
бинокль	binókl	opera glasses. Hiring opera glasses at the cloakroom (20 k.) usually helps get coats back quickly after the performance.
Программа	pragrámma	programme
ПАРТЕР	partér	stalls
ЛЕВАЯ СТОРОНА	lévaya staraná	left side
ПРАВАЯ СТОРОНА	právaya staraná	right side
СЕРЕДИНА	siridína	centre
БЕЛЬ-ЭТАЖ	bil-itásh	dress circle
ЛОЖА	lózha	box
ПЕРВЫЙ, 1-Й...	pérvy...	first...
ВТОРОЙ, 2-Й...	ftaróy...	second...
ТРЕТИЙ, 3-Й...	trétiy...	third...
...ЯРУС	...yárus	...circle
БАЛКОН	balkón	balcony
РЯД	ryat	row
МЕСТО	mésta	seat
КРЕСЛО	krésla	seat
АНТРАКТ	antrákt	interval
БУФЕТ	bufét	buffet

Cinemas. There are many cinemas in both Moscow and Leningrad. New films are shown in the big theatres on Tverskaya Ul. and Pr. Kalinina in Moscow and on Nevskiy Pr. in Leningrad. In cinemas the seat number is written on the ticket; there is no admission after the beginning of the performance.

Sports Facilities. Major facilities in Moscow include:

Army Sports Complex (Sportivnyy Kompleks TsSKA). Leningradskiy Pr., 39. Metro: Aeroport.

AZLK Sports Complex. Volgogradskiy Pr., 46. Metro: Tekstil'shchiki.

Central Chess Club (Tsentral'nyy Shakhmatnyy Klub). Gogolevskiy Bul'v., 14. Metro: Arbatskaya.

Chayka Swimming Pool (Plavatel'nyy Basseyn 'Chayka'). Turchaninov Per., 1/3. Metro: Park Kul'tury.

Dinamo Sports Complex (Universal'nyy Sportivnyy Kompleks 'Dinamo'). Leningradskiy Pr., 36. Metro: Dinamo.

Heavy Athletics Palace (Dvorets Tyazheloy Atletiki). Sirenevyy Bul'v., 4.

Hippodrome (Ippodrom). Begovaya Ul., 22.

Krylatskoye Olympic Sports Centre (Olympiyskiy Sportivnyy Tsentr Profsoyuzov 'Krylatskoye'). 5-ya Krylatskaya Ul., 10.

Kryl'ya Sovetov Sports Palace (Dvorets Sporta 'Kryl'ya Sovetov'). Leningradskiy Pr., 24a.

Lenin Stadium (Tsentral'nyy Stadion im. V.I. Lenina). Luzhniki Metro: Sportivnaya, Leninskiye Gory.

Moskva Swimming Pool (Plavatel'nyy Basseyn 'Moskva'). Kropotkinskaya nab., 37. Metro: Kropotkinskaya.

Olympic Sports Complex (Sportivnyy Kompleks 'Olimpiyskiy'). Olimpiyskiy Pr., n16/18. Metro: Prospekt Mira.

Olympic Water Sports Centre (Olimpiyskiy Tsentr Vodnovo Sporta). Mironovskaya Ul., 27.

Ski Jump (Lyzhnyy Tramplin). Leninskiye Gory. Metro: Leninskiye Gory.

Sokol'niki Sports Palace (Dvorets Sporta 'Sokol'niki'). Sokol'nicheskiy Val. 16.

Young Pioneers Stadium (Stadion 'Yunykh Pionerov'). Leningradskiy Pr., 31, Metro: Dinamo.

Znamensky Track and Field Stadium (Zimniy Legkoatleticheskiy Stadion im. Brat'yev Znamenskikh). Stromynka Ul., 8.

Major facilities in Leningrad include:

Kirov Stadium (Stadion im. S. M. Kirova). Krestovskiy Island.

Lenin Sports-Concert Centre (Sportivno-Kontsertnyy Kompleks im. V. I. Lenina). Pr. Yu. Gagarina, 8.

Lenin Stadium (Stadion im. V. I. Lenina). Petrovskiy Island.

Palace of Sporting Competitions (Dvorets Sportivnykh Igr). Ul. Butlerov, 9.

Winter Stadium (Zimniy Stadion). Manezhnaya Pl., 6.

Yubileynyy Sports Palace (Dvorets Sporta 'Yubileynyy'). Pr. Dobrolyubova, 18.

VII   Museums

The museums in Moscow and Leningrad are divided here into two broad groups. Those which foreign tourists are most likely to visit are dealt with first. The many museums whose interest is less general, are categorised by theme. Page references are given to the main text, where further details are available.

Admission charges, where they exist, are not high; 30k is typical. Please note that opening times are quite liable to change, and that an institution may be closed for repairs. (At the time of writing the Historical Museum and the Tret'yakov Gallery in Moscow are closed for major modernisation work; the same is true of much of the Russian Museum in Leningrad.) Note also that ticket offices often close an hour before the museum itself. **Before making a long trip to a museum it is advisable to check for confirmation that it is open.** Hotel Service Bureaux should have a complete list of opening times.

Moscow: Major Museums

Arkhangel'skoye. Pl. 1. Closed Mon, Tues. p 227.

Armed Forces Museum. Ul. Sovetskoy Armii, 2. Pl. 3; 3. Closed Mon. p 173.

Armoury Palace Kremlin. Pl. 4; 6, Metro: Kalininskaya. Closed Thurs. p 105.

Chekhov House. Sadovaya-Kudrinskaya Ul., 6. Pl. 4; 3, Metro: Barrikadnaya. Closed Mon. p 180.

Museum of Early Russian Art (Andrey Rublyov Museum). Andronikov Monastery. Pl. Pryamikova, 10. Pl. 3; 3. Closed Wed. p 205.

Exhibition of Economic Achievements (VDNKh). Pr. Mira. Pl. 3; 1, Metro: VDNKh. p 196.

Historical Museum. Krasnaya Pl., 1/2. Pl. 4; 3, Metro: Prospekt Marksa. p 111.

Kolomenskoye. Proletarskiy Pr. Pl. 3; 7, Metro: Kolomenskaya. Closed Mon, Tues. p 221.

Kremlin cathedrals. Pl. 4; 6, Metro: Kalininskaya. Closed Thurs. p 82.

Krutitskoye Podvor'ye. 4-y Krutitskiy Per. Pl. 3; 5, Metro: Proletarskaya. Closed Tues. p 208.

Kuskovo (Ceramics Museum). Ul. Yunosti, 2. Pl. 3; 4. Closed Mon, Tues. p 219.

Lenin Museum. Pl. Revolyutsii, 2. Pl. 4; 4, Metro: Ploshchad' Revolyutsii. Closed Mon. p 125.

Lenin Mausoleum. Krasnaya Pl. Pl. 4; 4, Metro: Prospekt Marksa. p 112.

New Convent of the Virgin (Novodevichiy Convent). Novodevichiy Pr., 1. Pl. 6; 6, Metro: Sportivnaya. Closed Tues. p 146.

Ostankino (Museum of Serf Art). 1-ya Ostankinskaya Ul., 5. Pl. 3; 1. Closed Tues, Wed. p 199.

Pushkin Fine Art Museum. Volkhonka Ul., 12. Pl. 4; 6, Metro: Kropotkinskaya. Closed Mon. p 138.

St. Basil's Cathedral. Red Square. Pl. 5; 5. Closed Tues. Metro: Prospekt Marksa. p 114.

Armed Forces Museum

Museum of Seventeenth Century Life and Applied Art. Kremlin (Patriarch's Palace). Pl. 4; 6, Metro: Kalininskaya. Closed Thurs. p 89.

Theatre Museum (Bakhrushin Theatre Museum). Ul. Bakhrushina, 31/12. Pl. 5; 7, Metro: Paveletskaya. Closed Tues. p 178.

Tolstoy House. Ul. L'va Tolstovo, 21. Pl. 4; 7. Closed Mon. p 145.

Tret'yakov Gallery. Lavrushinskiy Per., 10. Pl. 4; 6, Metro: Tret'yakovskaya. p 163.

Church of the Trinity in Nikitniki (Museum of 17C Architecture and Painting). Nikitnikov Per., 3. Pl. 5; 5, Metro: Ploshchad' Nogina. Closed Tues. p 117.

Other Museums in Moscow.

Art and Architecture

Museum of Applied Folk Art. Delegatskaya Ul., 5. Closed Fri. p 173.

Architecture Museum (Shchusev Museum of Architecture). Pr. Kalinina. Closed Mon, Fri. p 149.

Architecture Museum (Shchusev Museum of Architecture). Branch. Don Monastery. Donskaya Pl., 1. Closed Mon, Fri. p 149.

Diamond Fund. Kremlin. Closed Thurs. p 109.

Museum of Folk Art. Ul. Stanislavskovo, 7. Closed Mon. p 158.

Church of the Intercession. Novozavodskaya Ul., 6, Metro: Fili. Closed Tues, Wed. p 188.

Museum of Oriental Art. Suvorovskiy Bul'v., 12a. Closed Mon. p 128.

Picture Gallery of the USSR (Kartinnaya Galeriya SSSR). Ul. Krymskiy Val, 10, Metro: Park Kul'tury. Closed Mon. p 171.

Town Planning Exhibition. Berezhkovskaya Nab., 4. Closed Wed. p 212.

Tropinin Museum (Museum of V. Tropinin and the Artists of His Time). Shchetininskiy Per., 10. Closed Tues, Wed. p 167.

A. M. Vasnetsov House. Furmannyy Per., 6. Closed Mon, Tues. p 177.

V. M. Vasnetsov House. Per Vasnetsova, 13. Closed Mon, Tues. p 175.

Exhibition Halls

Central Artists House. Ul. Krymskiy Val, 10, Metro: Park Kul'tury. p 171.

Central Exhibition Hall (Manezh). Pl. 50-letiya Oktyabrya. p 121.

Exhibition Hall of the Academy of Arts. Kropotkinskaya Ul., 21. p 143.

Exhibition Halls of the Union of Artists of the USSR. Kuznetskiy Most, 20; Tverskaya Ul., 25; Ural'skaya Ul., 6.

Exhibition Hall of the Union of Artists of the RSFSR (Moscow Section). Begovaya Ul., 7–9.

History

Borodino Panorama. Kutuzovskiy Pr., 38. Closed Fri. p 188.

Decembrist Museum. Ul. Karla Marksa, 23. Closed Tues. p 201.

Gorki Leninskiye (Lenin Museum in Gorki). Closed Tues. p 226.

Herzen Museum. Per. Sivtsev Vrazhek, 27/9. Closed Mon. p 127.

Museum of the History of Moscow . Novaya Pl., 12. Closed Mon. p 118.

Kalinin Museum. Pr. Marksa, 21. Closed Mon. p 121.

Kutuzov Hut. Kutuzovskiy Pr., 38. Closed Mon, Fri. p 188.

Lenin Funeral Train. Leninskaya Pl., 1. Closed Tues. p 178.

Lenin Museum (Lenin Museum in the Apartment of A. I. Ul'yanova-Yelizareva). Manezhskaya Ul., 9. Closed Tues. p 120.

Marx and Engels Museum. Ul. Marksa i Engel'sa, 5. p 138.

Ministry of the Interior Museum (Central Museum of the MVD). Seleznevskaya Ul., 11. (By arrangement) p 173.

Moscow Defence Museum [1941–42]. Ul. A. Ia. Pel'she. Closed Mon. p 186.

Palace of the 16C–17C in Zaryad'ye (Palace of the Romanov Boyars). Ul. Razina, 10. Closed Tues. p 116.

Red Presnya Museum (Krasnaya Presnya Museum). Bol'shevistkaya Ul., 4. Closed Mon. p 191.

Revolution Museum (Central Museum of the October Revolution). Tverskaya Ul., 21. Closed Mon. p 159.

Underground Press Museum (Underground Press of the Central Committee of the RSDRP, 1905–06). Lesnaya Ul., 55. Closed Mon. p 161.

Literature and Theatre

Dostoyevsky House. Ul. Dostoyevskovo, 2. Closed Mon, Tues. p 174.

Gorky House Ul. Kachalova, 6/2. Closed Mon, Tues. p 129.

Gorky Literary Museum. Ul. Vorovskovo, 25a. Closed Mon, Tues. p 154.

Lermontov House. Ul. Mal. Molchanovka, 2. Closed Mon, Tues. p 153.

Literary Museum. Ul. Petrovka, 28/2. Closed Mon. p 132.

Lunacharsky House. Ul. Vesnina, 9/5. Closed Sun–Tues, Thurs. p 144.

Mayakovsky House, Proyezd Serova, 3/6. p 126.

Mayakovsky House, Krasnaya Presnaya Ul., 36. p 190.

MKhAT Museum (Museum of the Moscow Arts Theatre). Proyezd Khudozhestvennovo Teatra, 3a. p 156.

Nemirovich-Danchenko House. Ul. Nemirovicha-Danchenko, 5/7. Closed Mon, Tues. p 158.

N. A. Ostrovsky Museum. Tverskaya Ul., 14. Closed Mon. p 158.

Pushkin House. Ul. Arbat, 53. Closed Mon, Tues. p 151.

Pushkin Museum. Kropotkinskaya Ul., 12/2. Closed Mon, Tues. p 143.

Stanislavsky House. Ul. Stanislavskovo, 6. Closed Mon, Tues. p 158.

Tolstoy Museum Kropotkinskaya Ul., 11. Closed Mon. p 143.

Yermolova Museum Tverskoy Bul'v., 11. Closed Tues. p 130.

Music

Music Museum (Central Museum of Musical Culture named after M. I. Glinka). Ul. Fadeyeva, 4. Closed Mon. p 172.

Scriabin Museum. Ul. Vakhtangov, 11. Closed Mon, Tues. p 153.

Science and Technology

Agriculture Museum. Main Building, Moscow University. Closed Sat, Sun.

Animal Husbandry Museum (Liskun Museum of Animal Husbandry). Timiryazevskaya Ul., 48, Korpus 11. Closed Sat, Sun.

Anthropology Museum. Pr. Marksa, 18. Closed Sat, Sun.

Aviation and Space Travel (Frunze Central House for Aviation and Space Travel). Krasnoarmeyskaya Ul., 4. Closed Mon.

Biology Museum. (Timiryazev Museum of Biology). Mal. Gruzinskaya Ul., 15. Closed Mon. p 190.

Construction Section of VDNKh. Frunzenskaya Nab., 30. p 213.

Darwin Museum. Mal. Pirogovskaya Ul., 1. p 146.
Horse-breeding Museum. Timiryazevskaya Ul., 44, Korpus 14.
Korolyov House. 6-y Ostankinskiy Per., 2/28. Closed Mon, Tues. p 196.
Metro Museum. Sportivnaya Metro Station. Closed Sat, Sun.
Mineralogy Museum. (Fersman Museum of Mineralogy). Leninskiy Pr., 18. (By arrangement) p 182.
Palaeontology Museum. Profsoyuznaya Ul., 123. (By arrangement).
Planetarium. Sadovaya-Kudrinskaya Ul., 5. p 180.
Polytechnical Museum. Novaya Pl., 3/4. Closed Mon. p 118.
Sport Museum. Lenin Stadium, Luzhniki. Closed Mon.
Soil Science—Agronomy Museum (Vil'yams Museum of Soil Science and Agronomy). Timiryazevskaya Ul., 55. Closed Sat, Sun.
Timiryazev House. Ul. Granovskovo, 2. Closed Sun, Mon. p 150.
Vernadsky Museum. Ul. A. N. Kosygina, 47a.
Zhukovsky Museum. Ul. Radio, 17. Closed Sun. p 202.
Zoo. Bol. Gruzinskaya Ul., 1. p 190.
Zoology Museum. Ul. Gertsena, 6. Closed Mon.

Leningrad: Major Museums

Avrora. Petrogradskaya Nab., 4. Pl. 10; 4. Closed Fri, Mon. p 309.
Cabin of Peter I. Petrovskaya Nab., 6. Pl. 10; 4. Metro: Gor'kovskaya. Closed Tues. p 308.
Dostoyevsky House. Kuznechnyy Per., 5/2. Pl. 10; 8. Metro: Vladimirskaya. Closed Mon. p 293.
Museum of Ethnography of the Peoples of the USSR. Inzhenernaya Ul., 4/1. Pl. 10; 6. Metro: Gostinyy Dvor. Closed Mon. p 272.
Hermitage. Dvortsovaya Nab., 34. Pl. 10; 5. Closed Mon. p 243.
History of Leningrad Museum. Nab. Krasnovo Flota, 44. Pl. 13; 3. Closed Wed. p 242.
History of St. Petersburg Museum (Museum of the History of St. Petersburg and Petrograd. 1703–1917). Peter-Paul Fortress. Pl. 10; 3. Metro: Gor'kovskaya. p 306.
October Revolution Museum. Ul. Kuybysheva, 4. Pl. 10; 3. Metro: Gor'kovskaya. Closed Thurs. p 309.
Pavlovsk. Pl. 1. Closed Fri. p 351.
Peter-Paul Fortress. Pl. 10; 3. Metro: Gor'kovskaya. Closed Wed. p 305.
Petrodvorets. Pl. 1. Closed Mon. p 336.
Piskaryovskoye Cemetery. Pr. Nepokorennykh, 74. Pl. 9; 1. p 317.
Pushkin (*Catherine Palace*). Pl. 1. Closed Tues. p 342.
Pushkin House. Nab. Reki Moyki 12. Pl. 10; 5. Closed Tues. p 331.
Russian Museum. Inzhenernaya Ul., 4. Pl. 10; 6. Metro: Nevskiy Prospekt. Closed Tues. p 267.
St. Isaac's Cathedral. Isaakiyevskaya Pl., 1. Pl. 10; 5. Closed Wed. p 238.
Summer Palace. Summer Gardens. Pl. 10; 4. Closed Tues. p 283.

Other Museums in Leningrad.

Art and Architecture

Academy of Arts Museum (Research Museum of the Academy of Arts). Universitetskaya Nab., 17. Closed Mon, Tues. p 302.
Applied Arts Museum. Solyanoy Per., 15.
Architecture Museum (Museum of the Architecture of St. Petersburg and Petrograd, 18C–early 20C). Peter-Paul Fortress. Pl. 10; 4. Metro: Gor'kovskaya. Closed Wed. p 242.

Benois Museum. Petrodvorets.
Brodsky House. Pl. Iskusstv, 3. p 267.
Repin Museum (Penaty). Ul. Repina, 63, Repino. Closed Tues. p 358.
Museum of Town Sculpture (Alexander Nevskiy Lavra). Pl. Aleksandra Nevskovo, 1. Closed Thurs. p 279.

Exhibition Halls
Central Exhibition Hall. Isaakiyevskaya Pl., 1.
Exhibition Halls of the Union of Artists of the RSFSR. Sverdlovskaya Nab., 64, and Ul. Gertsena, 38.

History
Artillery Museum (Museum of Artillery, Engineers, and Signals). Park im. Lenina, 7. Closed Mon, Tues. p 313.
Dzerzhinsky Museum. Admiralteyskiy Pr., 6. p 238.
Kirov House, Kirovskiy Pr., 26/28. Closed Wed. p 310.
Lenin Museum (Leningrad Branch of the Central Lenin Museum) Ul. Khalturina, 5/1. Closed Wed. p 286. There are museums, in flats where the Bolshevik leader stayed, at the following addresses: Per. Il'icha, 7/4, p 295; Ul. Lenina, 52/9, p 311; 10-ya Sovetskaya Ul., 17, p 296; Serdobol'skaya Ul., 1, p 316; Nab. Reki Karpovki, 32, p 311; Khersonskaya Ul., 5/7, p 278. Lenin's study in the Smolny is sometimes opened to visitors. There is a Museum devoted to Lenin and the 1917 'Pravda' newspaper at Nab. Reki Moyki, 32/2—p 331. Outside Leningrad, to the NW, are two further Lenin Museums. '*Saray*', (p 358) and '*Shalash*', (p 358). All these museums are closed on Wed. The *Museum of the Vyborg Side,* at Bolotnaya Ul., 13/17 (p 317), is the house where Lenin led the meeting at which the final decision to seize power was made.
Menshikov Palace. Universitetskaya Nab., 15. Closed Mon. p 301.
Monument to the Heroic Defenders of Leningrad. Pl. Pobedy. Closed Wed. p 322.
Naval Museum. Pushkinskaya Pl., 4. Closed Mon, Tues. p 300.
Museum of Religion and Atheism (Kazan Cathedral). Kazanskaya Pl., 2. Closed Wed. p 265.
Suvorov Museum. Ul. Saltykova-Shchedrina, 43. Closed Mon. p 296.

Literature and Theatre
Blok House. Ul. Dekabristov, 57. Closed Wed. p 290.
Literary Museum of the Institute of Russian Literature (Pushkinskiy Dom). Nab. Makarova, 4. Closed Mon, Tues. p 300.
Literatorskiye Mostki ('Literary Plot' of the Volkovskoye Cemetery). Rasstannaya Ul., 30. Closed Thurs. p 277.
Lycée Museum (Branch of the All-Union Pushkin Museum). Komsomol'skaya Ul., 2. Pushkin. Closed Tues. p 348.
Nekrasov House. Liteynyy Pr., 36. Closed Mon, Tues. p 292.
Pushkin Dacha. Pushkinskaya Ul., 2, Pushkin. Closed Mon, Tues. p 350.
Pushkin Museum. Komsomol'skaya Ul., 7, Pushkin. p 345.
Theatre and Music Museum. Pl. Ostrovskovo, 6a. Closed Tues. p 274.

Music
Rimsky-Korsakov House. Zagorodnyy Pr., 28. Closed Mon, Tues. p 294.
Russian Opera Museum. Ul. Graftio, 26. Closed Mon, Tues. p 311.

Science and Technology

Museum of Anthropology and Ethnography. Universitetskaya Nab., 3. Closed Fri, Sat. p 301.

Museum of the Arctic and Antarctic. Ul. Marata, 24a. Closed Mon, Tues. p 294.

Botany Museum. Ul. Professora Popova, 2. Closed Mon, Tues, Thurs, Fri. p 311.

Communications Museum (Popov Museum of Communications). Ul. Soyuza Svyazi, 7. p 240.

Leningrad Today and Tomorrow. Pl. Rastrelli (Smolny Convent). Closed Wed. p 297.

Mendeleyev House. Universitetskaya Nab., 7/9. Closed Sat, Sun.

Museum of Military Medicine. Lazaretnyy Per., 2. Closed Fri. p 295.

Mining Museum. 21-ya Liniya, 2.

Pavlov House. 7-ya Liniya, 2. Closed Sat, Sun. p 303.

Planetarium. Park Lenina, 4.

Railway Museum. Sadovaya Ul., 50. Closed Fri, Sat. p 288.

Soil Science Museum (Dokuchayev Museum of Soil Science). Birzhevoy Proyezd, 6. Closed Sat, Sun. p 300.

Zoo. Park im. Lenina, 1. p 310.

Zoology Museum. Universitetskaya Nab., 1. Closed Mon. p 300.

Vocabulary

МУЗЕЙ	muzéy	museum
ВЫСТАВКА	výstafka	exhibition
КАРТИННАЯ ГАЛЕРЕЯ	kartínnaya galiréya	picture gallery
КАССА	kássa	ticket office
ГАРДЕРОБ	gardiróp	cloakroom
КАМЕРА ХРАНЕНИЯ	kámera khranéniya	cloakroom, left luggage
У вас есть каталог?	U vas yest katalók?	Do you have a catalogue?
экскурсовод	ikskursavót	guide
тапочки	tápochki	special overshoes which must be worn in some museums.
ЗАЛ	zal	hall, room
НАЧАЛО ОСМОТРА	nachála asmótra	beginning of the exhibition
ПРОДОЛЖЕНИЕ ОСМОТРА	pradalzhéniye asmótra	continuation of the exhibition
НЕ ТРОГАТЬ	ni trógat	do not touch
ЗАКРЫТ	zakryt	closed
НА РЕМОНТ	na rimónt	closed for repairs
В котором часу закрывается музей?	F katórom chisú zakryváyitsa muzéy?	When does the museum close?
Когда у вас выходной?	Kagdá u vas vykhadnóy?	On what day are you closed?
санитарный день	sanitárny den	special monthly day of closure

VIII   Use of Time

The following itineraries group together some of the most important sights. It is important to check in advance whether a particular place is open on a given day; museums, etc. tend to close on Mondays or Tuesdays, but there are many exceptions. A number of major museums are temporary closed for renovation.

Moscow Itinerary

1ST DAY: (a) The *Kremlin*, including the *cathedrals* and the *Armoury Palace* (p 82): it may be most convenient to arrange this through Intourist. (b) *Red Square* (p 110) and perhaps the nearby *Church of the Trinity* in Nikitniki (p 117).

2ND DAY: (a) *Tret'yakov Gallery* of Russian art (p 163). (b) *Kolomenskoye* (p 221), a former royal estate with a magnificent 16C church.

3RD DAY: (a) *New Convent of the Virgin* (Novodevichiy Convent) (p 146), a 17C Moscow Baroque monastery. (b) The *Tolstoy House* (p 145) and the nearby *Church of St. Nicholas* in Khamovniki (p 145). (c) *Pushkin Fine Art Gallery*, Moscow's gallery for Western art (p 138). (d) Lenin Hills; from here there is panoramic view of Moscow.

4TH DAY: Either (a) *Arkhangel'skoye* (p 227), a large former aristocratic estate in the W outskirts; or (b) the *Exhibition of Economic Achievements* (VDNKh) (p 196) and *Ostankino* (p 199), an 18C mansion now housing the *Museum of Serf Art*.

Special Interests

POLITICAL AND HISTORICAL: (a) *Lenin Mausoleum* (p 112). (b) *Historical Museum* (p 111). (c) *Lenin Museum* (p 125). (d) *Borodino Panorama* (p 188).

ART AND ARCHITECTURE: (a) *Don Monastery*, which now contains part of the *Shchusev Museum of Architecture* (p 149). (b) *Andronikov Monastery*, now the *Museum of Early Russian Art* (p 205), with its rich collection of icons. (c) *Tsaritsyno*, an unfinished Gothic palace complex (p 223).

LITERATURE AND THEATRE: (a) *Chekhov House* (p 180). (b) *Mayakovsky House* (p 126). (c) *Theatre and Music Museum* (p 178).

Leningrad Itinerary

1ST DAY: (a) *Peter-Paul Fortress* (p 305). (b) *Cabin of Peter the Great* (p 308). (c) *State Hermitage Museum* (p 243).

2ND DAY: (a) *St. Isaac's Cathedral* (p 238); the observation platform in the dome provides the best view of the city. (b) The *Bronze Horseman* (Peter I) in Pl. Dekabristov (p 241). (c) The *Summer Gardens* and the *Summer Palace* (not in winter) (p 283). (d) *State Hermitage Museum* (second visit).

3RD DAY: (a) *Russian Museum* of Russian art (p 267). (b) *Nevskiy Prospekt* (p 262); of special interest is the attractive detour along the *Griboyedov Canal*, which may be followed on foot as far as the *Cathedral of St. Nicholas* (Nikol'skiy Sobor) and the *Kirov Theatre*; another detour is to *Ploshchad' Ostrovskovo* and *Ulitsa Rossi* (p 274). (c) *Alexander Nevskiy Lavra* (p 278), with the *Trinity Cathedral* and the *graves of Dostoyevsky, Tchaikovsky*, and many other important Russians.

4TH DAY: One of the suburban former Imperial palaces; either (a) *Pushkin* (Tsarkoye Selo) (p 342); or (b) *Petrodvorets* (Peterhof) (p 336) (the famous Samson Fountain does not work in winter); or (c) *Pavlovsk* (p 351).

Special Interests

POLITICAL AND HISTORICAL: (a) *Smolny Institute* (no adm.) (p 297). (b) *Tauride Palace* (no adm.) (p 298). (c) *History of Leningrad Museum* (pp 242, 306). (d) *Piskaryovskoye Cemetery* (p 317), where the 1941–44 Blockade victims were buried. (e) *October Revolution Museum* (p 309).

ART AND ARCHITECTURE: (a) *Architecture Museum* (p 306), in the Peter-Paul Fortress. (b) Il'ya Repin's country house at *Repino* (p 358). (c) *Smolny Convent* (p 297).

LITERATURE AND THEATRE: (a) *Pushkin House* (p 331). (b) *Dostoyevsky House* (p 293). (c) *Theatre Museum* (p 274).

IX   General Hints

Weather. Moscow and Leningrad have a generally similar climate, with a warm summer and an extremely cold winter. Winter lasts from November to March, with temperatures in January, the coldest month, averaging 12°–23°F (−11°−−5°C) in Leningrad and 5°–14°F (−15°−−10°C) in Moscow. There can be heavy rainfall in July and August, and the combination of rain and thaw in the spring and autumn makes waterproof footwear essential. The summer months are pleasant, with a high average temperature in July of 57°–71°F (14°–22°C) in Leningrad and 54°–71°F (12°–22°C) in Moscow.

Things to take. For hotel-based tourists on short visits of one to three weeks the basic clothing and toilet requirements are the same as elsewhere. Warm outer clothing, including a heavy coat, a warm hat covering the ears, and stout waterproof shoes or boots are necessary in winter. The interior of buildings tends to be quite warm; note that outer clothing and boots must be left in cloakrooms in most public buildings, except shops and cinemas. Galoshes or waterproof shoes are necessary during the spring thaw or in the autumn. There may be wet spells in summer, so rainwear should be taken.

Electric current is 220v volt, but sockets normally take Continental-type pins; electric razors and hairdryers may need a plug adaptor.

Western film, proprietary medicines, and such items as sanitary towels, paper tissues, etc. are still not readily available, and visitors should take an adequate supply. Although the water in Moscow and Leningrad is drinkable, it may be advisable to use water purification tablets. Lavatory paper is seldom available outside hotels. Public lavatories can be very public and the standard of hygiene in these facilities can be low.

Other useful items are a rubber sink-stopper, plastic carrier bags, and pad and pencil to write down numbers, prices, etc. Small gifts for guides, hotel staff, etc. are often appreciated. Children like felt-tipped pens, badges, and chewing gum. The guides are often students who appreciate books in English.

Money. The amount of money required will vary, but on entering the USSR a declaration must be made of the sum involved (as well as of other valuables, such as jewellery). The Currency Declaration which is filled in on this occasion must be retained for presentation when leaving the country. Western currency may be changed into rubles in banks at the airport or hotel; the exchange slips should be kept. (Note that Scottish banknotes are not always accepted.)

Rubles may be changed back into Western currency only when leaving the USSR (e.g. at the airport). For this reason it may be inconvenient to change too much currency into rubles. Western currency can be used to book theatre and excursion tickets through Intourist or the hotel service bureau and must be used in the 'hard currency' 'Beriozka' shops (see below). (Major Western credit cards are also accepted.) Because the Beriozka shops do not always have Western small change it is advisable to carry some. Please note that the exchange of currency with private citizens outside the official channels is illegal, as is the sale of clothing, etc. Tourists may be approached by people interested in initiating such transactions outside hotels and in the main streets.

The ruble (рубль) is divided into 100 kopeks; the smallest coin is worth one kopek (копейка). Coins of 5k are useful for transport (20k, 15k, and 10k coins can be changed in machines at Metro stations); 2k pieces are useful for the telephone.

The ruble was drastically devalued in the autumn of 1989. At the time of writing the official rate of exchange is about 10 rubles to £ or 6 rubles to \$1.

Visas and General Regulations. Western visitors to the USSR must normally have a valid visa. This can be obtained from a Soviet consulate or through the tour operator. Regulations vary but it will usually be necessary to apply for a visa several weeks in advance and to submit a passport and photographs.

Visitors are generally free to move around within the city limits of Moscow and Leningrad, but may not currently travel more than 40km from the centres of the two cities. If in doubt one should check with Intourist, the hotel, etc.

The rules on photography are strict, and forbidden objects include not only military installations and personnel, but also ports, railways, bridges, some factories, etc. When in doubt it is best to ask permission.

Medicine. Doctor's visits and first aid treatment are free of charge, but visitors must pay for medicine and special hospital treatment.

At the time of writing it is not necessary for visitors from most Western countries to have vaccinations or other types of inoculation to enter the Soviet Union.

Major Public Holidays. 1 January, 8 March (International Women's Day), 1–2 May (May Day), 9 May (VE Day), 7 October (Constitution Day), 7–8 November (Anniversary of the 1917 Bolshevik Revolution).

Communications. At the time of writing (early 1990) the rates for sending letters abroad are 45k air mail and 15k surface, and for postcards 35k air mail and 10k surface. For internal post, the rates for letters are 6k by air and 4k by surface; postcards are 4k and 3k.

Local calls from public telephones cost 2k (2k coin; some machines take two 1k coins). Place the coin in the slot, pick up the receiver, and dial the number. Long buzzes indicate that the number is ringing; short buzzes indicate that it is engaged. Long-distance calls and calls abroad can be booked through the hotel service bureau.

Shopping. Tourists will probably be most interested in the type of shop called a 'Beriozka' ('Little Birch Tree'). Here the selection of consumer goods and souvenirs is much better than in normal Soviet shops. Payment is in 'hard', Western, currency, and the staff normally speak English. Most of the Intourist hotels have their own small Beriozkas, as do the international airports. In Moscow the largest Beriozkas are at the Rossiya Hotel (E side), opposite the New Convent of the Virgin (Luzhnetskiy Proyezd, 25), and at Kutuzovskiy Pr., 9. There is a Beriozka which specialises in books at Kropotkinskaya Ul., 31. In Leningrad there is a large Beriozka opposite the Pribaltiyskaya Hotel and another nearer the centre of town at Ul. Gertsena, 36. The Beriozkas close for an hour at lunch-time (usually 1–2).

Large conventional (ruble) department stores in central Moscow include *GUM* (in Red Square) and *TsUM* (behind the Bolshoy Theatre at Ul. Petrovka, 2). The major Moscow shopping streets, Pr. Kalinina and Tverskaya Ul., are also of interest, and Arbat Ul. has many interesting new co-operative shops. In Leningrad the main shopping street is Nevskiy Pr., and the best department stores *Gostinyy Dvor* (Nevskiy Pr., 35), *DLT* (Ul. Zhelyabova, 21–23), and *Passazh* (Nevskiy Pr., 48). These shops open at 10 and close at 9. The system here, as in other Soviet shops (excluding Beriozkas and some new supermarkets), is that the purchaser must decide what he or she wants to buy, find out the price, pay for the item at a central cash desk (kassa, КАССА), return to the original counter with a receipt, and pick up the item; this can mean standing in three queues.

The largest bookshops in Moscow and Leningrad are both called *Dom Knigi* (literally, House of the Book). The Moscow *Dom Knigi* is at Pr. Kalinina, 26, the Leningrad one at Nevskiy Pr., 28. Both also have poster departments. In Moscow there is a good poster shop at Arbat Ul., 4. There are large specialist record shops at Pr. Kalinina, 40, in Moscow, and at Nevskiy Pr., 34, in Leningrad.

'Antiques' of various ages can be bought at a government-run Commission Shop (komissionnyy magazin. КОМИССИОННЫЙ МАГАЗИН). In Moscow there are Commission Shops at Tverskaya Ul., 46, and Arbat Ul., 19 and 32; in Leningrad there is one at Nevskiy Pr., 52. Valuable antiques may carry an export duty of 100 percent and this is also true of old books.

Vocabulary

ГАСТРОНОМ	gastranóm	food shop
БУЛОЧНАЯ	búlachnaya	bakery
ОДЕЖДА	adézhda	clothes
КНИЖНЫЙ МАГАЗИН	knízhnyy magazín	bookshop
КНИГИ	knígi	books, bookshop
ПЛАКАТЫ	plakáty	posters
ГРАМПЛАСТИНКИ	gramplastínki	records
СУВЕНИРЫ	suvíniry	souvenirs
ДИАПОЗИТИВЫ	diapazitívy	slides (photographic)
Сколько это стоит?	Skólka eta stóit?	How much does this cost?
Покажите, пожалуйста.	Pakazhítye, pazhálsta.	Show me that, please.
Напишите, пожалуйста, цену	Napishítye, pazhálsta, tsénu	Please write down the price
ПЕРЕРЫВ НА ОБЕД	Pirirýf na abét	Closed for lunch
ЗАКРЫТ НА УЧЁТ	Zakrýt na uchót	Closed for stocktaking

Further reading. The following list concentrates for the most part on recent books in English.

Mark Frankland, *The Sixth Continent* (1987), and Martin Walker, *The Walking Giant: The Soviet Union under Gorbachev* (1986), provide an introduction to the modern USSR, but the 'Gorbachev Industry' is leading to many other surveys. The 1914 edition of Baedeker's *Russia*, re-issued by David & Charles in 1971, presents the best view of Russia on the eve of Revolution; its modern equivalent is Victor and Jennifer Louis, *Louis' Motorist's Guide to the Soviet Union* (1987) with descriptions of most of the major cities. The *Companion to Russian Studies*, edited by Robert Auty and Dimitri Obolensky and published by Cambridge University Press, is useful for general background: Vol. 1—*Introduction to Russian History* (1976), Vol. 2—*Introduction to Russian Language and Literature* (1971), Vol. 3—*Introduction to Russian Art and Architecture* (1981). Timothy Ware, *The Orthodox Church* (1969) is a readable short introduction to the Eastern Church in general. Of the many works on Russian history, Richard Pipes, *Russia under the Old Regime* (1974) is particularly interesting. Two inexpensive surveys of art are Tamara Talbot Rice, *A Concise History of Russian Art* (1963) and Camilla Gray, *The Russian Experiment in Art* (1962). Hubert Faensen and Vladimir Ivanov, *Early Russian Architecture* (1972) is large and expensive but unsurpassed on the period before 1700. William Brumfield, *Gold and Azure: One Thousand Years of Russian Architecture* (1983) is a beautifully illustrated survey. Natalia Roslavleva, *Era of the Russian Ballet* (1966) provides a broad survey, as does Herbert Marshall, *The Pictorial History of the Theatre* (1977).

On Moscow the most complete treatment of architecture is in *Moscow: Architectural Monuments* (Moskva: Pamyatniki Arkhitektury) published in four volumes from 1973 to 1977; there are large photographs of most important pre-revolutionary buildings, with captions and parallel text in English. Kathleen Berton, *Moscow: An Architectural History* (1977) is also good. The best directory available is *Information Moscow*, published twice a year by Mrs V.E. Louis (Leninskiy Pr., 45, kv. 426); this contains useful addresses and telephone numbers but is mainly a directory of embassy personnel.

The most complete work on Leningrad architecture, *Architectural Monuments of Leningrad* (Pamyatniki Arkhitektury Leningrada) (1969), includes explanatory notes in English. Audrey Kennett's beautifully illustrated *The Palaces of Leningrad* (1973) will probably be of more interest to the tourist, as it includes material on the outlying palaces.

Accurate maps of Moscow and Leningrad are only now being published in the USSR. Of Western-published maps, the German *Falk Plans* are sufficient for most purposes.

X   Russian Language

Russian is a difficult language, but it is easy to master the Russian (Cyrillic) alphabet, and a visitor who has done so will be far more independent. It is also not difficult to learn a few basic phrases.

This is not the place to go into the complexities of Russian grammar, but a few points might be noted.

Russian is an inflected language, so the endings and stress of words vary with the rôle they are playing. A noun and its adjectives can be in one of six cases. The genitive case is particularly common. Dvorets (дворец) means 'palace' and sport (спорт) means 'sport'; 'palace of sport' is dvorets sporta (дворец спорта). In masculine and neuter nouns -a or -ya (-а, -я) usually forms the genitive. For feminine nouns the genitive is usually formed by removing the final -a or -ya and adding -y or -i (-ы, -и). Thus 'culture' is kul'tura (культура) but 'palace of culture' is dvorets kul'tury (дворец культуры). Many street names use the genitive; 'Avenue (Prospekt) of Marx (Marks)' is Prospekt Marksa (Проспект Маркса).

Plurals are formed by adding -y, -i, or -a (ы, -и, -а). Thus 'ticket' is bilet (билет), 'tickets' is bilety (билеты).

Adjectives usually agree with the noun they modify. The masculine ending is -yy or -iy (-ый, -ий), the neuter -oye or -eye (-ое, -ее) and the feminine -aya or -yaya (-ая, -яя). The genitive endings of adjectives are -ovo or -evo (-ого, -его) for masculine and -oy or -ey (-ой, -ей) for feminine nouns. Proper names are often treated like adjectives, thus 'Street (Ulitsa) of Dostoyevsky' becomes Ulitsa Dostoyevskovo (Улица Достоевского).

Note also that Russian has no equivalent to 'a' or 'the' and that the present tense of 'to be' is omitted. Thus, one says simply 'Gde restoran?' (Где ресторан?), literally 'Where restaurant?', instead of 'Where is the restaurant?'.

Visitors to the Soviet Union may wish to take a proper phrase book. A good example is the Berlitz *Russian Phrase Book* (1987). Those interested in further details or in studying the Russian language on their own will find that considerable material is available. The BBC Russian courses include books, cassettes, and records and there is a similar Linguaphone course. Also useful are Michael Frewin, *Russian* (Teach Yourself Books, 1977), William Harrison, *et al.*, *Colloquial Russian* (1973), and J.L.I. Fennell, *The Penguin Russian Course* (1970).

Transliteration. The following transliteration system is used in the main text (the 'Routes') to put written Cyrillic names of streets, buildings, etc., into an equivalent written form with Latin letters. Russian is not, however, always pronounced as it is spelt. In particular, the value of unstressed vowels can change as can that of final consonants. In the Practical Notes the rendering in Latin letters is, in some instances, somewhat closer to the actual pronunciation; it should be clear when this second system is being used, as the stress is indicated. Thus выход (exit) would be strictly transliterated as vykhod, but is given in places in the Practical Notes as výkhat. The value of sounds in the second system is roughly the equivalent of that given below in the 'Cyrillic equivalents of transliteration'.

А	а	a	a as in father
Б	б	b	b as in boy
В	в	v	v as in vote
Г	г	g	g as in grab
Д	д	d	d as in do
Е	е	ye/e	ye as in yes
Ё	ё	yo/o	yo as in yonder
Ж	ж	zh	s as in treasure
З	з	z	z as in zero
И	и	i	ee as in meet
Й	й	y	y as in toy

К	к		k	k as in *k*iln
Л	л		l	l as in *l*earn
М	м		m	m as in *m*en
Н	н		n	n as in *n*o
О	о		o	o as in n*o*r
П	п		p	p as in *p*in
Р	р		r	r as in *r*un
С	с		s	s as in *s*un
Т	т		t	t as in *t*on
У	у		u	oo as in l*oo*t
Ф	ф		f	f as in *f*ull
Х	х		kh	ch as in lo*ch*
Ц	ц		ts	ts as in ca*ts*
Ч	ч		ch	ch as in *ch*air
Ш	ш		sh	sh as in *sh*ort
Щ	щ		shch	shch as in fre*sh ch*eese
Ъ	ъ		''	(hard sign)
Ы	ы		y	i as in p*i*t
Ь	ь		''	(soft sign)
Э	э		e	e as in p*e*t
Ю	ю		yu	u (yoo) as in *u*sual
Я	я		ya	ya as in *ya*rd

Cyrillic equivalents of transliteration

a	a as in f*a*ther	А/а
b	b as in *b*oy	Б/б
ch	ch as in *ch*air	Ч/ч
d	d as in *d*o	Д/д
e	ye as in *ye*s or e as in p*e*t	Е/е or Э/э
f	f as in *f*ull	Ф/ф
g	g as in *g*rab	Г/г
i	ee as in m*ee*t	И/и
k	k as in *k*iln	К/к
kh	kh as in lo*ch*	Х/х
l	l as in *l*earn	Л/л
m	m as in *m*en	М/м
n	n as in *n*o	Н/н
o	o as in n*o*r	О/о or Ё/ё
p	p as in *p*in	П/п
r	r as in *r*un	Р/р
s	s as in *s*un	С/с
sh	sh as in *sh*ort	Ш/ш
shch	shch as in fre*sh ch*eese	Щ/щ
t	t as in *t*on	Т/т
ts	ts as in ca*ts*	Ц/ц
u	oo as in l*oo*t	У/у
v	v as in *v*ote	В/в (or Г/г in -oro)
y	y as in t*o*y or i as in b*i*t	Й/й or Ы/ы
ya	ya as in *ya*rd	Я/я
ye	ye as in *ye*s	Е/е
yo	yo as in *yo*nder	Ё/ё
yu	u (yoo) as in *u*sual	Ю/ю
z	z as in *z*ero	З/з
zh	s as in trea*s*ure	Ж/ж
'	(soft sign)	Ь/ь
''	(hard sign)	Б/ъ

It is impossible to create a transliteration system which is both simple and accurate. The system used in the routes is a compromise, a slightly modified version of a standard British one. Note that ye is written for Cyrillic e at the beginning of words, after vowels, and after ъ and в. The Latin o is used for ё after ж, ч, ш, and щ. For many proper names the final -ый or -ий is simplified to -y. The modification introduced here is the use of v for the Cyrillic г in the genitive ending of adjectives, when it is pronounced as v rather than the usual g; this is very common in street names, e.g. Ул. Бродского becomes Ul. Brodskovo and not Ul. Brodskogo. The change was made to help those not familiar with the Russian language.

The transliteration system has been quite rigidly adhered to for local street names, etc., where the reader may wish to compare the transliterated version with a sign. It has been simplified in other cases where there is a generally accepted form, e.g. Olga rather than Ol'ga; Gorky rather than Gor'kiy; Smolny rather than Smol'nyy; Kazan rather than Kazan', etc. Russian capitalisation style has not been rigidly adhered to; for the names of theatres, museums, streets, etc. a form more familiar to English-speaking readers has been used (thus, Bol'shoy Dramaticheskiy Teatr, not Bol'shoy dramaticheskiy teatr).

In addition, the English translation has been used in many cases to make things easier. The names of churches and other buildings are given in their English equivalents (but followed by a transliteration). The English version of Russian first names has been used when this is common practice, but not otherwise. Thus, monarchs are given in an English form and most other people in a transliterated from, e.g. Emperor Alexander III but Aleksandr Ul'yanov. This is awkward, but there is no perfect solution.

Basic vocabulary

я не говорю по-русски.	Ya ni gavaryú pa-rússki	I don't speak Russian.
Кто здесь говорит…	Kto zdes gavarít…	Who speaks…
…по-английски?	…pa-anglíyski?	…English?
…по-французски?	…pa-frantsúski?	…French?
…по-немецки?	…pa-nimétski?	…German?
Вы говорите…	Vy gavarítye…	Do you speak…
…по-английски?	…pa-anglíyski?	…English?
…по-французски?	…pa-frantsúski?	…French?
…по-немецки?	…pa-nimétski	…German?
Позовите, пожалуйста, переводчика.	Pazavítye, pazhálsta, pirivótchika.	Please call an interpreter.
Как по-русски…	Kak pa-rússki…	What is the Russian for…
Здравствуйте	Zdrástvuytye	Hello
Доброе утро	Dóbraya útra	Good morning
До свидания	Dasvidániya	Good-bye
Спокойной ночи	Spakóyni nóchi	Good night
пожалуйста	Pazhálsta	Please (also, You're welcome)
Спасибо	Spasíba	Thank you
Да	Da	Yes
Нет	Nyet	No
Извините	Izvinítye	Excuse me
Можно?	Mózhna?	May I; is this permitted?
где	gde	where (is the…)
когда	kagdá	when
как	kak	how
сколько	skólka	how many
направо	napráva	on the right
налево	naléva	on the left

прямо	pryáma	straight ahead
хорошо	kharashó	O.K., good
ничего	nichivó	nothing, it doesn't matter
я	ya	I
он, она	on, aná	he, she
мы	my	we
вы	vy	you
они	aní	they
Как вас зовут?	Kak vas zavút	What is your name?
Молодой человек!/Девушка!	Maladóy chilavék!/Dévushka!	Young man!/Miss! (used to get the attention of someone, and not only of young people)
ТУАЛЕТ	Tualét	Lavatory
М (Мужской)	M (Muzhskóy)	Gentlemen
Ж (Женский)	Zh (Zhénskiy)	Ladies
НЕ КУРИТЬ!	Ni kurít!	No smoking. Smoking is forbidden on public transport, and in shops, theatres, etc.)
НЕЛЬЗЯ КУРИТЬ!	Nilzyá kurít!	''
КУРИТЬ ВОСПРЕЩ-АЕТСЯ!	Kurít vasprishcháitsa!	''
У НАС НЕ КУРЯТ	U nas ni kuryát	''
ПРОСЬБА НЕ КУРИТЬ	Prósba ni kurít	''
КУРИТЕЛЬНАЯ	Kurítilnaya	Smoking Room
К СЕБЕ	K sibyé	Pull
ОТ СЕБЯ	At sibyá	Push
ВХОД ВОСПРЕЩЁН!	Fkhod vasprishchón!	No admittance
НЕ ВХОДИТЬ!	Ni fkhodít!	''
ХОДА НЕТ!	Khoda net!	''
ВХОДА НЕТ!	Fkhoda net!	''
ПОСТОРОННИМ ВХОД ВОСПРЕЩЁН!	Pastarónnim fkhot vasprishchón!	''
ОКРАШЕНО!	Akráshena!	Wet Paint
ПО ГАЗОНАМ НЕ ХОДИТЬ!	Pa gazónam ne khadít!	Keep off the grass.
СТОЙТЕ	Stóitye	Stop
ИДИТЕ	Idítye	Go, cross
ПЕРЕХОД	Pirikhót	Crossing
понедельник	panidélnik	Monday
вторник	ftórnik	Tuesday
среда	sridá	Wednesday
четверг	chitvérk	Thursday
пятница	pyátnitsa	Friday
суббота	subbóta	Saturday
воскресенье	vaskrisénye	Sunday
сегодня	sivódnya	today
вчера	fchirá	yesterday
завтра	záftra	tomorrow

один, одно, одна/ первый (-ое, ая)	adín, adnó, adná/ pérvy (-oye, -aya)	one/first
два, две/второй	dva, dye/ftaróy	two/second
трн/третий	tri/tréti	three/third
четыре/четвёртый	chitýrye/ chitvyórty	four/fourth
пять/пятый	pyat/pyáty	five/fifth
шесть/шестой	shest/shistóy	six/sixth
семь/седьмой	sem/sidmóy	seven/seventh
восемь/восьмой	vósim/vasmóy	eight/eighth
девять/девятый	dévyat/divyáty	nine/ninth
десять/десятый	désyat/disyáty	ten/tenth
одиннадцать	adínnatsat	eleven
двенадцать	dvinátsat	twelve
тринадцать	trinátsat	thirteen
четырнадцать	chitýrnatsat	fourteen
пятнадцать	pitnátsat	fifteen
шестнадцать	shestnátsat	sixteen
семнадцать	simnátsat	seventeen
восемнадцать	vasimnátsat	eighteen
девятнадцать	divitnátsat	nineteen
двадцать	dvátsat	twenty
двадцать один	dvátsat adín	twenty-one
тридцать	trítsat	thirty
сорок	sórak	forty
пятьдесят	pidisyát	fifty
шестьдесят	shezdisyát	sixty
семьдесят	sémdisit	seventy
восемьдесят	vósimdisit	eighty
девяносто	divyanósta	ninety
сто	sto	one hundred

Glossary of Architectural and Historical Terms

ATTIC. The upper storey of a Classical building.
BLIND ARCADE. Wall decoration in the form of an arcade.
BOYAR. A senior nobleman of the Pre-Petrine era.
CIBORIUM. A canopy supported by columns.
CONSTRUCTIVISM. The Soviet name for the avant-garde architecture of the 1920s. It was akin to the International Modern.
DEËSIS. The central picture of an iconostasis: Christ Enthroned with the Virgin Mary and John the Baptist.
DRUM. Cylindrical element supporting a dome.
EARLY RUSSIAN. Concerning the period before Peter the Great (1682–1725).
ECLECTICISM. Architectural style based on a selection of historical styles; also called Historicism.
EMPIRE. Late Classicism.
GALLERY. External arcade.
HIPPED ROOF. Roof with sloping ends.
ICONOSTASIS. An icon wall. A tall partition covered with icons which separates the main body of the church from the sanctuary.

KOKOSHNIK. Ornamental or blind gable, usually semi-circular or ogee-shaped.

KREMLIN. Fortress.

LAVRA. A senior monastery.

LOGGIA. A gallery, usually with columns, open on one side.

MOSCOW BAROQUE. Late 17C architectural style containing elements of Baroque decoration.

NEO-RUSSIAN. Architectural style of c 1900 which attempted to revive the spirit of Early Russian building.

OGEE. Double curved line seen in gables, portals etc.

PALATA. Early Russian palace or mansion.

PEDIMENT. Triangular upper part of Classical building, often above a portico.

PILASTER. A column which is connected to the wall.

PODKLET. Ground floor of an Early Russian building.

PORTICO. Porch with columns.

PRE-PETRINE. Before Peter the Great (1682–1725).

PRIKAZ. Pre-Petrine government department or office.

PSEUDO-RUSSIAN. A form of Eclecticism which emerged in the mid-19C. In it elements of Early Russian architecture were combined with other historical styles.

REFECTORY. A large room attached to a church and used as a dining room.

ROYAL DOOR. The middle door of an iconostasis through which only the priest may pass.

SHATYOR. See 'Tent Roof'.

STREL'TSY. Musketeer auxiliary units of the Pre-Petrine army.

STYLE MODERNE. Term used in Russia for the architectural style known elsewhere as *Art Nouveau*. Also called simply 'Moderne'.

TENT ROOF. Roof in the form of a steep pyramid.

TEREM. Attic of an Early Russian building. Traditionally used by women and children.

ZAKOMARA. Semi-circular gable above a section of a wall.

MOSCOW

1 The Kremlin

The **Kremlin**, Moscow's castle, was the kernel from which the great city developed. The churches and palaces here have long been of the greatest historical and cultural importance, and the Kremlin is also the modern seat of the Soviet government.

One entrance is through the Trinity Gate on the NW side (Pl. 4: 6). The exits of the BIBLIOTEKA IMENI LENINA, ARBATSKAYA, and KALININSKAYA METRO STATIONS are nearby, on the corner of Pr. Kalinina and Pr. Marksa. Visitors may also enter the Kremlin through the Borovitskiye Gate at the SW corner. Tickets for the cathedrals and museums can be bought at one of the ticket offices in the Alexander Gardens (next to the Trinity Gate), but visitors with limited time may prefer to book a conducted tour through Intourist.

Much of what Lermontov wrote about the Kremlin in 1833 remains true today: 'What can compare to the Kremlin which, having ringed itself with crenellated walls and adorned itself with the golden domes of the cathedrals, sits on a high hill like the crown of sovereignty on the brow of an awesome ruler.' 'No,' he concluded, 'neither the Kremlin, nor its crenellated walls, nor its dark passages, nor the splendid palaces can be described. They must be seen, they must be seen. One must feel all that they say to the heart and the imagination.'

History. The Borovitskiy Hill (Pine Grove Hill) at the confluence of the Moskva and Neglinnaya Rivers was well-suited to defence. There was considerable settlement of people here even before 1147—the first reference to Moscow in the chronicles—and this may date back to as early as 500 BC. In 1156 Prince Yury Dolgoruky extended the walls and despite many setbacks, most notably its sacking by the Mongols in 1237–38, the castle continued to develop. Soon after the arrival of Metropolitan Peter in the early 14C the first stone churches were built, none of which survives. The 'White Stone' Kremlin originated in the 1360s, during the minority of Dmitry Donskoy, when limestone walls replaced the existing oak ones. By this time the Kremlin had almost reached its present size of 28 ha.

The modern Kremlin dates from the end of the 15C and the beginning of the 16C, a time of remarkable building activity which coincided with the unification of Russia under Ivan III (1462–1505). Italian master-builders summoned by Ivan supervised the construction of the present walls and towers (1485–95); the Kremlin, with its rounded corner towers and swallow-tailed merlons, was really a North Italian fortress erected in the heart of Russia. Most of the Kremlin's surviving early buildings were also designed by Italians: Aristotle Fioravanti's Cathedral of the Assumption (1475–79), Marco Ruffo and Pietro Solario's Granovitaya Palace (1487–91), Alevisio Novi's Cathedral of the Archangel (1505–08), and Antonio Fryazin's Ivan the Great Bell Tower (1505–08, later enlarged). Two other churches date from this era, the Cathedral of the Annunciation (1484) and the Church of the Deposition of the Robe (1484–86); these were the work of master builders from Pskov.

The century which followed added little to the Kremlin. The great fire of 1547 was the worst of a series that ravaged the Kremlin, and at the beginning of the 17C came the Time of Troubles. In the last stages the Poles were besieged inside the Kremlin; they surrendered the ruins of the fortress in October 1612. The remainder of the 17C—the last century of Muscovy—was more stable, however, and the building of the Kremlin was resumed. The Terem Palace (1635–36) was built during the reign of Mikhail Romanov, and the Kremlin defences began to take on a more uniquely Russian appearance with the addition of a tent roof to the Saviour Tower (1628). Tent roofs were added to the other towers in the 1680s. The Patriarch's Palace and the last of the surviving great Kremlin churches, the Cathedral of the Twelve Apostles (1645–55), were added during the era of Patriarch Nikon.

With the transfer of the court to St. Petersburg at the start of the 18C the Kremlin fell into neglect. The Emperors and Empresses lived in the northern capital, and the Kremlin was used mainly for traditional ceremonies like the coronation. Nevertheless Catherine the Great, the most foreign of Russia's rulers, took an interest in the place and instructed her favourite architect V.I. Bazhenov to replan it completely. Bazhenov proposed the construction of a huge four-storey Classical palace and new administrative buildings. The palace was to stretch 630m along the brow of the Kremlin hill, overlooking the river and enclosing the existing cathedrals. A number of valuable buildings were knocked down to clear the site, but in 1775 the Empress lost interest and nothing was actually built. There is a large model of Bazhenov's project in the Don Monastery branch of the Shchusev Museum of Architecture. A more modest project was worked out by M.F. Kazakov in 1797, but this also was not realised. Earlier, however, Kazakov did complete the Classical building of the Senate (1776–90) to the E of the Arsenal.

The next great event in the history of the Kremlin was its occupation by the French in 1812. The buildings and palaces were looted, and when Napoleon decided to leave Moscow he ordered that the Kremlin be blown up. Fortunately, on the appointed night of 11 October a heavy downpour and the prompt arrival of Russian troops prevented many of the planned explosions, but three towers, part of the wall, and much of the Arsenal were destroyed; the Ivan the Great Bell Tower was badly damaged. Restoration work on the Kremlin began in 1815 and was only completed twenty years later. During these years the Kremlin lost part of its defences; the Neglinnaya River was buried in a conduit under the new Alexander Gardens, and the moat in Red Square was filled in.

The first half of the 19C saw the completion of the buildings which still dominate the SW part of the Kremlin, the Great Kremlin Palace (1838–49) and the new Armoury Palace (1844–51), but after the reign of Nicholas I the main work was in the sphere of restoration. The only new structure was a Gothic monument to Alexander II (1898), and this has been demolished.

The Bolshevik Revolution brought the Kremlin back to the centre of Russian history. The garrison were sympathetic to the new Soviet regime, but on 28 October troops loyal to the Kerensky government regained control of the vital fortress. The Kremlin was finally taken by storm at dawn on 3 November. The Reds had shelled the Kremlin for several days, and the first Soviet Commissar of Education, Lunacharsky, resigned in protest at this destruction of the national heritage. Fortunately the early reports of destruction turned out to be exaggerated, although several of the churches had been hit; Lunacharsky returned to his post.

The Soviet government moved to Moscow in March 1918 and made the Kremlin its central headquarters. The new situation naturally led to changes. Some were symbolic: the double-headed Romanov eagles were removed from the principal towers in 1935 and were replaced first by metal stars and then, in 1937, by huge illuminated stars made of red glass (the largest is 3.75m across and weighs 1.5 tons). Other changes were more substantial. The Nicholas Palace and the Monasteries of the Assumption and of the Miracles, which formed a complex of buildings on the E side of the Kremlin, were torn down in 1929 to make way for a military school, now the Presidium of the Supreme Soviet (1932–34). The interior of the Great Kremlin Palace was much altered to create a meeting place for the Supreme Soviet; the Church of the Saviour in the courtyard was destroyed for the same purpose. Finally, and most recently, the giant Palace of Congresses (1960–61) was built in the area NW of the Kremlin cathedrals.

As the centre of the Soviet government the Kremlin was for some years closed to the general public. It was reopened on 20 July 1955 and is now visited by as many as 60,000 people a day.

The Kremlin was built as a fortress, and the towers and walls are of great interest. The white **Kutaf'ya Tower** (Bashnya), in front of the Trinity Gate, is the last survivor of a number of watch-towers protecting the outer ends of the Kremlin bridges. It dates from the early 16C, but the decorative parapet which gives it a unique appearance was added in the 17C. A brick bridge was built across the Neglinnaya River here in 1516 by Alevisio Novi; the present version is a later reconstruction (1901). The bridge leads to the

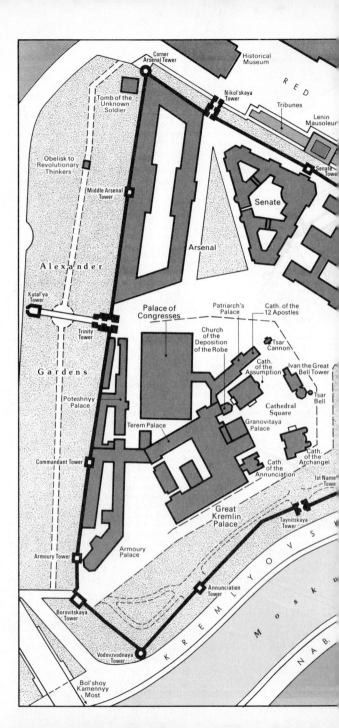

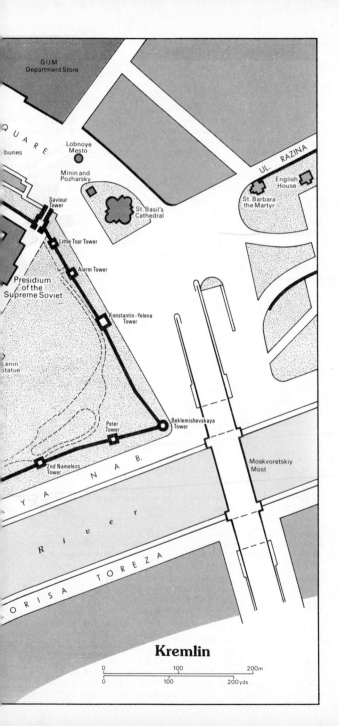

GUM
Department Store

QUARE

bunes

Lobnoye
Mesto

UL. RAZINA

Minin and
Pozharsky

English
House

Saviour
Tower

St. Basil's
Cathedral

St. Barbara
the Martyr

Little Tsar Tower

Alarm Tower

Presidium
of the
Supreme Soviet

Konstantin-Yelena
Tower

Lenin
Statue

Beklemishevskaya
Tower

Peter
Tower

Moskvoretskiy
Most

2nd Nameless
Tower

Y A   N A B.

R i v e r

R i

O R I S A   T O R E Z A

Kremlin

0   100   200m

0   100   200yds

***Trinity Tower** (Troitskaya Bashnya) (1495), which is 80m high and the tallest in the Kremlin; a tall tent roof rises from the rectangular brick mass of the base.

The approach to the Trinity Tower provides a good vantage point for looking at the W wall. The total length of the **Kremlin wall**, (including all sides of the triangle), is 2235m. It ranges in height from 5 to 19m and in thickness from 3.5 to 6.5m. There are 1045 swallow-tailed merlons running along the top of the wall, each from 2 to 2.5m high. These protected a walkway some 2 to 2.5m wide which until the great fire of 1737 was covered by a wooden roof. There are 19 towers along the Kremlin wall (excluding the outlying Kutaf'ya tower), of which six protected the W side. To the left of the Trinity Tower stands the smaller **Middle Arsenal Tower** (Alevisio Novi, 1495) and beyond, at the N corner, the round **Corner Arsenal Tower** or Sobakina Tower, begun by Pietro Solario in 1492. The **Commandant Tower** (1495) is to the right of the Trinity Tower and beyond it stands the **Armoury Tower** (Oruzheynaya Bashnya) (1495). In the SW corner rises Solario's tiered ***Borovitskaya Tower** (1490), where there is another entrance gate into the Kremlin grounds; the tower's name goes back to the pine-grove (bor) covered hillock where the Kremlin was first founded.

The Trinity Gate leads into the precincts of the Kremlin; Napoleon entered through here in 1812. To the right beyond the gates stands the giant **Palace of Congresses** (Kremlyovskiy Dvorets S''yezdov), built in 1960–61 by a team of architects led by M.V. Posokhin; the palace, in the International Modern style, makes extensive use of glass in the façade. The building with its great hall capable of seating 6000 people was intended to serve two major functions. First, it provided a long-needed purpose-built hall for major political meetings; the palace was opened for the 22nd Congress of the Communist Party of the Soviet Union (1961) and all subsequent Party congresses have been held here. This is the reason why the coat of arms of the Soviet Union is mounted at the top of the façade and why the foyer is decorated with the crests of the various republics. In 1989 the building was used for the first sessions of the Congress of Peoples Deputies. Second, the palace is normally open to the public as a theatre, and provides a second stage for the opera and ballet companies of the Bolshoy Theatre.

Plans for some great Palace of Soviets had been considered for decades, but only in the Khrushchev period were they realised, and then in the surprisingly short period of less than two years. Construction necessitated the demolition of a number of old Kremlin service buildings. The most notable were the former barracks of the Tsarist Yekaterinoslav Regiment, built originally in 1806–12 by Yegotov as the old Armoury Palace; also destroyed were the Officers Buildings, the Grenadier Building, the Kitchens, part of the Kavalerskiy Building, and an 18C wing of Kazakov's Synodal.

Several historically interesting buildings are visible down the narrow KOMMUNISTICHESKAYA UL., which runs between the Palace of Congresses and the Kremlin wall (no adm.). Part of the Kavalerskiy Building, used at one time by gentlemen-in-waiting, remains (left). Lenin stayed here from 19 to 28 March 1918 after he first moved into the Kremlin, and Trotsky lived here during the Civil War and in the early 1920s. Stalin had his private apartments in the **Poteshnyy Palace** across the road; here his wife Nadezhda Alliluyeva shot herself in 1932. The picturesque orange palace with a protruding bay at the fourth-storey level is a rare surviving example of mid-17C secular architecture and was once owned by the Miloslavsky boyars.

It was taken over and used for court 'amusements' (potekhi), including the first royal theatre, under Tsar Aleksey Mikhaylovich.

The N part of the Kremlin precincts, the zone to the left of the Trinity Gate, is closed to the general public. The buildings here include the former Arsenal and Senate, and also the Presidium of the Supreme Soviet. This is the centre of the Soviet government.

The NW part of the Kremlin was at one time full of the houses of boyars, churchmen, and monasteries, arranged haphazardly along the narrow Zhitnitskaya and Nikol'skaya Streets. These were gradually demolished and then, at the beginning of the 18C, Peter the Great began the construction of the **Arsenal** here. The successful outcome of the Great Northern War meant that an arsenal was not so urgently needed, and the work was only completed in 1736. This is one of Moscow's few surviving secular buildings from this period; it has, however, been rebuilt several times, most recently by Bove in the 1830s.

Ranged along the S façade are Russian artillery pieces from the 16C and 17C and the barrels of some 800 guns captured during the Napoleonic Wars. In 1927 a plaque was hung to the right of the entrance with 23 names and the following inscription: 'Here the officer cadets shot the comrade-soldiers of the Kremlin Arsenal during the defence of the Kremlin in the October Days (28 October 1917)'. To the left is another plaque commemorating members of the Kremlin garrison killed during German air raids in the Second World War.

The **Nikol'skaya Tower**, at the far end of the Arsenal, was built by Pietro Solario in 1491. Badly damaged by the French in 1812, it was rebuilt with a Gothic tower in 1817–18. The forces of Minin and Pozharsky broke into the Polish-occupied Kremlin through the Nikol'skiye Gate here in 1612, and three centuries later the Bolsheviks stormed the same gate to retake the citadel from the officer cadets defending it (the exterior of the tower was badly damaged during the bombardment). A monument by Vasnetsov in the shape of a Russian cross once stood just inside the gate. It commemorated Grand Duke Sergey Aleksandrovich (1857–1905), Governor-General of Moscow and uncle and brother-in-law of Nicholas II, who was blown to pieces here by a Socialist-Revolutionary's bomb.

The handsome yellow triangular building opposite the Arsenal was built for the *•Senate (more exactly, for its Moscow branch; the main Senate building was in St. Petersburg). Built to the plans of Kazakov between 1776 and 1790, and one of the first major commissions of that noted architect, the Senate is among Moscow's finest Classical buildings; Kazakov himself believed it to be his best work. The building served from the middle of the 19C as the *Court Offices* (Zdaniye Sudebnykh Ustanovleniy) and from March 1918 as the central headquarters of the Soviet government. Because of its important function it is not accessible to the public.

The four-columned portico on the W façade (opposite the Arsenal) contains an arch leading into a courtyard, and from here a path leads towards a rotunda in the E corner. The *Sverdlov Hall,* formerly the Catherine Hall, is located here, a round blue and white hall some 27m high. The rich decoration includes 18 bas-reliefs by G.T. Zamarayev flanked by Corinthian columns; a bust of Lenin by Merkurov is contained in a niche (earlier there was a bust of Alexander II here). The roof of the hall spans 25m, and the wide green dome above is visible from Red Square.

When the Soviet government moved to Moscow in March 1918 its cabinet, the Council of People's Commissars (Sovnarkom) (later the Council of Ministers), was established in the former Senate. The People's Commissars (Ministers) and the Politburo of the Communist Party met until 1958 in a long office on the top floor, near the S corner; the most important government and Party meetings are still held in this building. Lenin, as Chairman of the Council of People's Commissars, had offices in the Senate building and lived here with his wife and sister. These rooms, preserved as a museum, are only open to special groups, but there is a replica of Lenin's office in the Central Lenin Museum. On top of one of the interior wings is preserved a wooden veranda built for Lenin in 1923 after his illness. Stalin worked in this building and after 1932 had a cramped apartment on the 1st Floor (he also spent much time at a dacha in Kuntsevo). The Senate building housed the supreme command of the Red Army, the Stavka, during the Second World War; here Stalin, as Supreme Commander-in-Chief, worked out Soviet strategy with his marshals. Churchill and a number of other Allied leaders were received in this building during the war years.

The 8th (1919), 9th (1920), 10th (1921), and 11th (1922) Congresses of the Russian Communist Party were held in the *Sverdlov Hall*, which is named after the Communist leader who died in 1919. Important meetings are still held here, including sessions of the Council of Ministers and plena of the Central Committee of the Communist Party. In the *Oval Hall*, formerly the Mitrofan'yevskiy Hall, took place the 1st Congress of the Comintern in March 1919.

To the SE of the Senate, still in the closed part of the Kremlin, stands another Classical structure, built in 1932–34 by I.I. Rerberg for the *Military School of the Central Executive Committee* (Voyennaya Shkola im. VTsIK). The school was set up in December 1917 for the training of 'Red Commanders'; a small granite obelisk near the Arsenal commemorates young Red Commanders killed during the Civil War. In 1938, the building assumed its present function as the offices of the **Presidium of the Supreme Soviet** (no adm.). Here also is located the 1200-seat *Kremlin Theatre* (Kremlyovskiy Teatr), which was added in 1958.

A number of historic buildings were knocked down in 1929 to make room for the Military School. Near the NE wall of the Kremlin, by the Saviour Tower, stood the Convent of the Ascension (Voznesenskiy Monastyr'), founded in 1393 by Princess Yevdokiya, widow of Dmitry Donskoy. Many daughters of the royal family were forced to take vows here, as for centuries there were no foreign Orthodox rulers whom they could wed. In addition, the widows of the Moscow princes often withdrew to the Ascension Convent; among them was Yevdokiya herself.

The cathedral of the convent was rebuilt by Alevisio Novi in the early 16C on the burial place of the female members of the royal family. Here were buried Princess Yevdokiya, Sof'ya Paleologue (wife of Ivan III), Yelena Glinskaya (mother of Ivan the Terrible), and Natal'ya Naryshkina (mother of Peter the Great); their remains were transferred to the Archangel Cathedral after 1929. Just next to the Saviour Gate stood the striking Gothic Church of St. Catherine, built to the designs of Carlo Rossi in 1809–17.

To the W, and bounded on the N by the Senate, stood the Monastery of the Miracles (Chudov Monastery), founded in 1358 on what was said to be land occupied by the embassy of the Golden Horde. According to legend the first False Dmitry of the Time of Troubles was actually a monk named Grishka Otrep'yev from the Monastery of the Miracles; the first act of Mussorgsky's opera 'Boris Godunov' is set in Otrep'yev's cell. Later in this terrible period Tsar Vasily Shuysky was forced to enter the monastery after he had been deposed in 1610, and two years later Patriarch Hermogenes starved to death here while in Polish captivity. Another famous Patriarch, Nikon, was deposed by a church council which met here in 1667. Two great Russian Emperors, Peter I and Alexander II, were baptised in the Monastery of the Miracles. The outstanding building was the Cathedral of the Miracle of the Archangel Michael (Sobor Chuda Mikhaila Arkhangela), built in 1501–04.

The final building destroyed in this area was the Small Nicholas Palace, a Classical structure built by Kazakov in 1775–76 and intended as a bishop's residence. It was bought by the state, enlarged, and used as a residence by Grand Duke Nicholas Pavlovich, later Nicholas I; the future Alexander II was born here in 1818. The palace and the Church of St. Catherine (of the Ascension Convent) flanked the old ceremonial entrance into the Kremlin, the Saviour Gate.

The first historic feature of the southern, accessible, part of the Kremlin grounds is opposite the Senate—the *Tsar Cannon (Tsar'-Pushka). This was cast by the master Andrey Chokhov in 1586; on the barrel is a portrait of the reigning Tsar Fyodor, son of Ivan the Terrible. One of the largest cannon ever made, it weighs some 39,000kg and has a barrel 5.3m long and a bore of 890mm. It was intended to be part of the defences of the Kremlin's Saviour Gate, but it has probably never been fired. The ornate carriage dates from 1835.

The five-domed building behind the cannon is the ***Cathedral of the Twelve Apostles**** (Sobor Dvenadtsati Apostolov) which, with the former ***Patriarch's Palace** (Patriarshiye Palaty), forms one long structure running NE–SW and is the NW boundary of the most historic surviving part of the Kremlin, CATHEDRAL SQUARE (Dvortsovaya Pl.). The cathedral and palace contain the exhibits of the **Museum of 17th Century Life and Applied Art** (Muzey Prikladnovo Iskusstva i Byta XVII Veka).

Despite a certain similarity to the other Kremlin churches, the cathedral and palace were actually built a century and a half later. Nevertheless, the history of the two buildings goes back to the early 14C when Prince Ivan Kalita granted this plot of the Kremlin to Metropolitan Peter. The first stone palace was completed for Metropolitan Jonah in 1450, and after a Russian Patriarchate was established at the end of the 16C the Patriarch lived here.

Work on the present version actually began in the 1640s, but it is most closely associated with the man who became the head of the Russian Church in 1652, Patriarch Nikon (born 1605, died 1681). Nikon was a forceful character who attempted both to reform the Church and to assert its primacy over the state; the first policy helped precipitate the Schism and the second policy proved to be his undoing. Tsar Aleksey Mikhaylovich parried the threat to his autocracy, Nikon withdrew from Moscow (1658), and in 1666 he was deposed. Despite his short active reign Nikon had a considerable influence on architecture, partly because of his desire to project the power of the Church through building. This is evident in the cathedral and the Patriarch's Palace, whose scale and conservative design reflect Nikon's taste.

The buildings were begun in 1645 by the builder D.L. Okhlebinin; they were completed in 1655, but considerable alterations were made in 1680 after a serious fire. With the end of the Russian Patriarchate at the beginning of the 18C the palace was occupied by the Moscow offices of the Holy Synod and was known as the Sinodal'nyy Dom. It was altered over the years and only restored in the Soviet period.

The most notable features of the **Exterior** are the five silver domes and three rounded gables of the *Cathedral of the Twelve Apostles*. The 'conventional' appearance of the cathedral reflects Patriarch Nikon's desire to return to the traditional principles of church architecture embodied in the Kremlin by the Cathedral of the Assumption. It is set above two archways which once served as a ceremonial entrance to Cathedral Square from the N. The cathedral itself was at 1st Floor level, and it was regarded as improper to put the space beneath to residential or other worldly use. The S façade, on Cathedral Square, is more elaborate than that on the N and decorated with two rows of blind arcading. The gallery and arcade on the N side once extended around the building.

The former *Patriarch's Palace* to the SW is externally plain, and the Cathedral of the Assumption hides most of the S façade; the main decoration consists of the window surrounds. The palace is really two interconnected buildings, a three-storey part next to the cathedral, and a two-storey part farther W. The two-storey Sinodal'nyy Korpus, an extension to the NW, was demolished to make room for the Palace of Congresses; it had been built by M.F. Kazakov in the 18C.

The **Interior** of the palace and the cathedral may be entered through a door on the S side of the Patriarch's Palace and up stairs to the 1st Floor. To the left (W) at the top of the stairs is the *Krestovaya Palata* (Cross Chamber). It measures 19m by 13m and at the time of its construction was the largest room in Russia without supporting columns; the roof takes the form of a shallow vault. At first this magnificent room served for banquets and receptions, and later it was used for the preparation of miro or consecrated oil, hence its other name, the Mirovarnaya Palata. One prominent feature of the chamber is the large stove (mirovareniye) in which the oil was made; the stove was a gift from Catherine II. The chamber now houses most of the museum of applied art, with exhibits from the Armoury Palace collection. On display are objects of gold and silver, utensils, decorated Bibles, embroidery, etc. Many of these items were made in the Kremlin workshops although some, such as the clocks, came from Germany.

The *Cathedral of the Twelve Apostles* is located to the right of the stairs and past a small room with more applied art. The gold Moscow Baroque iconostasis dates from about 1700 and was moved here from the now-demolished Convent of the Ascension. A small window high on the W wall looks down on the cathedral from the Chapel of St. Philip on the 2nd Floor. From there the Patriarch could watch the service without entering the cathedral; his private chambers were located nearby. The robes of the Patriarch are on display in the cathedral, as well as a curious book-shaped cupboard used for storing holy wine.

The splendid white ***Ivan the Great Bell Tower** (Kolokol'nya Ivana Velikovo), with its two golden domes, forms the NE boundary of Cathedral Square. The main *Bell Tower* (Kolokol'nya) at the S end (nearest the river) is the oldest part of the structure. A stone church-cum-bell tower dedicated to St. John Climacus (Ivan Lestvichnik) was built on this site in 1329; it fell into disrepair and in 1505–08, just after the reign of Tsar Ivan III ('the Great') was replaced. The Italian architect Marco Bono (Bon Fryazin) created a tower in the form of two octagonal tiers crowned with a dome on a circular drum; this served not only as a place of worship but also as a strategic watch-tower.

The Bell Tower was increased to its final height of 81m by the ill-fated Boris Godunov in 1600. Around the top of the drum, gold letters spell out the following inscription: 'By the will of the Holy Trinity, by the command of the Great Lord, Tsar, and Grand Prince Boris Fyodorovich, Autocrat of All Russia, and of his son, the Orthodox Great Lord Fyodor Borisovich [1589–1605], Tsarevich and Prince of All Russia, this church was completed and gilded in the second year of their reign.' The extension of the Bell Tower was partly intended to provide work at a time of great economic crisis.

The third octagonal tier is crowned by two rows of kokoshnik gables, which make the transition to the circular drum. The gilded onion dome surmounted what was for many years the tallest structure in Russia. It could be seen from a distance of 30km and dominated the skyline of old Moscow. The name 'Ivan the Great' dates from the time of its completion. This is still one of Moscow's great landmarks.

The central part, or *Belfry* (Zvonnitsa), was added to the N of the original Bell Tower in 1532–43. Petrok Malyy created a four-storey structure along Novgorodian lines, but incorporating Italian Renaissance details in its external decoration (such as the window surrounds and pilasters). Below the onion dome with its drum and two tiers of columns hangs the 65,000kg 19C Voskresenskiy (Resurrection) Bell, the largest of 21. The tier below the bells contained the Church of the Nativity (Rozhdestvenskaya Ts.), which could be reached via the external staircase on the Cathedral Square (W) side. The rich Synodal Treasury or Sacristy (Riznitsa) once occupied the floor below. An exhibition hall in the base of the central part is sometimes used to display the treasures of the Kremlin museums.

The final (N) part, known as the *Filaret Annexe* (Filaretovskaya Pristroyka), dates from 1624 and was originally designed by Bazhen Ogurtsev. The rectangular tent-roofed annexe takes its name from the man who commissioned it, Patriarch Filaret (the father of Tsar Mikhail). In 1812, when the French left the Kremlin, they attempted to blow up the whole building, but fortunately only the Filaret Annexe was badly damaged (Napoleon's soldiers also tore down the great cross and left a crack in the Bell Tower). The present appearance of the annexe reflects its early 19C reconstruction to the plans of I.V. Yegotov and L. Rusca.

The **Tsar Bell** (Tsar'-Kolokol) is on display at the foot of the Bell Tower. At 201,900kg it is the world's largest bell (in comparison, London's 'Big Ben' weighs 13,700kg). On the bell, which measures 6.14m in height and 6.6m in diameter, are portrayed Tsar Aleksey Mikhaylovich and Empress Anna Ivanovna. The first, 130,000kg version was created in 1655, during Aleksey's reign; according to some sources, part of the metal used came from the Novgorod Vech' Bell. The great bell was actually rung, although it took 19 years from the time it was cast to discover a means of raising it to its special belfry and then in the fire of 1701 it fell to earth and shattered. Thirty years later Empress Anna decided to use the remains for a new and much larger bell. This was completed in 1735, the work of the masters Ivan and Mikhail Motorin. A new bell tower would have been required (as the bell was too large for the existing belfry) and the raising of the bell would have presented enormous engineering problems, but in fact more than a century was to pass before the Tsar Bell left the pit in which it had been cast. In 1737 fire again swept the Kremlin, and when water was poured on the still-hot bell it cracked, and an 11,500kg piece broke off. It was finally unearthed in 1836, at the instigation of the French architect Montferrand (who designed St. Isaac's Cathedral in Leningrad), and has been on display ever since.

The massive ****Cathedral of the Assumption** (Uspenskiy Sobor), with its five gilded domes, stands to the W of the Bell Tower, in the heart of Cathedral Square. This was the most important church in pre-revolutionary Russia, the burial place of Metropolitans and Patriarchs and the setting for the coronations of Grand Princes, Tsars, and Emperors.

One of the most important feasts of the Orthodox Church is that of the Uspeniye or Assumption (into heaven) of the Virgin Mary (this feast is also known as the Dormition). A small limestone Cathedral of the Assumption was erected on this site in 1326 by Grand Prince Ivan Kalita, at the suggestion of Metropolitan Peter. Although it housed the revered icon of the Virgin of Vladimir, this church had fallen into disrepair by the 1470s. Grand Prince Ivan III and Metropolitan Philip decided to replace it with a new cathedral, one which would be worthy of the growing might of Muscovy. A large church was duly begun under the supervision of two local craftsmen, but it collapsed before completion. The mortar used was too thin, and according to the Chronicles there was an earth tremor. After this fiasco Ivan III enlisted the services of an architect from Bologna known as Aristotle Fioravanti. The Italian arrived in 1475, bringing from the West both new engineering techniques and new architectural forms. Nevertheless, during the winter of 1475–76, having already laid the foundations some 4m deep, Fioravanti set out on a visit to the ancient Russian cities of Novgorod, Suzdal, and Vladimir to acquaint himself with the Russian architectural tradition. This tour was on the instructions of the Tsar himself, who had told his new architect to study in particular the Cathedral of the Assumption at Vladimir. It was to serve as a model for the new Kremlin cathedral and show that Moscow, now in the ascendant, intended to continue the tradition of the ancient Russian cities. The creation of the Cathedral of the Assumption took only four years (1475–79), and its design combined features of the Vladimir cathedral with some features of W European architecture. Fioravanti adapted to the tradition so well that two centuries later the traditionalist Patriarch Nikon told architects to use his cathedral as a model.

The Cathedral of the Assumption was the scene of many important events in the history of Russia. The coronations of her rulers took place here; the last of these great ceremonies, for Nicholas II, occurred in 1896. Here Ivan III publicly destroyed the charter under which the Russian princes paid taxes to the Tatar khans, and thus he symbolically brought to an end the Tatar Yoke. The final occasion when the cathedral was the centre of national attention came immediately after the outbreak of the First World War, when a Te Deum was sung here in the presence of the Imperial family, three Metropolitans, and 12 Archbishops.

The cathedral is rectangular in form with entrances on all but the E side. The **Exterior** is divided vertically by pilasters into equal sections, each ending in a semi-circular gable; there are four sections to the N and S, and three to the E and W. The façades are divided horizontally by blind arcading. Each vertical section has two slit-windows, the lower almost concealed in the blind arcading, the upper just under the gable.

The main *S façade* overlooking Cathedral Square has a fine arched portal surrounded by frescoes. These were painted in the 1660s and restored by artists from Palekh in 1952. Flanking the doorway itself are paintings of the archangels, and within the blind arcading are portraits of bishops; the Virgin Mary is depicted above. The royal processions came from the Granovitaya Palace (via the now-demolished Red Staircase) and entered the cathedral through this portal.

The five apses at the E end are well integrated into the overall symmetry, being partly concealed from Cathedral Square by one of the projecting corners. Murals cover the area between the apses and the roof.

The cathedral is crowned with five helmet-shaped golden domes; the central one is, by tradition, larger than the others. The domes are set on massive drums with slit windows.

The **Interior** is noted for its relative lightness and spaciousness, quite untypical of contemporary Russian churches. The number of windows, the absence of a choir gallery, and the distribution of four equidistant circular pillars help to explain this. The cathedral has been repainted and restored several times, having suffered particularly during the occupation by the Poles in the early 17C and by the French in 1812. The frescoes were cleaned and restored in 1949–50, and restoration work was continued throughout the 1960s and 1970s.

The original *Frescoes* were created by a group of painters led by the celebrated Dionysius (c 1440–1502/08). The work was completed in 1515, and a few frescoes from this period have survived. The row of saints on the stone altar screen and the fresco of the Adoration of

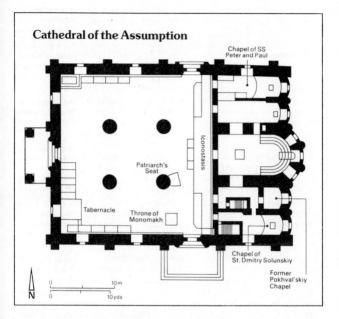

the Magi in the former *Pokhval'skiy Chapel* (in the second apse from the S) are attributed to Dionysius, while fragments in the *Chapel of SS. Peter and Paul* (Pridel Petra i Pavla) (the last apse to the N) date back to the early 16C; the chapel frescoes were revealed during early Soviet restoration work.

Most of the surviving wall paintings date from the 1640s when over 100 men under Ivan Paisein took part in large-scale restoration work. The walls were coated with gilt and the paintings added later; this method gave them the appearance of 'a magnificent old illuminated book', as Lady Londonderry noted in 1836. On the W wall are frescoes of the Last Judgement and scenes from the life of the Virgin Mary. The life of the Virgin is also depicted on the upper parts of the N and S walls, and on the lower parts are shown the seven ecumenical councils of the Church. Five rows of paintings of the early saints and martyrs decorate the massive round pillars. To emphasise the loftiness of the cathedral the height of each row decreases towards the roof. The paintings in the domes depict God the Father (in the central dome), the Lord of Hosts, Emmanuel, the Saviour, and the Virgin and Child. Below these are shown the prophets, apostles, and evangelists.

As Moscow consolidated its supremacy, the Cathedral of the Assumption became the repository for the finest and most revered *Icons* in Russia. On the S wall is an icon of the Life of Metropolitan Peter (c 1500), which is attributed to Dionysius. Peter, important both as a religious and political figure, paved the way for the removal of the Metropolitan's residence from Vladimir to Moscow. One of the scenes in the icon shows the foundation of the original Cathedral of the Assumption. Also attributed to Dionysius or his school is the huge icon of the Apocalypse on the W wall (c 1480).

The tall *Iconostasis* dates from 1652, although the richly engraved silver gilt frame was added later in the century (and restored in the late 19C). The most important icons are in the first row. 'All Creatures Rejoice in Thee' (O tebe raduyetsya) (left) depicts the Virgin Mary enthroned, and is attributed to Dionysius. 'The Saviour with the Angry Eye' (Spas 'Yaroye oko') dates from the 1340s. Immediately to the left of the Royal Door is the Virgin of Vladimir, a 15C copy by artists of the Rublyov School from an 11C–12C Byzantine original. The latter, now in the Tret'yakov Gallery, was traditionally believed to have been painted by St. Luke and was thought to have saved Moscow from the army of Timur (Tamerlane); no icon enjoyed greater renown. St. George the Victorious is depicted, clad in red, in an icon to the right of the S door of the iconostasis. This comes from 12C Novgorod and is one of the oldest surviving Russian icons.

The copper-plated *Doors* of the S portal, by the end of the iconostasis, were brought to Moscow from Suzdal in 1401 and show 20 scenes from ecclesiastical history. The *Throne of Monomakh* stands nearby, a splendid example of wood carving. Four pillars support an elaborately carved tent-roofed canopy; the canopy is adorned with kokoshnik gables and flower-and-goblet designs, and crowned with a double-headed eagle. The name derives from the 12 carvings on the throne (under the canopy) which depict the campaigns of Grand Prince Vladimir Monomakh (1113–25) and the presentation to him of the 'Crown of Monomakh' by the Byzantine Emperor Constantine IX Monomachus. The legend of the presentation of the crown was used in the 15C–16C to support Moscow's claim to be the 'Third Rome' and the heir to Byzantium; the crown can be seen in the Armoury Palace. This is also known as the Throne of Ivan IV ('the Terrible') as it was made for him in 1551. In front of the SE pillar is the white stone *Patriarch's Seat* (1653), and beyond is the *Seat of the Tsaritsa*.

The finely engraved open-work bronze *Tabernacle* in the SW corner (with a tent roof and kokoshniks) were made by D. Sverchkov (1625) and contained holy relics, including part of Christ's clothing and, from 1913, the remains of Patriarch Hermogenes, who starved to death in 1612 during the Polish occupation of the Kremlin. Most of the other Russian Patriarchs are buried nearby, including Adrian (died 1700), the last pre-Revolutionary Church leader to bear this title. Patriarch Nikon, an exception, was buried at the New Jerusalem Monastery, west of Moscow. The remains of Peter (died 1326), the first Metropolitan of Moscow, lie in the Chapel of SS. Peter and Paul behind the iconostasis (left).

During the French occupation of 1812 the cathedral (converted to a stable) was stripped of 5330kg of silver and 295kg of gold. Much of the silver was recaptured by the Cossacks, who presented the cathedral with a 46-branch silver and bronze *Chandelier* known as the Harvest. This is the central chandelier of 12 now illuminating the interior.

The rectangular ***Granovitaya Palace** juts out between the Cathedrals of the Assumption and the Annunciation. It was designed along Italian lines; begun by Marco Ruffo in 1487, the palace was completed four years later by Pietro Solario. The name, which might be translated as Faceted Palace, comes from the rusticated stone facing of the E side. The Italian influence would be more striking had the original Venetian windows not been replaced. Osip Startsev added the present beautiful window details, with their carvings and ornate columns, in 1682. The roof also has been changed; now hardly noticeable, it was once steeply pitched and perhaps even gilded. The so-called Red Staircase (Zolotaya Krasnaya Lestnitsa) once ran along the S wall of the palace. From the ceremonial rooms on the 1st Floor of the palace the Tsars and Emperors would proceed down the great stairs to weddings and coronations in the Cathedral of the Assumption. Artamon Matveyev and several members of the Naryshkin family were thrown from the top of the stairs onto the pikes of the strel'tsy during the revolt of 1682; a century and a half later Napoleon watched the burning of Moscow from here. The historic stairs were replaced in the 1930s by a two-storey dining-room annexe to the Great Kremlin Palace.

The Red Staircase of the Granovitaya Palace, in the Kremlin (engraving by M. Makhaev, 1760s). This was demolished in the Soviet period

The *Interior* of the Granovitaya Palace is, at the time of writing, *not open to tourists*. The great hall, on the 1st Floor, is supported by a thick central pillar; the room measures 22.1m by 22.4m and is 9m high at the top of the four groin vaults. The colourful religious paintings on a gold background are reproductions dating from 1881. This room served as the Tsar's audience chamber and as a banqueting hall. Here were held important church councils and meetings of the Boyar Duma and the Zemskiy Sobor. The only exit from this room is a splendid golden portal leading W to the *Holy Vestibule* (Svyatyye Seni), a rectangular room with four groin vaults and murals (the last by F.S. Zav'yalov, 1847). The door to the Red Staircase led from this vestibule. Above is the *Taynik*, or Secret Room, from which female members of the royal family were allowed to watch Court ceremonies.

A narrow space leads between the N wall of the Granovitaya Palace and the Church of the Deposition of the Robe. On the roof at the far end, eleven golden onion domes with ornate crosses are set on elongated drums. These are the cupolas of the **Terem Palace Churches**. The Terem Palace, part of the Great Kremlin Palace (see p 104), is *not open to the public*.

The *Golden Chamber of the Tsaritsa* (Zolotaya Tsaritsyna Palata) was built, under the present 11 domes, in the early 16C. Above it was added the present

Upper Cathedral of the Saviour (Verkhospasskiy Sobor) (1635) with, to the N, the *Chapel of John the Baptist* (Pridel Ionna Predtechi). (The small windows of an arcade to the E of the Cathedral of the Saviour are visible from Cathedral Square.) Above the chapel, in turn, is the *Church of the Crucifixion* (Ts. Raspyatiya). The *Church of St. Catherine* (Ts. Yekateriny) was built to the N of the Golden Chamber in 1627, and above it is the *Church of the Resurrection* (Ts. Voskreseniya Slovushchevo). In 1681 the three churches—the Saviour, Crucifixion, and Resurrection—were joined by a common roof. The 11 cupolas on the roof are really three sets of the traditional five, linked together. The gallery of the Church of St. Catherine, restored in the Soviet period, is visible from the N, by the SE corner of the Palace of Congresses.

The Golden Chamber, used as its name implies by the Tsaritsa, is dominated by two massive arches added as reinforcement in 1683. The murals date from the late 17C but have been much repainted. The Upper Cathedral of the Saviour became the domestic church of the royal family. The Baroque iconostasis was created in the mid-18C.

In the NW corner of Cathedral Square, hidden between the Cathedral of the Assumption and the Granovitaya Palace, stands the small white single-domed *Church of the Deposition of the Robe (Ts. Rizpolozheniya).

A church of this name was first erected here in 1451 to celebrate the prevention of a Tatar attack on Moscow. The church festival commemorating the day (2 July, o.s.) of the deposition (polozheniye) of the robe or veil (riza) of the Virgin Mary in a church in Constantinople (in 458) was much revered by Orthodox Christians, as the miraculous relic was believed to have saved Constantinople from capture by various enemies. The 1451 church was destroyed in the great

The Church of the Deposition of the Robe, in the Kremlin. In the background are the cupolas of the Terem Palace Palace churches

Kremlin fire of 1473, but in 1484–86 its foundations were used for a new Church of the Deposition of the Robe, which survives today. It was built by craftsmen from Pskov and Moscow.

At first the church served as the Metropolitan's private chapel (it adjoined his apartments); when the Russian church separated from Constantinople in the late 16C the church became the chapel of the Patriarch. In the mid-17C a new Patriarch's palace was built, and the Church of the Deposition of the Robe began to be used by the Tsar. Covered passages were built connecting the church with the Tsar's palace and the Cathedral of the Assumption; the female members of the royal family reached the cathedral by this route.

The church was set on a tall base to bring it level with the Metropolitan's quarters. The basic plan, typical of Moscow church architecture, is square with three apses on the E end. The other façades are divided by slender pilasters into three sections, each ending in an ogee gable; the middle sections are wider and taller than the others. The single silver dome with its cross is set on a tall drum with slit windows; this in turn stands on an octagonal base. On the S side a staircase climbs to the main ogee-shaped portal (portals were added to the N and W in the 17C). The external decoration is simple but refined, with bands of blind arcading on the apses and above the main portal. Intricate friezes run above the arcading of the apses, above the portal, and beneath the dome.

Interior. Four square pillars support the vaulted roof. In 1644 these pillars as well as the walls and ceilings, were covered with frescoes by Sidor Osipov and Ivan Borisov, who had also worked on the frescoes in the Cathedral of the Assumption. Christ, the Virgin Mary, and the prophets are portrayed on the ceiling. On the walls and pillars there are four rows of paintings: the top two rows depict scenes from the apocryphal life of the Virgin Mary, the bottom two illustrate the 25 stanzas of the Akafist (or Hymn to the Virgin Mary). There are also portraits of various rulers on the pillars, including Prince Vladimir and Alexander Nevskiy. The frescoes were painted over in the 18C and 19C. They were restored to their original appearance in the 1950s.

Also restored is the four-row *Iconostasis* originally created by Nazariy Istomin in 1627. The top row of icons depicts the prophets, the second shows the events and miracles of Christ's life on earth. The third and most important row, the deësis, includes the central icon of Christ Enthroned. The bottom row contains particularly revered 16C and 17C icons, including Istomin's 'Trinity' (left of the Royal Door). The iconostasis is famed for the painstaking execution of the figures and the refined, muted colours: pinks, olives, ochres, dark reds, and soft greens. Before it stand attractively painted candle holders.

The *Gallery* now houses a small exhibition of wooden handicrafts.

The *** * Cathedral of the Archangel Michael** (Arkhangel'skiy Sobor) with its one gold and four silver domes is situated on the brow of the Kremlin Hill—to the S of the Ivan the Great Bell Tower and to the E of the Cathedral of the Annunciation. It served as the burial place of the rulers of Muscovy.

The Italian architect Alevisio Novi created the cathedral in 1505–08 on a site where a church had stood since 1333. The Archangel Michael was regarded as the guardian of the Moscow princes.

The **Exterior** with its five domes adheres to the basic Russian architectural conventions, but Alevisio Novi employed many Renaissance decorative details. The walls are divided vertically by pilasters,

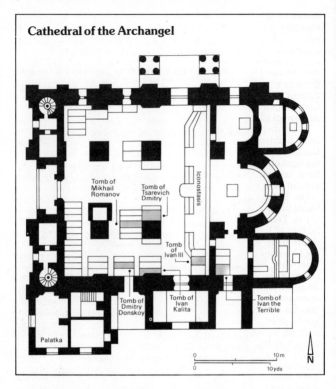

Cathedral of the Archangel

Tomb of Mikhail Romanov

Tomb of Tsarevich Dmitry

Iconostasis

Tomb of Ivan III

Tomb of Dmitry Donskoy

Tomb of Ivan Kalita

Tomb of Ivan the Terrible

Palatka

0   10 m
0   10 yds

N

their Corinthian capitals decorated with volutes. There are three
sections on the E and W walls and five on the N and S. The five
sections are rather unusual and are partly explained by the porch at
the W end (which was probably intended to allow the women of the
royal family to watch services in private); the result is a relatively
long building with the domes towards one end. The W pair of domes
have been made larger than the E pair to compensate for this
asymmetrical layout. Another imported feature relates to the horizontal division of the walls. Alevisio Novi employed two elaborate
cornices and, above the upper cornice, gables in the form of
Venetian-style scallops. The W portal is also Venetian in inspiration,
the archway being framed by elaborate carvings of plants and
fantastic animals. The fresco on the porch depicts the baptism of the
Russians at the time of Prince Vladimir.

The S wall (on the river side) retains traces of a gallery which once
surrounded the cathedral at the 1st Floor level. The buttresses were
added in 1773 when the walls developed a crack. To the SW is the
annexe or Palatka, added in 1826. Earlier, in the 16C, chapels were
added to the apses of the E end.

Interior. Six square pillars (four of them W of the iconostasis)
support the roof and create three W–E aisles. Little natural light
enters through the narrow windows, but there are also 17C gilded
chandeliers. In 1508 *frescoes* were painted on the walls, pillars, and

domes by Dionysius, but these were damaged or painted over as the centuries passed, and the only traces survive in the altar area. The existing paintings, the result of Soviet restoration, date back to the second half of the 17C. On the walls and pillars are depicted various rulers, not only those who are buried here, but also the founders of the Russian state and other rulers, such as the Emperor Constantine, through whom the Grand Princes and Tsars claimed to inherit their thrones. The upper part of the W wall is covered by a fresco of the Last Judgement, while to the N and S are depicted the deeds of Archangel Michael.

A four-tiered *Iconostasis* was originally created in 1680–81, with icons painted by Dorofey Yermolayev-Zolotarev (a pupil of Simon Ushakov) and others. The icon of St. Michael, in the bottom row to the right of the Royal Door, may date from the 14C and is said to have been commissioned by Yevdokiya, wife of Dmitry Donskoy. The present gold Baroque iconostasis dates from 1813.

The Cathedral of the Archangel Michael is most notable as the burial place of all the rulers of Russia from Prince Ivan Kalita (1328–41) to Tsar Ivan Alekseyevich (1682–96) (the feeble-minded half-brother of Peter the Great). The only exception was Boris Godunov, whose body was finally interred at Zagorsk. From the time of Peter the Great the Emperors and Empresses were buried in Leningrad's Peter-Paul Fortress. The remains of Emperor Peter II (1727–30), however, lie here in the Cathedral of the Archangel; the young Emperor died of smallpox while on a visit to Moscow. Altogether there are 46 tombs containing the remains of 56 individuals, and they take up much of the space in the aisles. The white stone sarcophagi were carved in the 17C and bronze covers added in 1903. Against the right (S) wall are those of Dmitry Donskoy, Ivan Kalita, and Ivan III (the great unifier of the Russian lands); against the left wall is that of Vasily Shuyskiy, who reigned during the Time of Troubles. The holy remains of Prince Mikhail of Chernigov and the Boyar Fyodor, who were murdered by the Tatars in 1246, were interred by the near right-hand (SW) pillar. Next to the far left-hand (NE) pillar lie Tsars Fyodor and Ivan Alekseyevich, and also Emperor Peter II. Beside the far right-hand (SE) pillar are the tombs of Tsar Mikhail Romanov and his son Tsar Aleksey Mikhaylovich, and also of Tsarevich Dmitry Ivanovich (1582–91). Dmitry was the son of Ivan the Terrible who died at Uglich, possibly murdered at the behest of Boris Godunov; he was the source of the two 'False Dmitrys' who appeared during the Time of Troubles. An attractive painted stone canopy was built above Dmitry's tomb; it encloses a fresco depicting Prince Andrey Bogolyubskiy. The tombs of Ivan the Terrible and two of his other sons are located together in the Sanctuary (right); Ivan Ivanovich was killed by his father, and Fyodor Ivanovich was the last Tsar of his dynasty. In 1963 the remains of Ivan the Terrible were exhumed and studied by a commission of experts.

On the W side of Cathedral Square, W of the Cathedral of the Archangel Michael and S of the Granovitaya Palace, stands the nine-domed **··Cathedral of the Annunciation** (Blagoveshchenskiy Sobor). Before 1917 this served as the Chapel Royal, a small private church where members of the ruling dynasty were christened, were married, and took Communion.

The first church here was founded by Grand Prince Vasily I (son of Dmitry Donskoy) in 1397, but by the 1480s this building had become dilapidated. Ivan III, having completed the Cathedral of the Assumption, commissioned a group of stonemasons from Pskov—some of the finest craftsmen in Russia—to recon-struct the church. From 1448 to 1489, using the foundations and tall basement-cum-treasure-house of the earlier building, they created a small cube-shaped church with three domes and three apses. An open gallery surrounded it on three sides, with stairs in the NE corner leading down to the square.

The evolution of the Cathedral of the Annunciation was more complex than that of the other Kremlin churches. The fire of 1547 seriously damaged the building, and during the reconstruction of 1562–64 Ivan the Terrible (who preferred elaborate churches, e.g. St. Basil's) ordered that four single-domed chapels be added, one to each corner. Two further false domes were added to the W part of the original roof to bring the grand total to nine, and the gallery was enclosed. Most remarkably, the domes, roof and the top of the apses were covered with gold sheet, thus earning the cathedral the name 'Gold-topped' (Zlatoverkhniy). (The gold apparently came from Novgorod, which was fully subjugated during Ivan's reign.) Ivan married for the fourth time in 1572. Under Orthodox law he was henceforth denied access to the cathedral by the way of the main entrance, and so he had an additional staircase, porch, and chapel built on the SE side. The Tsar entered the building by the porch, known as the 'Groznenskiy' (lit., 'Terrible's'), and remained behind a grille during the service.

The **Exterior** of the cathedral is rich in decorative detail. The band of blind arcading on the apses echoes the motif on the Cathedral of the Assumption. While the tiers of zakomara and kokoshnik gables above the apses, on the corner chapels, and around the base of the central drum show the influence of early Moscow architecture, the elaborately carved stone frieze just below the domes is typical of the architecture of Pskov.

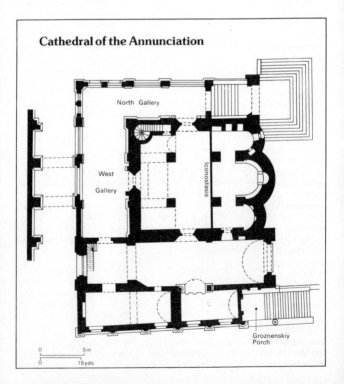

Cathedral of the Annunciation

North Gallery

West Gallery

Iconostasis

Groznenskiy Porch

0   5m
0   15yds

Interior. The *Gallery* was painted in the 1560s, and some of the frescoes have been well preserved. In the N Gallery, over the entrance door, are paintings of Jonah and the Whale (on the S wall) and the Veil of Veronica; the latter was restored by Ushakov in 1661. By the W Portal (W Gallery) are the Sign of the Virgin and the Trinity. The paintings on the ceiling of the gallery depict the Tree of Jesse (the ancestors of Christ); on the slopes of the vaults and on the pilasters are portraits of the Moscow princes as well as Classical philosophers and poets.

The limestone *Portals* to the N and W date from 1564. They feature elaborately carved late Renaissance motifs and are painted blue and gold. The copper-panelled double *Doors*, with biblical scenes and inscriptions engraved in gold, were brought from Rostov Velikiy in the 16C.

The *Frescoes* of the narrow but lofty cathedral itself were painted in 1508 by a 'brotherhood' of icon painters from the Iosifo-Volotskiy Monastery, led by the monk Feodosius (c 1470–early 16C)—son of the noted Dionysius (painter of the Cathedral of the Assumption). The paintings were renewed several times, but careful restoration by Soviet artists in 1945–47 revealed that some of the original murals had survived under the layers of paint. There is work attributed to Feodosius in the sanctuary (Eucharist, Breaking of Bread, Last Supper, Crucifixion, Descent into Hell), on the W pillars, and on the ceiling (40 Martyrs).

On the W wall and the ceiling are frescoes with scenes from the Last Judgement, while those on the N and S walls and on the apses portray the lives of Christ and the Virgin Mary. Angels, prophets, and patriarchs adorn the drum and arches around the central dome.

There are four pillars, two hidden behind the iconostasis and two in the nave itself. The W pillars support a choir gallery from which female members of the royal family could watch the service. The murals on the SW pillar show the Byzantine Emperors and their families, while the NW pillar has portraits of the Russian princes; Dmitry Donskoy and his son Vasily (founder of the original Cathedral of the Annunciation) are depicted on the N side.

The glory of the cathedral is the *Iconostasis*, perhaps the finest in existence. In 1405 the original building was decorated by three of the greatest Russian medieval artists, Theophanes the Greek (Feofan Grek) (c 1340–1405), Andrey Rublyov (c 1360–c 1430), and Prokhor of Gorodets (n.d.). Their murals perished when the cathedral was rebuilt, and for many years it was thought that the icons that they had painted had been destroyed by fire in 1547. In the 1920s, however, restorers working on the iconostasis discovered that a number of their icons had survived under layers of paint and varnish. Several of the other icons are also of artistic and historical interest.

The iconostasis has a late-19C engraved bronze-gilt frame designed by N.V. Sultanov, The (bottom) *1st Row* contains the oldest icon, Christ Enthroned, which was painted in 1337 and is only partly restored; it is to the right of the silver Royal Door. To the right of this is the Ustyug Annunciation, the central part of which is a 17C copy of a 12C icon which is now in the Tret'yakov Gallery. The 16C Hodigitria Virgin is to the left of the Royal Door and replaces another work that has been removed to the Tret'yakov Gallery, Theophanes' icon of the Virgin of the Don. Next to this, and only partially restored, is another icon of Christ Enthroned (17C). The tiny scenes surrounding the 16C icon of the Virgin of Tikhvin (far left) are rich in details of contemporary everyday life.

Between the bottom row and the Deësis is a row of miniatures illustrating the months. The Deësis (3rd Row) and the Festive Row above it include some of the finest icons in the world. In the *Deësis* the majestic central figure of Christ, and the icons of the Virgin Mary, John the Baptist, the Archangel Gabriel, and John Chrysostom are thought to be the work of Theophanes. The figure of the Archangel Michael (left of the Virgin Mary) is attributed to Andrey Rublyov. Andrey Rublyov is also thought to have painted several of the icons in the *Festive Row*, including the Annunciation, the Nativity, the Transfiguration, and the Raising of Lazarus (1st, 2nd, 6th, and 7th from left). Most of the remaining icons in the Festive Row, including the Last Supper, and the Crucifixion, are attributed to Prokhor.

The *5th Row*, depicting the prophets, was created after the fire of 1547 by artists from Pskov, while the *6th (top) Row* consists of small images of the Patriarchs. On the S wall, beside the iconostasis, is a four-part icon, also the work of Pskov artists. Its remarkably realistic depiction of human figures aroused controversy at the time it was painted, in the mid-16C.

The floor is a warm-toned, reddish-brown jasper, said to have been a gift to Tsar Aleksey Mikhaylovich from the Shah of Persia and originally used in Rostov Cathedral. Together with the glowing murals and superb silver-gilt framed iconostasis, it creates an impression of extraordinary richness in this most Russian of cathedrals.

To the E of the Kremlin cathedrals and surrounded by fir trees is a bronze **Statue of Lenin** by Pinchuk, erected in honour of the 50th anniversary of the Revolution. The site is part of the GREAT KREMLIN SQUARE where, on 1 May 1920, Lenin took part in the first Communist Subbotnik (Day of Voluntary Labour). A richly-decorated and very expensive Gothic monument to Alexander II by N.V. Sultanov was unveiled in 1898 here on the brow of the Kremlin hill. The statue of the Emperor (now demolished) was surmounted by a tent-roofed canopy and flanked on three sides by an arcade with mosaic portraits of Russian rulers.

The area to the W of the Lenin statue was one of the busiest squares of the old Kremlin, IVANOVSKAYA PLOSHCHAD'. This was bounded to the S (along the ridge) by the Prikazy (government offices), which were built in 1591, extended in 1675–80, and knocked down in the 1770s to make way for Bazhenov's Kremlin reconstruction project. Each Prikaz had its own entrance and staircase facing N onto the square. Government decrees were proclaimed in Ivanovskaya Pl., and executions were carried out. For a long time the Vech' Bell, brought from Novgorod in 1478 and a symbol of that city's ancient liberties, hung in a small bell tower here. On the E side of the square stood the Church of St. Nicholas (Ts. Nikoly Gostunskovo), built by Alevisio Novi in 1506. This revered church was demolished in one night in 1817 by Alexander I, who wanted to create a square to parade his troops but feared popular outrage at the church's destruction.

Below the Lenin statue, between the ridge and the NE and SE walls of the Kremlin, stretch the **Taynitskiy Gardens**, with many fir trees. The ridge provides an **excellent view** over the Moskva River and the S part of the city. The wall and towers around the NE and SE sides of the fortress are clearly visible.

The *Saviour Tower (Spasskaya, formerly Frolov Bashnya), is visible to the N beyond the front of the Presidium building. Perhaps the most handsome of the Kremlin towers, it was built by Pietro

Solario in 1491. The superstructure with its tent roof was added in 1625; it included a clock made by the Englishman Christopher Galloway. The present clock was installed under Nicholas I, and its chimes played 'The Preobrazhenskiy March' and the hymn 'Kol' slaven nash Gospod Sion'; after being damaged by a shell during the October Revolution the chimes were altered to play 'The Internationale'. The Tsars and Emperors entered the Kremlin by this gate, and all who passed under the sacred icon of the Saviour—from which the gate and tower derived their names—had to remove their hats. To the left of the Saviour Tower, hidden behind the Presidium and Senate buildings, is the **Senate Tower**.

Perched on the wall to the right of the Saviour Tower is the **Little Tsar Tower** (Tsarskaya Bashenka). The stone tower dates from 1680, but there is a legend that earlier Ivan the Terrible stood at this place on the wall to watch executions in Red Square. Next comes the **Alarm Tower** (Nabatnaya Bashnya) whose bell warned of fires. Catherine II ordered the bell's tongue removed after it had been used to summon a mob during the Plague Riot of 1771. The **Konstantin-Yelena Tower** (1490), to the right, was once popularly known as the 'Torture Tower' (Pytoshnaya Bashnya), as it was used as a prison in the early 17C. The **Beklemishevskaya Tower**, also called the Moskvoretskaya, was built in 1487 by Marco Ruffo. It stands in the E corner, which was often the first part of the fortress to be attacked.

There are a total of seven towers in the SE wall of the Kremlin, along the river. First comes the Beklemishevskaya, and after that three towers built in 1488–90: the **Peter** (Petrovskaya), **2nd Nameless** (2-ya Bezymyannaya), and **1st Nameless**. The next tower, the **Taynitskaya**, is the oldest; Antonio Fryazin supervised its construction in 1485. There was a storehouse or cache (taynik) here for use in sieges, hence the name of the tower. This gate was the most direct route from the cathedrals to the river, and the religious procession for the Blessing of the Waters passed through here. Next comes the **Annunciation Tower** (Blagoveshchenskaya Bashnya) which was used as a prison by Ivan the Terrible, and finally, in the SW corner, there is the tall round **Vodovzvodnaya Tower**, also called the Sviblova Tower. This last was built in 1489 by Antonio Fryazin and its name means Pump Tower, after a machine installed in it by Christopher Galloway in 1633.

Beyond the Cathedral of the Annunciation the huge façade of the **Great Kremlin Palace** stretches some 125m along the crest of the Kremlin hill. Built under Nicholas I in 1838–49, it was intended as the Imperial residence in Moscow. K.A. Thon, the architect, built it in what has been called the Russo-Byzantine style; the design is really Eclectic, combining a Classical regularity with Old Russian elements like the arcade, the Moscow Baroque window decorations, and the ogee-shaped gables. The palace now houses the Soviet 'parliament', the Supreme Soviet of the USSR, and is used for other important state occasions. *It is not open to the general public.*

The *State Entrance* (Paradnyy Vkhod), located to the right of centre in the S façade, leads into a white *Vestibule* with four grey granite columns. The private rooms of the royal family (Sobstvennaya Polovina) were to the left on this same Ground Floor. Beyond the Vestibule the wide *State Staircase*, its walls lined with artificial marble, climbs to the *Fore Hall* (Avanzal) on the 1st Floor. Behind tall golden doors to the right is the white *Hall of St. George* (Georgiyevskiy Zal). Intended as the largest room in the palace, it measures 61m long, 20.5m wide, and 17.5m high. The arched ceiling, with its decorated coffering, is supported by 18 pilasters; from it hang six gilded chandeliers. Above the entrance a bas-relief by P. Clodt von Jürgensburg depicts St. George slaying the dragon; the hall is dedicated to the Order of St. George, established in 1769 and the highest military decoration of Imperial Russia. The names of individuals and units awarded the medal are inscribed on the pilasters. In front of each pilaster is a twisted column and above it an allegorical statue of a Russian Victory (all the statues are by G. Vitali).

The St. George Hall runs N to S. Two other halls were built at right angles to it and running along the S façade of the palace, the St. Alexander Hall and the St. Andrew Hall. These were dedicated to the Orders of St. Alexander Nevskiy (est. 1725) and St. Andrew (est. 1695); the St. Andrew Hall also served as a throne-room. These richly decorated rooms were rebuilt and combined in 1932–34 (by I.A. Ivanov-Schitz) to form the large *Meeting Hall* (Zal Zasedaniy), which is 81m long and able to accommodate 3000 people. The decoration is austere and above the podium, at the W end, is a *Statue of Lenin* by S.D. Merkurov (1939). The Supreme Soviet meets here several times a year, and before the completion of the Kremlin Palace of Congresses this hall was used for congresses of Soviets and of the Communist Party. Several of the most important Party congresses—the 17th (1934), the 18th (1939), the 19th (1952), the 20th (1956), and the 21st (1959)—were held here.

The *W Wing* consists of a suite of ceremonial rooms. Beyond the white marble *Chevalier Guards* (Kavalergardskiy) *Hall* is the *Hall of St. Catherine*, with rose and silver walls—the colours of the Order of St. Catherine (est. 1714). The Hall of St. Catherine served as the throne-room of the Empress and was, until recently, the place where foreign ambassadors presented their credentials to the Soviet government. The 1963 nuclear test-ban treaty was signed here. The remaining rooms are the green *State Drawing Room* (Paradnaya Divannaya) and the raspberry-coloured *State Bedchamber* (Paradnaya Opochival'nya).

The mid-19C project for the construction of the Great Kremlin Palace was a complicated one. Several major buildings had to be demolished, including the palace's predecessor, the Kremlin Winter Palace built for Empress Elizabeth in 1749–53 by B.F. Rastrelli (Napoleon slept here briefly in 1812). The beautiful Cathedral of the Saviour 'in the Woods' (Sobor Spasa na Boru) was left standing, hidden in the courtyard of the palace; founded in 1333 under Ivan Kalita as one of the first stone churches in Moscow, it was largely rebuilt in the early 16C and again in the early 18C. The Cathedral of the Saviour was demolished in 1933 to make way for a service annexe to the palace. (There is a copy of this church, by Shchusev, in the former Martha-Mary Convent on Bol. Ordynka Ul.)

The *N Wing* of the Great Kremlin Palace consists of the **Terem Palace** (or Belvedere Palace), one of the most picturesque structures in the Kremlin. It is, unfortunately, difficult to see much of the exterior, which is between the 'new' façades of the Great Kremlin Palace (to the S) and the Palace of Congresses (to the N); the interior is still closed to tourists. The Ground Floor encloses, on the W, remains of the *Church of the Raising of Lazarus* (Ts. Voskresheniya Lazarya), built in 1393 by Princess Yevdokiya to commemorate the Battle of Kulikovo; the structure of the interior was restored in 1949–52. Alevisio Novi built a new church above in 1514, the *Church of the Nativity of the Virgin* (Ts. Rozhdestva Bogoroditsy). This was rebuilt in 1681, and its single gilded dome can be seen from the lane between the Great Kremlin Palace and the Armoury Palace. The first two floors of the Terem Palace served as an arcaded base (podklet) for the palace proper, which was built in 1635–36 for Tsar Mikhail Fyodorovich by Bazhen Ogurtsev, Trefil Sharutin, and others. The exterior, despite mid-19C alterations, retains the stepped appearance of the original—a series of layers piled on top of one another. The rows of windows are decorated with carved stone surrounds and separated by pilasters. One window in the second row from the top is more decorated than the others, with pillars and an ornate pediment containing a double-headed eagle. This is the so-called *Petition Window* of the Tsar's Throne-Room; from here on a rope hung a box into which people could place petitions.

The broad external Postel'naya Staircase once led along the S wall of the Terem Palace from the courtyard up to the Boyars' Terrace (Boyarskaya Ploshchadka) at the level of the 2nd Floor. Boyars and court officials would congregate on the platform to petition the Tsar and to receive orders; here were proclaimed official announcements. Then enclosed the E part of the Boyars' Terrace and made it into the *Hall of St. Vladimir* (for an Order founded in 1782); this hall adjoins to the E the Holy Vestibule of the Granovitaya Palace and to the S the Hall of St. George. The remaining open part of the Boyars' Terrace was converted into a large *Winter Garden* in 1959.

From the Boyars' Terrace the *Golden Staircase* (Zolotaya Lestnitsa) led up to the level of the 3rd Floor of the Terem Palace and the *Upper Saviour Terrace* (Verkhospasskaya Ploshchadka). The stairs and the terrace survive, but altered and no longer in the open air. At the top of the stairs the way onto the terrace—and towards the Tsar's chambers—was barred by the *Golden Gates* (Zolotaya Reshotka), a beautiful grille in the form of fantastic animals. Legend had it that the gates were made from the debased coinage which had caused the 'Copper Riot' of 1661 and been withdrawn from circulation; in fact they are made of iron. To the right (E) of the Upper Saviour Terrace, behind another grille, is the entrance to the Upper Cathedral of the Saviour (see p 96), also called the Church of the Saviour 'behind the Golden Grille' (Spas za Zolotoy Reshotkoy).

To the left (W) of the Upper Saviour Terrace a short flight of stairs flanked by carved lions leads up to a landing which is separated from the terrace by open arches, each with a suspended boss (gir'ka) (the tent roof of this landing is visible on the roof). Beyond the landing are the rooms used by the Tsars in the 17C. First comes the *Vestibule* (Prokhodnyye Seni), then the *Anteroom* (Perednyaya Palata, also called the Krestovaya Palata), which was used for discussions with the Boyars or the reception of foreign ambassadors. The third room is the *Throne Room* (Prestol'naya Komnata) and beyond it are the *Tsar's Bedchamber* (Opochival'nya) and *Oratory* (Molel'nya). The rooms are all low and vaulted; the decoration is most ornate, with murals, intricate mouldings, and tiled stoves, but these are actually reproductions from the 1830s and 1840s. Stairs, covered by a tent roof, lead to the quaint *Teremok* or garret. As a plaque above the ornate door indicates, the Teremok was built in 1637 by Tsar Mikhail for his sons Aleksey and Ivan. This small airy room with its richly painted ceilings was also used for meetings of the Boyar Duma. At the E end rises a quaint round belvedere. The high hipped roof of the Teremok is just visible from the front of the Armoury Palace; it is believed at one time to have been gilded.

The site just to the S and W of the Great Kremlin Palace was once occupied by the Zapasnyy Palace (lit. 'Reserve' Palace), built in 1601–03 by Boris Godunov as a means of providing work for the hungry. Boris himself lived in a wooden palace (khoromy) built on top. In 1605, during the Time of Troubles, the False Dmitry built a wooden palace here with a separate wing for his mistress, Marina Mnishek; the Pretender was soon replaced by Vasily Shuysky, who also built a palace on top of the Zapasnyy Palace. Under the first Romanov a roof-garden was built on top of the palace; in a pond here little Peter Alekseyevich, later the first Emperor, was said to have played with his toy boats—the ancestors of the Russian navy. The Zapasnyy Palace, like much else, was demolished in 1770 to make way for Bazhenov's Kremlin project.

The road in front of the Great Kremlin Palace leads to the Borovitskiye Gate. This area, nearest where the Moskva and Neglinnaya rivers once met, was the first part of the Kremlin to be settled. The earliest church stood on the site of the road, just in front of the Armoury Palace: the Church of the Nativity of John the Baptist (Ts. Rozhdestva Ionna Predtechi). The 'final' version was built in 1509 by Alevisio Novi, but demolished in 1848.

The ***Armoury Palace** (Gos. Oruzheynaya Palata) was built between the Great Kremlin Palace and the Kremlin wall by Konstantin Thon in 1844–51. It houses the oldest and one of the richest museums in Russia.

The Armoury Palace as an institution dates back to the mid-16C, and it later came to incorporate the gold and silver workshops of the Kremlin. In 1806 a building known as the Armoury Palace was begun to house the treasures accumulated over the centuries by the Russian state, but the wealth of the collection was such that Nicholas I soon had to commission the architect K.A. Thon to design a new museum building, which is the present home of the Armoury Palace. (The 'old' Armoury Palace was demolished in the 1950s to make way for the Palace of Congresses.) Thon constructed the new Armoury Palace in the same Russo-Byzantine style as the Great Kremlin Palace, with Early Russian windows and carved pilasters. The wing extending to the N was

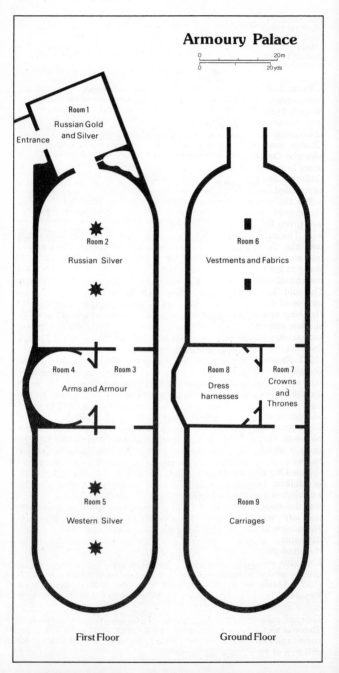

Armoury Palace

Room 1
Russian Gold and Silver

Entrance

Room 2
Russian Silver

Room 6
Vestments and Fabrics

Room 4   Room 3
Arms and Armour

Room 8
Dress harnesses

Room 7
Crowns and Thrones

Room 5
Western Silver

Room 9
Carriages

First Floor

Ground Floor

once occupied by the *Apartments* of the heir apparent; it is now used by important foreign guests. The galleried bridge between the Apartments and the Great Kremlin Palace contained a Winter Garden.

After the Revolution the treasures of the Kremlin cathedrals and of the Synodal Treasury (Riznitsa) were added to the collection of the Armoury Palace. A white marble staircase leads to the 1st Floor, where the exhibition begins.

Room 1. Russian Gold and Silver, 12C–16C. Many of the oldest items—rings, insignia, earrings, collars, etc.—were unearthed in Staraya Ryazan' in 1822 and date back to the 12C–13C. Silver work from this area is remarkable for its filigree, cloisonné enamel, and the abundance of precious stones. Also of interest is the 12C silver *Chalice* commissioned by Prince Yury Dolgoruky, the founder of Moscow. One of the gold covers of the icon of the Virgin of Vladimir dates from the 13C (the icon itself may be seen in the Tret'yakov Gallery). From the 15C are two gospel covers, including the bejewelled gold Morozov Gospel.

The 16C was perhaps the finest era of Russian craftsmanship. The round gold *Dish* with a swirling design and fine niello-work border was given by Ivan the Terrible as a wedding present to his second wife. The cover of the *'Measure icon'* (1554) for Tsarevich Ivan, son of Ivan the Terrible, is enamelled and decorated with a filigree of interwoven flowers. (When a tsarevich was born a 'measure icon' was made to his length.) Irina Godunova, daughter-in-law of Ivan, gave the church-shaped gold *Censer* to the Cathedral of the Archangel. The gold *Gospel Cover* by G. Ovdokimov (1631–32) is remarkable for its use of bright enamel, filigree, and gems. The gold and silver *Drinking vessels* are in the traditional Russian style. The graceful shallow swan-shaped scoop (kovsh) was traditionally used for mead; such scoops were sometimes presented as rewards for loyal service to the Tsar.

R.2. Russian Silver, 17C–early 20C. The gold *Gospel Cover* (G. Ovdokimov, 1631–32) is remarkable for its use of bright enamel, filigree, and gems. The late 17C gold and silver shows some of the finest Russian enamel work. The brightly enamelled and bejewelled gold *Chalice* (1664) was commissioned by the Boyarina Anna Morozova and presented to the Monastery of the Miracles. The *Loving-cup* decorated with enamelled flowers was given by Patriarch Nikon to Tsar Aleksey Mikhaylovich in 1653. 18C work includes a Rococo silver soup tureen, a tall silver beaker, platters, and snuff boxes.

Late 19C–early 20C work by leading jewellery firms, includes that of Sazikov, Ovchinnikov, and *Fabergé*. Gustav Fabergé (1814–93) established his firm in St. Petersburg in 1842, and the family tradition was developed by his son Carl (1846–1920). Included in the collection are several of the celebrated Fabergé Easter eggs. The *Heliotrope Egg* (1891), by M. Perkhin, is decorated with gold and diamonds. In 1899 Perkhin fashioned the yellow enamelled diamond-studded *Clock* topped with a bouquet of onyx lilies. Perkhin also worked on the large silver *Egg* supported by three golden griffins and engraved with a map of the Trans-Siberian Railway (1900); inside was a gold clockwork model of the Trans-Siberian Express. The music box *Model of the Kremlin*, centring around the dome of the Cathedral of the Assumption, was made in 1904. The Fabergé collection also contains a number of tiny *Carved Animals*. There is also a *Flower* fashioned from rock crystal with enamelled petals and gold leaves; the petals open to reveal tiny portraits of the children of Nicholas and Alexandra.

R.3. E and W European Arms and Armour, 15C–19C. Included is *Nuremberg armour* for knight and horse presented to Tsar Fyodor Ivanovich by King Stephen Bathory of Poland.

R.4. Russian Arms and Armour, 12C–early 19C. The remains of the *Helmet of Yaroslav Vsevolodovich* (father of Alexander Nevskiy), an iron helmet decorated with silver, were discovered in 1808 near the site of a 13C battle. The small spiked *Helmet* was commissioned by Ivan the Terrible for his three-year-old son Ivan. The *Armour of Boris Godunov* is displayed in the centre; each of the flat rings is inscribed 'God is with us, no one is against us'. The *Sabres of Kuz'ma Minin and Prince Dmitry Pozharsky* are relics of the men who led the Russian forces to final victory during the 'Time of Troubles' of the early 17C. The *Helmet of Tsar Mikhail* by tradition originally belonged to Alexander Nevskiy; it was restored in 1621 and inlaid with gold filigree and adorned with diamonds, emeralds, and rubies. The gold *'Saadak'* (weapons case) of Tsar Mikhail is also adorned with precious stones.

R.5. W European Silver, 13C–19C. Most of these items were brought to Russia as ambassadorial gifts. The museum has one of the finest collections of 16C–17C *English silver*; links were established with England in the 1550s, and silverware was brought to Russia in the decades that followed (much of the silver that remained in Britain was melted down under Cromwell). The Swedish collection is very large; the two large gilded bowls and the silver cornucopia-shaped goblet were given by Queen Christina to Tsar Aleksey Mikhaylovich in 1647 to commemorate his accession to the throne. The ingenious *Table fountain fruit dish* (P. Öhr) was presented in 1674.

There is a large amount of German work of the 16C–17C. The oldest article is the vessel in the shape of a *Cock* (late 15C), which belonged to Ivan III; it is thought that the body was originally made on an ostrich egg. The rock-crystal and gold *Goblet* was the work of the Nuremburg craftsman A. Jamnitzer (1555). A boyar is believed to have presented it to the False Dmitry on the day of his marriage to Marina Mnishek (1606). The *Pitcher and Tray*, decorated with rock crystal and precious stones (J.-H. Mannlich), was a gift from Emperor Leopold of Austria. French work on display includes part of the 3000-piece silver *Orlov Service* (J. Roëttiers and others); it was ordered by Catherine II in 1770 for her favourite Grigory Orlov. The 140-piece *Olympian Service* of Sèvres china was commissioned by Napoleon and presented to Alexander I.

R.6. Vestments and Fabrics, 14C–20C. Byzantine and Oriental work dates from the 14C–17C. The light blue and silver *Ceremonial robe* (sakkos) was made in 1322 for the first Metropolitan of Moscow, Peter. Other examples of the Byzantine sakkos were worn by Metropolitans Aleksey and Photius; that of the latter is richly decorated with portraits of the royal family. The red satin *Tunic of Mikhail Romanov* is on display, as well as caftans and boots worn by Peter the Great. Patriarch Nikon's *Ceremonial Vestment* was made in 1654 of Venetian velvet and lavishly adorned with gold embroidery, precious stones, and niello miniatures; it weighs 24kg. The sleeveless *Vestment* ('felon') was presented to Metropolitan Platon by Catherine II in 1770; the elaborate design is formed from over 150,000 pearls.

The red *Coronation gown of Catherine I* (widow of Peter) is on display, also the coronation gowns of Anna Ivanova (originally pink) and of Elizabeth Petrovna; the *Gown of Elizabeth* is the most impressive of the three, being richly embroidered in gold and wrapped with a silver lace mantle. The *Wedding dress of Catherine*

II (1745) is silver, while her *Coronation gown* is embroidered with gold two-headed eagles. The *Gown* that Alexandra Fyodorovna wore for the last Romanov coronation (1896) is in the traditional Russian style and decorated with pearls and silver embroidery.

R.7. *Crowns and Thrones. The ivory inlaid *Throne of Ivan the Terrible* is on display. The throne presented to Boris Godunov in 1604 by the Shah of Persia is covered in gold leaf and decorated with turquoises and other precious stones. The *Throne of Tsar Mikhail Fyodorovich*, the first Romanov Tsar, is the reworking of a throne that once belonged to Ivan the Terrible. The late 17C *Diamond Throne* is the most sumptuous; presented to Tsar Aleksey Mikhaylovich by an Armenian trading company in Persia, the decoration includes over 800 diamonds. The *Silver Throne* was made for the double coronation in 1682 of the 10-year-old Peter Alekseyevich and his feeble-minded 15-year-old half-brother Ivan; a curtain at the back concealed a secret compartment from which the young Tsars' elder sister told them what to say.

The Russian State Regalia. The famous **Crown (Cap) of Monomakh* in the centre was made in the 13C–14C from eight triangular gold plates; it is decorated with precious stones and trimmed with sable. This crown was used for coronations from the end of the 15C to 1682. According to legend it was much older, and had been given to Grand Prince Vladimir Monomakh by his grandfather, the Byzantine Emperor Constantine IX Monomachus. As such it was seen as the symbol of the continuation of authority from the Byzantine to the Russian state. A second 'Cap of Monomakh', also on display, was made for Peter before the dual coronation of 1682. Peter Alekseyevich became Peter the Great, and from his time a western style crown was used in coronations. The *Kazan Crown of Ivan the Terrible* was commissioned in 1552 to celebrate the taking of the Volga town of Kazan. The crown, sceptre, and orb of the first Romanov Tsar, Mikhail, were made in the Kremlin workshops in the 1620s. The diamond-encrusted *Crown of Empress Anna Ivanova* is of the W European type.

R.8. Dress harnesses. These items, as well as those in R.9, once belonged to the Stable Administration (Konyushennyy Prikaz). Outstanding is the *Velvet saddle* decorated with precious stones which the Shah gave to Mikhail Romanov in 1635; the yellow saddlecloth was made from over 400 parrot skins. The *Saddle of Ivan the Terrible* is covered with dark red velvet with gold embroidery, while the *Saddle of Boris Godunov* (1600) is embossed with lions' heads. Turkish harnesses include a gold and silver *Saddle* with dress harness presented to Catherine II by the Sultan in 1775; the set included silver horseshoes with silver nails.

R.9. Carriages. The oldest is the late 16C *English carriage* presented to Boris Godunov by King James I. The little *Summer and Winter Coaches* were made for the child Peter the Great in 1675; they were drawn by ponies, and dwarfs served as coachmen. Elizabeth Petrovna travelled from St. Petersburg to Moscow for her coronation in another *Winter coach* on display here. Elizabeth's daughter-in-law, Catherine II, was given the richly gilded open *Summer Coach* by her favourite, Grigory Orlov; it was made in London in 1779. The *Travelling coach of Catherine II* was built in France in 1765. The most elaborately-decorated *Coach* was built by the Frenchman Bournihall in 1757 and presented to Elizabeth Petrovna by Hetman Razumovsky; the paintings on the sides are by François Boucher.

The **USSR Diamond Fund** exhibition (Almaznyy Fond SSSR) is housed in the building of the Armoury Palace. Admission for foreign visitors can be arranged through Intourist.

The collection, established in 1922, contains diamonds and jewellery dating from the mid-18C to the present. On display is the diamond-encrusted crown made by J. Pozier for the coronation of Catherine II in 1762. Another exhibit linked with Catherine is the 190-carat *Orlov Diamond, which was given to her in 1774 by Count Grigory Orlov; the stone was found in India in the 17C. the 89-carat Shah Diamond, discovered in India in the 16C, also has an interesting history: it was presented to Nicholas I by the Shah of Persia as compensation for the assassination of the Russian diplomat (and noted poet) Aleksandr Griboyedov.

2   The Kitay-Gorod

This Rte runs through one of the oldest and most famous parts of Moscow, the Kitay-Gorod. It leads from the Historical Museum down through Red Square to St. Basil's Cathedral, E from St. Basil's along Ul. Razina, and N through Staraya and Novaya Pl. Finally, completing a rough square, it returns to the museum via Ul. 25 Oktyabrya. The basic Rte is some 3km long. The starting point is near PROSPEKT MARKSA, PLOSHCHAD' REVOLYUTSII, and PLOSHCHAD' SVERDLOVA METRO STATIONS.

The origin of the district's name is obscure, although historians agree that it does not mean literally 'China-' (Kitay) 'Town' (Gorod). It may come from the old word kita, meaning the wattle used in the earthen wall erected around what was an early 'suburb' of the Kremlin. One of the oldest parts of Moscow, the Kitay-Gorod was first settled in the 12C–13C. In the 1530s a 2.5km long brick wall connected to the Kremlin was built around it; the wall survived until the Soviet era. Nobles and merchants once lived here in this centre of Russian trade, but by the beginning of this century it had become mainly a commercial district with few dwelling-houses.

Red Square (Pl. 4; 4) takes up a great expanse of some 73,000 sq m to the E of the Kremlin. (A young West German, Mathias Rust, was able to land a light aircraft in the square in May 1987—after a violation of Soviet airspace which led to the retirement of the then Defence Minister.) The square was first opened up at the end of the 15C; since the 17C it has been called KRASNAYA PLOSHCHAD', the original meaning of which was 'Beautiful Square'.

Not only did the square develop as one of the commercial centres of Muscovy, it was also the scene of popular disturbances and manifestations and of state proclamations and repression. Here in 1550 the young Ivan the Terrible confessed his shortcomings to the people, but in the same place were perpetrated some of the worst excesses of his Oprichnina. During the Time of Troubles the body of the murdered False Dmitry was displayed in Red Square, and here Vasily Shuysky was both proclaimed Tsar and deposed. The late-17C was also a time of social unrest, and as an object lesson the Cossack rebel Stepan Razin was drawn and quartered here in 1671. The finale to this grim era came in 1698 when Peter I carried out a mass execution of the strel'tsy who had mutinied while he was visiting Western Europe.

Although Red Square was still used for religious and state processions in the 18C and 19C it had lost its political importance, and by 1914 it was used as a market only during the weekend before Easter. The year 1917 marked the return of the square to the centre of Russian history. The first shots of the Bolshevik rising in Moscow were exchanged here between rival army units on the evening of 27 October. Six days later Soviet forces massed here for the final attack on the Kremlin. Under the Communist regime Red Square has been world famous for the great popular demonstrations and military parades held on May Day and on 7 November, the anniversary of the Bolshevik Revolution. Particularly significant was the parade of 7 November 1941 when tanks rumbled through the square and then directly off to the front line. Four years after this, on 24 June 1945, a great victory parade took place in which captured Nazi standards were symbolically thrown to the ground.

The huge square has maintained its late-19C appearance except for the relatively unobtrusive Lenin Mausoleum. Various proposals to alter it fortunately remained unrealised. There was a pre-revolutionary project to route an elevated railway through Red Square, and later the visionary Soviet architect Leonidov suggested putting up here a 50-storey monumental building in the form of a huge factory chimney.

The red brick *Historical Museum (Gos. Istoricheskiy Muzey), built to the designs of Sherwood (1878–83), stands at the N end of the square. The site was the original location of Moscow University, established in 1775 as the first university in Russia. A product of the Pseudo-Russian school of architecture, the current building borrowed decorative details from a range of ill-matched sources, and the

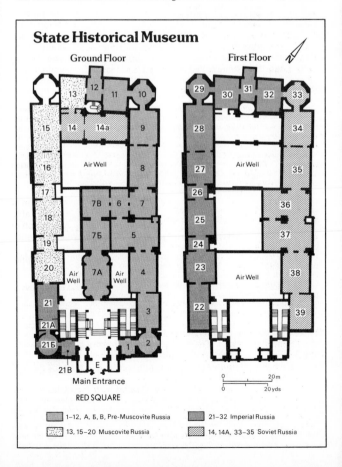

State Historical Museum

Ground Floor — First Floor

Main Entrance

RED SQUARE

▧ 1–12, A, Б, B, Pre-Muscovite Russia		▧ 21–32 Imperial Russia
▨ 13, 15–20 Muscovite Russia		▨ 14, 14A, 33–35 Soviet Russia

mechanical symmetry of the Red Square façade, with its twin towers, contrasted with the apparently anarchic splendour of St. Basil's Cathedral at the far end of the square. Sherwood wanted to use multi-coloured tiles here but had to settle for sombre red brick.

The layout of the museum is more functional than the exterior would suggest. The vast archaeological and numismatic collections help to illustrate the growth of the Early Russian towns and the early development of the various peoples of the present USSR. Original documents and artefacts show the rise of the Russian state after Peter the Great. Throughout this later period special attention is paid to economic development and the continuing social instability. The museum possesses a fine collection of arms, and much space is devoted to Russian military history. The museum is, at the time of writing, closed for renovation; the following is the layout before the closure.

Ground Floor. Rooms 1–7, 7-A, 7-Б, 7-B, Pre-Kievan Russia. R. 8. Kiev. RR. 9–11. Novgorod, Rostov, Suzdal, Vladimir. R. 12. Golden Horde. RR. 13, 15–20. Muscovite Russia, 14C–17C. RR. 14, 14-A. Second World War. RR. 21, 21-A, 21-Б, 21-B. 18C Russia.

1st Floor. RR. 22–27. Russia, 1750–1800. RR. 28–31. Revolutionary thinkers and movements. RR. 32–34. War and Revolution, 1914–21. R. 35 Soviet State. RR. 36–39. Temporary Exhibitions.

2nd Floor. R. 40. Temporary Exhibitions.

Until 1802 a moat ran down the W side of the square, and drawbridges extended from the Nikol'skiye and Saviour Gates of the Kremlin. Now the area in the shadow of the Kremlin wall is occupied by the **Lenin Mausoleum** (Mavzoley V.I. Lenina).

V.I. Lenin was the leader of the Bolshevik Party and the first prime minister of Soviet Russia. When Lenin died on 21 January 1924 his body was brought from suburban Gorki and interred next to the Kremlin wall in a temporary mausoleum which had been hastily designed by the architect A.V. Shchusev. Red Square was felt to be an appropriate place for Lenin's final resting place, as public demonstrations had been held here since 1918 and a number of revolutionary heroes already lay buried by the Kremlin wall.

A team of doctors led by Professors V.P. Vorob'yov and B.I. Zbarsky were able that spring to develop new methods of embalming which permitted the long-term preservation of the Communist leader's remains. From 1 August 1924 it was possible for visitors to see Lenin's body in a glass-topped coffin. By this time a new wooden mausoleum had been completed; it also was designed by Shchusev and incorporated the outline of the present version, a simple stepped-pyramid almost Pre-Columbian in style. Once it had become clear that the embalming method was effective a permanent granite building was erected to Shchusev's design. It was completed in October 1930, after 16 months' work. This mausoleum is faced with red, black and grey granite, with a mourning belt of black labradorite.

Lenin's body was maintained by a special Mausoleum Laboratory led by Zbarsky and later by S.R. Mardashov. The body was evacuated to the Urals in July 1941, but returned in April 1945 (meanwhile the Red Square Mausoleum was camouflaged to deceive the Luftwaffe). When Stalin died in 1953 his body (embalmed by Mardashov) was placed next to Lenin's, in what was known for eight years as the Lenin-Stalin Mausoleum. In October 1961 Stalin's remains were taken out and reburied nearby, under the Kremlin wall.

The entrance to the tomb is flanked by two soldiers manning the so-called Sentry Post No. 1. The guard is changed every hour; the relief sentries, with a corporal of the guard, leave the Saviour Gate of the Kremlin exactly 2 minutes and 45 seconds before, and march past the reviewing stands to the mausoleum.

Behind the sentries is a *Vestibule*, decorated with a coat of arms of the USSR. To the left a flight of granite steps descends between grey labradorite-faced walls. The *Funeral Hall* (Traurnyy Zal) is a cube measuring some 10m on each side. The black or grey labradorite-faced walls have red quartzite pilasters. In the centre, on a black base, lies *Lenin's Sarcophagus*. Visitors enter the hall, walk around three sides of the sarcophagus, and exit through a door in the opposite wall. The present sarcophagus was designed in 1939 by Shchusev and B. Yakovlev and installed in 1945. Special attention was paid to reducing reflection from the glass. The lighting in the room is indirect, and since 1964 the heating and humidity of the room have been electronically controlled.

Visitors emerge behind the Mausoleum into a kind of Soviet pantheon where for many years the most honoured dead have been buried.

On 10 November 1917, after the bitter fighting in Moscow during the Bolshevik rising, some 238 bodies were placed in two large common graves next to the Kremlin's Nikol'skiye Gate (which had been taken by storm seven days before). In the years that followed, other revolutionaries were buried by the Kremlin wall: 11 people killed by a bomb at the offices of the Communist Moscow Committee in 1919; A.V. Stankevich, a former Tsarist major-general who entered the Red service and was hanged by the Whites in 1919 after being captured; the American writer John Reed; Inessa Armand, an old personal friend of Lenin's, who (like Reed) died in one of the 1920 epidemics; the veteran Bolsheviks F.A. Artyom and V.P. Nogin; and V.V. Vorovsky and P.L. Voykov, two Soviet diplomats assassinated abroad.

In 1925, with the death abroad of the Commissar of Finance, M.K. Vladimirov, the practice began of burying the ashes of the deceased in the Kremlin wall. Each name is written in gold letters on a black granite plate.

Among the senior Soviet officials whose remains rest here are: L.B. Krasin; V.P. Menzhinsky; the historian M.N. Pokrovsky; Yu. Larin; G.M. Krzhizhanovsky; S.M. Kirov, the assassinated leader of the Leningrad Party organisation; V.V. Kuybyshev; G.K. Ordzhonikidze; A.V. Lunacharsky.

Also buried here are Nadezhda Krupskaya (Lenin's wife), M.I. Ul'yanova (Lenin's sister), and the writer Maxim Gorky.

Among foreign Communists are: Sen Katayami from Japan; Jenö Landler from Hungary; Fritz Heckert and Clara Zetkin from Germany; William D. 'Big Bill' Haywood (half of whose remains were buried in Chicago); Charles E. Ruthenberg, another early American Communist; Arthur MacManus, one of the founders of the British Communist Party; O.V. Kuusinen, the Finnish Comintern leader.

Individuals prominent in industry and science include: I.A. Likhachov, organiser of the Soviet motor industry; A.P. Karpinsky, head of the Academy of Sciences; I.V. Kurchatov, father of the Soviet atomic and hydrogen bombs; S.P. Korolyov, who organised the Soviet space programme.

Among military leaders: B.M. Shaposhnikov; F.I. Tolbukhin; L.A. Govorov; R.Ya. Malinovsky; K.K. Rokossovsky; I.S. Konev; G.K. Zhukov; and A.M. Vasilevsky (who replaced Shaposhnikov as Chief of the General Staff in 1942).

Among the other honoured dead are: the three-man crew of a stratospheric balloon which crashed in 1934; the test pilot V.P. Chkalov; Yury Gagarin, the first cosmonaut; V.M. Komarov, killed in Soyuz-1 in 1967; and the three cosmonauts who died during the re-entry of Soyuz-11 in 1971.

A small number of Communist leaders have been accorded the honour of burial in a special plot of ground behind the mausoleum: Ya.M. Sverdlov (1885–1919), first head of the Soviet state; M.V. Frunze (1885–1925), who succeeded Trotsky as Commissar for War; F.E. Dzerzhinsky (1877–1926), organiser of the Cheka (secret police); M.I. Kalinin (1875–1946), head of state from 1919; A.A. Zhdanov (1896–1948), Kirov's successor as head of the Leningrad Party organisation; Joseph Stalin (1879–1953); K.Ye. Voroshilov (1881–1969), Commissar of Defence (1925–40) and head of state (1953–60); S.M. Budyonny (1883–1973), a legendary Civil War commander; M.A.

Suslov (1902–81), prominent ideologist; L.I. Brezhnev (1906–82); Iu.V. Andropov (1914–84); and K.U. Chernenko (1911–85). However, nearly half these people have been deeply discredited by historical glasnost, and it would be surprising if there were not a number of re-interments.

Opposite the mausoleum extends the long façade ot **GUM** (Gos-udarstvennyy Universal'nyy Magazin or State Department Store). On this traditional market site Bove built a bazaar in the Classical style to replace the stalls that had been destroyed in the fire of 1812. This in turn was replaced in 1889–93 by the present GUM, then called the *Upper Trading Rows* (Verkhniye Torgovyye Ryady). The great build-ing designed by A.N. Pomerantsev originally contained over 1000 individual shops arranged along three parallel glass-roofed pas-sages. The revolutionary metal skeleton was hidden behind a 'tradi-tional' exterior which took motifs from Early Russian architecture. GUM is the largest department store in the Soviet Union, serving as many as 350,000 customers a day.

The architect R.I. Klein built the similar *Middle Trading Rows* to the S in 1891–93. Between the two buildings is UL. KUYBYSHEVA (Pl. 5; 3), leading E into the heart of the Kitay-Gorod.

Known as the Il'inka before the Revolution, this was one of the most important commercial streets in Moscow. It was the site of several major banks and also of the former **Stock Exchange** (Kupecheskaya Birzha) (M.D. Bykovsky, 1836–39; rebuilt by A.S. Kaminsky, 1873–75). The attractive Style Moderne building just to the N at PL. KUYBYSHEVA, left, was designed by Schechtel in 1904 as the *Ryabushinsky Bank*. Further down Ul. Kuybysheva are the *Ministry of Finance* (No. 9) and the *Ministry of Culture* (No. 10).

To the S of Red Square, on a terrace and surrounded by a wrought-iron fence, stands the Cathedral of the Virgin of the Intercession 'by the Moat' (Pokrovskiy Sobor 'chto na rvu') or, as it is better known, ****St. Basil's Cathedral** (Sobor Vasiliya Blazhennovo) (Pl. 4; 6). For many people this building with its celebrated cluster of multi-coloured onion domes epitomises 'Russia'. Ivan the Terrible com-missioned the church to commemorate his army's seizure of the Tatar stronghold of Kazan on 1 October 1552; this day was the Feast of the Intercession, hence the proper name of the church (the 'Moat', now filled in, ran along the NE wall of the Kremlin). The building was erected in 1555–60 on the site of the earlier Church of the Trinity. In 1588 an additional chapel was added to the NE corner over the grave of the Holy Fool (Yurodiviy) Basil (Vasily) the Blessed who had died in 1552 and been buried beside the former Trinity Church. His remains were transferred to the wall of the new cathedral, and since then it has been popularly known by his name.

For many years the church was thought to be the work of two architects, Posnik and Barma, but recent research suggests that there was only one—Posnik Yakovlev, nicknamed 'Barma' (Mumbler). According to legend Ivan had the architect(s) blinded so that he (they) might never again create a church of such splendour.

Lermontov described the domes as being 'scattered all over the building without symmetry or order like the offshoots of an old tree climbing over its bared roots'. Closer inspection, however, reveals the regularity of the design; this is best seen in the W (main) façade opposite the Kremlin wall. The Tsar originally wanted a cathedral with eight chapels. The main Chapel of the Intercession was to be surrounded by seven others to represent the number of attempts made by his army to capture Kazan. The architect(s), however, insisted that for the sake of symmetry there must be nine chapels, and so the basic ground plan resembles an eight-point star with eight domed chapels—four large and octagonal and four small and squarish. These are grouped alternately around the central chapel and connected by a covered gallery.

The central pillar-chapel has a very high tent roof crowned with an octagonal drum and a small cupola (like 'the cut-glass stopper of an antique carafe' according to Lermontov). The tent-roofed porches over the staircases (NW and SW corners) and the tent-roofed octagonal bell tower (SE corner) were erected in the late 17C. Amid the multitude of decorative detail certain motifs recur. The semi-circle used for the arcades and the top of the windows is repeated in the many gables higher up. The pointed arrow gables on the octagonal chapels echo the tent outline of the roof of the main chapel, the bell tower, and the roofs of the porches. It is colour more than anything else that creates the sense of irregularity. The building was originally red brick with white details, and at one time the walls were painted white and the domes gilded. Only in the 1670s did it assume its present appearance. While red prevails as the main colour, the gables are picked out in patterns. Most spectacularly, the domes were decorated with flamboyant moulded ribs and facets in various patterns and colours.

By comparison the **Interior** is simple. The lesser chapels, originally whitewashed, were decorated in the 17C with frescoes of entwined flowers. The main chapel, which is reached by an internal staircase, seems narrow but very high; the walls are brick, with painted pilasters, and inscriptions and frescoes under the dome. The Baroque iconostasis dates from the 19C with only a few of the icons surviving from the earlier period. The cathedral was badly damaged in the fire of 1739 and restored under Catherine II. In 1812 French troops plundered St. Basil's but fortunately failed to carry out Napoleon's instructions to blow it up. It was restored in 1817 and at the same time the houses around it were demolished. Further restoration work was started in 1921; two years later the cathedral was opened as a museum of art and architecture, and later it became a branch of the Historical Museum. The exhibition in the W chapel traces the stages in the Ivan IV's campaigns against the Tatars and including examples of 16C Russian and Tatar weaponry.

The **Monument to Minin and Pozharsky** (Martos, 1818), now just next to St. Basil's, stood originally in the middle of Red Square.

Moscow's first monumental sculpture, it commemorates the two heroes of the Time of Troubles (early 17C). The main inscription reads 'To Citizen Minin and Prince Pozharsky from a Grateful RUSSIA, 1818'. Bas-reliefs on the plinth depict (N) the citizens of Nizhniy Novgorod collecting funds for the patriotic struggle and (S) the expulsion of the Poles. The round structure between St. Basil's and GUM marks the **Lobnoye Mesto**, where state pronouncements were read; executions took place on wooden scaffolding erected nearby. The architect M.F. Kazakov designed the present version of the Lobnoye Mesto in the 1780s. The open space S of the cathedral and leading to the Moskvoretskiy Most was cleared in the 1930s by the wholesale demolition of the old buildings here.

Stepan (Stenka) Razin, who led a peasant revolt in 1670, was taken to his execution in Red Square by way of the road opposite the E façade of St. Basil's; from this comes its present name, UL. RAZINA (Pl. 5; 5). On the corner (right) stands the small red and white Classical **Church of St. Barbara the Martyr** (Ts. Velikomuchenitsy Varvary) (1795–1804). The origin of the street's old name, the Varvarka, was a 16C church on this site.

To the S of Ul. Razina, on a site once intended for the skyscraper of the People's Commissariat of Heavy Industry, rises the immense **Rossiya Hotel**. The hotel, with its glass and aluminium façade, measures 250m by 160m, towers 12 storeys, and can accommodate 5300 guests; it was designed by D.N. Chechulin and completed in 1971. One of the largest hard-currency *Beriozka Shops* is located here (at the E end), as well as the 3000 seat **Central Concert Hall** (Gos. Tsentral'nyy Kontsertnyy Zal) and the **Zaryad'ye Cinema**. The cinema perpetuates the name of the Zaryad'ye district, one of the oldest in Moscow and so-called for its position beyond (za) the trading rows (ryady) of Red Square. Latterly a poor area of artisans and Jews it was called 'Moscow's Whitechapel'.

A row of interesting old buildings stretches along the N side of the hotel. The so-called **English House** (Angliyskoye Podvor'ye), where English merchants lived in the mid-16C, was recently discovered next to the Church of St. Barbara; now restored, it is one of the few surviving secular buildings from this era. Next door, the yellow **Church of St. Maxim the Blessed** (Ts. Maksima Blazhennovo), with its central onion dome, dates from 1698; later builders added the bell tower (1829). The next bell tower, a pointed one, belonged to the former **Monastery of the Sign** (Znamenskiy Monastyr'), which continues beyond the access ramp to the Rossiya. The monastery was founded in 1634 on the estate of the Romanov family and includes a **Cathedral** (1677–84), monks' **Cells**, and the former *Palace of the Romanov Boyars* (a boyar was a member of one of the oldest noble families). This is now a museum known officially as the **Palace of the 16C–17C in Zaryad'ye** (Palaty XVI–XVIIvv. v Zaryad'ye).

The palace is one storey high on Ul. Razina but four-storeyed on the S side. It was built by the Boyar Nikita Romanov, brother-in-law of Ivan the Terrible, and is said to have been the birthplace of Mikhail Romanov, the first Tsar of the Romanov dynasty. The building was first restored in 1859, and further work has been carried out since. The interior gives a good idea of what life was like for a boyar family of this era. Clothes and items of furniture are on display, and of particular interest is the reconstructed boyar's study with its richly embossed and gilded leather wall-covering and its elaborate tiled stove. Russian pottery of the 17C–20C is exhibited on the top floor.

The **Old Gostinyy Dvor** occupies the N side of Ul. Razina between KHRUSTAL'NYY PER. and RYBNYY PER. Quarenghi's design (1790–1805) flanks the traditional arches of a bazaar with Corinthian columns. On the opposite side of Ul. Razina, is the small five-domed **Church of St. George** (Ts. Georgiya na Pskovskoy Gorke) completed in 1658. A stretch of the old Kitay-Gorod wall is visible behind it, running along KITAYSKIY PROYEZD. The top of the small grey and silver **Church of the Conception of St. Anna** (Ts. Zachatiya Anny) may also be seen, beyond the terrace of the Hotel Rossiya. This very old miniature church was completed in 1483 but altered after the great fire of 1547; the exterior was restored to its original appearance in the 1950s.

The Varvarka (Ul. Razina) once passed through the Kitay-Gorod wall by way of the Varvarskiye Gate (now demolished). A famous incident is connected with a supposedly miraculous icon of the Virgin which once hung above the gate. In the terrible plague year of 1771 it was taken down for use in crowded services, services which themselves helped to spread the pestilence. To prevent this the relatively enlightened Archbishop Amvrosiy (Ambrose), head of the church in Moscow, tried to have the revered image put back above the gate. The enraged mob turned on him, he was pursued to the Don Monastery, and there he was torn to pieces.

PL. NOGINA (Pl. 5; 3), at the foot of Ul. Razina, contains the **Delovoy Dvor** (lit. Business House), a five-storey building with large windows (No. 2/5); built in 1912–13 by I.S. Kuznetsov, it was the last word in pre-revolutionary office blocks. After the Revolution it served as a hostel (John Reed lived here in 1920) and later as the site of important government offices. Kuybyshev worked in this building as head of the Supreme Economic Council (VSNKh) from 1926–30, and Ordzhonikidze, Commissar for Heavy Industry, had his offices here from 1930–37. The Delovoy Dvor was built on the site of the Vasil'yevskiy Lug, one of the major markets of old Moscow. Nearby are the PLOSHCHAD' NOGINA METRO STATION and, in the SE corner of the square, the **Church of All Saints in Kulishki** (Ts. Vsekh Svyatykh na Kulishkakh) (1687), a picturesque brick building with Moscow Baroque details; the Church of All Saints is said to be the reconstruction of a church built by Dmitry Donskoy to celebrate the battle of Kulikovo (1380).

SOLYANKA UL. (Pl. 5; 5), one of the oldest in the city, leads E past the Church of All Saints. Its name comes from the Tsar's Salt Warehouse (Solyanoy Dvor) which was once situated here. The first street to the left off the Solyanka is UL. ARKHIPOVA with, at No. 8, a functioning **Jewish Synagogue**. The adjacent UL. ZABELINA, another side street off the Solyanka, climbs to STAROSADSKIY PER. Here, behind a fence (right) stands the **Church of St. Vladimir** (Ts. Vladimira v Starykh Sadekh) which was built by the Italian Alevisio Novi in 1510; it has been altered and truncated, hence its nickname 'bez glavy', 'without a dome'. Further up Starosadskiy Per. (right) is the yellow former Protestant **Church of St. Peter**. Opposite the Church of St. Vladimir, behind twin Gothic gate towers and yellow walls, are visible the remains of the **Ivanovskiy Convent**; this was founded in the 16C and rebuilt in 1861–78 by Bykovsky. A place with a gloomy history, the convent was once used for the detention and even torture of women prisoners. Among those held here at the end of the 18C was the infamous noblewoman Dariya Saltykova who had murdered scores of her serfs.

To the S of the Solyanka lies the giant complex of the former **Foundling Home** (Vospitatel'nyy Dom), which could accommodate several thousand children. It was built in 1764–70 by Karl Blank; the scale is best perceived from the river side. The grounds are inaccessible, as the *Dzerzhinsky Artillery and Engineering Academy* is now located here. The entrance on the Solyanka (No. 12) is flanked by statues of 'Mercy' and 'Education' by Vitali. The **Academy of Medical Sciences** stands next door at No. 14, a Classical structure with an eight-columned portico and a flat cupola. D. Gilardi built it in 1823–26, and it has been described as one of the finest 'Empire' style buildings in Moscow. Originally known as the **Opekunskiy Sovet** (lit. Guardianship Council), it was the institution in charge of financing the Foundling Home. The yellow **Church of the Nativity** (Ts. Rozhdestva) (1764) stands opposite the entrance to the Foundling Home on the corner of PODKOLOKOL'NYY PER. Up this street is visible the red belfry of the **Church of St. Nicholas the Wonder-Worker** (Ts. Nikoly Chudotvortsa) (1750), by the junction with PODKOPAYEVSSKIY PER.

Back in Pl. Nogina a lane in the SW corner, NIKITNIKOV PER., leads up to the striking *Church of the Trinity in Nikitniki** (Ts. Troitsy v Nikitnikakh). This was built in 1635–53 by the merchant Grigory Nikitnikov, who had premises nearby. Five domes and tiers of gables surmount the red brick building; on the NW corner, above an arcade, rises a beautiful tent-roofed belfry. The carved stonework and painted tiles of the exterior are particularly impressive. Restored in 1968, this is now one of the few 17C churches open to the public as a museum.

The frescoes and cast-iron doors of the interior are notable. The vestibule and the main nave are to the right of the main entrance. The richly-decorated *Iconostasis* dates from the 1640s and includes work by Simon Ushakov. The best fresco, of the Passion, is on the S wall, but there are fine scenes from the Gospels on the remaining walls. The *Chapel of St. Nikita the Martyr*, in the far right-hand corner, is reached through a splendid carved portal. It was built over the vault of the Nikitnikov family, some of whom are depicted in the wall-paintings.

The grey pre-revolutionary building which houses the **Central Committee of the Communist Party** is just to the N of Nikitnikov Per. The party's head-quarters face the long square N of Pl. Nogina, which is called STARAYA PL. The Regional (Oblast') and Town committees have offices nearby. In the square is displayed a **Roll of Honour** (Doska Pochota) of the best workers from the Moscow Region. At the N end of Staraya Pl. is the **Plevna Memorial** (Sherwood, 1887), commemorating the Russian Grenadiers who fell on 28 November 1878 during the capture of the Bulgarian town of Plevna from the Turks.

To the left of the Plevna Memorial the Il'inskiye Gate once led through the Kitay-Gorod wall to the present Ul. Kuybysheva (p 114); on the N side stood the Church of St. Nicholas (Ts. Nikoly 'Bol'shoy Krest') (1680–89), with its splen-didly decorated exterior. Both gate and church were destroyed in the 1930s.
   The E extension of Ul. Kuybysheva on the far (E) side of the Plevna Memorial is called UL. BOGDANA KHMEL'NITSKOVO (Pl. 5; 3) after the Cossack Hetman who transferred the Ukraine from Polish to Russian control in 1653; its former name, the Maroseyka, was a corruption of Malorosseyka, the Little Russian (Ukrainian) Office, which stood at No. 11. The Moscow Baroque **Church of St. Nicholas the Wonder-Worker** (Ts. Nikoly Chudotvortsa v Blinnikakh) is at No. 5 (left) and further down the street at No. 14 (right) stands the remarkable **Church of SS. Cosmas and Damian** (Ts. Kos'my i Damiana), built by M.F. Kazakov in 1791–1803. The design of this small church is unique: the central cylinder with a cupola is surrounded by several smaller cylinders, and the green exterior is virtually devoid of decoration. On the other side of this busy street are the headquarters of the Komsomol, the Communist Youth League (No. 13).

The **Polytechnical Museum** (Politekhnicheskiy Muzey) takes up a whole block between the Plevna Memorial and Pl. Dzerzhinskovo. The main façade, on NOVAYA PL. (Pl. 5; 3), was inspired by Early Russian wood carving and is an outstanding example of the Pseudo-Russian style; it was built by Monighetti in 1875–77 (the wings date from 1896 and 1907).

One of the first Russian purpose-built museums, this was originally called the Museum of Applied Knowledge (Muzey Prikladnykh Znaniy). Some exhibits trace the development of science and technology in Russia and others show the growth of the Soviet economy. Special attention is given to industry, with sections devoted to computers, automation, and aerospace developments.
   At a meeting of the Moscow Soviet in the museum's lecture hall on 25 October 1917 it was agreed to support the revolution in Petrograd. Here, on 12 March 1918, Lenin made his first post-revolutionary speech in Moscow.

The **Museum of the History of Moscow** (Muzey Istorii Goroda Moskvy) stands opposite the Polytechnical Museum, at Novaya Pl., 12; its Classical building was once the *Church of St. John the Divine* (Ts. Ioanna Bogoslova chto pod Vyazom) (1825). The history of the city is shown through a variety of exhibits, including archaeological discoveries and paintings. Special attention is paid to the Revolution and to the later development of Moscow.

To the N of the museums are Pl. Dzerzhinskovo (p 125), Ul. Kirova (p 134) and DZERZHINSKAYA METRO STATION (Pl. 5; 3). The continua-tion of the Rte leading back W to the Historical Museum is the ever-crowded UL. 25 OKTYABRYA, whose name commemorates the fight-ing here during the Bolshevik Revolution of 1917: formerly it was known as Nikol'skaya Ul. The street once began with the pictur-esque Vladimirskiye Gate of the Kitay-Gorod wall, but this was demolished between the wars; the domed Church of the Trinity just inside the gate (right) suffered the same fate. The **Childrens**

Musical Theatre (Moskovskiy Gos. Detskiy Muzykal'nyy Teatr) opened at No. 17 in 1965. The same building houses the new **Slavyanskiy Bazaar Restaurant**; iñ 1897 Nemirovich-Danchenko and Stanislavsky met in an earlier version of this establishment to plan the Moscow Arts Theatre. The green and white Gothic building at No. 15 was erected in 1810–14 as the **Synodal Printing House**. This was the site of the 16C Pechatnyy Dvor where, by tradition, Russian printing was begun with the production of the 'Apostol' in 1564. There is a statue of the printer, Fyodorov, nearby in Pr. Marksa. The press was attacked and burned by a superstitious mob and Fyodorov was forced to flee to Lithuania, but later the first Russian newspaper, 'Vedomosti' was printed here (1703). Next door stood the Greek Monastery of St. Nicholas (Nikol'skiy Grecheskiy Monastyr') from which the street derived its old name; it was founded in 1556 for monks from Mt Athos. Another monastery, the **Epiphany** (Bogoyavlenskiy) **Monastery**, once stood across the street on what is now the corner of KUYBYSHEVSKIY PROYEZD. Founded in the 13C, this was the second oldest monastic establishment in Moscow. The Moscow Baroque **Cathedral** survives, a brick structure with an octagonal tower which dates from 1693–96.

The **Zaikonospasskiy Monastery** (No. 7) was the third one in this street; Nikol'skaya Ul., behind (za) which the monastery stood, was traditionally a centre of the icon trade, hence the name. Boris Godunov founded the establishment in 1600, and from 1687 it housed the Slavo-Graeco-Latin Academy, the first higher school in Muscovy. Among the pupils of the school were Lomonosov, Kantemir, and the architect Bazhenov. The light octagonal spire of the

The Resurrection Gate (engraving by M. Makhaev, 1760s). This was the site of the Chapel of the Iberian Virgin. The gate stood at the north end of Red Square; it was demolished in the Soviet period

monastery's **Cathedral** is visible above the buildings facing Ul. 25 Oktyabrya. It was completed in 1661 and then extensively reconstructed by Zarudny in 1717–20.

Next to the monastery, on the corner of Red Square, once stood the tower of the Kazan Cathedral. The cathedral was built in 1635–36 and named after an icon of the Virgin from Kazan which Prince Pozharsky carried during the Time of Troubles. Pozharsky's copy of the icon was kept here until it was moved to the new Kazan Cathedral in St. Peterburg. The Moscow cathedral was demolished in the Soviet period, but in 1990 plans for rebuilding it were discussed.

The former *Provincial Administration* (Gubernskoye Upravleniye) stood opposite the Historical Museum in ISTORICHESKIY PROYEZD (No. 5/1). The Cossack rebel Pugachov and some of his followers were held here in the Yama ('Pit') prison in 1775 before their execution. The courtyard contains the former **Mint** (Monetnyy Dvor) (1697), an elaborately decorated building that has been restored.

At one time the remarkable Iberian (Iverskiye) or Resurrection (Voskresenskiye) Gate spanned Istoricheskiy Proyezd here. It was built in the reign of Tsar Fyodor with twin arches and twin tent-roofs. The Chapel of the Iberian Virgin (Iverskaya Chasovnya) was built in 1669 and stood on the N side of the gates, between the arches. It held a copy of a supposedly miraculous icon of the Virgin from the Iberian Monastery on Mt Athos; the copy was given to Tsar Aleksey in 1648. The chapel was regarded as a particularly holy place which the tsars and emperors traditionally visited as soon as they arrived in Moscow. The chapel and the gates were demolished in the 1920s and 1930s.

3   Prospekt Marksa

This Rte follows Pr. Marksa (Marx Prospekt) from Borovitskaya Pl. along the NW side of the Kremlin and beyond to Pl. Dzerzhinskovo, a distance of rather less than 2km. The starting point lies just to W of BIBLIOTEKA IM. LENINA METRO STATION.

One of the most important streets in the capital, the present PR. MARKSA (Pl. 4; 6) was much widened in the 1930s to form a great central avenue which was intended to lead to the projected Palace of Soviets. It was named in 1961 after the father of modern Communism. The first part of the avenue, as far as the foot of Tverskaya Ul., was formerly called the Mokhovaya after the 18C market where moss (mokh), used for insulation, was sold.

To the right, between MANEZHNAYA UL. and the walls of the Kremlin, is visible the green of the **Alexander Gardens** (Pl. 4; 6). The Neglinnaya River, once part of the Kremlin's defences, was buried in a conduit here, and above it in 1821–23 Bove laid out a park for Alexander I. Opposite the gardens, at Manezhnaya Ul., 11/1, was located in the 1920s and 1930s the Executive Committee of the Comintern. Lenin's sister Anna lived next door at No. 9 (1919–35) as did Inessa Armand (1919–20); there is a small *Lenin Museum* (Muzey V.I. Lenina v Kvartire A.I. Ul'yanovoy-Yelizarovoy) here.

Many people regard the **Pashkov House** at Pr. Marksa, 26 (left) as the finest Classical building in Moscow and the most impressive creation of its architect, V.I. Bazhenov. Built in 1784–87 for P.Ye. Pashkov, it stands on a hillock facing the Kremlin. The main façade includes three sets of four columns, one set in the centre on a high base and the other two in the wings. Bazhenov was not responsible for the existing belvedere which was rebuilt in the 1830s by A.I. Mel'nikov. In 1862 the building became the home of the Imperial

Rumyantsev Museum, an institution based on the collection of Count N.P. Rumyantsev (1754–1826), son of the famous Field Marshal. By 1914 the museum included a collection of national costume, an art gallery, and a library of a million volumes. In 1925 the library of the Rumyantsev Museum became the Lenin Library. The present main building of the **Lenin Library** (Gos. Biblioteka SSSR im. V.I. Lenina) stands next door, beyond the entrance to the Metro station.

This site, on the corner of the present Pr. Kalinina, was previously used for the archives of the Tsarist Foreign Ministry and before that for the palace of Natal'ya Naryshkina, Peter the Great's mother. The architects of the 'new building' of the Lenin Library were V.A. Shchuko and V.G. Gel'freykh who (with Iofan) were also to be the winners of the design competition for the Palace of Soviets. No attempt was made to blend the new library building with the Pashkov House and in fact the façade along Ul. Marksa is a repetition of the architects' unsuccessful project for the Dnepr Hydroelectric Power Station. Construction work began in 1928 and was finished only in the 1950s. The rich funds of the Lenin Library are second only to those of the US Library of Congress; many of the books are housed in the tall building in the rear of the site.

Mikhail Kalinin (1875–1946), a Bolshevik veteran, became head of state (Chairman of the VTsIK, later President of the Supreme Soviet) after Sverdlov's death in 1919. He remained in this post until 1946 and enjoyed considerable popularity as the 'All-Union Village Elder' (vsesoyuznyy starosta). The **Kalinin Museum** (Gos. Muzey M.I. Kalinina), with exhibits on Kalinin's life and activities, is the first building on the S side of Pr. Marksa, at No. 21. The **Reception Rooms of the Supreme Soviet** are on the opposite corner of Pr. Kalinina from the Lenin Library; Kalinin received delegations here throughout his career.

A long white Classical building lies to the right, between Pr. Kalinina and the Kutaf'ya Gate of the Kremlin. The **Manezh**, formerly a military riding-school (manège), has served since 1957 as the **Central Exhibition Hall** (Tsentral'nyy Vystavochnyy Zal).

Completed in 1825 by the French engineer Carbonnier to the design of Béthencourt, the Manezh represented a considerable technical achievement with its unsupported span of 45m. The architectural detail was handled by Bove. Khrushchev made his famous attack on abstract painting during an art exhibition here in December 1962.

The Classical buildings at Pr. Marksa, 20 (left), the 'new buildings' of **Moscow University**, were completed in 1836 to the designs of Ye.D. Tyurin. The columned rotunda, now a student club, once served as a chapel. In the courtyard is a *Statue of Lomonosov* (1957), the founder of the university. On the site was located Ivan the Terrible's Oprichnyy Dvor, the headquarters of his reign of terror in the 16C. Behind and to the left of the university buildings rises the tiered brick Moscow Baroque tower of the **Church of the Sign 'in the Sheremetev Courtyard'** (Ts. Znameniya na Sheremetevom Dvore) (1702). The 'old buildings' of the university, beyond UL. GERTSENA, are among the finest works of Russian Classicism. They were completed to M.F. Kazakov's design in 1793, destroyed by fire in 1812, and restored by D. Gilardi and A.G. Grigor'yev. The restorers kept the general form of the buildings but changed many details. In the centre stands an eight-columned portico and above it rises the low dome of the *Assembly Hall*. The *Statues of Herzen and Ogaryov* in the courtyard (N.A. Andreyev, 1922) depict two graduates of the university who were among the early 19C founders of the Russian radical tradition. The university had four faculties and nearly 11,000 students (all men) in 1914. The main campus is now situated around the skyscraper on the Lenin Hills.

The ornate Classical building next to the university, now the main offices of **Intourist** (No. 16) (left), occupies an important place in the history of Soviet architecture. I.V. Zholtovsky built it along the lines of a Palladian Renaissance palazzo in 1934, and it became a model for other builders; Constructivist architecture was now dead and the Classical revival dominated the next 20 years. From the 1930s to the 1950s this was the US Embassy. The **National Hotel** (Natsional'), one of the finest in Moscow since before the Revolution, is on the corner of TVERSKAYA UL.; it was built by A.I. Ivanov in 1903. Lenin stayed here for eight days in March 1918—after his arrival from Petrograd and before he moved into the Kremlin. The hotel later served as the '1st House of Soviets', a hostel for officials and delegates; John Reed lived here. (For details of Tverskaya Ul. see p 155.)

The vast asphalt space to the S of the university, the Zholtovsky building, and the National Hotel, is known as PL. 50-LETIYA OKTYABRYA (50th Anniversary of October Square) (Pl. 4; 4). It was created in 1938 when old buildings standing here were demolished. The grey bulk of the **Moskva Hotel** looms beyond. Shchusev produced the final version after a Constructivist design (already begun) had been abandoned; building work lasted from 1931 to 1938. Had the 1935 town plan been realised the curiously asymmetrical W façade would have faced the Palace of Soviets down a huge wide avenue; it looks out of scale facing the low building of the Manezh. With its new extension to the E, the hotel can accommodate 2000 guests.

The upper part of the Alexander Gardens occupies the space between the great square and the Kremlin Wall. The **Tomb of the Unknown Soldier**, an impressive war memorial at the NE end of the park, was dedicated on 8 May 1967 when the eternal flame was brought here from Marsovo Pole in Leningrad.

The Battle of Moscow was fought in December 1941, and 25 years later the remains of an unknown soldier who fell at Km. 41 of the Leningradskoye Shosse were reinterred here. On the tomb is the inscription 'Thy name is unknown. Thy victory is immortal'. To the left in red granite is written '1941 To those who fell for the Motherland 1945', to the right are the names of the 'Hero-Cities': Leningrad, Odessa, Sevastopol, Kiev, Volgograd (Stalingrad), Minsk, Novorossiysk, and Kerch (also the Hero-Fortress of Brest). A guard of honour stands by the grave, and newly-weds come here to lay flowers next to the eternal flame.

The Tomb of the Unknown Soldier was built on the site of an **Obelisk to Revolutionary Thinkers**, which has now been moved farther back into the gardens. The obelisk was originally erected in 1913 to commemorate 300 years of the Romanov dynasty. Five years later it became one of the first Soviet monuments when the inscribed names of the Tsars were removed and replaced by those of 20 theorists of revolution. Marx and Engels are included, as well as Thomas More and George Winstanley. Nearby in the park is an attractive Classical **Grotto** by Bove (1822).

The huge 11-storey grey and red **Gosplan Building**, the office of the State Planning Department, confronts the Moskva Hotel across Pr. Marksa. Built in 1932–35 by A.Ya. Langman for the Council of Labour and Defence (STO), it is also known as the **Council of Ministers Building**. The stretch of Pr. Marksa between it and the hotel was formerly known as Okhotnyy Ryad (Hunters Row) where fish and game were sold; this was one of the principal markets of old Moscow. The **House of Unions** (Dom Soyuzov) at No. 10 (left) is dwarfed by the Gosplan building next door. An outstanding example of Russian Classicism, with a four-columned portico facing Pr.

Marksa and a six-columned one in the main façade on Pushkinskaya Ul., it was rebuilt by M.F. Kazakov from an existing mansion in the 1780s.

The Moscow nobility purchased the building in 1784, and Kazakov undertook further work for them; major alterations were also made in 1896 and 1903–08. As the Club of the Nobility (Dom Blagorodnovo Sobraniya) the building was used for balls and concerts; the great ballroom of the club was Kazakov's *Hall of Columns*. After the Revolution the trade unions took over the building, hence its present name. Lenin's body lay in state in the Hall of Columns from 23 to 25 January 1924; it was here also that Stalin's body was placed in 1953. The Hall of Columns served for the trial of Bukharin and others in 1938. The public trials of 1936 (Zinoviev and Kamenev) and of 1937 were also held in the House of Unions, but in the smaller *October Hall*.

PUSHKINSKAYA UL. (Pl. 4; 4, formerly Bol. Dmitrovka Ul., contains at No. 6 (right), the **Moscow Operetta Theatre** (Moskovskiy Teatr Operetty). The building, although altered, is of interest as Savva Mamontov used it for his Private Opera in the 1890s. Chaliapin and Rachmaninov began their careers here, and Mamontov engaged a number of leading artists to design the sets and costumes. KUZNETSKIY MOST (Pl. 4; 4), which turns to the right off Pushkinskaya Ul., was one of the most fashionable shopping streets of pre-revolutionary Moscow, with many French- and German-owned premises selling luxury goods. The aristocracy would promenade here at four o'clock in the afternoon. The Revolution brought an end to the aristocratic way of life, but there are still some good bookshops here. Two impressive commercial buildings survive at No. 16 (A.E. Erikhson, 1912) and No. 15 (the former *International Merchant Bank*, 1898). The unusual name of the street derives from a bridge (most) which crossed the Neglinnaya River here until the early 19C, and from the fact that Ivan III established a district of smiths (kuznetsy) nearby.

Beyond Pushkinskaya Ul. and the entrance to PR. MARKSA METRO STATION the avenue opens out into one of the great squares of Moscow. PL. SVERDLOVA bears the name of Yakov Sverdlov (1885–1919), one of the key Bolshevik organisers of the Revolution and the first head of the Soviet state; a *Statue of Sverdlov* was unveiled on the S side of the square in 1978 (P.Ye. Ambartsumyan). Originally this area was a marshy extension of the Neglinnaya River, but after the fire of 1812 it was drained and turned into Teatral'naya Pl. (Theatre Square). A granite *Statue of Karl Marx* by L.Ye. Kerbel' (1961) stands in the middle of the square. Ground was broken by Lenin himself on May Day 1920 and the present statue was unveiled 41 years later. The inscription on the base reads 'Workers of the world, unite!' To the S is a fountain with cherubs by Vitali (1835).

The world-famous **Bolshoy Theatre** (Gos. Akademicheskiy Bol'shoy Teatr SSSR) (Pl. 4; 4) dominates the whole square. Bove and Andrey Mikhaylov built a great theatre here in 1821–24, but it burned down in 1853 and was rebuilt by Cavos. The existing massive eight-columned portico surmounted by the chariot of Apollo was part of the original design, but it is generally felt that the architectural quality of the theatre declined with Cavos' reconstruction.

The Bolshoy can trace its history back to 1776 when a company was founded by an English showman named Maddox. The first performances were given in a mansion on the present Ul. Frunze, but the company soon moved to new premises on the corner of Petrovka Ul. (the present site of the Bolshoy); the Petrovskiy Theatre, as it was then called, was the first permanent theatre in Moscow. Fire destroyed this theatre in 1805 and until the completion of what was originally called the Bol'shoy Petrovskiy Theatre the company had no permanent base. It was during this period, in 1806, that it came under state control as an Imperial theatre.

The company performed some of the first Russian operas at the end of the 18C and shared in the great national revival in the middle of the following century; Tchaikovsky's first opera, 'The Voyevoda' had its première at the Bolshoy in 1869. The best-known of the magnificent Russian operas of the 19C were, however, first produced in St. Petersburg, and for part of the century the theatre building was shared with an Italian company. Ballet developed in the 18C when the company drew on the talents of orphans from the Foundling Home, and a firm foundation was laid by Adam Gluszkowski (who led the company from 1812 to 1839). The Bolshoy tradition was developed by Carlo Blasis (1861–64) and, especially, by Aleksandr Gorsky (1898–1924). The greatest ballerina of the era was Yekaterina Gel'tser, who joined the company in 1894. But as was the case with the opera, the new Russian ballets tended to receive their first performances in St. Petersburg's Mariya Theatre. One notable exception was Tchaikovsky's 'Swan Lake', but the version produced at the Bolshoy in 1877 was not well received; Petipa and Minkus's 'Don Quixote' was also first performed at the Bolshoy (1869).

After 1917 the Bolshoy developed its repertoire with revolutionary works like the ballet 'The Red Poppy' (1927) and the opera 'Battleship Potemkin' (1938), but the greatest era came after the Second World War (during which the company had been evacuated to the city of Kuybyshev). The outstanding talents of the choreographer Leonid Lavrovsky and the ballerina Galina Ulanova were transferred from Leningrad's Kirov Theatre, new works like Prokofiev's 'Cinderella' (1945) and 'The Stone Flower' (1954) were introduced, and the company secured an international reputation with its triumphant tour to Britain in 1956. Both the ballet and opera companies made successful foreign visits in the 1950s and 1960s. In 1964 Yury Grigorovich became artistic director, producing Khachaturian's 'Spartacus' (1968) and Prokofiev's 'Ivan the Terrible' (1975). The leading dancers of this era, Maya Plisetskaya, Yekaterina Maksimova, and Vladimir Vasiliev contributed greatly to the success of the company.

The building of the Bolshoy Theatre also played an important role in Russian political life. The Moscow State Conference was held here in August 1917. The climax of this rallying of more conservative political forces was the ovation accorded to the supreme commander, General Kornilov; two weeks later Kornilov led an abortive coup. The great hall, with its capacity of over 2000 people, was used for many congresses of Soviets between 1918 and 1935 (the 5th to 9th All-Russian and the 1st to 7th All-Union Congresses). Of these, the most dramatic was the 5th All-Russian Congress of Soviets in July 1918. Not only did it accept the new Soviet constitution but it was also the occasion of the final split between the Communists and their Left Socialist-Revolutionary allies. The Left SRs attempted a coup d'état and their delegation, led by Mariya Spiridonova, was held prisoner in the Bolshoy Theatre while the revolt was put down.

When Teatral'naya Pl. (now Pl. Sverdlova) was created in the 1820s the Bolshoy Theatre was part of an ensemble of buildings; one other building remains, the **Maly Theatre** (Gos. Akademicheskiy Malyy Teatr). The Maly Theatre was built as a private mansion in the 1820s and converted by Thon in 1838–40. One of the finest dramatic companies in Moscow, the Maly can trace its history back to the university theatre founded in 1757. Two men were particularly identified with the evolution of the company; Mikhail Shchepkin (1788–1863), the actor who founded the Russian realist tradition, and the great playwright Aleksandr Ostrovsky (1823–86), who worked here from 1853 until his death; there is a *Statue of Ostrovsky* in front of the theatre (N.A. Andreyev, 1929). The noted actress Mariya Yermolova first appeared on the stage here in the 1870s and she was part of the company for over fifty years. Yermolova provided a continuity into the Soviet era, and she was the first person to be awarded the title 'People's Artist'. The **Central Childrens Theatre** (Tsentral'nyy Detskiy Teatr—TsDT) stands opposite the Maly. The company, which specialises in plays for children, was founded in 1921 and moved to the present building 15 years later.

PETROVKA UL. (Pl. 4; 4), which runs along the E side of the Bolshoy Theatre, was another of the fashionable shopping streets of pre-revolutionary Moscow. The old building of **TsUM** (Tsentral'nyy Universal'nyy Magazin or Central Department Store), at No. 2 (right), was built in 1909 by Klein as the first modern department store in Moscow—with the unlikely name of *Muir & Merrilees*. The Gothic exterior conceals pioneering use of reinforced concrete construction.

A six-storey glass extension was added in 1974. At No. 10 is the more traditional *Passazh* shopping complex (1903).

The E side of Pl. Sverdlova is occupied by the 400-room **Metropole Hotel** (Metropol'), long regarded as one of the best in Moscow. Built in 1899–1903 by the British architect Walcott, it represents a fine example of the Style Moderne. The decoration includes ornate grills and a mosaic by Vrubel', 'Printsessa Gryoza', based on E. Rostand's 'Princesse Lointaine'. After the Revolution the Metropole was for a time called the 2nd House of Soviets, and the Central Executive Committee (VTsIK) under Sverdlov met here in 1918 and 1919.

Voskresenskaya Pl. to the W of the Metropole (and to the S of the present Moskva Hotel) was the scene of bitter fighting during the Bolshevik uprising of 1917 and was renamed PL. REVOLYUTSII (Pl. 4; 4). In the square beyond the entrance to PLOSHCHAD' REVOLYUTSII METRO STATION stands an over-ornate red brick Pseudo-Russian building (1890–92) by D.N. Chichagov which once served as the *Town Duma*, or municipal council. The town dumas were set up as part of Alexander II's Great Reforms in 1870, but suffrage was always restricted; after the counter-reform of 1892 less than half of one per cent of the population had the vote. During the October Revolution the pro-government Committee of Public Safety was based here and the building had to be taken by storm by the Bolsheviks on 2 November 1917. The **Central Lenin Museum** (Tsentral'nyy. Muzey V.I. Lenina) is now housed here. Founded in 1924, the museum moved to its present building in 1936. The 34 halls contain a wealth of material pertaining to Lenin's career: personal effects, first editions, newspapers, paintings, and rare photographs. Also on show here are the Communist leader's Rolls-Royce 'Silver Ghost Alpine Eagle' and a replica of his office in the Kremlin.

NEGLINNAYA UL., runs N from the Metropole Hotel and Pr. Marksa, following the course of the buried Neglinnaya River. The sharp bend in the section of the 1538 *Kitay-Gorod Wall* which survives to the S and E of the hotel is explained by the fact that it also once followed the Neglinnaya. One crenellated tower remains at the E end, but the wall beyond was knocked down in the 1930s. The attractive archway next door marks the beginning of TRET'YAKOVSKIY PROYEZD, which leads via a second arch to UL. 25 OKTYABRYA (p 118). Built in 1871 to the plans of A.S. Kaminsky, the façade on Pr. Marksa combines tent roofs, Moscow Baroque windows, and swallow-tail battlements like those of the Kitay-Gorod wall.

The *Statue of Ivan Fyodorov*, set high on a bank to the right of Pr. Marksa, depicts the traditional founder of Russian printing. The date on the base, 19 April 1563, was when the printing of the 'Apostol' began in the nearby Pechatnyy Dvor. This monument, by S.M. Volnukhin (1909), is one of the most attractive in Moscow.

UL. ROZHDESTVENKA to the left (formerly Ul. Zhdanova) has recently had its historic Christian name restored, after the disgrace of Stalin's henchman Zhdanov. The **Savoy Hotel** at No. 3 is the former Berlin Hotel, reopened in 1989 after modernisation and run in partnership with the Finns.

This Rte ends with PL. DZERZHINSKOVO (Pl. 5; 3). The square was once called Lubyanskaya after people from NW Russia settled in this district in the 15C and 16C (there was a Lubyanitsa street in Novgorod). The present name dates from 1926, following the death of Feliks Dzerzhinsky; a *Statue of Dzerzhinsky* by Ye.V. Vuchetich was unveiled here in 1958. Dzerzhinsky, a veteran Polish Bolshevik, is best known as the founder of the secret police or Cheka. In 1918 the central headquarters of the Cheka was established here in Lubyanskaya Pl. between the present Ul. Dzerzhinskovo and Ul. Kirova in the former offices of the Rossiya Insurance Company; since that time the building has been known as the **'Lubyanka'**. The right half of the building, by Shchusev, was added in 1947. The square itself was much enlarged in the 1930s when the Vladimirskiye Gate and Kitay-Gorod wall were removed. There are now several entrances to the DZERZHINSKAYA METRO STATION here and, at the end of Pr. Marksa (left), the children's department store, *Detskiy Mir* (Childrens World). On the site of Detskiy Mir was the Pushechnyy Dvor or 'Cannon House' where the giant bronze Tsar Cannon in the Kremlin was cast.

UL. DZERZHINSKOVO (Pl. 5; 3) leads NW from the square towards the Bul'varnoye Kol'tso. By the junction with Kuznetskiy Most (No. 5/21, left) is a large grey apartment building (L.N. Benois and A.I. Gunst, 1905–07) which now serves as the Ministry of the Motor Car Industry. This was for a long time the Soviet Foreign Commissariat. In the courtyard stands a *Statue of V.V. Vorovsky* (M.I. Kats); it was unveiled in 1924, the year after this Soviet diplomat was assassinated in Switzerland. The house at Ul. Dzerzhinskovo, 14 (right), was in 1812 the residence of the governor, F.V. Rostopchin, who ordered the burning of Moscow. Here took place the episode in 'War and Peace' in which Rostopchin hands the prisoner Vereshchagin over to an angry mob in order to effect his own escape.

In the NE corner of Pl. Dzerzhinskovo, at the beginning of UL. KIROVA (p 134), is the **Mayakovsky Museum** (Gos. Muzey V.V. Maya-kovskovo). The museum, opened after reconstruction in 1974, occupies a corner site; the address is PROYEZD SEROVA, 3/6.

Vladimir Mayakovsky (1893–1930) is among the most highly esteemed of Soviet poets. He worked and lived in this building from 1919, producing much of his best poetry, and here, at the age of 37, he shot himself; his motives remain a point of contention. The museum contains, in addition to the poet's personal effects, a collection of the posters he produced for RosTA (the Soviet press agency). There is also a programme of films, including some in which May-akovsky himself took part.

4   The Bul'varnoye Kol'tso

The Bul'varnoye Kol'tso (Boulevard Ring) (Motor Route A) is the innermost of Moscow's ring roads. This Rte follows the Kol'tso clockwise from Kropotkinskaya Pl. (SW of the Kremlin) around centre of the town and on to the confluence of the rivers Yauza and Moskva (SE of Red Square). The basic Rte measures some 7.5km, more than a comfortable walk, but Trolleybuses No. 15 and 31 travel half-way around the Kol'tso to Trubnaya Pl. (Pl. 4; 2), and the final third of the way, from Turgenevskaya Pl. (Pl. 5; 3), is served by Trams No. A, 3, and 39. The Metro intersects the Rte at many places. The starting point is near KROPOTKINSKAYA METRO STATION.

The boulevards are among the most attractive parts of the city and evocative of 19C Moscow. For much of the way the centre of the avenue is occupied by wooded paths and decorated with iron railings and lamp-standards; statues stand among the trees. The buildings lining the avenue date mostly from the last century and are full of historical and architectural interest.

The history of the Bul'varnoye Kol'tso goes back to the late 14C, when an earthen rampart was erected here. In the last quarter of the 16C a white stone wall with 27 towers was built under the supervision of Fyodor Kon'. The area encircled, between these outer walls and the walls of the Kremlin and Kitay-Gorod, was known as the Belyy Gorod (White Town)—possibly after the colour of the wall. At the end of the 18C and the beginning of the 19C the Belyy Gorod fortifications were torn down and replaced by the existing boulevards. Some of the squares still bear the names of the old gate-towers, for example Nikitskiye

Vorota. The boulevards, unlike the outer Sadovoye Kol'tso, have survived without major change. In the mid-1920s there was one futuristic proposal by the artist El Lissitsky (1890–1941) to create buildings that would float like clouds above the compact squares of the Bul'varnoye Kol'tso (the supporting towers would take up a minimum of ground space). Happily for the preservation of the boulevards, this 'Wolkenbugel' scheme was never realised.

The Kol'tso leads to the N from KROPOTKINSKAYA PL. (Pl. 4; 6). (For details of the district S to the Moskva River see p 142.) Each segment of the Bul'varnoye Kol'tso has its own name. The first has been known since 1924 as GOGOLEVSKIY BUL'VAR (formerly Prechistenskiy Bul'v.), after the writer Nikolay Gogol (1809–52). There is a *Statue of Gogol* at the end of the boulevard; the present version, by N.V. Tomsky, was unveiled in 1952, but another monument had been erected here earlier, on the centenary of the writer's birth (see below).

This boulevard was in one of the wealthiest parts of old Moscow. S.M. Tret'yakov, a wealthy patron of the great gallery of Russian art, lived near the present Metro station at Gogolevskiy Bul'v. 6 (right). Across the boulevard, at No. 23, lived from 1910 to 1938 the actress Olga Knipper-Chekhova (1868–1959), widow of the playwright Chekhov.

On this left side UL. RYLEYEVA and SIVSTEV VRAZHEK PER. lead into an area where the homes of the gentry and the intelligentsia were concentrated. The writer Mikhail Bulgakov lived in 1934–40 in UL. FURMANOVA (to the right off Ul. Ryleyeva). In Sivtsev Vrazhek Per. Pasternak set the Gromeko House which plays an important part in 'Dr Zhivago'; Herzen lived as a student at No. 25 (where he was arrested) and in 1843–46 at No. 27. The latter is now the *Herzen Museum* (Dom-Muzey A.I. Gertsena). The Slavophile S.T. Aksakov (1791–1859) lived in 1849–51 in a lane to the right off Sivstev Vrazhek Per., at PER. AKSAKOVA, 9 (the building has been demolished). In the 1830s he held an important literary salon, the 'Aksakov Saturdays', in his house on the parallel UL. MYASKOVSKOVO (No. 12). The next two streets off Sivtsev Vrazhek Per. contain attractive wooden houses: the beautiful carved *Porokhovshchikov House* (A.L. Gun, 1872) in STAROKONYUSHENNYY PER., and, at UL. TANEYEVYKH, 5, a more Classical house (1816) typical of those built immediately after the great fire.

The block to the right of Gogolevskiy Bul'v. between UL. MARSHALA SHAPOSHNIKOVA and UL. FRUNZE is taken up by the former *Alexander Cadet Academy*, the main centre of resistance to the 1917 Bolshevik uprising in Moscow. This later became the headquarters of the Revolutionary Military Council (RVSR) (Ul. Frunze, 19) from which Trotsky led the Red Army during the Civil War; other early military leaders like Frunze and Budyonny also worked here. Beyond, the boulevard descends under Pr. Kalinina (Motor Route M1) at Arbatskaya Pl. (Pl. 4; 5) (p 150). The ARBATSKAYA METRO STATION is located here. The newly-pedestrianised Ul. Arbat (p 151) turns off to the left.

The Bul'varnoye Kol'tso emerges from the underpass as SUVOROVSKIY BUL'V.; Generalissimo A.V. Suvorov (1730–1800), one of Russia's greatest soldiers, lived near here in Ul. Gertsena. Gogol died at Suvorovskiy Bul'v., 7a (left) in 1852, and the *Statue of Gogol* (N.A. Andreyev, 1909) which originally stood in Gogolevskiy Bul'v. has been moved to the courtyard of this building, now a branch of the Literary Museum (Gos. Literaturnyy Muzey). Across the boulevard at No. 8a stands the *Central House of Journalists*, headquarters of their union. The imposing Classical *Lunin House* at No. 12a, with an eight-columned loggia and only one wing, was built by D. Gilardi in 1818–23 for General P.M. Lunin, the uncle of one of the Decembrists.

It is now the home of the **Museum of Oriental Art** (Muzey Iskusstva Narodov Vostoka).

The museum was founded in 1918 on the basis of the pre-revolutionary collections of P.N. Shchukin and others. On display is material from Transcaucasia and Soviet Central Asia as well as from non-Soviet Asia. Of special note are the Iranian ceramics (12C–13C), Chinese porcelain (13C–20C), Indian miniatures (16C–17C), and Japanese prints (18C–19C).

Suvorovskiy Bul'v., ends with NIKITSKIYE VOROTA (Pl. 4; 3), a square named after the demolished Nikitskiye Gate of the Belyy Gorod wall. A *Statue of K.A. Timiryazev* (1843–1920) stands in the centre of the next boulevard (S.D. Merkurov, 1923); Timiryazev, a noted botanist, is depicted wearing the academic gown of Cambridge University. The attractive building of the *TASS News Agency* (1977) stands to the right. On the other side of the square (left) is visible an austere white church with a green dome; the **Church of the Great Ascension** (Ts. Bol'shovo Vozneseniya) was built, probably by A.G. Grigor'yev, in the 1820s. Here in 1831 Pushkin married Natal'ya Goncharova. To the E stands the small **Church of St Fyodor Studit** (Ts. Fyodora Studita), built by Filaret Romanov in 1626.

The street which intersects the Bul'varnoye Kol'tso at Nikitskiye Vorota is called UL. GERTSENA (Pl. 4; 3) in honour of the radical thinker Aleksandr Herzen (1812–1870). Herzen often attended political salons at the home of his friend N.P. Ogaryov who lived in this street (formerly Bol. Nikitskaya Ul.), at No. 23 (right). Further E along Ul. Gertsena, in the direction of Pr. Marksa, is the Pseudo-Russian building of the **Mayakovsky Theatre** (Moskovskiy Akademicheskiy Teatr im. Vl. Mayakovskovo) (No. 19, right). This was originally the Potopkhin Operetta Theatre, which became after the Revolution the Theatre of Revolutionary Satire (TeRevSat). In 1923–24 Meyerhold was artistic director of what was then called the Theatre of Revolution, and later, as the Moscow Theatre of Drama, it was run by N.P. Okhlopkov. The **Tchaikovsky Conservatory** (Moskovskaya Gos. Konservatoriya im. P.I. Chaykovskovo) at No. 13 was founded in 1866 by N.G. Rubinstein (1835–81) and has been located in the present building since 1870.

Tchaikovsky (1840–93) played an important role in the new school, until 1878; a teaching post here provided the young composer with his first financial security. A *Statue of Tchaikovsky*, by Mukhina, was unveiled here in 1954. Among the most important musicians involved in the work of the Conservatory were S.I. Taneyev, Rachmaninov, Scriabin, and Khachaturian. The Tchaikovsky Conservatory (not to be confused with the Tchaikovsky Concert Hall) is now the largest music school in the Soviet Union. The international Tchaikovsky Piano Competition has been held here, in the Great Hall with its oval portraits of famous musicians, since 1958.

SOBINOVSKIY PER. turns right off Ul. Gertsena by the Mayakovsky Theatre; the opera singer L.V. Sobinov (1872–1934) trained at the academy of the Moscow Philharmonic Society, at No. 6. This building now houses the *Lunacharsky Institute of Theatre Art*, better known as *GITIS* (Gos. Institut Teatral'novo Iskusstva im. A.V. Lunacharskovo). The institute is one of the most important drama schools in the USSR.

The W part of Ul. Gertsena, to the left of Nikitskiye Vorota, is also of interest. The house at Ul. Gertsena, 42, has one of the oldest historical plaques in Moscow, with the laconic inscription, 'Here lived Suvorov'. V.I. Nemirovich-Danchenko (1858–1943), one of the founders of the Moscow Arts Theatre, lived at No. 50 from 1903 to 1938. The *Brazilian Embassy* is housed in an ornate blue and yellow tiled building at No. 54. Across the road (No. 53) stands the *Central House of Writers* (Tsentral'nyy Dom Literatorov).

Nearer to Nikitskiye Vorota is a *Statue of Aleksey Tolstoy* (1883–1945) (G.I. Motvilov, 1957). The Soviet writer lived beyond Ul. Kachalova in a street which now bears his name (No. 4). One of Schechtel's most striking Art Nouveau buildings, the *Ryabushinsky House (1902–06), stands behind an iron railing on the corner of Ul. Kachalova (No. 6/2) and UL. ALEKSEYA TOLSTOVO. Between the flat roof and the yellow glazed brick walls is an exotic floral mosaic frieze; a well-proportioned carved-stone porch protrudes in the front. The house was built for the wealthy industrialist Stepan Ryabushinsky, but the Soviet writer Maxim Gorky (1868–1936) lived here from 1931, after his return from emigration. There is now a **Gorky Museum** (Muzey-Kvartira A.M. Gor'kovo) here. It is possible to see the Schechtel interior with its Art Nouveau decoration and splendid carved-stone staircase. Ul. Alekseya Tolstovo, formerly Spiridon'yevskaya Ul., was in a very exclusive district at the turn of the century, and Schechtel had built in 1893 a mansion for another millionaire, Savva Morozov, at No. 17; this large attractive Gothic building was later owned by Mikhail Ryabushinsky, brother of Stepan. Zholtovsky's **Tarasov House** (1910) at No. 30 initiated yet another architectural style, the Neo-Classical revival of the early 20C. This architect was later to be largely responsible for the dominance of Classicism in the Soviet architecture of the 1930s, 1940s and 1950s.

Ryabushinsky House (Gorky Museum) (F. Schechtel, 1902–06). This Russian industrialist's mansion is one of the outstanding examples of Moscow Art Nouveau

UL. KACHALOVA (formerly Mal. Nikitskaya Ul.) is named after one of the leading actors of the Moscow Arts Theatre, V.I. Kachalov (1875–1948), who lived at No. 20 from 1915 to 1922. The handsome *Bobrinsky House* at No. 24 was built at the end of the 18C. This street was once the site of the Church of St. George, where Tchaikovsky began his disastrous marriage to Antonina Milyukova in 1877.

TVERSKOY BUL'V., beyond Nikitskiye Vorota, was the first of the boulevards to be laid out (1796). It has a number of theatrical associations. Mariya Yermolova (1853–1928), one of the finest Russian actresses, lived at No. 11 from 1889 to 1928; her flat has been made into a small **Yermolova Museum** (Muzey-Kvartira M.N. Yermolovoy). The **Malaya Bronnaya Theatre** (Moskovskiy Dramaticheskiy Teatr na Maloy Bronnoy) is located nearby in MALAYA BRONNAYA UL. at No. 2/4 (left) (the street's name derives from the quarter of armourers—bronniki—which existed here in the 16C–17C). The Malaya Bronnaya is one of the more adventurous theatre companies, and Anatoly Efros worked here as a director from 1967. The building once housed the *State Yiddish Theatre* (GosYet) which was run by the actor-director Solomon Mikhoels until the late 1940s. At Tverskoy Bul'v., 23, stands the **Pushkin Theatre** (Moskovskiy Dramaticheskiy Teatr im. A.S. Pushkina), established in 1950. The building formerly housed the *Kamernyy* (Chamber) *Theatre*, which A.Ya. Tairov (1885–1950) ran from 1914 until the end of his life. With Meyerhold, Tairov pioneered Expressionist drama, and he was the first to utilise Constructivism for stage design. The plays of Brecht, Shaw, and O'Neill were introduced to Russia by Tairov; later, in the changed intellectual climate of the 1930s, Vishnevsky's 'Optimistic Tragedy' was first produced at the Kamernyy Theatre (1933). On the other side of the boulevard (right), at No. 22, is the **Theatre of Peoples' Friendship** (Teatr Druzhby Narodov), which stages works by visiting Soviet companies. The striking theatre building (V. Kubasov and V. Ulyashov) with its towering reddish-brown superstructure and attractive lamps opened in 1973 and can accommodate an audience of 1400.

Bitter fighting occurred near this site during the Bolshevik Revolution as rebel forces stormed the nearby offices of the civil governor (gradonachal'nik). Herzen was born in 1812 near the end of the boulevard (left) in the Classical *Yakovlev House* (No. 25). This is now the *Gorky Literary Institute*, which was founded in 1933 on the initiative of Maxim Gorky as a centre for the training aspiring writers.

STRASTNOY BUL'V. (Pl. 4; 2) begins beyond the junction with Tverskaya Ul. (Motor Route M10) at Pushkinskaya Pl. (p 158). PUSHKINSKAYA METRO STATION is located here.

UL. CHEKHOVA turns to the left behind the building of the newspaper Izvestiya; the street takes its name from the writer Chekhov, who lived here at various addresses (Nos 11, 12, and 29). Ul. Chekhova contains one of the most delightful churches in Moscow, the white and green ***Church of the Nativity of Our Lady in Putinki** (Ts. Rozhdestva Bogoroditsy v Putinkakh). Built in 1649–52 with financial help from Tsar Aleksey Mikhaylovich, this is an outstanding example of a tent-roofed church (no adm.).

The builders produced an extremely complex design with four major elements: to the right the church itself with three graceful cupola-crowned steeples of uneven height; to the left (at right angles) the *Chapel of the Burning Bush*

*The Church of the Nativity in Putinki. This is one of the
most striking examples of use of the tent roof*

crowned with a pyramid of kokoshnik gables and a tent roof; a tent-shaped bell
tower linking church and chapel; and a one-storey refectory and porch. The
decoration is largely confined to the Ul. Chekhova side (the other façades were
originally masked by the Belyy Gorod wall—now demolished); this was once
the important road (put') to the town of Dmitrov (Mal. Dmitrovka Ul.), which
may explain the 'Putinki' in the name. The emphasis on external decoration and
the proliferation of tent roofs (Russian rather than Byzantine in origin) in this
and other churches met with the disapproval of the Church and especially of
Patriarch Nikon; in 1652, the year the Church of the Nativity was completed, an
edict was proclaimed banning the use of tent roofs for anything but bell towers.

The *Merchants Club* (Kupecheskoye Sobraniye) was built next door,
at Ul. Chekhova, 6, in 1908 (Ivanov-Schitz). After the Revolution the
building served first as a lecture hall for the Sverdlov Communist
University, then from 1927 as the Theatre of Worker Youth (TRAM).
It has been since 1928 the home of the **Leninskiy Komsomol Theatre**
(Moskovskiy Teatr im. Leninskovo Komsomola-TLK); the innovative
Anatoly Efros led the company from 1963 to 1967.

Rachmaninov lived from 1905 to 1917 near the beginning of Strastnoy Bul'v., at No. 3 (left); the *Novosti Press Agency* is now located here. The imposing yellow **Gagarin Mansion**, further along the boulevard on the same side (No. 15/29), was built in 1786–90 (possibly by M.F. Kazakov) and then rebuilt in 1826 by Bove.

The design includes an immense portico, the longest in Moscow, with 12 Ionic columns. Before the war with Napoleon this was the aristocratic *English Club*; here Tolstoy set a scene in 'War and Peace', the dinner for Bagration in 1806 where Pierre Bezukhov challenges Dolokhov to a duel. In 1833 the building became the New Catherine Hospital (the inscription '1775' on the pediment refers to the foundation of the original hospital); the building still serves the same function as *Municipal Clinical Hospital No. 24*.

The former *University Printing House*, on the corner of PUSH-KINSKAYA UL. (Pl. 4; 2), was built by D. Grigor'yev and N. Sobolevsky (1816–21). The **Stanislavsky and Nemirovich-Danchenko Musical Theatre** (Moskovskiy Akademicheskiy Muzykal'nyy Teatr im. K.S. Stanislavskovo i V.I. Nemirovicha-Danchenko) is situated down Pushkinskaya Ul. at No. 17 (right). This is Moscow's second theatre for opera and ballet (after the Bolshoy) and was established under its present name in 1941. UL. MOSKVINA which turns to the left (E) (parallel to the boulevard) contains at No. 3 (left) the **Branch of the Moscow Arts Theatre** (Filial Moskovskovo Khudozhestvennovo Akademicheskovo Teatra SSSR im. M. Gor'kovo). This was formerly the Korsh Theatre and was built to the plans of Chichagov in 1884–85 in the Pseudo-Russian style.

At the end of Strastnoy Bul'v. rise the cupolas of the *Upper Monastery of St. Peter** (Vysoko-Petrovskiy Monastyr'), the outstanding landmark of the district. Founded in the 1380s, it became in the early part of the following century one of the fortified monasteries protecting Moscow. The surviving buildings date from a later period, the end of the 17C, when a more or less coherent ensemble was laid out; in this way the monastery developed like the Don Monastery and the New Convent of the Virgin. The Naryshkin family were the major patrons of the St. Peter Monastery; many of them were buried here. Peter I, whose mother was a Naryshkin, took refuge in this monastery during the strel'tsy rising of 1682.

The principal **Church of the Icon of the Virgin of Bogolyubovo** (Ts. Bogolyubskoy Bogomateri) (1686) stands to the left past the entrance, a typical church of the period; the domes have now been removed. It commemorates three of Peter I's Naryshkin uncles who were killed in the revolt of 1682. A tall stepped Moscow Baroque **Bell Tower** with a green onion dome (late 17C) surmounts the old main entrance (right), now closed. Behind the Bogolyubovo Church Natal'ya Naryshkina had the **Church of Metropolitan Peter** (Ts. Petra-Mitropolita) erected in 1690 to celebrate the victory of her son Peter in the recent political struggle. In its existing form the small church consists of a ground storey and an octagonal domed tower. This brick church has some Moscow Baroque details but is particularly notable for the painted tracery around the windows. To the S lies the **Refectory Church** (1697) with five small cupolas set on tall drums above scalloped blind gables. Behind and running along Petrovka Ul. are the two-storey **Cells** (1680s) with their Moscow Baroque windows; a gallery connects them with the Refectory Church.

Petrovskiy Bul'v. and Petrovka Ul. both take their names from the monastery. At PETROVKA UL., 25, M.F. Kazakov built the Classical **Gubin House** in the 1790s. The current site of the **Literary Museum** (Gos. Literaturnyy Muzey) is at Petrovka Ul., 28. On display is material showing the history of Russian literature from the 18C to the 20C.

PETROVSKIY BUL'V. (Pl. 4; 2) runs downhill to the broad TRUBNAYA

PL. (Pl. 4; 2), named after the pipe (truba) which once carried the Neglinnaya River through the town walls at this point.

This district around Trubnaya Pl. had a reputation of being one of the most exotic in old Moscow. The best restaurant in the city before 1914 was held to be the *Hermitage* (Ermitazh) on the SW corner; there is still a restaurant here. The luxurious *Sandunov Baths*, a little way along NEGLINNAYA UL., were housed in a grandiose Beaux Arts style building by F.F. Freydenberg (1895) which is still considered an architectural monument of its era; the centre of the façade is formed by a great arch. Not far to the S on Neglinnaya Ul. is the *State Bank* (No. 12); it was built originally in 1893–95 by K.M. Bykovsky and modified in the 1930s by Zholtovsky. The market for flowers (tsvety) was located in TSVETNOY BUL'V., which runs N from the Bul'varnoye Kol'tso to the Sadovoye Kol'tso; this was also Moscow's centre for prostitution in the years before the Revolution (much of the Bul'varnoye Kol'tso, from Tverskoy Bul'v. on, was frequented by prostitutes and their clients in these years). Most of the houses in the notorious Sobolev Per. (now BOL. GOLOVIN PER.) nearby were brothels. Drachechka Ul. (now TRUBNAYA UL.), which ran parallel to Tsvetnoy Bul'v., was said to have been full of the most hardened criminals.

ROZHDESTVENSKIY BUL'V. (Pl. 5; 1) ascends from the former valley of the Neglinnaya River on the far side of Trubnaya Pl. The remains of the **Convent of the Nativity of the Virgin** (Rozhdestvenskiy Monastyr'), founded in 1386 and another of the fortified monasteries, are located above an embankment to the right. Access to the former convent can be gained from UL. ROZHDESTVENKA, once Ul. Zhdanova; the entrance lies beyond the white tiered **Bell Tower** (Kozlovsky, 1835). The grounds contain a small five-domed *Church* and some monks' *Cells*, but the most notable structure is the small grey **Cathedral** (1501–05). Recently restored, the cathedral is crowned by a complex series of gables and a single rounded dome.

Further up Ul. Rozhdestvenka, on the other side of the street (right), stands the green-domed **Church of St. Nicholas in Zvonari** (Ts. Nikoly v Zvonaryakh) (1762–81). It was built by Karl Blank on what was then the estate of Count I.D. Vorontsov and was intended as a household church.

The green building at Rozhdestvenskiy Bul'v., 12 (right), now the *Ministry of Fisheries*, was once the home of the Fonvizin family. Here in 1821 was held a conference of the 'Union of Welfare', a proto-Decembrist group based on the German Tugenbund; M.A. Fonvizin, one of the leading conspirators, was arrested here in 1826. The building is also of interest as the home of Nadezhda von Meck (1831–94), the patroness of Tchaikovsky, whom the composer never met. The Soviet poet Dem'yan Bedny (1883–1945) lived from 1933 to 1943 at No. 16, and across the boulevard, at No. 15, was the home of the ballerina Yekaterina Gel'tser from 1910 until the 1920s.

There are buildings in the centre of the boulevard where Rozhdestvenskiy Bul'v. meets Sretenskiy Bul'v. On the corner of UL. SRETENKA (left) stands the small white **Church of the Assumption in Pechatniki** (Ts. Uspeniya v Pechatnikakh), which was built in 1695 in the district where the master-printers (pechatniki) of the Pechatnyy Dvor lived. The interior has been converted into the **Merchant Navy Exhibition** (Vystavka 'Morskoy Flot SSSR'). The exhibition traces the development of the Soviet shipping industry with models, dioramas, photographs, etc.

The continuation of Ul. Sretenka S of the Bul'varnoye Kol'tso is UL. DZERZHINSKOVO. The cathedral of a third defensive monastery, the Sretenskiy, has been preserved a little way down the street (right). The **Sretenskiy Monastery** was founded in 1397 and its name is said to derive from a corruption of the word 'meeting' (vstrecha); the

population of Moscow 'met' the newly-arrived icon of the Virgin of
Vladimir here in 1395. The cathedral, a fairly small building with a
green dome, was built in 1679 in a rather conservative style.

An idealised *Statue of Nadezhda Krupskaya* (Ye. F. Belashova and
A.M. Belashov, 1976) stands adjacent to the former Church of the
Assumption, at the beginning of SRETENSKIY BUL'V. Krupskaya
(1869–1939), Lenin's wife, worked from 1920 to 1925 in the Commissariat of Education (Narkompros), which was then situated in a
block of flats at No. 6/1.

Sretenskiy Bul'v. ends with TURGENEVSKAYA PL. (Pl. 5; 3), where
UL. KIROVA crosses the Bul'varnoye Kol'tso. Situated at this intersec-
tion are the TURGENEVSKAYA and KIROVSKAYA METRO STATIONS.
The latter station is of historical interest as during the war it was the
communications centre and reserve headquarters for Stalin and his
GHQ.

Ul. Kirova was formerly called Myasnitskaya Ul. (after the local
community of butchers—myasniki). To the S of Turgenevskaya Pl.,
on the left side of the street, stands the **Main Post Office** (Glavnyy
Pochtamt), built just before the First World War by O.R. Munts. The
Vesnin brothers, who became well known architects in the 1920s,
were involved in the design, and inspired the Romanesque façade.
Opposite the Post Office, at No. 21, is Bazhenov's pink **Yushkov
House** (1793), distinguished by a semi-rotunda at the NE corner.
Here in 1844 was established the 'Academy of Painting and Sculpture' (Akademiya Zhivopisi i Vayaniya); an architectural section was
added later. The first Moscow exhibition of the Peredvizhniki group
of painters was held here in 1872. One of the members of the staff
was the artist L.O. Pasternak whose son Boris, late author of 'Dr
Zhivago', spent his childhood in a nearby annexe. After the Revolution the academy became the 'Higher Technical-Artistic Workshop'
or VKhuTeMas—the Soviet version of the Bauhaus. Next door, at Ul.
Kirova, 19, is a fantastic Pseudo-Chinese *Tea Shop* designed by Klein
(1893).

The lower part of Ul. Kirova, leading to Pl. Dzerzhinskovo (p 125),
is a busy shopping street. UL. MARKHLEVSKOVO, to the right, contains
a functioning Roman Catholic church, the **Church of St. Louis** (Ts.
Lyudovika); the simple Classical façade, by A. Gilardi (1830), looks
onto the narrow MALAYA LUBYANKA UL.

The NE part of Ul. Kirova, to the left of the Bul'varnoye Kol'tso,
contains several impressive large buildings. Beyond an early 19C
mansion by Bove (Ul. Kirova, 33–37) stands the glass façade of the
former **Tsentrosoyuz Building** now the *Central Statistical Administration*. Tsentrosoyuz was the Central Union of Consumer Societies
and its building was designed by one of the greatest architects of the
20C, Le Corbusier (construction was partly supervised by N.D. Kolli,
a Soviet architect). The building, erected in 1929–36, helped intro-
duce the International Modern style to Soviet Russia; it was, indeed,
one of the first of its kind anywhere. The façade on Ul. Kirova was
intended as the rear of the building; the main façade is on the NW
side where it has long been planned to build a major new avenue
called Novokirovskiy Pr. (running from Pl. Dzerzhinskovo to Komsomol'skaya Pl.). To get an adequate impression it is necessary to
view the building from ULANSKIY PER., which turns off Sretenskiy
Bul'v. just before Ul. Kirova.

The former *Baryshnikov Mansion*, a splendid Classical house by
M.F. Kazakov (1797–1802), stands at No. 42. There is another yellow

Classical building, dominated by a central arch, at No. 43; it was formerly the *Lobanov-Rostovsky Mansion* and dates from 1790. The *Gostorg Building* next door was built in the Constructivist style by B.M. Velikovsky. It dates from 1927 and pioneered the use of ferro-concrete and glass. The *Ministry of Trade* is now housed here.

CHISTOPRUDNYY BUL'V. (Pl. 5; 3) begins beyond Turgenevskaya Pl. The name of the boulevard comes from a pond at the far end. Formerly used for the waste from the butchers' suburb, it was cleaned in 1703 by Aleksandr Menshikov (who had acquired the land here) and became known as the Chistyye Prudy (Clean Ponds).

At the start of the boulevard, beyond the Metro pavilion and the tram loop, stands a *Statue of A.S. Griboyedov* (A.A. Manuilov, 1959), the writer (1795–1829) who lived for some time in what is now Ul. Kirova. The *Ministry of Education* is situated at Chistoprudnyy Bul'v., 6. Krupskaya, Lenin's widow, worked here from 1925 to 1939. One of the best-known churches in Moscow is hidden just off the boulevard (right) along TELEGRAFNYY PER. The **Church of the Archangel Gabriel* (Ts. Arkhangela Gavriila) is also known as the Menshikov Tower after the man who had it built in 1704–07, Aleksandr Menshikov (1673–1729); Menshikov, the most important associate of Peter the Great, had an estate here. The district was much built up in later years and the tall pink church now stands in an extraordinarily cramped site.

The church, designed by Ivan Zarudny, marked a new departure in Moscow's architecture. The original spire, similar in design to that of Leningrad's Peter-Paul Cathedral, was the tallest structure in Moscow, taller even than the Ivan the Great Bell Tower. It was, however, badly damaged by lightning and fire in 1723 and was restored, in a shortened and modified form, only in 1780; only two of the three octagonal tiers remain. The body of this Baroque building is richly decorated with stone carvings. On the W façade, giant volute buttresses flank the ornate main door. The church is still open for worship and much of Zarudny's interior survives. The adjacent small yellow **Church of St. Fyodor Stratilit** (Ts. Fyodora Stratilita) was built by I.V. Yegotov in 1806.

Since 1974 the home of the **Sovremennik Theatre** has been a white Classical former cinema (R.I. Klein, 1914) at Chistoprudnyy Bul'v., 19a (left). The company, established in 1956, was under the direction of Oleg Yefremov until 1971 and became one of the best in Moscow. The film director Sergey Eisenstein lived from 1920 to 1934 at No. 23. UL. MAKARENKO (left) contains at No. 5/16 the building of the former *Fiedler Academy* (Real'noye Uchilishche Fidlera) where, in December 1905, a Bolshevik conference decided to carry out an armed uprising; the hall was later shelled by government artillery. On the other side of the boulevard (right), at No. 18, is an early 20C block of flats by S.I. Vashkov, with extraordinary carvings of animals.

UL. CHERNYSHEVSKOVO (Pl. 5; 4) formerly Ul. Pokrovka, crosses the Bul'varnoye Kol'tso at this point; the square is called POKROVSKIYE VOROTA after the former gate-tower of the Belyy Gorod wall. By the corner (left) stands the aquamarine **Apraksin Mansion**, one of the finest (and one of the last) Baroque buildings in Moscow; it dates from 1766 and has recently been restored. The building once served as the *4th High School* (Gimnaziya), whose pupils included the director Konstantin Stanislavsky. After the Revolution it became the Industrial Academy; the exemplary 'shock-worker' Stakhanov and Nadezhda Alliluyeva, Stalin's wife, were among the students here, and Nikita Khrushchev was the school's Party secretary.

The much-altered *Church of the Resurrection in Barashi* (Ts. Voskreseniya v Barashakh) (1734), now a fire station, is situated at No. 26 (right); it is said that Empress Elizabeth Petrovna secretly married her lover Aleksey Razumovsky (1709–71) at this church in 1742. Behind, at No. 2 in PODSOSENSKIY PER., is the *Church of the Presentation in Barashi* (Ts. Vvedeniya v Barashakh), an elaborately-decorated structure built in 1701. This was the suburb where the

The Church of the Assumption in the Pokrovka (1696–99). This Moscow Baroque church stood in what is now Ul. Chernyshevskovo. It was demolished in the Soviet period

Tsar's tent-makers—barashi—lived from the 15C. Down this lane, at No. 18 (right), is a splendid Art Nouveau block of flats by F.I. Makayev (1903).

One of the finest Moscow Baroque buildings, the towering Church of the Assumption on the Pokrovka (Ts. Uspeniya na Pokrovke) (1696–99), once stood in the lower part of Ul. Chernyshevskovo, on the other (W) side of the Bul'varnoye Kol'tso (on the W corner of Potapovskiy Per.); it was destroyed in the Soviet period.

KHOKHLOVSKIY BUL'V. turns off to the right a little way beyond Ul. Chernyshevskovo; it contains (left) the small **Church of the Trinity** (Ts. Troitsy) (1696). POKROVSKIY BUL'V. (Pl. 5; 4) begins beyond this intersection, and to the left stretch the yellow blocks of the former *Pokrovskiye Barracks* (1798). At the end of the first street to the right, BOL. VUZOVSKIY PER., is the former *Morozov Mansion*, now a nursery (No. 1, right). The Left SR Party had their headquarters in this building in July 1918, and from here they launched their unsuccessful revolt against the Communists; Dzerzhinsky, head of the Cheka, was briefly held prisoner here. In quieter days, from 1892 to 1900, the painter I.I. Levitan worked in a studio in the courtyard. The next turn to the right off Pokrovskiy Bul'v. is PODKOLOKOL'NYY PER., which leads past gigantic statues of an armed worker and peasant into what was once the infamous Khitrov Rynok, a late-19C labour market full of the worst lodging-houses; Stanislavsky visited the Khitrov Rynok before staging Gorky's 'The Lower Depths' in 1902. The extension of Podkolokol'nyy Per. to the E of the boulevard is OBUKHA UL., which contains at No. 4 the building of the *Ministry of Justice* (1974).

The boulevards end with YAUZSKIY BUL'V. (Pl. 5; 5), from which PETROPAVLOVSKIY PER. climbs (right) to the **Church of SS. Peter and Paul in Kulishki** (Ts. Petra i Pavla na Kulishkakh). The 18C church stands on top of a hill and its blue domes are visible from a considerable distance.

The vast square extending from the end of the Bul'varnoye Kol'tso to the Moskva River, is bounded on the W by the former Foundling Home and to the E by the Yauza River. To the N of the square, on the corner of YAUZSKAYA UL. and SEREBRYANICHESKIY PER., stands the attractive blue **Church of the Trinity in Serebryaniki** (Ts. Troitsy v Serebryanikakh). A Classical building with a tiered bell tower, it was built in its present form by Karl Blank (1781) in the suburb of master silversmiths (serebryaniki). The western extension of Yauzskaya Ul. is SOLYANKA UL. (p 117); PLOSHCHAD' NOGINA METRO STATION (Pl. 5; 5) is not far along this road (400m).

5 Volkhonka Ulitsa to Lenin Stadium

This Rte leads W from the Kremlin via Volkhonka Ul., Kropotkinskaya Ul., and Bol. Pirogovskaya Ul. The starting point, BOROVITSKAYA PL. (Pl. 4; 6), at the W end of the Kremlin and of Pr. Marksa, is equidistant from the BIBLIOTEKA IMENI LENINA, KROPOTKINSKAYA, and BOROVITSKAYA METRO STATIONS. The full distance to Lenin Stadium totals 4.5km, but Trolleybus No. 5 follows the whole Rte.

UL. MARSHALA SHAPOSHNIKOVA is the first street to the right off
VOLKHONKA UL; on the corner of UL. MARKSA I ENGEL'SA is the 16C
Church of St. Antipiy (Ts. Antipiya 'chto na Kolymazhnom Dvore').
The large green Classical mansion building visible to the W along Ul.
Marksa i Engel'sa is the 18C Dolgoruky House. For a long time this
served as the Institute of Marxism-Leninism, but in 1962 the **Marx
and Engels Museum** (Muzey K. Marksa i F. Engel'sa) was opened
here. The museum is devoted to the life and work of the pioneers of
Communist doctrine. In addition to a wealth of documents and first
editions there are on display some of Marx's personal effects,
including the chair in which he died.

In front of the Marx-Engels Museum, on Volkhonka Ul. itself, is one
of the largest art galleries in the USSR, the ***Pushkin Fine Art
Museum** (Gos. Muzey Izobrazitel'nykh Iskusstv im. A.S. Pushkina).

The gallery was founded on the initiative of Professor I.V. Tsvetayev, a
specialist in art history at Moscow University (Professor Tsvetayev was the
father of the poetess Marina Tsvetayeva; 1892–1941). The basis of the original
collection were plaster casts of the finest Classical, Medieval, and Renaissance
sculptures. The elegant grey museum building is entered via a six-columned
portico. Above the entrance is a frieze of the Olympic Games. The building
dates from 1898–1912; it was built to the plans of R.I. Klein and paid for by
public subscription.
   The Pushkin Museum opened in 1912 as the 'Alexander III Fine Art
Museum'. Not long afterwards it acquired an important collection of Egyptian
antiquities which had been assembled by the Egyptologist V.S. Golenishchev.
The picture gallery was opened in 1924; most of the paintings had been
confiscated from private collections after the Revolution. The museum is
particularly renowned for its collection of French art, especially of the Impressionist and Post-Impressionist periods. Many of the best items had originally
been part of the Shchukin and Morozov collections and were transferred to the
Pushkin Museum from the Museum of New Western Art in 1948.

GROUND FLOOR. Entry is to the left through **Room 14**, with its plaster
casts of Greek sculpture of the 5C–4C BC. From here RR. 3, 4, and 2
lead to R. 1. **R. 1.** Art of Ancient Egypt. A very rich collection of
statues, busts, sarcophagi, tombstones, vases, jewellery, etc. **R. 2.** Art
of ancient civilisations of the Middle East. **R. 4.** Italian paintings,
13C–15C, many showing Byzantine influence. 13C Madonna and
Child, by an anonymous Pisan master. Late 13C Madonna and Child
Enthroned, by an anonymous Florentine artist. *Stefano di Giovanni
Sassetta* (c 1392–1450), SS. Lawrence and Stephen (altar panels). **R.
3.** Byzantine 14C icons. **R. 5.** Italian, German, and Netherlandish
paintings, 15C–16C. *Sandro Botticelli* (1455–1510). **The Annuncia-
tion. Pietro Perugino* (1445/50–1523), Madonna and Child. *Cima de
Conegliano* (1459–c 1518), Descent from the Cross. Works by *Jan
Mostaert* (1475–1555) and *Jan Gossaert (Mabuse)* (died 1533). *Lucas
Cranach the Elder* (1472–1553), The Virgin. *Master of the Castle of
Lichtenstein*, The Nativity.
   R. 6. NW corner. Italian paintings, 16C. *Sebastiano del Piombo*
(1485–1547), Portrait of a Cardinal. *Agnolo Bronzino* (1503–72), Holy
Family. *Paolo Veronese* (1528–88), Minerva. Works by *Giovanni
Boltraffio* (1467–1516), *Paris Bordone* (1500–71), and *Francesco Sal-
viati* (1510–63).
   The display of W European art continues on the other side of the
museum. Visitors should return through RR. 5, 4, and 3, past the large
R. 7 (with Classical antiquities), and on through RR. 11. **R. 10.** Dutch
paintings. 17C Landscapes by *Jan van Goyen* (1596–1656), *Salomon
van Ruysdael* (1600–70), and *Jacob van Ruisdael* (1628–82). Genre

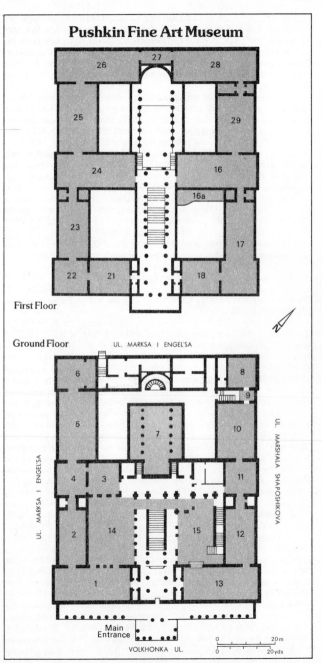

Pushkin Fine Art Museum

First Floor

Ground Floor

scenes and portraits by *Adriaen van Ostade* (1610–84), *Gerard Ter Borch* (1617–81), *Jan Steen* (1626–79). *Gabriel Metsu* (1629–67), and *Pieter de Hooch* (1629–c 1684). *Rembrandt* (1606–69), portraits of an old woman, of Adriaen van Rijn (Rembrandt's brother), and of Rembrandt's sister-in-law (1654); biblical scenes, Doubting Thomas (1634), and Ahasuerus, Haman, and Esther (1660). Paintings by *Carel Fabritius* (1622–54).

R. 11. Flemish and Spanish paintings. *Peter Paul Rubens* (1577–1640), Bacchanalia. Still lifes by *Frans Snyders* (1579–1657). Scenes of peasant life by *Jacob Jordaens* (1593–1678). Portraits by *Anthony van Dyck* (1599–1641). Works by *José Ribera* (1591–1652), *Francisco de Zubaran* (1598–1664), *Bartolome Murillo* (1617–82), and *Francisco Goya* (1746–1828). **R. 12.** Italian paintings, 17C–18C, including work by *Bernardo Strozzi* (1581–1644), *Giambattista Tiepolo* (1696–1770), *Canaletto* (1697–1768), and *Francesco Guardi* (1712–93). **R. 13.** French paintings, 17C–18C, including works by *Nicolas Poussin* (1594–1665), *Claude Lorrain* (1600–82), *Antoine Watteau* (1684–1721), *Nicolas Lancret* (1690–1745), *Jean Baptiste Pater* (1695–1736), *Jean Baptiste Chardin* (1699–1779), *François Boucher* (1703–70), *Jean Baptiste Greuze* (1725–1805), *Jean Honoré Fragonard* (1732–1806).

R. 15 contains copies of W European art of the Middle Ages and Renaissance. From this room a staircase leads to the 1st Floor.

1ST FLOOR. RR. 16, 24–29 contain plaster casts of the most important Classical and W European sculptures. **R. 16.** Greek, 5C BC. **R. 24** (to the W of the Main Staircase). 4C–1C BC. **R. 25.** Ancient Italy. **R. 26–27** (in the NW corner) Middle Ages. **R. 28.** Italian Renaissance. **R. 29.** Michelangelo.

The display of W European paintings continues in the S part of the 1st Floor. **R. 23.** European paintings and sculpture of the 1st half of the 19C. Paintings by *Jacques Louis David* (1748–1825), and *Théodore Géricault* (1791–1824). Fourteen landscapes by *J.B.C. Corot* (1796–1875), including A Gust of Wind (1870). *Eugène Delacroix* (1798–1863), After the shipwreck (1841). Landscapes by *Charles Daubigny* (1817–78). Landscapes by members of the Barbizon School, including *Diaz de la Pena* (1807–76), *Jean François Millet* (1814–75), and *Gustave Courbet* (1819–77). The English School includes landscapes by *J.M.W. Turner* (1775–1851) and *John Constable* (1776–1837), and portraits by *John Hoppner* (1758–1810) and *Thomas Lawrence* (1769–1830), including Au Café (1879). Eleven works by *Claude Monet* 1840–1926), including Déjeuner sur l'Herbe (1866), two versions of Rouen Cathedral, and Waterloo Bridge. *Auguste Renoir* (1841–1919), portraits of women, including the actress Jeanne Samary (1877). *Camille Pissarro* (1831–1903). *Edgar Degas* (1834–1917), including Dancers in Blue. *Albert Sisley* (1839–1899), including The Frost. Sculptures by *Auguste Rodin* (1840–1917), including versions of The Burghers of Calais and The Kiss.

*R. 18 (beyond the Main Staircase). French art of the 2nd half of the 19C. *Paul Cézanne* (1839–1906), Pierrot and Harlequin (1888), Man with a Pipe (c 1895), and one of the last versions of Montagne Ste.-Victoire; also still lifes. *Paul Gauguin* (1848–1903), including Café at Arles (1888) and Tahitian paintings. *Vincent van Gogh* (1853–90), Prisoners at Exercise (1890), landscapes. *Henri de Toulouse-Lautrec* (1864–1901), Portrait of Yvette Guilbert (1884). ***R. 17.** French art of the early 20C. Paintings by *Henri Rousseau* (1844–1910). Landscapes and interiors by *Pierre Bonnard* (1867–1947). Works by *Henri Matisse* (1869–1954), including The Artist's Studio (1911). Landscapes by *Albert Marquet* (1875–1947) and *Maurice*

Vlaminck (1876–1958). *Georges Rouault* (1871–1958), Bathing. Landscapes by *Raoul Dufy* (1877–1953) and *Maurice Utrillo* (1883–1955). *Fernand Léger* (1881–1955), Portrait of Nadia Lé Léger (1949). *Pablo Picasso* (1881–1973), Two Saltimbanques (1901), Acrobat on a Ball (1905), Woman from Majorca (1905), and Portrait of Sabartès (1913).

At Volkhonka Ul., 14/1, stood the *Knyazhiy Dvor Hotel*, where a number of prominent cultural figures stayed, including the writer Gorky and the painters Surikov and Repin; the dramatist A.N. Ostrovsky spent his last years here. In the early period of Soviet rule this is where the Communist Academy was situated. Ostrovsky, and also the prominent Communist Bukharin, were educated next door (No. 16) at the former *1st High School* (1-ya Moskovskaya Gimnaziya). On the corner of Gogolevskiy Bul'v., at No. 18/2, is the *Institute of Language and Literature* of the Academy of Sciences. Opposite this row of buildings is the huge **'Moskva' Swimming Pool**.

On this site was built between 1839 and 1883 the mammoth Cathedral of Christ the Redeemer (Khram Khrista Spasitelya); it was designed by K.A. Thon (architect of the Great Kremlin Palace) as a monument to the war with Napoleon. The cathedral was on nearly the same scale as Leningrad's St. Isaac's Cathedral. Its height was 103m and the central dome measured 30m in diameter. Inside it could accommodate 10,000 worshippers. The golden cupola of the Cathedral of Christ the Redeemer dominated the Moscow skyline until December 1931, when the whole building was blown up, probably the most remarkable act of self-inflicted architectural vandalism of the 20C. Some of the lavish interior decoration has been preserved at the Don Monastery. Another architectural monument which disappeared from this site was a large statue of Alexander III by A.M. Opekushin, which had been unveiled in 1912; the demolition figures in Eisenstein's film 'October'.

The Cathedral of the Saviour, seen from the Kremlin. This giant structure was demolished in the Soviet period. The site is now used for the 'Moskva' Swimming Pool

It was planned to erect an even more grandiose structure in place of the demolished cathedral, the 'Palace of Soviets' (Dvorets Sovetov). A variety of projects were put forward in the 1920s and early 1930s, including one by Le Corbusier (1931), but in 1932 it was decided to use the design of B.M. Iofan, V.A. Shchuko, and V.G. Gel'freykh. Their proposal for the headquarters of the new Soviet state envisaged an eight-tiered Classical building some 315m high and surmounted by a 100-m statue of Lenin. (The Empire State Building was then about 400m high; the Statue of Liberty 48m.) The main hall would have accommodated 20,000 people. Moscow was to be reconstructed with the palace as its architectural centre; a great avenue would run to the NE and SW. As things turned out, neither the new town plan nor the giant building were realised. The outbreak of war stopped construction, and in any event it was found that the water level of this riverside site was too high; the ground would not bear the colossal weight. A palace was completed, but it was the 1961 Palace of Congresses, built in the International Modern style and sunk fairly unobtrusively in the precincts of the Kremlin.

In 1958 construction of the 'Moskva' Swimming Pool began on the site between the Volkhonka and Kropotkinskaya Nab. It is on the same gigantic scale as the cathedral and the proposed Palace of Soviets: the pool has an area of 13,000 sq m and as many as 20,000 swimmers a day can use it. It is an outdoor pool but open all year round: the water is heated in winter.

The Volkhonka meets the Bul'varnoye Kol'tso (Motor Route A) at KROPOTKINSKAYA PL.; the KROPOTKINSKAYA METRO STATION is located here. The continuation of the Volkhonka is called KRO-POTKINSKAYA UL. (Pl. 7; 4). At the very beginning of this (left), on the W side of Kropotkinskaya Pl., stands a *Statue of Friedrich Engels* (I.I. Kozlovsky, 1975) and behind it the 17C *Palace* (Palata) *of Prince D. Golovin.*

SOYMONOVSKIY PROYEZD turns to the left off Kropotskinskaya Ul. The attractive Art Nouveau **Pertsov House** stands at No. 1. This house, with its steeply pitched roof, was built in 1905–1907 by B.N. Shnaubert and N.K. Zhukov; the artist Malyutin designed the striking mosaic panels. The artists Il'f and Petrov lived at Soymonovskiy Proyezd, 5, in the 1920s; a later resident was F.V. Gladkov, author of the novel 'Cement'.

Beyond the Golovin Palace OSTOZHENKA UL. (Pl. 7; 4) leads to the SW. This street was recently given back its pre-revolutionary name; for many years it was called Metrostroyevskaya Ul., or 'Metro-Builders' Street'. Ostozhenka Ul. was once a fashionable residential street. During the Revolution of 1917 the Ostozhenka was the scene of bitter fighting as the rebels tried to capture the headquarters of the Moscow Military District, the centre of the anti-Soviet forces (the front of this building is on Kropotkinskaya Ul., at No. 7). Not far along Ostozhenka Ul., 3-Y ZACHAT'YEVSKIY PER. turns to the left; the red Moscow Baroque **Gate-Church of the Saviour** (Ts. Nerukotvornovo Spasa) (1696) is visible at the end. This, and the E wall, are all that remain of the former *Convent of the Conception* (Zachat'yevskiy Monastyr'), which is said to have been founded in 1360 by Metropolitan Aleksey and his sisters Iulianiya and Yepraksiya. It was re-established by Tsar Fyodor Ivanovich who hoped by this gesture to cure his wife's barrenness.

Near the end of the street, at Ostozhenka Ul., 38, is a large yellow Classical building dating from the late 18C. Once known as the *Yeropkin House*, it served from 1804 as the *Commercial Academy* (Kommercheskoye Uchilishche); the historian S.M. Solov'yov was born here (1820), and the writer I.A. Goncharov was a student at the academy in the 1820s. The building now houses the *Thorez Foreign Languages Institute*; the French Communist Maurice Thorez once worked in this building. Ostozhenka Ul. continues SW beyond the Sadovoye Kol'tso as Komsomol'skiy Pr. (p 145).

Kropotkinskaya Ul. takes its name from the anarchist-prince, Pyotr Kropotkin (1842–1921). This was formerly Prechistenka Ul., and between it and Arbat Ul. to the N (Pl. 7; 2. p 151) was a unique quarter of old Moscow called the Staraya Konyushennaya.

The district's name indicates that it was once the site of the 'old stables', but by the beginning of the 19C it had an entirely different character. Prince Kropotkin, who was born near here, described it in his Memoirs: 'There lived in this quarter, and slowly died out, the old Moscow nobility, whose names were so frequently mentioned in the pages of Russian history before the time of Peter I, but who subsequently disappeared to make room for the newcomers ... Feeling themselves supplanted at the St. Petersburg court, these nobles of the old stock retired either to the Staraya Konyushennaya quarter in Moscow or to their picturesque estates in the countryside round about the capital, and they looked with a sort of contempt and secret jealousy upon the motley crown of families which came "from no one knew where" to take possession of the highest functions of the government...' The old aristocracy did die out during the 19C— its members were mostly buried in the Don Monastery—but a number of houses survive and the back streets retain that mood described by Kropotkin: 'Life went on quietly and peacefully ... in this Moscow Faubourg Saint-Germain'.

A.G. Grigor'yev, one of the most prolific architects of the Empire style, built the handsome mansion at Kropotkinskaya Ul., 12 (right) in 1814; the former *Khrushchov House* has six columns on Kropotkinskaya Ul. and four pairs of columns around the corner. The **Pushkin Museum** (Muzey A.S. Pushkina) was opened here in 1961.

The house had no historical connection with A.S. Pushkin (1799–1837), but now contains ten exhibition halls devoted to the life and work of the great Russian poet. On display are some of Pushkin's personal effects, as well as manuscripts and a number of his own sketches. There are portraits of friends and contemporaries and other material evoking the St. Petersburg and Moscow of the early 19C. Much space is devoted to the poet's published work, including many first editions.

The former *Lopukhin House* was also built by Grigor'yev (1817–22) and stands across the street at Kropotkinskaya Ul., 11. Here is situated the **Tolstoy Museum** (Gos. Muzey L.N. Tolstovo).

The museum, created in 1911, complements the Tolstoy House-Museum in nearby Ul. L'va Tolstovo (the Lopukhin House has no direct associations with Tolstoy). The eight rooms of the museum contain manuscripts, letters, and even sketches by Leo Tolstoy (1828–1910), the great Russian novelist. Included are notes for 'War and Peace' and 'Anna Karenina', various first editions, and other mementoes of Tolstoy's literary career. On display are paintings of Tolstoy, his relatives, and his contemporaries by leading artists of the late 19C and early 20C, as well as sculpture, photographs and even cinema film.

Denis Davydov, the famous partisan leader of 1812 and the prototype for Denisov in 'War and Peace', owned the *Bibikov House* at No. 17 (left). Another hero of the Napoleonic Wars, General A.P. Yermolov, owned the house at No. 20 (right); it later belonged to the vodka magnate Smirnov and in 1921 Isadora Duncan opened a school of dance here. The long building opposite, at No. 19 (left) is the former *Dolgorukov House*, and was built in the late 18C, possibly by M. Kazakov. The **Academy of Arts of the USSR** (Akademiya Khudozhestv SSSR) is now located here; there is an *Exhibition Hall* (Vystavochnyy Zal) next door. In a different style from the many Empire buildings is the yellow Art Nouveau *Isakov House* at No. 28 (right), built to the plans of L.N. Kekushev (1906); the grey-painted grillwork is particularly striking.

The building at No. 37 (left), on the corner of KROPOTKINSKIY PER. (Pl. 7; 4) is of historical interest as it was the headquarters of the Operations Department of the Red Military Commissariat during the Civil War; there is now a *Beriozka Shop* here which specialises in books and records. Not far along Kropotkinskiy Per. at No. 13 (right) is the splendid Art Nouveau *Derozhanskaya House* built by Schechtel in 1901 and now the *Australian Embassy*.

In the N part of Kropotkinskiy Per., to the right of Kropotkinskaya Ul., is the house at No. 26, where Kropotkin was born in 1842. At the end UL. SHCHUKINA leads right to UL. VESNINA (left), which contains at No. 5 the present *Italian Embassy*. In July 1918 this was the temporary embassy of Imperial Germany where the ambassador, Count Mirbach, was assassinated by a Left Socialist-Revolutionary terrorist; later it became the first headquarters of the Comintern. Lunacharsky, the first People's Commissar for Education, lived at Ul. Vesnina, 9; the wooden house here is a rare surviving example of the simple town houses built after the fire of 1812.

Kropotkinskaya Ul. ends at the Sadovoye Kol'tso (Motor Route Б), and the Rte continues for a short distance as ZUBOVSKAYA UL. and then as BOL. PIROGOVSKAYA UL. (Pl. 7; 4). The wooden triangular park to the right was originally part of the MAIDENS FIELD (Devich'ye Pole), where young girls were said to have been left as tribute for the Tatars; near here Tolstoy set the scene in 'War and Peace' in which

Pogodin Hut (N.V. Nikitin, 1850s). This traditional wooden dacha was the site of literary salons in the 19C

Pierre Bezukhov witnesses the execution of prisoners by the French. A new *Statue of Tolstoy* (A. Portyanko, 1972) stands in the E corner. The *Frunze Military Academy*, an impressive piece of 1930s architecture (L.V. Rudnev and V.O. Munts, 1932–37), faces the park from the N. To the W, on the corner of 2-Y TRUZHENIKOV PER., stands one of Mel'nikov's Constructivist workers clubs; this one was built for the Kauchuk Factory in 1929. POGODINSKAYA UL., which turns off to the left (parallel to Bol. Pirogovskaya Ul.), contains at No. 12 the *Pogodin Hut* (Izba) (N.V. Nikitin, 1850s), a small wooden dacha with attractive painted and carved details. It belonged to the journalist and historian M.P. Pogodin (1800–75) who was host here (at the now-demolished main house) to Gogol, Aksakov, Chaadayev, and other prominent intellectuals of the mid-19C.

Near the beginning of Bol. Pirogovskaya Ul., by the statue of Tolstoy, UL. L'VA TOLSTOVO turns to the left. The brown wooden house behind a long fence at No. 21 (right) is now the *Tolstoy House-Museum* (Muzey-Usad'ba L. N. Tolstovo).

The house and extensive grounds were bought by Leo Tolstoy (1828–1910) in 1882, and the writer spent his winters here until 1901. The estate was made into a museum in 1921, and 16 rooms of the main house have been preserved. They include the study where Tolstoy wrote 'Resurrection' and other important works, and where he received visitors. Tolstoy spent much of his time at his country estate of Yasnaya Polyana, which is situated some 200km S of Moscow.

At the foot of Ul. L'va Tolstovo is a broad new avenue which was laid out in the mid-1950s, KOMSOMOL'SKIY PR. (Pl. 7; 4); this is the continuation of Ostozhenka Ul. At the intersection is the striking *Church of St. Nicholas of the Weavers* (Ts. Nikoly v Khamovnikakh). This was the Khamovnicheskaya Sloboda, the 'Weavers Quarter', brought here from Tver at the beginning of the 17C (at the end of the 19C this area had become the centre of the silk industry). The church dates from 1676–82 and was commissioned by the local community of weavers. There is a Moscow Baroque tent-roofed bell tower at the W end, then a large refectory, and finally the beautiful main body of the church surmounted by five golden cupolas. The red and green trim and the diamond-shaped tiles stand out against the white of the walls. This church is open for worship.

The yellow buildings of the former *Khamovnicheskiye Barracks* stretch to the W along Komsomol'skiy Pr. They were built in 1807–08, possibly to the plans of M.F. Kazakov. At the far end of the barracks, by FRUNZENSKAYA METRO STATION, 2-YA FRUNZENSKAYA UL. turns to the right off Komsomol'skiy Pr. Here are the modern white buildings of the *Choreographic Academy* (Moskovskoye Khoreograficheskoye Uchilishche), which was opened in 1968. The institution dates back to 1773 and trained for the Bolshoy Ballet such great dancers as Yekaterina Gel'tser, Maya Plisetskaya, and Natal'ya Bessmertnova; it currently trains about six hundred students.

The middle part of Bol. Pirogovskaya Ul. is a centre of medical and other research. The *1st (Sechenov) Medical Institute* (K.M. Bykovsky, 1886–90), originally the Medical Faculty of Moscow University, occupies the N side of Bol. Pirogovskaya Ul. beyond the Maidens Field. I.M. Sechenov (1829–1905) was a pioneering physiologist; a *Statue of Sechenov* by L.Ye Kerbel' (1958) stands next to the institute that bears his name. Nearby is a *Statue of N.I. Pirogov* (1810–81) by V.O. Sherwood; unveiled in 1897, this statue of the surgeon and anatomist Pirogov was the first Russian monument to a man of science.

Another major centre of learning is located in this district on the parallel MALAYA PIROGOVSKAYA UL. (Pl. 7; 3), the *Lenin Pedagogical Institute*, one of the largest in the country. The Classical main building, completed in 1913, was designed by S.U. Solov'yov for the so-called Higher Women's Courses—the women's equivalent of Moscow University. In the courtyard are the *2nd*

(Pirogov) Medical Institute and the *Darwin Museum* (Darvinovskiy Muzey); the museum was founded in 1907 by Professor A.F. Koss. Across the road is the *Central Archive of the October Revolution* (TsGAOR), one of the most important in the country and containing over three million documents; the *Central Archive of Ancient Documents* (TsGADA) and the *Central Army Archive* (TsGASA) are also located here.

Further to the SW, at the end of Bol. Pirogovskaya Ul. (No. 2), is one of the most interesting and attractive places in Moscow, the ***New Convent of the Virgin** or Novodevichiy Convent (Novodevichiy Monastyr') (Pl. 6; 6). The convent may also be reached by Metro train to SPORTIVNAYA METRO STATION; from the S exit FRUNZENSKIY VAL UL. leads (right) to the convent.

Tsar Vasily III founded the New Convent of the Virgin in 1524 to commemorate his capture of Smolensk from the Poles. From the time of its foundation the convent had a high standing, and the nuns were often of noble or even royal birth. Irina Godunova, wife of Tsar Fyodor Ivanovich, retired to the New Convent of the Virgin at the end of the 16C; her brother Boris was proclaimed Tsar here in 1598. The present appearance comes from a later era, as the convent was badly damaged in the Time of Troubles and then extensively rebuilt in the last decades of the 17C. The great reconstruction was inspired by Tsarevna Sof'ya Alekseyevna, who lived here in the 1680s when she was the de facto ruler of Russia. When Peter the Great came to power in 1689 he had Sof'ya confined to the convent. A century later, in 1812, the French planted explosives to blow up the buildings here, but the monks were able to extinguish the fuses.

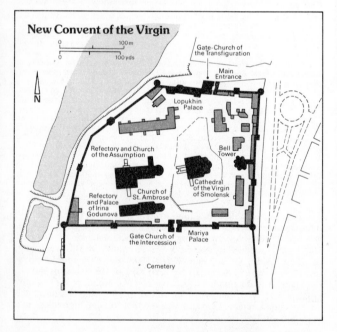

Like many of the other Moscow monasteries, the New Convent of the Virgin is well-protected. A high crenellated brick wall surrounds the convent precincts, and there are 12 richly ornamented defensive towers. The continuation of Bol. Pirogovskaya Ul. runs along the E wall; in the N wall is set the ***Gate-Church of the Transfiguration** (Preobrazhenskaya Ts.). A tall church with window surrounds, pilasters, and gables of white carved stone, it was built in 1687–89 and is one of the finest examples of the Moscow Baroque. Next to it, inside the walls, stands the **Lopukhin Palace** (Lopukhinskiy Korpus) (1687–89); Peter the Great made his first wife, Yevdokiya Lopukhina, live here after he had grown tired of her. The long brick palace is notable for the stone carving around the windows. In the opposite (S) wall of the convent are two buildings dating from 1683–88: the **Gate-Church of the Intercession** (Pokrovskaya Ts.) and the **Mariya Palace** (Mariiskiy Korpus). Tsarevna Sof'ya was forced to live in the Mariya Palace, and Peter is said to have hanged some of her supporters outside her windows. This was depicted by Repin in a painting now in the Tret'yakov Gallery.

The ***Cathedral of the Virgin of Smolensk** (Sobor Smolenskoy Bogomateri) is both the central edifice of the ensemble and the oldest. It was built in 1524–25 along the lines of the Kremlin Cathedral of the Assumption, which predates it by 50 years; the resemblance would be even stronger were it not for the bulbous onion domes, which were added in the 17C. The *Interior* is striking, the walls and pillars being covered with late-16C frescoes.

The enormous five-tiered gilded *Iconostasis* dates from the time of Tsarevna Sof'ya, as do most of the icons. Also notable are a wooden *Ciborium* (1653) and a large copper *Font* (c 1685). Sof'ya and two other sisters of Peter the Great were buried here.

To the W of the Smolensk Cathedral are the **Refectory** (Trapeznaya) and the single-domed **Church of the Assumption** (Uspenskaya Ts.). They date from 1685–87, and the church is open for worship. Between this long structure and the S wall stands the **Church of St. Ambrose** (Amvrosiyevskaya Ts.) (16C), with its **Refectory** and the **Palace of Irina Godunova**. The ***Bell Tower**, with six beautifully-decorated tiers and a golden dome, rises next to the E wall. It is generally regarded as the finest structure of its type in Moscow.

The ***Novodevich'ye Cemetery** (Novodevich'ye Kladbishche) lies beyond the S wall of the convent. It is one of the most famous in Russia, and many well-known people are buried here.

Among writers: N.V. Gogol, S.T. Aksakov, A.P. Chekhov, V.Ya. Bryusov, V.V. Mayakovsky, N.A. Ostrovsky, A.N. Tolstoy, A.A. Fadeyev, S.Ya. Marshak, I.G. Ehrenburg, and A.T. Tvardovsky. From theatre and cinema: K.S. Stanislavsky, V.I. Nemirovich-Danchenko, Ye.B. Vakhtangov, M.N. Yermolova, and S.M. Eisenstein. Among musicians: N.G. Rubinstein, S.I. Taneyev, A.N. Scriabin, L.V. Sobinov, and S.S. Prokofiev. Among painters: I.I. Levitan and V.A. Serov.

Among political thinkers: N.P. Ogar'yov and A.F. Pisemsky. Among statesmen: N.A. and D.A. Milyutin, G.V. Chicherin, V.D. Bonch-Bruyevich, A.M. Kollontay, M.M. Litvinov, N.S. Khrushchev, A.I. Mikoyan, and A.A. Gromyko.

Also the historian S.M. Solov'yov, General A.A. Brusilov, N.S. Alliluyeva (Stalin's second wife), and the partisan-heroine Z.A. Kosmodem'yanskaya.

Opposite the cemetery, at LUZHNETSKIY PROYEZD, 25, is one of the largest hard-currency *Beriozka* shops.

The area beyond the elevated railway line was once waste ground known as Luzhniki (the Marshes). In the 1950s, however, the district was transformed into a 180-ha sports complex, the **Lenin Central Stadium** (Tsentral'nyy Stadion im. V.I. Lenina) (Pl. 6; 8). This was chosen to be the main site for the 1980 Olympic Games. The Luzhniki complex may be reached directly by Metro; near it are the S exit of

*Monument to N.S. Khrushchev, Novodevich'ye Cemetery.
Khrushchev, who died in political disgrace in 1971, was
not granted a place behind Lenin's Tomb*

SPORTIVNAYA METRO STATION and the N exit of LENINSKIYE GORY
METRO STATION.

The central structure is the **Large Sports Arena** (Bol'shaya Sportivnaya Arena), which is capable of seating 103,000 spectators. It was
opened in 1956 and was modernised for the Olympic Games. Within
the building are extensive training facilities, as well as restaurants,
cafés, and a cinema. In front is a *Statue of Lenin* by M.G. Manizer
which was first shown at the Brussels World Fair of 1958.

In the same axis as the Large Arena are the **Small Sports Arena**
(Malaya Sportivnaya Arena) (NW) and the **Swimming Pool**

(Plavatel'nyy Basseyn) (SE). The Small Arena can accommodate 14,400 people and was intended for tennis and similar sports. The Pool, which was architecturally the most successful of the original buildings, has seats for 12,000. To the NW of the Small Arena stands the 13,000-seat **Palace of Sport** (Dvorets Sporta); it is also used for concerts and other non-sports events. Nearby are the **Museum of Physical Culture and Sport** (Muzey Fizicheskoy Kul'tury i Sporta) and the **Kristall Ice Rink** (Ledyanoy Katok 'Kristall').

Many new facilities were erected for the 1980 Olympics, of which the most striking is the '*Druzhba' Multi-Purpose Gymnasium* (Universal'nyy Sportivnyy Zal 'Druzhba'), with accommodation for 4000 spectators. Built to the E of Komsomol'skiy Pr. by a team of architects led by Bol'shakov (1979), it was nicknamed 'the golden tortoise' on account of its shape and the gold-coloured epoxy coating applied to it.

The Luzhniki complex includes dozens of smaller facilities, among which is a **Childrens Stadium** (Detskiy Stadion).

6   Prospekt Kalinina

Pr. Kalinina (Motor Route M1) leads W from Pr. Marksa to the Sadovoye Kol'tso and beyond to the Moskva River, a distance of some 2.5km. The starting point, near the Kremlin, is served by KALININSKAYA and BIBLIOTEKA IM. LENINA METRO STATIONS. Bus No. 89 and Trolleybus No. 2 follow Pr. Kalinina.

The avenue may be divided into three parts: from Pr. Marksa to the Bul'varnoye Kol'tso; from the Bul'varnoye Kol'tso to the Sadovoye Kol'tso; and from the Sadovoye Kol'tso to the Moskva River. The first part, the oldest, was once called Vozdvizhenka Ul. after the 16C Krestovozdvizhenskiy Convent (or Convent of the Raising of the Cross); a fine Moscow Baroque Church (1711) from the convent survived on the SE corner of what is now Per. Yanysheva until the Soviet period. In the early 1920s the street was renamed Ul. Kominterna in honour of the Communist International, which had its headquarters nearby. It became Ul. Kalinina in 1946 after the death of Mikhail Kalinin (1875–1946), the long-time Soviet head of state (the Comintern had been dissolved in 1943).

The Lenin Library (p 121) stands on the NW corner of Pr. Marksa and Pr. Kalinina (Pl. 4; 6). The next building on the left (No. 5) is the **Shchusev Museum of Architecture** (Nauchno-Issledovatel'skiy Muzey Arkhitektury im. A.V. Shchuseva).

The yellow museum building is the former *Talyzin House*, a Classical mansion built in 1787 by the school of M.F. Kazakov (it was rebuilt after 1812 and a third storey was added). After the Revolution the Secretariat of the Communist Party's Central Committee had its offices here in 1920–24.

The museum is named after the Soviet architect A.V. Shchusev who designed, among other things, the Lenin Mausoleum. There is a special room devoted to Shchusev's work. On display in the other rooms are plans, sketches, photographs, and models tracing the development of Russian and Soviet architecture. The Don Monastery houses a branch of the Shchusev Museum.

On the NW corner of Pr. Marksa, opposite the Lenin Library, is a building containing the *Reception Rooms of the Supreme Soviet* (No. 4/22). The Red Army's General Staff Academy was located at No. 6 in 1919–20. In the courtyard is the former *Sheremetev House* built in the 1770s, probably by Bazhenov, for Hetman K.G. Razumovskiy. The Moscow Town Duma met here, and later the Hunting Club took over the premises. Under the auspices of the latter the amateur

'Society of Art and Literature' gave regular performances directed by Stanislavsky. When the society became the Moscow Arts Theatre (MKhAT) it continued to rehearse here.

UL. GRANOVSKOVO, the first street to the right off Pr. Kalinina, takes its name from T.N. Granovsky (1813–55), an influential professor of history at nearby Moscow University.

Ul. Granovskovo, 2 and 4 (right) were given over to staff from the university. Flat No. 29 in the former building belonged to the biologist K.A. Timiryazev (1843–1920) and now contains a small *Timiryazev Museum* (Muzey-Kvartira K.A. Timiryazeva), devoted to his life and work. From the courtyard of this building one can get a good view of the *Church of the Sign 'in the Sheremetev Courtyard'* (Ts. Znameniya na Sheremetevom Dvore), a Moscow Baroque structure dating from 1702.

The composer A.S. Arensky lived in the 1880s and 1890s in the ornate, pink, 'U'-shaped block of flats at No. 3 (left). After the Revolution this became the '5th House of Soviets' for senior Soviet officials; M.V. Frunze and K.Ye. Voroshilov were among those who had flats here.

The building with the semi-circular colonnade that stands on the NE corner of Pr. Kalinina and Ul. Granovskovo (No. 8/1) was once owned by Count N.P. Sheremetev (N.A. L'vov, 1780). No. 10 houses *Voyentorg*, the 'Central Military Department Store', which was built for the officers of the Imperial army (S.B. Zalessky, 1913); Bela Kun (1886–1939), the leader of the 1919 Hungarian revolution, lived here from 1923–37. Further along Pr. Kalinina, beyond UL. SEMASHKO, are two buildings connected with international cultural relations. The headquarters of the 'Union of Soviet Societies of Friendship and Cultural Relations with Peoples of Foreign Countries' is at No. 14; the organisation unites 70 Soviet Friendship Associations with similar organisations in over 130 countries. Next door (No. 16) is the *House of Friendship with Peoples of Foreign Countries* (Dom Druzhby), a club where foreign visitors can meet Muscovites; receptions, exhibitions, and concerts are held here.

The former mansion with its lace-trimmed towers and walls decorated with sculptured sea shells is one of the curiosities of Moscow. V.A. Mazyrin built it in 1894–98 for the eccentric millionaire factory-owner A.A. Morozov; it was inspired by the 16C Casa de las Conchas in Salamanca, which Morozov had seen during his travels. In the early years of Soviet power the Morozov Mansion was a centre of 'Proletkul't', an organisation involving Lunacharsky, Mayakovsky, and Yesenin; the aim of Proletkul't was to train workers and peasants to become poets and novelists.

The left side of this part of Pr. Kalinina is of little interest. No. 9, the beige two-storey building on the corner of Per. Yanysheva was, however, the home of Prince N.S. Volkonsky, Leo Tolstoy's grandfather; it is considered to be the prototype for Prince Nikolay Bolkonsky's 'gloomy house on the Vozdvizhenka' in 'War and Peace'.

Beyond the public gardens on the left, Pr. Kalinina opens onto ARBATSKAYA PL. (Pl. 4; 5), a square which has undergone a vast reconstruction programme. An underpass was created for the Bul'varnoye Kol'tso, which intersects Pr. Kalinina at this point. Even before this, many of the old buildings in the square had been demolished including, unfortunately, the handsome Church of SS. Boris and Gleb (Ts. Borisa i Gleba) (1763–67) and the smaller Church of St. Tikhon (Ts. Tikhona) (1689/early 19C). The *Khudozhestvennyy Cinema* (left) is, however, a survival from the pre-revolutionary era, as it was built in 1912 by Schechtel. This is one of Moscow's oldest cinemas; the first Soviet 'talkie', 'Putyovka v zhizn'' had its première here in 1930. The **Praga Restaurant**, the large three-storey yellow building on the far side of the square, also dates from before the Revolution, although it was largely reconstructed in 1954. The Praga contains a number of small dining-rooms and two winter gardens, with a total capacity of 1500. Despite its name (Prague), this restaurant does not specialise in Czechoslovak food; it is, nevertheless, regarded as one of the best in Moscow.

On the left side of Pr. Kalinina, opposite the Praga, rises the seven-storey, concrete, glass, and metal block of *Dom Svyazi* (Communications House). Built in 1968, it serves as a post office and telephone exchange. On the near side of the Bul'varnoye Kol'tso, in the centre of the square, is the star-shaped pavilion of the ARBATSKAYA METRO STATION.

The name 'Arbat' comes from the Arabic word for 'suburbs' and in the 15C–16C the term was applied not just to the square and the street beyond, but to the whole suburb W of the Kremlin. Arbatskaya Pl. was the site of one of the gate-towers in the Belyy-Gorod wall; the Arbatskiye Gate was in fact the last to be demolished, in 1792. This was long an important part of Moscow's defences; here in 1612, during the 'Time of Troubles', the Russian militia fought a decisive skirmish which prevented the relief of the Polish garrison in the Kremlin. In similar confused street fighting three centuries later, during the revolutions of 1905 and 1917, Arbatskaya Pl. was a bitterly contested strategic point.

*UL. ARBAT (Pl. 4; 5) leads SW from Arbatskaya Pl., to the left of the Praga Restaurant. This was formerly part of the main route to the West, the Smolensk Road; Ul. Arbat is about 1200m long and ends at Smolenskaya Pl. on the Sadovoye Kol'tso. The street has recently been made into a pedestrian precinct, with a large number of co-operative shops. Many street musicians and actors perform here. Pushkin lived at Ul. Arbat, 53, for several months in 1831, and it was during this period that he married Natal'ya Goncharova. Pushkin's rooms are now a **Pushkin Musem** (Muzey-Kvartira A.S. Pushkina).

The whole district from the modern Ul. Arbat N to Ul Gertsena was full of the 16C settlements (slobody) of the royal servants; Ivan the Terrible had cleared the original residents out of the district and made it part of his 'Oprichnina'. Many of the local street names recall an era when the inhabitants served at the Tsar's court. Some of these are off Ul. Arbat: Serebryanyy Per. (Silver Lane), Starokonyushennyy Per. (Old Stables Lane), Kalashnyy Per. (Biscuit Lane), Plotnikov Per. (Carpenters Lane). Later, in the second half of the 18C, the streets around Ul. Arbat became a fashionable aristocratic district; the wooden mansions which burned down in 1812 were replaced by more permanent Empire-style residences. The quarter from Kropotkinskaya Ul. to Ul. Arbat was known as Staraya Konyushennaya, or the 'Moscow Faubourg Saint-Germain'.

The charm of the Arbat district survived even the massive reconstruction of the 1960s. A well-known song by the poet-singer Bulat Okudzhava (b 1924) expresses the feelings of many Muscovites: 'Oh, Arbat, my Arbat, you are my fatherland,/ And I'll never wander enough over you!' The quiet streets on either side of the busy Ul. Arbat still contain some of the old houses of the aristocracy; they passed to Moscow merchants and members of the intelligentsia in the later 19C, and some now serve as foreign embassies. Starokonyushennyy Per., for example, is the site of the Austrian (No. 1) and Canadian (No. 23) embassies. The residence of the American ambassador is the former *Vtorov House*, a Neo-Classical mansion in Spasopeksovskaya Ploshchadka (right) (V. Mart and V. Adamovich,

1900); the artist Vasily Polenov set his well-loved painting 'Moscow Courtyard' (1878) near this square.

The massive grey bulk of the **Vakhtangov Theatre** (Gos. Akademicheskiy Teatr im. Yevg. Vakhtangova), with its gallery of columns, stands half-way along Ul. Arbat. The company can trace its history back to 1914, when it was founded as a training studio for the Arts Theatre (MKhAT). The actor-director Ye.B. Vakhtangov (1883–1922), one of the influential figures of the modern Russian theatre, developed productions which combined elements of both the Meyerhold style and Realism. Vakhtangov's company moved to its

The Mel'nikov House (K.S. Mel'nikov, 1927). Mel'nikov was one of the oustanding Constructivist architects; this cylindrical house, built for his own use, was one of his most daring buildings

own theatre in 1921; the present building dates from after the Second World War.

UL. VAKHTANGOVA turns to the right off Ul. Arbat next to the theatre, and contains the *Shchukin Theatrical Academy*, the *Opera Studio of the Moscow Conservatory*, and the **Scriabin Museum** (Muzey A.N. Skyrabina). The last is the former flat of the composer A.N. Scriabin (1872–1915).

Opposite Ul. Vakhtangova begins the 'L'-shaped KRIVOARBATSKIY PER., which runs from Ul. Arbat to PLOTNIKOV PER. At Krivoarbatskiy Per., 10 (right), stands a unique building, the ***Mel'nikov House**. Konstantin Mel'nikov (1890–1974) was perhaps the most prolific and original of the Constructivist architects. The house he built for himself here in 1927 was one of his most daring projects; it consists of two interlocking white cylinders, their walls pierced by dozens of hexagonal windows. Mel'nikov built very little after the early 1930s, when Constructivism fell out of official favour, but this building remains a memorial to him, with its inscription; 'Konstantin Mel'nikov/Arkhitektor'.

The newly-widened Pr. Kalinina continues W beyond Dom Svyazi. On the corner of UL. VOROVSKOVO, stands a building which contrasts strikingly with the avenue's new multi-storey blocks, the **Church of St. Simeon the Stylite** (Ts. Simeona Stolpnika). This mid-17C pillar-less church is modelled on the Church of the Trinity in Nikitniki. Above the central cube are three tiers of kokoshnik gables topped with five graceful green domes. There is a chapel with a single dome and also a tent-roofed bell tower. The building was restored in 1965–68, but none of the original decoration of the interior survives; inside is the exhibition hall of the All-Russian Society for the Preservation of Nature.

UL. VOROVSKOVO (Pl. 4; 3) runs NW from Pr. Kalinina to the Sadovoye Kol'tso; its length is about 1km. This is another of the picturesque streets of W Moscow. It was formerly Povarskaya Ul. (Cook Street), because in the 17C the Tsar's cooks stayed here. Nearby streets, like those off the Arbat, have similar links with the servants of the royal household: Khlebnyy Per. (Bread Lane), Skat-ertnyy Per. (Table-cloth Lane), Stolovyy Per. (Table Lane). The modern name commemorates V.V. Vorovsky (1871–1923), a revolutionary and diplomat who was killed by an émigré in Lausanne. The link with Vorovsky seems appropriate as some of the 19C former aristocratic mansions lining the street now serve as embassies; those of Norway, Sudan, Cameroon, and New Zealand are located at Nos 7, 9, 40, and 44, and there are many others in the nearby streets. Before the Second World War the British Embassy stood at Ul. Vorovskovo, 46.

MAL. MOLCHANOVKA UL., which turns left off Ul. Vorovskovo, just beyond the Church of St. Simeon the Stylite, contains at No. 2 the low cream-coloured building where Lermontov lived in 1830–32; here he wrote an early draft of his poem 'The Demon'. The *Lermontov Museum* (Dom-Muzey M. Yu. Lermontova) is now located here. Another poet, Mayakovsky, studied before the First World War at the former *5th High School*, which stands at Ul. Vorovskovo, 3; it still serves as a school. No. 30 is the four-storey *Gnesin Music Teacher Training Institute*. This was set up in 1944 on the basis of an earlier music school established at the end of the 19C by the Gnesin family. The Armenian composer Khachaturian studied here. In 1958 a

600-seat concert hall was opened in the building; here students from the Moscow music schools give concerts.

The **Gorky Literary Museum** (Literaturnyy Muzey A.M. Gor'kovo) stands behind a courtyard at No. 25a. D. Gilardi built this in the Empire style in 1820 for one of the Gagarins: it later served as the *Konnozavodstvo* (or centre for horse-breeding). The middle of the main façade is articulated not by the usual colonnade but by three identical arched recesses, in which are set Doric columns. In front is a *Statue of Gorky* by Mukhina (1956). The museum contains a wealth of material on the life and creative work of the writer Maxim Gorky (1868–1936); there are letters, manuscripts, and photographs, and also various versions of Gorky's writings.

The *Film Actors' Theatre Studio* (Teatr-Studiya Kinoaktyora), which stands opposite the Gorky Museum at Ul. Vorovskovo, 33, is one of the outstanding examples of Constructivist architecture. The asymmetrical and angular building was created in 1931–34 by the Vesnin brothers for the Society of Former Political Prisoners (Obshchestvo Politkatorzhan); it became a club and theatre for cinema actors in 1940, after the society was disbanded. Another professional organisation is located at No. 50, the *Fadeyev Writers Club* (Tsentral'nyy Dom Literatorov im. Fadeyeva); here receptions are held for Soviet and foreign literary figures.

The 19C mansion at No. 52 was built for Count V.A. Sollogub and was for a long time thought to be Tolstoy's model for the Rostovs' house in 'War and Peace'. Recent research suggests that the 'Rostov House' was nearer Arbatskaya Pl., and has been demolished. It is certain, however, that Tolstoy visited the house at No. 52 while writing his epic novel, and a *Statue of Tolstoy* (G.N. Novokreshchenova, 1956) stands in the courtyard. This is now the headquarters of the *Union of Writers*.

The second and most striking section of Pr. Kalinina (Pl. 4; 5) runs for about 1km between the Bul'varnoye Kol'tso and the Sadovoye Kol'tso. The narrow Ul. Arbat had for years been unable to cope with the volume of motor traffic moving to and from the Kiev Station and the West. A proposal for a new avenue had been included in the 1935 General Plan, and in 1962–67 the giant Prospekt Kalinina development was created, by a team of architects led by M.V. Posokhin. A wide avenue was laid out, flanked by broad pavements, a large number of shops, restaurants, and cinemas, and nine tower blocks.

The development was known during its construction (and is still sometimes referred to) as Novyy Arbat or New Arbat. The name was appropriate as it transformed the district between Ul. Arbat and Ul. Vorovskovo; a swath 1000m long and 175m wide was cut through a quaint if run-down district of old Moscow. A number of old streets disappeared, including the picturesquely-named Sobach'aya Ploshchadka or 'Dog Square'.

On the left stand four 26-storey buildings, each shaped rather like an open book; these house a number of economic ministries. The base of these administrative blocks consists of a two-storey gallery some 850m long with shops and cafés. Among these is the *Novoarbatskiy* supermarket and the *Podarki* gift shop. Eating-places include the *Valday*, *Pechora*, and *Angara* cafés, the *Metelitsa* ice-cream parlour, and the *Arbat Restaurant*. The *Arbat* can accommodate 2000 diners and is among the largest in Moscow; it stands at the W end of the new development and is surmounted by an illuminated globe advertising Aeroflot.

Five 24-storey apartment blocks line the opposite (right) side of Pr. Kalinina. Each contains 280 flats, and on the ground floor are shops; other shops have been built between the towers. Moscow's largest bookshop, *Dom Knigi* is located near the beginning (No. 26) (books in foreign languages are sold on the 1st Floor). The *Malakhitovaya Shkatulka* jewellery shop is adjacent. The *Melodiya* record shop is further up the avenue, at No. 40. Next door stands one of the largest cinemas in the USSR, the **Oktyabr'**; the outside is decorated with revolutionary mosaics and inside are two halls, one seating 2450 spectators and the other 440.

The final 600m section of Pr. Kalinina (Pl. 7; 1) runs from the Sadovoye Kol'tso to the Moskva River. It was laid out beginning in 1957 along what had previously been Bol. Novinskiy Per. At the end rises the 32-storey Comecon Building (p 210). Further on, the road crosses the Moskva River and continues E as Kutuzovskiy Pr. (p 187).

7 Tverskaya Ulitsa

Tverskaya Ul. (Motor Route M10), from 1932 to 1990 called Ul. Gor'kovo (Gorky St.) runs NW from Pr. Marksa (at Pl. 50-letiya Oktyabrya) Pl. 4; 4) to Pl. Belorusskovo Vokzala (beyond the Sadovoye Kol'tso), a distance of 3km. Trolleybus No. 1 travels the length of Tverskaya Ul.. The starting point of this Rte is near one entrance to PROSPEKT MARKSA METRO STATION.

This has long been one of the busiest avenues of the city. Until 1932 the street was known as Tverskaya Ul. as it was the road to the old Russian town of Tver; from Tver the road continued to Novgorod and, from the 18C, to the new capital at St. Petersburg. It was renamed in honour of the writer Maxim Gorky. In the summer of 1990 the Moscow City Soviet decided to restore the original name.

Although the main street of Moscow, the Tverskaya was narrow and twisting, quite unable to meet the needs of 20C city transport. Little had changed since the early 19C when the critic V.G. Belinsky described how one house 'has run several steps into the street to have a look at what's going on there, while another has run back a few steps as if out of arrogance or modesty'. In the mid-1930s a mammoth reconstruction programme was undertaken. Many of the old houses were demolished and others were moved back to allow for the widening of the street. The Tverskaya had been 16–18m wide; the straight new avenue was 40–60m wide. The rebuilding of Tverskaya Ul. began under the direction of the architect A.G. Mordvinov, who designed many of the monumental buildings that line the street.

The 22-storey **Intourist Hotel** (Inturist), completed in 1969, stands at the foot of Tverskaya Ul. (No. 3). The corner building is the National Hotel, on Pr. Marksa (p 122); between these two hotels is located the **Intourist Service Bureau**. At Tverskaya Ul., 5, is the **Yermolova Theatre** (Moskovskiy Teatr im. M.N. Yermolovoy), which takes its name from the actress Mariya Yermolova (1853–1928) and was founded in 1937. This block ends at UL. OGARYOVA (left), named after N.P. Ogaryov (1813–77), revolutionary poet and friend of Herzen. The large grey building on the corner, with a rounded façade and rotating electric globe, was built by I.I. Rerberg in 1927 as the **Central Telegraph Office** (Tsentral'nyy Telegraf).

The opposite (right) side of Tverskaya Ul., as it climbs up to Sovetskaya Pl., is occupied by a line of massive 8-storey apartment buildings. They were the first part of the Tverskaya Ul. reconstruction plan to be completed (1938). These vast solemn blocks with their small windows and balconies and their huge archways leading to the (often charming) side streets are typical of the architecture of the period.

GEORGIYEVSKIY PER. is hidden behind the first arch; the name comes from the Convent of St. George which was located here from the 16C to the early 19C. The new 15-storey skyscraper of *Gosplan* and *Gosstroy* occupies the S side of the street, and beyond is the *Palace of the Boyar Troyekurov*. Troyekurov's palace is a rare surviving example of a 17C town house. The 1st Floor window surrounds and cornices, picked out in white against the dark pink of the walls, are characteristic of the mid-17C; the more intricate white stone designs of the 2nd Floor belong to the later part of the century.

The next street to the right off Tverskaya Ul. (opposite Ul. Ogaryova) bears the name PROYEZD KHUDOZHESTVENNOVO TEATRA or 'Arts Theatre Lane' (Pl. 4; 4) in honour of the **Moscow Arts Theatre**.

The MKhAT building, at No. 3 (left) was used in the 1880s by both the Korsh Theatre and Savva Mamontov's Opera Theatre. In 1902 it was quickly converted by the architect Schechtel for MKhAT, which had been founded four years earlier by K.S. Stanislavsky and V.I. Nemirovich-Danchenko. Schechtel concentrated his attention on the interior: backstage much modern equipment, including a revolving stage, was introduced. The foyer and auditorium, at the instigation of Stanislavsky, were extremely simple in design so as not to distract the spectator from the activity on stage. The façade was left largely unchanged, except that the entrance was moved from the centre of the building to the right side and given an Art Nouveau doorway (with a bas-relief, 'The Wave', by A.S. Golubkina); also of note are the Art Nouveau lanterns.

Although MKhAT is named after Maxim Gorky, whose early plays—including 'The Lower Depths'—were first performed here, the history of the company is even more closely associated with the name of Anton Chekhov. Chekhov's later plays, 'Uncle Vanya', 'Three Sisters' and 'The Cherry Orchard', were given their premières by MKhAT. The company also staged the first successful performance of 'The Seagull', which was a particular triumph; a stylized seagull, now the emblem of MKhAT, adorns the front of the theatre. Also on display are the awards won by the company. On the 3rd Floor of the building next door (No. 5) is the **MKhAT Museum**. Photographs, sketches, costumes, and props are used to illustrate the history of the theatre.

The *Artisticheskoye Cafe* on the opposite side of the lane (No. 6) was famed in the 1960s for poetry readings given by Akhmadulina and others. The composer S.S. Prokofiev (1891–1953) lived in this building from 1947 until his death.

Through the archway in the apartment block at Tverskaya Ul., 6, is visible the remarkable *Savvinskoye Podvor'ye* (I.S. Kuznetsov, 1905–07). This pale green building is decorated with floral tiles; dominant features of the design are the tiered rows of arches and tent-roofed silver towers at either end.

On the left side of Tverskaya Ul. beyond Ul. Ogaryova are two apartment blocks built in 1947–50 (Nos 9 and 11). The brown granite facing of the lower storeys is said to have been intended originally for a Nazi victory monument. An archway in one of these blocks leads to UL. NEZHDANOVOY (Pl. 4; 4) a quiet and delightful side street with several small parks.

In the 1920s several blocks of flats were put up here for people working at the Bolshoy Theatre, MKhAT, and the Operetta Theatre. The street is named after one such resident, the Bolshoy singer Antonina Nezhdanova, who lived at No. 7. The old name of this lane, Bryusovskiy Per., derived from the Bruce family, descendants of Jacob Bruce, one of Peter I's foreign helpers. The internationally-renowned theatrical director V.E. Meyerhold lived at No. 12 from 1928 until 1939, the year of his arrest, and No. 17 was the home of the celebrated MKhAT actors V.I. Kachalov and I.M. Moskvin and also of the one-time leading Moscow ballerina, Yekaterina Gel'tser. The poet Yesenin lived in 1914 at the far end of the street (No. 2), near Ul. Gertsena.

Ul. Nezhdanovoy, 10, is the headquarters of the USSR Composers Union, or *Dom Kompozitorov*. Across the street, on the corner with YELISEYEVSKIY PER., stands an attractive yellow church with a single dome and a bell tower; the **Church of the Resurrection** (Ts. Voskreseniya) (1629) is still open for worship. Yeliseyevskiy Per. leads to UL. STANKEVICHA, which is parallel to Ul. Nezhdanovoy and contains an unusual building, the red sandstone English *Church of St. Andrew* (now a recording studio).

At the top of the hill Tverskaya Ul.opens into SOVETSKAYA PL. or 'Soviet Square' (Pl. 4; 4); the Moscow Soviet meets in a building here. Earlier the square was called Tverskaya Pl. and then Skobelevskaya Pl., after a statue of the conqueror of Central Asia, Gen. M.D. Skobelev (1843–82), which was unveiled here in 1912. After the Revolution a statue of an Imperial general was regarded as unsuitable, and in 1919 an Obelisk to the Soviet Constitution designed by D.P. Osipov replaced it; the monument incorporated N.A. Andreyev's statue of 'Freedom'. This monument, too, was removed (in the late 1930s), and it is an equestrian *Statue of Grand Prince Yury Dolgoruky* (c 1090–1157) which now dominates the square. Prince Yury is traditionally considered the founder of Moscow, and the statue, by S.M. Orlov and others, was unveiled in 1954, shortly after the city had celebrated its 800th anniversary (1947).

The **Moscow Soviet of Working People's Deputies**, the 'town hall', is located in a dark red and white building which faces the statue of Yury Dolgoruky across Tverskaya Ul..

Formerly the residence of the Governor-General, the building was originally designed in 1782 by M.F. Kazakov. After the overthrow of the Tsar the Moscow Soviet of Workers' and Soldiers' Deputies was housed here; during the Bolshevik uprising this was the headquarters of the Soviet's Military-Revolutionary Committee.

The building was moved 14m back to its present site during the reconstruction of Tverskaya Ul. in the late 1930s, and in 1945–46 Kazakov's design was altered almost beyond recognition by D.N. Chechulin. The wings and porch were removed, two storeys were added, the six-columned portico was raised and given two further columns, and a monumental entrance was built below.

The S side of the square (Sovetskaya Pl., 2/6) was once the site of the Dresden Hotel (now reconstructed). Nekrasov, Turgenev, Robert Schumann, and Chekhov were among those who stayed here at various times. In 1917 the hotel became the headquarters of the Bolshevik's Moscow Committee, the editorial offices of some of their newspapers, and the 'Central Staff' of the Moscow Red Guard. The *Aragvi* Restaurant, famed for its Georgian cuisine, is now located here. The continuation of the S side of Sovetskaya Pl., STOLESHNIKOV PER., contains the *Almaz* jewellery shop (No. 14) and a shop which specialises in amber goods, *Yantar'*.

The dark grey monumental Constructivist building of the *Central Party Archives of the Institute of Marxism-Leninism* (S.Ye. Chernyshev, 1927) occupies the E side of Sovetskaya Pl. Here are stored some of the basic documents of Communism, including manuscripts of Marx, Engels, and Lenin. A granite *Statue of Lenin* stands in front of the Archives (S.D. Merkurov, 1938).

At the N side of Sovetskaya Pl. (Tverskaya Ul., 8) is a large block containing the *Moskva* and *Akademicheskaya Kniga* bookshops. Among those who lived in this building were the poet Dem'yan Bedny and, in 1947–67, the writer Il'ya Ehrenburg. The block opposite, Tverskaya Ul., 15, has several interesting shops; the *Druzhba* bookshop specialises in books from the countries of the

Communist bloc, and the *Beriozka* shop in glass and crystal. An archway on this side of Tverskaya Ul. leads to another of the charming streets behind the new buildings, UL. STANISLAVSKOVO (Pl. 4; 4).

The name of the street derives from the fact that from 1920 to 1938 the celebrated actor-director Konstantin Stanislavsky (1863–1938) lived in the late-18C building at No. 6. The flat is now open as the **Stanislavsky Museum** (Dom-Muzey K.S. Stanislavskovo). Opposite, at No. 7, stands the Pseudo-Russian **Museum of Folk Art** (Muzey Narodnovo Iskusstva), which was founded in 1885 by Savva Morozov. The museum is devoted to Russian popular art from the 17C to the present. A plaque at No. 18 commemorates the 19 people killed here in September 1919 when terrorists threw a bomb into the offices of the Communists' Moscow Committee. Among those killed was V.M. Zagorsky, Secretary of the committee, after whom the town of Zagorsk (formerly Ser-giyevo) is named.

UL. NEMIROVICHA-DANCHENKO turns right off Tverskaya Ul. beyond Ul. Stanislavskovo. The director V.I. Nemirovich-Danchenko (1858–1943), one of the founders of the Moscow Arts Theatre, lived at No. 5/7 from 1938 until his death. A **Nemirovich-Danchenko Museum** (Muzey-Kvartira V.I. Nemirovicha-Danchenko) has been established here. The *Central Hotel* (Tsentral'naya) (Tverskaya Ul., 10) is situated beyond this street. Dimitrov, Gottwald, Togliatti, Thorez, and many other leaders of the Comintern lived here before the Second World War, when the hotel was known as the Luxe. Next door, at No. 12, is the *Poeziya Hall*, which is used for poetry readings and similar events.

Gastronom (Food Shop) *No. 1* at Tverskaya Ul., 14, is still known unofficially by its pre-revolutionary name, 'Yeliseyev's'. While the shop stocks a wider range of goods than others of its type, the tourist is more likely to be interested in the elaborate turn-of-the-century décor, with its chandeliers, engraved pillars, stained glass, and abundance of gilt. No. 14 also houses the **N.A. Ostrovsky Museum** (Gos. Muzey N.A. Ostrovskovo). Nikolay Ostrovsky (1904–36) spent his last months here as an invalid; his novel, 'How the Steel was Tempered' is still considered to be a model of Socialist Realism.

The *All-Russian Theatrical Society* (VTO) and the *Yablochkina Actors Club* are situated at Tverskaya Ul., 16. Opposite (No. 17) is the popular *Armeniya* shop, which stocks Armenian products, including wines and confectionary.

Beyond, Tverskaya Ul. crosses the Bul'varnoye Kol'tso (see Rte 4); to the left is Tverskoy Bul'v., to the right Strastnoy Bul'v. This intersection forms one of the best-known squares in Moscow, PUSH-KINSKAYA PL. (Pl. 4; 4). PUSHKINSKAYA METRO STATION is located here. The square has been the site of important unofficial political demonstrations, especially in the 1980s. A well-loved bronze *Statue of Pushkin stands in a small park to the right of Tverskaya Ul.; this monument is one of Moscow's landmarks.

The statue, by A.M. Opekushin, was paid for by public subscription and erected in 1880. It originally stood on the other side of Tverskaya Ul., in Tverskoy Bul'v., and was moved to the present site only in 1950. At the original unveiling the novelist Turgenev paid tribute to A.S. Pushkin (1799–1837), crediting him with two achievements which elsewhere had been separated by at least a century: the establishment of a language and the founding of a literature. Pushkin is very dear to Russians and there are always floral tributes at the base of the statue.

Behind the Pushkin monument are first a fountain, and then the glass façade of the *Rossiya Cinema*. The cinema, built by a team led by Yu. Sheverdyayev in 1961, was one of the first daringly modern buildings in post-war Moscow. It contains three theatres with a combined total of 3000 seats.

This square was originally called Strastnaya Pl. after the Strastnoy Convent or Convent of the Passion, which once occupied the site of the Rossiya Cinema. The Convent of the Passion was founded by Tsar Aleksey Mikhaylovich in 1654, but its final form was the result of reconstruction by the architect M.D. Bykovsky in 1849–55. After the Revolution the building served for a time as the Central Museum of Atheism, but it was demolished in 1937 to create the present Pushkinskaya Pl.

Pushkinskaya Pl. is one of the main centres of the Soviet press. In the SE corner are the offices of 'Moscow News', which is published in many languages. The offices of the 'state' newspaper, 'Izvestiya', occupy the NE corner of Pushkinskaya Pl. The original 'Izvestiya' building dates from 1927 and was designed by G.B. Barkhin. With its asymmetrical balconies and circular top floor windows, it is a fine example of Constructivist architecture. The extension along Tverskaya Ul. was completed in the mid-1970s. The final newspaper with its offices in this district is the trade union newspaper 'Trud' (Labour), at Tverskaya Ul., 18. The building was designed in the Style Moderne by A.E. Erikhson at the beginning of this century; originally the *Sytin Printing House*, in the early years of Soviet power it housed the Communist Party newspaper 'Pravda'.

On the opposite (left) side of Tverskaya Ul., at No. 21, is a salmon-pink Classical mansion with an eight-columned portico; this is now the **Central Museum of the Revolution** (Tsentral'nyy Muzey Revolyutsii SSSR).

Built for the Kheraskov family in 1780, the mansion was badly damaged during the fire of 1812 and was rebuilt by the architect A.A. Menelaws. The wings were removed during the reconstruction of Tverskaya Ul. in the 1930s. The stone lions on top of the gatehouses at either end of the handsome iron railing are mentioned in Pushkin's 'Yevgeny Onegin'. From 1831 to 1917 the building housed the so-called *English Club* (Angliyskiy Klub), a very select meeting place of the nobility.

The Central Museum of the Revolution was opened here in 1923. There are now 11 rooms of exhibits tracing the history of the revolutionary movement from 1905 to 1917 and showing the later fruits of socialism. On display are various objects connected with the Revolution, as well as documents, photographs, and paintings. A 6-in gun used to bombard the Kremlin during the October Revolution is on show in the forecourt, as well as part of the gun deck of the cruiser 'Avrora'.

The **Stanislavsky Theatre** (Moskovskiy Dramaticheskiy Teatr im. K.S. Stanislavskovo) is next door, on the corner of PER. SADOVSKIKH. The company was founded in 1948 on the basis of an opera and drama studio set up by Stanislavsky in 1935. Nearby, in Per. Sadovskikh, stands the **Moscow Theatre of Young Spectators** (Moskovskiy Teatr Yunovo Zritelya), known as MTYuZ. The history of this theatre goes back to 1927. It specialises in plays for children, and only children may attend performances. On the opposite side of the street is the *Ophthalmic Hospital*, an architectural monument from the late 18C; it was moved around 90° from Tverskaya Ul. during the reconstruction. The lane takes its name from the Sadovsky family of actors whose founder, P.M. Sadovsky (1818–72), once lived at the far end (No. 1).

There is an *Exhibition Hall of the Artists Union* in the block of flats at Tverskaya Ul., 25 (A.K. Burov, 1938). A.A. Fadeyev (1901–56), author of the novel 'The Young Guard' and long-time head of the

Writers Union, lived next door at No. 27–29 (from 1948). On the right side of Tverskaya Ul., at No. 22, is the 400-bed **Minsk Hotel** (1964).

At PL. MAYAKOVSKOVO (Pl. 4; 1), Tverskaya Ul. passes over the busy Sadovoye Kol'tso (p 171). To the left is Bol. Sadovaya Ul., to the right Sadovaya-Triumfal'naya Ul. An underpass completed in 1960 allows traffic on the Sadovoye Kol'tso to avoid Tverskaya Ul. and prevents the former congestion at this point. The **Statue of Vladimir Mayakovsky** which dominates the square (to the left of Tverskaya Ul.) is by A.P. Kibal'nikov and was unveiled in 1958. The square has often been the site of outdoor poetry readings. It was renamed after the poet-dramatist Mayakovsky in 1935, five years after his suicide. The old name was Pl. Starykh Triumfal'nykh Vorot or Square of the Old Triumphal Arches; temporary triumphal arches were erected on this spot in the 18C for the arrival of the Emperor or for other state holidays.

Pl. Mayakovskovo is sometimes known as Moscow's second Theatre Square' (the first being Pl. Sverdlova). In the SE corner stands the **Tchaikovsky Concert Hall** (Kontsertnyy Zal im. P.E. Chaykovskovo) (not to be confused with the Tchaikovsky Conservatory). The massive structure was built in 1938–40 to the plans of D.N. Chechulin and K.K. Orlov, and can seat 1650 people. The USSR State Symphony Orchestra regularly performs in the Tchaikovsky Concert Hall; many other concerts and cultural events are held here.

'Stalin at the Ceremony for the 24th Anniversary of the October Revolution' (I. Toidze, 1947). The ceremony, held at the time of greatest danger to Moscow in 1941, took place underground in the Mayakovskaya Metro Station

The MAYAKOVSKAYA METRO STATION lies under the hall. The design of the subterranean station, by A.N. Dushkin (1938), is architecturally one of the most successful on the Metro. The station is also of note for a political rally which Stalin addressed here on 6 November 1941 at the height of the Battle of Moscow; it was the eve of the Revolution's anniversary and the meeting had to be held underground due to the danger of German air raids.

The **Theatre of Satire** (Akademicheskii Teatr Satiry) is situated at Bol. Sadovaya Ul., 2. The theatre was established in 1924 and is one of the most popular in the capital. In the **Aquarium Gardens**, stands the **Mossovet Theatre** (Gos. Akademicheskiy Teatr im. Mossoveta). Founded in 1922, the company moved to its present building in 1959. The *Moskva Cinema* can be seen on the N side of Pl. Mayakovskovo. One of the landmarks of Pl. Mayakovskovo is the ornate tiered tower of the *Peking Hotel*, which was built by Chechulin in 1946–50. The *Peking Restaurant*, which was opened in a period of close Soviet-Chinese friendship, still serves some Chinese dishes. Another restaurant with a foreign flavour is the *Sofia*, on the E side of the square. It specialises in Bulgarian cuisine.

The short stretch of Tverskaya Ul. beyond the Sadovoye Kol'tso is undergoing extensive reconstruction. A *Komissionnyy Magazin* or second-hand shop specialising in china and graphics is located at No. 46. On the other side of the street (No. 49) stands the *Yakor' Restaurant*, which specialises in seafood.

UL. GOTVAL'DA, to the right, bears the name of the Czechoslovak Communist leader Klement Gottwald (1896–1953) who master-minded the 1948 coup and then died in Moscow after catching a cold at Stalin's funeral. Ul. Gotval'da leads to MIUSSKAYA PL., site of what is now the *Higher Party School*. The building dates from 1910–13 and was created by I.A. Ivanov-Schitz for the so-called *Shanyavsky People's University*. The university was founded and financed by A.L. Shanyavsky and by 1914 had 4000 students. After the Revolution, the Sverdlov Communist University was housed here. In the centre of the square stands a *Statue of A.A. Fadeyev*, the Soviet writer. Fadeyev is depicted surrounded by a group of partisans (V. Fedorov, 1972).

PL. BELORUSSKOVO VOKZALA (Pl. 4; 1), at the end of Tverskaya Ul., was formerly known as Tverskaya Zastava after the barrier (zastava) in the Kamer–Kollezhskiy Rampart that was erected in the mid-18C. Here in 1827–34 Bove built a Triumphal Arch through which the Emperors rode when they arrived in Moscow from St. Petersburg; the arch was demolished in the 1930s, but later re-erected on Kutuzovskiy Pr. In its place now stands a *Statue of Maxim Gorky*; the monument, by Vera Mukhina, was unveiled in 1951. After the Revolution Gorky decided to live in Italy; he returned to Soviet Russia in 1928 and arrived at Moscow at the nearby BELORUSSIAN STATION (Belorusskiy Vokzal). The station, which runs around the N and W sides of the square, was originally built in 1870s, as the Smolensk Station. BELORUSSKAYA METRO STATION is located near the square.

The large white *Church of St. Nicholas the Wonder Worker* (Ts. Nikolaya Chudotvortsa) stands in the SE corner of the square, at Butyrskiy Val, 4. Although built in the Byzantine style it dates from 1914 (A. Gorzhienko). Intended for the Old Believers, war and revolution prevented its opening as a church. The building is now to be converted into a concert hall.

LESNAYA UL., next to the church, leads to the right. Not far along, at No. 18 (right), stands the **Zuyev Workers Club**, one of Moscow's best Constructivist buildings. The club was designed by I.A. Golosov and completed in 1926. It is distinguished by a giant glazed cylinder on the left side, which houses the staircase. One of the Bolshevik's underground printing presses is preserved as *Underground Press Museum* at Lesnaya Ul., 55. (Muzey 'Podpol'naya

*Church of St. Nicholas the Wonder Worker
(A. Gorzhienko, 1914)*

Tipografiya TsK RSDRP 1905–1906 gg.') It originally operated in 1905–06, when it was disguised as a fruit shop.

The continuation of Tverskaya Ulitsa to the NW is Leningradskiy Pr. (p 191).

8   Zamoskvorech'ye

Zamoskvorech'ye is the part of old Moscow lying S of the Kremlin and contained within the bend of the Moskva River; the name might be translated as 'Trans-Moskva district'. The present Rte begins at the MOSKVORETSKIY MOST (Pl. 5; 5), at the SE corner of the Kremlin, and leads S down Bol. Ordynka Ul. (Motor Route M4); Trolleybus No. 25 and Bus No. 25 run along this street. At the Sadovoye Kol'tso the Rte turns sharply to the NW along Bol. Polyanka Ul. (Bus No. 3), back to the river. The length of the basic Rte is about 4km. NOVOKUZNETSKAYA and TRET'YAKOVSKAYA METRO STATIONS (Pl. 5; 7) are in the middle of Zamoskvorech'ye.

The district traditionally had a character all of its own. It was settled early in the city's history, and by the 17C included a mixed population. There were various 'slobody', suburbs charged with supplying the Court; these became much less important once the new capital was established in St. Petersburg. The S side of the city was usually the first to be attacked by the Tatars, and as a result the defensive forces were settled in Zamoskvorech'ye; by the time of Tsar Aleksey there were some twenty companies (prikazy) of the strel'tsy, or musketeers, concentrated here. The end of the Tatar threat and Peter the Great's liquidation of the strel'tsy ended this part of the history of Zamoskvorech'ye, but traces remain in the names of streets and churches. The final major group of inhabitants were the merchants, who moved their homes here while keeping their shops in the Kitay-Gorod.

After the establishment of St. Petersburg the merchants stayed on as the dominant group in Zamoskvorech'ye in the 18C and 19C. There was, however, some influx of nobles, and then of factory workers; by the eve of the Revolution this had become the most central of the industrial districts, with a fifth of Moscow's factories and a third of the workers.

The area just S of Moskvoretskiy Most is an artificial island formed by the DRAINAGE CANAL. UL. OSIPENKO turns off to the left with, at No. 6 (right), the attractive **Church of St. George** (Ts. Georgiya v Yendove) (1654); the church has five silver domes and a detached yellow belfry.

On the far side of the drainage canal BOL'SHAYA ORDYNKA UL. leads S into Zamoskvorech'ye; the narrow street lined with two-and three-storey buildings is evocative of the old Moscow of the 19C. The name of the street derives from the 'Golden Horde' (Zolotaya Orda), the state the Mongols and Tatars founded on the lower Volga in the 13C; this part of Moscow was the beginning of the road to the Golden Horde, and the ambassadors of the Tatars lived near here.

To the right, KADASHOVSKAYA NABEREZHNAYA leads along the canal to LAVRUSHINSKIY PER. (left). The world-famous * *Tret'yakov Gallery** (Gos. Tret'yakovskaya Galereya) is situated here (Pl. 4; 6). The nearest Metro station is TRET'YAKOVSKAYA.

The attractive Neo-Russian museum building was created in 1900–05 to the plans of the artist V.M. Vasnetsov. The inscription at the top of the main façade, written in large ornate Early Russian letters, reads: 'The Moscow Municipal Art Gallery named after Pavel Mikhaylovich and Sergey Mikhaylovich Tret'yakov, which was founded by P.M. Tret'yakov in 1856 and presented by him as a gift to the town of Moscow in 1892 along with the collection which S.M. Tret'yakov bequeathed to the town'; there is a statue of P.M. Tret'yakov nearby (A.P. Kibal'nikov, 1980). The ogee-shaped gable in the centre of the façade contains a bas-relief of St. George. The Tret'yakov brothers, who belonged to a wealthy family of Moscow merchants, were great patrons of the arts and founded here what was to become the largest collection of Russian art. After the Revolution the holdings of private galleries were added and a new wing was built; by the 1970s there were some 45,000 works in the collection.

Regrettably the museum was closed for renovation and extension at the time of writing. It is also not clear which works will be displayed in the new Picture Gallery of the USSR (p 171); this gallery specialises in the Soviet period. The following is an outline of the most important holdings of the two galleries. For Notes on Russian Art see p 42.

*Early Russian Art.** The Tret'yakov Gallery has the finest collection of Russian icons in the world.

Kiev School. Few icons of this school have survived. Mosaic of St. Demetrius of Thessalonika (1113). St. Demetrius of Thessalonika (late 12C); the background details were added later.

Byzantine School. *The Virgin of Vladimir. Traditionally this icon was believed to have been painted by St. Luke. It is now thought to be the work of an early-12C Byzantine artist. The icon was brought to Kiev around 1135 and transferred to Vladimir in 1155. In 1390 it was moved to the Cathedral of the Assumption in the Moscow Kremlin, where it remained until 1930.

School of Vladimir-Suzdal. The Virgin Great Panagia (the Virgin Orans) (Yaroslavl, 12C).

Pskov School. The Prophet Elijah in the Wilderness, with scenes from his life (13C).

Novgorod School. *Ustyug Annunciation (12C); this icon was

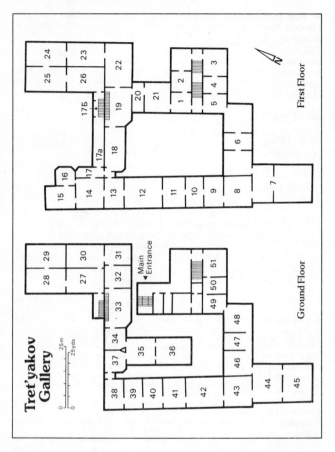

transferred by Ivan the Terrible from the Cathedral of St. Sophia in
Novgorod to the Cathedral of the Assumption in the Moscow
Kremlin. *St. Nicholas (13C) (the pictures of saints on the border
were added in the 16C); this was brought to the New Convent of the
Virgin in Moscow by Ivan the Terrible. *St. George (15C). *Last
Judgement (mid 15C). *SS. Florus and Laurus (late 15C). *Laying in
the Tomb (late 15C).

Moscow School. SS. Boris and Gleb on horseback (1340). *Theophanes the Greek* (Feofan Grek) (c 1340–1405), *Virgin of the Don
(late 14C). This icon by the Byzantine-trained Theophanes is said to
have been taken by Dmitry Donskoy to the Battle of Kulikovo; it was
formerly in the Kremlin Cathedral of the Annunciation. Also
attributed to Theophanes are The Assumption (late 14C), on the
reverse side of the above, and The Transfiguration (1403) (from the
Cathedral of the Transfiguration at Pereslavl-Zalesskiy). *Andrey
Rublyov* (c 1360–c 1430): **Old Testament Trinity (early 15C), from
the Cathedral of the Trinity at Zagorsk; *Archangel Michael, Christ,

St. Paul (half-length deësis row) (early 15C), from Zvenigorod; St. John, St. Gregory, the Virgin, Christ, John the Baptist, St. John the Evangelist, St. Andrew (deësis row) (early 15C). *Dionysius* (c 1440–1502/08): The Virgin with John the Baptist (late 15C) (this icon was painted by Dionysius and his sons and was brought here from the Feropontov Monastery); The Life of Metropolitan Aleksey (late 15C–early 16C); *The Crucifixion (1500). Icons by members of the late Moscow School, including *Simon Ushakov* (1626–86).

Art of the 18C and the First Half of the 19C. Portraits by *A.P. Antropov* (1716–95), *I.P. Argunov* (1727–1802), and *F.S. Rokotov* (1735–1808); Argunov's work includes the first Western-style portrait of a peasant. Paintings on Classical themes by *A.P. Losenko* (1737–73). *D.G. Levitsky* (1735–1822), portraits, including P.A. Demidov (1773) and Diderot (1774). *V.L. Borovikovsky* (1757–1825), portraits, including Catherine II (1794) and M.I. Lopukhina (1797). *F.Ya. Alekseyev* (1753–1824), Views of Moscow. *O.A. Kiprensky* (1782–1836), portraits, including *Pushkin (1827), and Self-Portrait (1809). *V.A. Tropinin* (1776–1857), Lace-maker (1823) and portraits. *K.P. Bryullov* (1799–1852), Horsewoman (1832) and other portraits. *A.A. Ivanov* (1806–58), *Christ Appearing before the People (1857), portraits, and scenes from mythology. Genre scenes of peasant life by *A.G. Venetsianov* (1780–1847). Seascapes by *I.K. Ayvazovsky* (1817–1900). *P.A. Fedotov* (1815–52), Courting of the Major (1848), Aristocrat's Breakfast (1849), and other satirical genre scenes.

Sculpture by *F.I. Shubin* (1740–1805) and *I.P. Martos* (1754–1835).

Art of the Second Half of the 19C. *V.G. Perov* (1833–82), Arrival of the Governess (1866) and other 'socially conscious' genre scenes; *Portrait of Dostoyevsky (1872). *K.D. Flavitsky* (1830–66), Princess Tarakanova (1864). *A.K. Savrasov* (1830–97), The Rooks have Arrived (1871) and other landscapes. *V.V. Pukirev* (1832–90), Més-alliance (1862). Landscapes by *M.K. Clodt von Jürgensburg* (1832–1902), *L.L. Kamenev* (1833–86), and *I.I. Shishkin* (1832–98).

I.N. Kramskoy (1837–87), portraits of *Tolstoy (1873) and of Unknown Lady (1883); the latter was said to be a prototype for Anna Karenina. *N.N. Gay* (1831–94), Peter I Interrogating Tsarevich Aleksey (1871) and other historical and religious works. *I.M. Pryanishnikov* (1840–94). *V.V. Vereshchagin* (1842–1904), Apotheosis of War (1872) and other anti-war paintings; paintings of the East. *A.I. Kuindzhi* (1842–1910), Birch Grove (1879) and other landscapes with dramatic lighting effects. *V.D. Polenov* (1844–1927), Moscow Courtyard (1878) and other landscapes.

I.Ye. Repin (1844–1930): Ivan the Terrible and His Son (1885) and other historical paintings; *Religious Procession in Kursk Province (1883) and other social themes; portraits, including P.M. Tret'yakov (1883) and Tolstoy (1887). Genre scenes by *V.Ye. Makovsky* (1846–1920). *V.I. Surikov* (1848–1916), historical paintings, including Morning of the Execution of the Strel'tsy (1881), Menshikov in Beryozovo (1883), and Boyarina Morozova (1887); portraits. Genre works and scenes from Russian mythology by *V.M. Vasnetsov* (1848–1926); Alyonushka (1881). Landscapes by *F.A. Vasil'yev* (1850–73) and *I.I. Levitan* (1860–1900).

Art of the Early 20C. Paintings of the fantastic by *M.A. Vrubel'* (1856–1910), including *Seated Demon (1890) and Swan Princess (1900); portrait of S.I. Mamontov (1897). *S.V. Malyutin* (1859–1937),

D.A. Furmanov (1922) and other portraits. Portraits by *K.A. Korovin* (1861–1939) and *A.Ya. Golovin* (1863–1930). Historical paintings by *S.V. Ivanov* (1864–1910). *V.A. Serov* (1865–1911): Peter the Great (1907) and other historical paintings; Girl with Peaches (1887), and portraits, including Mika Morozov (1901) and Chaliapin (1905). *K.A. Somov* (1869–1939), Portrait of Yelizaveta Martynova (1900). Genre scenes by *F.Z. Malyavin* (1869–1940). *A.N. Benois* (1870–1905), Reservoir (1902). Landscapes and still lifes by *I.E. Grabar'* (1871–1960).

Soviet Art. Portraits by *M.V. Nesterov* (1862–1942). Seascapes by *A.A. Rylov* (1870–1939) and landscapes by *K.F. Yuon* (1874–1958). Still lifes and portraits by *P.P. Konchalovsky* (1876–1956). Paintings, some of them inspired by the Revolution, by *K.S. Petrov-Vodkin* (1878–1939). Scenes of country life and revolutionary action by *B.M. Kustodiyev* (1878–1927). *P.V. Kuznetsov* (1878–1968). Landscapes and still lifes by *A.V. Kuprin* (1880–1960). *M.S. Sar'yan* (1880–1972), scenes of Armenia. Civil War paintings by *M.B. Grekov* (1882–1934).

Portraits by *I.I. Brodsky* (1884–1939), including Lenin in the Smolny (1930). *S.V. Gerasimov* (1885–1964), Partisan's Mother (1950) and other war scenes. Socialist Realist historical paintings by *B.V. Ioganson* (1893–1973). Scenes of war and country life by *A.A. Deyneka* (1899–1969). Oriental canvases by *S.A. Chuykov* (born 1902). *V.A. Serov* (1910–68), The Winter Palace is Taken (1954) and other revolutionary paintings. Sculptures by *S.T. Konyonkov* (1874–1971), *I.D. Shadr* (1887–1941), and *V.I. Mukhina* (1889–1953).

The holdings will presumably also include the works of the avant garde artists of the first part of the 20C, of 'emigre' artists like Marc Chagall, and perhaps even of 'unofficial' artists of the Soviet period.

The first street to the right off Bol. Ordynka Ul., after Kadashovskaya Nab., is 2-Y KADASHOVSKIY PER.; this contains the remarkable *Church of the Resurrection (Ts. Voskresenii v Kadashakh). Several levels of white stone window-surrounds stand out against the brick walls of this remarkable Moscow Baroque building. In some ways the Church of the Resurrection resembles other Moscow suburban churches, but in others it betrays its late-17C reconstruction (the church was rebuilt in 1687 from its original mid-17C form). The five green domes are on tall decorated drums, and the line of the roof is straight and lavishly ornamented; gone are the conventional rows of ogee-shaped gables. The light bell tower, topped by a tent roof, dates from 1696.

At Bol Ordynka Ul., 20 (right), near one entrance to NOVOKUZNETSKAYA METRO STATION, stands the yellow **Church of the Virgin of All Sorrows** (Ts. Bogomateri Vsekh Skorbyashchikh Radosti). In the 1780s Bazhenov added the round tiered belfry and the refectory with its four-columned porticoes to an existing church. The latter was replaced fifty years later (1828–33) by the present church with its small domed-rotunda; the architect was Bove.

To the left, KLIMENTOVSKIY PER. leads to UL. A.N. OSTROVSKOVO (right). The playwright Aleksandr Ostrovsky (1823–86) was born here at No. 9; a monument has been erected to him (G.I. Motovilov, 1954). Ostrovsky grew up here and once described himself as the 'discoverer' of the 'country' of Zamoskvorech'ye; many of his plays are devoted to describing the lives of the local residents, the merchants and petty officials.

Just beyond the All Sorrows Church on Bol. Ordynka Ul., BOL.

TOLMACHEVSKIY PER. turns right. (The tolmachi were the Tatar and Russian interpreters, who once lived near here.) Not far along (left) a striking Baroque wrought-iron fence separates the *Demidov Mansion* (No. 3) from the road. The yellow Classical building with a six-columned portico was once owned by the Demidovs, an enormously wealthy family with iron foundries in the Urals. A similar great house is located nearby, in Bol. Ordynka Ul. itself (No. 21, left); the *Dolgov-Zhemochkin Mansion* was built in 1779, possibly by Bazhenov, and was rebuilt in the early 19C by Bove. The *Latin American Institute* is now housed here.

The brick *Church of St. Nicholas in Pyzhi* (Ts. Nikoly v Pyzhakh), built in 1657–70, stands at Bol. Ordynka Ul., 27a (left). It is a typical five-domed church of its era. The little crowns on the crosses indicate that it was built with funds donated by the strel'tsy; in this case the donors were the Pyzhkov Prikaz (Company). Opposite, at No. 34a, was founded a much later religious institution, the *Convent of SS. Martha and Mary* (Marfo-Mariinskaya Obitel').

The abbess and patron of the convent was Grand Duchess Yelizaveta Fyodorovna (1864–1918), the sister of the last Empress; she established it in 1910, after the assassination of her husband, Grand Duke Sergey. The nuns' habits were designed by the painter Nesterov, and the buildings by Shchusev—who 15 years later built the Lenin Mausoleum. The white *Church of the Intercession* (Ts. Pokrova) (1908–12), with its large grey dome, is visible from the street through an archway; Shchusev carried out much historical research for this building and constructed it along the lines of the Church of the Saviour in the Kremlin (now demolished). The former convent is now a workshop for art restoration.

1-Y KAZACH'IY PER. turns to the right off Bol. Ordynka Ul. The first street to the left off 1-y Kazach'iy Per. is SHCHETININSKIY PER. with, at No. 10, the **Tropinin Museum** (Muzey V. Tropinina i Moskovskikh Khudozhnikov yevo Vremeni). This comprises a collection of early-19C Russian art, mainly paintings by V.A. Tropinin (1776–1857). The collection, originally built up by F.Ye. Vishnevsky, is now a branch of the Ostankino Museum. Shchetininskiy Per. continues to POGOREL'SKIY PER., and at the intersection of Pogorel'skiy Per. and Bol. Ordynka Ul. (No. 60/2) stands Karl Blank's **Church of St. Catherine** (Ts. Yekateriny) (1765–70). Across Bol. Ordynka Ul., and near its S end, is a **Branch of the Maly Theatre** (Filial Malovo Teatra) No. 69).

PYATNITSKAYA UL. (Pl. 5; 7) runs parallel to Bol. Ordynka Ul., and a little to the E. Vehicle traffic is one-way, to the S. At the N end, at No. 4, rises the green belfry of the **Church of John the Baptist** (Ts. Ionna Predtechi 'pod Borom') (1753); the church itself, which dates from the late 17C, is situated in the side street, CHERNIGOVSKIY PER. The **Church of SS. Mikhail and Fyodor** (Ts. Mikhaila i Fyodora) (late 17C) faces it across the narrow lane.

The Classical mansion at Pyatnitskaya Ul., 18 (Bove, early 19C), is one of several attractive buildings in this street. On the corner of KLIMENTOVSKIY PER. stands the tall red **Church of St. Clement, Pope of Rome** (Ts. Klimenta Papy Rimskovo). The two-storey church is crowned by five cupolas—a gold one in the centre surrounded by four blue ones with stars; architecturally the building is an interesting combination of Russian tradition and Rococo. The bell tower was completed in 1758, but the construction of the church itself lasted from 1754–74. The nearby pavilion of NOVOKUZNETSKAYA METRO STATION is located on the site of the demolished 16C Church of St. Paraskeva Pyatnitsa (Ts. Paraskevy Pyatnitsy), from which the street takes its name. The pink **Church of the Trinity in Vishnyaki** (Ts. Troitsy v Vishnyakakh) at No. 51 (left) was built in the Empire style by A.G. Grigor'yev in 1824–26; Vishnyakov was the name of the colonel of one of the strel'tsy companies quartered in this neighbourhood. A little further along, on the other side of the street, is the over-decorated *Rekk Mansion*

(No. 64), built by S.V. Sherwood in 1897 and dominated by a huge four-columned portico.

Bol Ordynka Ul. and Pyatnitskaya Ul. meet the Sadovoye Kol'tso at DOBRYNINSKAYA PL. (Pl. 4; 8), the main square of Zamoskvorech'ye. Formerly called Serpukhovskaya Pl. (and even earlier called Serpukhovskiye Gate after a a major gate in the town wall here), it was renamed in 1918 in honour of a young local Red Guard killed during the October Revolution—P.G. Dobrynin. In the square is DOBRYNINSKAYA METRO STATION.

The extension of Bol. Ordynka Ul. continues S as LYUSINOVSKAYA UL., BOL. TUL'SKAYA UL., and then as VARSHAVSKOYE SHOSSE (Warsaw Highway) (Pl. 3; 5). About 7km from Dobryninskaya Pl., the KASHIRSKOYE SHOSSE (Motor Route M4) forks off (left). Varshavskoye Shosse continues a further 11km through SOVETSKIY (right) and KRASNOGVARDEYSKIY (left) DISTRICTS as Motor Route M2 to the RING MOTORWAY and Domodedovo Airport.

Just to the E of Lyusinovskaya Ul. is BOL. SERPUKHOVSKAYA UL. (Pl. 3; 5) with (right) the large but truncated **Church of the Ascension** (Ts. Voznesenii za Serpukhovskimi Vorotami). Work began on this church in 1709 under the sponsorship of Peter I's son Aleksey, but with his disgrace and execution it was not completed until 1763. STREMYANNYY PER., which turns off Bol. Serpukhovskaya Ul. to the left, contains at No. 28 the *Plekhanov Economic Institute*, founded in 1904 as the *Commercial Institute*. The institute, which was then in the centre of a working-class district, was the headquarters of the Bolsheviks' Moscow Committee during the critical days of 29 October to 2 November 1917. The huge 17-storey building at Bol. Serpukhovskaya Ul., 27 (left), was completed in 1971 for the *Vishnevsky Surgical Institute*; this is one of the most important medical institutes in the Soviet Union.

At the end of Bol. Serpukhovskaya Ul. several roads diverge. To the left are a *Statue of Lenin* (V.B. Topuridze, 1967) and a smaller red granite *Monument* (1922) marking the spot where on 30 August 1918 the Communist leader was nearly killed. Lenin was visiting the Mikhel'son Factory (now the Vladimir II'ich Factory) when an assassin fired several shots, badly wounding him. A woman named Fanya Kaplan was executed for the attack, and other reprisals marked the beginning of the infamous 'Red Terror'. In the continuation of Bol. Serpukhovskaya Ul., PAVLOVSKAYA UL., is the former **Paul Hospital**, at No. 25 (left). The handsome yellow building stands behind an iron railing; it was built to the plans of M.F. Kazakov in 1802–07. Originally named after Emperor Paul I, it is now *Municipal Hospital No. 4*.

Just S of the hospital, and about 2km S of the Sadovoye Kol'tso, is the **'Danilov Monastery** (Moskovsko Svyato-Danilov Monastyr') (Pl. 3; 5). *Tul'skaya Metro Station* is just to the SW, in Bol. Tul'skaya Ul., a major avenue running N to the Sadovoye Kol'tso. TUL'SKAYA VAL UL. leads E from the avenue to the monastery; the name indicates that this was once part of the Kamer-Kollezhskiy Rampart.

The monastery was founded in 1272 by the first Prince of Moscow, Daniil (son of Alexander Nevskiy), and served as part of the southern defences of the town. After a period of decline it was rebuilt in stone by Ivan the Terrible in the 16C. Although it was not as wealthy as some of the other Moscow monasteries, additions were made as late as the 19C. The monastery fell into decay after the Revolution, when it was converted to a factory and a borstal, but in 1983 the decision was made to restore the complex as a centre for the Orthodox Church. The work was basically completed in time for the Millennium celebrations in

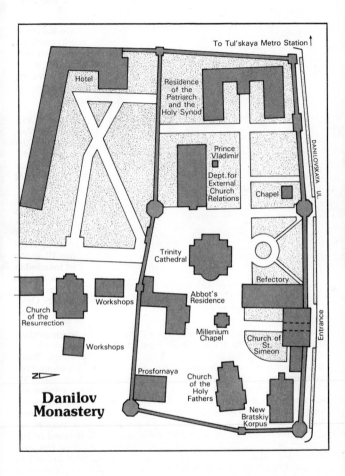

To Tul'skaya Metro Station ↑

Hotel

Residence of the Patriarch and the Holy Synod

DANILOVSKAYA UL.

Prince Vladimir

Dept. for External Church Relations

Chapel

Trinity Cathedral

Refectory

Workshops

Abbot's Residence

Church of the Resurrection

Millenium Chapel

Church of St. Simeon

Entrance

Workshops

Prosfornaya

Church of the Holy Fathers

New Bratskiy Korpus

2◁▷

Danilov Monastery

1988. The Patriarch of the Russian Orthodox Church now has his residence here.

The monastery is surrounded by a white crenellated wall with 10 turrets. The main entrance is through the gold-domed gate towards the E end of the N side, the *Gateway Church of Simeon the Pillar Saint* (Nadvodyashiy Ts. Simeona Stolpnika). The most important churches in the main part of the monastery are, to the right, the orange **Trinity Cathedral** and to the left the white **Church of the Holy Fathers** (Khram vo imya Svyatykh Ottsov Semi Vselenskikh Soborov). The former was build by Bove in 1833–38, the latter in the late 17C. Directly beyond the entrance is a tiny *Chapel* commemorating the Millennium. In the W end of the grounds, beyond the cathedral, are the headquarters of the Department of External Church Relations (OVTsS) and, in the NW corner, the *Residence of the Patriarch* and a new statue of Prince Vladimir. To the S of the main complex, beyond a wall, are the green-domed 19C *Church of the Resurrection* (Ts. Voskresenii Slovushchevo). Nearby are administrative buildings, workshops, and new hotel built to serve the complex.

Chapel commemorating the Millennium of Russian Orthodoxy, 1988. It is located in the recently restored Danilov Monastery

Returning to the main Rte, BOL. POLYANKA UL. (Pl. 4; 8) leads from Dobryninskaya Pl. back towards the Moskva; it is roughly parallel to Bol. Ordynka Ul., but to the W. This area was once a wide field or 'pole', hence the name of the street. The orange **Church of the Assumption** (Ts. Uspenii), with a Romanesque bell tower, stands at No. 39 (right), and further along, at No. 29, is the striking *Church of St. Gregory of Neocaesarea** (Ts. Grigoriya Neokesariiskovo). Another example of a late-17C suburban church, it was built by Tsar Aleksey Mikhaylovich in 1667–69; the building, with its five domes and the delightful bell tower (tent-roofed, light in design, and gaily painted), is notable for its frieze of coloured tiles by Polubes. Nearby, and on the other side of the street (No. 20), is the attractive Neo-Russian *Church* of the former *Iverskaya Nurses Community*. It was built in 1896 (probably by I.Ye. Bondarenko) and stands behind an arch in the grounds of a hospital.

UL. DIMITROVA (Pl. 4; 8) runs more or less parallel to Bol. Polyanka Ul. and two blocks to the W. The streets converge near the Drainage Canal, and set in a square here is a *Statue of G.M. Dimitrov* (1882–1949), the Bulgarian leader of the Comintern and famous defendant in the Reichstag fire trial; Dimitrov lived near here from 1934 to 1945. This old street was formerly called Bol. Yakimanka Ul.

The *Church of St. John the Warrior** (Ts. Ivana Voina) is located at Ul. Dimitrova, 46 (left), not far from the Sadovoye Kol'tso and the OKTYABR'SKAYA METRO STATION. Legend has it that Peter the Great took part in planning the church as he liked the idea of a church dedicated to a warrior saint; the actual construction (1709–13) has been attributed to the architect Ivan Zarudny. The body of the church is painted a deep red, against which stand out the white details; the design mixes the Moscow Baroque (tiered construction, octagonal bell tower) with the new styles of the 18C (lavish ornamentation, semi-circular pediments). This is a working church; the fine carved *Iconostasis* was formerly that of the Church of the Resurrection in 2-y Kadashovskiy Per. Opposite the Church, at No. 43, is the **French Embassy**, an ornate Pseudo-Russian building formerly called the *Igumnov Mansion* (N.I. Pozdeyev, 1892).

At the W end of Yakimovskiy Per., which runs off Ul. Dimitrova, is the **Picture Gallery of the USSR** (Kartinnaya Galereya SSSR) (Pl. 4; 8). The nearest Metro station is PARK KUL'TURY, on the other side of the Moskva River.

The huge building extends for more than 250m along the embankment. The S part of the building houses the *Exhibition Hall of the Central House of Artists* (Vystavochnyi Zal Tsentral'novo Doma Khudozhnikov), which is used for temporary exhibitions. Other facilities include 'rest zones', lecture halls and restoration workshops. The Picture Gallery of the USSR is in the N and E part of the building. At the time of writing it is still not clear what its permanent holdings will be. Presumably they will be Soviet art; see the listing for the Tret'yakov Gallery (p 163).

The continuation of Bol. Polyanka Ul., N between the Drainage Canal and the Moskva River, is called UL. SERAFIMOVICHA (Pl. 4; 6). On the left rises the grey and silver roof of the *Udarnik Cinema*, built in the Constructivist style at the end of the 1920s. It is part of a huge block of flats built by Iofan in 1928–31 and known unofficially as **'Government House'** (Dom Pravitel'stva) because it was intended for senior Soviet officials. It is said to have more commemorative plaques than any other building in Moscow. Among those honoured is A.S. Serafimovich (1863–1949), author of 'The Iron Flood', a classic novel of Socialist Realism, and the man after whom this street is named. Other plaques give the names of further former residents: Marshal Tukhachevsky; the Comintern leader Dimitrov; the historian Ye.V. Tarle; A.I. Mikoyan, designer of the MiG fighters; and a number of Party and state officials including G.I. Petrovsky, N.M. Shvernik, N.I. Podvoysky, and P.P. Postyshev. Among other people who lived here were Bukharin and Svetlana Alliliyeva, Stalin's daughter. The N part of the complex includes the **Variety Theatre** (Moskovskiy Gos. Teatr Estrady).

Opposite the Udarnik Cinema is PL. REPINA, named after the artist I.Ye. Repin; a *Statue of Repin* by M.G. Manizer was unveiled here in 1958. This square was formerly known as Bolotnaya (Swamp) Pl.; the Cossack rebel Yemel'yan Pugachov was executed here in 1775.

BOL'SHOY KAMENNYY MOST crosses the Moskva River back to the centre of town. For details of the interesting streets along the embankment see p 213. The nearest station is BIBLIOTEKA IM. LENINA, beyond the SW corner of the Kremlin, on Pr. Marksa.

9   The Sadovoye Kol'tso

The Sadovoye Kol'tso (Motor Route Б), the second Moscow ring road, encircles the city centre at a radius of 2 to 3km from the Kremlin. The length of the Sadovoye Kol'tso amounts to over 16km; it is unsuited, in its entirety at least, to pedestrians. On the other hand, bus No. Б follows the whole Rte and provides an inexpensive means of obtaining an overview of Moscow. A convenient starting point is Pl.

Mayakovskovo (Pl. 4; 1) on Tverskaya Ul.; this is served by MAYA-KOVSKAYA METRO STATION.

The multi-lane motor road runs along the course of the Earthen Rampart or Zemlyanoy Val, which was erected at the end of the 16C after a dangerous Tatar raid. The defences included the rampart, a ditch, and a wooden wall with towers; the names of some of the gateway towers survive in modern Moscow. The rampart marked for a long time the boundaries of the city, and the area enclosed between it and the Belyy Gorod wall was known as Zemlyanoy Gorod (lit., 'Earthen Town'). Another name was 'Skorodom' which, in Russian, indicates the frequency with which wooden houses were built in this district, burned down, and rebuilt. Companies of strel'tsy or musketeers were quartered near the main gates in the 17C.

The rampart gradually lost its military value, and after the fire of 1812 it was removed. In its place there appeared a tree-lined boulevard, one of the most attractive parts of 19C Moscow; the name Sadovoye Kol'tso, or 'Garden Ring', dates from this period. The ring road became a boundary of social division; inside were the fashionable and affluent residential districts, outside sprawled the new industrial suburbs. In 1905 and 1917 there was fighting along the Sadovoye Kol'tso as detachments of workers tried to break into the centre or as government forces counter-attacked. In the 1930s and afterwards massive new buildings (including three of Moscow's skyscrapers) were erected on either side to create a grand avenue. The trees were cut down to permit the widening of the road, and in the process the Sadovoye Kol'tso lost its 19C charm. A dramatic moment in the Soviet period came on 17 June 1944 when a parade of tens of thousands of German prisoners was held; they were herded along the northern part of the ring road in transit between two railway stations.

Each sector of the Sadovoye Kol'tso has its own name. Clockwise from Pl. Mayakovskovo begins SADOVAYA-TRIUMFAL'NAYA UL. (Pl. 4; 1), named after the Triumphal Arch which once marked the entrance to Moscow.

Ul. Fadeyeva, which turns to the left off Sadovaya-Triumfal'naya Ul., contains, at No. 4, the **Glinka Museum of Musical Culture** (Gos. Tsentral'nyy Muzey Muzykal'noy Kul'tury im. M.I. Glinki).

The museum has a fine collection of musical instruments from all over the world. Special attention is devoted to instruments from the republics of the USSR. Also on exhibit are musical scores and letters from Great Western composers, including Brahms, Wagner, Berlioz, and Debussy. The museum possesses a valuable collection of recordings. Temporary exhibitions devoted to individual composers and performers are held on the 2nd Floor.

KALAYEVSKAYA UL. (Motor Route A104) (Pl. 4; 2) turns to the left at the end of Sadovaya-Triumfal'naya Ul. The present street is named after I.P. Kalyayev, a Socialist-Revolutionary terrorist who in 1905 assassinated Grand Duke Sergey Aleksandrovich.

The next section of the Sadovoye Kol'tso is called SADOVAYA-KARETNAYA UL. (Pl. 4; 2). To the right are the **Hermitage Gardens**, with the **Theatre of Miniatures** (Moskovskiy Teatr Miniatyur), which was founded here in 1959. The Moscow Arts Theatre (MKhAT) performed in the Hermitage Gardens at the turn of the century, and there are still a number of summer theatres here. KARETNYY RYAD UL. runs along the E side of the gardens. In this street the builders of coaches (karety) once had their workshops.

SADOVAYA-SAMOTYOCHNAYA UL. (Pl. 4; 2) is the northernmost sector of the Sadovoye Kol'tso. The new building of the **Central Puppet Theatre** (Gos. Tsentral'nyy Teatr Kukol or GTsTK) is located at No. 3; the director of the theatre is S.V. Obraztsov. There is a small museum of puppets in the foyer and, on the building's façade, a splendid puppet clock which plays at noon. The functioning Roman Catholic *Church of Our Lady of Hope* is located on the S side of Sadovaya-Samotyochnaya Ul., at No. 12/24.

DELEGATSKAYA UL. runs (left) off Sadovaya-Samotyochnaya Ul. behind the Puppet Theatre and contains the **Museum of Russian Folk Art** (Vserossiyskiy Muzey Dekorativno-Prikladnovo i Narodnovo Iskusstva).

The museum displays the works of Russian craftsmen from the 17C to the present. The building is the late-18C *Osterman Mansion*. Once used as the *Moscow Seminary*, it served after the Revolution as the '3rd House of Soviets', a hostel for congress delegates. From this came the street's name; earlier it was known as Bozhedomskiy Per. after the morgue where unclaimed corpses were brought. The Osterman Mansion for many years housed the Council of Ministers and Supreme Soviet of the Russian Republic (RSFSR) of the USSR; these institutions are now housed in the RSFSR Soviet Building on the Moskva River. Boris Pasternak was born in 1890 in a house (now demolished) opposite the Seminary.

A 677m long flyover carries the Sadovoye Kol'tso across the old valley of the Neglinnaya River at SAMOTYOCHNAYA PL.; the river flowed through the Samotyochnyy Pond here. Visible on the right is the broad green TSVETNOY BUL'VAR (Pl. 4; 2), formerly the site of the Tsvetochnyy (Flower) Market. The wide-screen *Mir Cinema* and the *Central Market* line the W side of the boulevard.

SAMOTYOCHNAYA UL. runs left from the Sadovoye Kol'tso. At the N end of Samotyochnaya Ul. UL. DUROVA leads to the right. It contains at No. 4 the so-called **Durov Theatre** (Teatr Zverey im. V.L. Durova), a theatre of performing animals named after the trainer V.L. Durov (1863–1934). VYPOLZOV PER. runs into Ul. Durova; the **Mosque** is located here, at No. 7.

PL. KOMMUNY, at the N end of Samotyochnaya Ul., was named in 1919 after the Paris Commune of 1870. The square has strong military connections, and there is a *Monument to Suvorov* (O.K. Komov, 1982) here. To the right of the square is the green Classical former *Catherine Institute*, once a school for well-born girls and now the *Frunze Central Soviet Army House* (TsDSA im. Frunze). The institute, with its ten-columned portico, was converted from an earlier building by G. Gilardi in 1802, then restored by his son D. Gilardi and A.G. Grigor'yev after the fire of 1812. The giant buff and white **Soviet Army Theatre** (Tsentral'nyy Akademicheskiy Teatr Sovetskoy Armii) is situated in the middle of Pl. Kommuny. The theatre was built in 1940 to the plans of K.S. Alabyan and V.N. Simbirtsev; the design has been criticised, but at least it was imaginative in the use of Classical forms to create a building in the shape of the five-pointed Red Army star. The 1840-seat theatre is used for normal public performances. Just behind the theatre, at No. 2 in UL. SOVETSKOY ARMII, is the **Central Armed Forces Museum** (Tsentral'nyy Muzey Vooruzhonnykh Sil SSSR), opened in 1965.

The museum traces the history and development of the Soviet Army, Navy, and Air Force since the Revolution. The 25 halls contain photographs, documents, personal effects, weapons, models, and an exhibition of oil-paintings. Among the items on display are the captured German standards paraded in Red Square in 1945 and also parts of the American U-2 reconnaissance aircraft brought down over the Urals in 1960. Outside is a large collection of Soviet tanks, artillery pieces, aircraft, and even an armoured train.

The **Ministry of the Interior Museum** (Tsentral'nyi Muzey MVD SSSR) is located at No. 11 in Seleznevskaya Ul., which runs W from Pl. Kommuny; in the 1930s the Ministry was known as the NKVD.

UL. DOSTOYEVSKOVO runs NW (left) from Pl. Kommuny. The

Dostoyevsky Hospital, a pale buff Classical building by Andrey Mikhaylov (1803–05), stands at No. 2 (right). This was formerly the *Mariya Hospital*, and the writer F.M. Dostoyevsky (1821–81) was born in a wing on the left, now the **Dostoyevsky Museum** (Muzey-Kvartira F.M. Dostoyevskovo).

Dostoyevsky's father was a doctor at the Mariya Hospital, and the young Dostoyevsky spent the first 16 years of his life here. The museum, established in 1928, contains some of his personal effects as well as furniture from his father's apartment. Also on display are portraits of Dostoyevsky, autographs, documents, and first editions. A *Statue of Dostoyevsky* by S.D. Merkurov was unveiled in the courtyard of the hospital in 1918.

The former *Alexander Institute* stands behind an iron fence at Ul. Dostoyevskovo, 4. Built by G. Gilardi in 1804–05 and formerly a school for girls, it is now the *Tuberculosis Institute*.

School in the Art Nouveau style (A.U. Zelenko, early 20C)

A remarkable Art Nouveau former *School* by A.U. Zelenko is located about 15 minutes walk from here at No. 3 in VADKOVSKIY PER. To get to Vadkovskiy Per. follow Ul. Dostoyevskovo to PL. BOR'BY. Just beyond Pl. Bor'by, TIKHVINSKAYA UL. runs 700m N (right), past the derelict *Church of the Virgin of Tikhvin* to Vadkovskiy Per. (left).

OLIMPIYSKIY PR., named after the 1980 Olympic Games, is the first street (N) off the Sadovoye Kol'tso beyond Samotyochnaya Ul.; the huge *Olympic Sports Complex* can been seen in the distance

TROITSKAYA UL. turns right near the beginning of Olimpiyskiy Pr. and leads to PER. VASNETSOVA (left). The painter V.M. Vasnetsov (1848–1926) lived from 1894 until his death at Per. Vasnetsova, 13, in a quaint Neo-Russian wooden house he designed himself; there is a small *Vasnetsov Museum* (Dom-Muzey Khudozhnika V.M. Vasnetsova) here, accessible by prior permission.

SADOVAYA-SUKHAREVSKAYA UL. (Pl. 5; 1), the next part of the Sadovoye Kol'tso, is named after the Sukharev Tower (Sukhareva Bashnya) of the Zemlyanoy Val, which once stood at the far end of the street. The Sukharev Tower was 64m high; built by M.I. Choglokov in 1692–95, it was one of the largest structures in Petrine Moscow. The name came from Sukharev's company of strel'tsy which, quartered near here at the end of the 17C, was among the first military units to support Peter I against his half-sister Sof'ya. One of Russia's earliest higher institutions of learning, the 'Navigation School', was housed here, but in the 19C the Sukharev Tower had been reduced to a water tank. It was demolished in the 1930s, despite appeals to Stalin by leading architects, when the Sadovoye Kol'tso was widened; a small replica rises above one of the buildings on the N side.

The tower was situated at what is now the busy intersection of the Sadovoye Kol'tso with Sretenka Ul. (right) and Pr. Mira (left) (Motor Route M8). Below the tower in Sukharevskaya Pl. was held the outdoor Sukharevskiy Market, the busiest in old Moscow. The association with agriculture continues with the present name of the square, KOLKHOZNAYA PL. (Pl. 5; 1) or 'Collective Farm Square'. Nearby is the KOLKHOZNAYA METRO STATION.

One of Moscow's most impressive Classical buildings is situated to the left at Kolkhoznaya Pl., 3. The *Sklifosovsky First Aid Institute*, originally the **Sheremetev Hospital**, was built for N.P. Sheremetev, who also commissioned the estates at Kuskovo and Ostankino. Construction began in 1794 under the serf-architect Ye.S. Nazarov, but the death in 1803 of Sheremetev's wife, the actress Praskov'ya Zhemchugova-Kovalyova, led to a change in the design; the great house became a memorial to her, and Quarenghi added a unique semi-circular colonnade to the front of the building. The giant horseshoe-shaped hospital was completed in 1807. It is now named in honour of N.V. Sklifosovsky (1836–1904), a pioneer of modern surgery.

SADOVAYA-SPASSKAYA UL. is the segment of the Sadovoye Kol'tso beginning beyond Kolkhoznaya Pl. The *Novikov House* at No. 1 (left), built by Bazhenov in the late 18C, was at one time used by the 'Friendly Learned Society' (Druzheskoye Uchonoye Obshchestvo); the moving spirit behind the society was N.I. Novikov (1744–1818), a Freemason and one of Russia's first radical intellectuals. Next door were the *Spasskiye Barracks*. The art patron S.I. Mamontov lived across the avenue, at Sadovaya-Spasskaya Ul., 6. At the end of Sadovaya-Spasskaya Ul. (left) stands the **Ministry of Agriculture**, built in 1928–33 by Shchusev, the architect of Lenin's tomb. The most notable feature of the design is the seven-storey circular bay projecting from the S corner; the ministry, with its flat walls and strip windows, was one of the last Constructivist buildings in Moscow. Beyond is another busy intersection, this time with NOVOKIROVSKIY PR. (Pl. 5; 2).

Novokirovskiy Pr. leads to the NE to KOMSOMOL'SKAYA PL., now named in honour of the Communist Youth League, whose members helped to save the Metro from a flood here. Earlier this was Kalanchovskaya Pl., where a small royal palace with a high tower (kalancha) stood in the 17C.

The busy Komsomol'skaya Pl. contains three of Moscow's most important railway stations, which serve over half a million passengers a day. The **Leningrad Station** (Leningradskiy Vokzal) (left) is the oldest in Moscow, having been built by K.A. Thon in 1851 as the Nicholas (Nikolayevskiy) Station. With its high clock tower and Eclectic details, the building is similar to the Moscow Station in Leningrad; these were the twin termini of the Nicholas Railway. The Soviet government travelled along this line when it moved from Petrograd, and Lenin and his comrades arrived at what is now the Leningrad Station on 11 March 1918. Next door stands the pavilion of the KOMSOMOL'SKAYA METRO STATION, one of the largest built; the design incorporates a six-columned portico, a ribbed dome, and a tall spire. The *Yaroslavl Station (Yaroslavskiy Vokzal) is the final building on the left side of the square, a striking Art Nouveau structure by Schechtel (1902–04). The colourful building with its towers and steeply pitched roof is unique; regrettably, little of the original interior has survived modernisation. The Yaroslavl Station is the terminus for the Trans-Siberian Railway, and also for lines to Arkhangel'sk and the Far North. The *Central Railway Passenger Service Bureau* (Tsentral'noye Zheleznodorozhnoye Byuro Obsluzhivaniya Passazhirov) is located next to this station. At the beginning of the square, next to the Leningrad Station, stands the *International Post Office* (Mezhdunarodnyy Pochtamt) (No. 1a).

The *Kazan Station (Kazanskiy Vokzal), on the opposite (right) side, was begun in 1912 to the designs of Shchusev, who attempted to create a railway station in the Early Russian style. Completed after a long delay in 1926, the station is intended to resemble a picturesque collection of component buildings, known in medieval times as a khoromy. The general impression is increased by the application of Moscow Baroque details such as the window-surrounds. The 70m tower with its spire is based on the Syuyumbekin Tower of the kremlin at Kazan, the Volga town which was the original destination of this railway line. Trains from this station now also travel to the Urals, Western Siberia, and Central Asia.

Motor Route A103 continues to the NE as Krasnoprudnaya Ul., Rusakovskaya Ul., Stromynka Ul., Bol. Cherkizovskaya Ul., and Shcholkovskoye Shosse (Pl. 3; 3. 3; 1. 3; 2). The distance to the Ring Motorway is some 13km.

Returning to the Sadovoye Kol'tso, the square at the end of Sadovaya-Spasskaya Ul. is called LERMONTOVSKAYA PL. (Pl. 5; 2) after the writer M.Yu. Lermontov (1814–41), who was born at what is now the site of the 24-storey *Ministry of Transport Construction*, one of Moscow's post-war skyscrapers (A.N. Dushkin and B.S. Mezentsev, 1947–53); there is a *Statue of Lermontov* to the right of the skyscraper (I.D. Brodsky, 1965). Another high building rises to the N, the 26-storey *Leningradskaya Hotel* (Kalanchovskaya Ul., 21/40) (L.M. Polyakov and A.B. Boretsky, 1949–53).

Lermontovskaya Pl. was earlier known as Kransyye Vorota or 'Beautiful Arch', after a splendid triumphal arch erected by the Moscow merchants for the entry into the city of Empress Elizabeth Petrovna in 1742. A permanent stone Baroque version was completed by Ukhtomsky in 1757, but this unique architectural monument was demolished in 1928. The name survives with the KRASNYYE VOROTA METRO STATION.

NOVAYA BASMANNAYA UL. (Pl. 5; 2) turns off the Sadovoye Kol'tso (left) beyond the ministry skyscraper. This was formerly a district of the aristocracy, and the street contains a number of great houses, including the late-18C *Kurakin Mansion* at No. 6 (right). At No. 11 (left), beyond the hump of the railway bridge, stands the **Church of SS. Peter and Paul** (Ts. Petra i Pavla), an interesting and rare example of a Petrine church. It dates from 1705–17; the Tsar himself is said to have taken a hand in the design, which combines a traditional Russian arcaded base with a high Dutch-inspired steeple. The tiered bell tower was erected in 1740–44 and foreshadowed a number of similar structures elsewhere.

SADOVAYA-CHERNOGRYAZSKAYA UL. (Pl. 5; 2), the next section of the Sadovoye Kol'tso, takes its name from the Chernogryazka River, a tributary of the Yauza which is now buried underground; the name Chernogryazka means, literally, 'Black and Muddy'. To the right is BOL. KHARITON'YEVSKIY PER., which contains at No. 21 (right) the **Palace of the Boyar Volkov**, now part of the *Lenin All-Union Agricultural Academy*. This Moscow Baroque mansion with red brick walls and white trim is one of the few late-17C secular buildings in Moscow. The palace was for a long time owned by the Yusupov family; Pushkin spent part of his childhood here, in a wooden wing which no longer exists. UL. GRIBOYEDOVA intersects the street nearby; at No. 10 is the *Moscow Palace of Weddings* (Moskovskiy Dvorets Brakosochetaniya). At No. 6 in FURMANNYY PER. (which turns right off Sadovaya-Chernogryazskaya Ul. beyond Bol. Khariton'yevskiy Per.) is the **Vasnetsov Museum** (Muzey-Kvartira Khudozhnika A.M. Vasnetsova). This was the flat of the artist A.M. Vasnetsov (1856–1933), who lived here from 1903 until his death.

Beyond the intersection with Ul. Chernyshevskovo (right) and Ul. Karla Marksa (left) the Sadovoye Kol'tso continues as UL. CHKALOVA (Pl. 5; 4). This segment of the Sadovoye Kol'tso was renamed in honour of V.P. Chkalov (1904–38), who was Soviet Russia's best known airman. Chkalov completed a series of epic flights in the 1930s, the most famous of which was the first flight from Moscow to the USA over the North Pole (1937). The block of flats at Ul. Chkalova, 14–16 (right), is where Chkalov lived; Prokofiev stayed in this same building from 1936 to 1941, after his return from emigration, and other residents were the artist K.R. Yuon and the poet S.Ya. Marshak.

The **Kursk Station** (Kurskiy Vokzal) (Pl. 5; 4), visible behind a square to the left, is the largest in Moscow; in the 1930s it was planned to erect a huge terminus here incorporating all of the capital's main line stations, but nothing came of this. The Kursk Station was opened in 1896, and Lenin left from here for his Siberian exile a year later. The building was reconstructed in 1972. From here trains depart for the Crimea, the Caucasus, and the E Ukraine. KURSKAYA METRO STATION is located next to the railway station.

On the left side of the Sadovoye Kol'tso, and just before it crosses over the Yauza River, is a park, formerly the estate of the Usachov merchant family. Here D. Gilardi built for the Naydyonovs one of the finest Empire-style mansions in Moscow, **Vysokiye Gory** (High Hills); this is now a sanatorium of the same name. The main façade, with eight columns, faces Ul. Chkalova (No. 53), but a novel ramp (right) leads up from the riverside. The grounds behind contain attractive follies.

Ul. Chkalova passes over the Yauza River and Ul'yanovskaya Ul. (Motor Route M7) and then enters a 600m tunnel which leads under Taganskaya Pl.; in the square is the entrance to TAGANSKAYA METRO STATION. The Sadovoye Kol'tso then crosses the Moskva River via the Krasnokholmskiy Most and becomes ZATSEPSKIY VAL UL. To the left is situated LENINSKAYA PL. (Pl. 5; 7) with the **Pavelets Station** (Paveletskiy Vokzal), formerly the Saratov Station, from which trains leave for Saratov, Astrakhan, and other towns in SE Russia. Lenin's body was brought here from suburban Gorki on 23 January 1924. The **Lenin Funeral Train** has been preserved in a small park to the E of the station (Pavil'on-Muzey 'Traurnyy Poyezd V.I. Lenina').

PAVELETSKAYA METRO STATION is the nearest to the railway station and to the **Bakhrushin Theatre Museum** (Gos. Tsentral'nyy Teatral'nyy Muzey im. A.A. Bakhrushina) (Pl. 5; 7). The museum, founded in 1894 by the theatre-lover A.A. Bakhrushin (1865–1929), stands just to the N of the Sadovoye Kol'tso, at No. 31/12 in UL. BAKHRUSHINA.

The museum, which is the finest of its kind in the Soviet Union, contains a rich display of articles from the world of the theatre, including paintings, busts, photographs, and personal effects of famous artists. The collection of original props and costumes includes Nijinsky's ballet shoes and the costumes worn by Chaliapin as Mephistopheles and Boris Godunov. It is possible to get an idea of the greatest productions of Russian drama from the many photographs and models; included in the exhibition are programmes and tickets from these productions.

The Zatsepskiy Val Ul. part of the Sadovoye Kol'tso becomes VALOVAYA UL. ('Rampart Street'), which leads a short distance to DOBRYNINSKAYA PL. (Pl. 4; 8). Here, Bol. Ordynka Ul. (right) and Lyusinovskaya Ul. (left) (Motor Route M3), intersect the Sadovoye Kol'tso (see p 168). Nearby is DOBRYNINSKAYA METRO STATION. Beyond Dobryninskaya Pl. the Sadovoye Kol'tso becomes ZHITNAYA UL. The street is named after the Zhitnyy Dvor or Royal Granary, which was moved to a site near here from the Kremlin at the beginning of the 18C. Zhitnaya Ul. enters a tunnel to pass beneath Oktyabr'skaya Pl., where Ul. Dimitrova (right) and Leninskiy Pr. (left) (Motor Route M2) meet (see pp 170, 181). OKTYABR'SKAYA METRO STATION is situated in the square (Pl. 4; 8).

From Oktyabr'skaya Pl. to the Krymskiy Most over the Moskva, the Sadovoye Kol'tso is called KRYMSKIY VAL UL. (Pl. 4; 8); the embassy of the Crimean (Krymskiy) Khan was located near here. To the left stands the massive colonnade of the main entrance to Gorky Park, to the right the long white building of the Picture Gallery of the USSR.

On the far side of the Krymskiy suspension bridge (right) is the *Institute of International Relations* (MIMO), a centre for training Soviet diplomats. In 1918 this was the Commissariat of Education, which occupied the building of the former *Tsarevich Nikolay Lycée* (Litsey); the Lycée was founded by M.N. Katkov in 1868 and named after Nikolay Aleksandrovich (1843–65), son of Alexander II. Just beyond the institute, Moscow's first flyover (estakada)—completed in 1960—carries Ostozhenka Ul. over the Sadovoye Kol'tso (Pl. 4; 7); to the left the street becomes Komsomol'skiy Pr. PARK KUL'TURY METRO

STATION, which is named after Gorky Park, is situated next to this intersection.

Beyond the flyover the Sadovoye Kol'tso is called ZUBOVSKIY BUL'V. (Pl. 4; 7), after a 17C strel'tsy commander named Zubov whose company was quartered here. Another relic of the past are the three **Provisions Warehouses** (Provianstskiye Sklady), built to the plans of V.P. Stasov in 1832–35; these elegant and simple buildings stretch along the first part of the street (right) at Zubovskiy Bul'v., 2. Beyond the warehouses, at No. 4, are the long new offices of the Novosti Press Agency and the Union of Journalists. Opposite stands the early-19C *Gagarin House* (No. 27), where Pushkin attended the salon of the actress Ye.S. Semyonova-Gagarina.

Kropotkinskaya Ul. and Bol. Pirogovskaya Ul. (p 144) cross the Rte at ZUBOVSKAYA PL., after which the Sadovoye Kol'tso continues as SMOLENSKIY BUL'V. (Pl. 4; 7) and then SMOLENSKAYA PL. The square was once a busy market-place, but it was completely altered in the 1940s when one of Moscow's skyscrapers, the 27-storey **Ministry of Foreign Affairs**, was erected here (V.G. Gelfreykh and M.A. Minkus, 1948–51). On the other side of the square (left) rise the twin-storey towers of the *Belgrad Hotel*. They flank the E end of SMOLENSKAYA UL. which, from the end of the 16C, was the main road to the town of Smolensk. Not far along this part of the Sadovoye Kol'tso is the entrance to SMOLENSKAYA METRO STATION.

The Sadovoye Kol'tso enters a tunnel under Pr. Kalinina (Motor Route M1) (p 149) and emerges as UL. CHAYKOVSKOVO (Pl. 4; 3). The composer Tchaikovsky lived in the neighbouring Pl. Vosstaniya (No. 46) in 1872–73. Before this stretch of the road was named after him— on the 100th anniversary of his birth in 1940—it was called Novinskiy Bul'v., after the former Novinskiy Convent.

As Ul. Chaykovskovo rises from the tunnel it passes a monumental red Classical building at No. 11 (left). Constructed between 1911 and 1913 as a mansion-cum-block of flats for Prince S.A. Shcherbatov, it anticipated the monumental Soviet architecture of the 1930s and 1940s. After the Revolution the builder, A.I. Tamanyan, went on to design many official buildings in his native Armenia. The dramatist A.S. Griboyedov (1795–1829) grew up at No. 17 (left). Beyond, in BOL. DEVYATINSKIY PER. (left), is the yellow 18C **Church of the Nine Martyrs** (Ts. Devyati Muchenikov). The massive yellow building standing at Ul. Chaykovskovo, 19 (left) is the **United States Embassy**. Although an agreement was reached in 1963 to construct a new embassy, this has been delayed by various issues, including that of electronic bugging; the new embassy building, when opened, will be on a site behind the existing one. The singer Chaliapin lived from 1910 to 1922 in the small house next door to the present embassy, at No. 25. At the far end of the lane between the two buildings, and invisible at the moment from Ul. Chaykovskovo, is one of the outstanding Constructivist buildings, the *Narkomfin Building. Narkomfin was the 'ministry' of finance, and this block of flats was designed for its employees. It was intended to pioneer both new construction techniques and a new communal life-style. The strip windows emphasise the horizontal axis of the long six-storey structure and, apart from its dilapidated condition, the Narkomfin Building might seem to date from the 1960s; in reality it was completed in 1929. M.Ya. Ginzburg, the main architect, lived in a flat leading to the balcony at the S end.

PL. VOSSTANIYA, with its skyscraper apartment building, is at the end of Ul. Chaykovskovo. To the right are Ul. Vorovskovo and Ul.

Gertsena, to the left is Barrikadnaya Ul. Beyond the square begins
SADOVAYA-KUDRINSKAYA UL. Set back some distance from the street
at No. 5 (left) is the **Planetarium** (Moskovskiy Planetariy), built in
1928 by M.O. Barshch and M.I. Sinyavsky; at the time the ferro-
concrete and aluminium structure was revolutionary. Intended as a
monument to technology, it is dominated by a great silver dome
spanning 29m. Farther along on the same side of Sadovaya-
Kudrinskaya Ul., at No. 15, is the *Filatov Childrens Hospital*. It is set
in extensive grounds; there is a former mansion dating from 1792
and, on the street, a smaller house typical of those built in the early
decades of the 19C.

The two-storey terracotta coloured house at Sadovaya-
Kudrinskaya Ul., 6 (right) is dwarfed by the surrounding buildings. A
path leads through attractive wrought-iron gates; at the door is a
polished brass name-plate with the inscription 'Doctor A.P.
Chekhov'. The writer Anton Chekhov (1860–1904) lived here from
1886 to 1890 in what is now the ***Chekhov House-Museum** (Dom-
Muzey A.P. Chekhova).

In his years at this house the newly-qualified doctor developed into a serious
writer and created, among other works, his first play, 'Ivanov' (1887). As he
became more well known he was visited by many of the leading figures of the
Russian cultural world.
  The Chekhovs called this picturesque building the 'cupboard house' (dom-
komod). The personal effects of Chekhov and his family, as well as typical
furniture of the 1880s, have been used to create an impression of what the
interior looked like when they occupied it. The display includes manuscripts,
letters, and first editions. There are photographs of Chekhov and his contemporaries and also of various productions of Chekhov plays. The writer's sister,
Mariya Pavlovna Chekhova, provided material and advice for the creation of

Pionerskiy Pond (formerly Patriarshiy Pond)

the museum. Ol'ga Knipper-Chekhova (the actress whom Chekhov married in 1901) also took part and attended the opening of the museum in 1954.

Situated to the right of what is now the end of Sadovaya-Kudrinskaya Ul., by the junction with Mal. Bronnaya Ul., was territory owned by the Patriarch, the so-called Patriarshaya Sloboda. From this came the old name of the Patriarshiy Prud, the beautiful pond which still survives here, hidden behind the tall buildings of the Sadovoye Kol'tso; it is now called the *Pionerskiy Pond*. The district nearby, also S of the Sadovoye Kol'tso, was a place where many students lived in the 19C, and it came to be known as Moscow's 'Latin Quarter'.

The final segment of the Sadovoye Kol'tso before Tverskaya Ul. (the starting point of this Rte) is called BOL. SADOVAYA UL. (Pl. 4; 1). A **Bulgakov Centre** is planned for No. 10 (right). The Soviet satirist Mikhail Bulgakov (1891–1940), rehabilitated in the era of glasnost, lived in this block of flats from 1921 to 1924; the centre will include the restored flat and a museum. The *Lenin Military-Political Academy* is located here at No. 14 (right), and beyond are the theatres of Pl. Mayakovskovo.

10 Leninskiy Prospekt to Moscow University

Leninskiy Pr. (Motor Route M3) begins at Oktyabr'skaya Pl. on the Sadovoye Kol'tso and runs to the SW. Beyond Pl. Gagarina, Ul. A.N. Kosygina turns off (right) towards the university. The starting point is served by OKTYABR'SKAYA METRO STATION. This Rte is some 5.5km long, but Trolleybus No. 7 runs the whole distance.

OKTYABR'SKAYA PL. (Pl. 4; 8) is now a major road junction through which traffic travelling to the centre of Moscow along Leninskiy Pr. (and later Ul. Dimitrova) passes over the Sadovoye Kol'tso. Overlooking the square are the *Varshava Hotel* and the tower block of the *Hotel of the Academy of Sciences*. A *Statue of Lenin* (L.Ye. Kerbel' and V.A. Fedorov, 1985) stands here.

LENINSKIY PR. was until 1957 called Bol. Kaluzhskaya Ul. after the 15C road to the town of Kaluga. Napoleon travelled along this route as his army began its disastrous withdrawal from Russia. The avenue was extensively developed from the 1930s as one of the main approaches to the capital. Two examples of the grandiose buildings erected here are the apartment blocks at No. 11 and No. 13 built, respectively, by Zholtovsky (1949) and Shchusev (1939). Shchusev, the architect of the Lenin Mausoleum, lived at No. 13, as did the historian B.D. Grekov. The expanse of territory between the avenue and the river (right) is taken up by **Gorky Park** (Tsentral'nyy Park Kul'tury i Otdykha im. A.M. Gor'kovo).

Opened in 1928, this was the first 'Park of Culture and Rest' in the Soviet Union; with an area of about 300ha it is still the largest. The NE third of the park, up to KRYMSKIY VAL UL. (i.e. the Sadovoye Kol'tso) was originally laid out in 1923 at the height of the New Economic Policy as the '1st All-Union Agricultural and Artisan Exhibition'; the pavilions for the exhibition (now demolished) provided some of the first projects for architects in the Soviet period. The main entrance, a massive colonnade, is in this section of the park, on Krymskiy Val Ul. PARK

KUL'TURY METRO STATION is near here, but on the other side of the bridge across the Moskva.

The central zone of Gorky Park was originally the *Golitsyn Gardens*, created by Kazakov in the late 18C when he built the nearby Golitsyn Hospital. The final and largest section of the park, to the SW, was pre-revolutionary Moscow's best park, the *Neskuchnyy Sad* or 'Pleasure Gardens'. Here has been built a 10,000-seat outdoor *Green Theatre* (Zelyonyy Teatr). Gorky Park provides extensive walks in attractive riverside surroundings. There are also facilities for recreation and entertainment: boating ponds, a cinema, sports pavilions, and a fairground with a large Ferris wheel. A number of restaurants and cafés have been provided, of which the best known is the *Pl'zenskiy Restaurant* (the name comes from the Czech town of Pilsen (Plzen) and the establishment specialises in beer and sausages). The park featured in the best-selling thriller of the same name by Martin Cruz Smith.

A number of institutes and other important buildings are located in the strip of land between Leninskiy Pr. and Gorky Park. Two impressive Classical buildings stand next door to one another at Leninskiy Pr., 8, hospitals erected in what were once the sparsely-settled suburbs. The first was built in 1828–33 by Bove as the **1st Municipal Hospital** (1-ya Gradskaya Bol'nitsa); its façade is dominated by a great portico with eight Ionic columns. Bove was a very prolific architect, but this is regarded by many as his finest building. Next door is M.F. Kazakov's **Golitsyn Hospital** (1796–1801), one of the architect's best works. Above the Classical central building is a large dome which was once the roof of the hospital chapel: the smaller cupolas in front create the illusion of a five-domed Russian church. These buildings are now part of the *1st (Pirogov) Municipal Hospital*, the largest in Moscow. The gardens behind, now in Gorky Park, contain paths and ponds laid out by Kazakov, as well as attractive outbuildings.

Further along Leninskiy Pr., at No. 14, twin pylons flank the entrance path to the headquarters of the **Academy of Sciences of the USSR**, the building was formerly the *Alexander Palace* of the *Neskuchnoye Estate*.

The Neskuchnoye Estate originally belonged to the Trubetskoy family, but it was owned by the industrialist Demidov when the main building was commissioned (1756). This was later brought and substantially altered by Count Aleksey Orlov—who had master-minded the accession of Catherine II but later fallen from favour. In 1826 the new Tsar Nicholas I purchased the estate, and in the 1830s it was extensively developed by the architect Ye.D. Tyurin. The unconventional Empire façade of the great house, with half-rotundas on either side, is Tyurin's work, as are the entrance pylons, the *Guardhouse* (Gauptvakht) and several other outbuildings. The sculptures ('Abundance') on the *Pylons* are by Vitali, as is the *Fountain* in front of the palace; the fountain was moved here in the Soviet period from Pl. Dzerzhinskovo. In 1934 the Academy of Sciences transferred its main offices here from Leningrad.

Several attractive late-18C pavilions stand in the former grounds of Neskuchnoye. In addition there are the *Riding-School* (Manezh) and *Stables* (Konyushni), both built by Tyurin in the 1830s. The **Mineralogy Museum** (Mineralogicheskiy Muzey im A.Ye. Fersmana) is located here, at Leninskiy Pr., 14/16. The museum possesses an extensive collection, including many unusual gems and rare stones.

On the other side of Leninskiy Pr. (left), UL. STASOVY leads to the ***Don Monastery** (Donskoy Monastyr'), which contains a branch of the **Shchusev Museum of Architecture** (Pl. 7; 8).

This was the last of Moscow's fortified monasteries to be founded and dates from 1591, a year in which the Crimean Tatars attacked Moscow. After skirmishing with the defenders the Tatars withdrew, and as they retreated the

Muscovite army under Boris Godunov inflicted a sharp defeat on them; this was to be the last Crimean Tatar raid to reach Moscow. The happy outcome of the campaign was thought to have been due to the miraculous intervention of the icon of the Virgin of the Don; this was an icon which Dmitry Donskoy was said to have carried in *his* campaign of 1380 against the Tatars. To commemorate the victory and to house the icon a monastery was founded at the place where the Russian army had made its camp.

The Don Monastery remained fairly small until the end of the following century, when there was a revival of interest in warfare against the Crimean Tatars (this time offensive warfare). Tsarevna Sof'ya Alekseyevna (patroness of the New Convent of the Virgin) and her lover Prince V.V. Golitsyn began a major building programme, and this was continued by Sof'ya's half-brother, Peter the Great. The walls and the main cathedral were built during a comparatively short period (1684–1733), and so the Don Monastery is more of a coherent 'ensemble' than many other monasteries. Latterly the monastery became very prosperous; before secularisation in 1764 it possessed nearly 7000 serfs. After the Revolution it served for some time as an anti-religious museum, but in 1935 it became the Museum of Architecture.

The grounds are surrounded by 12 towers, set at regular intervals in the square brick wall; these substantial fortifications were erected between 1686 and 1711. There are two impressive gates. On the W side (facing Ul. Stasovoy) is a handsome **Bell Tower**; the gateway itself (1730–33) was built to the plans of D. Trezzini, but the three-tiered belfry was added twenty years later (1750–53) by A.P. Yevlashev. The *Gate-Church of the Virgin of Tikhvin** (Ts. Tikhvinskoy Bogomateri) (1713–14), in the N wall, is one of the last examples of the Moscow Baroque.

Within the walls are two cathedrals. The *Old Cathedral (Staryy Sobor, also called the Malyy (Small) Sobor), dates from 1591–93, the time of the monastery's foundation. It is an unimposing but attractive single-domed church with three tiers of round gables. The chapels, refectory, and belfry were added considerably later (1678–79). The white trim of the carved stonework stands out sharply against the red-painted walls. This is a functioning church; inside are 17C wall-paintings.

The massive brick *New Cathedral (Novyy Sobor), built in 1684–93, was one of the largest structures of its time.

It stands on a high base in the exact centre of the monastery precincts, and each of the four rounded apses points towards one of the walls; the four smaller domes are on these axes, which is unusual. There is a contrast between the generally austere style of the cathedral and the Moscow Baroque window-surrounds above the gallery.

The *Interior* is well lit and contains an impressive iconostasis (1699). Archbishop Amvrosiy, the head of the Church in Moscow, was killed here by an enraged mob in 1771; he had angered the population during a plague epidemic and was discovered hiding in the cathedral.

The New Cathedral now serves as a branch of the **Shchusev Museum of Architecture** and comprises the pre-Soviet section of that museum. (The main part of the museum is on Pr. Kalinina.) On display in the cathedral is a rich collection of original plans and drawings. The development of Russian architecture is illustrated with unique photographs and builders' models.

The former *Abbot's House* (Nastoyatel'skiy Korpus) (18C–19C), to the left of the New Cathedral, is used for temporary exhibitions. Another interesting structure, to the right of the main entrance, is the long mid-18C building of the *Cells* (Bratskiye Kel'i).

One of the most remarkable aspects of the Don Monastery is the **Cemetery**. In 1771, after the epidemic of plague, Catherine II forbade burials in the centre of Moscow, and thereafter the monastery became a very 'fashionable' burial ground for the aristocracy. Many impressive Empire-style headstones and monuments were erected here, designed by such outstanding sculptors as Martos and Vitali. Some of the finest examples are on display in the **Church of the Archangel Michael** (Ts. Mikhayla Arkhangela), to the right of the Old Cathedral; this was built in 1806–09 as the private chapel of the Golitsyn family. Other impressive family chapels include the round *Church of St. Aleksandr Svirskiy* (Ts. Aleksandra Svirskovo) (1796) of the Zubovs, the Pervushins' Neo-Byzantine *Church of St. John Chrysostom* (Ts. Ioanna Zlatousta) (A. Venson, 1891), and the Neo-Russian *Chapel of the Tereshchenkos* (1899).

Among those buried in the cemetery are: A.P. Sumarokov, one of the founders of the Russian theatre; the architect O.I. Bove; P.D. Kiselyov, a reforming official of Nicholas I; the philosopher P.Ya. Chaadayev; the historian V.O. Klyuchevsky; and N.Ye. Zhukovsky, 'the father of Russian aviation'.

To the N of the monastery, at No. 56 in DONSKAYA UL., is the *Church of the Deposition of the Robe (Ts. Rizpolozheniya) (1701), which is still used for worship; it is an elegant building in the Moscow Baroque style and has a well-preserved interior. SHABOLOVKA UL., E of the monastery, contains at No. 53 a structure in complete contrast, the lattice-work **Radio Tower**. The 160m high antenna was built in 1922 by the engineer V.G. Shukhov, who designed several similar structures before the Revolution; the first Soviet TV broadcasts were made from here just after the Second World War. Along the S side of the monastery runs UL. ORDZHONIKIDZE; No. 3 here is **Patrice Lumumba University** (Universitet Druzhby Narodov im. Patrisa Lumumby). This was founded in 1960 for the training of 'Third World' students, and the first class graduated in 1965; it is named after a murdered leader of the independence movement in the

Belgian Congo. To the S of the present site of the university, on DUKHOVSKOY PER. (No. 1), is the *Danilovskoye Cemetery*. The *Church of the Holy Spirit* (Dukhovskaya Ts.) (F.M. Shestakov, 1832) stands in the cemetery. **Golubyatnya**, the former country-house of the Orlov family, is situated near here, at 2-Y VERKHNIY MIKHAYLOVSKIY PROYEZD, 4. It was built at the turn of the 19C and was one of the most unusual buildings of Classical Moscow; it takes the form of a wide circular columned rotunda set on a square base and surmounted by another smaller rotunda.

At Leninskiy Pr., 27 (left) stands *Hospital No. 5*; its buildings include the former Medvednikov Almshouse, an interesting Neo-Russian structure by S.U. Solov'yov (1902–03). Beyond, the avenue opens out into PL. GAGARINA (Pl. 7; 8). At one time this was called Pl. Kaluzhskoy Zastavy after the 'Kaluga Gate' of the Kamer-Kollezhskiy Rampart, Moscow's outer boundary from the end of the 18C. As late as 1940 the square was still on the SW boundary of the built-up city, and to mark this two great eight-storey semi-circular apartment blocks were erected like a wall on the NE side of the square. Begun in 1940, the imposing ensemble was completed in the mid-1950s. Yury Gagarin was greeted here by thousands of cheering Muscovites after his first space flight in 1961. Seven years later the square was renamed in his honour, and in 1980 a monument was erected here; a titanium statue of Gagarin (P.I. Bondarenko) stands at the top of a tall column. PR. LENINA METRO STATION is situated here.

After Pl. Gagarina the avenue crosses the Loop Railway and divides into three parts; Ul. A.N. Kosygina leads right to the Lenin Hills, while Leninskiy Pr. and PROFSOYUZNAYA UL. (Motor Route A101) continue to the SW.

Under the 1935 Town Plan for Moscow the South-West was designated as the first area for general development. The German invasion postponed the work, but in the post-war years what amounts to a whole new city has appeared on either side of Leninskiy Pr. in GAGARINSKIY DISTRICT (Rayon) (right) and CHERYOMUSHKINSKII DISTRICT (left). (Gagarinskii district is named after the first cosmonaut; Cheryomushkinskii District was once called Brezhnevskii District after the now disgraced Party leader.) One of the first major housing schemes NOVYYE CHERYOMUSHKI was built along Profsoyuznaya Ul., with simple relatively inexpensive blocks of flats created from prefabricated material. Today the 11km from Pl. Gagarina to the Ring Motorway is full of such houses. The area is served by two Metro lines, and Bus No. 144 follows Leninskiy Pr.

Among the buildings along Leninskiy Pr. are the *Sputnik Hotel* (No. 38) and the *Gavana* (Havana) restaurant (No. 88). At the far end is the **Central House of Tourists** (Tsentral'nyy Dom Turista), an angular 36-storey skyscraper with accommodation for 1300 guests; beyond it, at the junction of Leninskiy Pr. and Pr. Vernadskovo, stands the 22-storey *Salyut Hotel*. Not far away, on the W side of Pr. Vernadskovo and within sight of YUGO-ZAPADNAYA METRO STATION (Pl. 2; 7), is the **Church of the Archangel Michael** (Ts. Mikhayla Arkhangela). This church was built in 1693 in the village of TROPARYOVO, which was then owned by the New Convent of the Virgin. Like the convent itself, the Church of the Archangel Michael incorporates many Moscow Baroque details; this is unusual in a 'country' church.

Leninskiy Pr. is notable for the large number of modern research institutes situated along it. To the E of the avenue, in UL. KRASIKOVA (the extension of Lomonosovskii Pr.), at No. 28/45, is the elegant low building of the *Social Sciences Institute Library* or INION (Biblioteka Instituta Nauchnoy Informatsii po Obshchestvennym Naukam AN SSSR) (1976). The library is situated near PROFSOYUZNAYA METRO STATION.

PROFSOYUZNAYA UL. (Pl. 2; 6) or 'Trade Union Street' runs to the SW parallel to Leninskiy Pr. At Nos 90 and 91 on BOL. CHERYOMUSHKINSKAYA UL., which is not far to the E, can be found the former **Cheryomushki Estate**. The main house is a modest 18C Classical structure, but the *Stables* (Konnyy Dvor) feature unique twin pagoda-like towers. Several attractive pavilions are set in the former parkland of the estate. The name of the village of Cheryomushki was given to one of the first post-Second World War housing schemes, NOVYYE CHERYOMUSHKI.

VORONTSOVO, on KALUZHSKAYA SHOSSE is situated to the W of Profsoyuznaya Ul. and not far from KALUZHSKAYA METRO STATION. Here survives a country estate built for the Repnins in the late 18C. The main entrance is flanked by two Pseudo-Gothic turrets dating from the 1770s and 1780s; it has been suggested that the architect Bazhenov was responsible for their design. Another former village was KON'KOVO, located near Profsoyuznaya Ul. to the S of the present BELYAYEVO METRO STATION (Pl. 2; 8). Here to the right of the avenue can be seen a simple but attractive estate *Church*, built in 1694 in the Moscow Baroque style.

UL. A. N. KOSYGINA (Pl. 7; 7), named after a Soviet prime minister, leads from Pl. Gagarina into the Lenin Hills (Leninskiye Gory), which were known until 1935 as the Vorob'yovskiye Gory (Sparrow Hills). The hills command the finest view of Moscow. Herzen and Ogaryov, who became the pioneers of the the early 19C radical movement, are said to have made a vow here to fight to the end against oppression. During the Revolution of 1917 rebel guns were emplaced on the Sparrow Hills to bombard the government forces in the city below.

The highway curves past the Classical *Dmitriyev-Mamonov Palace* (1756–61) (right) and the *Orlenok Hotel*. Further on (left) is the 49-ha site of the **Palace of Pioneers** (1958–62), an impressive complex built to serve the Soviet children's organisation. The road passes over PR. VERNADSKOVO (Pl. 2; 6), the extension of Komsomol'skiy Pr., at this point.

Pr. Vernadskovo avenue is named after the geochemist V.I. Vernadsky (1863–1945), and is one of the main thoroughfares of SW Moscow. To the right of Pr. Vernadskovo is the stadium of Moscow University. Behind trees to the left at No. 5 is the low building of the *Children's Musical Theatre* (Gos. Detskiy Muzykal'nyi Teatr) (V. Krasilnikov and A. Velikanov, 1979); the bluebird symbol of the company can be seen on the roof. The building of The **State Circus** (Gos. Tsirk) is located to the left at No. 17, near the intersection with Lomonosovskiy Pr.; the 3400-seat arena, completed in 1971, is set on a broad plaza and is shaped like a huge wide-brimmed hat. The building of the *Humanities Faculties* of Moscow University is located opposite, and nearby is UNIVERSITET METRO STATION. Pr. Vernadskovo runs out into the suburbs and parallel to Leninskiy Pr. The *Druzhba Hotel* stands at No. 53 (left), not far S of PR. VERNADSKOVO METRO STATION. The *Olympic Village* for the 1980 Games was built to the W of Pr. Vernadskovo and is now a model housing estate. The **Museum of the Defence of Moscow** (Gos. Muzey Oborony Moskvy) was set up in 1981 in the former office of the village (Ul. Pel'she, 3). The three halls of the museum contain historical material from the 1941–42 Battle of Moscow.

To the right of Ul. Kosygina, beyond Pr. Vernadskovo, an escalator descends to LENINSKIYE GORY METRO STATION. The artificial **Ski Jump** (Lyzhnyy Tramplin), built in 1963, is a few hundred metres further along. Across the road (left) rises the enormous skyscraper of **Moscow University** (Moskovskiy Gos. Universitet im. M.V. Lomonosova or MGU) (Pl. 2; 6).

The 240m high, 36-storey building was the tallest of seven skyscrapers erected in the late 1940s and early 1950s. Even today it is surpassed only by the Ostankino TV Tower, and with its prominent site it dominates the whole city. It was built between 1949 and 1953 by the team of L.V. Rudnev, S.Ye. Chernyshev, P.V. Abrosimov, and A.F. Khryakov.

Beyond the main university building (right) the green-domed **Church of the Trinity** (Ts. Troitsy) (1811) overlooks the river.

Parallel to Pr. Vernadskovo, but about 2.5km to the NW, is MOSFIL'MOVSKAYA UL. and the site of the largest film studio in the USSR—**Mosfilm**. Construction of the studio began in 1927, and the first film was produced three years later. Some of the finest Soviet directors worked here: Pudovkin, Dovzhenko, Eisenstein ('Alexander Nevskiy'), Chukhray ('Ballad of a Soldier'), Tarkovsky ('Andrey Rublyov'), and Bondarchuk ('War and Peace').

The old village of *Troitskoye-Golenishchevo*, once owned by the central authorities of the Orthodox Church, was situated beyond the present Mosfil'movskaya Ul. Here, above the valley of the lower Setun' River, stands an early stone *Church* with three tent roofs; it dates from 1647.

11 Kutuzovskiy Prospekt to Fili

Beginning from the Moskva River at the W end of Pr. Kalinina, this Rte follows KUTUZOVSKIY PR. (Motor Route M1) to the SW. A side road leads to the former suburb of Fili, which is 6km from the start. Buses No. 45, 157, 505, and 567 follow Kutuzovskiy Pr. The Rte begins not far from KIYEVSKAYA METRO STATION (Pl. 7; 1).

The district contained within the loop of the Moskva River was one of the poorer suburbs of 19C Moscow, the Dorogomilovskaya Sloboda. Extensive rebuilding took place here in the Soviet period, especially in the 1950s, when the present Kalininskiy Most was constructed (1957) and a new avenue, Kutuzovskiy Pr., created.

The dominant landmark of the district is the 29-storey **Ukraina Hotel**, completed in 1956 (A.G. Mordvinov); the Ukraina contains over 1000 rooms and a restaurant. A *Statue of Taras Shevchenko*, the Ukrainian national poet, was unveiled in front of the hotel in 1964.

Kutuzovskiy Pr. is lined with shops and blocks of flats. There is a *Beriozka* hard-currency shop at No. 7. The poet A.T. Tvardovskiy, editor of 'Novyy Mir', lived at No. 7/11 from 1950–61 and the film director Dovzhenko lived at No. 22.

At the junction with BOL'SHAYA DOROGOMILOVSKAYA UL. (left) is a recently erected **Obelisk to Moscow the 'Hero-City'** (1976).

The main route to and from the West, the Smolensk Road, began at Smolenskaya Pl. on the present Sadovoye Kol'tso and ran along Smolenskaya Ul., Bol. Dorogomilovskaya Ul., and what is now called Kutuzovskiy Pr. The stretch of Kutuzovskiy Pr. beyond the obelisk was once known as the Mozhayskoye Highway, and in the critical last months of 1941 it served as one of the main roads used by the defenders of the capital as they marched W to fight the German invaders.

Not far from the obelisk, Kutuzovskiy Pr. is carried by a long bridge across railway and surface Metro lines. The entrance to KUTUZOVSKAYA METRO STATION is situated on the S side. Visible farther along the avenue is a Triumphal Arch (Pl. 6; 3) which commemorates another famous episode in the history of the strategically important Smolensk Road—the campaign of 1812.

The area around the arch, now built up, was once known as the Poklonnaya Gora (lit., 'Hill of Greeting'), from which travellers entering and leaving Moscow could give a greeting (poklon) to the town. It was from this hill that Napoleon on 2 September 1812 (o.s.) had his first view of Moscow, and here he waited in vain for a Russian delegation ready to surrender the city. The French Emperor rode into Moscow without any formal surrender; that night began the great fire which was to consume the city and dash his hopes of victory.

The name of the avenue commemorates Field Marshal M.I. Kutuzov (1745–1813), who was in command of the armies defending Moscow. After the indecisive Battle of Borodino (16 August) the

Russian forces retreated E along the Smolensk Road, and on 1
September 1812 a Council of War was held in the village of Fili to
decide the future course of action; this dramatic meeting of Kutuzov
and his generals in the hut (izba) of a peasant named Frolov was
portrayed by Tolstoy in 'War and Peace'. Kutuzuv resolved that
Moscow could not be defended and the city was abandoned to the
French. A supposedly exact copy of the hut, the **Kutuzovskaya Izba**
(1887), stands to the right of the avenue just before the arch (the
original hut burned down in 1868). Nearby, a grey marble *Obelisk*
marks the common grave of 300 officers and men killed in the
campaign, and next to the main road is a new equestrian *Statue of
Kutuzov* (N.V. Tomsky, 1973).

The centre of the museum complex is the cylindrical building of
the **Borodino Panorama** (Muzey-Panorama 'Borodinskaya Bitva').
Inside the building is an enormous painting of the Battle of Borodino,
fought 129km W of Moscow on 26 August 1812; the battle did not
prevent the French entry into Moscow, but serious losses were
inflicted on the invaders. The panorama is 115m long and 14m high
and was created by F.A. Roubaud (1856–1928) in 1912. The panorama was originally situated on Chistoprudnyy Bul'v. After damage
and years of neglect it was restored in the 1950s and moved to the
present glass and aluminium building (A.R. Korabel'nikov). The
Borodino Panorama reopened in 1962, the 150th anniversary of the
battle.

The **Triumphal Arch** was transferred to this site relatively recently.
It was designed by Bove and erected in 1827–34 as a monument to
the victory over Napoleon; above the arch with its paired Corinthian
columns is a chariot drawn by six horses and driven by an allegorical
winged figure of 'Glory'. The chariot and other sculptures and bas-
reliefs were the work of Vitali and I.T. Timofeyev. The arch originally
stood at the point where the road from St. Petersburg entered
Moscow, in what is now the square in front of the Belorussian Station
(at the N end of Tverskaya Ul.). During Imperial visits to Moscow the
procession of the Tsar passed through the Triumphal Arch and along
Tverskaya Ul. to the Kremlin. Like the 'Moscow' Triumphal Arch in
Leningrad it was demolished (in 1934) as a relic of the past and an
impediment to motor traffic, but it was re-erected in the upsurge of
patriotism after the Second World War. The rebuilding of the
Triumphal Arch on Kutuzovskiy Pr. was completed in 1968 and made
use of the original sculptures, which had been preserved at the Don
Monastery.

A 110ha site was cleared on the Poklonnaya Hill for a great complex honouring
the Soviet victory in the Second World War. There was to be a Victory Park, a
Central Museum of the Great Fatherland War, and a Monument to Victory. A
huge project, designed by N.V. Tomsky, was approved by the Politburo in 1983.
Such was the public outcry (possible for the first time in the era of glasnost) at
the scale and bad taste of the project that at the time of writing work on the
domed museum has been greatly delayed, and the fate of the monument is
uncertain.

Not far beyond the Triumphal Arch, UL. 1812 GODA (Pl. 6; 3) turns to
the right. After about 1km the road passes the FILI METRO STATION
(left), from which one of the most striking Moscow Baroque churches,
the *Church of the Intercession** in Fili (Ts. Pokrova v Filyakh), is
visible on the other side of Ul. 1812 Goda—at the intersection with
BOL. FILEVSKAYA UL. (It is easiest to take the Metro from
Kutuzovskaya Station to Fili Station.)

The Church of the Intercession was commissioned by Prince L.K. Naryshkin, an uncle of Peter I, and erected in about 1693. It is set on a high arched base with three sets of stairs leading up to a terrace. The red brick church itself takes the form of a Greek cross with short rounded arms; each arm is surmounted by a ribbed gold dome. Above the central part of the building are two octagonal tiers and finally another dome; each layer is decorated with elaborate white stone cornices, pilasters, and window-surrounds.

Motor Route M1 continues SW beyond the end of Kutuzovskiy Pr. as PR. MARSHALA GRECHKO and then as MOZHAYSKOYE SHOSSE. The distance from the Triumphal Arch to the Ring Motorway is some 9km; on either side of the road stretch the new housing estates and factories of the KUNTSEVSKIY DISTRICT. The former village of KUNTSEVO (right) was the location of Stalin's suburban dacha, 'Blizhnoye'. In his later years the Soviet leader spent much of his time at this dacha, commuting to and from the Kremlin in a convoy of ZIS limousines; he died here in 1953. Before the Revolution Kuntsevo was a popular resort area frequented by figures from Moscow's cultural world: Turgenev, Dostoyevsky, Nekrasov, Tolstoy, and Tchaikovsky are among those who spent time here.

The former Troyekurovo Estate was located to the S of the present Mozhayskoye Shosse, on the Setun' River (Pl. 2; 5). From this survives the **Church of the Intercession** (Ts. Pokrova), which was built in the Petrine era (1699–1706). The church is architecturally unusual for its time in that it has two storeys and is surmounted by a rotunda (the Baroque belfry was added in 1745). It is within sight of Mozhayskoye Shosse and may be reached by DOR-OGOBUZHSKAYA UL. and RYABINOVAYA UL. Bus No. 11 travels here from KUNTSEVSKAYA METRO STATION.

12 Krasnaya Presnya

This Rte takes in the area W of the Sadovoye Kol'tso and N of the Moskva River. The starting point is Pl. Vosstaniya on the Sadovoye Kol'tso, near the BARRIKADNAYA METRO STATION (Pl. 4; 3). From here begins Barrikadnaya Ul., which continues as Krasnaya Presnya Ul.; Ul. 1905 Goda forks off to the right. Bus No. 6 follows these roads.

This Rte cuts through the industrial KRASNOPRESNENSKIY DISTRICT, which was formerly called simply Presnya. The name derives from the Presnya River, a tributary of the Moskva (the Presnya was buried in an underground channel in 1908). Since the uprising of 1905 the district has been known as 'Red' (Krasnaya) Presnya.

At the beginning of the 20C Presnya was one of Moscow's squalid industrial suburbs. Several important early factories had been established here, beginning with a textile mill founded in 1799 by a wealthy serf named Prokhorov; by 1905 the Prokhorovskaya Manufaktura (now Tryokhgornaya Manufaktura) was the largest textile works in Moscow and employed 7000 people. Bad working conditions and inadequate, insanitary housing made Presnya fertile ground for Marxist and Socialist-Revolutionary agitation. The workers of the district responded eagerly to the appeal of the Moscow Soviet of 6 December 1905 for an uprising against the Tsarist government (the St. Petersburg Soviet had been arrested three days before). The 'December Uprising' was not well-organised and its participants had few arms and little training. There was sporadic fighting in many parts of Moscow, but government forces were gradually able to gain control of the situation. Presnya was one of the firmest rebel strongholds and the last district to be subdued, on 18 December. The district was subjected to an artillery bombardment for several days and as the government troops closed in they carried out savage reprisals against the defenders.

PL. VOSSTANIYA (Pl. 4; 3) is situated on the Sadovoye Kol'tso by the W end of Ul. Gertsena. It was originally known as Kudrinskaya Pl. after the one-time royal village of Kudrino, but in 1919 it was renamed 'Uprising Square' in commemoration of the heavy fighting which took place here in December 1905 and October–November 1917; Kudrinskaya Pl. commanded the route between the centre of Moscow and the revolutionary suburb of Presnya. The square has been completely rebuilt and is now occupied by one of Moscow's skyscrapers (M.N. Posokhin and A.A. Mindoyants). The building is 22 storeys tall and contains 480 flats, a number of shops, and a cinema; it was completed in 1954. The Classical façade of the former **Widows Home** (Vdoviy Dom) runs along the right side of the square. It was built to the plans of G. Gilardi in 1809–11 and served as a hospital during 1812; hundreds of wounded Russian soldiers perished here during the great fire. The building was restored from a shell by Gilardi's son Domenico and served in the 19C as a home for the widows and orphans of soldiers and civil servants.

BARRIKADNAYA UL. leads W from the square; it is intended that this will eventually form part of a planned Krasnopresnenskiy Prospekt leading from the Nikitskiye Vorota (Pl. 4; 3) on the Bul'varnoye Kol'tso to Serebryanyy Bor (Pl. 2; 3) on the western outskirts of Moscow. To the right of the present road is the BARRIKADNAYA METRO STATION, which makes use of revolutionary themes in its decoration. The older KRASNOPRESNENSKAYA METRO STATION is located nearby and connected by an underground tunnel. A statue (A.F. Zelinsky) in front of the circular columned station building depicts a member of the workers' militia (druzhinnik), and on the station platform are bas-reliefs with scenes from the Revolution of 1905.

BOL'SHAYA GRUZINSKAYA UL. (left) meets Barrikadnaya Ul. between the two Metro stations. The name, which means 'Georgia Street', derives from the 'Georgian Suburb' (Gruzinskaya Sloboda) founded here in the early 18C. King Vakhtang of Georgia (1675–1737), who had been forced to flee from his own country by the Turks and Persians, was granted the local village of Voskresenskoye.

The **Moscow Zoo** (Moskovskiy Zoopark) is on the NW corner, at Bol. Gruzinskaya Ul., 1. Founded in 1864 and nationalised in 1919, the Moscow Zoo contains over 3000 animals, representing some 550 species. The larger mammals are kept in relatively extensive enclosures. The pond by the corner of Bol. Gruzinskaya Ul. is the only part of the Presnya River which is still visible. The *German Embassy* stands in this street at No. 17 (left).

Beyond the intersection Barrikadnaya Ul. becomes KRASNAYA PRESNYA UL.

The first street to the left, DRUZHINNIKOVSKAYA UL., was in 1905 the site of the Schmidt Furniture Factory, destroyed in 1905. The former grounds are now part of the *Pavlik Morozov Childrens Park*. Pavlik Morozov (1918–32), a member of the Soviet children's organisation, was killed by peasants after he had denounced his father to the authorities during the collectivisation campaign; he became a model for Soviet youth. There is a *Statue of Pavlik Morozov* in the park (I. Rabinovich, 1948). ROCHDEL'SKAYA UL., which joins Druzhinnikovskaya Ul. near the Morozov Park, is named after the Rochdale weavers who founded the Co-operative Movement in 1844.

The first street to the right off Krasnaya Presnya Ul. is MALAYA GRUZINSKAYA UL. with, at No. 15, the **Timiryazev Biology Museum** (Gos. Biologicheskiy Muzey im. K.A. Timiryazeva). Founded in 1922, the Biology Museum has been located on this site since 1934. The museum's 17 halls trace the development of life from the earliest times. There are also special displays on Darwin and the Russian biologists K.A. Timiryazev, I.V. Michurin, and I.P. Pavlov.

The poet Mayakovsky lived as a child with his family near here in 1913–15. Their flat was situated near the end of Krasnaya Presnya Ul., at No. 36; in 1978 this was made into a **Mayakovsky House-Museum** (Muzey-Kvartira V.V.

Mayakovskovo). The original appearance of the flat was recreated with the help of the poet's relatives and friends; also on display are letters, first editions, and photographs.

The square beyond is called PL. KRASNOPRESNENSKOY ZASTAVY, which recalls that here was once a barrier (zastava) in the Kamer-Kollezhskiy Rampart (the city limits in the 18C). The square contains the ULITSA 1905 GODA METRO STATION, a *Monument to the Revolution of 1905–07* (O.A. Ikonnikov, V. A. Fedorov, 1981), and the Constructivist *Krasnopresnenskiy Univermag* (Department Store), built by the Vesnin brothers in 1928.

To the left is PRESNENSKIY VAL UL. (on the site of the 'val' or 'rampart'). BOL'-SHEVISTSKAYA UL. turns off this (left) and runs E parallel to Krasnaya Presnya Ul. The simple single-storey wooden building at No. 4 served as the local Bolshevik headquarters in 1917. It now houses the **Red Presnya Museum** (Istoriko-Revolyutsionnyy Muzey 'Krasnaya Presnya'), with its exhibits on the revolutionary history of the district.

In the future Krasnopresnenskiy Pr. will run along what is now the left fork beyond Pl. Krasnopresnenskoy Zastavy, ZVENIGORODSKOYE SHOSSE (Pl. 2; 4). Traffic at present takes the right fork and follows UL. 1905 GODA. Not far along and to the left stretches the **Vagan'kovskoye Cemetery**; near the entrance on MALAYA DEKABR'SKAYA UL. stands the *Church of the Resurrection* (Ts. Voskreseniya), built by Grigor'yev in the early 19C. The poet Yesenin is buried here, as well as Galina Benislavskaya, a long-time friend of Yesenin who shot herself on his grave in 1926. Also buried in this cemetery is the Bolshevik N.E. Bauman, who was assassinated by a right-wing terrorist in 1905. The Vagan'kovskoye Cemetery was used for the mass grave of the 1500 people killed in the Khodynka Field catastrophe of 1896 (see p 192).

Ul. 1905 Goda continues beyond the railway bridge and BEGOVAYA METRO STATION (Pl. 2; 4) as KHOROSHOVSKOYE SHOSSE (left). From the POL-EZHAYEVSKAYA METRO STATION the road is named PR. MARSHALA ZHUKOVA, after the famous Second World War general. A parallel street to the N commemorates an earlier commander of the Red Army, Marshal M.N. Tukhachevsky, who was executed in 1937, during the Purges. Ul. Zorge, off Khoroshovskoye Shosse, bears the name of Richard Sorge, the famous Soviet spy who provided—unheeded—advance warning of the Nazi invasion. There is a monument to Sorge (V.Ye. Tsigal, 1985) at the start of the street.

At the W end of Pr. Marshala Zhukova, in the former lands of the Godunov and Naryshkin families, extend the vast new housing estates of the KHOROSHOVSKIY DISTRICT, including KHOROSHOVO-MNEVNIKI. The village of Khoroshovo belonged at the end of the 16C to Boris Godunov, who built the attractive **Church of the Trinity** (Ts. Troitsy) (1598), a highly decorated building with rows of kokoshniki around the main dome and its satellites. The church has recently been restored to its original appearance and is visible to the left of Pr. Marshala Zhukova (near No. 60). It stands on a high bluff and commands a fine view of the upper reaches of the Moskva River. Pr. Marshal Zhukova ends at the Moskva River near the resort of Serebryanyy Bor.

13 Leningradskiy Prospekt

LENINGRADSKIY PR. (Motor Route M10) is the NW extension of Tverskaya Ul. The starting point of this Rte is near BELORUSSKAYA METRO STATION. Trolleybus No. 12 follows Leningradskiy Pr. from beginning to end, a distance of some 6km.

Leningradskiy Pr. was known before the Revolution as Peterburgskoye Shosse (Petersburg Highway), the main road from Moscow to the Imperial capital. It has been extensively developed in the Soviet period, especially in the 1940s, when new multi-storey buildings were erected on either side and the broad tree-lined avenue which exists today was created.

UL. PRAVDY (right) contains the headquarters of the Communist Party newspaper 'Pravda' ('Truth'), first published in 1912. The present **Pravda Building** (No. 24) was designed by P.A. Golosov and built in 1929–35. This large eight-storey block is a major example of Constructivist architecture.

The *Sovetskaya Hotel* (Pl. 2; 2)is not far along on the same side of Leningradskiy Pr. (No. 32). The hotel was extensively rebuilt in 1948–50, but it dates from the years just before the First World War when this was the site of the fashionable Yar Restaurant; Rasputin caused such a scandal here one evening in April 1915 that his behaviour was reported to the Tsar. The modern successor to the Yar, the *Sovetskiy*, is regarded as one of Moscow's best restaurants.

The entrance to BEGOVAYA ALLEYA (left) is marked by a pair of statues of horses; these were inspired by the statues on the Anichkov Bridge in Leningrad and executed by K.A. Clodt von Jürgensburg and S.M. Volnukhin. The next street, BEGOVAYA UL., leads to the *Hippodrome* (Ippodrom) (No. 22), the centre in Moscow for horseracing—including troyka-racing. The Hippodrome was first built in 1883 and reconstructed in 1955 by Zholtovsky. Above the massive portico, with its 12 Corinthian columns, are statues of rearing horses. The grandstand can accommodate 3500 spectators.

The *Botkin Hospital*, one of the largest in Moscow, is located to the right off Begovaya Ul. in 2-Y BOTKINSKIY PROYEZD; it was founded in 1911. Here in April 1922 Lenin underwent an operation to remove a bullet which had remained in his body after the assassination attempt of 1918.

The **Young Pioneers Sports Complex** (Tsentral'nyy Detskiy Uchebno-Sportivnyy Kombinat 'Yunyye Pionery') was founded in 1932 on the corner of Begovaya Ul., at Leningradskiy Pr., 31. The complex, the largest of its kind in the world, comprises a variety of sports facilities, including a 7000-seat *Football Stadium*, a *Track and Field Hall*, and the first artificial ice rink in the USSR (built 1955).

The sports complex was built on part of the historic Khodynka Field (Khodynskoye Pole), which once covered the wide expanse to the left of the Peterburgskoye Shosse as far as the Moskva River. The field was used for the training of the Moscow garrison and for popular festivities. In 1882 an 'All-Russian exhibition' was held here, and one of the pavilions survives in the Young Pioneers complex. The Khodynka Field is best known, however, for the disastrous panic of 18 May 1896 during the coronation festivities for Nicholas II. Some 1500 people were crushed to death when the crowd suddenly surged forward to receive the gifts that were being distributed. The Tsar was criticised for continuing the programme of coronation celebrations afterwards, and the disaster was a bad omen for his reign.

After the October Revolution Khodynka Field was used for the first parades of the new Red Army. It also served as a centre for Soviet aviation. The first regular civil air service began from here in 1923 (the destination was Nizhniy Novgorod, now Gor'kiy). Later, in 1931, it became the first proper airport (aerovokzal) in Soviet Russia. For a long time the Frunze Central Aerodrome (Leningradskiy Pr., 41) was Moscow's main airport. A military aircraft carrying the German surrender documents landed here in 1945. There are now new airports beyond the Ring Motorway. Khodynka Field was renamed 'October Field' (OKTYABR'SKOYE POLE) and has been partly built up with new housing estates.

The Petrovskiy Park once ran along the right side of the present Leningradskiy Pr., opposite the Young Pioneers complex. The **Dinamo Sports Complex** (Universal'nyy Sportivnyy Kompleks

'Dinamo') (Pl. 2; 2) now occupies a 40-ha site here (No. 36). It is served by DINAMO METRO STATION. The sports complex was begun in 1928, and when the main *Stadium* was rebuilt in 1935 it was the largest in Moscow, seating 55,000 people. The *Small Arena*, virtually rebuilt in 1978, is now equipped with a 5000-seat grandstand containing a variety of training facilities including a gymnastics hall and an ice rink. A large new building enclosing a football ground and running track is situated nearby, and the Dinamo complex has a number of other facilities, including an *Indoor Swimming Pool* (1957).

The **Peter Palace** (Petrovskiy Putevoy Dvorets) (No. 40) was built in 1775–82, one of the first major projects of the architect M.F. Kazakov.

The palace is a large brick structure with carved stone details; the main building is sheltered by a semi-circular courtyard. The general style is an original mixture of Pseudo-Gothic and Early Russian. The inspiration for the design was in part a group of pavilions built by Bazhenov, Kazakov's mentor, across the road in Khodynka Field, and the palace also has much in common with Bazhenov's Tsaritsyno project (p 223). Nevertheless, the originality of the design did much to make Kazakov's name as a leading architect.

The Peter Palace was used by the Imperial family when travelling by road from St. Petersburg to Moscow, but its most famous visitor was probably Napoleon, who moved here from the Kremlin at the height of the great fire. The building has for a long time housed the *Zhukovsky Air Force Engineering Academy*. Among those who studied here were the designers Mikoyan, Yakovlev, and Il'yushin; later students included the cosmonauts Yury Gagarin and Valentina Tereshkova. Flanking the palace are statues of the Russian aerospace pioneers N.Ye. Zhukovsky (right) and K.E. Tsiolkovsky (left).

To the left of Leningradskiy Pr., at No. 37, stand the twin 12-storey towers of the *Ministry of Civil Aviation* and the 560-bed **Aeroflot Hotel**. Between the two buildings stretches the long glass **Air Terminal** (Aerovokzal), which entered service in 1966. From here buses leave for the Vnukovo, Sheremet'yevo, Domededovo, and Bykovo airports, which are situated beyond the Ring Motorway.

The **Central Army Sports Club** (Tsentral'nyy Sportivnyy Klub Armii or TsSKA) (Pl. 2; 2) is situated at No. 39. The utilitarian **Palace of Sports** (Dvorets Sporta), with its low arched roof, was completed in 1962. Nearby is the 320m long **Football and Athletics Hall** (Futbol'no-Legkoatleticheskiy Manezh) (Yu. Krivushchenko, 1979); it seats 5000. The entrance to AEROPORT METRO STATION is not far away.

The end of Leningradskiy Pr. is marked by the 27-storey tower of the *Gidroproyekt Institute* (1965–69), an organisation responsible for planning canals, dams, and other hydraulic projects.

The left fork beyond the Gidroproyekt tower is VOLOKOLAMSKOYE SHOSSE (Pl. 2; 1) (Motor Route M9), leading W to the Ring Motorway (8km). The highway passes through a tunnel under the Moscow Canal and emerges among the new housing estates of TUSHINO (right). Tushino is famous in Russian history as the base of the so-called 'Scoundrel of Tushino' (Tushinskiy Vor), the pretender known as the Second False Dmitry. The *First* False Dmitry had in 1603 declared himself to be Dmitry Ivanovich, the son of Ivan the Terrible and rightful holder of the Muscovite throne; taking advantage of the unpopularity of Tsar Boris Godunov he was able to install himself on the throne in 1605, but he was killed by the boyars a year later. The Second False Dmitry emerged in 1607, and entered Russia at the head of a Polish-Lithuanian army. The Moscow government of Tsar Vasily Shuysky was unpopular and paralysed by the crisis of the Time of Troubles. The new pretender was unable to take the capital, but he created an alternative centre of power at his headquarters in Tushino, some 15km NW of the Kremlin. The Second False Dmitry was driven from Tushino at the beginning of 1610 (and was murdered in December), but for a year and a half he had attracted the support of many opponents of Shuysky, including

Filaret Romanov, father of the future first Romanov Tsar. The lair of the
'Scoundrel of Tushino' was situated on a hill by the left bank of the lower
SKHODNYA RIVER, and some of its remains have recently been unearthed.

To the left, on the low ground between the highway and the Moskva River, is
Tushino Airport. The surrounding area is becoming built up and the field is now
used only by flying clubs, but in the 1950s it was famous for air displays where
the Soviet public and foreign observers were first shown new jet aircraft.

The delightfully ornate **Bratsevo Estate** is situated to the right of Volokolamskoye Shosse, on high ground by the left bank of the Skhodnya River. It
was built at the end of the 18C for one of the Stroganovs, who wanted to 'exile'
his wife here. The architect was A.N. Voronikhin, who later designed the Kazan
Cathedral in St. Petersburg.

Volokolamskoye Shosse was the scene of heavy fighting during the Battle of
Moscow in late 1941. On 16 November at Dubosekovo, only 95km W of the
present Ring Motorway, soldiers of the 316th Rifle Division prevented a
breakthrough of German armour down the highway to the capital.

The right fork at the end of Leningradskiy Pr. is the continuation of
Motor Route M10 and is known as LENINGRADSKOYE SHOSSE (Pl. 2;
1). The distance from the junction to the Ring Motorway is 9km.

UL. ZOI I ALEKSANDRA KOSMODEM'YANSKIKH turns to the right
after the VOYKOVSKAYA METRO STATION. The name of the street
commemorates two young wartime heroes of the Komsomol. Zoya
Kosmodem'yanskaya was an eighteen-year-old partisan executed by
the Germans in 1941; her younger brother, a tank officer, was killed
in 1945. The Kosmodem'yansky children studied in School No. 201 in
this street, and there is a monument marking the place nearby where
their house once stood. The street leads via BOL. AKADEMICHESKAYA
UL. to the park of the *Timiryazev Agricultural Academy* (Pl. 2; 2)
(about 2km).

This is one of the oldest institutions of higher education in Moscow and was
originally founded in 1865 as the Peter (Petrovskaya) Agricultural Academy.
For a long time the academy was a centre of revolutionary ferment; in 1869 the
populist Nechayev had a suspected informer murdered in the grounds of the
academy. The botanist K.A. Timiryazev (1843–1920) taught at the academy for
22 years, and in 1923 it was renamed in his honour. A *Statue of Timiryazev*
stands in front of the main building. There are now some 5000 students at the
Timiryazev Academy, many from abroad.

The **Mikhalkovo Estate** is located not far away, about 1.5km to the NW at No.
66 in MIKHALKOVSKAYA UL. In the 1770s the new owner of the estate, P.I. Panin,
commissioned the architect V.I. Bazhenov to redesign it. Bazhenov's project
incorporated features from the Turkish fortresses which the Panins had played
an important role in capturing during the recent Russo-Turkish War. The great
house has not survived, but the crescent-shaped plan of the courtyard is still
evident. Particularly noteworthy are the brick turrets by the main entrance
which recall both the Kremlin and similar structures by Bazhenov at Tsaritsyno.

The KHIMKINSKIY RESERVOIR lies to the left of Leningradskoye
Shosse. It is part of the Moscow Canal and is served by the **Northern
River Terminal** (Severnyy Rechnoy Vokzal) (Pl. 1), a striking build-
ing with a high pointed spire (A.M. Rukhlyadev, 1937). From here
ships leave for Leningrad, Rostov, Astrakhan, Volgograd, and
Gor'kiy. The RECHNOY VOKZAL METRO STATION is nearby. To the
right, behind *Druzhba Park*, sprawls the huge housing estate of
KHIMKI-KHOVRINO, begun in 1961.

In UL. LAVOCHKINA, to the E of Leningradskoye Shosse, stands the new **Dinamo
Sports Palace** (Dvorets Sporta 'Dinamo') (1979). An octagonal structure with an
angular concave roof sits on the broad terrace of a two-storey base. Inside are
two grandstands capable of seating 3400.

The route to Sheremet'yevo Airport continues along Leningradskoye

Shosse for some distance beyond the Ring Motorway. To the left of the highway at the 23km line is an unusual *Monument 'To the Defenders of Moscow'* (1966); it takes the form of a set of anti-tank obstacles some 6m high. Here was one of the last lines of defence protecting Moscow in November–December 1941. There was heavy fighting further out along Leningradskoye Shosse as the Germans came as close as they ever did to Moscow. The Unknown Soldier who lies buried next to the Kremlin fell in action near the 41km line; a 58m tall *Obelisk* (1974) marks the site of a mass grave of Red Army soldiers.

14 Prospekt Mira

This Rte follows Prospekt Mira (Motor Route M8) N from Kolkhoznaya Pl. (Pl. 5; 1) on the Sadovoye Kol'tso to the Exhibition of Economic Achievements (VDNKh) (6km); from the area of the VDNKh a side road leads W to Ostankino (2.5km). A Metro line runs underneath Pr. Mira, and KOLKHOZNAYA METRO STATION is located near the start of the Rte. It is possible to take Bus No. 85 along much of Pr. Mira (although the bus route begins a block N of Kolkhoznaya Pl.).

PR. MIRA is the continuation N of the Sadovoye Kol'tso of Ul. Dzerzhinskovo and Sretenka Ul. The avenue, which was extensively developed from the 1930s onwards, follows the ancient road to such historic places as the Troitse-Sergiyeva Lavra (Zagorsk), Rostov Velikiy, and Yaroslavl; from the middle of the 16C this was also the road to Russia's northern port at Arkhangel'sk (Archangel). The present name of Pr. Mira or 'Avenue of Peace' derives from the '6th World Festival of Youth and Students', which was held in the Soviet capital in 1957 and had peace as one of its major themes. The earlier name, 1-ya Meshchanskaya Ul., dated from the establishment here in the 17C of the Meshchanskaya Suburb where townspeople (meshchane) from W Russia were settled.

The house of one of Peter the Great's closest collaborators, Jacob Bruce, was situated at Pr. Mira, 12 (right). Another relic from Peter's time is at No. 26, the branch of the **Botanic Gardens** of Moscow University (Filial Botanicheskovo Sada); it was founded in 1706 as a source of medicinal herbs, and is the oldest such institution in the country. The Symbolist poet V.Ya. Bryusov lived from 1914 to 1921 in the attractive Art Nouveau house at No. 30 (V.I. Chagin, 1909).

The giant cylindrical structure visible to the left of Pr. Mira (No. 33–41) is the *Indoor Stadium* of the **Olympic Sports Complex** (Sportivnyy Kompleks 'Olimpiyskiy'), built for the 1980 Olympics by Posokhin. This has an outside diameter of 224m, an overall height of 40m, and seating capacity for 47,000 spectators at sporting and other events; there are 30,000 sq m of playing space under the concave transparent roof. Also part of the complex is the nearby *Indoor Swimming Pool*, a large glass-walled structure with a saddle-like roof.

Also visible to the W of Pr. Mira is the yellow **Church of Metropolitan Filipp** (Ts. Filippa-Mitropolita), built in 1777–88 by Kazakov; this served as the domestic church of Metropolitan Platon. Kazakov designed the building in the shape of a tiered rotunda with four-columned porticoes to the N and S. The interior is richly decorated, with a dome supported by columns. The church stands at No. 35 in

UL. GILYAROVSKOVO, which runs parallel with Pr. Mira and bears the name of an expert on old Moscow, V.A. Gilyarovsky (1853–1935).

TRIFONOVSKAYA UL. turns off to the left not far beyond the stadium complex. The street takes its name from the tiny **Church of St. Trifon** (Ts. Trifona v Naprudnom) which stands 600m to the W at No. 38 (left). This church was founded in the suburban village of Naprud-noye as early as the end of the 15C and is probably the oldest surviving 'posadskaya' (suburban) church in Moscow. Although much altered over the years, St. Trifon's has recently been restored to its original appearance: it is a simple building of white limestone construction which is crowned by a dome and an unusual belfry.

Pr. Mira passes the *Riga Station* (Rizhskiy Vokzal) (Pl. 3; 1) just to the N of Trifonovskaya Ul.; the RIZHSKAYA METRO STATION is nearby. The square here was once the point where 1-ya Mesh-chanskaya Ul. passed through the Kamer-Kollezhskiy Rampart. Beyond the railway line it is possible to see (right) the *Pyatnitskoye Cemetery*; the yellow **Church of the Trinity** (Ts. Troitsy) here was built by A.G. Grigor'yev in the early 19C.

The next stretch of Pr. Mira contains many buildings erected in the 1940s and 1950s. To the right is the vestibule of SHCHER-BAKOVSKAYA METRO STATION. By the *Kosmos Cinema* (left) (Pr. Mira, 109) the avenue turns to the right and passes near (right) the **Church of the Virgin of Tikhvin** (Ts. Tikhvinskoy Bogomateri). The red brick church is set on a galleried base and surmounted by five blue domes. It was built in 1680 on high ground at Alekseyevskoye. In this village the pious Tsar Aleksey Fyodorovich (the father of Peter the Great) rested on his trips to and from the Troitse-Sergiyev Monastery (Zagorsk); a wooden palace once stood here. The 27-storey 'U'-shaped building nearby is the French-designed *Kosmos Hotel* (1979), which has accommodation for 3500 guests.

One of modern Moscow's landmarks, the 100m high titanium **Space Obelisk**, soars into the sky on the other side of the road. Built in 1964 to the designs of A.P. Faydysh-Krandiyevsky, it is dedicated to Soviet achievements in the field of space flight. Here too is a bust of K.E. Tsiolkovsky (1857–1934), one of the first Russians to develop ideas on rocketry and space flight. The *Avenue of Cosmonauts* extends from in front of the obelisk and is lined with bronze busts of the early Soviet cosmonauts Gagarin, Tereshkova, Belyayev, Leonov, and Komarov as well as Academician S.P. Korolyov (1907–66). Korolyov led the design team which produced the great Soviet space triumphs of the 1950s and 1960s. He lived from 1960 to 1966 at No. 2/28 in 6-Y OSTANKINSKIY PER., a side-street off UL. AKADEMIKA KOROLYOVA which begins near the obelisk). The house has been made into the **Korolyov Museum** (Memorial'nyy Dom-Muzey S.P. Korolyova).

Next to the Space Obelisk lies the 211-ha site of the **Exhibition of Economic Achievements of the USSR** (Vystavka Dostizheniy Narod-novo Khozyaystva SSSR), generally known by its Russian initials as **VDNKh** (pronounced Vey-Dey-En-Kha).

VDNKh is one of the best-known tourist attractions in Moscow and takes the form of a constantly changing display of the economic plans and progress of the Soviet Union. The 'All-Union Agricultural Exhibition' was opened on this site in 1939 to show the supposed results of ten years of collectivised agriculture. This was transformed in 1959 into the VDNKh, and since then the display has undergone constant modernisation.

To the right of the Main Gate and still outside VDNKh proper stands the famous steel statue *'Worker and Woman Collective-Farmer'*, which was created by V.I. Mukhina in 1937 and displayed at the Paris Exhibition of that year. It is well-known as the symbol of Mosfilm. Behind the statue is a large aluminium and glass building that originally served as the USSR Pavilion at the 1967 Montreal World Fair; this is now the *General Exhibition Pavilion No. 3* (Pavil'on Mezhotraslevykh Tematicheskikh Vystavok No. 3). Adjacent is the pavilion devoted to *Consumer Goods* (Tovary Narodnovo Potrebleniya i Uslugi Naseleniyu).

The MAIN ENTRANCE (Glavnyy Vkhod) is a giant triumphal arch surmounted by gilded figures of a tractor-driver and a woman collective farmer. Beyond this begins the central axis of the VDNKh, the ALLEY OF FOUNTAINS. The *Central Pavilion* (Tsentral'nyy Pavil'on), by Yu.V. Shchuko and Ye.A. Stolyarov, is surmounted by a 35m tall spire and surrounded by colonnades. The exhibition in this pavilion traces the history of the Soviet Union and the various republics.

The **Friendship of Peoples Square** lies beyond the Central Pavilion and contains two elaborate fountains by K.T. Topuridze and G.D. Konstantinovsky. The first is called the *Friendship of Peoples Fountain* and is decorated with statues of maidens representing the various republics of the USSR. Beyond is the complex *Stone Flower Fountain*. The square is surrounded by a number of pavilions. To the left are pavilions devoted to *Education* (Narodnoye Obrazovaniye), *Biology* (Biologiya), *Physics* (Fizika), *Chemistry* (Khimiya), *Weights and Measures* (Standarty SSSR), *Metallurgy* (Metallurgiya), *Health* (Zdravookhraneniye), *Computers and Information Technology* (Vychislitel'naya Tekhnika i Informatika), *Radio Electronics and Communications* (Radioelektronika i Sviaz'), and *Electrical Engineering* (Elektrotekhnika).

The pavilions on the right of the fountains include *Atomic Energy* (Atomnaya Energiya), *Coal Industry* (Ugol'naya Promyshlennost'), *Soviet Press* (Sovetskaya Pechat'), *Soviet Culture* (Sovetskaya Kul'tura), and *Technical Education* (Proftekhobrazovaniye). The pavilions at the end, beyond the Stone Flower Fountain, are devoted to *Agriculture* (Zemledeliye) and *Grain* (Zerno).

On the far side of the Agriculture pavilion lies **Industry Square**. On either side of the path into the square is the *Roll of Honour* (Doska Pochota), commemorating the best workers in the USSR. In the square itself, to the left, are *General Exhibition Pavilion No. 2* (Pavil'on Mezhotraslevykh Tematicheskikh Vystavok No. 2) and the *Transport* (Transport) pavilion. One of the most popular pavilions, *Space* (Kosmos), forms an extension of the main axis of VDNKh; it contains examples of Soviet spacecraft from the first Sputnik. Here also is the *Engineering* (Mashinostroyeniye) pavilion. To the right in Industry Square are the *Electrification* (Elektrifikatsiya) *Pavilion* and the long *General Exhibition Pavilion No. 1* (Pavil'on Mezhotraslevykh Tematicheskikh Vystavok No. 1).

There are various pavilions at the far (W) end of the pathway, around the Space Pavilion. Some of these are devoted to animal husbandry and include displays on Soviet livestock. To the left lie the *Michurin Gardens*, which were originally laid out by the biologist I.V. Michurin (1855–1935). There is an *Outdoor Theatre* (Zelyonyy Teatr) near here.

The *Circlarama Cinema* (Krugovaya Kinopanorama), where special films are projected onto a 360° screen, is situated to the left of the Alley of Fountains, near the SOUTH ENTRANCE (Yuzhnyy Vkhod).

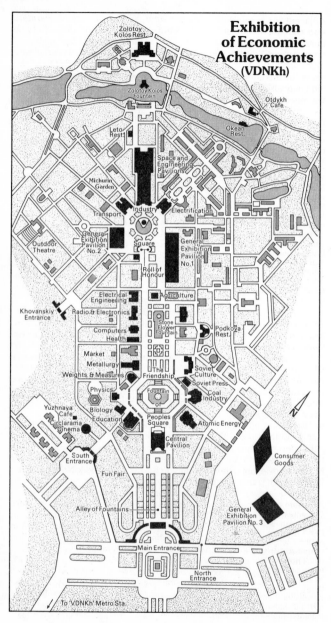

**Exhibition
of Economic
Achievements
(VDNKh)**

Zolotoy Kolos Rest.

Zolotoy Kolos Fountain

Otdykh Cafe

Okean Rest.

Leto Rest.

Space and Engineering Pavilions

Michurin Garden

Transport

Industry

Electrification

Outdoor Theatre

General Exibition Pavilion No.2

Square

General Exhibition Pavilion No.1

Roll of Honour

Electrical Engineering

Agriculture

Khovanskiy Entrance

Radio & Electronics

Stone Flower Fountain

Podkova Rest.

Computers

Health

Market

Metallurgy

The Friendship

Weights & Measures

Soviet Culture

Physics

Soviet Press

Yuzhnaya Cafe

Biology

Fountain of Peoples Square

Coal Industry

Circlarama Cinema

Education

Atomic Energy

South Entrance

Central Pavilion

Consumer Goods

Fun Fair

Alley of Fountains

General Exhibition Pavilion No.3

Main Entrance

North Entrance

To 'VDNKh' Metro Sta.

Adjacent is the *Fun Fair* (Attraktsiony). The S (left) part of VDNKh also contains the *Market* (Yarmarka), where various items may be purchased. Here, and scattered throughout the exhibition, are restaurants and buffets. The most important restaurant is the *Zolotoy Kolos* or Golden Sheaf, which is located near the fountain of the same name, at the end of the Alley of Fountains. The diversity of Soviet food may also be sampled at the *Podkova* and *Leto* restaurants and at various cafés.

Pr. Mira continues beyond VDNKh. Not far to the N it crosses over the Yauza River, and from the bridge the white stone *Mytishchinskiy Aqueduct* is visible to the right; it was built in 1775–85. Another bridge carries the avenue across railway lines, and from this point Motor Route M8 is known as the YAROSLAVSKOYE SHOSSE. It is some 9km from VDNKh to the Ring Motorway.

UL. SERGEYA EYZENSHTEYNA turns left off Pr. Mira even before it reaches the Yauza. The street is named after the film director S.M. Eisenstein; the *All-Union State Institute of Cinematography* (VGIK), a film school with which Eisenstein was long associated, is situated to the right, at No. 3 in 3-Y SEL'SKOKHOZYAYST-VENNYY PROYEZD. The austere columned building opposite (No. 4) houses the *Institute of Marxism-Leninism*; it is also notable as the last Moscow headquarters of the Comintern.

Near the old village of MEDVEDKOVO, to the W of KOL'SKAYA UL., is a unique white church with a high tent-roof and black domes. This is the **Church of the Intercession** (Ts. Pokrova) (Pl. 1), which was built here on the right bank of the Yauza River in 1627 by Prince Dmitry Pozharsky, the hero of the Time of Troubles; it was intended to commemorate the victory over the Poles. The design is similar to that of St. Basil's Cathedral in Red Square (which celebrates an earlier Russian victory). The church is about 6km N of VDNKh and not far from SVIBLOVO METRO STATION.

OSTANKINO (Pl. 3; 1) lies just to the W of VDNKh; it is quite near the KHOVANSKIY ENTRANCE. Trams No. 7 and 11 travel here from VDNKH METRO STATION.

The old village of Ostankino became the property of the Princes Cherkassky in 1620, and in 1687–88 the serf-architect Pavel Potekhin built for them the **Church of the Trinity** (Ts. Troitsy). Brick was used to create a remarkable decorative effect which anticipated the Moscow Baroque. The five main green domes on long drums accentuate the vertical axis; the belfry is much more recent and was added in 1877–78.

In 1743 the estate passed to the Sheremetevs, and in 1790 Count N.P. Sheremetev decided to rebuild the manor-house (to the right of the church). The result of the reconstruction is now the *Ostankino Museum of Serf Art* (Ostankinskiy Dvorets-Muzey Tvorchestva Krepostnykh) (Pl. 3; 1).

A number of architects took part in planning the Ostankino Palace, including Camporesi and Quarenghi, but the final design was entrusted to the Sheremetev family architects, who were in fact serfs; the most gifted of these was Pavel Argunov. Construction continued from 1791–98, and the result was the existing large wooden Classical palace. The main (S) façade with its six-columned portico is set behind a broad courtyard and an iron railing. A low dome on a drum crowns the central part of the building; below this is the main feature of the interior, the elegant ballroom-cum-theatre. The theatre was used by the large troupe of serf-actors which the Sheremetevs maintained. Among those who performed here was the serf-actress Praskov'ya Zhemchugova-Kovalyova, whom Nikolay Sheremetev was to marry; the Sheremetev Hospital, now the Sklifosovsky First Aid Hospital on the Sadovoye Kol'tso, became a memorial to Zhemchugova-Kovalyova after her death. The theatre hall could be rapidly transformed into a ballroom. There are a number of splendidly-decorated public rooms, with chandeliers and fine parquet floors. On display are furniture, china, crystal, and other items from the 18C, the 'golden age' of the Russian nobility.

The grounds of the palace are now the **Dzerzhinsky Park**, and to the N lie the 361-ha **Main Botanic Gardens** (Glavnyy Botanicheskiy Sad AN SSSR) (Pl. 3; 1). Founded in 1945, the gardens contain the finest collection of flora in the Soviet Union. There are an arboretum, extensive flower beds, tropical greenhouses, and a rock-garden; the centre of the gardens is a grove of one and even two-hundred-year-old oaks.

The great landmark of the district stands across a pond from the Ostankino Museum, the 540m high **Ostankino Tower**, known officially as the 'All-Union Radio-Television Station named after the 50th Anniversary of October'. The giant ferro-concrete structure was completed in 1967 and has three observation platforms; at the 328m level there is a three-storey restaurant called **'Seventh Heaven'** (Sed'moye Nebo), which revolves once every 40 minutes. Less dramatic, but still one of the largest buildings in Moscow, is the *All-Union Television Centre*, a modern glass building at the end of the Ostankino pond. Completed in 1972, it contains over a million cubic metres of space.

15   North-East Moscow

The Rte to the NE from the Sadovoye Kol'tso may conveniently be broken into two sections. Rte 15A starts as Ul. Karla Marksa, which continues as Spartakovskaya Ul. and Bakuninskaya Ul. Trolleybus No. 25 and Bus No. 3 follow this route. Rte 15B begins as Ul. Kazakova and continues along Ul. Radio; Bus No. 78 runs along here. From Ul. Radio, Tram No. 24 travels across the Yauza to Lefortovo.

The starting points of Rtes 15A and 15B may be reached by Bus No. 10 or Б from KURSKAYA or KRASNYYE VOROTA METRO STATION.

Although industrial and relatively hard to reach, this district has much of historic interest. In the middle of the 17C the foreigners' quarter, the so-called Nemetskaya Sloboda, was moved from near the E wall of the Kitay-Gorod to a remote new site here, 4km NE of the Kremlin on the Yauza River (Pl. 3; 3). 'Nemetskaya' today means 'German', but the word originally meant 'mute' and was applied to all those who could not speak the Russian language. Tsar Mikhail, the first Romanov, objected to the presence of so many 'unbelievers' in the centre of Moscow, and this sentiment was shared by many of his xenophobic countrymen. In 1652 Tsar Aleksey Mikhaylovich ordered the foreigners to move, but his victory was short-lived; the Nemetskaya Sloboda had an irresistible attraction for his son Peter, who spent much of his youth here and became the westernising Emperor Peter the Great.

Later the district between the Earthen Rampart (Sadovoye Kol'tso) and the Yauza was settled by the nobility and wealthy merchants; there are a number of great houses and large churches here. However, by the end of the 19C the NE, especially the Lefortovo District beyond the Yauza, had become the centre of Moscow's engineering industry; it also shared with Zamoskvorech'ye in the production of textiles.

A. Ulitsa Karla Marksa

UL. KARLA MARKSA (Pl. 5; 4) or Karl Marx Street is the extension beyond the Sadovoye Kol'tso of Ul. Chernyshevskovo, and is the central street of the BAUMANSKIY DISTRICT. It was formerly known as Staraya Basmannaya Ul., and the whole district between the Sadovoye Kol'tso and the Yauza formed the Basmannaya District before the Revolution; here in medieval times was the Basmannaya Sloboda where lived the basmanniki, who served the Court either as bakers or as silversmiths.

The large red **Church of St. Nikita the Martyr** (Ts. Nikity Muchenika) at Ul. Karla Marksa, 16 (right), was built in 1751, one of the first major buildings erected in Moscow after the time of Peter the Great. It has been suggested that Prince Dmitry Ukhtomsky was the architect of this Baroque church. The free-standing columns in the tiered bell tower are an interesting feature of the design. Opposite is the entrance to the *Bauman Gardens*. The philosopher P.Ya. Chaadayev (1794–1856) lived for twenty years in a small house on this site.

Directly behind St. Nikita's, at No. 4 in GOROKHOVSKIY PER., stands the yellow former **Demidov House** built in 1789–91 by M.F. Kazakov. A six-columned portico dominates the main façade. The interior includes three beautifully decorated 'Golden Rooms', but as the building now houses a scientific institute they are not open to the casual visitor. Another former mansion stands at Ul. Karla Marksa, 23 (left). It was built for I.M. Murav'yev-Apostol, whose son was a leader of the 1825 Decembrist Uprising; the building now houses the **Decembrist Museum** (Muzey Dekabristov).

TOKMAKOV PER. turns to the right not far beyond the Decembrist Museum. Behind the modern flats at Tokmakov Per., 13/15, stands an architecturally unique *Old Believer church* built in 1907–08 by I.Ye. Bondarenko; above the church rises a steeply pitched belfry with a painted gable. Unfortunately, the building is in a bad state of repair. At the end of the lane, about 500m from Ul. Karla Marksa, is the intersection with Ul. Radio and Ul. Kazakova (Rte 15B).

Ul. Karla Marksa becomes SPARTAKOVSKAYA UL. not far beyond Tokmakov Per. The former **Musin-Pushkin House** stands at Spartakovskaya Ul., 2 (right). The library of A.I. Musin-Pushkin was located in this late-18C house and contained, among other treasures, the original manuscript of the epic poem 'The Lay of the Host of Igor', which was destroyed by fire in 1812.

The long narrow BAUMANSKAYA PL. runs along the left side of Spartakovskaya Ul. A *Statue of N.E. Bauman*, the murdered Bolshevik leader (see below), was unveiled here in 1931 (B.D. Korolyov).

The *•**Church of the Epiphany** (Ts. Bogoyavleniya v Yelokhove) (Pl. 3; 3), also known as the Yelokhovskiy Cathedral, was for some time the main church in Moscow and, from 1943, the seat of the Russian Patriarch; it stands to the left at Spartakovskaya Ul., 15. This large church, now painted aquamarine, was built by Tyurin in 1837–45. It is an early example of the Russian Eclectic style: the five grey domes are Classical and the façades include Renaissance and Baroque decoration (the Classical bell tower dates from the early 18C). The post-revolutionary Patriarchs are buried here.

The birth of the poet Alexander Pushkin was registered at an earlier version of the Church of the Epiphany. Pushkin was born near here in 1799, on the site of No. 40 in BAUMANSKAYA UL. A *Bust of*

Pushkin as a child (Ye.F. Belashova, 1967) has been erected in a grove of trees here, opposite the BAUMANSKAYA METRO STATION (Pl. 3; 3). Baumanskaya Ul., which turns right off Spartakovskaya Ul. just beyond the Church of the Epiphany, was once called Nemetskaya Ul. after the local Nemetskaya Sloboda (German Settlement).

Not far along Baumanskaya Ul., in front of No. 60, is the spot where the Bolshevik N.E. Bauman was beaten to death by a member of the ultra-nationalist Black Hundreds in 1905, while leading a procession; this part of Moscow, the BAUMANSKIY DISTRICT, is named in his honour. STARO-KIROCHNAYA UL. (left) contains a small house (No. 6) where the young Peter the Great is said to have visited his lover, Anna Mons.

Spartakovskaya Ul. becomes BAKUNINSKAYA UL. beyond Baumanskaya Ul. The **Church of the Intercession** at Rubtsovo (Ts. Pokrova v Rubtsove) (Pl. 3; 3) is located about 1500m along (left), just before the railway underpass. The squat white pyramid-shaped church with a central green dome was built in 1619–26 on the royal estates of the new Romanov Tsar, Mikhail Fyodorovich; the design of the church was evidently inspired by the 'Old' Cathedral of the Don Monastery (completed in 1593). From the church it is only a short walk across the Yauza to the ELEKTROZAVODSKAYA METRO STATION.

B.   Ulitsa Kazakova to Lefortovo

UL. KAZAKOVA (Pl. 5; 4) leading E from the Sadovoye Kol'tso, was formerly called Gorokhovskaya Ul. It was renamed in honour of the great architect M.F. Kazakov (1738–1812), to mark the 200th anniversary of his birth; several major Kazakov buildings are located near here.

At Ul. Kazakova, 18–20 (right), are the extensive grounds of the former **Razumovsky House**. This great wooden manor-house was built in 1801–03 by the British architect Menelaws, with a large arch in the centre of the façade. It survived the fire in 1812, and the Polish poet Mickiewicz lived here in the 1820s. The building serves as the *Central Institute for Physical Culture* (TsIFK), where Soviet athletes are trained. (There is a new TsIFK complex in the NE suburbs, near Izmaylovo). The **Gogol Theatre** (Moskovskiy Dramaticheskiy Teatr im. N.V. Gogolya), which dates back to 1938, is at No. 8a.

The large yellow **Church of the Ascension** (Ts. Vozneseniya) stands at the end of the street, at the intersection with Tokmakov Per. (left) and Ul. Radio (right). It was built by M.F. Kazakov in 1790–93 with the main part of the church taking the form of a rotunda encircled by a colonnade. This is one of the architect's best churches.

UL. RADIO, running E, towards the Yauza River, commemorates the construction here of the first Soviet-built wireless station, which went on the air in 1922. Early research in another technical field, aviation, was conducted near this street by N.Ye Zhukovsky (1847–1921). There is a small *Zhukovsky Museum* (Nauchno-Memorial'nyy Muzey N.Ye. Zhukovskovo) at No. 17, the house where the Russian aviation pioneer lived and worked from 1915 to 1920. Next door is the building of the *Central Aerodynamics and Hydrodynamics Institute* (TsAGI) (A.V. Kuznetsov and A.Ya. Movchan, 1925–31), an institution founded by Zhukovsky; many of the first Soviet aircraft were designed here. (The adjacent Naberezhnaya Akademika Tupoleva on the Yauza commemorates Academician A.N. Tupolev, the long-time head of TsAGI, who was responsible for a number of important aeroplanes.)

To the left of Ul. Radio is 2-YA BAUMANSKAYA UL. which is the site of the former **Suburban Palace** (Slobodskiy Dvorets). This is now the centre of the *Bauman Higher Technical Academy* (MVTU im. Baumana) (Pl. 3; 3), one of Moscow's largest institutions of higher education, with over 17,000 students.

The building was originally completed in 1749 as the mansion of A.P. Bestuzhev-Ryumin, but it has since been rebuilt several times. Quarenghi carried out extensive work in 1788–89 and 1801 (the half-rotunda in the rear—facing the Yauza—is his work), and as the Suburban Palace the building was presented to the Emperor Paul I by A.A. Bezborodko. After being damaged in the great fire, it was in 1826 again reconstructed by Domenico Gilardi. Gilardi's façade survives behind an iron railing, with three loggias, each containing two columns. In the centre of the roof is a sculpture group by Vitali. After this reconstruction the palace became the Technical Academy (Remeslennoye Uchebnoye Zavedeniye), one of the first such schools in Russia. Later, when it was known as the *Imperial Moscow Technical Academy*, it became a centre of revolutionary activity. In 1905 the Bolsheviks' Moscow Committee met at the academy and the body of N.E. Bauman, murdered nearby, lay in state here.

Further along the street (No. 3, right) is an even more historic building, the **Lefort Palace** (Pl. 3; 3), built in 1697–99 by D. Aksamitov and presented by Peter I to his Swiss advisor Franz Lefort (1656–99). On Lefort's death the palace passed to Prince Menshikov, the Tsar's closest confidant, who commissioned G.M. Fontana to surround the courtyard with new buildings; the Classical gateway was added at this time. The Lefort Palace, in its original form, was the scene of many of Peter's notorious drunken orgies. The building now serves as an archive.

Beyond 2-ya Baumanskaya Ul., Ul. Radio reaches the Yauza; the road crosses the river and becomes KRASNOKAZARMENNAYA UL. To the left on the river bank is a park, once the grounds of Annenhof Palace (the palace, built by B.F. Rastrelli for the Empress Anna, was destroyed by fire in 1746). The yellow building to the right, at Krasnokazarmennaya Ul., 2, is the former *Aleksey Military Academy*, built by Bove in the early 19C. This was the scene of bitter fighting during the October Revolution, when it served as a loyalist strong-hold. The former *3rd Cadet Corps* was located just down the street, at No. 4 (left).

The most impressive building in the district is situated in KRASNOKURSANTSKIY PROYEZD, a street leading to the left (parallel to the Yauza). This is the former **Catherine Palace** (Yekaterininskiy Dvorets) (left) (Pl. 3; 3), built in the second half of the 18C; three prominent architects were involved, Quarenghi, Rinaldi, and Camporesi. Although partially rebuilt, the palace is remarkable for the columns set in the loggia; there are 16 in all, forming the longest colonnade in Moscow. Before the Revolution the *1st and 2nd Cadet Corps* were housed here; the palace now serves as the *Malinovsky Tank Academy* (formerly the Stalin Tank Academy). The **Church of SS. Peter and Paul** (Ts. Petra i Pavla) (1711), a white building with blue domes, stands just to the N, on the corner of Krasnokursantskiy Proyezd and SOLDATSKAYA UL. The latter street continues towards the Yauza as GOSPITAL'NAYA UL. and contains (right) the Classical former *1st Military Hospital* (now named after N.N. Burdenko). The central building, by Yegotov, dates from 1798–1802, but the hospital was originally founded here under Peter I in 1706. The name of Soldatskaya Ul. commemorates the fact that here was the 'Sol-datskaya Sloboda', the quarters of the Preobrazhenskiy Regiment. This was one of the first 'modern' units in the army of Peter the Great, and the commander of the regiment was Lefort.

From Gospital'naya Ul., Tram No. 50 returns across the Yauza to
BAUMANSKAYA METRO STATION.

16 South-East Moscow

A convenient starting point for Routes in the SE is Taganskaya Pl. (Pl.
5; 8), on the Sadovoye Kol'tso; this is served by the TAGANSKAYA
METRO STATION. From here Rte 16A leads NE to the Andronikov
Monastery (1.5km), Rte 16B leads N to the Yauza River (1km), while
Rte 16C leads S to the former Simonov Monastery (3km).

TAGANSKAYA PL. takes its name from the Tagannaya Sloboda, a
suburb which specialised in making the tagany or kettles used by the
Muscovite armies in their campaigns against the Tatars. The main
building in the square is the **Taganka Theatre** (Moskovskiy Teatr
Dramy i Komedii na Taganke). The company, one of the best-known
in the city, is noted for its adventurous repertoire. Its work is closely
linked with the director Yu.P. Lyubimov, who founded the theatre in
1964. The original theatre building was the Vulkan Cinema; the
angular brick extension housing the new auditorium was completed
in 1981. In the centre of the square is the **Church of St. Nicholas** (Ts.
Nikoly na Bolvanovke), a dark-red Baroque building crowned with
green domes. The church dates from 1712 and may have been the
work of Osip Startsev.

Taganskaya Pl. is an important road junction. To the E is TAGANSKAYA UL.,
leading to NIZHEGORODSKAYA UL. and then RYAZANSKIY PR.; these roads are
designated together as Motor Route A102, which runs some 12km to the Ring
Motorway. Motor Route M6, leading SW 13km to the Ring Motorway, begins as
MARKSISTSKAYA UL. and continues as VOLGOGRADSKIY PR. These two avenues,
which pass through the suburban TAGANSKIY, VOLGOGRADSKIY, and
LYUBLINSKIY DISTRICTS, are not in themselves of interest to the tourist.

A. Taganskaya Ploshchad' to the
Andronikov Monastery

BOL. KOMMUNISTICHESKAYA UL. (Pl. 5; 6), which runs to the NE from
Taganskaya Pl., was originally Bol. Alekseyevskaya Ul. and a centre
of the Old Believers, many of whom had risen to prominence in the
commercial world of old Moscow. Konstantin Alekseyev-
Stanislavsky, later the world famous theatre director, was born into
one of these families at No. 29 in 1863. A number of large houses
remain in this street, but the most impressive building is at No. 15
(left), the **Church of St. Martin the Confessor** (Ts. Martina Ispoved-
nika) (1782–93), which is the work of R.R. Kazakov (no relation to the
more famous M.F. Kazakov); the church has a high belfry and
rotunda.
   Bol. Kommunisticheskaya Ul. ends at PL. PRYAMIKOVA.

To the left is UL'YANOVSKAYA UL., to the right TULINSKAYA UL. Together with
Shosse Entuziastov (the continuation to the W, beyond Pl. Il'icha) these roads
make up Motor Route M7. Several of these street names are linked with Lenin,
whose real name was Ul'yanov and who once used the pseudonym K. Tulin;

the Bolshevik leader was affectionately known by his patronymic, Il'ich. Pl. Il'icha (Pl. 3; 3), 750m E of Pl. Pryamikova, was formerly the Rogozhskaya Barrier (zastava) of the Kamer-Kollezhskiy Rampart. Before the Revolution this industrial suburb on the left bank of the Moskva was called the Rogozhskaya District; the name comes from the fact that coaches left from here for the post station at the village of Rogozhi (now Noginsk). To the N of Pl. Il'icha stretches the *Serp i Molot* (Hammer and Sickle) *Factory*, founded in 1884 as the Goujon Works. The revolutionary workers of this large metallurgical plant took an active part in the revolutions of 1905 and 1917. SHOSSE ENTUZIASTOV (Pl. 3; 4) continues the road 11km E to the Ring Motorway; to the left of the latter half of the highway is Izmaylovo Park. This avenue was originally the Vladimirskoye Shosse, leading to the provincial town of Vladimir; the present name derives from the fact that it was the road along which from the 16C to the mid-19C prisoners, including revolutionary 'enthusiasts', were marched in chains to exile in Siberia.

On the NW side of Pl. Pryamikova, at Ul'yanovskaya Ul., 59, stands the large derelict **Church of St. Sergey** (Ts. Sergeya v Rogozhskoy) (1796–1838). The old **Church of the Metropolitan Aleksey** (Ts. Alekseya-Mitropolita) is situated a little farther to the W, at No. 54 (left); it dates from 1748–51, and Prince Ukhtomsky is thought to have been involved in the construction.

Just N of Pr. Pryamikova, on the high bank of the Yauza River, is the **Andronikov Monastery** (Spaso-Andronikov Monastyr'), now the **Andrey Rublyov Museum of Early Russian Art** (Muzey Drevnerusskovo Iskusstva im. Andreya Rublyova). (Pl. 3; 3).

One of the earliest of the chain of monastery-fortresses built for the defence of Moscow, it was founded in 1360 on a site said to have been chosen by Metropolitan Aleksey (1290s–1378). The monastery takes its name from its first abbot, Andronik, who was a disciple of St. Sergiy of Radonezh. The original wooden fortifications, churches, and monks' cells were gradually rebuilt in stone.

The most famous of the Andronikov's monks was the great icon painter Andrey Rublyov (who was also associated with the Troitse-Sergiyeva Lavra). Little is known about Rublyov's life; in Soviet Russia the 600th anniversary of his birth was celebrated in 1960—the museum at the Andronikov was opened at this time—but the artist may have been born some time later. He died in about 1430, probably at the Andronikov Monastery. Rublyov helped to paint the icons in the Kremlin Cathedral of the Annunciation, and he also worked at Vladimir and elsewhere. He is perhaps best known for his icon of 'The Old Testament Trinity', painted in the early 15C for the Troitse-Sergiyev Monastery; fine examples of Rublyov's work are on display at the Tret'yakov Gallery.

Rublyov was probably buried at the Andronikov, as were many of the men who fell fighting the Tatars at the great Battle of Kulikovo (1380). Here also was the grave of F.G. Volkov (1729–63), who founded at Yaroslavl the first Russian theatre.

The Museum of Early Russian Art, which is housed in several of the monastery buildings, was opened in 1960. There are no icons by Rublyov here, but the exhibition contains a rich and growing collection of 14C–17C icons, as well as some ancient embroideries.

Whitewashed stone walls, laid out on a roughly rectangular plan, surround the monastery. Part of the 16C–17C walls had been removed over the years, and they were rebuilt in the 1950s. There are attractive turrets at three of the corners; the one to the SW is a restoration. Visitors enter the monastery through the **Holy Gate** (Svyatyye Vorota) on the S side; the entrance path is flanked by picturesque turrets with wooden cone-shaped roofs. This gate is a reconstruction dating from the 1950s. The other monastery buildings were dwarfed by a 72m four-tiered Classical bell tower which once stood here. It was built in 1795–1803 by R.R. Kazakov and demolished in the 1930s.

To the left of the gate and connected to it is the restored oblong **Abbot's Residence** (Nastoyatel'skiye Pokoi) (c 1690). To the right

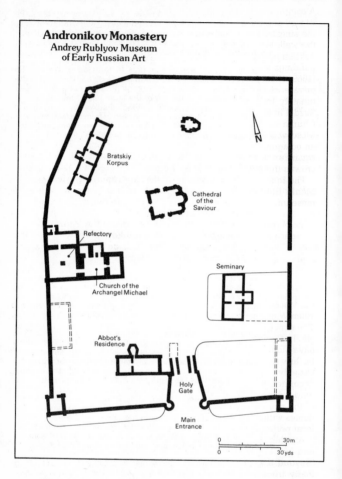

Andronikov Monastery
Andrey Rublyov Museum
of Early Russian Art

Bratskiy
Korpus

Cathedral
of the
Saviour

Refectory

Seminary

Church of the
Archangel Michael

Abbot's
Residence

Holy
Gate

Main
Entrance

stands a Classical building (1810–14) which once served as the
Seminary (Dukhovnoye Uchilishche).

In the centre of the monastery is the *Cathedral of the Saviour**
(Spasskiy Sobor), which was built in 1425–27—in Rublyov's era—and
is the oldest extant stone building in Moscow.

Fire destroyed the upper part of the cathedral in 1812, and during the
rebuilding the original design was drastically altered by the addition of side
chapels and a tent-shaped roof. Painstaking work over the period 1930–60 has
returned the building to its original appearance.

The influence of Vladimir architecture can be seen in the three apses and in
the helmet-shaped dome; this is set on a tall drum with blind arcading and slit
windows. Other features are more characteristic of the early Moscow style,
including the picturesque pyramid of zakomara and kokoshnik gables which
constitute the main architectural interest of the building. The interior, now
largely bare, was painted by Rublyov and Daniil Chornyy. Fragments of the
original frescoes have survived by the altar windows.

A complex structure, created over several centuries, is set against the W wall of the monastery, to the left of the cathedral. The oldest part, the simple two-storey pyramid-roofed **Refectory** (1504–06), adjoins the wall. Next to it rises the **Church of the Archangel Michael** (Ts. Arkhangela Mikhaila) (1691–1739) (the architects combined the two buildings with an elaborate cornice). Tsaritsa Yevdokiya Lopukhina (1669–1731), the first wife of Peter the Great, commissioned it as the private church and burial-place of the Lopukhin family. Unfortunately for Yevdokiya, Peter had her confined to a monastery at Suzdal in the late 1690s, before her church could be completed. The Church of the Archangel Michael is a restrained example of the Moscow Baroque. It has the typical tiered construction of the period; an octagonal storey with scalloped arches and pilasters is set above square and rectangular tiers. An octagonal tower with an onion dome crowns the whole structure.

The long building behind the church is the **Bratskiy Korpus** (lit. Monks Building); it dates from the 18C and now houses part of the museum.

B. Taganskaya Ploshchad' to the Yauza River

UL. VOLODARSKOVO (Pl. 5: 6), which runs N–S, is situated about 100m W of the Taganka Theatre, beyond the Church of St. Nicholas. The street now bears the name of an assassinated Petrograd Bolshevik, but it was originally called Goncharnaya Ul. after the Goncharnaya Sloboda or 'Potters Settlement'. Easily visible from Taganskaya Pl. are the onion-domes of the *Church of the Assumption (Ts. Uspeniya v Goncharakh), at Ul. Volodarskovo, 20. This richly-decorated and recently renovated pink church was built from the funds of the local community of potters in 1654. Above the main part of the church is a central golden dome surrounded by four smaller domes with stars. The 17C tile frieze on the refectory was the work of local potters. The belfry on the corner dates from the mid-18C.

Another suburban church is perched on the top of a hill at the N end of Ul. Volodarskovo (No. 4). This is the **Church of St. Nikita 'Beyond the Yauza'** (Ts. Nikity chto za Yauzoy), which dates originally from 1595. The chapel, belfry, gallery, and staircase were added in 1684–85, and the building was restored in 1958–60. The small white church is dwarfed by one of the Moscow skyscrapers which was built in the early 1950s between it and the Yauza (p 214). From the church, a road descends past the E wing of the skyscraper to the ASTAKHOVSKIY MOST over the Yauza. Several roads converge at the bridge.

UL'YANOVSKAYA UL. (Motor Route M7) leads E and passes under the Sadovoye Kol'tso. No. 1 (left), in the space between the street and the embankment of the Yauza, is the building of the *Library of Foreign Literature* (BIL); No. 10 (right) is the **Church of St. Simeon the Stylite** (Ts. Simeona Stolpnika), built in 1798, possibly by R.R. Kazakov. INTERNATSIONAL'NAYA UL. returns S to Taganskaya Pl; the final parts of this road are named VERKHNYAYA and NIZHNYAYA RADISHCHEVSKAYA UL. The richly-decorated yellow Classical building at Internatsional'naya Ul., 9–11 (left), is the former **Batashov**

House, commissioned by a rich factory-owner for his daughter and built by R.R. Kazakov in 1798–1802. The mansion with its eight-columned portico is set behind an attractive iron railing; the entrance is flanked by twin gate houses surmounted by lions. Marshal Murat occupied the building in 1812 and it was little damaged by fire; later it was turned into a hospital and it is now known as the *Medsantrud Hospital*.

C. Taganskaya Ploshchad' to the Simonov Monastery

BOL'SHIYE KAMENSHCHIKI UL. (Pl. 5; 8) leads to the S from the lower part of Taganskaya Pl. It begins near one entrance to TAGANSKAYA METRO STATION (on the Tagansko-Krasnopresnenskaya Line, not the Circle Line), and at the S end of Ul. Volodarskovo. Bol. Kamenshchiki Ul. derives its name from the two royal slobodas (settlements) of masons (kamenshchiki) which existed here in the 17C. To the left is PER. MAYAKOVSKOVO with, at No 15/13, the house where the poet Mayakovsky lived with Lili and Osip Brik from 1926 to 1930, at the height of his literary success. Here he first read many of his best-known poems at gatherings of Moscow's cultural élite. There is now a small *Mayakovsky Museum* here, but the main exhibits and the Mayakovsky library have since 1974 been located at the main Mayakovsky Museum in Proyezd Serova (near Red Square).

The ***New Monastery of the Saviour** (Novospasskiy Monastyr') (Pl. 5; 8) is visible at the S end of Bol. Kamenshchiki Ul. The monastery was established here at the end of the 15C, after having been moved out of the Kremlin (hence the 'new' in the name). The site, next to the river, was of great strategic importance, and the New Monastery of the Saviour became part of the outer defences of Moscow. The existing massive walls and towers date from 1640–42.

The most prominent feature of the monastery complex and one of the district's landmarks is the giant four-tiered **Bell Tower**, with its golden dome. Built in 1759–84 to the design of Zherebtsov, it bears a strong resemblance to the bell tower at Zagorsk. The **Cathedral of the Saviour** (Sobor Spasa Preobrazheniya) was erected in 1645 on the site of the original 15C cathedral. It is a massive five-domed building in the traditional style, as befitted its intended role as a burial place for the Romanov family. The **Refectory**, built in 1673–75, is situated to the E of the cathedral. The small **Church of St. Nicholas** (Nikol'skaya Ts.) dates from the same period (1676) and is situated in the NW corner. Nearby is the **Church of Sign** (Znamenskaya Ts.), built by Ye. Nazarov in 1791–95 and intended as a burial place for the Sheremetev family; the serf-actress Praskov'ya Zhemchugova-Kovalyova, wife of N.P. Sheremetev, was buried here. Restoration work on the monastery has been going on since 1965.

KREST'YANSKAYA PL. is situated by the SE corner of the monastery. SARINSKIY PROYEZD, running W towards the Novospasskiy Most, is named after the Sara River, which once flowed into the Moskva here (it is now buried under the street). PROLETARSKAYA METRO STATION is 300m to the E. The motor route continues S beyond this point at KRUTITSKIY VAL UL. and then as SIMONOVSKIY VAL UL. (As their names suggest, these streets run along the site of the 18C Kamer-Kollezhskiy Rampart (Val).)

The shortest route to the next place of interest, the ***Krutitskoye**

Podvor'ye (Pl. 3; 5), is 4-Y KRUTITSKIY PER., which begins to the S of Krest'yanskaya Pl. and is in effect the continuation of Bol. Kamenshchiki Ul. The complex of 17C church buildings is visible at the end of the lane.

The name derives from the fact that the banks of the Moskva River here are very steep (krutoy). There was once a small monastery on this site, but the real importance of the place derived from the fact that the senior Metropolitan of the Russian Church moved here from the Kremlin in the 16C, after the Patriarchate was established. The existing structures were built a century later. In later centuries the complex fell into disrepair, being used in the 19C as a barracks and a prison. In 1966 it was decided to restore these buildings to their original condition.

At the N end stands the small brick **Cathedral of the Assumption** (Uspenskiy Sobor). It dates from 1685 and has five domes and a tent-roofed belfry. A long covered *Arcade* leads from the cathedral to the so-called *Teremok, one of the finest surviving examples of Moscow Baroque civil architecture. The hipped-roofed teremok was built above the entrance archways of the Krutitskoye Podvor'ye by Osip Startsev in 1694 for Metropolitan Jonah (Iona). It is notable for the stone-carving around the windows and for the outstanding ceramic tile decoration on one wall. The arcade and the teremok were intended for the use of the Metropolitan as he walked in procession from the cathedral to his residence on the river bank. Little of the Metropolitan's house remains.

The Rte continues S along SIMONOVSKIY VAL UL., a broad avenue with blocks of flats on either side. About 1km along, VOSTOCHNAYA UL. (Pl. 3; 5) turns off to the SW. This street contains two interestingly juxtaposed groups of buildings, the **Palace of Culture of the Likhachov Motor Works** (No. 4, right) and, next door, the remains of the **Simonov Monastery**. The AVTOZAVODSKAYA METRO STATION is within walking distance, to the S of the monastery.

The Simonov Monastery was founded here by the Moskva in the 1370s. It served as a vital part of Moscow's defences, and the site was said to have been chosen by Grand Prince Dmitry (Donskoy); the monk Simon donated the land (hence the name). The first head of the monastery was Fyodor, a nephew and pupil of St. Sergiy of Radonezh (c 1321–91), founder of the Troitse-Sergiyeva Lavra; St. Sergiy stayed here during his visits to Moscow. The legendary 14C warrior-monks Peresvet and Oslyabya were reputed to have been interred here, and later the monastery became the burial place of a number of notable figures, including Prince Simeon Bekbulatovich (the mock 'tsar' of Ivan the Terrible) and the Slavophile Aksakov brothers.

Unfortunately, the greater part of the monastery was blown up in 1934 to make way for the expansion of the adjacent motor works. The main churches were destroyed at this time, as was a 93m five-tiered bell tower by Thon (1839). The Moscow Baroque *Refectory* survives, one of the oldest and most lavish of its type; it was completed in the 1680s under the supervision of Osip Startsev. Most easily seen is the *S Wall* with its massive towers. On the SW corner overlooking the river stands the 16C **Dulo Tower**, evidently the work of Fyodor Kon'. The other towers, the **Kuznechnaya** and **Solevaya**, were built, along with the surviving wall, in the 1640s after the original defences had been devastated in the Times of Troubles.

The *Likhachov Motor Works* (Avtozavod im. I.A. Likhachova), the oldest in Russia, was originally founded in 1916 as the AMO Factory. The first example of a Soviet lorry (a modified Fiat) was completed here in 1924. In the 1930s the plant was greatly expanded and renamed the Stalin Works (Zavod im. Stalina); it produced large numbers of ZIS–5 and ZIS–150 lorries, as well as the ZIS–101 and ZIS–110 limousines. The factory was again renamed in 1956 after I.A. Likhachov (the director from 1926 to 1950), and its products now bear the name 'ZIL'; the ZIL–164 and ZIL–130 lorries were manufactured in great quantity and the ZIL–115 limousines are used by the most senior officials. The *Palace of Culture* of the motor works was built on the site of the Simonov Monastery in 1930–37 by the Vesnin brothers, and is one of the outstanding works of the Constructivist era. The grey 'L'-shaped building includes a 1200-seat theatre.

The nearby AVTOZAVODSKAYA METRO STATION, to the S, stands on the site of the Lizin Prud, a pond in which the heroine of Karamzin's novel 'Bednaya Liza' (Poor Liza) (1792) drowns herself. The Metro is the quickest route back to the centre of Moscow. A motor route continues S beyond Vostochnaya Ul. as VELOZAVODSKAYA UL., SAYKINA UL., and PROLETARSKIY PR. (Pl. 3; 5); this is the road to Kolomenskoye.

17 The Moskva River

The Rtes for the Moskva River begin at the embankment near KIYEVSKAYA METRO STATION (Pl. 7; 1). From here in summer excursion boats sail upstream (NW) to Kuntsevo and Krylatskoye or downstream (SE) past the Kremlin to the Novospasskiy Most. On holidays the boats sail from the pier at Gorky Park, near PARK KUL'TURY METRO STATION (Pl. 7; 6), and travel all the way to the Southern River Terminal. Rte 17A runs upstream from the Kiev Station; Rte 17B follows the river downstream from the Kiev Station.

The MOSKVA RIVER rises 280km W of the city that bears its name, winds for 71km through the sprawling Soviet capital, and then continues SE for 151km to Kolomna on the Oka River. The Oka in turn flows E to Gor'kiy (formerly Nizhniy Novgorod) on the Volga River. One reason for the ascendancy of Moscow in the 14C was its geographical position at the centre of the Russian river system; these natural advantages were increased in 1937 by the completion of the Moscow Canal (Kanal im. Moskvy) from the Moskva River (W of Moscow) to Dubna on the upper Volga. Moscow became the 'Port of Five Seas' with river and canal links to the Baltic, the White Sea, the Caspian, the Sea of Azov, and the Black Sea. The completion of the canal also raised the level of the river 3m and necessitated the reconstruction of the embankments and bridges.

A.   Upstream from the Kiev Station

The river boats depart from a pier in front of the **Kiev Station** (Kiyevskiy Vokzal). The station was built by I.I. Rerberg in 1912–17 as the Bryansk Station; it is a structure of simple Classical design reminiscent of the Pushkin Museum. The square next to the Kiev Station was cleared only in the 1950s.

The first bridge upstream from the station is the BORODINSKIY MOST (Pl. 7; 1) (1909–13), The obelisks and colonnades, designed by R.I. Klein, commemorated the centenary of the Battle of Borodino; this bridge carries the main road from Moscow to the battlefield, the Smolensk Road. To the E of the bridge (right) rise the twin towers of the Belgrad Hotel and the Gothic skyscraper of the Foreign Ministry. Just upstream is the first post-revolutionary bridge across the Moskva, built in 1937 for the Metro. The embankments on either side, NAB. TARASA SHEVCHENKO (left) and SMOLENSKAYA NAB. (right) are lined with impressive buildings from the 1930s, 1940s and 1950s.

The KALININSKIY MOST (Pl. 7; 1), completed in 1957, connects Pr. Kalinina (right) with Kutuzovskiy Pr. (left). Tall buildings stand on either side of the river at this point. To the right is the modern tower of the **Comecon Building**, which was designed by M.V. Posokhin, A.A. Mindoyants, and V.A. Svirsky and completed in 1969; Comecon, or the Council for Mutual Economic Assistance (CMEA) (known by its Russian initials as SEV) co-ordinates the economic policies of the Soviet bloc states. Further upstream is the white marble **RSFSR Soviet Building** (Dom Sovetov RSFSR) (D.N. Chechulin, 1981), the administrative headquarters of the Russian Republic (the largest of the 15 republics of the USSR). The Gothic skyscraper of the Ukraina Hotel is opposite (left). The river swings sharply to the left beyond the hotel. The industrial KRASNOPRESNENSKIY DISTRICT lies to the right, with the green *Krasnaya Presnya Park*, formerly the estate of the Princes Gagarin, behind KRASNOPRESNENSKAYA NAB. The **International Trade Centre** (Tsentr Mezhdunarodnoy Torgovli i Nauchno-Tekhnicheskikh Svyazey s Zarubezhnymi Stranami), housing the office of many foreign firms based in Moscow, and also used for major exhibitions, is on a 100-ha site here. The complex includes the 600 bed **Mezhdunarodnaya Hotel** with 600 beds.

After a relatively long straight stretch the river turns sharply to the right (N) as it passes under a bridge of the Loop Railway. To the left, past a second railway bridge, are the docks and cranes of the *Western Port* (Zapadnyy Port); the golden cupolas of the **Church of the Intercession** at Fili are visible beyond. The road bridge here is the KRASNOPRESNENSKIY MOST (1965) (Pl. 6; 1). The river passes a number of factories and then zigzags left (S) to the **Fili Park** (Filevskiy Park Kul'tury i Otdykha) and the pier at KUNTSEVO (Pl. 2; 3).

From Kuntsevo there are boats which continue N to the beaches at Plyazh. The TATAROVO FLATS (Tatarovskaya Poyma) extend to the left, with the giant artificial **Rowing Canal** (Grebnoy Kanal) at KRYLATSKOYE (1973) (Pl. 2; 3).

This 130-ha sports complex includes two rowing courses some 2300m long and a grandstand for 3400 spectators. Other parts of the Krylatskoye complex were developed for the Olympic cycling events. The **Indoor Cycle Track** (Velotrek) (1979) is shaped like a huge silvery-white butterfly and seats 6000 people; a 13.5km *Cycle Track* (Velotrassa) was created nearby. The Krylatskoye facilities can be reached by bus from MOLODYOZHNAYA METRO STATION.

The boats pass through *Lock No. 9* of the Moscow Canal (also called the Karamyshevskiy Lock). The nearby *Karamyshevskaya Dam* (plotina) controls the flow of water to the lower part of the river. The modern housing scheme of KHOROSHOVO-MNEVNIKI, begun in 1857, extends to the N. The little *Church of the Trinity at Khoroshovo* (1598) is visible on a bluff to the right.

Not far upstream is located the popular recreation area called SEREBRYANYY BOR or Silver Pine Grove (Pl. 2; 3) after the giant pines found here, some of them over 200 years old.

Many suburban dachas were built at Serebryanyy Bor before 1917, and now this island resort with its beaches and clear water attracts as many as half a million visitors a day in summer. It is possible to take a motor boat up the natural course of the river, around three sides of Serebryanyy Bor. In addition to giving a view of this pleasant reach of the river, the boat also sails past the handsome *Church of the Trinity (Ts Troitsy) (Pl. 2; 1) at TROITSE-LYKOVO (opposite the NW corner of Serebryanyy Bor). This tiered structure with a high central dome and two flanking domes was built in 1698–1704 for the Naryshkin family, who owned the village. This is an outstanding example of the Moscow Baroque, and a building which the art historian M.A. Il'in has described as 'the swan-song' of Early Russian architecture. An alternative route to Troitse-Lykovo is Bus No. 137 from TUSHINSKAYA METRO STATION.

A canal separates Serebryanyy Bor from Khoroshovo-Mnevniki, and boats pass through by a straight route to the upper part of the Moskva. Upstream, to the left, is the PLYAZH pier, and beyond are the parks and beaches around STROGINO (Pl. 2; 1). At SHCHUKINO the river bends sharply to the left (W), while the MOSCOW CANAL from the Volga joins it on the right (NE).

When the 128km long canal was built in 1932–37 (during the 2nd Five-Year Plan) it opened Moscow up to larger ships and provided essential supplies of drinking-water. The canal rises some 30m through Locks No. 8 and No. 7 to the KHIMKINSKOYE RESERVOIR and the Northern River Terminal (Pl. 1).

The upper Moskva River is to the NW. The SKHODNYA RIVER enters the Moskva (right) just before it passes under the Ring Motorway.

B. Downstream from the Kiev Station

Opposite the Kiev Station is ROSTOVSKAYA NAB. (the territory of which once belonged to the diocese of Rostov Velikiy). BEREZHKOVSKAYA NAB. runs along the right (W) bank, with a number of post-war buildings. The permanent **Town Planning Exhibition** (Vystavka po Gradostroitel'stvu) at No. 4 uses models and plans to illustrate projects for future urban development. At the end of this straight reach of the river the spires and cupolas of the **New Convent of the Virgin** rise to the left (p 146).

After the cantilevered *Krasnoluzhskiy Most* (1903–08) of the Loop Railway the SETUN' RIVER joins the Moskva (right). Beyond this the river bends sharply to the left, reversing its direction. On the right are the Lenin Hills with the *Church of the Trinity*, the *Ski Jump*, and the skyscraper of **Moscow University**. On the left the bend of the Moskva encloses the great sports complex of **Luzhniki**, the main site of the 1980 Olympics (p 147) (Pl. 6; 8). Ahead a striking two-tiered bridge (1958) carries both road traffic and the Metro across the river.

The *Palace of Pioneers* is visible above the steep river bank to the right, followed, after the river turns ninety degrees, by the buildings of the former **Monastery of St. Andrew** (Andreyevskiy Monastyr').

The monastery dates from 1648, and here one of the earliest influential 'Westernizers', Afanasiy Ordyn-Nashchokin, sponsored the first state school in Muscovy, where secular subjects were taught. Thereafter it served a variety of roles, including (in the 1770s) that of Moscow's first mental hospital; latterly there was a charitable institution for merchants' families here. The buildings have been much altered, but the *Church of Andrey Stratilat* (Ts. Andreya Stratilata) (1675), the *Church of the Resurrection* (Ts. Voskreseniya) (1689–1703), and the *Church of St. John* (Ts. Ioanna Bogoslova) (1648) are currently being restored.

The monastery gave its name to the nearby *Andreyevskiy Most* of the Loop Railway; this is identical to the bridge on the other side of Luzhniki. The long straight segment of the river beyond the railway bridge is flanked on the right by **Gorky Park** (Pl. 7; 6). Near the embankment are some attractive domed follies by M.F. Kazakov, as well as a pier from which excursion boats and 'Raketa' hydrofoils leave for trips on the river. The embankment, PUSHKINSKAYA NAB., is so called because the poet Pushkin visited the pleasure gardens here in 1830. FRUNZENSKAYA NAB. runs along the opposite shore; the embankment, named in honour of the Red Army leader M.V. Frunze (1885–1925), was sheathed in granite in the 1930s, and after 1945 an impressive row of flats was completed here. The **Construction**

Section (Razdel Stroitel'stva) **of the Exhibition of Economic Achievements** (VDNKh) is situated in the middle of this embankment, at No. 30.

The KRYMSKIY MOST (Pl. 4; 7) or Crimean Bridge is an attractive suspension bridge carrying the Sadovoye Kol'tso; it dates from 1936–38, when the completion of the Moscow–Volga canal and the consequent deepening of the river necessitated the reconstruction of many bridges. Beyond the bridge is KROPOTKINSKAYA NAB., with the *Chayka Swimming-Pool*. The even larger *Moskva Swimming-Pool* is located further downstream among trees. To the left of this pool runs SOYMONOVSKIY PROYEZD, once the site of the Belyy Gorod wall; here was the 16C anchor of Moscow's defences, the Semiverkhaya Tower.

The long white building of the **Picture Gallery of the USSR** occupies the embankment to the right, after the Krymskiy Most. Two of the lanes near the museum share the picturesque name of BAB'YEGORODSKIY PER, which recalls that this was once the Babiy Gorodok where, according to legend, the women of the town beat off a 14C attack by the Tatars. Beyond this begins the 4km long DRAINAGE CANAL (Vodootvodnyy Kanal), which was developed from a branch of the river in 1783–86 and served to prevent disastrous spring floods in the centre of Moscow. From 1836 to 1937 the canal contained a weir and two locks.

BERSENEVSKAYA NAB. (Pl. 4; 6) runs along the N side of the long narrow 'island' created by the Drainage Canal. The white **Church of St. Nicholas** (Ts. Nikoly na Bersenevke) (1656) is located on the embankment.

The rectangular central part of the church is crowned by a pyramid of gables and five green domes. This was the private church of Averiky Kirillov (1622–82), whose *Mansion* (palata) stands next door (right); the two buildings were once connected by an arcade. The mansion was modified in Petrine times by the addition of an elaborate Dutch-style gable. The Boyar Kirillov was one of the closest advisors of the early Romanov tsars; he was murdered during the Strel'tsy Uprising of 1682.

The Church of St. Nicholas is now dwarfed by the grey mass of the Variety Theatre next door. In front of the theatre is the BOL'SHOY KAMENNYY MOST or Great Stone Bridge (Pl. 4; 6); the name derives from the first stone bridge across the Moskva, which was erected here in the late 17C. The present bridge dates from 1936–38 and was designed by a team led by Shchuko and Gel'frekh, the architects of the Lenin Library.

The next stretch of the river is the most striking. Just beyond the Bol. Kamennyy Most is visible in the embankment (left) an outlet through which the Neglinnaya River once flowed into the Moskva. Before the Neglinnaya was buried underground (in the early 19C) it was valuable as a moat and here, at the confluence of the two rivers, the first wooden Kremlin was founded by Prince Yury Dolgoruky in 1156. Now the left bank is taken up by the *splendid panorama of the **Kremlin**, with its brick walls and towers, and above them the Armoury Palace, the long façade of the Great Kremlin Palace, the cathedrals, the Ivan the Great Bell Tower, and the Classical Presidium of the Supreme Soviet.

Facing the Kremlin, on the embankment named after the French Communist Maurice Thorez (NAB. MORISA TOREZA) (Pl. 4; 6), is the **British Embassy** (No. 14); this was once the mansion of a wealthy merchant. The attractive Pseudo-Russian bell tower of the **Church of**

St. Sophia (Ts. Sof'i), further along the embankment, was built by N.I. Kozlovsky in 1862–68. Nearby is the MOSKVORETSKIY MOST a handsome structure faced with pink granite; the bridge was built in 1936–38, and the design team included Shchusev, builder of the Lenin Mausoleum.

Beyond the Moskvoretskiy Most there is an excellent view (left) of **Red Square** with St. Basil's Cathedral and, in the distance, the Lenin Mausoleum and the Historical Museum. MOSKVORETSKAYA NAB. runs along the side of the river, and behind it rises the gigantic **Hotel Rossiya** (Pl. 5; 5); clearly visible on the embankment and level with the W (near) end of the hotel is the outlet through which the subterranean Neglinnaya River now enters the Moskva. Next to the other end of the Rossiya is the tiny *Church of St. Anna*. A restored segment of the Kitay-Gorod wall is visible to the right of the church, and beyond it stands the yellow former **Foundling Home**, now a military academy, a building on almost the same scale as the Rossiya Hotel.

The right shore of the river is bounded by RAUSHSKAYA NAB., which ends with the BOL'SHOY UST'INSKIY MOST (1938). The bridge spans the river at the end of the Bul'varnoye Kol'tso. The mouth (ust'ye) of the Yauza River is located just downstream from the Bol. Ust'inskiy Most; the MALYY UST'INSKIY MOST (1938) carries the Moskva embankment across the Yauza.

The YAUZA RIVER is the largest tributary of the Moskva within the Moscow city limits. It runs 34km from springs near Mytishchi and was once part of the great trade route from the Baltic to the Volga and beyond; later the young Peter I sailed his boat on the Yauza. In the 19C factories appeared along the banks of the upper Yauza creating a serious problem of pollution; the Yauza became known as 'the river of seven colours' (semitsvetnaya). There is still industry here, but in the Soviet period work has been carried out to improve the conditions of the river; beginning in 1937 a granite embankment was built, along with a walkway and attractive arched bridges.

The left bank of the Yauza, as it flows into the Moskva, is dominated by Moscow's first **Skyscraper**, a 33-storey block of flats built on KOTEL'NICHESKAYA NAB. in 1948–52 by D.N. Chechulin and A.K. Rostkovsky.

The building is perhaps seen to best advantage from the Kremlin. From the central spired tower, 176m high, radiate three 22-storey wings; two 11-storey wings run along the Yauza and the Moskva. Among those who lived in the 800 flats here were the ballerina Ulanova and the writer K.G. Paustovsky. The *Illyuzion Cinema*, Moscow's theatre for classic films, is located in this building.

More new flats have been built along the right bank of the Moskva, on NAB. MAKSIMA GOR'KOVO (Pl. 5; 5); this is on the island formed by the Drainage Canal. Standing on the embankment at No. 24–26 is the so-called **Krigskomissariat**, a Classical building with domed rotundas at each corner; it was built to the plans of N.N. Legrand in 1778–80 and served as an army supply centre.

The BOL'SHOY KRASNOKHOLMSKIY MOST (1938) crosses the Moskva at a marked angle, carrying the Sadovoye Kol'tso. Beyond it (right) the emerging Drainage Canal is spanned by the SHLYUZOVSKIY MOST (1965), a suspension bridge. The embankment on the left is now called KRASNOKHOLMSKAYA NAB., behind which are clearly visible the cathedral and tiered bell tower of the **New Monastery of the Saviour**. Just downstream from the monastery are the NOVOSPASSKIY MOST (1911/37) and a terminal for river boats.

Excursion boats do cruise further downstream, but there is little of interest to the tourist in the industrial zones and housing estates of PROLETARSKIY, KRASNOGVARDEYSKIY, and LYUBLINSKIY DISTRICTS. To the left, behind KRUTITSKAYA NAB. and SIMONOVSKAYA NAB., are visible the cathedral and teremok of the **Krutitskoye Podvor'ye** and then the surviving fortifications of the **Simonov Monastery**, once the key to the SE defences of the city. Then, after a series of bends, comes the AVTOZAVODSKIY MOST (Pl. 3; 5), and the sprawling Likhachov Motor Works (left). To the right, by the old Southern River Terminal, is the point where the channelled CHURA RIVER enters the Moskva. Beyond this the DANILOVSKY MOST, the fourth of the bridges carrying the Loop Railway, crosses the river. After the railway bridge the river bends sharply left (E) and passes into an artificial channel created in 1968 at NAGATINO, now a large and growing housing scheme. Here the NAGATINSKIY MOST (Pl. 3; 5), the longest in the city, carries PR. ANDROPOVA across the Moskva.

The new **Southern River Terminal** (Yuzhnyy Rechnoy Vokzal) (Pl. 3; 5), which was opened in 1972, is located just downstream from the Nagatinskiy Most; from here passenger boats sail to a number of inland river towns. The largest river freight terminal in Moscow, the *Southern Port* (Yuzhnyy Port), is located near here on the opposite bank. As the river bends to the right (S) it passes the pier at PECHATNIKI (left) and, on the same side of the river, the huge *Leninskiy Komsomol Motor Works* (AZLK). The original factory was set up in 1947 on the basis of the Opel works (transferred from Brandenburg to Moscow after the German defeat) and was greatly enlarged in the 1960s. Here are produced Moskvich motor cars; the original Moskvich-400 was a copy of the Opel Kadett but the current Moskvich-412 is Soviet-designed and has been made in large numbers for home sale and export.

Boats pass through a canal and *Lock No. 10* as the river continues towards the south. The *Church of the Ascension* at Kolomenskoye and the nearby *Church of John the Baptist* at D'yakovo (Pl. 3; 7) stand on a high bluff to the right. The Moskva then flows E and S through the suburbs before passing under the Ring Motorway.

18 Moscow Outskirts

The outskirts of Moscow encompass a number of interesting places suitable for day trips. Most are near the Ring Motorway (Moskovskaya Kol'tsevaya Avtomobil'naya Doroga), which is some 109km long and encircles Moscow at an average of about 20km from the Kremlin. Work began in 1956 and the highway was opened to traffic six years later.

Although it is possible to visit some places just beyond the Ring Motorway without getting special permission (e.g. Leninskiye Gorki and Arkhangel'skoye), more distant places are closed to foreign visitors with visas for Moscow only. The last section of this Rte lists places which lie *outside* the regions normally open, but it may be possible to arrange a day trip through Intourist.

If there is any doubt as to whether a particular trip outside the city is permitted *tourists should check the arrangements with Intourist or other authorities.*

A. Sokol'niki and Preobrazhenskoye

The **Sokol'niki Park** (Park Kul'tury i Otdykha 'Sokol'niki') (Pl. 3; 1) is
located about 4km NE of the Sadovoye Kol'tso off STROMYNKA UL.
(Motor Route A103). SOKOL'NIKI METRO STATION, which serves the
district, was completed in 1935 as the eastern terminus of the first
line of the Moscow Metro. The name comes from the falconers
(sokol'niki) who lived here in the 17C. The 'Park of Culture and Rest'
was opened in 1931, but the Sokol'niki Woods had long been a place
of relaxation for Muscovites. The first Young Pioneers rally took
place here in 1922; an obelisk now marks the spot. The 600ha of
parkland include many pavilions, an outdoor theatre, playing fields,
and the **Sokol'niki Palace of Sports** (Dvorets Sporta 'Sokol'niki')
(1973). The *Exhibition Pavilions* (Vystavochnyye Pavil'ony) are used
for international trade fairs and similar events; here took place in
1959 the famous 'washing-machine debate' between Khrushchev
and the then Vice-President Nixon.

The working **Church of the Resurrection** (Ts. Voskreseniya
Kristova), a handsome green and white tent-roofed building (P.A.
Tolstykh, 1909–13), is situated on the right side of the road which
leads from the park to the Metro station. Not far to the left (E) along
Stromynka Ul., at No. 10 (right) in STROMYNSKAYA PL., is one of the
outstanding Constructivist workers clubs built by K.S. Mel'nikov, the
Rusakov House of Culture (Dom Kul'tury im. I.V. Rusakova) (1929).

About 1.5km NE of Sokol'niki Metro Station, Stromynka Ul.
crosses the Yauza River; not far beyond are PREOBRAZHENSKAYA PL.
and PREOBRAZHENSKAYA PL. METRO STATION (Pl. 3; 1). In the late
17C Preobrazhenskoye was a village on the upper Yauza where in
1657 a summer palace (now demolished) had been built for Tsar
Aleksey Mikhaylovich. Preobrazheniye means 'Transfiguration' in
Russian. Here Peter the Great (Aleksey's son), spent much of his
childhood, especially after 1682 when his half-sister Sof'ya became
Regent. The famous 'toy regiments' were formed at Preobrazhenskoye from the friends and servants of the boy-Tsar; these
grew into the first 'modern' units of the Imperial Russian Army, the
Preobrazhenskiy and Semyonovskiy Guards Regiments. The
Semyonovskiy Regiment was originally quartered at the village of
Semyonovskoye, which was located about 2km down the Yauza near
the present SEMYONOVSKAYA METRO STATION (Pl. 3; 4).

Preobrazhenskaya Pl. was formerly the Preobrazhenskaya Barrier
(zastava) of the 18C Kamer-Kollezhskiy Rampart (val), which ran S
along what is now PREOBRAZHENSKIY VAL UL. (right). The district
was once inhabited mainly by 'priestless' sectarians, the so-called
'bezpopovtsy', many of them wealthy merchants, and two religious
centres survive in this street, beyond the *Preobrazhenskoye Cemetery*. The **Preobrazhenskaya Old Believers Commune** (Preobrazhenskaya Staroobryadcheskaya Obshchina) at No. 17 (left)
contains a number of churches and dormitories from the late 18C and
early 19C. Nearby, at No. 25, is the **Monastery of St. Nicholas**
(Nikol'skiy Yedinovercheskiy Monastyr') with, among other structures, the *Church of St. Nicholas* (Ts. Nikoly) (1790) and a *Bell Tower*
(1830).

Motor Route A103 becomes BOL'SHAYA CHERKIZOVSKAYA UL. beyond Preobrazhenskaya Pl. After the recently improved CHERKIZOVSKIY POND the road is
known as SHCHOLKOVSKOYE SHOSSE (Pl. 3; 2). The new **Central Institute of
Physical Culture** (Tsentral'nyy Institut Fizicheskoy Kul'tury or TsIFK) is located

on a 200ha site at the junction with SIRENEVYY BUL'VAR. The *General Sports Complex*, is a striking building with a concave roof (I. Gunst, 1979). Other TsIFK facilities include the largest indoor *Track and Field Hall* in Europe, an *Aquatics Centre*, and a number of teaching blocks. The nearby *Stadium*, completed in 1979, occupies the site where before the Second World War it was planned to build Moscow's central stadium; in the 1950s Luzhniki was chosen instead.

B.   Izmaylovo

Izmaylovo (Pl. 3; 2) is located some 8km NE of the Sadovoye Kol'tso and can be reached via the road extending E from Ul. Bogdana Khmel'nitskovo. The most convenient way to get to Izmaylovo is via IZMAYLOVSKIY PARK or IZMAYLOVSKAYA METRO STATIONS.

The Izmaylovs once owned this land, but in the 16C it passed to another boyar family, the Romanovs. In the middle of the following century, after the foundation of the Romanov dynasty, Izmaylovo became a favourite royal country estate where Tsars Fyodor Mikhaylovich and Aleksey Fyodorovich spent their summers; under Aleksey both a kind of model farm and a primitive zoo were created here. Peter the Great spent much of his childhood at Izmaylovo. Here was discovered a little boat, the 'Grandfather of the Russian Navy', which the Dutchman Brand taught Peter to sail on the nearby ponds, and here were held manoeuvres of the 'Toy Regiments'. The Izmaylovskiy Guards Regiment, formed in 1730, took its name from the village.

The **Izmaylovo Hotel** stands next to Izmaylovskiy Park Metro Station. The five 28-storey towers have a total of 10,000 beds.

On the other side of the Metro Station, beyond IZMAYLOVSKOYE SHOSSE, is the NW corner of **Izmaylovo Park** (Park Kul'tury i Otdykha 'Izmaylovo') (Pl. 3; 4), which occupies 330ha and includes cafés and a variety of recreation facilities. It was established as a 'Park of Culture and Rest' in 1930 and was at one time called 'Stalin Park'. (This area was then the Stalinskiy District of Moscow; Izmaylovskiy Park Metro Station was opened in 1944 as 'Stalinskaya'.) To the E stretches the *Izmaylovo Forest Park* (Izmaylovskiy Lesopark). The two parks form a combined 1480ha of wooded parkland which is bounded on the S by Shosse Entuziastov and on the E by the Ring Motorway. The woods were used for the royal hunt in the 17C and became a popular place of relaxation in the years before the Revolution.

The remains of the **Royal Estate** (Pl. 3; 2) are located on an island in a small pond about 1km E of Izmaylovskiy Park Metro Station and just to the N of Izmaylovskoye Shosse. (Buses No. 20, 211, and 509, which begin at the station, travel past here before turning right (S) through the park.) The five massive green domes of the **Cathedral of the Intercession** (Sobor Pokrova) (1679) are clearly visible above trees to the left (N) of the road.

A small bridge with an iron gate at the far end leads to the island. To the right is a small tiered building with a tent roof, the **Bridge Tower** (Mostovaya Bashnya) (1671). The large cathedral stands behind; the most striking feature of its decoration are the elaborately tiled gables. Almshouses were added to the N and S in the middle of the 19C. Opposite the cathedral, on the left side of the complex, are the former ***Ceremonial** (Paradnyye) **Gates**, built in 1682 by Terentiy Makarov. This handsome white structure with a triple archway and a high tent roof is reminiscent of similar gates at Kolomenskoye and anticipated the Moscow Baroque. The wooden palace that was the centre of the 17C estate has not survived.

Ceremonial Gates, Izmaylovo Royal Estate (T. Makarov, 1682)

C.   The Rogozhskaya Commune

The former **Rogozhskaya Old Believers Commune** (Staro-obryadcheskaya Obshchina) (Pl. 3; 3) is located just N of NIZHEGORODSKAYA UL. Trolleybuses No. 16 and 26 travel here from Taganskaya Pl. and TAGANSKAYA METRO STATION, a distance of some 3km; the green-domed bell tower is visible to the left beyond the railway line.

The Old Believers broke away from the Russian Orthodox Church in the latter part of the 17C in protest against the reform of the church ritual. The dissenting movement split into a number of sects, but the most important group had its centre here, at the Rogozhskaya Commune, from the 1770s. In the middle of the 19C the dissenters suffered considerable persecution, and the tall **Bell Tower** at the Rogozhskaya complex was erected in 1912–13 (F.I. Gornostayev) to celebrate the liberalisation of 1905 and the reopening of churches.

The **Cathedral of the Intercession** (Pokrovskiy Sobor) was built in 1790–92 as a 'summer church', possibly by M.F. Kazakov; it is a yellow Classical building with a golden cupola above a wider dome. The 'winter church' is the **Church of the Nativity** (Ts. Rozhdestva) (1804). Also located here is the working Orthodox **Church of St. Nicholas** (Ts. Nikoly) (late 18C–early 19C), an attractively painted structure. The *Rogozhskoye Cemetery*, established in the plague year of 1771, lies beyond.

On the S side of Nizhegorodskaya Ul., and before the railway line, is the
Kalitnikovskoye Cemetery. BOL'SHAYA KALITNIKOVSKAYA UL., running parallel
to Nizhegorodskaya Ul., is the site of the Sunday-morning open-air pet market,
or **Ptichiy Rynok**.

D. Kuskovo

Kuskovo (Pl. 3; 4) was the country estate of the Sheremetevs; its
extensive grounds are open to the public and contain the **Ceramics
Museum** (Gos. Muzey Keramik i 'Usad'ba Kuskovo XVIII v.').

The former estate is situated in the eastern suburbs of Moscow; it
lies 2km N of RYAZANSKIY PR. (Motor Route A102) and about 10km
from the Sadovoye Kol'tso. A convenient route by public transport is
Metro to RYAZANSKIY PR. METRO STATION (Pl. 3; 6) and then Bus No.
208.

En route to Kuskovo the bus from Ryazanskiy Pr. passes near VESHNYAKI
RAILWAY STATION an old suburban church. This was built by the Sheremetev
boyars in 1646.

The land at Kuskovo belonged to the Sheremetev family from 1623 to 1917;
the estate as it exists today was created in the middle of the 18C by Field
Marshal P.B. Sheremetev.

The palace stands to the N of a large rectangular pond (which runs
roughly E–W). A canal enters the pond opposite the house; the two
white columns flanking it were once used to illuminate the pond. The
entrance to the grounds is by the NE corner of the main pond. There
is a smaller square pond to the right beyond the entrance, with two
pavilions. The **Italian Cottage**, built in the form of an Italian villa by
Yu. Kologrivov and F.S. Argunov (1754–55), stands on the N side of
the small pond; to the W is Argunov's splendid domed Baroque
Grotto (1756–75). The path to the palace leads past the **Kitchens**
(1755–56) and the attractive **Church** (1737) with its wooden **Bell
Tower** (1792).

The wooden **Palace**, the centre of the estate, was built between
1769 and 1777 by the serf-architects F.S. Argunov and A.F. Mironov.
It is a moderate-sized structure in the Early Classical style. To the S,
facing the pond, are three porticoes and an entry ramp. A four-
columned portico on the N side faces the main lane of the gardens.
The *Interior* is richly decorated and includes the **Ceramics Museum**
with its collection of Russian and imported china of the pre-
revolutionary period, as well as some Soviet-made china. The palace
also contains many other kinds of applied art. At the end of a long
corridor of rooms is the lavishly decorated *White Hall*, which served
as a ballroom; beautiful chandeliers hang above the parquet floor,
and the walls are decorated with mirrors and bas-reliefs.

Kuskovo is set in 32ha grounds with *Formal Gardens* that contemporaries called the 'Moscow Versailles'. The main lane runs N from
the palace past statues and an obelisk to the stone **Orangery** (1761–
62), a long building designed by Argunov and D. Antipov. In the
centre of the gardens to the W is the cross-shaped **Hermitage**, by
Karl Blank (1765–67). The **Dutch Cottage** (1749) stands in the SW
corner; its simple façade is reflected in a small pond. On the other
side of the central lane, N of the Italian Cottage is an outdoor *Green
Theatre*.

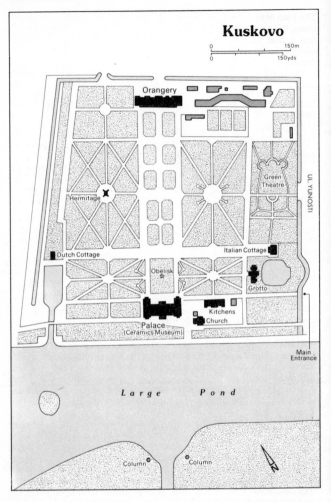

E. Lyublino and Kuz'minki

The former estate of **Lyublino** (Pl. 3; 6) is located about 8km SE of the
Sadovoye Kol'tso and 2km S of KUZ'MINKI METRO STATION, which is
on VOLGOGRADSKIY PR. (Motor Route M5). Trolleybus No. 74 and
Bus No. 613 run S from the Metro Station; LETNYAYA UL. leads (right)
to the estate from KRASNODONSKAYA UL. An alternative route is by
suburban train from Kursk Station to LYUBLINO RAILWAY STATION.

Lyublino was the country estate of the Durasov family, and N.A.
Durasov had a mansion built here in 1801, possibly by I.V. Yegotov.

The plan of the house is unique; two intersecting wings form a Greek cross, the arms of which are joined by a circular colonnade. Legend has it that this unusual design came from the owner's desire to commemorate his being awarded the similarly-shaped Cross of St. Anne.

The building is now occupied by the *Institute of Oceanography* (no adm.).

Bus No. 29 runs to **Kuz'minskiy Park** (Pl. 3; 6) from RYAZANSKIY PROSPEKT METRO STATION. The park is located about 2km S of Volgogradskiy Pr., beyond Kuz'minki Metro Station (and about 2km E of Lyublino).

Kuz'minskiy Park was formerly owned by the Golitsyns. The Kuz'minki Estate dates from the mid-18C, but it was substantially rebuilt early in the following century. The main house burned down in 1915, and of the central buildings only the so-called *Egyptian Pavilion* by Voronikhin, survives (1811). There are, however, several notable pavilions near the long pond around which the estate was built. The **Konnyy Dvor** (lit. Stables) is a splendid music pavilion built in 1793 by R.R. Kazakov and rebuilt by D. Gilardi (1819). It consists of a row of Doric columns with a great arch; the sculptured horses flanking the entrance steps are by P. Clodt von Jürgensburg (who created the similar sculptures on the Anichkov Bridge in Leningrad). A number of other outbuildings, by Zherebtsov, Yegotov, and others, stand in the English gardens; the *Church of the Virgin* (Ts. Vlakhernskoy Bogomateri) was begun by Bazhenov but much altered. There is also a fine iron railing.

The 24-year-old Lenin spent the summer of 1894 at a dacha near Kuz'minki; the following year the first small Moscow May Day rally was held here.

F.   Kolomenskoye

Kolomenskoye (Muzey-Zapovednik XVI–XVII vv. 'Kolomenskoye') is a former royal estate on the right bank of the lower Moskva River, about 10km SE of the Kremlin (Pl. 3; 7). It lies between the river and PR. ANDROPOVA which continues a motor route which begins off the Sadovoye Kol'tso near Taganskaya Pl. The churches are within ten minutes walk of KOLOMENSKAYA METRO STATION.

The name Kolomenskoye may derive from refugees from the town of Kolomna who fled here in the early 13C at the time of the Mongol onslaught. In the 16C this pleasantly-sited village above the Moskva became a favourite royal country estate, the summer residence of the Tsars; the main Church of the Ascension and the nearby church at D'yakovo date from this period. In the troubled 17C Kolomenskoye was a centre of activity. Ivan Bolotnikov, leader of a horde of rebellious peasants, set up his main base at Kolomenskoye in 1606; here he fought a battle with the forces of Tsar Vasily Shuyskiy and was forced to flee. Crowds of discontented Muscovites came here to appeal to Tsar Aleksey Mikhaylovich during the 1648 disturbances and in the 'Copper Riots' of 1662; on the latter occasion many of the protesters were massacred by government troops.

The same Tsar Aleksey greatly expanded the estate. The gates and the Kazan Church were constructed, as well as a splendid wooden palace. The palace, built in 1667–71, was demolished by Catherine the Great; there is a model in the museum. As a child, Peter the Great (son of Aleksey) fled to Kolomenskoye during the Strel'tsy Uprising of 1682; later he held manoeuvres of his 'Toy Regiments' here. The location lost none of its attraction in the following centuries, and Catherine II and Alexander I built small palaces here. These, however, no longer exist.

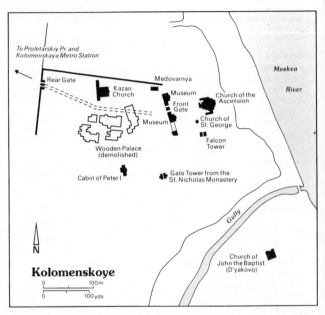

To Proletarskiy Pr. and
Kolomenskaya Metro Station

Moskva
River

Rear Gate

Kazan
Church

Medovarnya

Museum

Front
Gate

Church of the
Ascension

Museum

Church of
St. George

Falcon
Tower

Wooden Palace
(demolished)

Cabin of Peter I

Gate Tower from the
St. Nicholas Monastery

Gully

N

Kolomenskoye

0   100m

0   100 yds

Church of
John the Baptist
(D'yakovo)

The grounds are now part of a 400ha conservation area with 600-year-old oaks, and several buildings were moved here from other parts of Russia.

A little way beyond the **Rear Gate** and the remains of the walls, the path passes (left) the **Kazan Church** (Kazanskaya Ts.); this attractive white church with blue domes was built in 1649–50 and is still used for services. The wooden palace of Aleksey Mikhaylovich once stood on the other side of the path, opposite the Kazan Church. About 100m along is the **Front Gate**, a white tiered structure with two archways and a high tent roof; the gate dates from 1672 and served as the main entrance to the palace compound. The Kolomenskoye administration and **Museum** are now housed in the wings of the Front Gate. The museum contains Russian wood-carving and tiles; other exhibits are devoted to the popular rebellions of the 17C in which Kolomenskoye played a prominent part.

The *Church of the Ascension** is the most striking building at the Kolomenskoye complex and one of the most important in Moscow.

The composer Berlioz wrote that this church had impressed him more than anything else he had ever seen. It stands on a splendid natural site, on a bluff overlooking the Moskva. The church was built in 1530–32 by Tsar Vasily III, apparently to celebrate the birth of an heir, Ivan Vasil'yevich—later known as Ivan the Terrible. Architecturally, the church marked an important development, the application of Russian wooden forms (especially the tent roof or shatyor) to stone buildings. The essentially cubic base is surrounded by an arcaded porch with three sets of stairs. From the roof of the porch soars first the upper part of the base with square pilasters and then rows of ogee-shaped gables surmounted by an octagonal tier. The church is crowned by the steep pyramid of the tent roof, with, at the very top, a small drum and a cross. All told, the Church of the Ascension is 70m high (the little drum served as an observation post to give warning of sudden Tatar attacks on Moscow from the S). The red brick exterior is decorated with white limestone details; the most impressive aspect of this is the fine tracing on the tent roof. The *Interior* of the church is small because the walls had to be very thick. The vertical axis is accentuated by the tall roof, narrow windows, and pilasters. There is little internal decoration.

Opposite the great church were built the **Church of St. George** (Ts. Georgiya) (16C) and the so-called **Falcon Tower** (Sokolinaya Bashnya) (1630–40). The white church served also as a bell tower. The Falcon Tower, brick and angular, was intended as a gateway and also housed the falcons of the Tsar.

A path leads down to the river. This is also a convenient route to the **Church of John the Baptist** (Ts. Ionna Predtechi) at D'yakovo, which is separated from Kolomenskoye by a steep gully. The D'yakovo church is about 350m S of the Church of the Ascension.

The tall brick church with its low dome was built in the late 1540s or early 1550s by Ivan the Terrible. The placing of chapels at the four corners around the central tower anticipated what would be done a decade later at St. Basil's Cathedral in Red Square; the total effect is more austere and regular, with flat domes and little use of colour. Notable features of the exterior are the angular arches and gables, as well as the cylinders around the central drum.

From behind the Falcon Tower paths lead SW into a conservation area; a number of interesting wooden buildings have been moved here. The tent-roofed **Gate Tower** is from the St. Nicholas Monastery in Karelia (Nikolo-Karel'skiy Monastyr'); it was built in 1690 on the shores of the White Sea and moved here in 1932. The cubic **Watchtower** from the Bratskiy Ostrog in Siberia also dates from the 17C. The long wooden building is the **Cabin of Peter I**, transferred in 1934 from Arkhangel'sk (Archangel), where it was built in 1702. Peter lived in this structure for several months while supervising ship-building and fortification work at the mouth of the Northern Dvina; the interior, with the Tsar's study, has been restored. The first wooden building to arrive at Kolomenskoye (in 1930) is located on the far side of the entry path, near the Front Gate; the 17C **Medovarnya**, a building used for making honey, came from the suburban Moscow village of Preobrazhenskoye.

G.   Tsaritsyno

Tsaritsyno (Pl. 3; 7) is an unfinished Imperial palace situated in a 100-ha park (Tsaritsynskiy Dvorets i Park) some 15km SE of the Kremlin, beyond Kolomenskoye. LENINO METRO STATION is just to the W of the park. Motorists can take Motor Route M4 (through Zamoskvorech'ye) or the motor route through the SE and past Kolomenskoye; both routes lead to the KASHIRSKOYE SHOSSE (Motor Route M4) which passes just N of Tsaritsyno.

In 1775 Empress Catherine II bought an estate called Chornaya Gryaz' (Black Mud) and renamed it Tsaritsyno. The architect V.I. Bazhenov was commissioned to build the palace and outbuildings and created a unique style which combined the Classical orders, traditional Russian motifs, and the Pseudo-Gothic. In 1785, after Bazhenov had worked on the project for some ten years, Catherine decided that his plans were unsatisfactory and had him dismissed. She apparently resented the fact that the design (which she had earlier approved) included a twin palace for Grand Duke Paul, who had fallen out of her favour. The outbuildings which Bazhenov had completed were left

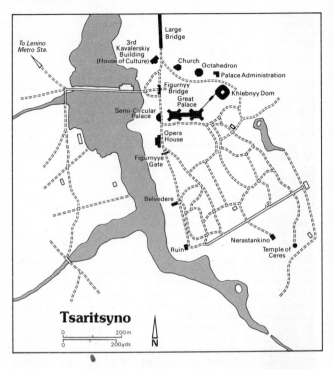

To Lenino
Metro Sta.

Large
Bridge

3rd
Kavalerskiy
Building
(House of Culture)

Church

Octahedron

Palace Administration

Figurnyy
Bridge

Khlebnyy Dom

Great
Palace

Semi-Circular
Palace

Opera
House

Figurnyye
Gate

Belvedere

Nerastankino

Temple of
Ceres

Ruin

Tsaritsyno

0   200 m
0   200 yds

N

standing and the other great Moscow architect of the period, M.F. Kazakov, was
brought in to complete the palace. Kazakov's project was less ambitious, but it,
too, was never finished. The cause was partly restrictions on government
expenditure during the war with Turkey, and partly the waning enthusiasm of
the aging Empress for a Moscow suburban estate.

A causeway carries the entry road across the TSARITSYNSKIYE
PONDS, which were formed by damming the GORODNYA RIVER. (This
took place in the 16C when this land was the property of Irina, sister
of Boris Godunov.) Beyond, and just before the brick Gothic **Figurnyy Bridge** (lit. 'Patterned Bridge') (1786), a footpath climbs to the
right. At the top of the steps the uncompleted shell of the **Great
Palace** is visible to the right. What exists today was built by Kazakov
in 1787–93 on the remains of Bazhenov's earlier project (1779–82).
Notable features of the design are the white-stone details in the red
brick walls, especially the rows of pointed arches. There are turrets at
the four corners, each of them framed by pilasters. To the left (E) of
the palace is the carved stone **Khlebnyy Gate**, leading into what
was to have been the palace courtyard. Beyond it, and in the same
axis as the palace, is the **Khlebnyy Dom** (the Kitchens). Both the Gate
and the Khlebnyy Dom were built by Bazhenov in 1784.

A path leads to the right (S) (parallel to the pond) between the
Great Palace and the semi-circular **Small Palace** (Bazhenov, 1776),
which was intended for Gentlemen-in-Waiting. Beyond (right) is the
Opera House (Opernyy Dom) (Bazhenov, 1776) with its fantastic
stone-carving. Next to the Opera House stands one of the landmarks

Figurnyye Gate, Tsaritsyno (V.I. Bazhenov, 1790s). This was the entrance to an uncompleted Gothic suburban palace intended for Catherine the Great

of Tsaritsyno, the ***Figurnyye Gate** (lit. Patterned Gate) (Bazhenov, 1780s), a turreted Gothic arch with geometrical stone-carving; this marked the entrance into the park.

The path through the park continues S past the **Belvedere** (Milovida), a yellow Classical archway-pavilion with a splendid view of the pond. This was built by Yegotov in 1803, some time after the palace complex. An artificial **Ruin**, an essential element of an 18C park, was built by Bazhenov a little farther along. Here the path turns sharply to the left (E). To the right (S) of this path, in the woods, are two follies built by Yegotov (1803); **Nerastankino** and the **Temple of Ceres** (Khram Tserery). Near the perimeter of the park another path turns to the left through the woods back to the palace.

A path around the E end of the Palace-Courtyard-Khlebnyy Dom complex leads to a row of former service buildings. The **Palace Administration** (Upravitel'skiy Dom) (now a music school) is Bazhenov's work (1782–83), as is the extraordinary ruined servants quarters called the **Octahedron** (Vos'migrannik) (1782–83). The

Baroque **Church**, just beside the Figurnyy Most, dates from 1722 when this estate was owned by the Kantemirs; the poet A.D. Kantemir spent his childhood here.

The path behind the church leads N (in line with the Figurnyy Most) past Bazhenov's **3rd Kavalerskiy Building** (1776), now a 'House of Culture', to the striking Gothic ***Large Bridge** which Bazhenov constructed across a deep ravine (1784).

H.   Bittsa

Near **Bittsevskiy Forest Park** (Bittsevskiy Lesopark) is the **Trade Union Equestrian Complex** (Konnosportivnyy Kompleks Prof-soyuzov) (Pl. 2; 8). The 45ha complex includes a show-jumping stadium with accommodation for 12,000 spectators, a steeplechase ring, a dressage field, and an indoor riding hall. The nearby *Sevastopol*" *Hotel*, at KAKHOVSKAYA METRO STATION, consists of four 16-storey tower blocks with rooms for 4000 guests.

The **Church of SS. Boris and Gleb** (Ts. Borisa i Gleba) nearby at ZYUZINO (Pl. 2; 8) was begun in 1688 by the Boyar Prozorovsky and is one of the oldest surviving Moscow Baroque buildings. As it is similar to the church at Troitse-Lykovo it has been suggested that the same architect, Yakov Bukhvostov, was involved. The church is visible from SEVASTOPOL'SKIY PR. and is situated between Kakhovskaya and Kaluzhskaya Metro Stations. There is another Moscow Baroque church to the SW in what was once the village of Uzkoye, to the E of PROFSOYUZNAYA UL. It was built by the Streshnev boyars in 1698 and shows a strong Ukrainian influence.

The Bittsevskiy Forest Park straddles the Ring Motorway. To the S beyond the motorway flows the BITTSA RIVER (a tributary of the Pakhra which in turn enters the Moskva SE of the capital). The **Znamenskoye-Sadki Estate**, with its large manor house, was built near here in the middle of the 18C by the Princes Trubetskoy; the estate is now occupied by a veterinary institute. Znamenskoye-Sadki is not far from BITTSA RAILWAY STATION, which is served by suburban trains from Kursk Station.

I.   Gorki Leninskiye

Gorki Leninskiye, the suburban estate where Lenin died, has been preserved as a **Lenin Museum** (Dom-Muzey V.I. Lenina v Gorkakh) (Pl. 1). It is located 32km S of the Kremlin, beyond the Ring Motorway. Suburban trains from the Pavelets Station travel to LENINSKAYA STATION (30–40 minutes); from here it is a short trip on Bus No. 27 or 28 to the museum.

Gorki is situated on a hill by the left bank of the Pakhra River. The Classical yellow *Manor House* with its six-columned portico dates from the late 18C; before the Revolution it belonged to the mayor of Moscow. Lenin began to travel to Gorki for short rests in September 1918, after he had narrowly escaped death at the hands of a terrorist. As his health declined Lenin was forced to spend more and more time here. In May 1922 he suffered a stroke which caused him temporarily to lose his faculties of speech and movement. Lenin returned to the Kremlin in October 1922 but then suffered two incapacitating strokes.

He returned to Gorki in May 1923 and, apart from a short trip to Moscow in October, remained there as an invalid. Lenin died at Gorki on the evening of 21 January 1924.

The Lenin Museum was opened in 1949. The house is maintained as it was in the early 1920s. From the summer of 1921 Lenin and his wife and sister stayed in the Manor House; here is preserved the telephone he used to contact the outside world and, on the 1st Floor, his study and bedroom. (In earlier visits to Gorki, Lenin occupied the detached North Wing.)

J. Arkhangel'skoye

Arkhangel'skoye (Muzey-Usad'ba 'Arkhangel'skoye') is one of the finest aristocratic country estates in the Moscow area (Pl. 1). It is situated some 26km W of the Kremlin, beyond the Ring Motorway and off VOLOKOLAMSKOYE SHOSSE. The nearest Metro station is TUSHINSKAYA. From here Buses No. 541 and 549 travel to Arkhangel'skoye.

The Arkhangel'skoye Estate and village take their name from the **Church of the Archangel Michael** (Ts. Mikhaila Arkhangela), which dates from 1667. The white-painted stone church is distinguished by rows of kokoshnik gables and silver-aspen onion domes. Tyurin's Classical *Holy Gate* (1823–24) marks the beginning of the path to the church.

In 1703 the estate became the property of the Golitsyns, and in the middle of the century a palace was built and a garden landscaped 'à la française'. In the 1780s, after the palace had fallen into disrepair, N.A. Golitsyn ordered its demolition and commissioned the building of a replacement. The plans were drawn up in Paris by the French architect Chevalier de Guerney, but the actual construction was overseen by local serf-craftsmen. At the same time the Italian G. Trombara designed the terraces and park. In 1810, before the final completion of all this work, the estate was bought by the Director of the Imperial Museums, N.B. Yusupov (1751–1831); Yusupov was a renowned art collector and one of the richest men in Russia. Soon after it changed hands, the palace was severely damaged, first during the war of 1812 and in a subsequent serf uprising, and then by fire in 1820. Restoration work was carried out by Bove, Tyurin, and S.P. Mel'nikov, along with the serf-architect V.Ya. Strizhakov. It was at this point that the triumphal arch was added by the entrance and the theatre built. In 1829 the terraces in the gardens were replanned by V.G. Dregalov.

The ***Palace**, a fine example of stucco-covered wooden architecture, is long and ochre-coloured. The main (N) façade is approached through a triumphal arch with beautiful wrought-iron gates. Flanking the courtyard are colonnades which link the wings on either side of the arch to the main building. The lower part of the wings is painted to create the illusion of a continuous colonnade. Standing in a flower-bed in the centre of the courtyard is a *Statue of Menelaus with the Body of Patroclus*—an 18C Italian copy of an ancient original. The side of the palace which faces the courtyard is sparsely decorated with only a central four-columned portico and a white stone band dividing the two storeys. A high circular belvedere with paired columns rises above the portico. The S façade, looking onto the gardens, has a central semi-circular bay with pilasters. Each suite of rooms on the ground floor has access to the gardens through the French windows.

The *Interior* is decorated as it was before the Revolution. Much of the furniture, fabrics, china, and crystal was manufactured by serfs in the estate's factories. The sumptuously furnished public rooms on the

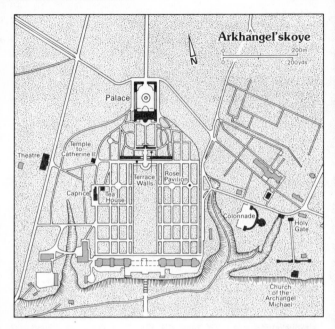

Ground Floor house part of N.B. Yusupov's collection of W European art.

Beyond the *Vestibule* and the *Fore Hall* is the compositional centre of the palace, the elegant *Oval Hall*; this was intended for balls and receptions. There is a musicians gallery above the eight pairs of Corinthian columns. The chandelier, the work of local craftsmen, is made of papier mâché on a wire base. The *Imperial Hall*, to the right, contains portraits of the Tsars and their families. Beyond the pale blue *Main Bedroom* is the W end of the palace. The two corner rooms named after the French painter *Hubert Robert* (1733–1808) contain 18C French landscapes reflecting the surrounding countryside; these are linked by the *Antique Hall* with its Classical sculpture.

To the E of the 2nd Hubert Robert Hall, on the courtyard side of the palace, is a room devoted to paintings by *G.B. Tiepolo* (1696–1770); the figure of the major domo (left) in 'Cleopatra's Feast' is a self-portrait of the Venetian master.

To the left of the Oval Hall is the *Salon*, with 18C French paintings. The *Music Salon*, beyond, contains many of the finest works from the Yusupov collection, including 'Portrait of an Unknown Woman' by Van Dyck (1599–1641). The adjacent *Rotari Salon* (in the SE corner) has on display female portraits by *Pietro Rotari* (1707–62). The *Winter Study*, also at the E end of the building, contains a portrait of Prince N.B. Yusupov as a child.

The smaller rooms on the *1st Floor* house an exhibition tracing the history of the palace and showing the work of serf-craftsmen. Here too is Yusupov's library of 16,000 volumes; an oddity on display in the library is a papier mâché model of the dying J.-J. Rousseau.

The palace stands at the top of a slope, and below are two terraces and a lawn. The terraces are decorated with a fountain, Classical statues, urns, and flower-beds; the lawn is flanked by rows of trimmed lime trees decorated with sculpture. To the E of the lawn stands the *Rose Pavilion*, while to the W are two 18C pavilions, the yellow and white *Caprice* (Kapriz)—actually a miniature palace—and the domed *Tea House* (Chaynyy Domik). Nearby, and just below the lower terrace, stands the little *Temple to Catherine II* (Khram Yekaterine), built by Tyurin in 1819. (After Pushkin visited Arkhangel'skoye he wrote to Yusupov: 'I am suddenly transported to the days of Catherine'.) Not far to the W is the oblong **Theatre**, built in 1818 by P.G. Gonzaga for Yusupov's troupe of serf-actors. Some of Gonzaga's splendid stage decorations are on display here, as well as an exhibition on the history of this theatre. To the E of the lawn is the mid-19C *Rose Fountain*. The last 'pavilion' at Arkhangel'skoye was the *Colonnade* (Kolonnada), a large domed Classical structure intended as a chapel; it was built in 1909–16 by R.I. Klein, who was then one of the most important Moscow architects.

K. The Moscow Region

Visitors to Moscow must stay in the city and its immediate outskirts. *Trips outside this area may only be made with special permission.* This involves obtaining a visa, which is difficult to do on an individual basis during a short stay. For this reason, and because this book is primarily concerned with the city of Moscow, the intention here is to simply outline some of the main places which are being developed for tourists in the Moscow Region (Moskovskaya Oblast').

RYAZANSKOYE SHOSSE leads to the SE from Moscow. The ancient town of **Kolomna** is situated 115km from Moscow at the point where the Moskva River flows into the Oka. In Kolomna are the remains of a kremlin, as well as a number of churches and monasteries. The brick *Cathedral of the Assumption* (Uspenskiy Sobor) dates from 1672–82. **Zaraysk**, 165km from Moscow and to the SW of Ryazanskoye Shosse, has a kremlin dating from the early 16C.

SIMFEROPOL'SKOYE SHOSSE, which extends S from the Varshavskoye Shosse in Moscow, is the main road to Kiev. At CHEKHOV (formerly Lopasnya), which is 49km from Moscow, a road leads 12km E to the **Chekhov Museum** at the former **Melikhovo Estate** (Gos. Literaturnyy Muzey-Zapovednik A.P. Chekhova 'Melikhovo'). The writer Anton Chekhov (1860–1904) lived here in the 1890s.

The main road to the western border at Brest begins as the MOZHAYSKOYE SHOSSE in SW Moscow. To the N of this road and 53km W of the capital is the Moskva River town of **Zvenigorod**, one of the oldest in the region. The *Cathedral of the Assumption* (Uspenskiy Sobor 'na Gorodke') dates from 1399. Nearby is the **Savvin-Storozhevskiy Monastery**, which was founded in the late 14C and now houses the **Zvenigorod Historical Museum** (Zvenigorodskiy Istoriko-Arkhitekturnyy Muzey). The partisan-heroine Zoya Kosmodem'yanskaya was executed by the Germans on 29 November 1941 in the village of PETRISHCHEVO, which is S of the main road to the west and about 7km from DOROKHOVO. An *Obelisk* marks the place where she died, and there is a **Zoya**

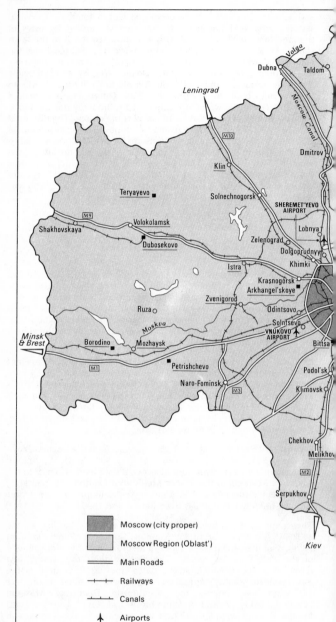

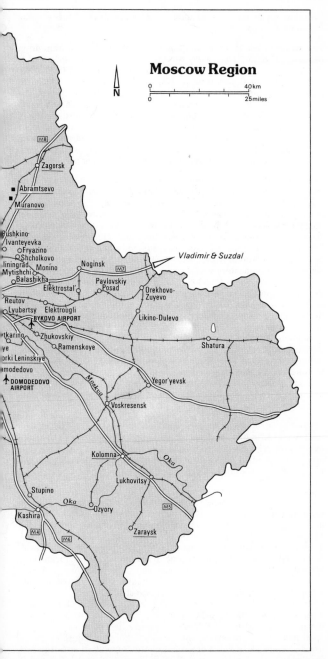

Moscow Region

Kosmodem'yanskaya   Museum   (Memorial'nyy   Muzey   Zoi
Kosmodem'yanskoy).

The town of MOZHAYSK, on the upper Moskva, is 113km from
Moscow. The 15C *Luzhetskiy Monastery* contains the *Cathedral of
the Nativity of the Virgin* (Sobor Rozhdestva Bogorditsy) (mid-16C).

One of the great battles of the Napoleonic Wars was fought on 26
August 1812 near the village of BORODINO and just SW of the
Moskva River; the French called this the Bataille de la Moskova.
Borodino is located some 16km W of Mozhaysk and there are many
monuments marking the places where the forces of the two sides
were deployed. The battlefield, now part of the **Borodino Museum**
(Gos. Borodinskiy Voyenno-Istoricheskiy Muzey-Zapovednik), con-
tains much of interest and has been developed as a centre of tourism.

One continuation of Leningradskiy Pr. leads NW as VOL-
OKOLAMSKOYE SHOSSE. The town of **Istra**, 56km from Moscow, is the
site of the former **New Jerusalem Monastery** (Voskresenskiy
Novoiyerusalimskiy Monastyr'), now the **Moscow Region Local
History Museum** (Moskovskiy Oblastnoy Krayevedcheskiy Muzey).
The New Jerusalem Monastery was built on an impressive scale by
Patriarch Nikon (1652–67), and was intended as an expression of the
power of the Church. Nikon, who died in 1681, was buried here. The
centre of the monastery was the giant *Cathedral of the Resurrection*
(Voskresenskiy Sobor (1658–85), which was based on the Church of
the Holy Sepulchre in Jerusalem. The cathedral and other monastery
buildings were very badly damaged during the Second World War,
but extensive restoration work has been carried out recently. There is
also an outdoor museum of wooden architecture here. **Volokolamsk**
is a town situated some 118km W of Moscow; within the local
kremlin stands the 15C *Cathedral of the Resurrection* (Voskresenskiy
Sobor). At TERYAYEVO, 26km NE of Volokolamsk, is the **Joseph of
Volokolamsk Monastery** (Iosifo-Volokolamskiy Monastyr'). The
monastery was founded in 1479 by Joseph of Volokolamsk (1439/40–
1515), but the picturesque buildings which survive today date
primarily from the late 17C.

On the main highway to Leningrad, LENINGRADSKOYE SHOSSE, is
the town of **Klin** (87km). The composer Pyotr Tchaikovsky (1840–93)
lived in the Klin district from 1885. His last house, in Klin itself, has
been preserved as a **Tchaikovsky Museum** (Gos. Dom-Muzey P.I.
Chaykovskovo v Klinu).

The extension of Pr. Mira to the NE of Moscow is called
YAROSLAVSKOYE SHOSSE. The poet Fyodor Tyutchev (1803–73)
spent much time at MURANOVO, which is about 50km from Moscow
and to the W of Yaroslavskoye Shosse. The main house of the
Muranovo Estate was built in 1841 and has been made into a
Tyutchev Museum (Muzey-Usad'ba 'Muranovo' im. F.I. Tyutcheva).
About 60km from Moscow and near Muranovo is the **Abramtsevo
Museum** (Muzey-Usad'ba 'Abramtsevo'). The Abramtsevo Estate
was purchased in 1870 by Savva Mamontov, who invited leading
artists to work here. The revival of interest in Russian art and folk
crafts at the end of the 19C was centred at Abramtsevo. Of particular
interest is the little Neo-Russian *Church* built in 1881–82 to the
designs of the artists V.M. Vasnetsov and V.D. Polenov.

Further along Yaroslavskoye Shosse, 75km from Moscow, is the
town of **Zagorsk**. It was known before the Revolution as Sergiyevo,

but was renamed in honour of a Bolshevik named V.M. Zagorsky who was assassinated in 1919. The main focus of interest in Zagorsk is the *Troitse-Sergiyeva Lavra (Trinity Monastery of St. Sergiy), which has been preserved as the **Zagorsk Historical and Art Museum** (Zagorskiy Gos. Istoriko-Khudozhestvennyy Muzey-Zapovednik); the Lavra remains an important centre of the Russian Orthodox Church.

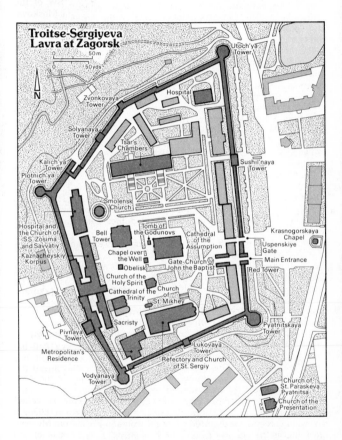

The monastery was founded by St. Sergiy of Radonezh (c 1321–91) in 1345. Early in the following century the district was laid waste by a Tatar army, and the miraculous survival of the body of St. Sergiy in the ruins of the monastery he had founded made it a place of pilgrimage. The Troitse-Sergiyev Monastery became one of the most important monastic institutions, and in 1744 was given the rank of a lavra (laura). A Theological College was established here in 1749, and this remains today as a seminary for training priests.

Since the mid-14C, when St. Sergiy advised Dmitry Donskoy and blessed the army which defeated the Tatars at Kulikovo, the monastery has had an important place in Russian history. In 1608–10, during the Time of Troubles, the monks withstood a 16-month siege by the Poles. The young Tsars Peter and Ivan sheltered here in the 1680s during the uprisings of the strel'tsy in Moscow. Other Russian rulers came on pilgrimages over the centuries.

Outside the walled monastery, to the E and SE, are the *Church of the Presentation* (Vvedenskaya Ts.), the *Church of St. Paraskeva Pyatnitsa* (Pyatnitskaya Ts.) (both completed in 1547), and the *Krasnogorskaya Chapel* (1770). The massive *Wall* and *Towers* of the monastery-fortress were built of brick in 1540–50, and reconstructed in the middle of the following century. The main entrance, formed by the *Red Tower* and the **Gate-Church of John the Baptist** (Nadvratnaya Ts. Ionna Predtechi), is on the E side. The terracotta-coloured church dates from 1693–99 and was paid for by the Stroganov family. The second tier is decorated with Venetian scallops and crowned with a small dome. There are frescoes above the gateway itself.

The large church in the centre of the monastery, with five bulbous domes decorated with gold stars, is the *Cathedral of the Assumption** (Uspenskiy Sobor). The cathedral was built in 1559–85 on the orders of Ivan the Terrible and commemorates the taking of Kazan and Astrakhan. The design of the building was inspired by the Kremlin Cathedral of the Assumption. The frescoes of the interior date from 1684. Outside the W door of the cathedral are the low *Tomb of the Godunovs* (Usypal'nitsa Godunovykh) (1605/1780), where Tsar Boris Godunov and his family were buried, and also the so-called *Chapel over the Well* (Nadkladeznaya Chasovnya). The chapel was built in the late 17C over a holy well.

The **Church of the Holy Spirit** (Dukhovskaya Ts.), just to the SW of the cathedral, was built by craftsmen from Pskov in 1476. The church was unusual, as it served as a watch-tower and a belfry. The tower with its single blue dome and gold bands was once used by sentries, and around its base is a row of kokoshnik gables, each one containing a bell.

The oldest church in the monastery is not far away, and nearer the W wall. This is a relatively small structure with a single gold dome, the *Cathedral of the Trinity** (Troitskiy Sobor). It was built in 1422 on the site of an earlier wooden church. The original frescoes of the new cathedral were the work of Andrey Rublyov and Daniil Chornyy but the walls were repainted in the 16C. The well-lit *Iconostasis*, by the same artists, has survived. The most celebrated icon, Rublyov's Old Testament Trinity, is now in the Tret'yakov Gallery. The cathedral was the burial place of St. Sergiy. It has several chapels, the most important of which is the *Chapel of St. Nikon* (Nikonovskiy Pridel) 1548/1623), by the SE corner.

The southern part of the monastery is occupied by several interesting buildings. The two-storey *Metropolitan's Residence* (Mitropolich'i Pokoi) (1778) is in the SW corner. Adjacent is the great building of the *Refectory** (Trapeznaya) (1685–92). The exterior is brightly painted with a checkerboard pattern, and decorated with carved pillars and a sculptured frieze incorporating scallop shells. At the E end is the massive *Church of St. Sergiy* (Ts. Sergiya) with its single golden dome. The interior of the refectory building includes a vast richly-decorated two-storey hall. The little *Church of St. Mikhey* (Mikheyevskaya Ts.) next to the NW corner of the Refectory was built in 1734.

In the northern part of the monastery are the *Hospital* (Bol'nichnyy Korpus) (1835/84), a number of seminary buildings, and the former **Tsar's Chambers** (Tsarskiye Chertogi). The Tsar's Chambers were constructed in the late 17C, decorated in the early 18C, and now serve as part of the *Theological College* and the *Ecclesiastical Academy*.

The remaining buildings of interest are in the western part of the grounds, near the great five-tiered *Bell Tower**. This blue and white

Refectory, Zagorsk (1685–92)

Baroque structure was built between 1740 and 1770, and the architects I.F. Michurin and D.V. Ukhtomsky took part in the work. To the S is an *Obelisk* (1792), with bas-reliefs showing the history of the monastery, and to the NW the round *Smolensk Church* (Smolenskaya Ts.) (1745–48).

The row of buildings between the Bell Tower and the W wall includes the *Sacristy* (Riznitsa) (1781) (behind the Cathedral of the Trinity), the *Kaznacheyskiy Korpus* (16C/17C/1859), and the *Hospital* (Bol'nichnyye Palaty); the hospital, built in 1635–38, incorporates the white tent-roofed *Church of SS. Zosima and Savvatiy* (Ts. Zosimy i Savvatiya). Several of these structures have been made into a **Museum** (Ekspozitsiya). On display are icons, portraits from the 18C–19C, furniture, pottery, china, glass, Russian and foreign fabrics, and examples of Russian handicrafts.

LENINGRAD

19 Dvortsovaya Ploshchad' to Novaya Gollandiya

This Rte takes in one of the most important parts of old St. Petersburg, the former Admiralty District, which contained the administrative centre of Imperial Russia. The imposing architecture of the Admiralty District reflected its political importance. The starting point is the main square of the city, Dvortsovaya Pl., which is only a few hundred metres from NEVSKIY PROSPEKT METRO STATION. The Rte then runs W along the Neva River.

DVORTSOVAYA PL., or Palace Square (Pl. 13; 4), lies to the S of the former Winter Palace (now part of the State Hermitage, Rte 20), from which it takes its name. The opposite (S) side of the square is taken up by the splendid 600m curve of the former *Main Staff (Glavnyy Shtab) of the Russian Army. Carlo Rossi built the Main Staff in 1819–29, two massive blocks joined by an arch over Ul. Gertsena. The arch was intended to commemorate the war against Napoleon and is surmounted by the *Chariot of Victory* and flanked by statues of warriors (S.S. Pimenov and V.I. Demut-Malinovsky).

The Main Staff was partly created by the reconstruction of older buildings. In 1845–46 the former headquarters of the Free Economic Society (by the junction with Nevskiy Pr.) were incorporated to form an extension of the main façade. The building housed important Imperial offices until the Revolution; on the right (W) was the Army's Main Staff, in the centre, behind the arch, the Ministry of Finance, and on the left the Foreign Ministry. Here on 19 July 1914 (o.s.) the German ambassador presented the declaration of war which began the world conflict of 1914–18. Three years later the government offices were taken over by new Soviet institutions. The Bolshevik M.S. Uritsky, head of the Petrograd Cheka (secret police), was assassinated in this building by a Socialist-Revolutionary in August 1918; for a long time Dvortsovaya Pl. was known as Pl. Uritskovo.

Dvortsovaya Pl. has witnessed many dramatic events. Great military parades were held here in the Imperial period, and the square is still the focal point of the 1 May and 7 November parades. One of the most memorable popular manifestations took place on the first anniversary of the October Revolution (7 November 1918) when young avant-garde artists used nearly 15,000m of canvas to decorate the square with enormous Cubist and Futurist paintings. The connection with the revolutionary tradition was a real one. In April 1879 a terrorist from 'People's Will' fired several shots at Alexander II as he returned through the square from his morning walk. A more famous incident occurred on 'Bloody Sunday', 9 January 1905, when crowds demonstrating on the W side of the square were fired on by troops. As many as 30 people were killed or wounded; the incident, along with other shootings in St. Petersburg, marked the start of the 1905 Revolution. Although a huge crowd gathered in Dvortsovaya Pl. for a patriotic demonstration at the beginning of the First World War, within three years the square served as the cockpit of the Bolshevik uprising. The great charge across the square depicted in Eisenstein's film 'October' and elsewhere is a myth, but there was a good deal of gun-fire back and forth before the Bolshevik-led forces broke into the last government 'redoubt', the Winter Palace. In November 1920 revolutionary artists staged a re-enactment of the October Revolution here.

The centrepiece of Dvortsovaya Pl., the 47.5m tall **Alexander Column**, commemorates the war against Napoleon. It was completed in August 1834; on the base was the inscription 'To Alexander the First from a Grateful Russia'. The 707-ton granite monolith was brought by ship from the Pyuterlaks quarry near Vyborg in S Finland and winched to a vertical position in August 1832 by 2000 soldiers and 400 workers; the pillar is supported only by its own weight. The angel on the top, holding a cross, was created by the sculptor B.I. Orlovsky. There are allegorical bas-reliefs on the pedestal.

Dedication of the Alexander Column, 30 August 1834 (V.E. Raev, 1834). The column was a monument to the Napoleonic Wars. The painting gives a sense of the vistas that the town planners of Imperial St. Petersburg had created

The Classical building which forms the E side of Dvortsovaya Pl., the former *Guards Headquarters* (Shtab Gvardeyskovo Korpusa), was built in 1837–43 to the plans of A.P. Bryullov. In 1917 this building was the headquarters of the Petrograd Military District; it was captured by the October insurgents and the extensive communications facilities were used to co-ordinate the uprising.

The *Admiralty (Pl. 13; 4), to the W of Dvortsovaya Pl., is one of the great landmarks of Leningrad. The building forms the architectural centre of the city; three of the original avenues converge on it: Nevskiy Pr., Ul. Dzerzhinskovo, and Pr. Mayorova.

The Admiralty began as a fortified shipyard in 1704; seven years later the first primitive Admiralty building appeared, and by 1738 this had been rebuilt with a spire. The present version, however, dates from 1806–23 and was the work of the architect A.D. Zakharov. This is a superb example of the Classical style in Russia. Rows of white columns surround the corners of the building, the entrances, and the tower which supports the spire. This gilded spire can be seen from many parts of the city. The weather-vane is set 72m above the ground; it takes the form of a sailing-ship and has become one of the symbols of Leningrad.

The extensive use of sculpture is another remarkable feature of Zakharov's design. I.I. Terebenev created the relief 'The Establishment of the Russian Fleet' on the base of the central tower (on the attic above the main entrance); Neptune is depicted handing Peter the Great a trident. Statues of Alexander the Great, Achilles, Ajax, and Pyrrhus sit on the corners of the attic, and above the tower's colonnade there are a further 28 allegorical statues. Nymphs holding globes frame the archway of the main entrance. The archways of the twin flanking pavilions on the Neva side are decorated with anchors and bas-reliefs. Regrettably, the view of the river façade of this massive 'U'-shaped building was spoiled in the late 19C by the construction of houses along Admiralteyskaya Nab. Until the middle of the 19C the area contained by the three sides of the Admiralty building was used as a shipyard.

Before the Revolution the Admiralty housed the Ministry of the Navy and also the Naval Museum. This building was the last, weak, rallying point of the Tsarist forces during February 1917. The *Dzerzhinsky Higher Naval Engineering Academy* is now located here.

The *Gorky Gardens*, (formerly the Alexander Gardens) extend along the S side of the Main Admiralty. These were laid out in 1872–74, in place of the wide esplanade between Dvortsovaya Pl. and Isaakiyevskaya Pl. Statues of the writers Gogol, Lermontov, and Zhukovsky, the composer Glinka, and the Central Asian explorer N.M. Przheval'sky (1839–88) were erected here in the 1890s. ADMIRALTEYSKIY PR. forms the boundary of the park to the S. At No. 6, on the corner of Ul. Dzerzhinskovo, was the pre-revolutionary *Office of the City Governor* (Dom Gubernskikh Prisutstvennykh Mest), a rectangular Classical structure by Quarenghi (late 18C). Here, in December 1917, Feliks Dzerzhinsky established the first offices of the Cheka, the Soviet secret police. There is now a small **Dzerzhinsky Museum** (Memorial'nyy Muzey-Kabinet F.E. Dzerzhinskovo) here.

The next street to the W is one of the original Petersburg avenues, PR. MAYOROVA, formerly Voznesenskiy Pr. The old name came from the Church of Ascension (Voznesenskaya Ts.) (A. Rinaldi, 1769), which stood by this street (next to the Griboyedov Canal) until its demolition in 1936; P.V. Mayorov was a Petrograd worker killed in 1919 while serving as a Red Army commissar. The French architect Montferrand designed the triangular building on the far side of Pr. Mayorova; the two white marble lions in front of the eight-columned portico on Admiralteyskiy Pr. were the work of P. Triscornia. Originally built as the Lobanov-Rostovsky House (1817–20), it housed before the Revolution the Imperial *Ministry of War*.

Montferrand's most famous building, however, lies just beyond, **ˑSt. Isaac's Cathedral** (Isaakiyevskiy Sobor) (Pl. 13; 4). This huge and lavishly-decorated church is now open as a museum. In addition, from the vantage point of the gallery (in the drum of the great dome) one can get an unrivalled view of central Leningrad. *No photography is permitted.*

The first wooden Church of St. Isaac was built near here in 1710 and replaced in 1727 by a stone version. St. Isaac of Dalmatia was a Byzantine monk whose feast day fell on 30 May, the birthday of Peter I. A stone cathedral to the design of Rinaldi was begun on the present site in 1768, but in general this structure was unsatisfactory; shortly after its completion in 1802 a competition was held to design a replacement. The Napoleonic wars delayed a decision, but in 1818 the project of the young French architect Auguste de Montferrand (1786–1858) was approved.

Construction proceeded slowly, as might be expected given the size of the project and the inexperience of the architect. A particular feature of the project was the 48 largest pillars, each weighing 114 tons. Special ships and tackle, as well as a small railway, had to be constructed to transport the columns and the huge granite blocks from the Pyuterlaks quarry in Finland. The main columns were erected between March 1828 and August 1830, and the basic structure was completed in 1842, but the cathedral had not been decorated. It was consecrated only in 1858—the year of Montferrand's death and 40 years after he had begun work. One estimate of the total cost is 23,256,000 silver rubles. Inside is a small display showing how the cathedral was built and, in particular, how some of the great engineering problems were overcome.

The overall height of the cathedral is 101.5m. The dominant feature, the huge dome, may be seen from a great distance and nearly 100kg of gold were used to cover it. The 24 statues encircling the dome (above the colonnade) are copies of Antique originals by J. Hermann. The four smaller gilded cupolas served as bell towers. Statues of angels by Vitali adorn each corner of the roof; these were equipped with gas torches that could be lit at Easter.

The pediments of the four enormous porticoes constitute another notable feature of the exterior. The reliefs to the S and W were created by Vitali, while those to the N and E are the work of P. Lemaire. Episodes from the life of St. Isaac are illustrated on the E and W pediments, to the S is the Adoration of the Magi, and to the N the the Resurrection. On the extreme left of the pediment of the W portico can be seen a statue of Montferrand himself, wearing a toga, kneeling, and holding a model of the cathedral.

The three huge *Doors*, made of oak and bronze, were decorated with biblical scenes by Vitali. Beyond is the vast **Interior**, which could hold as many as 14,000 worshippers. K.P. Bryullov created the huge painting in the cupola; it covers 800sq m and depicts the Virgin Mary surrounded by saints and angels. Lower down the walls are murals of the Apostles and evangelists; the walls themselves are faced with marble in many different colours. F. Bruni, T. Neff, C. von Steuben, C. Mussini, and others painted the monumental murals around the pillars and arches; the gilded sculptures here are the work of Vitali, Clodt, and Pimenov.

Ten malachite and two lazurite columns decorate the three-tiered white marble *Iconostasis*. The two lower tiers are mosaics designed by Neff and F.P. Bryullov, while the upper tier consists of paintings by S.A. Zhivago. The gilded bronze Royal Doors weigh 5 tons; above, a statue by Clodt depicts 'Christ in Glory'. The stained-glass window in the depth of the sanctuary, a rarity in an Orthodox cathedral, was made in Munich to the design of Leo von Klenze (builder of the New Hermitage).

Another unusual feature is the 93m long Foucault pendulum which hangs from the dome and demonstrates the earth's rotation. It was installed in 1931 when the cathedral was being used as the 'State Anti-Religious Museum'.

ISAAKIYEVSKAYA PL., S of the cathedral, contains a bronze equestrian **Statue of Emperor Nicholas I** (1825–55) unveiled in 1859. Montferrand was in charge of the whole project, while Clodt created the figures of the Emperor and his horse; N.A. Ramazanov and R. Saleman were responsible for the decoration of the base, which includes allegorical statues and bas-reliefs of episodes from the Emperor's life.

The *Leningradskaya Hotel* (formerly the Angliya), on the corner of Ul. Gogolya, was where the poet Yesenin hanged himself in 1925. To the S, on the corner of Ul. Gertsena, is the **Astoriya Hotel**. Built by Lidval in the Style Moderne (1910–12), it is regarded as one of the finest hotels in the city. Across the street to the S stands one of the buildings of the former *Ministry of State Domains*, later the Ministry of Agriculture. This, and a similar three-storey ministry building on the opposite (W) side of the square, were designed in an Italian Renaissance style by N.Ye. Yefimov (1844–53). Two important streets lead E back to Nevskiy Pr. from here. Ul. Gogolya and Ul. Gertsena (formerly Morskaya Ul.) were centres of commerce and aristocratic society before the Revolution; the élite Imperial Yacht

Club was located at No. 31 on the Morskaya (just beyond the Astoriya).

The S side of Isaakiyevskaya Pl. is taken up by the Siniy (Blue) Most across the Moyka River and, beyond it, by the *Mariya Palace (Mariinskiy Dvorets) (Pl. 13; 4).

The palace was built in 1839–44 for Grand Duchess Mariya (1819–76), daughter of Nicholas I. Stakenschneider, the architect, incorporated in this new building part of Vallin de la Mothe's earlier Chernyshev Palace. The main façade is lined by columns and pilasters and divided into several major components; the high attic of the central section dominates the design.

From late in the 19C the Mariya Palace was used for meetings of the State Council and the Committee of Ministers. Repin's painting of the State Council in session (1903)—now in the Russian Museum—depicts the Rotunda Hall of the Mariya Palace. The palace was to play a considerable role in the political turmoil of the early 20C. In April 1902 Sipyagin, the Minister of the Interior, was assassinated in the Vestibule by a revolutionary.

The last meetings of the Tsar's Council of Ministers were held in the palace in February 1917, and after the new Provisional Government moved out of the Tauride Palace it made its first headquarters here; the April (1917) Demonstrations against Milyukov, the Foreign Minister, were concentrated around the Mariya Palace. In the autumn the so-called Pre-Parliament met here until it was dispersed by the Bolsheviks.

After the Revolution the Mariya Palace housed a number of institutions, including the Stalin Industrial Academy, but since 1948 it has been the headquarters of the Executive Committee of the Leningrad City Soviet. The palace serves in effect as the town hall; it is for this reason that the various medals won by Leningrad are displayed on the front of the building.

The massive building of the former *German Embassy* stands on the W side of Isaakiyevskaya Pl., on the corner of Ul. Gertsena. It dates from 1912, and one of the outstanding 20C German architects, Peter Behrens, was responsible for the design; the young Mies van der Rohe also worked on the project. A patriotic mob attacked the building on the outbreak of war in July 1914. It is now the offices of Intourist. Ul. Gertsena, 43, once served as the Italian Embassy; Montferrand built this in 1840 as a mansion for the great industrialist P.N. Demidov. Montferrand also designed the mansion at No. 45. Formerly owned by Princess Gagarina, it is now occupied by the Composers Union as *Dom Kompozitorov*. Next door, at No. 47, lived the Kadet (liberal) politician V.D. Nabokov, a minister in the Provisional Government; his son was to become the émigré writer Vladimir Nabokov, best known for his novel 'Lolita'.

UL. SOYUZA SVYAZI, the first street N of Ul. Gertsena, contains at No. 9 (about 150m along) the **Main Post Office** (Glavnyy Pochtamt), a Classical structure built by N.A. L'vov in 1782–89; the arch across Ul. Soyuza Svyazi (formerly Pochtamtskaya Ul.) was designed by A.K. Cavos and added in 1859. At Ul. Soyuza Svyazi, 4, is the **Popov Museum of Communications** (Tsentral'nyy Muzey Svyazi im. A.S. Popova).

The building was at one time the Palace of A.A. Bezborodko, a late-18C statesman, for whom Quarenghi designed the interior (1780s). The museum, founded in 1877, shows the development of telegraph, telephone, wireless and television systems in Russia.

The long Classical structure to the NW of St. Isaac's served as the *Horse Guards Riding-School* (Konnogvardeyskiy Manezh), which explains the statues of the Dioscuri flanking the entrance (these are copies by P. Triscornia of statues in front of Rome's Quirinal Palace). the Riding-School dates from 1804–07 and was the work of Quarenghi.

The wide boulevard leading W beyond the Riding-School was originally an extension of the Admiralty Canal (dug in 1717). After the canal was covered over (1842), Konnogvardeyskiy Bul'v. or Horse Guards Boulevard—named after the nearby Horse Guards Barracks (No. 4)—replaced it. The marble columns on either side were erected at this time, with *Statues of Victory* designed by Christian Rauch. The modern name, BUL'V. PROFSOYUZOV or Trade Union Boulevard, derives from the nearby union headquarters in Pl. Truda.

PL. DEKABRISTOV (Pl. 13; 4), the third of the great squares around the Admiralty, was laid out in the 1760s in the space between the present St. Isaac's Cathedral and the river. It was formerly called Senatskaya Pl. or Senate Square; the Senate, a key judicial-administrative institution, was from 1763 housed in the mansion of A.P. Bestuzhev-Ryumin on the W side of the square. The handsome Classical buildings of the **Senate and Synod** which stand here today, connected by an arch and richly-decorated with sculpture, were created in 1829–34, when it was decided to build a structure that would harmonise with the Admiralty on the E side of the square; the architect was Carlo Rossi. The Senate occupied the building to the N, while the Holy Synod (responsible for the administration of the Church) occupied the S building. The *Central Historical Archive* is now located here.

The present name, Pl. Dekabristov or Square of the Decembrists, comes from one of the most dramatic events in 19C Russian history, the Decembrist Uprising of 1825. On the early morning of 14 December (Dekabr') revolutionary-minded young officers of the St. Petersburg garrison tried to carry out a coup d'état against the new Emperor, Nicholas I. They marshalled their troops here, in Senatskaya Pl., but at the critical moment the leaders faltered and Nicholas was able to rally loyal forces and disperse the rebels with grape-shot. Despite this failure the rising of the Decembrists (Dekabristy) marked the first spark of the Russian revolutionary movement, and on the centenary of 1825 the square was renamed in their honour.

One of the best-known symbols of Leningrad stands in the centre of Pl. Dekabristov, the ***Bronze Horseman**, an equestrian statue of Peter the Great by the French sculptor Etienne Falconet; this was unveiled in 1782.

The rearing horse of the Emperor is seen riding over the Serpent of Treason. The inscription on the wave-like granite base reads: 'To Peter the First from Catherine the Second. MDCCLXXXII'. The statue is well-known to Russians from the poem 'The Bronze Horseman' (Mednyy Vsadnik), written by Pushkin in 1833. The poet describes the great flood of 1824 and tells how a poor clerk named Yevgeny imagines himself to be pursued by the horse and rider, which symbolise the domineering Russian state: 'He knew ... the one/Who, without motion, held high/ In the darkness his bronze head,/ Whose fateful will/ Had founded the city on the sea./ How terrible he was in the surrounding gloom!/ What thought upon his brow!/ What strength contained within him!/ And in this steed what fire!/ Where are you galloping, proud steed,/ And where do your hoofs fall?/ Oh mighty master of destiny!/ Was it not thus that you, above the very abyss,/ Aloft, with curb of iron,/ Made Russia rear up?'

NAB. KRASNOVO FLOTA, an embankment lined with former aristocratic mansions, leads W from Pl. Dekabristov and commands a fine view of the lower Neva. The Decembrist S.N. Trubetskoy lived at No. 4, which had been rebuilt in 1804–10 by Thomas de Thomon. The great impresario Diaghilev, when he was an employee of the Imperial Theatres, lived at No. 22. The mansion at No. 28, now a **Palace of Weddings** (Dvorets Brakosochetaniya), formerly belonged to Grand Duke Andrey Vladimirovich (1879–1956) and served as the headquarters of the Socialist-Revolutionary Party in 1917. The General Staff Academy of the Imperial Army occupied No. 32.

Nab. Krasnovo Flota continues W beyond MOST LEYTENANTA

SHMIDTA (right) and Pl. Truda (left). A plaque next to the river notes that the cruiser 'Avrora' and other warships were moored here during the October 1917 Revolution. The cruiser controlled movement over the vital bridge and later fired a blank shot during the attack on the Winter Palace. The embankment was renamed Nab. Krasnovo Flota (Red Fleet Embankment) to commemorate these events.

It was formerly called Angliyskaya Nab. or English Embankment, because it was a centre of the British community. The British Embassy and the *English Church* were at one time located here; the latter (No. 56), a handsome Classical structure with Corinthian columns and pilasters and three statues on the roof, was built to the plans of Quarenghi (1814). The *Palace of Grand Duke Pavel Aleksandrovich* (1860–1919) was situated near the end of Nab. Krasnovo Flota, at No. 68.

The ***Museum of the History of Leningrad** (Gos. Muzey Istorii Leningrada), at Nab. Krasnovo Flota, 44, was founded in the Soviet period and is devoted to the post-revolutionary history of the city.

N.P. Rumyantsev, son of the Field Marshal, bought this house from a British merchant named Barr in 1802, and created one of the earliest Russian museums here. The Rumyantsev Museum of art, manuscripts, and coins was moved to Moscow in 1861, and later formed the nucleus of the Lenin Library. The present museum contains a wealth of material on the city since 1917. There are displays on the Revolution and on the early years of Soviet power, but perhaps the most moving section is that devoted to the Blockade of 1941–44. Photographs, documents, models, dioramas, weapons, uniforms, and items of everyday life are used to show how Leningraders lived and died during the siege.

PL. TRUDA (Pl. 13; 3), S of the embankment and Most Leytenanta Shmidta, is dominated by the large *Nikolay Palace* (left), built originally for Grand Duke Nikolay Nikolayevich (1831–91). The palace was erected in 1853–61, the last major project of the architect Stakenschneider. The main (W) façade, behind an iron railing, has wings projecting forward at the corners. There are three storeys, each decorated by rows of pilasters. From 1894–1917 the palace housed the Kseniya (Xenia) Institute, a school for daughters of the aristocracy, but since the Revolution it has been used by the Leningrad trade unions and called the *Palace of Labour* (Dvorets Truda). From this came the name of Pl. Truda; the square was formerly known as Blagoveshchenskaya Pl. after the Church of the Annunciation (Blagoveshchenskaya Ts.), which occupied what is now its S part. The tall church, built by Thon in 1843 and one of the landmarks of old Petersburg, was demolished in 1929.

UL. KRYUKOVA continues S from Pl. Truda, with the Kryukov Canal and the triangular island known as **Novaya Gollandiya** on the right. Novaya Gollandiya (Pl. 13; 3) surrounded by the Kryukov Canal (E), the Moyka River (S), and the Krushteyn Canal (N), was originally used for storing and seasoning ship timber. In 1917 the powerful naval wireless station here broadcast both news of the successful Bolshevik uprising and the first Soviet decrees. The handsome *Arch* of Novaya Gollandiya, by Vallin de la Mothe (1765–80s), may be seen from the tree-lined NAB. REKI MOYKI.

Nearly opposite the arch, on the S side of the Moyka (Nab. Reki Moyki, 106), was the *Palace of Grand Duchess Kseniya Aleksandrovna* (1875–1960), sister of Nicholas II; this now houses the *Lesgaft Institute of Physical Culture*, one of the largest sports training institutions in the USSR. Another member of the Imperial family lived a little farther down the Moyka; the *Palace of Grand Duke Aleksey Aleksandrovich* was created in its present picturesque form with Baroque details and a high tent-roofed tower in the 1880s (M.Ye. Mesmakher). Aleksey

Aleksandrovich (1850–1908), as 'General-Admiral', bore responsibility for the poor state of the Russian Navy before the 1904–05 war with Japan. Aleksandr Benois, the designer for the Ballets Russes, lived to the N of Novaya Gollandiya at NAB. KANALA KRUSHTEYNA, 31.

20 The State Hermitage

The ★★State Hermitage (Gosudarstvennyy Ermitazh) (Pl. 13; 2) is one of the world's finest art museums. The collection is partly housed in the former Imperial Winter Palace, a building rich in historical significance.

The NEVSKIY PROSPEKT METRO STATION is the nearest Metro stop to the State Hermitage. From here there is a 15-minute walk along NEVSKIY PR. (p 262) towards the Admiralty; the museum building is clearly visible (right) from the end of Nevskiy Pr. Buses No. 7, 44, and 45 and Trolleybuses No. 1, 7, and 10, which run along Nevskiy Pr., follow this route. They stop opposite the W end of the museum, just before the Neva. The main entrance to the State Hermitage is in the middle of the N side, on DVORTSOVAYA NAB., the Neva embankment.

The layout of the State Hermitage is easier to follow once it is realised that the museum consists of a line of three interconnected buildings: (1) the Winter Palace (farthest W), then; (2) the Small Hermitage; and (3) the Large Hermitage. The main entrance gives access to the first part, the Winter Palace.

Because of the diversity of the museum's collections and the great number of rooms, it is useful to summarise here the principal points of interest. The general location of the main collections is as follows (the compass directions assume the museum buildings are oriented exactly E–W, while they are actually more NE–SW):

Classical Antiquities	Large Hermitage, Ground Floor
	Small Hermitage, Ground Floor
	Winter Palace, Ground Floor, E
Western European Art	Large Hermitage, 1st Floor, N, NE,
Italian, 13C–18C	Centre
Dutch and Flemish,	Large Hermitage, 1st Floor, NW, W,
15C–18C	SW, S
	Small Hermitage, 1st Floor, E, S, W
German, 15C–18C	Winter Palace, 1st Floor, SE
French, 15C–18C	Winter Palace, 1st Floor, SE, S
Spanish, 16C–18C	Large Hermitage, 1st Floor, W
British, 17C–19C	Winter Palace, 1st Floor, SW
French Impressionists and	Winter Palace, 2nd Floor, S, SE
other Modern	
Primitive Culture and Art	Winter Palace, Ground Floor, W, NW
Culture and Art of Soviet Asia	Winter Palace, Ground Floor, SW
Culture and Art of Non-	Winter Palace, Ground Floor, E
Soviet Asia	Winter Palace, 2nd Floor, W, NW
Russian Culture	Winter Palace, 1st Floor, E, N, W
Numismatic Collection	Winter Palace, 2nd Floor, N
Special Collection	Large Hermitage, Ground Floor,
(Jewellery)	Centre

From the point of view of architectural and historical importance the most interesting parts of the State Hermitage are:

Winter Palace	Rastrelli Gallery (Ground Floor, N)
	Jordan Staircase (Ground Floor, NE)
	Hall of Peter I (R. 194: 1st Floor, E)
	Armorial Hall (R. 195: 1st Floor, E)
	Gallery of 1812 (R. 197: 1st Floor, E)
	Hall of St. George (R. 198: 1st Floor, E)
	Cathedral (R. 271: 1st Floor, SE)
	Gold Drawing Room (R. 304: 1st Floor, SW)
	Malachite Hall (R. 189: 1st Floor, NW)
Small Hermitage	Pavilion Hall (R. 204: 1st Floor, N)
	Hanging Garden (1st Floor)
Large Hermitage	State Staircase (RR. 110 and 242: Ground and 1st Floor, S)
	Hall of Twenty Columns (R. 130: Ground Floor, NE)
	Loggia of Raphael (R. 227: 1st Floor, E)

HISTORY AND ARCHITECTURE OF THE MUSEUM BUILDINGS

The **Winter Palace** (Zimniy Dvorets), the W part of the State Hermitage complex, was the winter residence of the Imperial family.

Construction of the Winter Palace. The existing Winter Palace was preceded by three earlier versions. The first was completed in 1711, between what are now Dvortsovaya Nab. and Ul. Khalturina (S of the present Hermitage Theatre). It was soon replaced by a second Winter Palace, built to the plans of G.J. Mattarnovi in 1716–20; this stood nearer the Neva. Peter the Great died here on 28 January 1725. The third Winter Palace was built for the Empress Anna in the early 1730s on the site of the W wing of the present building. The architect was the young Bartolomew Francesco Rastrelli (1700–71). This third version was extensively developed in the 1740s, but still did not satisfy the reigning Empress Elizabeth. On her instructions Rastrelli began work in 1754 on what was to be the fourth and final Winter Palace.

As construction work proceeded Rastrelli built temporary quarters for the Empress, the so-called Wooden Winter Palace. Completed in 1755, it was situated some distance from the present State Hermitage at the point where Nevskiy Pr. crosses the Moyka River; the Barrikada Cinema (Nevskiy Pr., 15/14) now occupies the site. Elizabeth Petrovna died there on 25 December 1761, without seeing the completion of the great palace. The first resident of the Winter Palace was to be her nephew, the ill-fated Emperor Peter III, who moved in during the spring of 1762. Peter presented Rastrelli with a Holstein medal and awarded him the rank of Major-General (in lieu of a cash payment).

The Baroque **Exterior** of Rastrelli's Winter Palace has changed little in the course of two centuries. The three visible façades are similar; each is divided into two tiers, the horizontal axis is broken by regularly-spaced pilasters, and there are statues on the parapets. Nevertheless, Rastrelli did succeed in giving each façade a character of its own. The S façade, looking into Dvortsovaya Pl., was intended to be the main one. It is broken into several sections, three of which jut out and contain arched entrances. The central part, with its triple archway, is most prominent; on 20 July 1914 (o.s.), after the outbreak of war with Germany, a huge patriotic crowd gathered in Dvortsovaya Pl., and Nicholas II appeared before them, standing on the balcony here (on the 1st Floor, above the central arch, by the left-hand window). The ornate iron gates were added in the 1880s. The W façade, facing the Admiralty, is distinguished by the projecting masses at the corners. At this end of the palace there was once an attractive wrought-iron fence, installed in 1901 and enclosing a royal garden. The design of the N façade, along the embankment, incorporates a large number of pilasters, especially in the outer sections.

The **Interior** of the Winter Palace has undergone drastic alteration. Rastrelli's Baroque interiors were not to the taste of Catherine II, who early in her reign commissioned Vallin de la Mothe, Rinaldi, and Velten to make changes. (Rastrelli went abroad in the summer of 1762, when Catherine came to power.) Quarenghi made further alterations for Catherine, and in the first third of the 19C Rossi and Montferrand created a number of new interiors. By 1837 practically the whole inside of the palace had been redecorated in the Classical style; the major exceptions were the Jordan Staircase and the Cathedral.

In December 1837 a fire broke out in a heating shaft of the Hall of Field Marshals (R. 193). The conflagration raged for 30 hours and most of the interior of the Winter Palace was destroyed. Nevertheless work on the restoration of the main ceremonial rooms was completed for Easter 1839, by employing as many as ten thousand workers at a time. This mammoth task was supervised by V.P. Stasov and A.P. Bryullov who recreated the interior, on the whole, as it had been before the disaster. Iron construction and an improved heating system were introduced to reduce the risk of fire. The main state rooms have changed little since this restoration.

History of the Winter Palace. Peter III had only three months in the Winter Palace, in 1762. He occupied the SE corner of the 1st Floor and installed his mistress, Countess Ye.R. Vorontsova, nearby; Catherine, his disgraced wife, had rooms on the far side of the courtyard, in the W wing. The Winter Palace was the scene of the famous dinner at which Peter publicly humiliated his wife; her response was to take part that summer in the overthrow of the Emperor. After she became sole ruler the Empress lived in the redecorated rooms in the SE corner of the 1st Floor; Grigory Orlov, her favourite and one of the organisers of the palace coup, was given rooms directly underneath. The W wing was used in 1767–68 for the Petersburg deliberations of the Legislative Commission, a body created by Catherine to draft a new law code.

After Catherine's death in 1796 her son, Paul I, placed the remains of the murdered Peter III in the Armorial Hall. Paul built a new Imperial residence, the Michael Castle, but after his assassination in 1801 Alexander I returned to the Winter Palace, which remained the home of the Imperial family for a hundred years. Both Nicholas I and Alexander II died in the reconstructed Winter Palace, but in the last decades of Tsardom the building was not much used. Alexander III had rooms in the NW section, on the 1st and 2nd Floors, but preferred to spend his winters in the Anichkov Palace. Nicholas II lived at the beginning of his reign in the same part of the palace, but from 1904 he and his family had their main residence at the Alexander Palace in suburban Tsarskoye Selo (Pushkin) (p 349).

During the Great War part of the palace was used as a hospital. Then came the Revolution, and in July 1917 the Provisional Government moved here from the Mariya Palace. Alexander Kerensky, the Prime Minister, had his offices in the former Imperial apartments in the W wing, on the 1st and 2nd Floors. The cabinet met in the Malachite Room (R. 189) and was arrested in the nearby White Dining-Room (R. 188) on the morning of 26 October. The Winter Palace had been the last stronghold of the Provisional Government, defended by the Women's Battalion. It was besieged by revolutionary forces, and fortunately it was hit by only two shells. Afterwards there was some looting of the Imperial apartments and the wine cellars, but the palace suffered surprisingly little damage.

In 1922 the building was transferred to the Hermitage art gallery for use as exhibition space. The Imperial Hermitage had originally been an annexe of the palace; now the Winter Palace was incorporated into the State Hermitage, and it has been identified with it ever since. In the inter-war years part of the palace also served as the Museum of the Revolution.

The present **Small Hermitage** (Malyy Ermitazh) was begun a decade after the Winter Palace, in the second year of Catherine's reign (1764). The project, by Vallin de la Mothe, was completed in 1767, a narrow building running along the E side of the palace and perpendicular to its main axis. At one time the only entrance was through Catherine's Winter Palace apartments, as it was intended as a retreat for the Empress; inspired by the Hermitage pavilion at Tsarskoye Selo (Pushkin), it was given the same name. Of greater long-term importance, the Small Hermitage was also used to house the rapidly-expanding Imperial art collection. The interior of the building was extensively altered by Stasov and Stakenschneider in the 1840s and 1850s.

The **Large Hermitage** (Bol'shoy Ermitazh) of today was built in stages over almost a century. The N part, along the river, is sometimes called the 'Old Hermitage' (Staryy Ermitazh) and was constructed to the plans of Velten (1771–87); Velten and Quarenghi produced the interiors, but these were replaced by those of Stakenschneider in 1851–60. In the late 1820s the Ground Floor of the Old Hermitage became the meeting place for the State Council and the Committee of ministers. These important government bodies held sessions here until 1885.

The S part of the building was added eighty years after the Old Hermitage (1838–52) as Russia's first purpose-built art gallery. The splendid 'New Hermitage' (Novyy Ermitazh) was the work of the German Leo von Klenze (1784–1864), one of the best-known architects in Europe; von Klenze also produced the similar Glyptothek and Pinakothek in Munich for Ludwig I of Bavaria. The exterior, composed of large natural-coloured blocks, is relatively austere but impressive. The main façade, to the S, is notable for a porch supported by atlantes. Set in niches on this and the E and W façades are statues of the great Classical and Renaissance artists. The lavish interiors created by von Klenze have survived.

The New Hermitage and the Old Hermitage (together forming the 'Large Hermitage') were joined to the Small Hermitage, and with it made up the 'Imperial Hermitage' (Imperatorskiy Ermitazh), the finest art gallery in Tsarist Russia.

The final building in the State Hermitage complex is the **Hermitage Theatre** (Ermitazhnyy Teatr). It is used for lectures, but is not open to casual visitors. The Hermitage Theatre was designed by Quarenghi (1783–87) and was one of that prolific architect's favourite buildings. The simple main façade, to the N, has eight pilasters set in a loggia; on the right-hand side is an arched bridge leading over a canal to the Large Hermitage. The theatre is blocked off from Ul. Khalturina by the former Preobrazhenskiy Guards Barracks. The Classical interior of the auditorium is very impressive. The stage is framed by pink Corinthian marble columns and statues, and similar columns and statues are arranged around the semicircular area where the audience sits. The first performance here took place in 1785, before the final completion of the building, and in the following century it was used extensively as a Court theatre (the hall was also used for ceremonies and even, on occasion, for drilling troops). One of the most interesting companies to use the hall was the Diaghilev ballet, which held its first rehearsal here in 1909, thanks to the patronage of Grand Duke Vladimir Aleksandrovich.

History of the Collection. The transition from palace to museum was a gradual one. The origins of the collection go back to 1764 when Catherine II began to acquire works of art from Western Europe, beginning with Dutch and Flemish paintings. Catherine bought individual works and also whole collections; in addition, she commissioned a number of paintings.

Gallery of 1812, the Winter Palace (State Hermitage) (G.S. Alekseev, 1835)

The example of Catherine the Great was followed by her grandsons Alexander I and Nicholas I. The last was particularly important as he extended the collection and, after commissioning the 'New Hermitage', opened the museum to the public in 1852. In the later part of the 19C the holdings of the Imperial Hermitage became even more diversified. The great expansion of the collection of Classical antiquities began in 1861 with the purchase of many pieces formerly owned by the Marquis G.P. Campana. The museum also acquired exhibits from Egypt and the Near East, as well as Greek and Scythian objects unearthed in South Russia.

The collection of Western art grew considerably in the 20C. Some works were purchased from private owners in the years before 1917, but it was the Revolution, with the centralisation of the state museums and the nationalisation of private collections, that transformed the holdings of what was now the 'State Hermitage'. The Stroganov, Shuvalov, Yusupov, and other aristocratic collections greatly increased the number of old masters owned by the museum. More remarkable was the transfer to the Hermitage in 1948 of Impressionist and Post-Impressionist paintings from the Shchukin and Morozov collections (p 260).

In 1922 the Winter Palace was made into part of the art museum. New

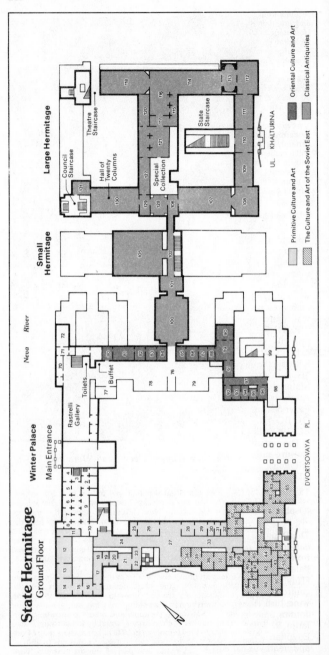

State Hermitage
Ground Floor

Winter Palace

Small Hermitage

Large Hermitage

Neva River

Main Entrance

Rastrelli Gallery

Toilets

Buffet

Council Staircase

Theatre Staircase

Hall of Twenty Columns

Special Collection

State Staircase

UL. KHALTURINA

DVORTSOVAYA PL.

Oriental Culture and Art

Classical Antiquities

Primitive Culture and Art

The Culture and Art of the Soviet East

sections were added, on Russian culture, primitive cultures, and oriental culture and art. It must also be added that, having expanded so much, the State Hermitage now suffered from the sale abroad of a great many important works, including paintings by Rembrandt, Rubens, Titian, and the Van Eycks, as well as a large number of prints. This was partly due to a lack of exhibition space, but even more because of Soviet Russia's pressing need in the 1920s and 1930s for foreign currency to pay for the import of machinery. At the beginning of war with Germany in 1941 the treasures of the Hermitage were evacuated to Sverdlovsk in the Urals. During the Blockade the museum buildings were hit by 30 shells and two bombs, and they also suffered from a lack of heat and maintenance. Despite this, part of the State Hermitage was reopened as early as 4 November 1945.

At the time of writing the State Hermitage is beginning a long-term major modernisation programme; the aim is to bring its facilities up to world class, certainly by the time of the tercentenary of Leningrad in 2003. This programme will include conversion of adjoining buildings to exhibition and technical space and, in the existing buildings, the rearrangement of exhibition halls and the provision of better visitor services. The description below was accurate as of autumn 1990, but presumably the 1990s will see a period first of limited access and, in the longer term, altered and improved facilities.

WINTER PALACE, GROUND FLOOR

Beyond the main entrance is a foyer containing ticket kiosks; cloakrooms are to the right. To the left extends the long, columned Rastrelli Gallery, the main route into the palace and to the state rooms and exhibits on the 1st floor (see below, p 255).

To the right, through R. 2, is a second entrance leading to the W wing and the **Department of Primitive Culture and Art**. The department which specialises in primitive cultures in what is now the USSR was founded in 1931.

R. 11. Palaeolithic and Mesolithic artefacts, including tools and primitive figures. **RR. 12–14, and 24.** Neolithic, Bronze, and Iron Age exhibits. **RR. 15–18.** The culture and art of the Scythians, who lived in S Russia from the 7C to the 3C BC; the collection contains the 6C BC *Golden Stag* found near the village of Kostromskoye. **RR. 19–20.** Material from the forest steppe region (7C to 4C BC). **RR. 21–23.** Artefacts from the Tuektinskiye Kurgans. **R. 26.** Artefacts from the Pazyrykskiye Kurgans. **R. 24.** Finno-Ugric, Baltic, and Slavic cultures (7C BC–12C AD). **R. 33.** Culture and art of the southern steppe (3C BC–10C AD).

The remaining part of the W wing houses the **Department of the Culture and Art of the Soviet East**, which was founded in 1920 by the orientalist I.A. Orbeli. **RR. 34–39.** Central Asia (4C BC–early 20C AD); of special note is a huge 14C bronze cauldron commissioned by Tamerlane. **RR. 55–61, 66.** Caucasus (10C BC–19C AD). **RR. 67–69.** Golden Horde (13C–14C AD). **RR. 41–45.** *Oriental Special Collection* (Osobaya Kladovaya Vostoka).

The **Department of Oriental Culture and Art** includes material from eastern cultures which are not part of the present USSR. Material from this department is on exhibition in the E wing of the Winter Palace. This may be reached via the foyer and the Rastrelli Gallery. (This is the main entrance to the State Hermitage, with a ticket control point; souvenir kiosks are situated in the hall.) To reach the E wing turn right at the end of the Rastrelli Gallery, just before the Jordan Staircase. Between RR. 84 and 85 a corridor leads into the large **R. 100.**, which lies directly under the Hall of St. George: Egyptian antiquities, 4C BC–3C AD. **RR. 89–91.** Babylon, Assyria, and nearby areas of the Middle East (4C BC–3C AD).

SMALL HERMITAGE, GROUND FLOOR

This floor, which begins beyond a short flight of stairs at the end of R. 100, originally housed the palace stables and riding-school. A long hall (R. 102) leads to the Large Hermitage.

LARGE HERMITAGE, GROUND FLOOR

This floor is devoted to the **Department of Classical Antiquities**. The logical starting point for viewing the collection is R. 111 in the SE corner of the building (turn right from R. 106 and continue through the sequence of rooms).

R. 111–114, 121. Ancient Greece (8C AD–2C AD). (R. 112, in the SE corner, is an especially impressive room with grey columns and pilasters.) Vase by *Euphronius*, The Swallow's Arrival (late 6C BC). Statue by *Pythagorus of Rhegium*, Hyacinth (early 5C BC). Roman copies of Greek 5C BC sculptures by Myron, Polyclitus, and Phidias. Roman copies of Greek 4C BC sculptures by Scopas, Praxiteles, and Lysippus (Heracles Fighting the Lion). Hellenistic art, including the Gonzaga Cameo (3C BC). **R. 115–117, 121.** The Greek Black Sea colonies (7C BC–3C AD): especially those near the Straits of Kerch, the Cimmerian Bosporus: Sphinx from Phanagoreia (5C BC), Attic vases, and other ceramics. (RR. 115–117 are an interconnected series of rooms, with walls painted a striking red.)

The entrance to the *Special Collection (Osobaya Kladovaya) of the State Hermitage is in R. 121. Founded in 1925, but based on pre-revolutionary Hermitage collections, the Special Collection comprises some of the most precious items in the museum, made of gold, silver, and precious stones. The collection falls into two sections. The first is golden artefacts discovered on what is now Soviet territory and originating in various ancient cultures, of which the most important are the Greek Black Sea colonies and the Scythian and Sarmatian tribes. The second section comprises W European and Russian items from the Renaissance to the 19C. Included are jewellery, snuff boxes, and church ornaments. It is normally necessary to arrange a visit in advance through Intourist; visitors are taken around in groups by an English-speaking guide; the cost is about £5.00.

RR. 130–131 Ancient Italy (7C–2C BC) R. 130, which may be reached from R. 121 via RR. 127 and 129, is one of the finest in the museum and is known as the *Hall of Twenty Columns. Designed by von Klenze, it contains elaborately painted beams and two long rows of granite columns. In R. 130 and in **R. 131** beyond are Etruscan ceramics of the 7C–6C BC, including the black Queen of Vases, found in Cumae in the 19C.

RR. 106–109, 127–129 Ancient Rome (1C BC–4C AD). RR. 108–109 are located in the SW corner, and may be reached through RR. 121, 127, and 129 and the W wing. **R. 108.**, with four pairs of fluted columns, was intended by von Klenze to represent the courtyard of a Hellenistic or Roman house. Graeco-Roman decorative art. The Tauride Venus (**R. 109.**) is a 1C–2C AD copy of a 3C BC statue. It was acquired by Peter the Great from Pope Clement XI as Russia's first Classical sculpture; the name derives from Petersburg's Tauride Palace, where it was kept until the mid-19C.

R. 127. Rome, 1C BC–1C AD. Portraits, including statues of Octavian Augustus (1C AD), Gaius Caesar (1C AD), and Philip the Arabian (3C AD). **R. 129.** Roman decorative art. **R. 128.** Roman architectural fragments. In the middle of this cross-shaped room stands the jasper Kolyvanskaya Vase; this is the largest in the museum and was created in 1829–43 at the Kolyvanskaya Lapidary Works in W Siberia. **R. 106.** (by the corridor leading from the Small Hermitage). Fragments from the Forum of Trajan. **R. 107.** Roman sculpture, 1C–4C AD. Giant (3.5m) statue of Jupiter (1C AD) from the Villa of Domitian.

LARGE HERMITAGE, 1ST FLOOR

This floor is devoted to the collections of the **Department of Western European Art**. The most convenient route from R. 107 and the Roman collection on the Ground Floor is via RR. 106 and 128–131 and up the **Council Staircase** (Sovetskaya Lestnitsa) to R. 206, which is next to the beginning of the Italian section. The Council Staircase is in a white hall with fluted pillars and is notable for its iron railings. It was designed by Stakenschneider in the mid-19C and takes its name from its use by members of the State Council.

The collection of **Italian art** occupies some 30 rooms in the N and central parts of this floor. **R. 207**, in the NW corner. 13C–14C. *Simone Martini* (c 1284–1344). Virgin of the Annunciation (1330s). **RR. 208** and **209**. 15C *Fra Angelico* (1387–1455), Virgin and Child with St. Dominic and St. Thomas Aquinas (c 1440). **R. 210.** Florentine sculpture of the 15C. **RR. 211–213.** 15C–early 16C. *Cima da Conegliano* (1459–c 1518), Annunciation. *Sandro Botticelli* (1445–1510).

R. 214. *Leonardo da Vinci* (1452–1519). The only two Soviet Leonardos are in the Hermitage collection. The so-called Benois Madonna (c 1478) takes its name from the family which once owned it. Madonna Litta (c 1490). **R. 215.** Pupils of Leonardo. **R. 216.** Mannerist paintings of the early 16C.

The inner corridor of the N wing has work of the Venetian School. **R. 217** is off R. 207 and near the NW corner and the Council Staircase. 15C–early 16C. *Giorgione* (c 1478–1510), Judith (c 1504). **RR. 218–219.** 16C paintings. **R. 220.** 16C bas-reliefs. **R. 221.** *Titian* (c 1487/90–1576), including Portrait of a Young Woman (c 1530s), Danaë (1550s). **R. 222.** *Paolo Veronese* (1528–88), Mourning of Christ (1582). There is more work by Veronese in R. 237 in the central wing; this may be reached via RR. 216, 224, and 227.

To the right of R. 224 is the **Theatre Staircase**, intended as the entrance to the Hermitage Theatre. The attractive **Foyer** of the theatre, designed by L.N. Benois in 1902–04 and now used for temporary exhibitions, is to the left (above the Zimnyaya Kanavka, or Winter Canal). **R. 227**, beyond RR. 224 and 226, is the *Loggia of **Raphael** (Lodzhii Rafaelya), built by Quarenghi along the Zimnyaya Kanavka in the 1780s. This is a copy of a similarly-named gallery which was installed in the Vatican in the early 16C with murals designed by Raphael; the murals here were produced for Catherine the Great in 1778–85 by a group of artists led by the Tyrolese *Christopher Unterberger* (1732–93). **R. 229**, running parallel to the gallery, contains original works by *Raphael* (1483–1520): Madonna Conestabile (c 1500), Holy Family (1505).

The central section of the Large Hermitage begins with **R. 230**, which contains the only work by *Michelangelo* (1475–1564) in the Soviet Union, the statue of a Crouching Youth (early 1530s). Frescoes by the School of Raphael. **R. 231.** Late-16C–early-17C paintings. **R. 232.** *Caravaggio* (1573–1610), The Lute-Player (1595). Sculpture by *Gianlorenzo Bernini* (1598–1680). **R. 233.** Baroque paintings of the

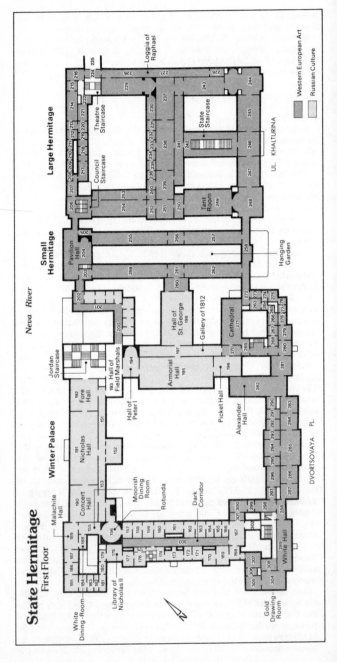

State Hermitage
First Floor

Winter Palace

Small Hermitage

Large Hermitage

Neva River

White Dining-Room

Malachite Hall

Concert Hall

Library of Nicholas II

Gold Drawing-Room

Nicholas Hall

Fore Hall

Jordan Staircase

Hall of Field Marshals

Hall of Peter I

Moorish Dining Room

Rotunda

Dark Corridor

Armorial Hall

Hall of St. George

Gallery of 1812

Picket Hall

Alexander Hall

Cathedral

White Hall

Pavilion Hall

Hanging Garden

Tent Room

Council Staircase

Theatre Staircase

Loggia of Raphael

State Staircase

UL. KHALTURINA

DVORTSOVAYA PL.

Western European Art

Russian Culture

School of Genoa. **R. 234.** School of Naples. **R. 235.** 18C, various schools. **R. 236.** Venice, 18C.

R. 238 is von Klenze's impressive central hall. Monumental Italian paintings of the 17C–18C. *Giambattista Tiepolo* (1696–1770), *Canaletto* (1697–1768) and others. **R. 237**, to the E, is similar. Paintings by *Paolo Veronese, Jacopo Tintoretto* (1518–94), and the School of Bologna. **R. 241** contains a curious collection of panels by *I.G. Hiltenschperger* (1806–90) on the development of Greek Classical painting. Sculptures by *Antonio Canova* (1757–1822) and *Bertel Thorvaldsen* (1770–1844).

Beyond R. 241 is the splendid **State Staircase** (Paradnaya Lestnitsa), **R. 242.** The stairs are flanked by walls of yellow marble; at the 1st Floor level are two rows of ten columns and a gallery with many pieces of 19C sculpture.

The collection of **Spanish art** is contained in only two rooms, but it is very rich. **R. 240** is near the W end of the central section of the Large Hermitage. Paintings by *Luis de Morales* (1509–86) and others. *El Greco* (1541–1614), St. Peter and St. Paul (1614). **R. 239**, next to the central hall. 17C and 19C. *Diego Velázquez* (1599–1660), The Breakfast (c 1617). *Bartolomé Murillo* (1617–82), Boy with a Dog (1650s). *Francisco de Zurbaran* (1598–1664), Girlhood of the Madonna (c 1660). Paintings by *José Ribera* (1591–1652) and *Goya* (1746–1828).

The exhibition of art from the Low Countries actually begins in R. 261 of the Small Hermitage (p 254). The first related room in the Large Hermitage is **R. 247**, near the SW corner, which is the start of a section on **Flemish 17C art**. *Peter Paul Rubens* (1577–1640), Descent from the Cross (c 1615), Portrait of a Chambermaid (c 1625), and a number of other paintings. **R. 246**, next to the State Staircase. *Anthony van Dyck* (1599–1641), Self-Portrait (1620s). **R. 245.** Flemish painters, including *Jacob Jordaens* (1593–1678), *Frans Snyders* (1579–1657), and *David Teniers the Younger* (1610–90).

Before continuing the exhibition of art from the Low Countries (in R. 249) it may be convenient to examine the rooms next to R. 245. **R. 244** (in the SE corner). A splendid room with two tiers of columns which is used for temporary exhibits. **R. 243.** W European arms and armour of the 15C–17C.

The exhibition from the great period of **Dutch art** is situated in the W wing of the Large Hermitage. **RR. 249–252.** R. 249, near the SW corner, was given a unique pitched roof by von Klenze, and is called the **Tent Room** (Shatrovyy Zal). *Jan van Goyen* (1596–1656), *Salomon van Ruysdael* (1600/02–70), *Frans Hals* (1580/85–1666), *Bartholomeus van der Helst* (1613–70). **R. 254.** *Rembrandt* (1606–69). The State Hermitage possesses 26 canvases by this master, including Flora (1634), Abraham's Sacrifice of Isaac (1635), Danaë (1636), and The Holy Family (1645). **R. 253.** Pupils of Rembrandt.

SMALL HERMITAGE, 1ST FLOOR

The most striking room in the Small Hermitage is situated at the N end, the *Pavilion Hall** (Pavil'onnyy Zal) or **R. 204.** Stakenschneider designed this white galleried room in the 1850s; a two-tiered row of fluted columns runs down the middle, and in the walls at either end are apses with fountains. Splendid chandeliers hang from the ceiling, but the natural light is excellent: to the right windows look onto the Neva, to the left is the Hanging Garden created in Catherine's time. In front of the French windows leading to the garden is a mosaic floor panel copied from a Roman bath. A large case on the Neva side

contains the remarkable Peacock Clock with several ingenious
mechanical animals. The Englishman James Cox made the clock and
Potyomkin presented it to Catherine II.

The long row of rooms on the E side, **RR. 255–257**, was once called
the Peter Gallery, as it housed an exhibit of the personal possessions
of Peter I. The similar rooms on the W side were known as the
Romanov Gallery, and the walls were hung with paintings of the
Imperial family. **R. 259**, the N part of the former Romanov Gallery,
now contains **W European applied art of the 11C–15C**.

The display of **Netherlandish art** of the 15C–16C is partly situated
in the W gallery, but begins in the adjacent R. 260 (next to the Hall of
St. George). **R. 260** is also known as the Apollo Room. Altar paintings.
R. 261, the central part of the W gallery. *Robert Campin* (c 1380–
1444) and *Rogier van der Weyden* (c 1400–1464). **RR. 262, 258, 248**
(the last is in the SW corner of the Large Hermitage). Paintings by
Lucas van Leyden (1494–1533) and *Pieter Bruegel the Younger*
(c 1564–1638), The Fair (a copy of a work by his father), as well as a
number of portraits. The long corridor of R. 258 was in an earlier form
the only entrance to Catherine's Hermitage from the Winter Palace.
By the door the Empress hung her 'Rules' calling for informality
among those who met here: 'Leave all ranks at the door, along with
hats and swords'.

WINTER PALACE, 1ST FLOOR

The rooms on this floor were the most impressive part of the Imperial
palace, especially the two suites in the N and E wings. These rooms,
however, will be discussed later; the present section continues the
description of the Department of Western European Art in the S
wing, which may be reached directly from R. 258 of the Small
Hermitage.

The SE corner of the Winter Palace has an interesting history. Here were
located the rooms of the first resident, Emperor Peter III, and later of his widow;
Catherine the Great died near her bedroom here in 1796. Later this became the
IInd Guest Suite (II-ya Zapasnaya Polovina) where high dignitaries stayed.

German art is now on display here. **RR. 263–266.** 15C–16C portraits,
including work by *Lucas Cranach the Elder* (1472–1553). Etchings by
Albrecht Dürer (1471–1528) and Hans Holbein the Younger (1497–
1543). **RR. 267–268.** German applied art and 17C–18C paintings.

Western European porcelain of the 18C–20C is exhibited in **RR.
269–271**, which lie to the right of the exit from R. 268. The centre of
the collection is in R. 271, which was the former ***Cathedral** of the
palace and of the Imperial family, a centre of Court ceremony. Many
royal weddings took place here including, in 1894, that of Nicholas II
and Alice of Hesse. The cathedral was rebuilt after the great fire of
1837 by Stasov, who retained Rastrelli's lavish Baroque design with
its gilt pillars and moulding.

Most of the S wing of the Winter Palace is devoted to **French art.
RR. 273–274** are in the SE corner next to the beginning of the
German collection and off the corridor from the Small Hermitage.
15C–16C. Limoges enamels, Court art of the Fontainebleau School,
porcelain by *Bernard Palissy* (1510–89). **RR. 275–278.** Early and
middle 17C. *Louis Le Nain* (c 1593–1648). **R. 279.** *Nicolas Poussin*
(1594–1665). **R. 280.** *Claude Lorrain* (1600–82). **R. 281.** Late 17C.

The white **Alexander Hall** (R. 282), with its richly-decorated
arched ceiling, was designed in 1838 by Bryullov to commemorate

the victory of 1812. Scenes from the war are depicted in bas-reliefs, and at the far end is an image of Alexander I in the guise of a Slavic warrior (a large painting of the Emperor once hung underneath). The room now contains a collection of W European silver. The section of the palace from here to R. 289, as the 1st Guest Suite (I-ya Zapasnaya Polovina), was used for such distinguished foreign visitors as the Kaiser, the King of Italy, and the French President.

The exhibition of **French art** continues. In the corridor on the courtyard side (**RR. 290–297**) is a rich display of French applied art. **R. 283** (in the parallel corridor on the side of Dvortsovaya Pl.). 17C portraits and 18C furniture. **R. 284.** *Antoine Watteau* (1684–1721). **R. 285.** Rococo paintings by *François Boucher* (1703–70). Sculpture by *Etienne Maurice Falconet* (1716–91) (creator of the Bronze Horseman). **R. 286.** 18C portraits, sculpture by Falconet. **R. 287.** Paintings by *J.B.S. Chardin* (1689–1779). *Jean-Antoine Houdon* (1741–1828), statue of Voltaire (1781). **R. 288.** *Jean Baptiste Greuze* (1725–1805) and *Jean Honoré Fragonard* (1732–1806). **R. 289.** Painting, sculpture, and applied art of the late 18C. (Further French art may be found on the 2nd Floor, beginning in R. 314.) R. 289 is known as the **White Hall** and was created by Bryullov in 1838 using the model of a Roman bath; the high arched ceiling has elaborate carving.

The exhibition of **British art** begins off R. 288 (left). **R. 298.** 17C–early 18C. **R. 299.** *Joshua Reynolds* (1723–92). **R. 300.** *Thomas Gainsborough* (1727–88), Portrait of a Lady (Duchess of Beaufort?) (late 1770s). **R. 301.** 19C paintings. **R. 302** (off R. 167, left). *William Morris* (1834–96) tapestry, Adoration, after sketches by Edward Burne-Jones (1833–98).

The great state rooms on the 1st Floor of the Winter Palace begin at the top of the magnificent *Jordan Staircase (Iordanskaya Lestnitsa), which is also the main route from the Rastrelli Gallery (R. 1) on the Ground Floor. The name of the staircase came from the annual Jordan Festival or the 'Blessing of the Waters'; on 6 January (o.s.) the Imperial family descended these stairs to take part in the ceremonial blessing of the Neva. It is also called the State (Paradnaya) or Main (Glavnaya) Staircase, and was used by foreign ambassadors presenting their credentials. The Baroque staircase was designed by Rastrelli and restored by Stasov after the fire of 1837. The overall effect is one of lightness: on the N and E sides are windows, with mirrors set opposite them. The walls and staircase present an expanse of white Carrara marble, with gilded moulding and allegorical statues. On the W side are paired columns of grey granite (Rastrelli's originals were pink). The painting on the ceiling depicts Olympus.

The state rooms consist of two suites, the Neva Enfilade (Nevskaya Anfilada) running parallel to the river, and the Great Enfilade (Bol'shaya Anfilada) which meets it at right angles at the Jordan Staircase. Here took place the Great Court ceremonies. An example was the New Year celebrations on the late morning of 1 January 1900 when the Imperial family walked in procession from the Malachite Hall (R. 189) (next to their private apartments) through the Neva and Great Enfilades to the Cathedral (R. 271). The assembled guests were positioned by rank, with the more honoured categories being nearer to the apartments of the Tsar. The members of the Court stood in the Concert Hall (R. 190), and next came the Nicholas Hall (R. 191) and the Fore Hall (R. 192), both full of military officers. In the Hall of Field Marshals (R. 193), S of the Jordan Staircase, were gathered mayors and important merchants, and in the Armorial Hall (R. 195) were lesser officials and wives (the latter in Russian national costume). The procession consisted of the Court (in pairs, with the most junior in front), the Imperial family, and the ladies-in-waiting and maids of honour. After the church service the Emperor received greetings in the Hall of St. George

*'The Winter Palace has been Taken!' (V.A. Serov, 1954).
The revolutionary soldier and worker stand at the bottom
of the Jordan Staircase*

(R. 198). The guard of honour was positioned along the route: Grenadier Guards
in the Picket Hall (R. 196) (next to the Cathedral), Cossack Guards in the Hall of
Field Marshals, and Chevalier Guards in the Nicholas Hall. In another annual
ceremony, the Blessing of the Waters, élite Guards units were drawn up in these
halls, with arms and regimental standards.

The **Fore Hall** (Aванzal) (**R. 192**), directly at the top of the Jordan
Staircase, is the first room in the **Neva Enfilade**. Stasov rebuilt it after

the fire of 1837, a large, square, and relatively simply-decorated hall. Like the hall which follows, it is now used for temporary exhibitions.

The **Nicholas Hall (R. 191)** is one of the largest in the palace. As many as 5000 people gathered here for the great Imperial balls of the winter season; a champagne buffet was held in the Fore Hall, the Rotunda (R. 156) and the Gallery of 1812 (R. 197), and after the dancing there was a meal in the Hall of St. George. The Nicholas Hall was rebuilt by Stasov; massive Corinthian columns run along the walls and hanging from the ceiling is a row of chandeliers. The name dates from 1856 when Alexander II installed a portrait of his father (Nicholas I) here; the room is also known as the Great Hall (Bol'shoy Zal). Here, soon after his accession, Nicholas II delivered an address rejecting the 'senseless dreams' of those who wanted to limit the autocracy.

The last great room in the suit is the **Concert Hall** (Kontsertnyy Zal) **(R. 190)**, where smaller balls of the Imperial era were held. This room also was restored by Stasov; set on the cornice above the colonnade are statues of Muses. On display here is Russian silver of the 17C–20C, including the 18C coffin of Alexander Nevskiy.

The Imperial family gathered for ceremonies in the ***Malachite Hall** (Malakhitovyy Zal) **(R. 189)**, which is smaller and lower than the preceding halls, but gorgeously decorated with columns and pilasters faced with a bright green malachite. It was designed after the fire of 1837 by Bryullov. The room now houses a collection of objects decorated with malachite, but in the latter part of 1917 it was used for cabinet meetings of Kerensky's Provisional Government. On the night of 25–26 October 1917, when the palace was being fired at from the Peter-Paul Fortress across the river, the ministers withdrew to the adjacent **White Dining-Room R. 188**), where they were arrested.

To see the other great rooms, return through the Neva Enfilade to the Jordan Staircase.

The **Great Enfilade** begins with the **Hall of Field Marshals** (Fel'dmarshal'skiy Zal) **(R. 193)**, to the left of the Jordan Staircase. The room was originally designed in the 1830s by Montferrand, the builder of St. Isaac's Cathedral; the disastrous fire of 1837 broke out here, and Montferrand's construction may have been partly to blame. It once contained portraits of Russian generals, and some military themes survive in the decoration.

Montferrand's second room was the **Hall of Peter the Great** (Petrovskiy Zal) or Small Throne Room **(R. 194)**. It dates from 1833 and was rebuilt after the 1837 fire; a nearby shell explosion during the Blockade caused much damage and necessitated further restoration. The room is relatively small but lavishly decorated, with deep red velvet-covered walls and gilded columns and, above, an elaborate arched ceiling. In the niche hangs a painting of Peter the Great and Minerva by *Jacopo Amigoni* (c 1682–1752); the oak and silver Tsarist throne was made in London.

The **Armorial Hall** (Gerbovyy Zal) **(R. 195)** takes its name from the coat of arms of Russian provinces borne by sculptured groups of warriors in the corners. Around the room, to the level of the cornice, are pairs of gilded columns. The main architect of the hall was Stasov, who rebuilt it after 1837. W European silver (17C–18C) is now displayed here. The final room of the Great Enfilade is known as the **Picket Hall** (Piketnyy Zal) **(R. 196)**, as here the sentries or 'pickets' were mustered. A small room decorated with martial themes, it is also the work of Stasov.

The *Gallery of 1812 (Galereya 1812 goda) (R. 197) runs parallel to the Armorial Hall. The long arched room was designed by Rossi and intended for portraits of the victors in the campaign against Napoleon; originally opened in 1826, it was restored by Stasov after the fire.

The inspiration for the gallery was the Waterloo Chamber at Windsor Castle and it was in Englishman, George Dawe (1781–1829), who was commissioned to produce most of the paintings of Russian generals (and also a portrait of Wellington). The equestrian portrait of Alexander I at the end of the gallery (right) is by Franz Krüger (1797–1857), who also painted King Friedrich Wilhelm III; the third ally, Franz I of Austria, was portrayed by Peter Krafft (1780–1856). The gallery also contains large paintings of Kutuzov, Barclay de Tolly, and Grand Duke Konstantin Pavlovich, as well as over 300 smaller portraits.

The giant **Hall of St. George** (Georgiyevskiy Zal) (R. 198) is also known as the Great Throne Room. Originally designed by Quarenghi, it was part of an extension added to the palace in the late 1780s (Rastrelli had intended the throne room to be in the NW corner). The room was officially opened on St. George's Day, 1795. At the far end was the Imperial throne, now replaced, rather incongruously, by a mosaic map of the USSR once displayed at the Paris and New York World Fairs in the 1930s; above is a bas-relief of St. George slaying the dragon. Quarenghi's original hall perished in 1837, but it was rebuilt by Stasov and Yefimov along generally similar lines. The overall effect is more austere, as the walls and the paired columns which rise to cornice level are now faced with white Carrara marble. The Hall of St. George was used for the great occasions of state, such as receptions for distinguished subjects or the diplomatic corps. Here in 1906 the Emperor delivered an address at the opening of the State Duma (parliament), the body which represented the first check to his autocratic powers.

To see the smaller rooms of the N and W wings, return to the Hall of Field Marshals (R. 193).

The NE corner of the Winter Palace once served as the VIIth Guest Suite (VII-ya Zapasnaya Polovina) where Eastern potentates like the Shah of Persia, the Emir of Bokhara, and the Khan of Khiva stayed. The corridor leading to the right (E) from the Hall of Field Marshals towards the Small Hermitage now contains W European tapestries (**RR. 200–202**).

The exhibition halls of the **Department of Russian Culture** (est. 1941) begin to the right of R. 202, in the outer corridor of rooms, **RR. 147–150**. Applied art, arms, and utensils from Early Russia, 5C–15C.

The exhibition continues beyond R. 193 in the corridor running along the courtyard side of the Neva Enfilade; this was once known as the Eastern Gallery. **RR. 151–152.** Icons, manuscripts, and applied art from Muscovy, 15C–17C; R. 152 was formerly a Winter Garden. **RR. 153, 155–161.** Russian culture, late 17C–early 18C, the pivotal period of Peter the Great. **R. 156**, the **Rotunda**, was originally hung with portraits of Russian rulers. It was redesigned by Bryullov after Montferrand's original was destroyed by fire. The handsome domed room now contains the uniform worn by Peter at the Battle of Poltava (1709). **R. 155** (right), the **Moorish Dining-Room** (Arapskaya Stolovaya), was created by Bryullov in 1838–39; on display here now are busts of Peter and Menshikov by *B.C. Rastrelli* (1675–1744), father of the architect of the Winter Palace. **R. 157**, to the S of the Rotunda. Engravings of St. Petersburg. **RR. 158–160.** Early 18C furniture, lathes used by Peter, and a striking effigy of the Emperor by B.C. Rastrelli (1725).

R. 161 was once the Dining-Room of Alexander II. In 1880 there was an attempt to assassinate the Tsar by exploding a dynamite bomb in the room directly below. Eleven soldiers perished, but Alexander was unhurt; he was in another room at the time of the explosion. The man who planted the bomb was a member of 'People's Will', Stepan Khalturin, and the street to the S of the Large Hermitage now bears his name. A carriage used by Peter I is now on display in this room. **RR. 162–167.** Russian portraits and applied art from the latter half of the 18C.

The centre of the W wing of the Winter Palace is occupied by **R. 303**, which has no windows and is known as the **Dark Corridor**. Before the Revolution the walls were lined with portraits of knights of the Order of St. Andrew. The corridor now contains an impressive number of tapestries from the Low Countries and France.

Emperor Alexander II and his wife Mariya Aleksandrovna (1824–80, formerly Princess of Hesse-Darmstadt) lived in the W and SW part of the palace from the time of their marriage in 1841. Here in 1861 the 'Tsar-Liberator' signed the decree ending serfdom and here, twenty years later, he was brought to die after the bomb attack on the Griboyedov Embankment. The suite of rooms used by the Empress has survived. **R. 307**, to the left of R. 168, is the **Blue Bedroom, R. 306** the **Boudoir**, and **R. 305** the **Raspberry Drawing-Room** (Malinaya Gostinaya). **R. 304** in the SW corner is one of the most lavishly decorated in the palace, the **'Gold Drawing-Room**. This room, with its gold walls and arched ceiling, was designed in 1853, probably by V.A. Schreiber; on display here now is a collection of gems.

The display of Russian culture continues in the suite of rooms in the W wing facing the Admiralty (formerly the private apartments of Alexander II). **RR. 168–173.** Watches, portraits, and applied art from the late 18C.

R. 175 begins the suite of rooms occupied by the last Imperial family; the suite ran around the NW corner of the palace as far as the Malachite Hall. The interiors which had been created here by Bryullov and Stakenschneider for Alexandra Fyodorovna, the wife of Nicholas I, were replaced. **R. 178** is the wood-panelled Gothic **Library of Nicholas II**, created by Meltzer in 1894. For the White Dining Room and the Malachite Hall (RR. 188–189) see p 257. The other rooms in the NW corner (RR. 175–187) contain displays mainly on Russian interior design.

To reach the 2nd Floor and French art of the 19C–20C pass through the Neva and Great Enfilades (RR. 190–196) and ascend the stairs next to R. 269. (An alternative route to the Oriental and Numismatic Collections on the 2nd Floor is by way of the staircase next to R. 174.)

WINTER PALACE, 2ND FLOOR

This is the only part of the State Hermitage at 2nd Floor level which is open to the public. Before the Revolution this was a labyrinth of small rooms used by pages and maids of honour; extensive alterations were required to create exhibition space. Among other exhibits, the world-famous collection of **French art of the 19C–20C** is now housed here. The direct route from the main entrance is along the Rastrelli Gallery (R. 1), up the Jordan Staircase, and through the suite made

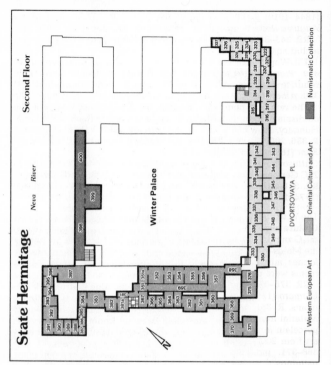

up of RR. 193–196. The staircase next to R. 269 leads up to the beginning of the French section. **R. 314.** Early Classicism. **R. 332** (left). *Jacques-Louis David* (1748–1825) and *François Gérard* (1770–1837). **R. 331.** Paintings by *Eugène Delacroix* (1798–1863) and *J.A.D. Ingres* (1780–1867). Bronzes by *Antoine Barye* (1796–1875). **RR. 329, 328, 325, 322,** and **321.** Barbizon School, including *Théodore Rousseau* (1812–67) and *Jean François Millet* (1814–75). Landscapes by *J.B.C. Corot* (1796–1875) and *Gustave Courbet* (1819–77).

Before describing the collection of work from the later 19C and early 20C mention should be made of the two men who did most to establish it: the Moscow industrialists S.I. Shchukin (1854–1937) and I.A. Morozov (1871–1921). Shchukin began his collection in 1897 and by the time of the Revolution had accumulated over 200 canvases; his taste was daring, and he was an early patron of Matisse and Picasso. Morozov gathered more than a hundred works and took a special interest in the Impressionists, especially Cézanne. Shchukin and Morozov emigrated after 1917 and their collections were nationalised. For a time the collections were held in a Museum of New Western Art in Moscow (now the Academy of Arts), but in 1948 they were divided between the State Hermitage and Moscow's Pushkin Museum.

R. 320. *Edgar Degas* (1834–1917) and *Auguste Renoir* (1841–1919). **R. 319.** *Claude Monet* (1840–1926), Women in a Garden (1860s). **R. 318.** Paintings by *Camille Pissarro* (1830–1903) and *Paul Cézanne* (1839–1906), The Banks of the Marne (1888), Still Life (1890). **R. 317.** *Vincent van Gogh* (1853–90), The Bush (1888). *Henri Rousseau*

(1844–1910). **R. 316.** *Paul Gauguin* (1848–1903). **R. 315.** Sculpture by *Auguste Rodin* (1840–1917).

RR. 343–345. Thirty-five canvases by *Henri Matisse* (1869–1954), including The Dance (1910). **RR. 346–347.** (*Pablo Picasso* (1881–1973). Work from the artist's Blue, Rose, and Cubist periods. **RR. 348–349.** *Pierre Bonnard* (1867–1947), *Edouard Vuillard* (1868–1940), *Maurice Vlaminck* (1876–1958), and *André Derain* (1880–1954). **R. 350.** *Albert Marquet* (1875–1947).

The remaining parts of the collection of modern W European art, on display in the inner corridor, are not so outstanding. **R. 334.** 20C Hungary, Poland, Romania, and Czechoslovakia. **R. 335.** Germany. **R. 336.** 20C USA, including a large collection presented by *Rockwell Kent* (1882–1971). **R. 337.** 20C Finland and Belgium. **R. 338.** *Renato Guttuso* (born 1912) and other 20C Italian painters. **R. 339.** 19C–early 20C Germany, Finland, and Spain. **R. 340.** 19C Belgium and Holland. **RR. 341–342.** 19C Germany, including paintings by *C.D. Friedrich* (1774–1840) and *Max Liebermann* (1847–1935).

The W wing is occupied by exhibits from the **Department of Oriental Culture and Art** (material from Soviet Asia, Egypt, and Babylon is on the Ground Floor). The central R. 359 was once part of the Corridor of the Maids of Honour (Freylinskiy Koridor). Alexander II installed his former mistress, Princess Yur'yevskaya, here and in 1917 these rooms were used by Kerensky's adjutants.

RR. 376–375. **Japanese art** of the 17C–20C, including woodcuts by *Utamaro* (1753–1806). The display of **Chinese art** occupies several rooms. **R. 351.** Sculpture and wall-paintings of the 6C–9C. **R. 352.** Material from Khara-Khoto. **RR. 354–362.** Sculpture, paintings, and porcelain from China, 14C–19C. **RR. 363–364.** Fine art and applied art from 20C China. **RR. 365–367.** Mongolia, 1C BC–19C AD. **RR. 368–371.** Indian art of the 17C–20C, including some modern paintings.

The rich collection of **Byzantine art** begins beyond the staircase in **R. 381.** Early Byzantine items, including some unearthed at Khersones in the Crimea. **R. 381a.** Silver and ivory of the 6C–7C. **R. 382.** 10C–12C decorated caskets. 12C–14C icons.

Nicholas I occupied a suite in the NW corner of this floor, as did Alexander III, when he was staying at the Winter Palace. These rooms were also used by Alexander Kerensky, the Prime Minister, during the last months of the Provisional Government in 1917.

The NW corner is now occupied by a display of art from the Middle East. The largest section is devoted to **Persian art. R. 383.** Sassanian silver, mostly discovered in the Ural and Kama regions. **R. 384.** Bronze artefacts. **RR. 385–387.** Ceramics from the 12C–15C. **RR. 391–394.** Persian miniatures, art and handicrafts from the 16C–18C. **R. 388.** Syria and Iraq, 13C–15C. **RR. 389–390.** Egypt, 7C AD–15C. **RR. 395–397.** Turkey, 15C–18C.

The **Numismatic Collection** is located in the courtyard side of the N wing (RR. 398–400), and comprises a rich collection of coins and medals from Russia and abroad.

21 Nevskiy Prospekt

This Rte follows the most important part of NEVSKIY PROSPEKT, Leningrad's main thoroughfare, from the Admiralty to Pl. Vosstaniya, a distance of nearly 3km. The starting point is near NEVSKIY PROSPEKT METRO STATION, while PLOSHCHAD' VOSSTANIYA METRO STATION is located at the far end. Bus No. 44, and Trolleybuses No. 1, 7 and 10 follow the whole Rte.

Nevskiy Pr. is probably the most famous street in all of Russia, and has witnessed many important events in the country's history. For many years it has been the main shopping and entertainment centre in the city. From the point of view of architecture it is a great success, with a careful balance maintained between the width of the avenue and the height of the buildings; around the Nevskiy were created most of the great town planning ensembles, including Dvortsovaya Pl., Pl. Iskusstv, and Pl. Ostrovskovo. The range of styles goes from the mid-18C Baroque to the Art Nouveau of the early 20C, but with a predominance of excellent Classical buildings.

The avenue was laid out in the earliest years of St Petersburg as a link between the Admiralty and the old Novgorod Road (now Ligovskiy Pr., Pl. 10; 8). As it grew it became known as the Great Perspective Road (Bol. Pershpektivnaya Doroga) and took its present name after the completion of the Alexander Nevskiy Monastery at the far end. (From the Revolution until 1944 it was called Pr. 25-vo Oktyabrya or Avenue of 25 October—after the date of the Bolshevik uprising—but this never found popular acceptance.)

Nevskiy Pr., 1 (right), was built in 1910–11 as the *Private Commercial Bank*, one of the many financial institutions concentrated on the Nevskiy and on what are now Ul. Gogolya and Ul. Gertsena; the district was known before the Revolution as the 'Petersburg City'. The Imperial Ministry of Finance was nearby, in the Main Staff building, and half of the city's banks were situated on the Nevskiy. No. 7/9, for example, now the *Leningrad Air Terminal*, was built in 1911–12 as the *St. Petersburg Commercial Bank*. The architect, M.M. Peretyatkovich, utilised a mixture of Italian Renaissance styles, and the two rows of arches along the avenue recall the Doge's Palace in Venice.

The first street to the right, UL. GOGOLYA (Pl. 10; 5), takes its name from the writer Nikolay Gogol, who lived from 1833–36 at No. 17; here he wrote 'The Government Inspector' and the first chapters of 'Dead Souls'. (Mal. Morskaya Ul. was renamed Ul. Gogolya in 1902.) The house at Ul. Gogolya, 10, also has a connection with Russian literature as it was the home of Princess N.P. Golitsyna, upon whom Pushkin is said to have based the old Countess in his 'Queen of Spades'. The composer Tchaikovsky died on 25 October 1893 at No. 13/8, the home of his brother Modest, after contracting cholera from drinking unboiled water. This address was also that of the *Vienna Restaurant*, where writers and artists gathered; Lenin came here to meet Bolshevik comrades in 1905–06.

The Free Economic Society, a learned institution founded by Catherine II in 1765, was located until 1844 at Nevskiy Pr., 2 (left); the building was rebuilt to merge in with the Main Staff in Dvortsovaya Pl. The *International Post Office* is at Nevskiy Pr., 6. The buildings at Nos 8 and 10 are interesting examples of early Classicism, built by A.V. Kvasov in the 1760s in accordance with the guidelines of the 'Commission on Masonry Construction'; No. 8 now houses a shop exhibiting for sale the work of Leningrad artists (Lavka Khudozhnikov). *School No. 210*, at Nevskiy Pr., 14, was completed 180 years later, in 1939 (B.R. Rubenenko). (The 18C house here had been demolished in 1915 to make way for yet another bank—never completed.) The wall still carries a grim reminder of the Blockade, a blue and white stencilled sign originally painted in 1941; 'Citizens! During artillery bombardment this side of the street is very dangerous.'

UL. GERTSENA, which begins at the arch of the Main Staff and intersects Nevskiy Pr., is named after the 19C radical thinker A.I. Herzen. The pre-revolutionary name, Bol. Morskaya Ul., came from the Morskaya Sloboda or Naval Settlement, where employees of the nearby Admiralty lived in the 18C. Bol. Morskaya Ul. was among the most fashionable streets in St Petersburg, with banks, jewellers, expensive restaurants and, at the far end, the Imperial Yacht Club and the Hotel Astoriya. Ul. Gertsena, 3–5, to the left of the Nevskiy, was rebuilt by Lidval in 1908–09 as the *Azov-Don Commercial Bank*; the grey Style Moderne building now houses the *Long-Distance Telephone Exchange*. To the right of the Nevskiy, at Ul. Gertsena, 15, is a building with rusticated granite blocks and eight pillars. This was built by M.M. Peretyatkovich in 1910–15 as the *Russian Bank of Trade and Industry* (Russkiy Torgovo-Promyshlennyy Bank; the initials RTPB can still be seen above the door). The *Kirov Institute of Textile and Light Industry*, a looming grey structure at Ul. Gertsena, 18, was also begun before the Revolution as a bank, although it was only completed in 1931 (L.V. Rudnev and Ya.O. Svirskiy). Aleksey Kosygin, the former Soviet premier, was a student here. The shop of the best-known Russian jewellers, Fabergé, was located at No. 24. A hard-currency *Beriozka Shop* is now located next door, on the corner of Ul. Dzerzhinskovo.

Politseiskii Bridge (engraving by B. Paterson, early 19C). The bridge carrying Nevskiy Prospekt across the Moyka River at this point is now called the Narodnyy Bridge

The large peach-coloured building of the *Barrikada Cinema* (Nevskiy Pr., 15), in the block between Ul. Gertsena and Moyka River, was built in 1768–71 for General-Polizeimeister N.I. Chicherin. A dominant feature of this early Classical structure are the two tiers of columns in the centre of the façade and on the corners; the architect was probably Vallin de la Mothe. Later, in the 19C, it housed the *Blagorodnoye Sobraniye* (or Club of the Nobility). Before the construction of the Chicherin House, this site had been occupied by the Wooden Winter Palace, which Rastrelli built for the Empress Elizabeth in 1755, pending completion of the permanent Winter Palace. On the opposite side of the street, at No. 18, stands the Kotomin House, which V.P. Stasov rebuilt in 1812–15. Located here was the Café Wulf et Beranger, where the poet Pushkin met his second en route to the fatal duel with d'Anthès.

Nevskiy Pr. crosses the Moyka River by the Narodnyy Most (p 331). On the opposite bank, at No. 17 (right), stands one of the finest buildings on the avenue, the dark-green and white *Stroganov Palace* (Pl. 10; 5).

The Stroganovs were one of the leading Russian families, and S.G. Stroganov commissioned Rastrelli to build this great mansion; the work was carried out in 1752–54. The overall appearance is Baroque, with elegant window-surrounds and an abundance of moulding. One can enter the courtyard through the archway on the Nevskiy. The little garden here is decorated with sculpture. The interior is still closed, which must be regretted as some of the fine rooms decorated by A.N. Voronikhin survive. The Stroganovs kept the palace until the Revolution and assembled here one of the finest private art collections in Russia. This was later transferred to the State Hermitage.

The building of the **Dutch Church** (Gollandskaya Ts.) (1830–33) (No. 20) is of interest as the architect P. Jacot combined the church itself (behind the portico) with a much larger structure. Here were located the editorial offices of the early-19C journal 'Notes of the Fatherland'. The many churches of different denominations on this part of the Nevskiy led to its being known as the 'Street of Tolerance'.

UL. ZHELYABOVA (Pl. 10; 5), a tree-lined boulevard which turns left off the Nevskiy, was named after A.I. Zhelyabov, one of the 'People's Will' terrorists who organised the assassination of Alexander II. The first Petersburg theatre founded in 1723 on the site of No. 27 (left), now the **Variety Theatre** (Teatr Estrady). Also located here is the *Leningrad Tourist and Excursion Bureau* (Leningradskoye Byuro Puteshestviy i Ekskursii). The **DLT Department Store** at the end of the block (left) is one of the largest in the city. It was built in 1908–10 as the department store of the Guards Economic Society. Opposite (Ul. Zhelyabova, 6-a) stands the grey and white Classical *Finnish Church* (Finskaya Ts.), built in 1803–05 by G. Paulson. This street was among the most fashionable in pre-revolutionary St. Petersburg. A number of famous people lived here: at No. 15, Chernyshevsky (1850s); at No. 13, both Turgenev (1858–59) and the dancer Nijinsky (early 20C); and at No. 11, Rimsky-Korsakov (1889–93). The Court Stables (Konyushni) were located at the end of the street, and from this came its old name, Bol. Konyushennaya Ul.

The pale yellow Lutheran **Church of St. Peter** (Ts. Sv. Petra), set back from Nevskiy Pr. at No. 22–24, was built in its present form by A.P. Bryullov (1832–38). The exterior with its rounded arches and simple towers owed much to the Romanesque style and marked a new departure in Russian architecture. The two buildings which flank the entrance path date back to the earliest (18C) Lutheran church on this site, and behind the present version is the Baroque mid-18C *Peterschule* (now *School No. 222*); the architect Carlo Rossi and the composer M.P. Mussorgsky were among those who studied here.

On the right the Nevskiy opens onto the site of one of the finest buildings in Leningrad, the *Kazan Cathedral** (Kazanskiy Sobor). (Pl. 10; 5). The first stone church here was demolished to make way for the present structure. The project was first conceived in the reign of Emperor Paul, but work began only after his death, in August 1801, and was completed in 1811. Andrey Voronikhin (1760–1814) was the architect finally chosen for the project. Perhaps the most remarkable feature of Voronikhin's design is the great arc of Corinthian columns, 96 in number and four deep, which stretches for 111m on the N side, facing Nevskiy Pr.; this was inspired by Bernini's colonnade of St. Peter's in Rome. Voronikhin wanted a similar colonnade on the S side of the cathedral, but this was never built. The church itself, oriented at right angles to the colonnade, is surmounted by a dome set on a tall drum with 16 pilasters and 16 windows; the total height is 80m. The decoration of the exterior includes a wealth of sculpture. The bas-reliefs of biblical scenes are the work of I.P. Martos, I.P. Prokof'yev, D. Rachette, and F.G. Gordeyev; set in niches are large bronze statues of St. Vladimir, Alexander Nevskiy (both by S.S. Pimenov), John the Baptist (Martos), and St. Andrew (V.I. Demut-Malinovsky). The N doors are copies of Ghiberti's Gates of Paradise from the Baptistery in Florence.

Since 1932 the Kazan Cathedral has housed the **Museum of the History of Religion and Atheism** (Muzey Istorii Religii i Ateizma). The museum is primarily devoted to anti-religious propaganda, showing the supposed excesses of religious movements from all over the world. Included are documents, paintings, sculpture, false relics, and dioramas (for example, a torture chamber from the Spanish Inquisition).

Despite the presence of the museum, it is possible to get some sense of the original *Interior*. The cathedral takes the shape of a Latin cross. The great dome is supported by four massive pillars, from which extend in all directions pairs of pink granite columns with bronze capitals and bases. The most sacred object in the cathedral, and the source of its name, was the icon of the Virgin of Kazan which Prince Pozharsky carried when he drove the foreign invaders out of Moscow in 1612, during the Time of Troubles. This was said to be a copy of the original icon which had appeared miraculously in the Volga town of Kazan in 1579. The cathedral had many other connections with the history of Russian arms, and before the Revolution was hung with the standards captured in 1812–15. In addition, it is the burial place of Field Marshal M.I. Kutuzov, who commanded the Russian armies in 1812. The grave is in the crypt of the N chapel.

At either end of the great colonnade stand statues of outstanding commanders from the campaign of 1812, *M.I. Kutuzov* (left) and *M.B. Barclay de Tolly* (right). They are both the work of B.I. Orlovsky, and were unveiled in 1837. The square between these statues, in front of the Kazan Cathedral, is associated with Russian political history, beginning with a demonstration in 1876 when G.V. Plekhanov (later one of the founders of Russian Marxism) delivered a fiery speech. The tradition developed with the student and worker demonstrations of 1897, 1901, and 1906, and in February 1917 this square was a centre of the great popular manifestations that culminated in the overthrow of the Romanovs. In the era of glasnost' in the 1980s the square again became a place for informal meetings.

UL. PLEKHANOVA, on the W side of the cathedral, leads past the fine railings designed by Voronikhin. The intricately designed railings are supported by 14 squat Doric columns. The composer A.K. Glazunov lived for most of his life at Ul. Plekhanova, 8–10.

Dom Knigi or House of the Book, the largest bookshop in Leningrad, stands opposite the Kazan Cathedral (Nevskiy Pr., 28). It occupies the former building of the Singer Sewing Machine Co., built, with Art Nouveau details, by P.Yu. Syuzor in 1902–04. The glass globe on the roof, the Singer trademark, is one of Leningrad's landmarks.

The Kazanskiy Most carries Nevskiy Pr. over the Griboyedov Canal (p 334). To the left on the far side is an entrance to NEVSKIY PROSPEKT METRO STATION and, in the same building (Nevskiy Pr., 30), the **Glinka Hall** (Malyy Zal im. M.I. Glinki) of the Philharmonia. This has been a centre of the city's musical life since the early 19C, when the Philharmonic Society organised concerts with outstanding W European musicians. The pianist Anton Rubinstein made his debut here in 1843. Further up the Griboyedov Canal can be seen the cupolas of the Church of the Resurrection, built on the site of Alexander II's assassination (p 334). The Roman Catholic **Church of St. Catherine** (Kostyol Sv. Yekateriny) at Nevskiy Pr., 32–34, was built by Vallin de la Mothe and Rinaldi; construction began in 1762 and was completed only in 1783. The Nevskiy façade, with its arches and columns, represents an interesting mixture of Baroque and Classical styles. Among those buried here were Stanislas Poniatowski (1732–98), lover of Catherine II and last King of Poland, and General J.V.M. Moreau, a French officer who turned against Napoleon and fell at the Battle of Dresden (1813). The Melodiya record shop is located at No. 34.

The so-called 'Silver Row' (Serebryanyye Ryady), built by Quarenghi (1784–87) on the site of the jewellers' stalls, faces the Church of St. Catherine across Nevskiy Pr. (No. 31). The tower next door was part of the **Town Duma**, the pre-revolutionary centre of municipal government. The Duma building, which extends S of the Nevskiy along DUMSKAYA UL., was built in 1799–1804; it has been much extended over the years. In October–November 1917 the Town Duma was a rallying point for the forces which opposed the Soviet take-over. The Classical building beyond the Duma (No. 33-a) was known as the *Portico of the Perinnaya Linaya*; this also has been much altered, but the Portico was basically the work of Rusca (1802–06).

The longest frontage on the Nevskiy (220m) is occupied by the great yellow and white building of the **Gostinyy Dvor Department Store** (Pl. 10; 6).

A 'gostinyy dvor' meant a bazaar, and there were several such establishments in St. Petersburg, some of which survive; this one was known as the Bol'shoy (Great) Gostinyy Dvor. It was begun in 1757 by Rastrelli and completed only in 1785. The façade, with two tiers of arches separated by pilasters, was the work of Vallin de la Mothe. The simple yet practical plan served as a model for several provincial bazaars. Alterations have been carried out over the years, most recently in 1955–67 when the many small shops were incorporated into one huge store, the largest in Leningrad. The main entrance to GOSTINYY DVOR METRO STATION is located in the corner at the far end.

UL. BRODSKOVO (Pl. 10; 6) turns left (N) off the Nevskiy opposite the tower of the Town Duma. It was laid out in 1834 as part of Rossi's ensemble in the square known as Mikhaylovskaya Pl. (now Pl. Iskusstv), and the Russian Museum (the former Mikhail Palace) may be seen down the street. Ul. Brodskovo was formerly Mikhaylovskaya Ul. The present name comes from the painter I.I.

Brodsky, who lived nearby (in the 1920s and 1930s the street was called Ul. Lassalya after the 19C German socialist Ferdinand Lassalle). The *Sadko Restaurant* occupies the first part of the street (left) and beyond stands one of the finest pre-revolutionary hotels, the **Yevropeyskaya**, once known as the Hôtel de l'Europe. It was built in 1873–75 and redecorated by Lidval (1908–10). The **Shostakovich Philharmonia** (Gos. Filarmoniya im. D.D. Shostakovicha) stands opposite the hotel, at the far end of Ul. Brodskovo (No. 2).

This was originally the *Club of the Gentry* (Dvoryanskoye Sobraniye), built in 1834–39 by P. Jacot. Rossi designed the façades and the building was enlarged in the late 19C. Many famous performances have taken place in the Large Hall. Isadora Duncan made her Russian début here in 1904, but the hall is best known for its connection with classical music. The Russian Musical Society, organised by Anton Rubinstein in 1859, staged many concerts of the works of Russian composers in the Club of the Gentry, and great foreign musicians like Wagner, Liszt, and Berlioz appeared here. The Leningrad Philharmonic Orchestra was founded in the early 1920s, on the basis of the Imperial Court Orchestra. One of its most moving concerts was given on 9 August 1942; here, 13km from the front line, the depleted orchestra gave the first Leningrad performance of Shostakovich's 7th (Leningrad) Symphony.

Pl. Iskusstv (Pl. 10; 6) or Square of the Arts (so called after the many cultural institutions here) is one of the finest examples of town planning in Leningrad. It was created by Rossi as Mikhaylovskaya Pl., an ensemble grouped around the Mikhail Palace. The site had formerly been occupied by the wooden orangeries of the 3rd Summer Gardens. In the centre of the oval square stands a **Statue of Pushkin** by M.K. Anikushin, which was unveiled in 1957.

The buildings on the W (left) side of the square begin with the *Jacot House* (No. 5) and the *Golenishchev-Kutuzov* House (No. 3). The latter now houses the **Brodsky House-Museum** (Kvartira-Muzey I.I. Brodskovo).

The artist I.I. Brodsky (1883–1939) lived here from 1924 until his death. Brodsky's portraits and paintings of revolutionary scenes are well known, and many of them are exhibited in the museum. Also on display are some 500 works by Brodsky's teachers and contemporaries, including Repin, Kustodiyev, Yuon, Kramskoy, Surikov, Kuindzhi, and Levitan.

The **Maly Theatre** (Gos. Akademicheskiy Malyy Teatr Opery i Baleta), next to the Brodsky Museum, is Leningrad's second opera and ballet theatre (after the Kirov Theatre).

The building of the Maly (Small) Theatre, which seats 1200, dates from 1831–33. The main architect was A.P. Bryullov, although Rossi designed the façade. Like the Bolshoy Theatre in Moscow and the Kirov Theatre, it was rebuilt in the mid-19C by Cavos. The *Mikhail* (Mikhaylovskiy) *Theatre*, as the Maly was originally known, was used before the Revolution for Russian and French drama and for opera. It was renamed in 1918, and continued to be a centre for opera; Shostakovich's controversial 'Lady Macbeth of Mtsensk' was first performed here in 1934. The ballet company was organised in the Soviet period by F.V. Lopukhov. In the 1970s, under the direction of O.M. Vinogradov, it gained a reputation as an experimental company.

The handsome yellow building of the ***Russian Museum** (Gos. Russkiy Muzey) dominates the square.

Rossi built this in 1819–24 as the *Mikhail* (Mikhaylovskiy) *Palace* for Grand Duke Mikhail Pavlovich (1798–1849), the younger brother of Alexander I and Nicholas I. The main façade looks S onto Pl. Iskusstv. Before the central portico, with eight Corinthian columns, lies a large courtyard with an attractive iron railing. Pimenov and Demut-Malinovsky were responsible for the many reliefs which decorate the building. The N side (rear) of the palace, facing the Mikhail Gardens, is also impressive, with 12 columns set in a broad loggia.

Grand Duke Mikhail's wife was the liberal Yelena Pavlovna (1806–73), Princess of Württemburg, who became a patron of the most enlightened state officials and held a salon here. Later, in 1896–97, Nicholas II had the palace converted into the 'Russian Museum of Emperor Alexander III' in memory of his father; the late Emperor had taken an interest in Russian art, and the new museum which opened its doors in 1898 was intended to be the national collection of such work. The museum was expanded after 1917 by the confiscation of rich private collections. It is now second only to Moscow's Tret'yakov Gallery. The holdings of the Russian Museum provide a comprehensive view of Russian art from Kievan times; they also give interesting insights into the Russian past.

The exhibition halls are spread over three buildings, the first of which is the **Mikhail Palace**. The second is the *Rossi Wing* (Fligel' Rossi) to the left, which was originally the service quarters of the palace. The *Benois Building* (Korpus Benua) is further to the W, on the Griboyedov Canal; it was built in 1912–16 (L.N. Benois).

The entrance is through a basement door on the right side of the main façade of the Mikhail Palace. The basement contains the ticket office, cloakrooms, a buffet, and toilets. A maze of corridors ends with stairs ascending to the **State Vestibule**, a great white central hall. Surrounding the grand staircase at 1st Floor level are 18 Corinthian columns and a gallery with classical sculptures. The **White Hall** (R. 11 on the N side of the palace on the 1st Floor) is the finest room in the palace; an oblong hall with two pairs of Corinthian columns and murals by A. Vighi (1764–1844) (left), it contains a rich collection of period furniture designed (like the hall itself) by Rossi.

Regrettably a large part of the museum—the Rossi Wing and the Benois Building—is at the time of writing under repair and closed for an indefinite period. That relatively small part of the collection which is on show is displayed in a temporary arrangement in the Mikhail Palace. The following is an outline of the most important holdings of the museum without any attempt to show physical layout; hopefully this will be possible in a future edition. (See also 'Notes on History and Culture: Art', p 42.)

*Early Russian Art. Icons from the Novgorod, Pskov, Tver and Moscow Schools. Especially outstanding are: Angel with Golden Hair (12C), Battle between the Men of Suzdal and the Men of Novgorod (15C), Trinity (1671) by *S. Ushakov* (1626–86). Some of the Moscow icons are attributed to *Andrey Rublyov* (c 1360–c 1430) and his pupils.

18C Painting and Sculpture. There is an abrupt change from icons to secular works. Court portraits by *I.N. Nikitin* (1688–1741) and *A. Matveyev* (1701–39). *B.C. Rastrelli* (1675–1744), Life Mask of Peter I (1719). Mid-18C paintings by *A. P. Antropov* (1716–95), *I.P. Argunov* (1727–1802) and others. Portraits by foreign artists working in Russia in the 18C. Large statue of Anna Ivanovna (1741) by B.C. Rastrelli. Portraits, including one of V.N. Surovtseva (late-1780s) by *F.S. Rokotov* (1735–1808). Religious and historical paintings by *A.P. Losenko* (1737–73). Sculptures by *F.I. Shubin* (1740–1805). Paintings by **D.G. Levitsky* (1735–1822) ('the Russian Gainsborough') including portraits of Khrushchova and Kovanskaya (1773).

Early and Middle 19C Painting and Sculpture. Portraits by *V.L. Borovikovsky* (1757–1825). Sculpture by *I.P. Martos* (1754–1835); monument to Ye.S. Kurakina. Large Academic canvases by *F.A. Bruni* (1801–74), *G.I. Ugryumov* (1764–1823) and *K.P. Bryullov* (1799–1852), including the latter's *Last Days of Pompeii (1833).

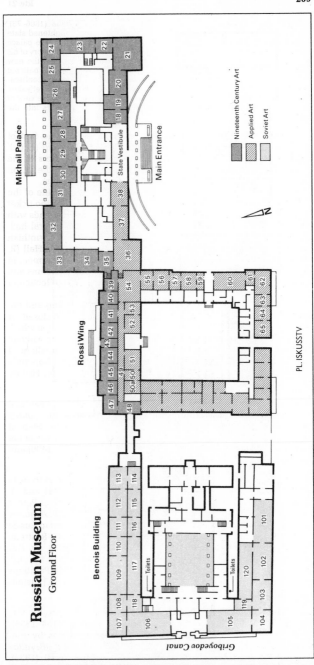

Russian Museum
Ground Floor

Mikhail Palace

State Vestibule

Main Entrance

Nineteenth Century Art
Applied Art
Soviet Art

N

Rossi Wing

PL. ISKUSSTV

Benois Building

Toilets

Toilets

Griboyedov Canal

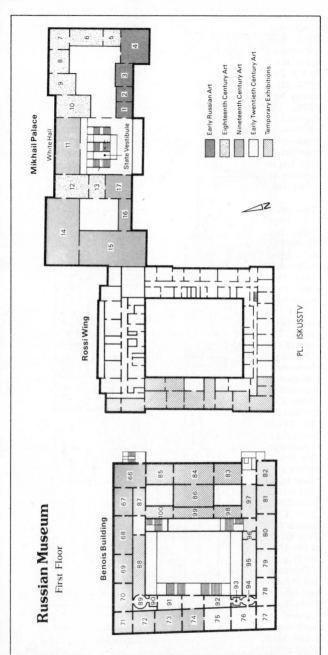

Russian Museum
First Floor

Mikhail Palace

White Hall

State Vestibule

Rossi Wing

Benois Building

Early Russian Art

Eighteenth Century Art

Nineteenth Century Art

Early Twentieth Century Art

Temporary Exhibitions

PL. ISKUSSTV

Giant seascape, The Wave (1889) by *I.K. Ayvazovsky* (1817–1900). Landscapes by *F.M. Matveyev* (1758–1826) and *S.F. Shchedrin* (1791–1830). Portraits by *O.A. Kiprensky* (1782–1836).

Portraits and genre scenes by *A.G. Venetsianov* (1780–1847) and his pupils. Paintings by *A.A. Ivanov* (1806–58). Romantic paintings by *V.A. Tropinin* (1776–1857). Early Realist canvases by *P.A. Fedotov* (1815–52) and *A.F. Chernyshev* (1824–63). Socially-conscious genre scenes by *V.G. Perov* (1833–82), including Monastery Refectory (1876). The First Step (1864), appealing genre statue by *F.F. Kamensky* (1836–1913). Religious and historical works by *N.N. Gay* (1831–94). Fine portraits by *I.N. Kramskoy* (1837–87), including Mina Moiseyev (1882). Landscapes by *A.K. Savrasov* (1830–97), *F.A. Vasil'yev* (1850–73), and *I.I. Shishkin* (1832–98), including Shishkin's Ship-Timber Grove (1898). Portraits and genre scenes by *N.A. Yaroshenko* (1846–98), *I.M. Pryanishnikov* (1840–94), and *K.A. Savitsky* (1845–1905).

*Late 19C and Early 20C Painting and Sculpture. Large canvases by *V.V. Vereshchagin* (1842–1904). Landscapes by *A.I. Kuindzhi* (1842–1910), including Evening in the Ukraine (1878). Paintings by *A.D. Kivshenko* (1851–95); Council of War at Fili (1880). Landscapes by *A.P. Bogolyubov* (1824–96). Large Realist canvases by *K.Ye. Makovsky* (1839–1915); The Fair (1869). Statue of Ivan the Terrible (1871) by *M.M. Antokol'sky* (1843–1902). Christ and the Sinner (1888) by *V.D. Polenov* (1844–1927). Death of Nero (1888) by *V.S. Smirnov* (1858–90).

**I.Ye. Repin* (1844–1930), probably the best-known Russian painter. Among the canvases in the museum are The Volga Boatmen (1873), The Zaporozhets Cossacks (1891), Meeting of the State Council (1903), and portraits of Stasov (1883) and Glazunov (1887).

Paintings by *V.M. Vasnetsov* (1848–1926) including Knight at the Crossroads (1882). Historical canvases by *V.I. Surikov* (1848–1916); Conquest of Siberia by Yermak (1895), Suvorov's Army Crossing the Alps (1899), Stepan Razin (1906). Landscapes by *I.I. Levitan* (1860–1900), *S.A. Korovin* (1858–1908) and *A.Ye. Arkhipov* (1862–1930). Striking portraits by *V.A. Serov* (1865–1911) of Ida Rubinstein (1910), O.K. Orlova (1911), and Princess Z.N. Yusupova (1902) (the last being the mother of Feliks Yusupov, assassin of Rasputin).

Paintings of the fantastic by *M.A. Vrubel'* (1856–1910), including The Knight (1898) and Six-Winged Seraph (1904). Religious and historical paintings by *M.V. Nesterov* (1862–1942). Works by painters, many of them connected with Mir Iskusstva. Winter, Skating (1915) by *K.A. Somov* (1869–1939). Portraits of Diaghilev by *L. S. Bakst* (1866–1924) and of Chaliapin (1912) by *A.Ya. Golovin* (1863–1930). Ghostly canvases by *V.E. Borisov-Musatov* (1870–1905). *A.N. Benois* (1870–1960), Parade under Paul I (1907). Work by *K.A. Korovin* (1861–1939), *N.K. Roerich* (1874–1947), and *F.A. Malyavin* (1869–1940). Landscapes and portraits by *B.M. Kustodiyev* (1878–1927) and *K.F. Yuon* (1875–1958).

Paintings by *S.A. Vinogradov* (1869–1938), landscapes by *A.A. Rylov* (1870–1939). Works by *Z.Ye. Serebryakova* (1884–1967) and still lifes by the painter and art historian *I.E. Grabar'* (1871–1960). Work by *M.F. Larionov* (1881–1964) including A Corner of the Garden (1905) from his Impressionist period. Works by *S.Yu. Sudeykin* (1882–1946), *P.P. Konchalovsky* (1876–1956), *M.S. Sar'yan* (1880–1972), and *P.V. Kuznetsov* (1878–1968). Still lifes by *I.I. Mashkov* (1881–1944). A few works by **N.S. Goncharova* (1881–

1962). Paintings by *K. S. Petrov-Vodkin* (1878–1939). Canvases by *V.V. Kandinsky* (1866–1944), *V.Ye. Tatlin* (1885–1953), and *A.V. Shevchenko* (1882–1948). Paintings by *K.S. Malevich* (1878–1935). Portrait of Akhmatova (1915) by *N.I. Al'tman* (1889–1970). Paintings by *B.D. Grigor'yev* (1886–1939).

In the courtyard, visible from the passageway between the Rossi Wing and the Benois Building, is the huge equestrian statue of Alexander III (1909) which once stood in Pl. Vosstaniya—the sculptor was *P.P. Trubetskoy* (1866–1938).

Soviet Period. Monumental sculpture, some of it dating back to the Civil War period. The paintings include The Defence of Sevastopol (1942) by *A.A. Deyneka* (1899–1969) and the triptych Communists (1960) by *G.M. Korzhev* (born 1925). Among the other important Soviet artists represented are *Yu. I. Pimenov* (1903–77), *A.A. Plastov* (1893–1972), the portraitist *P.D. Korin* (1892–1967), and *I.A. Serebryany* (born 1907–79).

Applied art of the 18C and 19C. Russian and imported furniture, tapestries, china, glass, gold and silver work.

Soviet applied art. Mostly porcelain.

Handicrafts. On display are folk costumes, weaving, lace, pottery, Palekh boxes, and wood carving; in the last category there is even the complete carved pediment of a wooden house (1888).

The building of the *Museum of Ethnography of the Peoples of the USSR (Muzey Etnografii Narodov SSSR), to the right of the Russian Museum, does not entirely fit into the ensemble of Pl. Iskusstv. It was built (1901–11) in place of the E Wing, Stables, and Laundry of the Mikhail Palace and was intended to house the ethnographical collection of the Russian Museum. This became an independent museum in 1934.

The exhibition spaces extend from either side of the central hall, with its marble walls and sculptured frieze depicting 'The Peoples of Russia' (M.Ya. Kharlamov). The most interesting rooms show the way of life of the various national groups in the 19C and early 20C. There is an extensive collection of clothes, tools, handicrafts, folk art, etc., as well as photographs and models. Other sections are devoted to life in the modern USSR.

In the SE part of the square, on the corner of Ul. Rakova, stands the *Viyel'gorsky House* (Pl. Iskusstv. 4), one of several owned in this square by the great patron of the arts M.Yu. Viyel'gorsky (he lived earlier at No. 3 and No. 5). Liszt, Berlioz, and Schumann performed at Viyel'gorsky's 'Evenings'. UL. RAKOVA, now named after a Civil War hero, was originally Ital'yanskaya Ul. after the Italian Palace at its E end (on the Fontanka). General N.V. Mezentsov, chief of the security police, was stabbed to death in the street here in 1878 by the terrorist Kravchinsky (Stepniak). The **Theatre of Musical Comedy** (Gos. Teatr Muzykal'noy Komedii), at Ul. Rakova, 13, was founded in 1929; the building was formerly the Palace Theatre (Palas-Teatr). Further along Ul. Rakova, at No. 19, is the **Komissarzhevskaya Theatre** (Gos. Dramaticheskiy Teatr im. V.F. Komissarzhevskoy), which was established during the Blockade (October 1942) as a drama company.

It moved here to the rear of the Passage Department Store in 1944, but this theatre had existed for many years. In 1904–06 it was rented to the New Drama

Theatre, which had been organised by the famous actress Vera Komissarzhevskaya (1864–1909). The Soviet company was given Komissarzhevskaya's name in 1959.

Nevskiy Pr. continues beyond Ul. Brodskovo with, at No. 40–42, Velten's white and blue **Armenian Church** (Armyanskaya Ts.) (1771–80). This fine example of the early Classical style, incorporating a portico and dome, is set back from the avenue. The 19C poet F.I. Tyutchev lived for many years in one of the buildings in front of the church (No. 40), while the early-19C statesman M.M. Speransky lived in the other (No. 42); the latter building is now the *Central Theatre Booking Office* (Tsentral'naya Kassa). The ground floor of No. 46 is occupied by the *Sever Café* and patisserie; upstairs is the *Neva Restaurant*.

The **Passage Department Store**, at No. 48, was built in 1846–48. The narrow arcade with its glass roof stretches some 180m N from the Nevskiy.

Sadovaya Ul. (pp 281, 287) crosses Nevskiy Pr. beyond Passage and the Gostinyy Dvor. One of the best known photographs of the 1917 Revolution shows crowds of demonstrators scattering under fire at this intersection. The **Puppet Theatre** (Gos. Kukol'nyy Teatr), beyond Sadovaya Ul. (Nevskiy Pr., 52), was founded in 1918 and directed for forty years by Ye.S. Demmeni, one of the great Russian puppeteers; the writers Ye.L. Shvarts and S.Ya. Marshak produced many works especially for this small theatre. *Gastronom No. 1*, at Nevskiy Pr., 58, is a food shop built by the architect G.V. Baranovsky for the merchant Yeliseyev. Like its counterpart in Moscow, it is still renowned for its extravagant Art Nouveau décor; the stained glass and chandeliers are particularly noteworthy. The same building contains the Leningrad **Comedy Theatre** (Gos. Akademicheskiy Teatr Komedii). The company, founded in 1929, was for several decades (until 1968) directed by N.P. Akimov. A number of plays were written for the Comedy Theatre by Ye.L. Shvarts.

Twenty years before Yeliseyev's was built, the 'People's Will' group used the building on this site for an elaborate conspiracy against Alexander II. From a shop they had set up here in January 1881 the terrorists began tunnelling under the adjacent MAL. SADOVAYA UL., along which the Emperor frequently travelled. A mine was to have been planted, but in the meantime Alexander was killed elsewhere.

The **Saltykov-Shchedrin Public Library** (Gos. Publichnaya Biblioteka im. M.Ye. Saltykova-Shchedrina), formerly the Imperial Public Library and known as the 'Publichka', is the second largest institution of its kind in Russia, after Moscow's Lenin Library, and contains over 20 million items. The first part of the library, on the SE corner of Sadovaya Ul. and Nevskiy Pr., was built in 1796–1801. The extension to the E dates from 30 years later (1828–34) and formed part of the ensemble that Rossi created in Aleksandrinskaya Pl., now PL. OSTROVSKOVO (Pl. 10; 6). The original name came from the wife of Nicholas I, Alexandra Fyodorovna (1798–1860); A.N. Ostrovsky (1823–86) was a prominent Russian dramatist. Set between the 18 columns of the library are statues of great men by Pimenov, Demut-Malinovsky, and others; Demut-Malinovsky also created the bas-reliefs and the statue of Minerva on the roof.

Pl. Ostrovskovo was laid out by Rossi in the 1820s and 1830s. The central point was Rossi's handsome Alexandra (Aleksandrinskiy) Theatre, now the **•Pushkin Theatre** (Gos. Akademicheskiy Teatr Dramy im. A.S. Pushkina), but still known popularly as the 'Aleksandrinka'. The elegant yellow theatre was constructed in

1828–32; above the six Corinthian columns of the main (N) façade are figures of Glory and a Chariot of Apollo, drawn by four horses. The Muses Terpsichore and Melpomene are set in niches on either side of the colonnade and a sculptured frieze surrounds the building. Pimenov, Demut-Malinovsky, and A. Triscornia were responsible for this decoration. Flanking the oblong building are twin eight-columned porticoes.

The Pushkin, the oldest dramatic theatre company in Russia, can trace its history back to 1756. The Imperial Alexandra Theatre was one of the most important centres of Russian drama; Gogol's 'The Government Inspector' had its première here (1836). The theatre was renamed after Pushkin on the centenary of the poet's death, in 1937.

The *Statue of Catherine II* between Nevskiy Pr. and the Pushkin Theatre was unveiled in 1873. The towering figure of the Empress stands above her close associates: Suvorov, Rumyantsev, Derzhavin, Betsky, Dashkova, Orlov, Bezborodko, Potyomkin, and Chichagov. The statue of Catherine was the work of M.A. Chizhov, her nine colleagues that of A.M. Opekushin; the overall design was by M.O. Mikeshin.

Rossi's ensemble continues behind the theatre with the marvellous *UL. ZODCHEVO ROSSI (Pl. 10; 8) or 'Street of Rossi the Master Builder', formerly Teatral'naya Ul. (Theatre St). The perfectly proportioned street, 22m wide and flanked on either side by symmetrical colonnades of buildings 22m high, leads 220m S to Pl. Lomonosova on the Fontanka River. The building on the right was the Ministry of Education, while that on the left was intended for the Director of the Imperial Theatres and for the Theatre Academy. The latter building now houses the *Theatre and Music Museum (Muzey Teatral'novo i Muzykal'novo Isskustva).

The museum was founded in 1918 on the initiative of Lunacharsky, the People's Commissar of Education. The exhibits, from a collection of 300,000 items and including paintings, sculpture, photographs, models of sets, programmes, posters, and other memorabilia, trace the history of the dramatic and musical theatre of Russia from its beginning to the present day. The museum also has a large library of books on theatre, as well as a collection of recordings of the voices of outstanding actors and singers.

The **Vaganova Choreographic School** (Leningradskoye Gos. Akademicheskoye Khoreograficheskoye Uchilishche im. Prof. A. Ya. Vaganovoy) (no adm.), on the left side of Ul. Zodchevo Rossi, beyond the Theatre Museum, is still probably the finest ballet school in the world and offers superb classical training. The history of the school goes back to 1738 when J.B. Landé began to train the children of the palace servants to take part in Court entertainments. Perhaps the most significant period in the early history of the school came in 1801–11; during these years Charles Didelot reformed the teaching to incorporate the best features of the French School. The Imperial Ballet School, which moved to its present quarters in 1836, continued to flourish at a time when Western ballet was in decline. Some of the world's most celebrated dancers were trained by the school in the early 20C: Pavlova, Karsavina, Nijinsky, and the choreographer Fokine. (Karsavina's memoirs were entitled 'Theatre Street'—the old name of Ul. Zodchevo Rossi.) The traditions were kept alive after the Revolution by fine teachers, most notably Agrippina Vaganova (Director in 1934–41). Vaganova developed a teaching method now used throughout the Soviet Union. Post-revolutionary graduates of the school have included Ulanova, Kolpakova, Nureyev, Makarova, Baryshnikov, and the Bol'shoy ballerina Semenyaka.

Pl. Ostrovskovo was laid out in place of the gardens of the **Anichkov Palace** (Anichkovskiy Dvorets), which survives today on the Nevskiy as the *Palace of Pioneers* (no adm.). The remaining part of the gardens runs along the E side of Pl. Ostrovskovo, behind a railing and two of Rossi's Classical *Pavilions* (the sculptures and bas-reliefs of the latter were designed by Pimenov).

The palace (Nevskiy Pr., 39) took its name from a military engineer named M.O. Anichkov, who had been in charge of developing this district of early St. Petersburg. The oldest part (1741–1750s) faced E onto the Fontanka River. M.G. Zemtsov drew the original plans, but the palace was rebuilt several times, by I.Ye. Starov (1778–79), Rusca (1809–10), and Rossi (1817–18); the last of these added the *Service Wing* to the S. The handsome colonnade between the Fontanka and the original palace was built by Quarenghi in 1803–05. This was originally intended as an arcade where the products of the Imperial factories would be sold, but it was soon enlarged by Rusca and converted into royal offices, known as the *Kabinet.*

The Anichkov Palace was built for Aleksey Razumovsky, the favourite of Empress Elizabeth; after Razumovsky's death, Catherine II presented it to Potyomkin. In the 19C the palace served as the residence of the heirs to the throne, beginning with Nicholas Pavlovich in 1817. Grand Duke Alexander Nikolayevich lived here, as did Alexander Aleksandrovich. After the latter became Emperor Alexander III he kept the Anichkov Palace as a residence (using the Winter Palace for ceremonial functions); his wife, the Dowager Empress Mariya Fyodorovna (1854–1928), stayed on here until the Revolution. In 1937 the palace was given to the Soviet youth organisation, the Pioneers.

The *Anichkovskiy Most** (Pl. 10; 6) across the Fontanka River (p 328) is one of the finest bridges in Leningrad. The first stone bridge here was a drawbridge with four towers (like the Chernyshev Most visible to the right). This proved inadequate for the heavy traffic on the Nevskiy and was replaced by the present structure, with its three arches, in 1839–41. The outstanding feature of the Anichkovskiy Most is the four statues of rearing horses and trainers cast to the designs of P.K. Clodt von Jürgensburg in the 1840s.

The **Belosel'sky-Belozersky Palace** (no adm.), now the head-quarters of a local Party organisation, is the large red building (No. 41) to the right on the far side of the Fontanka. It was created in its present Baroque form by Stakenschneider in 1846–48 and is similar to Rastrelli's Stroganov Palace at the other end of the Nevskiy. Originally built for Prince K.Ye. Belosel'sky-Belozersky, the palace became in 1884 the residence of Grand Duke Sergey Aleksandrovich (1857–1905).

Not far beyond, Liteynyy Pr. (p 291) turns left off Nevskiy Pr., while Vladimirskiy Pr. (p 293) turns to the right. Between this intersection and Pl. Vosstaniya (700m) there is little of interest except for the Classical *Yusupov House* (No. 96), built in the 1820s and 1830s by M.A. Ovsyannikov and G. Fossati. Several large cinemas are located near here, including the *Avrora* (No. 60), *Khudozhestvennyy* (No. 67), *Znaniye* (No. 72), *Oktyabr'* (No. 80), *Novosti Dnya* (No. 88), and *Neva* (No. 108). Ul. Marata and Ul. Mayakovskovo are side-streets to right and left respectively. The MAYAKOVSKAYA METRO STATION is at the end of this part of Nevskiy Pr., next to Leningrad's largest restaurant, the *Nevskiy* (No. 71). This Rte ends at Pl. Vosstaniya (see next Rte), with the PLOSHCHAD' VOSSTANIYA METRO STATION.

22   South-East Leningrad

This Rte covers the SE part of the city, beyond the main part of
Nevskiy Pr. The starting point is Pl. Vosstaniya, which is served by
PLOSHCHAD' VOSSTANIYA METRO STATION. From here Rte A follows
Ligovskiy Pr., which runs perpendicular to Nevskiy Pr., while Rte B is
the continuation of Nevskiy Pr. to the Alexander Nevskiy Lavra.

PL. VOSSTANIYA or 'Uprising Square' (Pl. 11; 7) takes its name from
the fact that it was a centre of the February 1917 uprising against the
Tsarist government. Troops and mounted police tried and failed for
several days to win back control of the square from the demonstrating crowds. Here on 25 February occurred the portentous incident
when Cossack troops sympathetic to the demonstrators killed a
policeman; within two days the whole garrison had gone over to the
Revolution. In the centre of the square stands the granite **Obelisk to
the Hero City of Leningrad** (A.I. Alymov and V.M. Ivanov), erected
in honour of the fortieth anniversary of 1945.

Earlier this important square was called Znamenskaya Pl. after the Church of
the Sign (Ts. Znameniya), built by F.I. Demertsev in 1794–1804. The church was
demolished in 1940, and its place is now occupied by the ornate spired rotunda
of the Ploshchad' Vosstaniya Metro Station. For several decades a statue of
Alexander III stood in the centre of the square. It was unveiled in 1911; the
sculptor P.P. Trubetskoy portrayed the reactionary Emperor as a huge barrel-
chested figure riding on a small horse. The new regime kept the statue, but
added a mocking inscription by Demyan Bedny: 'My son [Nicholas II] and my
father [Alexander II] were executed in their prime,/ But I have attained
posthumous glory:/ I stand here as an iron scarecrow for the country/ Which has
forever thrown off the yoke of autocracy.' By 1937 the joke had worn thin and
the big statue was removed; it may now be seen standing forlorn in the
courtyard of the Russian Museum.

The **Moscow Station** (Moskovskiy Vokzal) forms the S side of Pl.
Vosstaniya; from here trains travel to Moscow and the North. The
architect K.A. Thon built identical terminals at either end of what
was once called the 'Nicholas Railway' (now the 'October Railway');
they shared the name 'Nicholas Station'. The St. Petersburg version
dated from 1843–51, but behind the green façade it has been
modernised.

The NE side of the square is occupied by the **Oktyabr'skaya Hotel**,
one of the largest in the city. The hotel dates from 1845–47 and was
earlier known as the 'Znamenskaya' and then as the 'Severnaya' (or
'Grand-Hôtel du Nord'). In the mid-18C the Elephant House
(Slonovvy Dvor) of Empress Anna Ivanovna stood here.

The main façade of the Oktyabr'skaya Hotel extends along the N
part of LIGOVSKIY PR. Not far beyond, at No. 6 (right), stands the
modern white **Oktyabr'skiy Concert Hall** (Bol'shoy Kontsertnyy Zal
'Oktyabr'skiy'). Completed in 1967 with a capacity of 4000, this is
one of the largest theatres in the USSR.

KOVENSKIY PER., which turns left off Ligovskiy Pr. about 300m
beyond the Oktyabr'skiy Concert Hall, contains at No. 7 a functioning *Roman Catholic Church*. This was built in 1908–09 by L.N. Benois
and M.M. Peretyatkovich as the Chapel of the French Embassy.

A.   Ligovskiy Prospekt

The main part of LIGOVSKIY PR. (Pl. 10; 8) runs SW for about 5km from Pl. Vosstaniya, and ends at Moskovskiy Pr. by the Moscow Triumphal Arch. Along this route ran part of the 20km canal dug in 1718–25 to feed the fountains of the Summer Gardens. As its source was the Liga River, the canal was called Ligovskiy; from this came the name of the tree-lined boulevard which remained after the canal was covered over at the end of the last century.

Before the Revolution considerable residential and industrial development had taken place along Ligovskiy Pr. In 1917 the printing-press of the 'yellow' newspaper 'Kopeyka' was located at No. 34 (left), and this is where the first issue of the 'Izvestiya' (Bulletin) of the Petrograd Soviet was printed. The most striking building on the avenue stands at No. 128, the **Church of the Raising of the Cross** (Krestovozdvizhenskaya Ts.). The prominent Classical bell tower, with its pointed spire and semicircular colonnade, was created by the architect A.I. Postnikov in 1810–12. Although the first stone church was built here in 1749, the Baroque church behind the bell tower dates from 1851. The earlier *Church of the Virgin of Tikhvin* (Tikhvinskaya Ts.) survives nearby (1764–68/1842–44).

Ligovskiy Pr. crosses the OBVODNYY CANAL or 'Bypass Canal' (Pl. 9; 5) just beyond the Church of the Raising of the Cross. The canal, like the similarly-named Vodootvodnyy Canal in Moscow, was designed partly to prevent flooding; it was also used for the transport of freight. French military engineers supervised the construction of the 8km canal between 1803 and 1835. For a long time it marked the southern boundary of St. Petersburg.

S of the Obvodnyy Canal and E of Ligovskiy Pr. lies the so-called **Literatorskiye Mostki** (Nekropol' 'Literatorskiye Mostki'), the NW part of the **Volkovskoye Cemetery** (Pl. 9; 5). Trams No. 10 and 44 travel here from Pl. Vosstaniya.

The Volkovskoye Cemetery was opened in 1756; the name comes from the Volkovka River, which flows 4.5km from Kupchino to the Obvodnyy Canal. The small and rather angular *Church of the Resurrection* (Voskresenskaya Ts.) was built here in 1782–85, possibly by I.Ye. Starov; it now houses an exhibition on the cemetery's history.

Among the cultural figures buried at the Literatorskiye Mostki are the writers I.S. Turgenev, M.Ye. Saltykov-Shchedrin, N.S. Leskov, V.M. Garshin, G.I. Uspensky, L.N. Andreyev, A.I. Kuprin, A.A. Blok, and O.F. Berggol'ts, the architect K.A. Thon, the ballerina A.Ya. Vaganova, and the film director G.M. Kozinstev. Among scientists are D.I. Mendeleyev, I.P. Pavlov, and A.S. Popov.

The early Russian radical A.N. Radishchev was buried here, but the precise location of his grave is unknown. Among the later 19C political thinkers and activists here are V.G. Belinsky, N.A. Dobrolyubov, D.I. Pisarev, N.K. Mikhaylovsky, and V.I. Zasulich.

G.V. Plekhanov, one of the founders of Russian Marxism, is buried here, as well as several of Lenin's close relatives: his mother Mariya Aleksandrovna Ul'yanova, his sisters Olga and Anna, and his brother-in-law Mark Yelizarov (Anna's husband).

One of the streets leading S from the far end of Ligovskiy Pr. bears the curious name Vozdukhoplavatel'naya Ul., which means 'Air Navigation Street'. The name commemorates the first Russian military flights. This former artillery proving ground was used for balloon flights in the 1880s, and the first powered airship in Russia flew here in 1909.

B.   The Alexander Nevskiy Lavra

Nevskiy Pr. continues beyond Pl. Vosstaniya to the Alexander
Nevskiy Lavra, a distance of some 2km. Suvorovskiy Pr. (p 296) turns
off to the left and, not far beyond, POLTAVSKAYA UL. turns to the
right. At Poltavskaya Ul., 9, is the *Dzerzhinsky Palace of Culture*,
once the Kalashnikov Grain Exchange. Stalin was arrested here in
February 1913 at a benefit meeting for the newspaper 'Pravda'; he
remained in prison or exile until the Revolution of 1917. The
extraordinary grey Pseudo-Russian church at the end of Poltavskaya
Ul. was built to celebrate the Romanov tercentenary (S.S. Krichinsky,
1913).

PEREKUPNOY PER. leads left off Nevskiy Pr. to KHERSONSKAYA UL.
No. 5 in this last street is a small **Lenin Museum** (Kvartira-Muzey V.I.
Lenina).

V.D. Bonch-Bruyevich, a close associate of Lenin's, lived here, and his flat was
used for an important meeting on 4 April 1917 when the recently returned Lenin
explained his political strategy to the Bolshevik leaders. Lenin also stayed with
Bonch-Bruyevich on the crucial night of 24–25 October, as the Bolsheviks
began their uprising; here he drafted the decree which gave land to the
peasants.

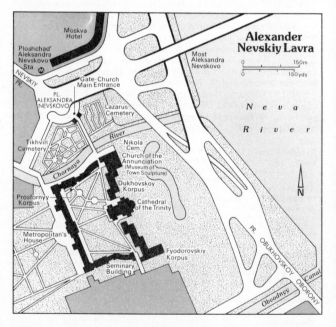

Nevskiy Pr. ends at PL. ALEKSANDRA NEVSKOVO (Pl. 11; 7). The N
side is occupied by the PLOSHCHAD' ALEKSANDRA NEVSKOVO
METRO STATION and the **Moskva Hotel**. The hotel, which accom-
modates nearly 1500 guests, extends around the corner along the
Neva embankment.

The Classical domed archway (I.Ye. Starov, 1783–85) on the S side of the square is the entrance to the *Alexander Nevskiy Lavra. A short path leads to a bridge over the little Chornaya River (now a branch of the Obvodnyy Canal); beyond, the buildings of the Lavra form a rough rectangle surrounding a large wooden courtyard.

The monastery was founded by Peter the Great in 1713. He believed that this site was where in 1240 young Prince Alexander of Novgorod (1220–63) defeated the Swedes in battle and earned the title 'Alexander of the Neva' or Alexander Nevskiy. (The battle was actually fought some 20km upstream at the point where the Izhora River enters the Neva; this should not be confused with Alexander's other famous victory, over the Teutonic Knights, which was won two years later on the ice of Lake Peipus.) In 1724 the Emperor had the remains of the recently canonised St. Alexander Nevskiy transferred from Vladimir to the new monastery. By these gestures Peter was trying to legitimise both his policies and his new capital. At the end of the century, in 1797, the monastery was elevated to the rank of a laura (laura), a senior monastery and one of only four in all Russia. The 'Aleksandro-Nevskaya Lavra' is still a functioning religious establishment, although the grounds are open to the public and contain several museums.

Domenico Trezzini began the work of planning, and his *Church of the Annunciation* (Blagoveshchenskaya Ts.)—just to the left of the main entrance—was built in 1717–22. Because of the richly-decorated tombstones inside, the building has been made into the **Museum of Town Sculpture** (Muzey Gorodskoy Skul'ptury).

Like the Don Monastery in Moscow, the Alexander Nevskiy Lavra became in the 18C and 19C a burial place for the Russian upper classes and in consequence a centre for the outstanding sculpture-monuments of that era. Among the many prominent soldiers and statesman buried in the Church of the Annunciation are Generalissimo Suvorov, Imperial Russia's most gifted commander, and Count N.I. Panin, the foreign minister of Catherine the Great; the stone on Suvorov's grave bears the laconic inscription—'Here lies Suvorov'. A fine collection of sculpture was gathered here in the Soviet period after the church was made into a museum. Among the outstanding monuments are those to Field Marshal Prince A.M. Golitsyn (by F.G. Gordeyev) and to Ye.S. Kurakina and Ye.I. Gagarina (both by I.P. Martos).

The real centre of the Lavra, beyond the Church of the Annunciation and the so-called *Dukhovskoy Korpus*, is the *Cathedral of the Trinity* (Troitskiy Sobor). This building is in the Classical style, unlike the rest of the essentially Baroque ensemble. It was begun only in 1776 and completed in 1790; the architect was I.Ye. Starov. The site of the cathedral was chosen by Trezzini, but as he proposed to put the entrance on the river (E) side and this went against the normal Russian Orthodox custom, his project was not realised. The German T. Schwertfeger designed the next version, but this was demolished in 1755 when the walls cracked.

The exterior of Starov's final design is dominated by the dome mounted high on a drum and the two square bell towers; the entrance is framed by a six-columned portico. The *Interior* is open; this is a functioning Orthodox church, not a museum. The wide nave, flanked by Corinthian columns with gilded capitals and statues of saints (by F.I. Shubin), leads to the gorgeous gilded iconostasis. The splendid frescoes above date from 1806. A silver reliquary containing the remains of St. Alexander Nevskiy once stood on the right, but it has been transferred to the Hermitage.

The building to the right of the cathedral is the *Fyodorovskiy Korpus*, built in the 1740s by Pietro Antonio Trezzini, the son of Domenico. The other buildings, proceeding clockwise around the central square of the monastery, are the *Seminary Building*, the *Metropolitan's House*, and—back opposite the Church of the

Annunciation—the *Prosfornyy Korpus*; all were erected between 1756 and 1771 to the designs of M.D. Rastorguyev. The Metropolitan's House was the residence of the Metropolitan of St. Petersburg, one of the most senior Russian churchmen.

The monastery complex includes several important cemeteries. The one in the central courtyard contains, incongruously, the so-called '*Communist Plot'* (Kommunisticheskaya Ploshchadka) where some prominent Soviet personalities, including Eino Rahja (Lenin's bodyguard), were buried. Among the 'headstones' are giant aeroplane propellers marking the graves of Soviet fliers killed in the last war.

Every effort should be made to visit the two cemeteries which flank the entrance path: they are among the most important in Russia. On the left (E) as one enters the monastery grounds from Pl. Aleksandra Nevskovo is the **Lazarus Cemetery* (Lazarevskoye Kladbishche), founded in 1716 when Peter I's favourite sister Natal'ya Alekseyevna was buried here. Among the famous sculptors interred here are F.I. Shubin, F.F. Shchedrin, and I.P. Martos; among the architects are I.Ye. Starov, A.N. Voronikhin, G. Quarenghi, A.D. Zakharov, T. de Thomon, and C. Rossi. The graves of the scientist M.V. Lomonosov, the Swiss mathematician Leonhard Euler, and the satirist D.I. Fonvizin are also located here.

The **Tikhvin Cemetery* (Tikhvinskoye Kladbishche) on the right (W) of the entrance path was founded in 1823 and is the burial place of some of the greatest Russians of the 19C.

Among writers: N.M. Karamzin, V.A. Zhukovskiy, I.A. Krylov, and F.M. Dostoyevsky. Among musicians: M.I. Glinka, M.P. Mussorgsky, P.I. Tchaikovsky, N.A. Rimsky-Korsakov, and A.P. Borodin. Among artists and sculptors: V.I. Demut-Malinovskiy, S.S. Pimenov, P. Clodt von Jürgensburg, and A.I. Kuindzhi. Others buried here are M.M. Speransky (one of the most important state officials of the early 19C), the choreographer M.I. Petipa, and the actors V.F. Komissarzhevskaya, and N.K. Cherkasov (who portrayed Alexander Nevskiy in Eisenstein's film).

To the E, between the lavra and the Neva embankment, lies the smaller *Nikola Cemetery* (Nikol'skoye Kladbishche).

MOST ALEKSANDRA NEVSKOVO (Pl. 11; 8) crosses the Neva from the E side of Pl. Aleksandra Nevskovo. It had long been planned to build a bridge from the S end of Nevskiy Pr., but the present handsome 628m long structure was completed only in 1965. The district of Malaya Okhta lies at the other end of the bridge.

The area on the left bank of the Neva, SE of the Alexander Nevskiy Monastery, had not been much developed before the Revolution, although the Aleksandro-Nevskaya District, also known as the Nevskaya Zastava, extended for 3 or 4km S of the Obvodnyy Canal. In the 18C great nobles like Potyomkin, Kurakin, and Vyazemsky built country mansions here, but in later years the district became an industrial suburb. The big Nevskiy and Obukhov Factories were established in the middle of the 19C, and the district's workers took part in the revolutionary movement.

One of the main routes to the SE is called PR. OBUKHOVSKOY OBORONY (lit., 'Obukhov Defence Avenue') (Pl. 9; 5), after a violent strike at the Obukhov Factory in 1901. (The pre-revolutionary name was Shlissel'burgskiy Pr.)

Some construction took place in the 1920s, but real developments came only in the following decade, as part of the 1935–36 General

Plan for Leningrad. Work centred on the Shchemilovka area, some 5 or 6km S of the Obvodnyy Canal. An impressive series of buildings were laid out in 1936–41 along IVANOVSKAYA UL. (Pl. 9; 5), to the designs of Ye.A. Levinson, I.I. Fomin, and S.I. Yevdokimov; the new street was to have been the E end of the planned Central Ring Road (Tsentral'naya Dugovaya Magistral') extending W to the Kirovskiy District. At the E end of Ivanovskaya Ul., by the river and Pr. Obukhovskoy Oborony, is a large square with (N) the *Nevskiy District Soviet* built in 1939–40 by Levinson, Fomin, and T.Ye. Gedike. One of the first Soviet monuments in Leningrad (1925) stands just to the S of Ivanovskaya Ul., and marks the spot where the Communist leader V. Volodarsky was assassinated by an SR terrorist in June 1918. (The whole area was at one time known as the Volodarsky District.) Nearby is LOMONOSOVSKAYA METRO STATION.

Ivanovskaya Ul. leads E to the VOLODARSKIY MOST, completed in 1936. On the other side of the river is an impressive square with two 18-storey buildings erected in the 1960s; these are intended to mark the beginning of the E–W ring road.

A further 2km S on the left bank is the site of the former Obukhov Factory, now the Bolshevik Factory. Along the way Pr. Obukhovskoy Oborony passes the *River Passenger Terminal* (Rechnoy Passazhirskiy Vokzal) (left) (No. 195); from the terminal, opened in 1970, river boats travel along the inland waterways to ports as far away as Astrakhan on the Caspian. The *Church of the Trinity* (Troitskaya Ts.), once part of the Aleksandrovskoye Estate of Prince A.A. Vyazemsky, stands at No. 235. It was given a fanciful design by the architect N.A. L'vov (1785) and is known as 'Kulich i Paskha'; the domed rotunda of the church and the pyramidal belfry resemble the traditional Russian Easter cakes known as kulich and paskha.

The *'9 January' Cemetery* (Kladbishche im. Zhertv 9 Yanvarya) (Pl. 9; 5), formerly the Preobrazhenskoye Cemetery, is where the victims of 'Bloody Sunday' (9 January 1905) were buried, secretly and at night, by the police. A large monument by M.G. Manizer was unveiled above the common grave in 1931. The cemetery lies to the W of the Trinity Church, near OBUKHOVO METRO STATION.

23 Sadovaya Ulitsa (North)

Part of Sadovaya Ul. runs N from Nevskiy Pr. (Pl. 10: 6) to Marsovo Pole and the Summer Gardens, a distance of about 1km. From the end of the main Rte it is possible to walk back to Nevskiy Pr. by way of Ul. Khalturina and Dvortsovaya Pl. (1.5km). The starting point is near GOSTINYY DVOR METRO STATION.

SADOVAYA UL. or Garden St originally ran S from the Nevskiy (for this part of the street see Rte 24). The extension to the N was added in the late 18C. On the right side in the first block are the *Baku Restaurant* and the *Molodyozhnyy Cinema*; the Imperial *Ministry of Justice* was once located here. Ul. Rakova, leading to Pl. Iskusstv (p 267), crosses Sadovaya Ul. here, and the next cross street, Inzhenernaya Ul., contains the Museum of Ethnography of the Peoples of the USSR (p 272). Beyond (left) lies an attractive park, the *Mikhail Gardens*.

To the right, opposite the park, stands a large brick red building with a tall gilded spire. The so-called *Engineers Castle (Inzhenernyy Zamok) (Pl. 10; 6) was intended to be a palace for Emperor Paul I (1796–1801).

This site, bordered by the Moyka River (N) and Fontanka River (E), was once occupied by a wooden Summer Palace which Rastrelli built in 1741–45 for Elizabeth Petrovna. Paul was born here in 1754, the son of Grand Duchess Catherine (later Catherine the Great), and it is said that the Archangel Michael appeared in a dream and told him to build a church on his birthplace. This Paul did, demolishing the attractive Summer Palace and replacing it with not only a church but also a new royal residence called the *Michael Castle* (Mikhaylovskiy Zamok). The general design was by Bazhenov, but Brenna supervised the construction; work began in 1797 and the castle was completed on the Feast of the Archangel Michael (8 November) in 1800. Paul lived in fear of assassination, a fear which became increasingly more justified as his regime grew stricter. The Michael Castle resembled a medieval fortress; it was surrounded by water, with moats dug to the W and S and spanned by drawbridges. Paul's precautions were in vain, however, and a mere forty days after he moved in, on 11 March 1801, the Emperor was smothered in his bed; the conspirators were led by the Governor-General of St. Petersburg, Count P.A. Pahlen. From the reign of Alexander II until the Revolution the room where Paul died was preserved as a chapel.

For twenty years after this incident the castle lay empty, but in 1823 it became the Military Engineering Academy (hence the modern name, Engineers Castle). Among those who studied here was the young Dostoyevsky. In October 1917 the cadets of the *Nicholas Engineering Academy* (as it was then called) resisted the Bolshevik take-over, and there was serious fighting here between them and revolutionary forces.

The Engineers Castle, square in plan and with an octagonal courtyard, is a fine example of late-18C architecture. Each façade is different, and appropriate to its setting. The main façade, to the S, has a grey stone portico with obelisks and paired Ionic columns; above is a bas-relief depicting the glories of Russia. The N façade, overlooking the Summer Gardens, features a row of paired Ionic columns supporting a terrace; broad steps lead towards the gardens. The moats to the W and S were drained in the 19C. Some of the richly-decorated interior survives, but this is not open to the public.

During Paul's brief reign the square to the S of the castle was used for his favourite occupation, drilling troops. Paul also had erected the equestrian **Statue of Peter I**, which still stands here; on the base is the inscription 'Pradedu Pravnuk (To the Great Grandfather from the Great-Grandson) 1800' (Paul's paternal grandmother was a daughter of Peter I). The statue has an interesting history. It was designed by B.C. Rastrelli (father of the great architect) during Peter's lifetime, and the original intention was to place it next to the Twelve Colleges on Vasil'yevskiy Island. In fact this first Russian equestrian statue was cast only in 1745–47, and then remained in storage for half a century before it was erected in front of the Michael Castle. The bronze statue depicts the Emperor in Roman armour and crowned with a laurel wreath. On the sides of the base are bas-reliefs of Peter's two great victories against the Swedes, at Poltava and Gangut.

The *Maple Alley* (Klenovaya Alleya) was laid out by Rossi on the site of Paul's parade-ground in the 1820s. This was obstructed by later buildings, but after 1945 Rossi's original conception was restored. The oval *Pavilions* which flank the middle of the Alley (on Inzhenernaya Ul.) were designed by Bazhenov (1798–1800). Bordering the lower part of the Alley are the former *Stables* (Konyushni) (E) and the *Mikhail Riding-School* (Mikhaylovskiy Manezh) (W). Both of these were rebuilt and decorated by Rossi in 1823–24, when he was working on the Mikhail Palace (now the Russian Museum). The Riding-School served in 1917 as the depot of the Armoured Car Detachment (Bronevoy Divizion), an important military unit, and

Lenin spoke here several times. In 1948 the Riding-School was converted into the *Winter Stadium* (Zimniy Stadion).

After crossing the Moyka River (p 332). Sadovaya Ul. is flanked to the left by Marsovo Pole and to the right by the Lebyazhiy Canal with the *Summer Gardens (Letniy Sad) beyond it (Pl. 10; 6).

The Summer Gardens occupy an area of nearly 12ha bounded on all sides by rivers and canals. They contain about 3000 trees, mostly lime trees, which with the numerous statues, the pavilions, and the wide alleys make the gardens the finest park in Leningrad.

The first part of the Summer Gardens were laid out in 1704, only a year after the foundation of St. Petersburg. Peter I dreamt of having gardens better than those at Versailles. He had trees imported from all over Russia and from abroad, laid out fountains and ponds, constructed pavilions, and purchased or commissioned works of sculpture (mostly from Italy). In the early 18C the gardens were used for Court events, such as the reception of important guests or the celebration of military victories.

Gradually the character of the gardens changed. The splendid system of fountains, some 50 in number, was destroyed in the great storm and flood of 1777, many pavilions disappeared, and the formal gardens evolved into the kind of landscaped park that was fashionable in the Romantic era. The Summer Gardens became a walking place for the privileged classes of St. Petersburg. Writers frequented the park in the early 19C, including Pushkin, who wrote to his wife that 'the Summer Gardens are my kitchen garden (ogorod). Having risen from my slumbers I go there in dressing-gown and slippers. After lunch I sleep in it, I read and write. In it I am at home'.

The railings along the S edge of the gardens, decorated with shields and Medusa heads, were made in 1826, to the design of L.I. Charlemagne. The giant pink porphyry vase inside the S entrance was a gift from the King of Sweden (1839); behind it lies the large geometrical *Karpiyev Prud* or Carp Pond (after the fish bred here).

From the pond the Main Alley leads to the N. The statues arranged on either side, white against the dark greenery, constitute a unique museum of decorative park sculpture. There are more than 80 statues, and they may be divided by themes into three groups: historical (including Alexander the Great, Julius Caesar, Nero, Trajan, the Polish King Jan Sobieski, and Queen Christina), allegorical (Beauty, Truth, Nobility, Architecture, Glory, Navigation, etc.), and mythological (Minerva, Flora, Mercury, etc.). These are not the statues that Peter commissioned in the early 18C, they were erected in the late 19C. (All the statues, incidentally, are covered by individual wooden cases in winter to protect them from the bitter cold.)

Rossi Alley, to the right, ends at the Fontanka with the *Coffee House* (Kofeynyy Domik), a pavilion rebuilt by Carlo Rossi in 1826. It is decorated with stucco bas-reliefs by Demut-Malinovsky, and now serves as a reading-room. Another path to the right of the Main Alley leads to the large *Statue of I.A. Krylov* (1768–1844) by P. Clodt von Jürgensburg which was paid for by public subscription and unveiled in 1855. Krylov is depicted in a thoughtful pose; the granite pedestal is decorated with bronze reliefs of some of the most famous of Krylov's fables, including 'The Fox and the Grapes' and 'The Crow and the Fox'. Beyond stands the wooden *Tea House* (Chaynyy Domik) (L.I. Charlemagne, 1827), now a café.

The modest *Summer Palace (Letniy Dvorets-Muzey Petra I), in the NE corner of the Summer Gardens, was the first proper royal residence in St. Petersburg. Domenico Trezzini built the Summer Palace for Peter I in 1710, and the building survives without major alteration. In 1934 it became a museum.

The Summer Palace is a two-storey rectangular structure with a steep hipped roof. The walls, stucco-covered brick, are painted primrose yellow. The 29 rectangular bas-reliefs between the two storeys, probably by Schlüter, were added soon after completion and celebrate in allegorical form the victories of the Russian Navy.

The decoration of the *Interior* has been altered over the years, but some rooms retain their original Petrine from, and many items of early-18C furniture have been installed; the result is that it is possible to imagine how the Tsar lived in the first years of St. Petersburg. Peter occupied the *Ground Floor*. The *Lower Vestibule* contains an original carved oak panel of Minerva (1710), and the *Staircase* behind it is also authentic. The *Reception-Room, Study, Tokarnaya, Dining-Room, Kitchen* and *Bedroom* include a wealth of early furniture and paintings. The Tokarnaya or Workshop is where Peter worked with his lathe; it contains a fascinating German machine for measuring the wind. Of the rooms on the *1st Floor* where Peter's second wife Catherine lived, the *Upper Vestibule* and the *Green Study* are of particular interest. Both are original, and the latter is the best decorated room in the palace; the built-in cupboards were the first home of Peter's Chamber of Curiosities or Kunstkamera (p 301). The other rooms on the 1st Floor comprise the *Reception Room, Throne Room, Bedroom, Nursery, Ballroom,* and *Kitchen.* The Kitchens on both floors are authentic, with remarkable tiled stoves and early-18C utensils.

Near the Summer Palace is one of the most interesting statues in the park, Baratta's 'Peace and Plenty' (1722), which Peter I commissioned to celebrate the Peace of Nystadt (1721). The seated figure of 'Russia' is crowned with a laurel wreath by 'Victory'; the expiring lion at her feet represents Sweden.

The *'**Railing**' on the Neva side of the park is one of the finest in Russia. Designed by Velten and erected in 1770–84, this is an outstanding example of 18C Classicism. Supporting the gold-tipped spears of the railing are 36 pink granite columns. Near the elaborate Gate is a plaque commemorating Karakazov's attack on Alexander II here in April 1866; Karakazov's shot missed and he was later hanged. Until 1930 there was a chapel on this spot, built in gratitude for the Emperor's escape.

The Neva Embankment at the Summer Gardens in the 1820s

Marsovo Pole (Field of Mars or Champ-de-Mars) (Pl. 10; 6), to the W of Sadovaya Ul. and the Summer Gardens, is one of the largest open spaces in central Leningrad.

When St. Petersburg was founded this place was a marsh, the source of what are now the Moyka River and the Griboyedov Canal. Peter had the marsh drained, and as the Great Field (Bol'shoy Lug), the Amusement Field (Poteshnoye Pole), and the Field of the Tsaritsa (Tsaritsyn Lug) it was used for popular celebrations, promenades, and military manoeuvres. The present name came from the great army parades that were held here in the early 19C and from the construction nearby of the Pavlovskiy Barracks. Later the sandy expanse of the parade ground was called the 'Petersburg Sahara'. Before the First World War there were proposals to use this site for a new State Duma building.

The present appearance of Marsovo Pole dates from the Revolution. The whole character of the square changed in early 1917 when the numerous victims of the February Revolution were buried here with great ceremony. Later, people killed in the October Revolution and the Civil War were interred in Marsovo Pole, including the Communist leaders Volodarsky and Uritsky. The last person to be buried here, in 1933, was the Secretary of the Leningrad Town Committee, I.I. Gaza. On 7 November 1919 the existing *Monument to Revolutionary Fighters* (Pamyatnik Bortsam Revolyutsii) was unveiled. Designed by L.V. Rudnev, it represented one of the first major architectural projects of the Soviet era. (Thirty years later Rudnev led the team that built the Moscow University skyscraper.) Granite blocks form a massive square wall, and on this are inscribed verses by A.V. Lunacharsky commemorating those who lie buried here. The Eternal Flame in the centre was first lit on the 40th anniversary of the October Revolution. In 1920 Marsovo Pole was replanned by I.A. Fomin with paths, lawns, and gardens; 16,000 people took part in a day of voluntary labour (subbotnik) on May Day 1920 to beautify the square.

Most of the W side of Marsovo Pole is occupied by the vast former **Barracks of the Pavlovskiy Guards Regiment**, an expression of Russian military might in the early 19C. The architect V.P. Stasov created the building in its present form in 1817–19. The long E façade, with its central twelve-columned portico and flanking six-columned porticoes, is particularly impressive. The Pavlovskiy Regiment, formed in 1796, had distinguished itself in 1812. (The regiment was said to have recruited only men with snub noses, a tradition established by Paul I, who wanted guardsmen resembling himself.) In February 1917 soldiers of the Pavlovskiy Regiment were among the first to turn their guns against the Tsarist government. To the S of the barracks, and completing the W side of Marsovo Pole, is another large Classical structure (D. Adamini, 1823–27); this formerly housed the *Department of the Imperial Domains* (Vedomstvo Udelov).

The area between Marsovo Pole and the Neva was built up in the reign of Catherine II. The building nearest the Summer Gardens (Dvortsovaya Nab., 2) was built in 1784–87 and once belonged to I.I. Betsky, who supervised Catherine's building programme. The fabulist I.A. Krylov lived here from 1791–96. Quarenghi designed the mansion next door (No. 4) for a wealthy merchant in 1784–88. In the 19C this building housed first the Austrian Embassy and then from 1863–1918, the *British Embassy*. The *Krupskaya Institute of Culture*, a school for librarians, is now located here.

SUVOROVSKAYA PL., directly N of Marsovo Pole, was laid out by Rossi in 1818. The **Suvorov Monument**, a statue of Generalissimo

Suvorov (1730–1800), honours a great Russian soldier. It was designed by M.I. Kozlovsky, unveiled in 1801, and originally stood in the S part of Marsovo Pole. Suvorov is depicted as a classical warrior. With his shield (decorated with the Russian crest) he protects the Papal tiara and the Sardinian and Neapolitan crowns, an allegory on his campaigns against Napoleon in Italy in 1799.

The **Marble Palace** (Mramornyy Dvorets) (Pl. 10; 5), to the N of Marsovo Pole, was commissioned by Catherine II for her favourite, Grigory Orlov. Construction began in 1768, under the supervision of the architect Rinaldi, and was finally completed in 1785, several years after Orlov's death. The name derives from the pale pink marble facing on the pilasters and elsewhere. Other parts of the building are covered with pink or grey granite, which made this one of the few St. Petersburg buildings to be faced with natural stone. This was an early example of the Classical style in Russia. The main façade, set back in a courtyard, is decorated with four columns and statues by Shubin. The building next to Suvorovskaya Pl., the *Service Wing*, was built in its present form in the 1840s. In the last decades of the old regime the Marble Palace was the residence of Grand Duke Konstantin Konstantinovich (1858–1915); since 1937 it has housed the **Leningrad Branch of the Central Lenin Museum** (Leningradskiy Filial Tsentral'novo Muzeya V.I. Lenina).

Like the main Lenin Museum in Moscow, this contains material on Lenin and the revolutionary movement. Included are personal effects, examples of Lenin's writings, photographs, and Soviet applied art. Perhaps the single most interesting exhibit stands in the lobby, the Austin armoured car (bronevik) from which Lenin made his first speech after returning to Russia in April 1917.

The lavish interior decoration of the palace is also of interest. The *State Staircase* and the *Marble Hall*, with bas-reliefs by Shubin and M.I. Kozlovskiy, are original; other rooms were decorated by A.P. Bryullov in the 1840s.

UL. KHALTURINA (Pl. 10; 5) leads W from the Marble Palace to Dvortsovaya Pl. (800m), by the State Hermitage. The name comes from S.N. Khalturin, who planted a bomb in the Winter Palace in 1880. Before the 1917 Revolution some of the wealthiest people in St. Petersburg lived here, and the street was known as Millionnaya Ul.

Quarenghi rebuilt the former *Glavnaya Apteka* (lit., 'Main Chemist's Shop') in the 1790s (Ul. Khalturina, 4) (left); this institution had first been established here in 1732. No. 10 further down the street, was the house which the architect A.I. Stakenschneider built for himself in 1852–54; it was a centre of St. Petersburg's cultural life in the mid-19C. The former house of Princess Putyatin, at No. 12, is of particular historical interest. Here, on 3 March 1917, Grand Duke Mikhail Aleksandrovich (1878–1918), the brother and designated successor of Nicholas II, renounced his right to the throne. With this ended the Romanov dynasty.

The buildings on the right (N) side of Ul. Khalturina tend to have their main façades looking onto the Neva on DVORTSOVAYA NAB., or Palace Embankment. The embankment runs parallel to Ul. Khalturina and may be reached via ZAPOROZHSKIY PER. The *New Mikhail Palace* (Novo-Mikhaylovskiy Dvorets) at Dvortsovaya Nab., 18, was built by Stakenschneider in 1857–61 for Grand Duke Nikolay Mikhaylovich (1832–1919). No. 16, further E along the embankment, was the exclusive *English Club* (Angliyskoye Sobraniye) and No. 14 was the similar *New Club*. To the W of Zaporozhskiy Per., at Dvortsovaya Nab., 26, stands the former *Palace of Grand Duke Vladimir Aleksandrovich* (1847–1909), which was created in the style of the Florentine Renaissance by A.I. Rezanov in the 1860s and 1870s. The wife of Vladimir Aleksandrovich, Grand Duchess Mariya Pavlovna (1854–1923), made this a centre of Court life in the last years of the Old Regime, especially after the Empress withdrew more and more from society. Several members of the Romanov family met here secretly in December 1916 and drafted a letter of warning to Nicholas II.

From Dvortsovaya Pl., at the end of Ul. Khalturina, it is about a 15-minute walk to NEVSKIY PROSPEKT METRO STATION (Pl. 10; 5).

24 Sadovaya Ulitsa (South)

This Rte follows that part of Sadovaya Ul. which lies S of Nevskiy Pr. (Pl. 10; 6). The main section of the Rte turns right at the Cathedral of St. Nicholas and continues N to Teatral'naya Pl.; the distance is about 3km. Tram No. 5 runs along this Rte, and GOSTINYY DVOR METRO STATION is next to the starting point.

This is the original part of SADOVAYA UL. or Garden St, which was created in the 1730s and took its name from the suburban estates and gardens that bordered it. In the 19C the Sadovaya became one of the city's most important trading streets. The section of Sadovaya Ul. N of the Nevskiy is dealt with in Rte 23.

On the corners of the intersection with Nevskiy Pr. (pp 273, 281) are the Gostinyy Dvor (right) and the Saltykov-Shchedrin Library (left). A little way beyond the library stands the **Vorontsov Palace** (No. 26), built in 1749–57 by Rastrelli for Vice-Chancellor M.I. Vorontsov (no adm.).

This outstanding town house dates from the time when the district was still not built up, and it stands back from the road in its own grounds like a country mansion. The graceful railings in front of the palace, also Rastrelli's, are one of the earliest examples of Russian artistic wrought-iron work. From 1810 the palace housed the *Pazheskiy Korpus* (Corps of Pages), the most select military school in the Empire. Pestel and a number of other Decembrists studied here, as did Kropotkin, the anarchist philosopher. The building is now one of the Suvorov Military Academies. In 1798–1800 Quarenghi added the *Maltese Chapel* for Paul I, who had become Grand Master of the Knights of Malta. It is unfortunate that the chapel is inaccessible, because it is regarded as one of the architect's finest buildings.

Further along (No. 21) (right) stands the former **State Bank** (Assignatsionnyy Bank) (1783–90), now the *Voznesensky Economic Institute*. The three-storey Classical main building stands in a courtyard formed by the horseshoe-shaped depositories. The architect was Quarenghi, and a bust was unveiled here in 1867 to commemorate the 150th anniversary of his death. The row of shops opposite the bank were part of the former *Apraksin Market*.

At the intersection with Ul. Dzerzhinskovo two contrasting buildings can be seen in the distance: the Admiralty (N) and the Theatre of Young Spectators (TYuZ) (S). The 'L'-shaped mansion on the corner (Sadovaya Ul., 38) was built for the millionaire factory-owner Savva Yakovlev in the 1780s. A little farther on the Sadovaya opens into PL. MIRA or Peace Square (Pl. 10; 7).

This area was known as Sennaya Pl. ('Hay Square' or 'Haymarket') from the 1730s, when a market was opened for the sale of livestock, oats, and hay. It was then on the outskirts of the city, at the start of the Moscow road. For a long time the square was also used for the public punishment of serfs. In the 19C the Haymarket was not only St. Petersburg's chief market, where goods could be bought more cheaply than elsewhere, but was also the centre of the worst slums in the city. Stolyarnyy Per. ('Joiners' Lane', now UL. PRZHEVAL'SKOVO) achieved particular notoriety. In 1865 it was reported that in the street's 16 houses there were no fewer than 18 establishments selling drink. The satirist Saltykov-Shchedrin remarked that 'the Haymarket was the only place in the centre of town where the police did not demand even an outward semblance of

View of the Haymarket (K.P. Beggrov, 1820). The Baroque Church of the Assumption was finally demolished as late as 1961

respectability'. This was the setting for 'Crime and Punishment' by Dostoyevsky, who in 1864–67 lived at KAZNECHEYSKAYA UL., 7 (beyond the Griboyedov Canal, and not far from the NW corner of Pl. Mira). Dostoyevsky wrote that Raskolnikov, the hero of his novel, liked to wander aimlessly around the lanes here, mixing with the 'many different sorts of tradespeople and rag-and-bone men' who 'crowded around the eating-houses in the lower storeys, in the dirty evil-smelling courtyards ... and especially in the pubs'. Raskolnikov's house may have been patterned on Dostoyevsky's own; another possibility was the building at GRAZHDANSKAYA UL., 19, on the corner of Ul. Przheval'skovo. The model for the house of the money-lender whom Raskolnikov murders is believed to have been the building at NAB. KANALA GRIBOYEDOVA, 104.

The Haymarket Square was transformed in the late 1930s. The market stalls were removed and trees planted. After the war new apartment blocks replaced those destroyed by bombing, and in 1953 the square received its present name. PLOSHCHAD' MIRA METRO STATION, in the SE corner, occupies the site of one of the landmarks of the old Haymarket, the Baroque Church of the Assumption (Uspenskaya Ts.). The church was completed in 1765 but destroyed in 1961. **Bus Terminal No. 1** (Avtobusnyy Vokzal No. 1) is nearby at Sadovaya Ul., 37.

The **Railway Museum** (Muzey Zheleznodorozhnovo Transporta) is located about 200m to the W of Pl. Mira (Sadovaya Ul., 50).

This is one of the oldest museums in the country, and can trace its history back to 1813. Models and photographs are used to show the development of the Russian railway system, especially in the Soviet period.

The *Children's Park of the Oktyabr'skiy District*, next to the Railway Museum, was formerly the Yusupov Gardens (the Yusupov Palace stands near the SE corner, see p 330).

The writer M.Yu. Lermontov lived in 1836–37 at Sadovaya Ul., 61. On the opposite side of the street (No. 62) is the long arcade of the former *Nikol'skiy Market*, built in 1788–89. In the 19C the market also served as an informal labour exchange; people seeking work would gather in large wooden sheds here. The GRIBOYEDOV CANAL (p 335) flows to the right of Sadovaya Ul. at this point. Beyond the Nikol'skiy Market both are intersected by the KRYUKOV CANAL (Pl. 13; 6).

Sadovaya Ul. runs for some distance beyond the Kryukov Canal. In PL. TURGENEVA, on the site now occupied by Sadovaya Ul., 111 and 112, lived M.V. Butashevich-Petrashevsky. He held here on Friday nights in the late 1840s one of the earliest political salons of the intelligentsia. The 'Petrashevsky Circle' believed in utopian socialism, and many of its members—including the young Dostoyevsky—were arrested in 1849 and condemned to death; they were reprieved at the last moment and exiled to Siberia. The avenue leading north from Pl. Turgeneva has the unlikely name PR. MAKLINA. Formerly Angliyskiy (English) Pr., it was renamed in 1918 after one of the leaders of 'Red Clydeside', John Maclean. Sadovaya Ul. ends at Pl. Repina (Pl. 13; 5), near which come together the Griboyedov Canal, the Fontanka River, and Pr. Gaza.

N of the Nikol'skiy Market and bounded by the intersecting Gri-boyedov and Kryukov Canals is PL. KOMMUNAROV. Here, in the gardens, stands the *Cathedral of St. Nicholas (Nikol'skiy Sobor), also known as the 'Sailors' Church'. The cathedral was built in 1753–62 by S.I. Chevakinsky and represents a fine example of the Russian Baroque, recalling Rastrelli's Smolny Cathedral. Particularly impressive is the light airy 'upper' church, with its rich decoration, carved iconostasis, and icons. The church is open for worship. Nearby, on the Kryukov Canal, stands the *Bell Tower*, an elegant four-tiered structure also by Chevakinsky.

UL. GLINKI leads N from the cathedral and very soon opens into TEATRAL'NAYA PL. or Theatre Square (Pl. 13; 5). In the square are two of the most important cultural institutions in Russia, (left) the *Kirov Theatre (Gos. Akademicheskiy Teatr Opery i Baleta imeni S.M. Kirova) and (right) the **Rimsky-Korsakov Conservatory** (Gos. Kon-servatoriya imeni N.A. Rimskovo-Korsakova).

From the middle of the 18C this area beside the Kryukov Canal was a place of public entertainment, with fairground booths, shows, swings, and roundabouts; from this came its original name, Karusel'naya Pl.

In 1783 the Kamennyy (lit. 'Stone') Theatre, later called the Bolshoy Theatre, was completed on the site of the present Conservatory. Drama, opera, and ballet were presented here, in what was for many years the leading theatre in the capital as well as the largest in Europe. The first performance of Glinka's 'A Life for the Tsar' ('Ivan Susanin') took place here in 1836. By the middle of the 19C, however, the Bolshoy had become a centre of Italian rather than Russian opera.

In 1889 the old building was declared unsafe and was replaced (1896) by the Conservatory, which had been founded three decades earlier (1862) on the initiative of A.G. Rubinstein. Among those associated with the work of the Conservatory have been Tchaikovsky, Glazunov, Prokofiev, and Shostakovich. In 1944 the Conservatory was renamed after Rimskiy-Korsakov, who had taught there for 37 years. The Conservatory incorporates a large theatre used for various public performances, the **Opera Studio** (Opernaya Studiya Konser-vatorii im. N.A. Rimskovo-Korsakova).

Flanking the Conservatory building are statues of (right) Glinka (R.R. Bach, 1906) and (left) Rimsky-Korsakov (V.Ya. Bogolyubov and V.I. Ingal, 1952).

Opposite the old Bolshoy Theatre was a circus-theatre. This burned down in 1859 and was replaced by the Mariya (Mariinskiy) Theatre, now the famous Kirov Theatre. The building was designed by A. Cavos and named after Mariya Aleksandrovna (1824–80), wife of Alexander II. After the Revolution the Mariinskiy became the Akademicheskiy (Academic) Theatre, and in 1935 it was renamed in honour of S.M. Kirov, the Party leader killed in the previous year. Despite these changes, the building is still known affectionately as the 'Mariinka'. It was badly damaged by bombing during the last war, but such was the importance of the theatre that it was one of the first buildings to be repaired. The theatre seats about 1800. Its foyer is surprisingly small, but the auditorium is beautifully decorated in blue and gold.

Many of the finest Russian operas and ballets were first performed at the Mariya Theatre, including Mussorgsky's 'Boris Godunov' (1874), Borodin's 'Prince Igor' (1890), and Tchaikovsky's 'Sleeping Beauty' (1890) and 'Nutcracker' (1892). Verdi's 'La Forza del Destino' also received its première here, in 1862. More recent works created by the Kirov company are Prokofiev's 'Romeo and Juliet' (1940) and Khachaturian's 'Spartacus' (1956).

Among the Russian dancers who made their debuts on the stage of the Mariya/Kirov Theatre were Kschessinska, Preobrazhenska, Pavlova, Karsavina, Nijinsky, and Ulanova. Their tradition was continued by such artists as Irina Kolpakova (and in the West by Rudolf Nureyev, Natalia Makarova, and Mikhail Baryshnikov, former members of the Kirov). Also associated with this ballet company were the choreographers Marius Petipa, M.M. Fokine, and K.M. Sergeyev and the dancer-teacher A.Ya. Vaganova. Chaliapin often sang at the Mariya Theatre and the history of the opera company continued into the modern period with such singers as S.P. Preobrazhenskaya, B.T. Shtokolov, and G.A. Kovalyova.

Teatral'naya Pl. serves as the terminus from which Buses No. 3, 27, and 43 travel to Nevskiy Pr.

Many important figures from the world of theatre and music lived around Teatral'naya Pl. The choreographer M.M. Fokine (1880–1942) had a flat just to the SE of the Conservatory, on the canal embankment (Nab. Kanala Griboyedova, 109), while Igor Stravinsky (1882–1971) lived as a young man at Ul. Glinki, 3–5. Of the great ballerinas. Tamara Karsavina (1885–1978) owned a house facing the Kryukov Canal (Nab. Kryukova Kanala, 8) (NW of the Kirov Theatre), and Anna Pavlova (1881–1931) lived about 600m W of the Kryukov Canal in a six-storey apartment building which still stands at UL. DEKABRISTOV, 60/21 (on the SW corner of the intersection with Pr. Maklina).

The district to the W of the Kryukov Canal and N of the Fontanka River was known as KOLOMNA. The name derives from a corruption of a foreign word. One source may be 'kolonna', the name of the straight avenues (proseki) laid out through this swampy district by G. Trezzini in the 1730s (including the present Ul. Dekabristov and Ul. Soyuza Pechatnikov). Another source might have been the extensive foreign colony (koloniya) here in the 18C.
The 'First Five-Year Plan' Palace of Culture (Dvorets Kul'tury im. Pervoy Pyatiletki), at Ul. Dekabristov, 34 (left), just beyond the Kryukov Canal, was built in 1930 on the site of the former Lithuanian Market (Litovskiy Rynok). The so-called Lithuanian Castle (Litovskiy Zamok), a prison burned down in 1917, once stood on the opposite side of the street. The elaborately-decorated **Synagogue** is located around the corner (left) at LERMONTOVSKIY PER., 2. Another interesting place of worship survives nearby at No. 22 in UL. SOYUZA PECHATNIKOV, the **Chapel of St. Stanislav** (Kostyol Sv. Stanislava). This austere square-shaped Classical structure was built in 1823–25 to the plans of D.I. Visconti.
The poet A.A. Blok lived from 1912 at the end of Ul. Dekabristov (No. 57/25), in an apartment building on the Pryazhka River embankment; he died here in 1921. A **Blok Museum** (Muzey-Kvartira A.A. Bloka) has been established here, containing many of his personal effects.

25 Liteynyy Prospekt and Vladimirskiy Prospekt

Liteynyy Pr. and Vladimirskiy Pr. form, with Zagorodnyy Pr., a long avenue cutting across the city from the Neva to Moskovskiy Pr. For the sake of convenience, the avenue is here divided into two parts. The common starting point is the intersection of the avenue with Nevskiy Pr., some 200m E of the Fontanka River (Pl. 10; 6). Rte A follows Liteynyy Pr. N to the Neva, while Rte B leads in the opposite direction along Vladimirskiy Pr.

A. Liteynyy Prospekt

The name of this avenue is one of the oldest in the city and derives from the 'Liteynyy Dvor' (Smelting House), a cannon foundry established on the left bank of the Neva in 1711. The avenue later became one of the most important in the city, and a major shopping street.

Among those who lived in the part of the Liteynyy nearest Nevskiy Pr. were K.P. Pobedonostsev, the conservative mentor of the last two Emperors (at No. 62) and the satirist M.Ye. Saltykov-Schedrin (No. 60). The *Kuybyshev Hospital* is set back from the road at No. 56; this large Classical structure was built by Quarenghi in 1803–05 as the Mariya Hospital. Beyond (right) is UL. ZHUKOVSKOVO, formerly a centre of Russian journalism. The pre-revolutionary newspaper 'Rech'', often described as the equivalent of 'The Times', was edited at No. 21, and the offices of 'Novoye Vremya' stood in the first street to the left UL. CHEKHOVA (No. 6).

The short UL. BELINSKOVO leads left from Liteynyy Pr. to the Fontanka River and contains (right) the very old **Church of SS. Simeon and Anna** (Ts. Sv. Simeoniya i Anny) (1731–34) (no adm.). This two-storey church with its ribbed dome, spired bell-tower, and decorative pilasters was originally the work of M.G. Zemtsov. (For the nearby embankment of the Fontanka see p 333.) Zemtsov's church stands on the corner of MOKHOVAYA UL., which runs parallel to the Liteynyy. Further up this street (right) stand the *Mussorgsky Academy of Music* (No. 36) and the *Institute of Theatre, Music, and Cinematography* (No. 34); during the First World War the latter building was the home of the octogenarian prime minister, I.L. Goremykin. The institute's *Practice Theatre* at No. 33 (opposite) was from 1922 to 1962 the home of the Theatre of Young Spectators (TYuZ) (now located on Zagorodnyy Pr.). Before the Revolution this was the liberal Tenishev Commercial Academy to which many children of the intelligentsia were sent, including the future writer Vladimir Nabokov. Among the famous people who lived in Mokhovaya Ul. were the critic V.V. Stasov (1854–73) (No. 26), Admiral S.O. Makarov (1892–98) (No. 7), and the writer I.A. Goncharov; Goncharov lived for 34 years at No. 3, where he wrote his celebrated novel 'Oblomov'.

Returning to Liteynyy Pr., the **Leningrad Theatre of Drama and Comedy** (Teatr Dramy i Komedii) is situated at No. 51 (left). The building was owned before 1917 by the Theatrical Society. It was destroyed during the last war, rebuilt, and since 1963 has housed this touring company for the Leningrad Region. In the late 1890s Diaghilev lived at No. 45 and established here the editorial offices of the 'World of Art' (Mir Iskusstva) magazine. The red sandstone Pseudo-Baroque building at No. 42 was built in the 1850s as the *Yusupov Mansion* and is now used for the public lectures of the

'Znaniye' organisation. The poet N.A. Nekrasov (1821–77) spent the last twenty years of his life at No. 36/2; here he worked on the journals 'The Contemporary' and 'Notes of the Fatherland'. The poet's flat was made into a small **Nekrasov Museum** (Muzey-Kvartira N.A. Nekrasova) in 1946. The adjacent street was renamed in his honour; at No. 10 in UL. NEKRASOVA is located the Leningrad **Bolshoy Puppet Theatre** (Bol'shoy Teatr Kukol), founded in 1931. There is a statue of Nekrasov in the small park at the end of the street (1200m). P.N. Milyukov, the historian and liberal leader, lived before the Revolution in the big grey seven-storey block of flats overlooking this park (Ul. Nekrasova, 60).

Just to the right of Liteynyy Pr., in PL. RADISHCHEVA (Pl. 10; 6), may be seen the fine ***Cathedral of the Transfiguration** (Preobrazhenskiy Sobor), with its five domes and Classical portico.

This site was originally the headquarters of the Grenadier Company of the Preobrazhenskiy Guards Regiment. In 1741 Elizabeth Petrovna came here to rally guards' support for her successful coup, and in commemoration the new Empress commissioned a regimental church here. This Baroque building burned down in 1825 and was restored in the Classical style by V.P. Stasov (1827–29). An unusual feature is the circle of Turkish cannon around the little wooded square in which the church is set; these were captured in the Russo-Turkish War of 1828. The cathedral is open for worship and contains a splendid carved wooden iconostasis designed by Stasov.

UL. MAYAKOVSKOVO is the first major road behind the square. It runs N–S (parallel to the Liteynyy) and takes its name from the poet Mayakovsky, who lived with Lili and Osip Brik at No. 52. The artist Léon Bakst, who worked with Diaghilev, had a flat at the same address.

The Pseudo-Russian building on the corner of Liteynyy Pr. and UL. SALTYKOVA-SHCHEDRINA (Pl. 10; 6) was opened by Nicholas II as the *Officers Club* (Ofitserskoye Sobraniye) (1895–98); it fulfils the same function for the Soviet Army of today. Earlier this site was occupied by the house of Count A.A. Arakcheyev, the reactionary advisor to Alexander I; next door were the headquarters of Arakcheyev's infamous Military Colonies.

Velten's interesting Classical **Church of St. Anna** (Ts. Sv. Anny) (1775–79) may be found not far along Ul. Saltykova-Shchedrina, at No. 8 (left). The N end (on Ul. Petra Lavrova) takes the form of a semi-circle of Ionic columns crowned with a cupola. In 1939 the former Lutheran church was converted into a cinema, the *Spartak* or Spartacus.

The next turn to the right off the Liteynyy is UL. PETRA LAVROVA, named after the radical thinker P.L. Lavrov, who lived at No. 12/4. This handsome boulevard was once, as Furshtadtskaya Ul., a fashionable residential street.

Here during the First World War lived two of the most prominent Duma politicians, M.V. Rodzyanko (No. 20) and A.I. Guchkov (No. 36). One of the mainstays of the Bolshevik organisation, D.V. Stasova, lived in the same building as Rodzyanko, and Lenin was a frequent visitor. The *United States Consulate* stands across the street, at No. 15. There are two impressive mansions at the far end of the street: the former house of Count P.N. Ignat'yev (No. 52) now serves as a *Palace of Weddings* (Dvorets Brakosochetaniya) (A.I. Gogen, 1896) while the Spiridonov town house (A.N. Pomerantsev, 1897) is used for the ceremonial registration of births.

UL. CHAYKOVSKOVO is named in honour of the composer Tchaikovsky who studied here at the Law School (No. 1/16) and lived briefly (1852–53) at No. 41. Formerly Sergiyevskaya Ul., it was lined with the homes of the wealthy, including the Neo-Rococo *Buturlin House* at No. 10 (G.A. Bosse, 1857–60).

On the right side of the Liteynyy, beyond Ul. Chaykovskovo, stands a massive seven-storey administrative block, which is of interest as one of the few large buildings erected in central Leningrad between the two world wars. It was built for the OGPU (secret police) in 1931–32 by A.I. Gegello, A.A. Ol', and N.A. Trotsky.

This site was once occupied by the St. Petersburg Regional Court (Okruzhnyy Sud). The building of the old Arsenal was converted into a court in 1865–66, and was used for some of the most famous trials in Russian history. The leading Populists of the 1870s were tried here (the trials of 'the 50' and 'the 193'), and also the assassins of Alexander II (1881), Lenin's elder brother (condemned to death in 1887), and the leaders of the 1905 St. Petersburg Soviet, including Leon Trotsky. The Regional Court was regarded as one of the most outstanding symbols of Tsarist oppression, and it was burned down by rioters on 27 February 1917.

The Liteynyy ends at the river; near here was located the 'Liteynyy Dvor' from which the avenue took its name. The embankment to the right is called NAB. ROBESP'YERA, that to the left NAB. KUTUZOVA. The first is named after Ròbespierre, the second after Field Marshal M.I. Kutuzov, the hero of 1812, who lived at No. 30.

The French Embassy used to be at Nab. Kutuzova, 10. At the height of the Franco-Russian entente, after a state visit by President Faure in 1897, Gagarinskaya Nab. was renamed Frantsuzskaya (French) Nab. The embankment was renamed again after the Revolution, this time in honour of the French socialist Jaurès. The present name dates from after the Second World War. The Kuleshov-Bezborodko House, a marble-faced Italian Renaissance mansion, stands at UL. FURMANOVA, 3 (by the intersection with Nab. Kutuzova). It was once occupied by the mistress (from 1880 morganatic wife) of Alexander II, Princess Yekaterina Dolgorukaya—later Princes Yur'yevskaya (1847–1922).

B.   Vladimirskiy Prospekt

VLADIMIRSKIY PR. (Pl. 10; 8) extends for only 400m S of Nevskiy Pr. Masons and carpenters from the town of Vladimir settled here in the early 18C, and from this came the name of the present avenue.

The **Lensovet Theatre** (Leningradskiy Gos. Teatr im. Lensoveta), at No. 12 (left), was formerly the *Merchants Club* (Kupecheskoye Sobraniye). An impressive Classical structure with a central row of ten pilasters, it was built by A.A. Mikhaylov in 1826–28. The Lensovet company was founded in 1933 (but was known until 1953 as the Novyy Theatre). Dostoyevsky lived from 1842–45 at No. 11 across the street.

Vladimirskiy Pr. ends with VLADIMIRSKAYA PL. (Pl. 10; 8), the site of the large yellow *Vladimir Church (Vladimirskaya Ts.). The two-storey church with its onion domes set on high drums is the work of an unknown architect (1761–69); the Classical vestibule was added to the W end by A.I. Mel'nikov in 1831. Quarenghi designed a detached bell tower in 1783 (the fourth tier is a later addition).

The entrance to VLADIMIRSKAYA METRO STATION occupies the S side of the square. To the left is KUZNECHNYY PER., with the *Kuznechnyy Market*. The market was built in the Soviet period in a mixture of Baroque and Renaissance styles (S.I. Ovsyannikov and A.S. Pronin, 1925–27). Dostoyevsky rented a flat at No. 5 in this street from 1878, and he died here on 28 January 1881. A **Dostoyevsky Museum** (Muzey-Kvartira F.M. Dostoyevskovo) was opened here in 1971, the 150th anniversary of the writer's birth.

Several rooms have been recreated as they were in Dostoyevsky's time, including the Study where he wrote 'The Brothers Karamazov' and the

Drawing-Room where he received visitors. One room has been made into an exhibition hall tracing the great writer's life and displaying various editions of his work.

The **Museum of the Arctic and Antarctic** (Muzey Arktiki i Antarktiki) is situated a little farther down Kuznechnyy Per., at the intersection with UL. MARATA.

This striking building is basically cubic in shape but with six-columned porticoes on each side and a dome on a square base above. It was built in 1820–26 by A.I. Mel'nikov as the *Church of St. Nicholas* (Nikol'skaya Yedinovercheskaya Ts.). The present museum, opened in 1937, has extensive displays on Soviet exploration of the polar regions, including various mementoes, models, and dioramas.

Meetings of the Bolsheviks' 'April Conference' (1917) were held across the street, at Kuznechnyy Per., 9/27; originally a women's university (Vysshiye Zhenskiye Kursy) (est. 1914), the building now houses the *Togliatti Engineering Institute*. A.N. Radishchev wrote his celebrated radical work 'Journey from St. Petersburg to Moscow' when he was living at what is now Ul. Marata, 14 (to the left). In the opposite direction (right) along Ul. Marata can be found the architecturally interesting *Yamskoy Market* (No. 53); V.P. Stasov designed a triangular building surrounded on each side by a long Doric colonnade (1817–19).

ZAGORODNYY PR. (or 'Suburban Avenue') (Pl. 10; 8) turns to the SW beyond Vladimirskaya Pl. and continues in a straight line for 2km to Moskovskiy Pr. A number of figures from the world of music lived here: A.G. Rubinstein at No. 9 (1887–91), and Tchaikovsky at 14/25 (1863–65). A small **Rimsky-Korsakov Museum** (Muzey-Kvartira N.A. Rimskovo-Korsakova) was opened in 1973 at No. 28. M.A. Balakirev lived down a side street, RAZ"EZZHAYA UL., at No. 11 (1879–82). Alexander Kerensky, leader of the 1917 Provisional Government, lived before the Revolution at Zagorodnyy Pr., 23.

As in other peripheral areas of old St. Petersburg, there were barracks here. The Semyonovskiy Guards Regiment was quartered along the S side of Zagorodnyy Pr. and to the W of ZVENIGORODSKAYA UL. In October 1820 there was a mutiny in this regiment which foreshadowed the later Decembrist rising; the Semyonovskiy Mutiny made a strong impression on Emperor Alexander I, as he had once been the regimental commander.

The parade ground of the Semyonovskiy Regiment, or the Semyonovskiy Platz, stretched from Zagorodnyy Pr. (at the S end of the modern Ul. Dzerzhinskovo) to the Obvodnyy Canal and was the scene of several grim episodes. Here took place in 1849 the cruel mock-execution of the members of the Petrashevsky Circle; 21 people, including the writer Dostoyevsky, were sentenced to be shot, and only at the last moment were they told that their actual punishment would be a prison term. In 1881, five 'People's Will' terrorists who had organised the assassination of Alexander II were hanged in the Semyonovskiy Platz; among the five were Andrey Zhelyabov and Sof'ya Perovskaya.

In the latter part of the 19C the parade ground was made into a race track or hippodrome. A large part of this site is now occupied by the **Bryantsev Theatre of Young Spectators** (Teatr Yunykh Zriteley im. A.A. Bryantseva), better known as TYuZ. The company was founded in 1922 by A.A. Bryantsev and was one of the first Russian youth theatres. Its first production, and one of the most popular, was P.P. Yershov's 'The Little Hunchbacked Pony' ('Konyok-Gorbunok'); this is still used as the symbol of TYuZ. The present 1000-seat theatre was opened in 1962, and here TYuZ continues its tradition of producing plays for children and young adults.

The Admiralty spire can be seen far away (right) at the end of UL. DZERZHINSKOVO. Rasputin lived nearby in this street (then

Gorokhovaya Ul.) at the height of his notoriety (No. 64). PER. IL'ICHA runs parallel to Ul. Dzerzhinskovo and a block to the W. From February 1894 to April 1895 the young Lenin lived in a flat here (No. 7/4. This has now been made into a **Lenin Museum** (Kvartira-Muzey V.I. Lenina). The red Classical building located farther along Zagorodnyy Pr. and behind a square to the right is the *Military Medical Museum* (Voyenno-Meditsinskiy Muzey). The museum contains a large collection of material on the history of medicine in the Russian armed forces and particularly in the Second World War.

Rasputin's House on Gorokhovaya Ul. (now Ul. Dzerzhinskovo)

The **Vitebsk Railway Station** (Vitebskiy Vokzal) (Pl. 10; 7) stands on the opposite side of the street. This is of considerable historical interest as it was the first Russian railway station. The Viennese F.A. von Gerstner laid out the first experimental railway running 22km from St. Petersburg to Tsarskoye Selo (Pushkin); the St. Petersburg terminal was opened in 1837 and is now the Vitebsk Station. Suburban trains still leave here for Pushkin and Pavlovsk. The present building dates from 1904 (S.A. Brzzhovsky and S.I. Minash) and represents a remarkable example of Russian Art Nouveau.

The PUSHKINSKAYA METRO STATION is just to the left of the Vitebsk Station.

Zagorodnyy Pr. continues for another 700m to Moskovskiy Pr. (p 320).

26 The Smolny District

The extensive district E of Liteynyy Pr. and N of Nevskiy Pr. contains much of interest. This Rte leads NE from near Pl. Vosstaniya (by the Moscow Railway Station) along Suvorovskiy Pr. to the Smolny Institute. Trolleybus No. 5 follows this avenue from the region of PLOSHCHAD' VOSSTANIYA METRO STATION; Bus No. 26 follows it from the intersection of Suvorovskiy Pr. and Nevskiy Pr. From the Smolny, Buses No. 136, and 137 travel W past the Tauride Palace to Liteynyy Pr.

SUVOROVSKIY PR. (Pl. 11; 5) commemorates one of Russia's greatest soldiers, Generalissimo A.V. Suvorov; it received the name on the centenary of Suvorov's death, in 1900. The avenue runs 2.5km from Nevskiy Pr. to the Smolny. The streets crossing Suvorovskiy Pr. at right angles have the names 1-YA, -YA, etc. SOVETSKAYA UL. Formerly they were called 1-ya, 2-ya, etc. Rozhdestvenskaya Ul. The whole district was known as the Rozhdestvenskaya District, the name deriving from the Church of the Nativity (Ts. Rozhdestva) (P.Ye. Yegorov, 1781–89, demolished in 1934), which stood in a square (right) in 6-ya Sovetskaya Ul. Dostoevsky lived from 1875–78 at 5-ya Sovetskaya Ul., 6/6; here he began work on 'The Brothers Karamazov'. At 10-ya Sovetskaya Ul., 17 (reached from Suvorovskiy Pr. via UL. MOISEYENKO), lived the veteran Bolshevik S.Ya. Alliluyev. The Alliluyev flat has been preserved as a small **Lenin Museum** (Kvartira-Muzey V.I. Lenina). The Bolshevik leader stayed here from 7 to 9 July 1917 while hiding from the Provisional Government after the 'July Days' demonstrations. Nadezhda Alliluyeva, the daughter of the family, later married Joseph Stalin; she was to be the mother of Svetlana Alliluyeva.

The area to the left of Suvorovskiy Pr., beyond Ul Moiseyenko, and GOSPITAL'NAYA UL., was once the Preobrazhenskiy Platz, the parade ground of the Preobrazhenskiy Guards Regiment. The former Nicholas General Staff Academy was built on the S part of the parade ground in 1900 (A.I. Gogen), while the **Suvorov Museum** (Muzey A.V. Suvorova) was built on the N part. the Suvorov Museum stands at No. 43 on UL. SALTYKOVA-SHCHEDRINA, opposite the gardens of the Tauride Palace, and can be reached from Suvorovskiy Pr. via TAVRICHESKAYA UL.

Generalissimo A.V. Suvorov (1730–1800) was one of Imperial Russia's finest soldiers, excellent both as a strategist and as a leader of men. He is held in high regard in modern Soviet Russia as well, where several of the élite cadet schools bear his name. Suvorov is perhaps best known for his campaign in the Alps in 1799 against the French, but his greatest success came in the wars of Catherine II against the Turks; he also suppressed the Polish uprising of 1794. Part of the Suvorov Museum is devoted to the life and exploits of the famous general, with documents, paintings, dioramas, banners, war trophies and some of Suvorov's personal effects. The other part is concerned with the history of the Soviet officer corps, which is supposed to be trained in the tradition of Suvorov.

The sand-coloured brick museum, built by public subscription in 1901–04 to the design of A.I. Gogen and G.D. Grimm, is an interesting example of the

Pseudo-Russian style. To emphasise the military connection, the central part takes the form of a fortress tower. The wings are decorated with large mosaic panels by N.A. Shabunin: 'The Recall of Suvorov from Konchanskoye' (the village to which he had been retired by Paul I) and'Suvorov's Crossing of the Alps'.

The Preobrazhenskiy Guards, the senior regiment in the Imperial army, were quartered down the street (to the W), at Ul. Saltykova-Shchedrina, 31–39. The *Preobrazhenskiy Barracks* were built in the early 19C. The most impressive part of the complex is the large regimental hospital with its eight-columned portico.

Suvorovskiy Pr. ends with the Smolny Institute and, beyond, the Smolny Convent (Pl. 11; 4). The name 'Smolny' derives from the 'Smolny Dvor' (lit., 'Tar House') which was established here for the Admiralty by Peter I. The convent is flanked by two buildings originally designed as schools for young women. The ***Smolny Institute**, to the right, was intended for the nobility, and the *Alexander Institute*, to the left, for townspeople (meshchane). The Alexander Institute, a large yellow structure with a concave façade, was built by Velten in 1765–75 and is now used by Leningrad University.

The 'enlightened despot' Catherine II founded the first school for daughters of the gentry in 1764. At the start of the following century the school, known commonly as the Smolny Institute, moved from the nearby convent buildings to purpose-built accommodation. The 220m long three-storey yellow building was created by Quarenghi (1806–08) in a Classical style which contrasts with the Baroque convent. The Classical *Gatehouses* (propylaea) flanking the long entrance road are actually the post-revolutionary work (1923) of V.A. Shchuko and V.G. Gel'freykh—who went on to design some of Moscow's major buildings in the 1930s. A life-size *Statue of Lenin* by V.V. Kozlov stands in front of the eight-columned portico of the institute; unveiled in 1927, it was one of the first monuments to the Communist leader.

The Smolny Institute is one of the most famous buildings in the Soviet Union, as well as a symbol of Leningrad, because of its role in 1917. In August of that year the Central Executive Committee (VTsIK) and the Petrograd Soviet moved to the institute building from the nearby Tauride Palace. Two months later the city Soviet, now chaired by Trotsky and dominated by the Bolsheviks, led the October insurrection from the Smolny; here also was the headquarters of the Bolshevik Central Committee. Lenin arrived at the Smolny on the night of 24–25 October to take command of the rising. The 2nd All-Russian Congress of Soviets, the body which took power in the name of the slogan 'All Power to the Soviets!', met from 25–27 October in the *Lecture Hall* (Aktovvy Zal) and passed the famous decrees on land reform and peace. The Lecture Hall survives as an outstanding example of Classical architecture. It is sometimes possible, through Intourist, to arrange a visit to the Lecture Hall and to the modest room in the S wing where Lenin lived and worked from 27 October to 10 November 1917. The rooms used by Lenin from 10 November to 10 March 1918 and by Sovnarkom, the Bolshevik-dominated 'cabinet' which ran the country, are not opened to the public.

After the capital was moved to Moscow, the Smolny became the local Party headquarters. It was in the Smolny that L.V. Nikolayev assassinated Sergey Kirov, the head of the Leningrad Party organisation, in December 1934; the killing triggered off the Purges of the late 1930s.

The ***Smolny Convent**, a major architectural monument, now serves as an exhibition centre, **'Leningrad Today and Tomorrow'** (Ekspozitsiya 'Leningrad Sevodnya i Zavtra').

In 1748 Empress Elizabeth Petrovna founded here the 'Resurrection New Convent of the Virgin' (Voskresenskiy Novodevich'iy Monastyr') and commissioned Bartolomeo Francesco Rastrelli (future architect of the Winter Palace, etc.) to head the construction work. The building of the convent proceeded slowly after the first years. Russia's entry into the Seven Years' War (1757) reduced the funds available, and in 1761 Elizabeth died; Rastrelli went abroad after the accession of Catherine, leaving only the basic structure completed. The convent, as such, was closed in 1797, and made into a Widows Home, but in

1832–35 V.P. Stasov carried out the work of completing and decorating Rastrelli's project.

The towering blue and white buildings of the convent are a combination of traditional Russian forms with Baroque detail. The **Cathedral** is basically shaped like a Greek cross. The broad two-storey lower section serves as a base for the tall dome with its four interconnected satellite towers; crowning the edifice are five gilded Baroque cupolas. The cathedral is the main landmark of the district and can be seen at a considerable distance from the Neva or from Suvorovskiy Pr. and Ul. Voinova. The blue walls and towers are richly decorated with white pilasters and window-surrounds.

Rastrelli never completed the work on the interior, and Stasov kept the final version simple, with white walls and some sculptured detail. It is still possible to get some impression of what the 19C interior was like, although it now houses the 'Leningrad Today and Tomorrow' Exhibition. On display are the products of Leningrad's factories as well as the plans, architectural and otherwise, for the future developments of the city: there are numerous models, photographs, and dioramas.

The cathedral is surrounded by a square of *Convent Buildings*, which Rastrelli created in the same Baroque style. The cells, refectory, etc., are of a uniform two-storey design, and from the four internal corners rise tall domes and cupolas. Various Party organisations are now housed in these buildings (no adm.). Rastrelli's original design included a 140m six-tiered gateway bell tower on the W side, but this was never built; it would have been taller and more substantial than the 122m spire of the Peter-Paul Cathedral and 50m higher than the similar monastery bell towers in Moscow. (A model of the original convent project, complete with bell tower, is on display in the Museum of the Academy of Arts.) The existing W opening in the convent square was created by V.P. Stasov; the façades were designed in the 1860s by P.I. Tamansky in the spirit of the Rastrelli buildings.

UL. VOINOVA (Pl. 11; 3) runs W from the Smolny Convent to Liteynyy Pr. (2.5km). This street was originally called Shpalernaya Ul. after a factory manufacturing wallpaper (shpalera) that was located here until the mid-19C; the present name commemorates the Bolshevik I.A. Voinov who was killed at No. 28 by soldiers during the wave of anti-Bolshevik feeling which followed the 'July Days' demonstrations of 1917. Not far from the Smolny, on the corner of STAVROPOL'SKIY PER. (right), stands a handsome tan-coloured building with white trim, the **Kikin Palace** (Palaty Kikina). Although much rebuilt, this is one of the oldest structures in the city and dates from 1714. The first owner was A.V. Kikin, an associate of Peter the Great. Kikin fell from favour and was executed; his mansion became temporary home for Peter's Kunstkamera museum. After being damaged during the Blockade the Kikin Palace was restored to its original appearance.

Not far beyond, on the opposite side of Ul. Voinova (No. 47), is a building of even greater historical importance, the *Tauride Palace (Tavricheskiy Dvorets) (Pl. 11; 3). The architect I.Ye. Starov built the palace in 1783–89 for Catherine the Great's favourite, Grigory Potyomkin, who in 1783 had master-minded the annexation of the Crimea (Tauris or Tavriya). Erected in what was then a sparsely-settled district, it was one of the first Russian buildings in the Classical style. This long yellow palace, with its low dome set above the central six-columned portico and its handsome wings flanking the courtyard, now serves as the Leningrad Higher Party School (no. adm.).

Potyomkin hardly lived to enjoy his magnificent home, and within five years Catherine herself was dead. The Emperor Paul's violent reaction to his mother and her Court included the stripping of the Tauride Palace and its conversion into a barracks for the Horse Guards. Although the building was restored after Paul's death, it only became prominent after 1905 when the great Winter Garden was converted into the chamber of Russia's parliament, the State Duma.

In February and March 1917 the Tauride Palace was at the very centre of the Revolution which overthrew the Tsar; both the Provisional Government and the Petrograd Soviet first met here (although both moved out in the course of the year). The palace was again briefly the political centre of Russia in January 1918. The Constituent Assembly gathered here for one day and was then closed by the Bolsheviks, who in turn used the building for the 3rd Congress of Soviets and the 7th Party Congress. The 2nd Congress of the Comintern met here in the summer of 1920.

The yellow former *Barracks of the Chevalier Guards Regiment* (Ul. Voinova, 41/43) occupy most of the block W of the Tauride Palace. They were built at the very beginning of the 19C, to the plans of Luigi Rusca. The same architect also designed the nearby *Church of All Sorrows* (Ts. Vsekh Skorbyashchikh) (1817–18); the rectangular Classical building with its low dome and six-columned portico stands at Ul. Voinova, 35a.

The pre-revolutionary 'House of Preliminary Detention' (Dom Predvaritel'novo Zaklyucheniya), known to generations of political prisoners as the 'Predvarilka', is located at No. 25 in Ul. Voinova. It was the mistreatment of a political prisoner here that led to Vera Zasulich's attempt on the life of the governor-general. F.F. Trepov, in 1878. A plaque on the wall notes that Lenin spent 14 months in a cell here (December 1895–February 1897) before his exile to Siberia.

This Rte ends at Liteynyy Pr. (p 293), which is well served by public transport. CHERNYSHEVSKAYA METRO STATION (Pl. 10; 6) is not far away, to the S down Ul. Chernyshevskovo (400m); this street turns off Ul. Voinova by the Church of All Sorrows.

27 Vasil'yevskiy Island

Vasil'yevskiy Island (Vasil'yevskiy Ostrov) forms the NW part of central Leningrad. The most convenient route to the island runs over the DVORTSOVYY MOST (Pl. 13; 2), between the Hermitage and the Admiralty. Bus No. 44 and Trolleybuses No. 1, 7, and 10 follow this route from Nevskiy Pr.

This was one of the first areas of St. Petersburg to be built up. Because the island could be easily defended the first town planners considered making it the core of the new city. In the event, Vasil'yevskiy Island was soon surpassed by the districts on the left bank of the Neva. With the exception of the area around the SE tip it became a quiet residential district, notable for the many foreign—especially German—residents.

The *Strelka (Point) (Pl. 13; 2) at the E tip of Vasil'yevskiy Island affords one of the finest views of the city. The shore here was sheathed in granite in the early 19C. The present geometrical square was laid out in the 1920s; in 1937 it was given the name PUSH-KINSKAYA PL. A striking feature of the square and of the Strelka are the **Rostral Columns** (Rostral'nyye Kolonny), which were erected in 1810 to the plans of T. de Thomon. For a long time—until the 1880s—the shore around the Strelka was the main port of St. Petersburg, and the ships prows (rostra) emerging from the 34m Doric columns symbolise the port. The seated figures represent four great Russian rivers—the Volga, Dnieper, Neva, and Volkhov. The columns were designed to act as lighthouses, and the gas-fired torches are still lit on special occasions.

The Rostral Columns constitute part of a splendid ensemble centred on the present **Central Naval Museum** (Tsentral'nyy Voyenno-Morskoy Muzey), formerly the *Exchange* (Birzha).

The Exchange was designed by T. de Thomon and built in 1805–10. It was modelled on the Greek basilica at Paestum; the building is set on a granite stylobate and has ten Doric columns on the front and fourteen on the side. Sculpture groups stand in the attics; on the E. 'Neptune with Two Rivers', on the W 'Navigation with Mercury and Two Rivers'. The Exchange became redundant after the Revolution, and in 1940 the building was given to the naval museum; with its nautical themes de Thomon's building is an appropriate site.

The history of the museum can be traced back to 1709, and before the Revolution it was located in the Main Admiralty. The *Boat of Peter I*, the 'Grandfather of the Russian Navy', is among the exhibits. Also on display are a wealth of models, flags, paintings, photographs, and other items showing the development of the Russian fleet from the sailing ships of Petrine days to modern guided-missile submarines. Special attention is devoted to the 1917 Revolution and to the Second World War.

Two nearly identical buildings with twelve-columned porticoes flank the Naval Museum and complete the ensemble of the Strelka. These were originally built by Luchini in 1826–32 as *Warehouses* (Pakgauzy). The Warehouse to the N now houses the *Dokuchayev Museum of Soil Science* (Tsentral'nyy Muzey Pochvovedeniya im. V.V. Dokuchayeva). To the S is the **Zoology Museum** (Zoologicheskiy Muzey).

Founded in 1832, the Zoology Museum is the largest of its type in the USSR and one of the largest in the world. The collection, originally part of Peter I's Kunstkamera, has been expanded to include over 100,000 specimens from all over the world. It includes the best-preserved mammoth carcass extant, which was unearthed in Siberia in 1902, and there are many other examples of rare or extinct animals. Part of the collection is exhibited in the form of dioramas.

The *Institute of Russian Literature*, also known as Pushkinskiy Dom (Pushkin House) and formerly the *Custom-House* (Tamozhnya), stands behind and to the W of the Dokuchayev Museum, on the embankment of the MALAYA NEVA RIVER (NAB. MAKAROVA, 4). The Custom-House was built at the same time as the Warehouses, and by the same architect, but the style is late Classical, with Ionic columns and a dome and drum. Statues of Mercury, Neptune and Ceres decorate the roof. The institute is primarily intended for the use of specialists in Russian literature, and the handsome Classical interior includes the **Literary Museum** (Literaturnyy Muzey Instituta Russkoy Literatury). On display here are permanent exhibitions on Gogol, Lermontov, Tolstoy, Turgenev, Goncharov, and Gorky, with personal effects, photographs, portraits, manuscripts, and first editions.

A long utilitarian-looking group of buildings with staircases in the centre stands on the opposite side of the Malaya Neva (Bol'shoy Pr., 1-a). These are known as the *Tuchkov Buyan*. They were built in 1764–70 with the participation of Rinaldi as warehouses for hemp, one of Russia's leading exports.

Next to the Institute of Russian Literature a short road runs left and ends at a building with a long arcade, the former *Novobirzhevoy Gostinyy Dvor* (lit., 'New-Exchange Bazaar'). Designed in the early 19C by Quarenghi, it has been considerably altered, and now forms part of Leningrad University. Nearby, at BIRZHEVAYA LINIYA, 1 is the **Library of the Academy of Sciences** (Biblioteka Akademii Nauk SSSR or BAN); this is the third largest library in the USSR, although it was badly damaged by fire in 1988.

The W side of the Academy of Sciences Library is bounded by the

Mendeleyevskaya Liniya. (On Vasil'yevskiy Island each side of the N–S streets is called a 'line' or liniya.) The far side of Mendeleyevskaya Liniya is occupied by one of the oldest buildings in the city, the *Twelve Colleges (Dvenadtsat' Kollegii).

This 400m long building was designed as a major administrative centre. There are twelve detached façades, each of which was planned to house a Kollegiya, one of the collective-ministries which Peter the Great set up. The project was the subject of Russia's first architectural competition, but the final building was under construction for a very long time (1722–42) and a number of architects took part, including Schwertfeger, D. and G. Trezzini, and B.C. Rastrelli. The function of the building gradually changed. St. Petersburg University, which Alexander I founded in 1819, was housed here, and by 1835 had taken over the whole building. The great scientist D.I. Mendeleyev, inventor of the periodic table, worked in this building for 33 years—hence the name of the liniya.

Mendeleyevskaya Liniya ends at the embankment of the Neva, UNIVERSITETSKAYA NAB. To the left, on the short route back to the Strelka, is the building of the **Academy of Sciences** (Akademiya Nauk SSSR) (No. 5).

The Academy was set up in 1724 and began to function the following year—with 17 imported German scholars. The present building, designed by Quarenghi, was put up sixty years later (1783–89); it is an austere structure with an eight-columned portico. The building is still occupied by the Academy, but the central administration was moved in 1934 to Moscow. Behind the main façade and facing the Twelve Colleges is a separate building constructed (1826–31) by Luchini, the Academy's *Museum Wing* (Mendeleyevskaya Liniya, 1).

The long blue and white building between the Academy of Sciences and the Zoology Museum now houses the **Museum of Anthropology and Ethnography** (Muzey Antropologii i Etnografii), not to be confused with the Museum of Ethnography of the Peoples of the USSR in Inzhenernaya Ul. (p 272).

This was originally intended for the *Kunstkamera*, the Chamber of Curiosities (kunstkammer), which Peter the Great assembled in 1714. The building was designed by Matarnovi but other architects supervised the prolonged construction (1718–34). There are really two buildings linked by a central block; in the 18C the W wing housed a museum, the E wing a library, the central part an anatomical theatre, and the tower the first Russian observatory. The top of the tower was destroyed in 1747, and it was only restored 200 years later.
     The entrance is via the late-19C extension on TAMOZHENNYY PER. (left). The collection includes material gathered from all over the world, first by individual Russian explorers and then by the expeditions of the Academy of Sciences. There are also grisly remnants of the original Kunstkamera, including preserved freaks and human organs. On the 2nd Floor, under the tower, is a small museum devoted to the great scientist M.V. Lomonosov (1711–65), who worked in this building from 1741 until his death.

To the W along Universitetskaya Nab. (beyond the S end of the Twelve Colleges) are several buildings of **Leningrad State University** (Leningradskiy Gos. Universitet) (Pl. 13; 4). It was formerly called the Imperial University, and later Zhdanov University, after Andrey Zhdanov, the Leningrad Party leader who died in 1948.
     Universitetskaya Nab., 9, is the 'Rector's Wing' (Rektorskiy Fligel') (1834–35), where the poet Blok was born in 1880. No. 11, a long building with three storeys in the centre and two in the wings, was originally intended as a palace for Peter the Great's grandson, Peter II. The young Emperor reigned very briefly (1727–30) and the palace, begun in the year of his accession, was completed only in 1761. In the 19C it became part of the university.
     The *Menshikov Palace (Menshikovskiy Dvorets-Muzey), at Universitetskaya Nab., 15, is a very historic building. It was intended for

Aleksandr Menshikov, Peter I's closest associate, and built in 1710–16 by Fontana and Schädel; when completed it was the most splendid palace in the new capital.

The building has been much altered. In 1732 it became a school for training the sons of the aristocracy for an army career. This was at first known as the Sukhoputnyy Shlyakhetskiy Korpus (lit., 'Army Gentry Corps') and then as the *1st Cadet Corps* (1-y Kadetskiy Korpus). The palace soon proved to be too small for its new purpose, and in 1738–66 an extension was built running along S"YEZDOVSKAYA LINIYA. Among the students at the school were Field Marshal P.A. Rumyantsev and a number of the Decembrists. In June 1917 the building of the 1st Cadet Corps was used for meetings of the 1st All-Russian Congress (S"yezd) of Soviets; from this came the present name of the liniya. The former *Riding-School* (Manezh) of the 1st Cadet Corps, completed in 1759, stands at Universitetskaya Nab., 13.

In 1981 the Menshikov Palace re-opened as a branch of the State Hermitage Museum. The display focusses on Russian 18C art.

Beyond S"yezdovskaya Liniya is a small park, PL. SHEVCHENKO, also called Rumyantsev Square (Rumyantsevkiy Skver). This was laid out in the 1860s in honour of the 18C Field Marshal, P.A. Rumyantsev (1725–96), who was so successful in Catherine the Great's wars against the Turks. The 21m high *Obelisk* by Brenna was originally erected in Marsovo Pole in 1799. It was moved in 1818 to the present site, next to the cadet school where the marshal studied. The inscription reads: 'To the Victories of Rumyantsev'.

The last building on Universitetskaya Nab. (No. 17) is the *Academy of Arts* (Akademiya Khudozhestv) (Pl. 13; 3). The design, by Vallin de la Mothe, was one of the earliest examples of the Classical revival in Russia. Construction, which continued from 1764 to 1788, was supervised by A.F. Kokorinov. Within the central four-columned portico are statues of Hercules and Flora. The interior is richly decorated, and there is a circular courtyard 40m in diameter. The Academy was founded in 1757 and many of Russia's leading artists and architects were associated with it. The Ukrainian poet Taras Shevchenko was a student at the Academy; he died here in 1861. In 1947 the Academy was moved to Moscow. The building now houses the *Repin Institute of Painting, Sculpture, and Architecture*. Here also is the **Research Museum of the Academy of Arts** (Nauchno-Issledovatel'skiy Muzey Akademii Khudozhestv).

The Ground Floor includes a department with plaster casts of great Antique and W European sculpture. This, like the other parts of the museum, was intended as part of the Academy students' training. The department on the 1st Floor contains the work of teachers and students of the Academy from the 18C to the present; these included some of the most famous names in Russian art history, such as Bryullov, Repin, Polenov, and Surikov. The Department of Russian and Soviet Architecture, on the 2nd Floor, has a rich and unique collection of plans and models.

Around the corner (4-ya Liniya, 3) is the Academy's *Garden Building* (Sadovyy Korpus), built by Andrey Mikhaylov in 1819–21. The granite *Column* in the nearby park was originally installed in the central courtyard of the Academy; it was designed by Voronikhin who used a surplus column from the Kazan Cathedral as the basis. The column was re-erected on the present site in the 1840s.

On the embankment in front of the Academy is a granite quay with two **Sphinxes**. These 23-ton statues date from the 13C BC; they were found at Thebes in the 1820s and brought to St. Petersburg in 1832. The general design of the quay was worked out by K.A. Thon.

The embankment continues as NAB. LEYTENANTA SHMIDTA. Lieutenant P.P. Shmidt (1867–1906) was an SR naval officer who led a great mutiny in the Black Sea Fleet in 1905; he studied at the nearby Naval Academy. The Nikolayevskaya (Nicholas) Nab. was renamed in his honour in 1918. Tram No. 37 follows the embankment from the Academy of Arts to the Mining Institute, a distance of about 1.5km.

The bridge on the left is Most Leytenanta Shmidta. A few steps farther along (right), on the corner of 7-ya Liniya, is the **'Academicians' House'** (Dom Akademikov) with a large number of plaques giving the names of the scientists who lived here. Among these was the physiologist I.P. Pavlov, whose flat has been made into a museum (Muzey-Kvartira I.P. Pavlova). No. 17, on the corner of 12-ya Liniya, was the Tsarist **Naval Academy** (Morskoy Kadetskiy Korpus), now the *Frunze Naval Staff College*. One of the oldest educational institutions in Russia, it was founded in 1701 (in Moscow) as the 'Navigation School'. The present building is the work of F.I. Volkov and dates from 1796–98. Among those who studied here were Admiral Nakhimov, the defender of Sevastopol in the Crimean War, Admiral Rozhestvensky, who led the fleet to disaster at Tsu-Shima in 1905, and Admiral Kolchak, who headed the White government during the Civil War; Rimsky-Korsakov was also a gardemarin (cadet) here, before he turned to a musical career. In front of the Academy stands a *Statue of Admiral I.F. Kruzenshtern*, the first Russian to circumnavigate the globe (1803–06). The large church on the corner of 15-ya Liniya was formerly the *Church of the Nativity* (Ts. Rozhdestva), completed in 1898.

Beyond 21-ya Liniya is the **Plekhanov Mining Institute** (Gornyy Institut im. G.V. Plekhanova) (Pl. 13; 3), which was originally founded in 1773. The handsome Classical building of the Mining Institute was built in 1806–08 by Voronikhin, the architect of the Kazan Cathedral. The main façade consists of 12 Doric columns with statues and bas-reliefs by Demut-Malinovsky and Pimenov. In 1957 the institute was named in honour of G.V. Plekhanov, an early Russian Marxist, who had been a student here in 1874–76.

Further N, and parallel to the Neva embankment, is BOL'SHOY PR. (Pl. 13; 3). It runs for 3.5km from S''yezdovskaya Liniya to the Passenger Port. Trolleybuses No. 10 and 12 follow this avenue.

The block of flats at Bol'shoy Pr, 6/13, was the scene of one of the best-known tragedies of the Blockade. Tanya Savicheva, an eleven-year-old schoolgirl, lived here and between December 1941 and May 1942 recorded the deaths of her sister, grandmother, brother, uncles, and mother. Tanya's notebook, which was discovered later and preserved, ends with the following: 'The Savichevs have died. They have all died. Only Tanya remains.' The little girl survived to be evacuated, but she died in 1943.

The interior of Vasil'yevskiy Island contains a number of interesting 18C and 19C churches. On the N side of Bol'shoy Pr., at No. 1, stands the former Lutheran **Church of St. Catherine** (Ts. Sv. Yekateriny), an impressive Classical building with a four-columned portico and a cupola. It was built in 1768–71 by Velten. Three streets further along, on the corner of 6-YA LINIYA (right), is the large **Cathedral of St. Andrew** (Andreyevskiy Sobor), built in the 1760s and 1770s to the design of A.F. Vist. Next door is the **Church of the Three Holy Men** (Ts. Tryokh Svyatiteley), a modest structure dating from 1740–60 and intended for winter services. Also on 6-ya Liniya (No. 9), but S of Bol'shoy Pr., is the long arcade of the former

Andreyevskiy Market (1789–90). On the other side of the street, at 7-ya Liniya, 12, can be seen one of the oldest buildings in the city, the *Aleksandro-Nevskoye Podvor'ye*. The construction, in 1720–26, was supervised by D. Trezzini and Schwertfeger, and the design was that of the 'House for the Distinguished (Imenityye)', prepared by Le Blond in 1717.

The *Kirov Palace of Culture*, in the central part of Bol'shoy Pr. (No. 83), was planned to be the largest such institution in the USSR. Even though the whole project—by N.A. Trotsky—was not fully completed, the building remains an impressive example of 1930s architecture. It houses the *Kinematograf Cinema*, Leningrad's centre for classic films.

Bol'shoy Pr. ends at the **Passenger Port** (Morskoy Passazhirskiy Port) (Pl. 12; 3), which was opened in 1963. Passenger ships often berth here at the **Sea Terminal** (Morskoy Vokzal) (V.A. Sokhin, 1977–82), and adjacent is the **Morskaya Hotel**. This site was developed as a galley base by Peter for his successful war against the Swedes. The only reminders of those times are the **Guardhouses** (Kronshpitsy), originally built in wood by D. Trezzini, and later (1754) reconstructed in stone. Nearby is another reminder of Russia's naval past, a motor torpedo boat erected as a memorial to the Baltic Fleet in the Second World War.

SREDNIY PR. (Pl. 13; 1) runs parallel to Bol'shoy Pr. and a block inland. Bus No. 30 follows this avenue. Opposite the beginning of Sredniy Pr., at S''yezdovskaya Liniya, 27–29, stands the **Church of St. Catherine** (Ts. Sv. Yekateriny), built in 1811–23 by Andrey Mikhaylov. The tall bell tower and dome may be seen from far away.

Mikhaylov was also the architect of the former *Russian Academy* (Rossiyskaya Akademiya) (1802–04) on the W side of the street, at 1-ya Liniya, 52. Another Classical building extends along 1-ya Liniya (at No. 58), the *Vera Slutskaya Hospital*, formerly the *Mary Magdalene Hospital*; it was built as a mansion for a wealthy merchant in the late 18C.

The Gothic *Reformed Church* (1870) stands on the corner of Sredniy Pr. and 3-ya Liniya (left), a reminder of the large foreign community that once lived here. Nearby, between 5-ya and 6-ya Liniya, is VASILEOSTROVSKAYA METRO STATION. The so-called Higher Women's Courses (Vysshiye Zhenskiye Kursy), established in 1875 as the first university for women in Russia, was moved in 1885 to 10-ya Liniya, 33–35, near Sredniy Pr.

In 1917 Stalin lived at Sredniy Pr., 46, between 11-ya and 12-ya Liniya. By this time Vasil'yevskiy Island had become a centre of the workers' movement. The Laferme Tobacco Factory (now the Uritskiy Factory) was at Sredniy Pr., 36/40, and other industrial enterprises on the island included the shipyards to the SW and the Siemens & Halske and Trubochnyy factories to the N. The workers here were prominent in the revolutions of 1905 and 1917. The Smolensk Field (Smolenskoye Pole), which once occupied the sparsely-settled central part of Vasil'yevskiy Island (W of 25-ya Liniya), had a grim connection with the revolutionary tradition. Karakazov, who tried to shoot Alexander II, was publicly hanged here in 1866, and in the same year the radical N.A. Ishutin underwent a mock execution on this spot. Another unsuccessful assassin, A.K. Solov'yov was executed in the Smolensk Field in 1879.

GAVANSKAYA UL. crosses Sredniy Pr. near its W end; the unusual complex of buildings at No. 47 in this street was the 'Gavanskiy

Gorodok', built in 1903–07 as a model housing settlement for workers.

MALYY PR. (Pl. 13; 1) is the third of the three parallel avenues. Buses No. 44 and 47 travel here from the Strelka of Vasil'yevskiy Island. Off Malyy Pr., at 8-ya Liniya, 57-(left) stands the interesting *Church of the Annunciation* (Blagoveshchenskaya Ts.). It was built in 1750–65 along the lines of a 'traditional' 17C Muscovite church; the handsome bell tower dates from the 1780s. The *Smolenskoye Cemetery* one of the oldest in the city, lies to the right of Malyy Pr., beyond 19-ya Liniya. During the Blockade of 1941–44 the cemetery was used for mass burials.

A great deal of building has taken place recently at the NW-end of Vasil'yevskiy Island, beyond the end of Malyy Pr., and on the adjacent OSTROV DEKABRISTOV (Pl. 12; 2). The narrow SMOLENKA RIVER, which separates the two islands has been canalised at its lower end and made to run down a central esplanade. A green belt extends along the shore of the Gulf of Finland, and behind it high-rise blocks form the sea façade of Leningrad; there is an excellent view of the Gulf here. PRIMORSKAYA METRO STATION is in the centre of this district. The 17-storey **Pribaltiyskaya Hotel** (1976–78) is a short bus trip from the station.

Ostrov Dekabristov (Decembrists Island) was where the executed Decembrists—the officers who rose against the Tsar in 1825—were buried; a monument was erected to them here in 1926. Before the Revolution the island was called Goloday (possibly a corruption of Holiday, the name of an English family which owned land here). At the beginning of this century a major new region of the Imperial capital, called 'New Petersburg', was planned for the W part of Goloday; it was hoped that as many as 500,000 people might be housed here. I.A. Fomin worked out a grandiose architectural scheme, but in the end completed only one building, at PER. KAKHOVSKOVO, 2.

28 The Petrograd Side and Novaya Derevnya

The Petrograd Side (Petrogradskaya Storona) (Pl. 8; 4) N of the Neva consists of four islands. Three of these, Zayachiy, Petrovskiy, and Aptekarskiy, are appendages of the main Petrogradskiy Island and separated from it by narrow streams. To the N is the Novaya Derevnya area of the mainland. Kirovskiy Pr., which links these areas together and to the centre, is followed by Bus No. 46 and 65. GOR'KOVSKAYA, PETROGRADSKAYA and CHORNAYA RECHKA METRO STATIONS are on this avenue.

The ***Peter-Paul Fortress** (Petropavlovskaya Krepost') occupies ZAYACHIY I. (Pl. 10; 3), the southernmost part of the Petrograd Side.

The fortress is most easily reached by Metro. It is a short walk (500m) from Gor'kovskaya Metro Station S through Lenin Park to Pl. Revolyutsii and then across a pedestrian bridge to the main (E) entrance, the *Ivan Gate* (Ioannovskiye Vorota). To the right, beyond the gate, is a booking office where tickets for the various buildings of the fortress are sold. No ticket is needed to enter the fortress grounds. There is another entrance to the fortress from behind the Zoo, at the W end of Pr. Maksima Gor'kovo.

Peter the Great founded his fortress on Zayachiy (Hare) I. in May 1703. Russian forced labour and Swedish prisoners, working without proper tools, completed primitive earthworks by the end of the year. Later on, stone bastions were erected under the supervision of Domenico Trezzini. There were, in the end, six bastions, named after Peter (SE) and five of his generals—Menshikov (NE), Golovkin (N), Zotov (NW), Trubetskoy (SW), and Naryshkin (S). The fortress was never required for its original purpose, because the real defence of St. Petersburg soon became the fortresses at Kronstadt and Vyborg. Nevertheless, it was put to semi-military use in 1917. After the failure of the 'July Days' the last Bolshevik demonstrators took refuge here, and in October the fortress was a strategically important position, especially for the attack on the Winter Palace (directly across the river).

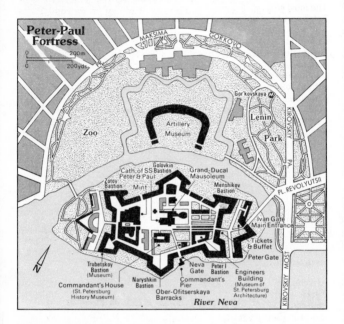

From the ticket office, the central part of the fortress is reached through the **Peter Gate** (Petrovskiye Vorota). The gate, built by D. Trezzini in 1717–18, served as a triumphal arch. Above the double-headed Romanov eagle is a wooden bas-relief showing the magician Simon cast down by St. Peter; lest the allegory to the defeat of Karl XII of Sweden be missed, Tsar Peter stands among the onlookers wearing a laurel wreath. Statues of Bellona (right) and Minerva (left) represent Peter's military and legislative virtues.

Through the gates and to the left of the main path stands the former *Engineers Building* (Inzhenernyy Dom) (1748–49). The former *Ober-Ofitserskaya Barracks* (Gauptvakhta), a small Classical building with a four-columned portico (1748–49), stands to the S of the path. Just beyond is the *Neva Gate* (Nevskiye Vorota), leading to the *Commandant's Pier with a *splendid view* of the Neva and Dvortsovaya Nab. on the far shore.

Opposite the cathedral, to the left of the main path, is another former fortress building, the *Commandant's House* (Ober-Komendantskiy Dom) (1743–46), now the **Museum of the History of St. Petersburg** (Ekspozitsiya 'Istoriya Peterburga-Petrograda 1703–1917 gg.').

This building was used in the 19C for major political trials, including those of the Decembrists, the Petrashevsky Circle (which involved Dostoyevsky), and Chernyshevsky. One of the rooms has been restored to its appearance in 1826, during the trial of the Decembrists (the aristocratic rebels who attempted to depose Nicholas I).

The extensive exhibits of this museum trace the history of the Neva region from the earliest settlement until 1917. Artefacts and photographs illustrate all aspects of life, including socio-economic development, culture, and the revolutionary movement.

The most striking building inside the fortress is the *Cathedral of SS. Peter and Paul (Petropavlovskiy Sobor).

A wooden church was built here in 1703, and work on a proper cathedral began nine years later, to the designs of D. Trezzini. Completed in 1733, the Cathedral of SS. Peter and Paul had little in common with earlier Russian churches. The thin gilded spire is reminiscent of Copenhagen's Exchange, built a century earlier. Peter set out to make it higher than the Ivan the Great Bell Tower in the Kremlin, and until the completion in the 1960s of the TV tower it was, at 122m, the tallest structure in Leningrad. The original spire was destroyed by lightning in 1756 and replaced first by a wooden spire and then, in 1858, by a metal one.

The *Interior*, too, with its long nave and massive Corinthian columns and pilasters, is foreign to the Russian tradition. The splendid Baroque *Iconostasis*, designed by Ivan Zarudny and carved by Moscow craftsmen in the 1720s, is gilded and dominated by figures of the Archangels Gabriel and Michael. Near the iconostasis are a pulpit (left) and the *Tsar's Throne* (right). The cathedral is the burial place of all the Emperors and Empresses—with the exception of Peter II, Ivan VI, and Nicholas II. (Earlier Russian rulers were interred in the Kremlin's Archangel Cathedral.) Most of the sarcophagi are of white marble, but those of Alexander II and his wife are carved from Altai jasper and Urals rhodonite (orlets). The tomb of Peter I (in front, right) is the only one on which flowers are now placed. It was on this site in 1725 that Feofan Prokopovich gave his funeral oration, describing Peter as 'he who—like a true father of the fatherland—has given birth to Russia and nursed her'.

Attached to the cathedral and to the NE is the former *Grand-Ducal Mausoleum* (Usypal'nitsa) (D.I. Grimm, 1896–1908). It now contains an exhibition on the fortress's history. Facing the main entrance to the cathedral is a small building (c 1761) which once housed Peter's boat (now in the Naval Museum). The female figure on the roof symbolises 'Navigation'. (To the NW, beyond the wall, there is a fine view of the moat. Paths lead (right) back to the main entrance and (left) to a bridge and to the W end of Pr. Maksima Gor'kovo.) The *Mint* (Monetnyy Dvor) (1798–1806) stands to the W across the square from the cathedral. Beyond the Mint, to the SW, was the most famous political prison in Tsarist Russia, the **Trubetskoy Bastion**, now a museum.

In 1718 the bastion became a prison for Aleksey, Peter's 28-year-old son. Here, in June of that year, Aleksey Petrovich was beaten to death—apparently with the active participation of his father. Later a special prison, the 'Secret House', was built in the Alekseyevskiy Ravelin, and many of the revolutionaries of the early and mid-19C were incarcerated here, including the Decembrists and others who dared to question the authority of the Romanovs, like Radishchev, Dostoyevsky, Nechayev, and Chernyshevsky. The Secret House was demolished, but in 1872 a new prison was built in the Trubetskoy Bastion. Here were held some of the terrorists of the 'People's Will' group, who assassinated Alexander II. Another condemned prisoner of the 1880s was Aleksandr Il'ch Ul'yanov, Lenin's elder brother. Trotsky and Gorky were among those held here in the wake of the 1905 Revolution. An unusual prisoner was General V.A. Sukhomlinov, the Minster of War, who was held in the fortress on charges of treason and corruption after the great Russian defeats of 1915.

The February Revolution did not end the history of the fortress-prison. The Provisional Government held a number of important Tsarist officials here, as well as Anna Vyrubova, the confidante of the Empress. When in its turn the Kerensky government fell, the ministers who had been arrested at the Winter Palace were transferred to the fortress. The Civil War years were probably the bloodiest in the history of the Peter-Paul Fortress. Hostages and other prisoners were kept in the fortress, and among those reported shot here in January 1919, were Grand Dukes Nikolay Mikhaylovich (born 1859), Pavel Aleksandrovich (born 1860), Dmitry Konstantinovich (born 1860), and Georgy Mikhaylovich (born 1863). The last political prisoners held in the Trubetskoy Bastion are said to have been the sailors who mutinied against the Communists at Kronstadt in 1921.

In 1924 the Trubetskoy Bastion was opened as a museum. Several of the cells have been restored to their 19C appearance, and visitors can get an impression of what conditions were like for political prisoners in Imperial Russia.

The most interesting route from the Trubetskoy Bastion back to the 'mainland' is S through the Neva Gates and around the E perimeter of the fortress. This leads to the pedestrian bridge by the Ivan Gate.

Beyond the moat was the northern defensive wall known as the Kronverk. An *Obelisk* (1975) marks the place near the Kronverk where the five leaders of the Decembrists were hanged in 1826. In the 1850s the Kronverk was replaced by an artillery arsenal which now houses the **Artillery Museum** (Voyenno-Istoricheskiy Muzey Artillerii, Inzhenernykh Voysk i Voysk Svyazi).

Founded in 1756 and moved to the present building in 1868, this is now the main army museum in Leningrad; the emphasis is on the artillery, engineer, and signals branches of the service. The extensive material on the pre-revolutionary army includes artillery, small arms, uniforms, medals, standards, etc., as well as models and dioramas. The display on the Soviet Army is similar, with special attention being given to the Second World War. The whole collection includes 600 artillery pieces, including the most modern.

The 'mainland' of the Petrograd Side NE of the Peter-Paul Fortress, on PETROGRADSKIY ISLAND, was an early centre of the city's population and construction at the beginning of the 18C. At this time it was known as 'Town Island' (Gorodskoy Ostrov). The area then stagnated until the end of the 19C, when it became the fastest-growing part of St. Petersburg; between 1890 and 1910 the population jumped from 75,000 to 210,000.

PL. REVOLYUTSII or Revolution Square, formerly Troitskaya Pl. (Pl. 10; 3), was one of the first districts to be built up. The old name came from the 18C Cathedral of the Trinity (Troitskiy Sobor), which was demolished in 1934. Perhaps the worst incidents of 'Bloody Sunday', 1905, took place in Troitskaya Pl., when nearly 40 people were killed by government troops.

PETROVSKAYA NAB., the embankment S of Pl. Revolyutsii, contains at No. 6 the *Cabin of Peter I (Muzey 'Domik Petra I').

This unique building, where Tsar Peter lived between 1703 and 1709, has been preserved as an historical museum. It is a log cabin which soldiers fashioned out of rough-hewn pine during three days in May 1703. There are just two rooms, a study and a dining room. After Peter's death the cottage was protected against the elements, and in 1784 a permanent stone structure was erected around it. Nicholas I made the study into a revered chapel for an apparently miraculous icon of the Redeemer which Peter had always carried. After 1917 the interior was restored to its original appearance. The simple furniture dates from the early 18C.

The steps down to the river in front of Peter's Cabin are flanked by mythical beasts, *Shi-Tsza*, brought from Kirin in Manchuria (1907). To the E of the cabin is a long apartment building, formerly the Intourist Hotel (Ye.A. Levinson and I.I. Fomin, 1938–44), and around the corner is the Bol'shaya Nevka river. The large blue building in the style of the Petrine Baroque which stands by the river was actually completed in 1912 (A.I. Dmitriyev) as a secondary school. It now serves as a 'Nakhimov Academy', for the education of aspiring naval officers. The modern building on the far shore is the Leningrad Hotel. Moored in front of the Nakhimov Academy is one of the most famous symbols of Leningrad, the cruiser ***'Avrora'**.

The 'Avrora' (6700 tons), built in St. Petersburg and completed in 1903, took part in the ill-fated voyage of the Baltic Fleet to the Far East in 1904–05 but, unlike most of the squadron, she escaped destruction at Tsu-Shima. By 1917 the ship was obsolete, but she happened to be refitting in the capital. The Bolsheviks won over the crew and deployed the old cruiser just downstream from what is now the Most Leytenanta Shmidta (Pl. 13; 3) on the night of 24–25 October. The following evening her forward 6in gun fired a blank shot to intimidate the last defenders of the Kerensky government in the Winter Palace. The ship was sunk in shallow water at Oranienbaum (now Lomonosov) in 1941, but seven years later she was raised and moved to her present position. In 1956 the 'Avrora' was opened as a museum.

UL. KUYBYSHEVA (Pl. 10; 3), to the NE of Pl. Revolyutsii, contains at No. 4 the **October Revolution Museum** (Muzey Velikoy Oktyabr'-skoy Sotsialisticheskoy Revolyutsii).

The main building of the museum was originally the town house of Mathilda Kschessinska (1872–1971), the greatest ballet dancer of her era. She had an affair with Tsarevich Nicholas Aleksandrovich (later Nicholas II) and in 1921 married Grand Duke Andrey Vladimirovich (1879–1956). The house was built in 1904–06 by A.I. Gogen and is a good example of the Style Moderne. It was a centre for St. Petersburg Society before the war, but in March 1917 the Bolsheviks 'confiscated' the building for use as Party headquarters. When Lenin returned to Russia it was here that he first put forward his famous 'April Theses'. The balcony on the W side was used by Lenin and others to address crowds of supporters. After the 'July Days', when the Bolsheviks had to go underground, their offices here were wrecked by government troops.

The museum contains a wealth of material on the Bolshevik Party and the events of the Revolution and Civil War. The display includes the personal effects of prominent Bolsheviks, as well as documents, posters, photographs, banners, etc.

PR. MAKSIMA GOR'KOVO or Maxim Gorky Avenue runs NW from the museum and then in an arc around the Peter-Paul Fortress. (Hence its old name, Kronverkskiy Pr.) The cupola of the **Mosque** (Mechet') (N.V. Vasil'yev, 1910–14) is based on the Mausoleum of Tamerlane in Samarkand. Beyond the Mosque, Pr. Maksima Gor'kovo crosses Kirovskiy Pr. and is then bordered on the S by LENIN PARK (Park im. V.I. Lenina), formerly the Alexander Park, which was laid out in 1845.

Near the road is the GOR'KOVSKAYA METRO STATION. The W side of the park contains many small pieces of modern sculpture. By Kirovskiy Pr. stands the 'Steregushchiy' Monument (1911), which is dedicated to the sailors of the destroyer 'Steregushchiy', who, in 1904, sank their ship rather than let a superior Japanese force capture her.

A *Statue of Maxim Gorky* (1868–1936) was erected on the centenary of his birth, at the intersection of Kirovskiy Pr. and Pr. Maksima Gor'kovo. Gorky lived in the latter street, at No. 23, from 1914 to 1921.

Further W along Pr. Maksima Gor'kovo, on the park side, is the *Leninskiy Komsomol Theatre* (Gos. Teatr im. Leninskovo Komsomola). The theatre was founded in 1936, after a merger of other companies; the present 1520-seat auditorium dates from 1939. Next door are the *Planetarium* (Planetariy) and the *Velikan Cinema*.

The Velikan (Giant) originated as the 'Nicholas II People's House' (Narodnyy Dom Imp. Nikolaya II) (1901). It became in 1917 one of the great forums of the Revolution, along with the nearby 'Cirque Moderne'. (The latter stood at Pr. Maksima Gor'kovo, 11—next to the Mosque—but burned down in 1919; the existing Constructivist building by G.A. Simonov dates from 1932.)

The **Zoo** (Leningradskiy Zoopark) (Pl. 10; 3) is located at the far end of Pr. Maksima Gor'kovo, about 1km from Gorky's statue. It was founded in 1865 and includes over 400 kinds of animal. Opposite, on the W corner of Pr. Dobrolyubova (No. 2), is a building which served from 1907 to 1917 as the Petersburg headquarters of the Tsarist political police, the Okhrana. From here it is only a short walk across the Most Stroiteley to Vasil'yevskiy Island (p 299).

From Gorky's statue, KIROVSKIY PR. runs N 2.5km across the Petrograd Side to Kamennyy Island (Ostrov); from this came its old name—Kamennoostrovskiy Pr. Many blocks of luxury flats were built here at the turn of the century. The building at No. 1/3 is an interesting example of Style Moderne (F. Lidval, 1902–04), while No. 5 was the villa of Count S.Yu. Witte, the great industrialiser of Imperial Russia. On the left at No. 10 is the *Lenfilm Studio*. This was the site of the very first film show in Russia; in May 1896 the Akvarium Summer Theatre presented films by the Lumière brothers. The present studio was established in 1918 and is among the busiest in the country. Here were made Pudovkin's early films, the Vasil'yevs' 'Chapayev' and, more recently, Kozintsev's Shakespeare films. Beyond Ul. Skorokhodova is a park and a building that once housed the élite *Alexander Lycée*, moved here from Tsarskoye Selo (Pushkin) in 1843. Kirovskiy Pr., 26/28, houses the **Kirov Museum** (Muzey S.M. Kirova). This is a good example of a pre-revolutionary block of luxury flats (Yu. Yu. Benois, 1911–1913). From 1926 to 1934 it was the home of the Secretary of the Leningrad Party organisation, S.M. Kirov; in 1957 his flat was opened to the public.

Kirovskiy Pr. is crossed by Bol'shoy Pr. at the striking PL. L'VA TOLSTOVO (Leo Tolstoy Square) (Pl. 10; 1). A multi-storey turreted block of flats (right) uses motifs from English medieval castles (A.Ye. Belogrud, 1913–1916). The square is also the location of *Fashion House* (Dom Mod), completed in 1968 as a centre for clothing design.

BOL'SHOY PR. (Pl. 10; 1) runs NE–SW across the Petrograd Side for 2km to Vasil'yevskiy Island. It is similar in character to Kirovskiy Pr. Three-quarters of the way along UL. KRASNOVO KURSANTA turns off to the right. (Pl. 8; 4). No. 14–18 in this street was the *2nd Cadet Crops* (2-y Kadetskiy Korpus), which was built in about 1800 for the training of army officers. This now houses part of the *Mozhaysky Military Engineering Institute*. In 1917, as the Vladimir Military Academy (Vladimirskoye Voyennoye Uchilishche), this was a centre of resistance to the Bolshevik uprising; a monument marks the spot from which Red artillery bombarded the building. The former Paul Military Academy (Pavlovskoye Voyennoye Uchilishche) was nearby; the military cadets here also fought the Bolsheviks in October 1917.

At the end of the Petrograd Side section of Bol'shoy Pr., PR. DOBROLYUBOVA leads (left) to the 18C **Prince Vladimir Cathedral** (Knyaz'-Vladimirskiy Sobor), the construction of which took from 1741 to 1789. Some of the best architects were involved including Zemtsov, P. Trezzini, and Rinaldi; the final stages of construction were supervised by I.Ye. Starov. The cathedral is an interesting mixture of Baroque and Classical styles. On the other (W) side of Pr. Dobrolyubova is the **Yubileynyy Sports Palace** (Dvorets Sporta 'Yubileynyy'), a large modern circular structure built to celebrate the jubilee (50th anniversary) of the October Revolution. It has arenas for ice hockey and other sports; the large hall is also used for concerts.

Nearby, across Bol'shoy Pr. and on the S tip of Petrovskiy I (Pl. 13; 1), is one of the oldest sports facilities in Leningrad, the **Lenin Stadium** (Stadion im. V.I. Lenina), which has opened in 1924.

To the E of Pl. L'va Tolstovo and Kirovskiy Pr. is Ul. L'va Tolstovo. About 500m along this (No. 6/8) is the *1st (Pavlov) Medical Institute*. Founded in 1897 as Russia's first institution for training women doctors, it has since become one of the largest medical centres in the USSR, educating both men and women. It was also the setting in April 1917 for part of the Bolshevik's 7th Conference, the first held legally in Russia.

Beyond Pl. L'va Tolstovo on Kirovskiy Pr. is (right) the PETROGRADSKAYA METRO STATION. Hidden by the trees of the park next door stands *Lensovet House*, a block of flats designed by Ye. A. Levinson and I.I. Fomin (1931–35) and one of the most attractive buildings of the 1930s. (Nab. Reki Karpovki, 13). The concave front of Lensovet House faces onto the Karpovka River. Levinson, with V.O. Munts, also designed the *Lensovet Palace of Culture* on the W side of Kirovskiy Pr. (No. 42) in 1933–39. The large house a little further on (No. 44–6) with central arches was built just before the First World War by S.S. Krichinsky for the Emir of Bukhara.

Kirovskiy Pr. crosses the narrow KARPOVKA RIVER, which flows for about 3km E–W from the Bol'shaya to the Malaya Nevka and separates Petrogradskiy and Aptekarskiy Islands.

The embankment S of the Karpovka leads W (500m) to Nab. Reki Karpovki, 32/1, where on the night of 10–11 October 1917 the Bolshevik Central Committee decided to overthrow the Kerensky government. The flat has been preserved as a **Lenin Museum** (Kvartira-Muzey V.I. Lenina). The big green-domed church on the opposite bank of the Karpovka belonged to the *Convent of St. John* (Ioannovskiy Monastyr'). Father John of Kronstadt, a famous late-19C preacher and friend of the Imperial family, was buried here. Another Lenin flat has been preserved nearby, UL. LENINA, 52/9 (Kvartira-Muzey V.I. Lenina). The Bolshevik Leader lived here with his sister Anna and her husband (Mark Yelizarov) from the time of his return to Russia in 1917 until the 'July Days'.

Near the E end of the Karpovka are the former *Grenadier Guards Regiment Barracks* (Nab. Reki Karpovki, 2), a group of Classical structures built in 1805–07 by L. Rusca. To the N of the Karpovka lies the 18ha site of the **Botanic Gardens** (Botanicheskiy Sad). The main entrance is at No. 2 in UL. PROFESSORA POPOVA. The gardens were founded at the time of Peter I as a source of medicinal herbs. From this came their original name, Aptekarskiy Ogorod (Apothecary Garden), and later the name of the Aptekarskiy I. In 1823 the Aptekarskiy Ogorod became the Imperial Botanic Gardens. On the opposite side of Ul. Professora Popova (No. 5) is the *Ul'yanov (Lenin) Electro-Technical Institute*, founded in 1891. The main building dates from 1900 and is a curious mixture of English Gothic and Style Moderne. The Dacha of Prime Minister P.A. Stolypin once stood at the E end of Ul. Professora Popova, by the river. Socialist-Revolutionary terrorists blew up the building in 1906; Stolypin survived, but 32 people were killed, including the terrorists.

Kirovskiy Pr. passes (right) UL. CHAPYGINA. The *Druzhba Hotel* or friendship Hotel at No. 4 is used for international youth exchanges. The adjacent *Television Centre*, with its 316m *Television Tower*, was completed in 1965. The singer Chaliapin lived a block further N, at UL. GRAFTIO, 2-6; his flat has been preserved as a small *Russian Opera Museum* (Russkiy Opernyy Teatr). Many of the houses in this part of Kirovskiy Pr. are particularly impressive, for example Nos 63 and 65, by V.A. Shchuko (1908–11). Shchuko went on to become one of the prominent architects of Soviet Moscow. The name of the last street on the right, UL. AKADEMIKA PAVLOVA, honours Academician Ivan Pavlov (1849–1936), the physiologist who developed the idea of the conditioned reflex and won the Nobel Prize (1904). The laboratory where Pavlov carried out his famous experiments with dogs was in this street (No. 12).

Between Ul. Akademika Pavlova and the Malaya Nevka are the pleasant DZERZHINSKY GARDENS. Kirovskiy Pr. then crosses the river onto the 'Island of the Working People' (Ostrov Trudyashchikhsya), generally known by its traditional name of KAMENNYY OSTROV (Stony Island) (Pl. 8; 2). On the E side of KAMENNOOSTROVSKIY PR. (as the continuation of Kirovskiy Pr. is called) stands the *Church of John the Baptist* (Ts. Sv. Ioanna Predtechi), built by Velten in the Gothic style in 1776–78. Behind it is the **Kamennoostrovskiy Palace**, now a sanatorium. The grounds are closed, but the palace can be seen from the other side of the Bol'shaya or Malaya Nevka. Catherine II had the palace built in 1776–81 for her son Paul; the original architect of this early Classical building is unknown, but the work was supervised by Velten. The roads to the W of Kamennoostrovskiy Pr. lead to the other KIROV ISLANDS (Pl. 8; 4).

Kamennyy, Yelagin, and Krestovskiy Islands received the collective name of the Kirov (Kirovskiye) Islands in 1934, after the death of S.M. Kirov. The three islands form the N part of the Neva delta, above Vasil'yevskiy Island and the Petrograd Side. They have for centuries been a place of relaxation and provide a contrast to the busy everyday life of Leningrad.

KAMENNYY ISLAND is served by CHORNAYA RECHKA METRO STATION. From Kamennoostrovskiy Pr. a number of roads lead W into the island. The route which Bus No. 134 follows to Krestovskiy Island is 2-YA BERYOZOVAYA ALLEYA. The road farthest N on Kamennyy I is NAB. BOL'SHOY NEVKI. No. 22, near the NW point (1.25km) is perhaps the finest example of the turn-of-the-century Classical revival. This was the dacha of Senator A.A. Polovtsev, built in 1912–16 by I.A. Fomin, who was to become one of the main architects of inter-war Leningrad. The building now serves as a sanatorium; it was, in fact, the first 'House of Rest' (Dom Otdykha) in Soviet Russia, and Lenin visited it on his last trip to Petrograd in July 1920. Fomin also designed the dacha at NAB. REKI KRESTOVKI, 2 (on the SW side of Kamennyy I); nearby is an oak supposedly planted by Peter I. There are a number of other pleasant dachas on the island.

At the W end of Kamennyy I stands the *Kamennoostrovskiy Theatre*. Put up very quickly in 1827 and rebuilt in 1844 by A. Cavos this unusual wooden building with eight columns was used as a summer theatre. It was restored in the 1960s, and now houses a Television Theatre.

The theatre faces a bridge leading to YELAGIN ISLAND (Pl. 8; 2). The island takes its name from one of Catherine II's Court officials, I.P. Yelagin, who owned it in the 1770s. It passed to the widow of Emperor Paul, Mariya Fyodorovna (1759–1828), who had the existing mansion reconstructed as the *Yelagin Palace* (Yelaginskiy Dvorets) and an ensemble of buildings created around it. The work was entrusted to Carlo Rossi, who was to become one of St. Petersburg's outstanding architects. The Classical palace was built in 1818–22. The rear façade, looking onto the Bol'shaya Nevka, is visible from as far away as the Ushakovskiy Most (Kamennoostrovskiy Pr.). Part of the palace is open for exhibitions, but most of the original interior was destroyed by fire during the last war. There are a number of interesting outbuildings, especially the *Kitchens* (Kukhonnyy Korpus), the *Orangery* (Bol'shaya Oranzhereya), and the *Stables* (Konyushennyy Korpus).

Yelagin Island was opened as the **Central Park of Culture and Rest** (Tsentral'nyy Park Kul'tury i Otdykha (TsPKiO) im. S.M. Kirova) in 1932. About 1km W of the palace a bridge leads N to the 'mainland' and Primorskiy Pr.; 1km further W is the **Strelka** (Point), with a granite wall and carved lions erected in the late 1920s. The Strelka is an excellent place to watch the sun set over the Gulf of Finland.

About 800m SW of the Yelagin Palace a bridge leads S to the third and largest (420ha) of the Kirov Islands, KRESTOVSKIY ISLAND (Pl. 8; 4). This island can be reached by bus from Kamennyy Island, and by Bus No. 45 or Trolleybus No. 9 from Nevskiy Pr.; it is also planned to build a Metro station here. The E end is built up, but the island is mostly parkland. The **Dinamo Stadium** in the SE part was opened in 1925. The marshy W tip of the island began to be filled in 1933 in preparation for an even bigger stadium. The outbreak of war stopped further work, but in 1945 the area became the **Coastal Victory Park** (Primorskiy Park Pobedy), and volunteer labour was brought in to raise an artificial hill 16m high. Within this the architects A.S. Nikol'skiy, K.I. Kashin, and N.N. Stepanov built a huge open stadium capable of seating 100,000 people. It was opened in 1950 as the **Kirov Stadium** (Stadion im. S.M. Kirova), and a giant statue of Kirov by V.B. Pinchuk (1950) stands before the main (E) entrance. The large park which was laid out on either side of MORSKOY PR. is notable for a large number of sports facilities and for its flowerbeds.

The BOL. PETROVSKIY MOST crosses the Malaya Nevka between Krestovskiy and Petrovskiy Islands. After Rasputin was murdered, in December 1916, the conspirators drove his body across the city and dumped it into the frozen river from this Bridge. BOL. KRESTOVSKIY MOST, further upstream, connects the SE extremity of Krestovskiy Island to the main part of the Petrograd Side. BOL. ZELENINA UL., to the S of the bridge, is the main route back to Bol'shoy Pr. and the centre of town.

Kamennoostrovskiy Pr. crosses the Bol'shaya Nevka River by way of the 255m long USHAKOVSKIY MOST (Pl. 8; 2) and continues as UL. AKADEMIKA KRYLOVA. CHORNAYA RECHKA METRO STATION is located near here. VYBORGSKAYA NAB. turns right in front of the massive *Grechko Naval Academy* (A.I. Vasil'yev, 1941) and follows the shore of the Bol'shaya Nevka upstream to the Leningrad Hotel (4km).

To the W of Ul. Akademika Krylova begins PRIMORSKIY PR., which follows the river downstream towards Primorskiy District (formerly Zhdanovskiy District). Primorskiy Pr., 79, is the small round *Church of the Annunciation* (Blagoveshchenskaya Ts.) (V.O. Mochul'sky, 1805–09), while the *Shishmarev Dacha* (A.I. Mel'nikov, 1824–25) at No. 87 typifies the Classical wooden country houses that the aristocracy built in this district, known as STARAYA DEREVNYA. The *Buddhist Temple*, at No. 91, was built in 1909–15 on the initiative of the Dalai Lama. The avenue runs into PRIMORSKOYE SHOSSE, the highway to Repino Camping Site.

The district N of the Ushakovskiy Most is known as NOVAYA DEREVNYA (lit., 'New Countryside or Village') formerly an area of country houses. A small river, the CHORNAYA RECHKA, winds through the district. Here on 27 January 1837 the poet Pushkin fought his duel with d'Anthès; he died of his wounds two days later. On the centenary of Pushkin's death a red granite **Obelisk** was erected on the site of the duel. This may be found at the N end of NOVOSIBIRSKAYA UL., which turns to the left off the main avenue of the district, PR. N.I. SMIRNOVA (Pl. 8; 2). Nearby is CHORNAYA RECHKA METRO STATION.

One of the streets to the W of Pl. N.I. Smirnova and N of the Chornaya Rechka is called AERODROMNAYA UL. The name recalls the Commandant's Aerodrome (Komendantskiy Aerodrom), which was used by pioneer aviators in the first decades of this century; Igor Sikorsky's giant four-engined 'Il'ya Muromets' made its test flights here. During the Blockade of 1941–44 the Aerodrome was used by transport aircraft ferrying in supplies. Not far away, on the S side of the Chornaya Rechka, is the **Serafimovskoye Cemetery**, where many victims of the Blockade were buried. An impressive monument was unveiled here in 1965.

29 The Vyborg Side

The Vyborg side (Vyborgskaya Storona) (Pl. 9; 3) is the name traditionally given to the area N of the Neva and E of the Bol'shaya Nevka River and the Petrograd Side. The starting point for the three Rtes in the Vyborg Side is PL. LENINA METRO STATION (Pl. 10; 4), at the Finland Railway Station. From here Rtes A and B lead N, the first along Pr. Karla Marksa and the second along Lesnoy Pr. Rte C begins with Ul. Komsomola and continues to the E.

The town of Vyborg (Viipuri in Finland from 1918–40) is situated some 174km W of Leningrad. The main road to Vyborg ran through the northern part of St. Petersburg, and from this came its name—the Vyborg Side.

The Vyborg District of St. Petersburg developed by the latter part of the 19C into a squalid industrial suburb and a centre of working class militancy. The Vyborg workers were important in 1905, they erected barricades during the great strike of July 1914, and they were among the leaders of the mass movement in February 1917. After the overthrow of the Tsar the Vyborg District became one of the Bolsheviks' main strongholds in Petrograd.

In the Soviet era the Vyborg Side has been much developed, and the built-up industrial and residential districts of the VYBORGSKIY AND KALININSKIY DIS-TRICTS now extend into what was once St. Petersburg's dacha region. This is one of the fastest-growing parts of the city.

The **Finland Station** (Finlyandskiy Vokzal) (Pl. 10; 4) is, as its name suggests, the terminus for trains to and from Finland. The original station building dated from 1870, when rail services to Finland began; it was badly damaged during the Second World War and the present bleakly-modern structure with its spire was completed in 1960. Part of the ornate old station may be seen on the W side.

Lenin arrived here on the evening of 3 April 1917. This was the end of his trip from Switzerland by 'sealed train' through Germany and then via Sweden and Finland to Petrograd. The Bolshevik leader emerged from the station (by way of the former Imperial Waiting Room) and delivered an impromptu speech from the roof of an Austin armoured car; this was his first statement in Russia of the revolution-ary tactics that were to bring his party to power less than seven months later.

To commemorate this historic event a monument, the first major **Statue of Lenin**, was unveiled near the Finland Station on 7 November 1926. The original design, by sculptor S.A. Yevseyev and architects Shchuko and Gel'freykh, depicts the Bolshevik leader speaking from the tiny turret roof of the Austin. The armoured car (bronevik) itself is now on display at the Lenin Museum (p 286).

Lenin had to return to Finland after the disaster of the 'July Days'. He left on 9 August (from Udel'naya Station, not the Finland Station) disguised as the fireman of *Locomotive No. 293* of Finland Railways; on 7 October he returned the same way. The original No. 293, a Baldwin 4–6–0 built in the United States in 1900, was presented to the USSR by the Finns and has been on display since 1961 in a glass case on the platform of the Finland Station.

The large square stretching from the front of the station to the Neva is called PL. LENINA. When it was laid out after the Second World War the 1926 statue of Lenin was moved from its original position adjacent to the station building to a new site nearer the river. The five-storey *Kalininskiy District Soviet*, built in 1954, forms the E side of Pl. Lenina; the building contains the 800-seat *Leningrad Concert Hall* (Leningradskiy Kontsertnyy Zal). Opposite, on the W side of the square, is the *Kalinin Artillery Academy*, which was rebuilt in the 1950s. This was earlier the Mikhail Artillery Academy, and among those who studied here were the radical theorist P.L. Lavrov and the terrorist S.M. Kravchinskiy (Stepniak).

A.   Prospekt Karla Marksa

The street which runs N from the Liteynyy Most (and Liteynyy Pr.) is UL. AKADEMIKA LEBEDEVA. This is located a block W of Pl. Lenina and the Finland Station.

The *Kirov Military Medical Academy* stands on the W side of the street. Its origins go back to the army and navy hospitals founded by Peter I in 1715–16. Later, as the Medical-Surgical Academy (Medikokhirurgicheskaya Akademiya), this was the largest medical institution in Imperial Russia. At Ul. Akademika Lebedeva, 6, stands the main building, a Classical structure dating from the 1790s. The long two-storey façade of the building on VYBORGSKAYA NAB. (Pl. 10; 4) can be seen from many points on the Neva; it was built in the 1860s.

The modern **Leningrad Hotel** stands to the W of the Kirov Academy at the point where the Bol'shaya Nevka branches off the Neva. The 11-storey hotel (S.B. Speransky, 1970) is one of the few large modern buildings on the river front, and affords a splendid view of the part of the Neva between the Liteynyy and Dvortsovyy bridges. The road between the hotel and the Kirov Academy is PR. KARLA MARKSA (Pl. 10; 4), one of the main avenues of the district. Barricades were set up here during the February Revolution of 1917, and the first legal Bolshevik meeting was held on 1 March at No. 37 (right), then a temperance hall and now the *'May 1st' Palace of Culture*. When the Bolsheviks were on the defensive after the abortive 'July Days' demonstration, their semi-secret 6th Congress opened here (26 July). This was a 'safe' industrial district with a line of factories extending along the Bol'shaya Nevka River; the Nobel Factory (est. 1849), now the *Russkiy Dizel' Factory* stood across the avenue.

The green *__Cathedral of St. Sampson__ (Sampsoniyevskiy Sobor), at No. 41, is one of the oldest buildings in the city. Work began in 1728 (on the site of a wooden church built in 1709) and the cathedral was finished in 1740. The feast day of St. Sampson is 27 June—the date of Peter's great victory over the Swedes at Poltava in 1709. Pr. Karla Marksa was once called Bol. Sampsoniyevskiy Pr. after the cathedral.

The design features a bell tower at the W end and five ribbed cupolas above the church; to N and S run unusual open galleries. In the grounds a monument (1885) marks the burial place of three officials of Anna Ivanovna who were executed on the orders of Biron, her favourite, in 1740. There is an unconfirmed story that a later Empress, Catherine the Great, secretly married her favourite, Potyomkin, at this church in 1774.

Among the many factories along Pr. Karla Marksa is one of the oldest in the city, the *Oktyabr'skaya Factory*, which was founded in 1837. The *Krasnaya Zarya Factory* (est. 1897, formerly the Erickson

Factory) and the *Karl Marx Combine* (formerly part of the Lessner engineering firm) also have a long tradition, including one of revolutionary activity. A Constructivist 'factory-kitchen' was built at No. 45 in 1929–30.

Pr. Karla Marksa, 61–63, now the *Military Institute of Physical Culture* (VIFK), was originally built in the 1830s as the barracks of the *Moscow Guards Regiment*. The temporary camp of a famous revolutionary unit, the 1st Machine-Gun Regiment, was established in mid-1917 on waste ground opposite No. 77 (then the Russkiy Renault Factory). The machine-gunners were among the worst-disciplined troops in Petrograd, and they initiated the 'July Days' demonstrations.

Pr. Karla Marksa becomes PR. ENGEL'SA (Pl. 8; 2) (formerly Vyborgskoye Shosse) beyond SERDOBOL'SKAYA UL. Lenin lived secretly at Serdobol'skaya Ul., 1, on the eve of the October Revolution. He returned from Finland on 7 October (via the nearby Udel'naya Station) and moved into the flat of Margarita Fofanova. He left here for the Smolny Institute by tram (along Lesnoy Pr.) on the night of 24–25 October as the Bolsheviks began their uprising. Fofanova's flat was later made into a *Lenin Museum* (Kvartira-Muzey V.I. Lenina).

The wooded area to the right of Pr. Engel'sa, just before Serdobol'skaya Ul. turns off to the left, is the *Park of the Kirov Forestry Academy*.

The Imperial predecessor of the Kirov Academy, the Lesnoy (Forestry) Institute, gave its name to the 19C dacha region of Lesnoy. In the woods here in 1879 a secret meeting of the 'People's Will' group passed their 'death sentence' on Emperor Alexander II. The former resort area of UDEL'NAYA, farther N along what is now Pr. Engel'sa, also has a connection with the radical movement. Father Gapon, instigator of the 'Bloody Sunday' demonstrations, was hanged in a dacha here in March 1906 by revolutionaries who believed him to be a traitor. Eight years later, in November 1914, the Bolshevik deputies to the State Duma, who had taken an anti-war stand, were arrested at Udel'naya. PARGOLOVO, on the northern edge of modern Leningrad, was the final burial place of Rasputin; after the February Revolution his body was taken here from Tsarskoye Selo (Pushkin).

B.   Lesnoy Prospekt to the Piskaryovskoye Cemetery

Pr. Akademika Lebedeva, W of the Finland Station, leads into LESNOY PR. (Pl. 10; 2). This is one of the major avenues of the Vyborg Side, running parallel to and E of Pr. Karla Marksa. Trolleybus No. 23 follows Lesnoy Pr. from PL. LENINA METRO STATION to Pl. Muzhestva.

Lesnoy Pr., 20, was the mansion of the oil magnate E.L. Nobel. It was built in the Style Moderne in 1910 by F.I. Lidval and is regarded as one of the best works of that architect. The stretch of Lesnoy Pr. to the N was extensively developed between the two world wars.

Lesnoy Pr. ends at the wooded parkland of the *Kirov Forestry Academy* (Lesotekhnicheskaya Akademiya im. S.M. Kirova) which originally moved here, as the Lesnoy (Forestry) Institute, in 1811. Timber played and still plays an important part in the Russian economy, and the Kirov Academy is one of Leningrad's largest institutions of higher education. A granite *Obelisk* in the woods marks the graves of men killed in the October Revolution and the Civil War.

The road around the S and E sides of the park passes under the railway line and leads to PL. MUZHESTVA (or Square of Courage) (Pl. 9; 1), a giant traffic circle which marks the beginning of a new housing area.

PLOSHCHAD' MUZHESTVA METRO STATION stands just to the N of the traffic circle on POLITEKHNICHESKAYA UL.. This wide avenue passes the *Kalinin Polytechnic Institute* (Leningradskiy Politekh-nicheskiy Institut im. M.I. Kalinina), which has over 20,000 students and is one of the largest Soviet institutions of higher education. The Polytechnical Institute was established in 1902. V.M. Molotov, one-time Soviet prime minister and Stalin's foreign minister, was among the leaders of the radical students here before the Revolution.

The N part of Kalininskiy District, along Pr. Nauki and Grazhdanskiy Pr., is one of new housing estates. This area was rural dacha country before 1917; the British community even established a golf course at MURINO on the upper Bol'shaya Okhta River.

The next 'spoke' counter-clockwise from Politekhnicheskaya Ul. is PR. TOREZ, which leads through new residential areas to the NW. The *Sputnik Hotel* stands at No. 34. PR. SHVERNIKA is the next road off Pl. Muzhestva. Not far along Pr. Shvernika, BOLOTNAYA UL. turns off to the right; here at No. 13/17 stands a picturesque brown wooden house which gives an idea what this region was like before its recent development. This is now the *Museum of the Vyborg Side* (Istoriko-Revolyutsionnyy Muzey Vyborgskoy Storony). Here on 16 October 1917 the Bolshevik Central Committee met and took the final decision to launch an uprising against the Kerensky government.

PR. NEPOKORYONNYKH (Avenue of the Unvanquished) leads to the E from Pl. Muzhestva. To the left off Pr. Nepokoryonnykh is UL. BUTLEROVA with, at No. 9, the indoor stadium known as the *'Zenit' Palace of Sporting Competitions* (Dvorets Sportivnykh Igr 'Zenit') (G.P. Morozov, 1974–76). About 2.5km to the E of Pl. Muzhestva along Pr. Nepokoryonnykh is the ***Piskaryovskoye Memorial Ceme-tery** (Piskaryovskoye Memorial'noye Kladbishche). Bus No. 75 travels to the cemetery from PLOSHCHAD' MUZHESTVA METRO STATION.

The name derives from the former village of Piskaryovka (which in turn comes from the early-19C owner of the land, the merchant Piskaryov). The place was of no significance until the dreadful winter of 1941–42, when it was used for the burial of those who died during the Blockade; from February 1942 it became the city's main burial place. About 600,000 Leningraders died from starvation, disease, shelling, and air raids; 470,000 of them were interred in 186 mass graves at Piskaryovka.

Although an architectural competition was held in 1945, work on the 16ha memorial complex did not begin until 1955; it was opened on 9 May 1960, the 15th anniversary of the Allied Victory. A.V. Vasil'yev and Ye.A. Levinson were the architects in charge of the project.

The entrance is flanked by twin propylaea, which contain a small museum. An external flame burns on the terrace beyond; it was lit from the eternal flame in Marsovo Pole. Steps descend to a 300m long alley. To either side are the mounds of the mass graves; on each is inscribed a year and either a star (for military dead) or a hammer and sickle (for civilians). At the end of the alley is a high wall and before it a 6m tall bronze *Statue of 'The Motherland'* (Mat'-Rodina)

(V.V. Isayeva and R.K. Taurit); the statue holds a garland of oak leaves, the symbol of immortal glory.

The poetess Olga Berggol'ts (1910–75), who herself lived through the Blockade and lost her husband, composed the inscription on the wall. It begins as follows: 'Here lie Leningraders./ Here are townspeople—men, women, and children,/ Beside them are the soldiers of the Red Army./ With their whole lives/ They defended thee, Leningrad,/ Cradle of the Revolution./ We cannot give here each of their noble names,/ There are so many under the granite./ But know as you look on these stones,/ That no one has been forgotten and nothing has been forgotten'.

PISKARYOVSKIY PR. turns right off Pr. Nepokoryonnykh just beyond the cemetery and runs 4km S to the Neva through new housing estates.

C. Ulitsa Komsomola and Sverdlovskaya Naberezhnaya

UL. KOMSOMOLA (Pl. 10; 4) runs in front of the Finland Station and continues to the E. To the right, a few blocks along, are the dirty orange buildings of the former *Kresty Prison*. The freeing of the political prisoners held in the 'Kresty' was one of the first acts of the February Revolution; after the 'July Days' Trotsky and other supporters of the Bolsheviks were held here. The brick buildings with rounded windows on the N side of the street (Ul. Komsomola, 1, 2, 3) are part of the former *Arsenal*, which was moved here from Liteynyy Pr. in the 1840s.

There are a number of major industrial enterprises in this SE part of the Vyborg Side, which is called POLYUSTROVO. Among them are the *Sverdlov Lathe Combine* (est. 1858, formerly the Rozenkrants Factory), and the *Leningrad Metal Factory*. The last, formerly the Stalin Metal Factory and founded in 1857 as the St. Petersburg Metal Factory, is still one of the most important plants in the city. In front of it, at No. 22 on SVERDLOVSKAYA NAB. (Pl. 11; 1), is a handsome ten-columned mansion known as the *Durnovo Dacha*. The dacha, created in its present form in 1813–14 by Andrey Mikhaylov, is perhaps best known as the headquarters of the Petrograd anarchists in 1917. An even more impressive villa is the *Bezborodko Dacha* (No. 40), which belonged to A.A. Bezborodko (foreign minister of Catherine II). The central part of the three-storey turreted mansion was planned by the Moscow architect Bazhenov (1773–77); Quarenghi added the semi-circular wings (1783–84). One of the most interesting features of the design is the row of 29 cast-iron lions which support the front railing.

Just beyond the Bezborodko Dacha, Sverdlovskaya Nab. meets PISKARYOVSKIY PR., which leads N to the Piskaryovskoye Cemetery (4km). At the turn of the century this avenue was named 'Emperor Peter the Great Avenue' (Pr. Imp. Petra Velikovo) and off it to the right was the Peter the Great Hospital, now the *Mechnikov Hospital*. Planning for the hospital began in 1903, and it was intended to celebrate the 200th anniversary of the foundation of St. Petersburg. The work was completed in 1924, and the hospital complex is of architectural interest as it was designed in the Petrine style.

The main avenue to the E beyond Sverdlovskaya Nab. (via Piskaryovskiy Pr.) is SHOSSE REVOLYUTSII. (Pl. 9; 3). This road, which cuts across KRASNOGVAR-DEYSKIY DISTRICT to the Bol'shaya Okhta River, was once known as

Porokhovskoye Shosse or 'Powder Highway' after the Okhta Gunpowder Factory, which was established here in 1715. Another relic of those days survives on Shosse Revolyutsii, the *Church of Elijah the Prophet in Porokhovyye* (Ts. Il'i-Proroka na Porokhovykh). Built in 1781–85, the Classical façade and tiered bell tower were added in 1804 by F.I. Demertsov. The building now houses a branch of the State Hermitage. The late-18C *Zhernovka Estate* is nearby, at the confluence of the Bol. Okhta and Zhernovka rivers. The buildings have been much altered, but Quarenghi was probably involved in their design.

Sverdlovskaya Nab. continues around the bend in the Neva, beyond Piskaryovskiy Pr., as far as the Bol. Okhta River. The handsome façade of buildings along the Neva embankment was completed in 1971, and forms a background to the Smolny across the river.

The BOL'SHAYA OKHTA RIVER (Pl. 9; 3) begins in the Lembolovskiye Hills and flows 86km to the Neva; it is the Neva's largest tributary near Leningrad. The area on the right (N) bank is called BOL'SHAYA OKHTA, that on the left (S) bank MALAYA OKHTA. The Swedes built their fort of Nyenschanz on the left bank of the Bol. Okhta where it enters the Neva. Nyenschanz was captured in 1703 by Peter the Great. Near here is the first permanent road bridge across the upper Neva, the 335m long BOL. OKHTINSKIY MOST. Built in 1911 as the 'Peter the Great Bridge', it crosses to the left bank of the Neva just upstream from the Smolny Institute.

30 Moskovskiy Prospekt

MOSKOVSKIY PR. is one of the major avenues of S Leningrad. It runs some 9km S from Pl. Mira (p 287) (Pl. 13: 6); the starting point is near PL. MIRA METRO STATION. Bus No. 50 follows Moskovskiy Pr., and there is a Metro line running underneath the avenue.

This has long been the main road to Moscow, hence the name. (An 18C milestone by the Fontanka River records that it is 673 versts—713km—to the old capital.) In 1878 the avenue became known as 'Trans-Balkan Prospekt' (Zabalkanskiy Pr.) in honour of the regiments which marched along it en route to the Russo-Turkish War of 1877–78. It received its present name in 1956, after having been called 'International' (Mezhdunarodnyy) Prospekt and then Stalin Prospekt (Pr. I.V. Stalina).

The stretch of Moskovskiy Pr. between Pl. Mira and the Obvodnyy Canal was built up in the 19C and contains several important institutions of higher education. The *Institute of Communications Engineers*, now the *Obraztsov Institute of Railway Transport Engineers* (No. 9, right), was founded in 1809. D.I. Mendeleyev (1834–1907), who devised the Periodic Table, taught at the institute. There is a *Statue of Mendeleyev* (I.Ya. Gintsburg) at Moskovskiy Pr., 19, by the *Chamber of Weights and Measures* which the world-famous scientist directed. He lived here from 1897 until his death.

The *'Red October' Higher Artillery Academy* occupies a Classical building beyond the Fontanka River (F.I. Demertsov, 1809). This has long been one of Russia's most important military schools; its 19C name was the *Konstantin Artillery Academy*. Plekhanov, the early Russian Marxist, was a cadet here in 1873–74. In 1917 the Konstantin Academy was one of the main centres of resistance to the Bolshevik uprising.

The **Technological Institute**, on the corner of Zagorodnyy Pr. (left), was founded in 1828 to train engineers for industry. TEKHNOLO-GICHESKIY INSTITUT METRO STATION occupies the opposite corner.

Projected Town Centre of Leningrad, 1930s. At the top right is 'Soviet House', where the projected Ring Road would have met Prospekt I.V. Stalina (now Moskovskii Pr.). Soviet House was actually completed, but not the rest of the scheme

The institute building dates from 1829–31 (A.I. Postnikov and E.K. Anert). A number of leading scientists worked or studied here, including Mendeleyev, but the institute is also known for its part in the revolutionary movement; because of its industrial character it attracted radical students. The St. Petersburg Soviet of Workers' Deputies held its first meeting in the Physics Lecture Theatre here on 13 October 1905; the building was captured by government troops after a short 'siege' on the 18th.

On the opposite side of Moskovskiy Pr., at No. 33/1, is a former estate (1806–10) which housed from 1844 the *Free Economic Society*. This was one of Russia's first learned societies, founded by Catherine II in 1765 (its original building was at the N end of Nevskiy Pr.). One wing now houses *'Plekhanov House'* (Dom Plekhanova), a branch of the Saltykov-Shchedrin Library.

G.V. Plekhanov (1856–1918) went abroad in the 1880s and formed the first Russian Social-Democratic group. Although he opposed the Bolsheviks in 1917 he is still regarded as the father of Russian Marxism. Plekhanov's archives and library were brought here from Switzerland in 1923; 'Plekhanov House' includes a replica of his study in Geneva. A *Statue of Plekhanov* was unveiled in front of the Technological Institute in 1925 (I.Ya. Gintsburg).
     The Executive Committee of the St. Petersburg Soviet, then chaired by the young Leon Trotsky, was arrested at the building of the Free Economic Society on 3 December 1905. This action of the government broke the back of the revolutionary movement in St. Petersburg and sparked off the unsuccessful December Uprising in Moscow. Another dramatic event of these tumultuous years occurred about 800m further S along Moskovskiy Pr., just before the

Obvodnyy Canal; here in July 1904 the Minister of the Interior, V.K. Pleve, was blown up in his carriage by a Socialist-Revolutionary (Ye.S. Sazonov).

The roads to the W of Moskovskiy Pr. beyond the Technological Institute, 1-YA, 2-YA, etc., KRASNOARMEYSKAYA UL. (1st, 2nd, etc., Red Army Street), were once called 1-ya, 2-ya, etc., 'Rota'. Each was named after a company (rota) of the Izmaylovskiy Guards Regiment. This unit, one of the most distinguished in the Imperial army, was quartered in these streets on both sides of IZMAYLOVSKIY PR., an avenue running parallel to Moskovskiy Pr. and about 600m to the W.

The Obvodnyy Canal (Pl. 13; 8) marked for many years the S limit of St. Petersburg. To the right, NAB. OBVODNOVO KANALA leads past the late-19C *Church of the Resurrection* (Ts. Voskreseniya) (now closed) to the **Warsaw Station** (Varshavskiy Vokzal) (600m) and the **Baltic Station** (Baltiyskiy Vokzal) (1100m).

BALTIYSKAYA METRO STATION stands next to the Baltic Station. The buildings of the Nicholas Cavalry Academy ran along the N bank of the canal opposite the stations. The writer M.Yu. Lermontov studied here, and that is why the avenue to the W of the academy was renamed in his honour in 1912 as LERMONTOVSKIY PR. Other cavalry cadets who became famous were the composer Mussorgsky and Marshal Mannerheim of Finland. About 600m to the N along Lermontovskiy Pr. (No. 43) is the 16-storey **Sovetskaya Hotel** (Pl. 13; 5).

The S part of Moskovskiy Pr., beyond the Obvodnyy Canal, was an industrial district even before 1917, but it was further developed in the Soviet period. The grandiose block of flats at No. 79 (right), now a listed building, was erected on the site of the Goryacheye Pole—the city's main rubbish tip. The architects were L.A. Il'in and A.M. Arnol'd; the central part dates from 1938, the S wing from 1951.

Across the avenue, at No. 96, stands the grey building of *Soyuzpushnina*, where international fur auctions are held. Next door, at No. 98, is the grey Pseudo-Russian building of the former *New Convent of the Virgin* (Voskresenskiy Novodevich'iy Monastyr'). N.Ye. Yefimov designed the present structure in 1845, but the first St. Petersburg convent of this name was founded at the Smolny in 1748.

A conspicuous landmark on Moskovskiy Pr. is the green 12-columned cast-iron **Moscow Triumphal Arch** (Pl. 8; 6). The arch was designed by V.P. Stasov but bears a strong resemblance to Berlin's Brandenburg Gate. It was completed in 1838 (50 years after the German version) and commemorates a series of victories over Persians, Turks, and Polish nationalists in the years 1826–31.

The arch stood at the junction of the Moscow highway and the former Ligovskiy Canal (now Ligovskiy Pr.), and was at one time the largest cast-iron structure in the world. Like the Triumphal Arch in Moscow it was demolished after the Revolution (1936), and during the war sections of the arch were used for fortifications. The arch was rebuilt on the old site in 1959–60 but with new columns and entablature.

The green building to the left of the arch (No. 116) is marked with the date '1925'. This was the first fire station built in Soviet Leningrad and is now a listed building. To the right of the arch is MOSKOVSKIYE VOROTA METRO STATION.

Some of Leningrad's most important factories are situated along this part of the avenue: the *Skorokhod Factory* (right), the *Yegorov Railway Wagon Factory* (right) and the *Elektrosila Factory* (formerly Siemens-Schuckert). Among these vast plants, at No. 129 (right), stands the massive grey cylinder of the *Moscow District Soviet* (I.I. Fomin and V.G. Dagul', 1930–35).

The more residential zone to the S contains the ten-storey *Rossiya Hotel* (1962) (No. 163, right). Nearby are two statues, one of the radical N.G. Chernyshevsky (V.V. Lishev, 1947), the other a symbolic female figure of 'Russia' (G.V. Kosov). The 70-ha **Moscow Victory Park** (Pl. 8; 6) was laid out in 1945 on the opposite side of the avenue.

PARK POBEDY METRO STATION is located here. The Victory Park includes an 'Alley of Heroes' with busts of six Leningraders who were twice awarded the title 'Hero of the Soviet Union'. There is also a bust of Prime Minister Aleksey Kosygin, who has twice received the 'Hero of Socialist Labour' medal.

Facing the eastern side of the park on PR. YU. GAGARINA is the vast round **Lenin Sports-Concert Centre** (Sportivno-Kontsertnyy Kompleks im. V.I. Lenina) (1980) with an indoor hall seating 25,000 spectators.

By the S end of the park a tall spire marks the beginning of a stretch of post-war buildings. Not far along, the *Zenit Cinema* can be seen to the left, on the corner of UL. GASTELLO. This side-street contains two interesting relics of the 18C. Velten built the **Chesma Palace** in 1774–77 as a place where Catherine II could rest on the way to Tsarskoye Selo (Pushkin). The name comes from the great naval victory of 1770 over the Turks in the Aegean at Chesma. The plan is unique: an equilateral triangle with turrets at each corner. The building was converted into a hospital for war veterans in the 1830s; this involved substantial alterations during which the wings were added and the Gothic battlements removed. Rasputin's body lay in state here in 1916 after it had been pulled out of the Neva.

The *Chesma Church (Chesmenskaya Ts.), a unique red and white Pseudo-Gothic structure by Velten (1777–80), stands behind the palace. The church was restored to its present excellent condition in 1968. The white moulded stripes on the red wall accentuate the vertical axis, as do the many spires. Beneath the fanciful design, however, the traditional five cupolas of the Russian church are still evident.

The 1935–36 General Plan for Leningrad envisaged the S part of what is now Moskovskiy Pr. as the centre of the whole city, replacing the old Imperial districts on the Neva. The heart of Leningrad was to be the present MOSKOVSKAYA PL., where the main N–S artery intersected the planned Central Ring Road. The enormous eight-storey building which now stands in the depth of the 13-ha square was known as *Soviet House (Dom Sovetov) (no adm.). It was begun in 1936 and designed by N.A. Trotsky on a monumental style consistent with its intended role as the administrative and Party headquarters of the city.

Above the 14 pilasters of the main (W) façade a frieze depicts scenes of economic development and national defence; in the centre is the crest of the USSR. The E façade is also of interest—a projecting semi-circular colonnade surrounds the giant Assembly Hall. The German invasion interrupted the final completion of Soviet House, and after the war the plan for a southern town centre was changed. Moskovskaya Pl. was nevertheless completed on a grand scale, with the flats on the W side of Moskovskiy Pr. echoing the forms of Soviet House opposite. A large bronze *Statue of Lenin* by M.K. Anikushin was unveiled in the centre of Moskovskaya Pl. in 1970. MOSKOVSKAYA METRO STATION is located here.

The final stretch of Moskovskiy Pr. was built up more recently. Not far beyond Moskovskaya Pl. are twin blocks distinguished by the large windows of artists' studios on the top floors. Adjacent 22-storey towers mark the gateway to the city. They flank PL. POBEDY (or Victory Square) (Pl. 8; 8), a giant traffic circle with, in the middle, the impressive **Monument to the Defenders of Leningrad**. On the W side of the square is the **Pulkovskaya Hotel** (1981).

This site, formerly called Srednyaya Rogatka, has a direct connection with the Blockade of 1941–44: it was one of the strong-points of Leningrad's defences. In July 1945 a temporary triumphal arch was erected here to welcome troops returning from conquered Germany. The present monument was designed by M.K. Anikushin, S.B. Speransky, and V.A. Kamensky and opened on the 30th anniversary of V-E Day in 1975. The remains of a small baroque Palace (Putevoi Dvorets) by Rastrelli (1751–53) on this site were dismantled.

The central feature on the monument complex is a 48m high red granite obelisk inscribed '1941–1945'; on either side stand stylised black figures of the defenders themselves. The monument is reached via pedestrian underpasses from the end of Moskovskiy Pr.; the northern part is a giant concrete broken ring symbolising the Blockade with, in the centre, an eternal flame. The subterranean memorial hall (Pamyatnyi Zal) south of the broken ring was opened in 1978. The vestibule is lit by 900 electric candles, one for each day of the Blockade. The central hall is decorated with giant mosaic panels ('Blockade' and 'Victory') and contains artefacts from the war.

From Pl. Pobedy, MOSKOVSKOYE SHOSSE leads left to Moscow. The continuation of Moskovskiy Pr., directly S of the square, is called PULKOVSKOYE SHOSSE; it leads to Pulkovo Airport and past the Pulkovo Observatory to Pushkin and Pavlovsk. The observatory, with its three silver domes, stands on high ground (the Pulkovo Heights) about 8km along Pulkovskoye Shosse. Founded in 1839 by Wilhelm von Struve and equipped with German instruments, the former Nicholas Observatory was one of the world's finest. The observatory was used for many years to determine the exact time and the 'Pulkovo Meridian' served as a baseline for Russian maps. The observatory buildings were destroyed during the Second World War and restored. Nearby, the Pulkovskiy Rubezh Monument (1967) marks the front line of 1941–44.

31 Prospekt Stachek

The main axis of the south-western KIROVSKIY DISTRICT is Pr. Stachek, which forms with Pr. Gaza a 6km Rte from Pl. Repina (Pl. 13; 5) on the Fontanka River to the new suburb of Avtovo.

From NARVSKAYA METRO STATION (Pl. 13; 7), Trams No. 13 and 33 and Bus No. 2 run N along Pr. Gaza to Pl. Repina. Trolleybus No. 20 and Bus No. 73 run S from Narvskaya Station to Avtovo Metro Station and beyond. The Metro follows the S part of this Rte, from Narvskaya Station to Pr. Veteranov station.

Before the Revolution this area was known as the Narvskaya District or the Narvskaya Zastava (gate). The town of Narva lies 147km to the W (on the border between Russia and Estonia), and the road there led through this suburb of St. Petersburg.

The Sea Port (Morskoy Port) forms the W side of this district. It was built up in the last quarter of the 19C, after the Sea Canal was dredged from near Kronstadt. (Earlier, goods had to be unloaded at Kronstadt and moved by lighter to the capital.) This is now the largest port in the Soviet Union. Many passenger ships, however, arrive at the Sea Terminal (Morskoy Vokzal) on Vasil'yevskiy Island.

Until the middle of the 19C this was a region of aristocratic estates and dachas, but only a few of these survive. The Russian Industrial Revolution led to the creation in the Narvskaya Zastava of some of the largest factories in the country.

I.I. Gaza (1894–1933) was a young worker from the Narvskaya Zastava who had a distinguished Civil War career and then became a secretary of the Leningrad Party Committee. After his premature death the name PR. GAZA (Pl. 13; 5) was given to what had formerly been Staro-Petergofskiy Pr. Pr. Gaza runs 2km from Pl. Repina to the Narva Triumphal Arch. One building of interest stands at No. 6, the lavish marble-faced Moskva Cinema. To the left beyond the

Obvodnyy Canal lies the *Krasnyy Treugol'nik* (Red Triangle) *Factory*; the workers here were important in the Russian revolutionary movement.

The ***Narva Triumphal Arch** (Pl. 13; 7), near NARVSKAYA METRO STATION, was erected in 1827–34 to commemorate the victories of the Imperial Guards in the Napoleonic Wars. Quarenghi created a wooden arch for the triumphal return of the Russian army in 1814, and this was later replaced by the existing permanent structure which V.P. Stasov designed. For many years the arch served as one of the main entrances to the city.

The structure of the arch is brick, covered with copper plates; copper was also used for the decoration. Between the columns are statues of Russian warriors, and above them allegorical winged figures. The triumphal chariot drawn by six horses surmounts the arch and contains a statue of Victory. The gilded inscription lists the Guards regiments and their victories. Among the sculptors involved in the project were S.S. Pimenov, V.I. Demut-Malinovsky, M.G. Krylov, N.A. Tokarev, and P. Clodt von Jürgensburg.

Just 200m NW of the arch along PEREKOPSKAYA UL., is the *Park im. 30-letiya VLKSM* (or 'Park named in honour of the 30th Anniversary of the Communist Youth League') (Pl. 12; 8), which lies between two canals. Here Peter the Great created the Yekateringof Estate for his wife Catherine (Yekaterina). The attractive wooden Yekateringof Palace, built in 1711, burned down in 1924.

Narvskaya Pl., now PL. STACHEK, was known for more than just the triumphal arch. One of the worst incidents of Bloody Sunday, 1905, occurred here as workers, led personally by Father Gapon, tried to break through into the town; as many as 40 people were killed by government troops. Because of this incident and because of the general militancy of the Narvskaya Zastava, the square was renamed in 1923 as Pl. Stachek or 'Square of Strikes'.

Petergofskoye Shosse, the highway to Peterhof (now Petrodvorets), was renamed PR. STACHEK at the same time. During the 1920s the stretch of Pr. Stachek immediately to the S of the Narva Arch was one of the first districts to be redeveloped, in an attempt to redress the imbalance between the formerly wealthy central districts and the squalid industrial suburbs.

The domed building to the left of the Narva Arch is from a later period (1956), the NARVSKAYA METRO STATION. Next door stands the ***Gorky Palace of Culture**, designed by A.I. Gegello and D.L. Krichevsky and opened on the tenth anniversary of the October Revolution.

This was one of the first purpose-built cultural and educational centres in Soviet Russia. The fan-shaped plan comes from the 1900-seat theatre inside; the large windows enable the theatre hall to be used for afternoon meetings. Some of the sessions of the Bolshevik 6th Party Congress took place in a school on this site (July–August 1917).

The handsome Constructivist building opposite (Pr. Stachek, 9) is the *Kirovskiy Univermag* (Kirov Department Store) (1929–31). It included a 'factory-kitchen' (fabrika-kukhnya), a means of socialised catering which produced 15,000 meals a day. Further down the avenue, beyond a modern block of flats, stands another relic of the inter-war years, the *'10th Anniversary of the October Revolution' School* (Shkola im. 10-letiya Oktyabrya) (No. 11/5).

Begun in 1925 and opened, as its name suggests, on 7 November 1927, this was one of the very first Soviet-built schools. It was designed by A.S. Nikol'sky with the overall plan of a stylised hammer and sickle. A total of 1000 pupils were to be trained here using the most progressive methods.

The turret of the school forms part of an architectural ensemble, as it is in line with TRAKTORNAYA UL. on the E side of Pr. Stachek. Traktornaya Ul. comprised the very first housing project in the Soviet Union; the modest row of houses was built in 1925–27 by the design team of Gegello, Nikol'sky, and G.A. Simonov. The name, 'Tractor Street', was given in honour of the Fordson Tractors produced under license at the nearby Krasnyy Putilovets (now Kirov) Factory; these were built from 1924, the first such machines in Russia.

The large square beyond Traktornaya Ul., KIROVSKAYA PL. (Pl 8; 6), dates from the following decade. Along the S side runs a long Constructivist building with an 11-storey tower, the *Kirovskiy District Soviet* (N.A. Trotsky, 1934); the circular bay at the W end now contains a cinema. Kirovskaya Pl. is dominated by a 16m high *Statue of S.M. Kirov*, the Leningrad party leader who was assassinated in 1934. N.V. Tomsky was the sculptor of the monument, which was unveiled in December 1938; Tomsky depicted a bold dynamic figure gesturing toward the Kirov Factory with outstretched arm.

The *'9 January' Childrens Park* (Detskiy Park im. 9 Yanvarya) (Pl. 8; 6) stretches along the left side of Pr. Stachek beyond the Soviet building. Father Gapon began his famous march from this site on 'Bloody Sunday', 9 January 1905; most of the demonstrators got no farther than the Narva Arch, and many died there. The park was laid out in 1924. The attractive railing was originally erected in 1901 around the W side of the Winter Palace, where another shooting incident took place on 'Bloody Sunday'; in 1928 the railing was moved to the present site.

Some distance along Pr. Stachek, at No. 45 (right), is an interesting anomaly in this industrial district, the yellow 18C *Dashkova Dacha*. Princess Yekaterina Dashkova (1743–1810) was an intimate of Catherine II's who helped master-mind her coup d'état and was later head of the St. Petersburg Academy of Sciences. The villa was built in the 1780s, possibly by Quarenghi. It was substantially altered in the 19C and now serves as a *Palace of Weddings*.

The Kirovskiy District is dominated by the huge plant which begins beyond the railway overpass, the **Kirov Factory**.

The St. Petersburg State Iron Works, established in 1801, was bought by N.I. Putilov in 1868. The Putilov Factory had as many as 40,000 workers; it was both one of the biggest industrial enterprises in Imperial Russia and a centre of the revolutionary labour movement. The 'Avenue of Strikes' (Pr. Stachek) took its name from the industrial militancy of the Putilov workers. The strike and lock-out at the factory in early 1917 contributed greatly to the mass movement which overthrew the Tsar, and the 'Putilovtsy' played an active role later in the year during the October Revolution. The works became known as the Krasnyy Putilovets (or Red Putilov Worker) Factory in 1922, but immediately after Kirov's assassination it was renamed in his honour. The plant specialised in heavy engineering and also produced the first license-built tractors. Although much equipment was evacuated in 1941, work continued here—only 4km from the front line—during the Blockade.

Opposite, on the left side of Pr. Stachek, stands the grey pavilion of KIROVSKIY ZAVOD METRO STATION, a large Classical structure. The *Gaza Palace of Culture* is next door, at No. 72; it was originally built in 1930–35 to the design of Gegello and Krichevsky.

Beyond the Kirov Factory, Pr. Stachek enters the impressive KOMSOMOL'SKAYA PL. (Pl. 8; 6), where three identical seven-storey apartment blocks (V.A. Kamensky and S.G. Mayofis, 1955–60). Just beyond the square the road divides into Krasnoputilovskaya Ul. and Pr. Stachek; the wedge-shaped park between contains a *Statue commemorating the 50th Anniversary of the Komsomol.* Kom-somol'skaya Pl. was the centre of the new district of AVTOVO, which was planned before the Second World War by A.A. Ol'. The name has nothing to do with motor cars; the Finnish village of Autovo was located here before the time of Peter I. The Classical domed pavilion of AVTOVO METRO STATION is located about 800m S along Pr. Stachek.

Pr. Stachek turns sharply to the right (W) beyond the Metro station. To the left a 'KV' tank has been preserved as a war memorial; Avtovo was in the Soviet front line during the Blockade.

The avenue continues for a short distance to the W as Pr. Stachek. To the right lie the innovative housing developments of the Krasnosel'skiy district, but *Aleksandrino*, the late-18C estate of Count I.G. Chernyshev, survives at No. 226. Beyond Pr. Marshala Zhukova, Pr. Stachek becomes PETERGOFSKOYE SHOSSE, the main road to Petrodvorets.

PR. MARSHALA ZHUKOVA, running from NE to SW, becomes TALLINSKOYE SHOSSE (Pl. 8; 7). This is the road to the suburban town of Krasnoye Selo, which was incorporated into Leningrad as a new district in 1973. The avenue continues to the Baltic port of Tallin (formerly Reval), some 358km W of Leningrad.

To the S of Pr. Stachek are the newly-developed regions of UL'YANKA and DACHNOYE, to which the Metro was extended in the late 1970s (PR. VETERANOV METRO STATION). The avenue to the S is Pr. Narodnovo Opolcheniya; the name commemorates the volunteers of the Narodnoye Opolcheniye (People's Militia) who held the line here against the Germans in 1941–44.

32 Leningrad Rivers and Canals

Much of Leningrad's special attraction comes from its location on the delta of the Neva River. The Neva and its embankments create, arguably, the grandest view of the city. Also of note is the network of rivers and canals which makes the central area a kind of northern Venice or Amsterdam. A tour of the most interesting parts of this water system may be divided into three Rtes. Rte A gives the main sights that can be seen from the Neva, while Rte B describes the course followed by excursion boats on the Moyka and Fontanka Rivers. The smaller Griboyedov Canal, which may be followed on foot, is described in Rte C.

A.   The Neva River

Excursion boats sail along the main part of the river. Moving upstream, there are piers at PL. DEKABRISTOV, the STATE HERMITAGE (Ermitazh), the SUMMER GARDENS (Letniy Sad), NAB. KUTUZOVA, and, near the SE edge of the city, at the RIVER TERMINAL (Rechnoy Vokzal) and the NEVA FOREST PARK (Nevskiy Lesopark). Other piers are at the SEA PIER (Morskaya Pristan') on the E shore of Vasil'yevskiy Island and at the KIROV PARK (TsPKiO im. S.M. Kirova) beyond; the park may also be reached via the Bol'shaya Nevka River.

The NEVA RIVER flows 74km from Lake Ladoga to the Gulf of Finland. Peter I built the Peter-Paul Fortress to command the W end of the Neva, and his new capital grew up around the river. Many of the most impressive buildings were constructed along the shore, and at the end of the 18C the banks of the river were sheathed in granite.

The westernmost bridge across the main channel of the Neva (or the Bol'shaya Neva) is the MOST LEYTENANTA SHMIDTA (Pl. 13; 3). This drawbridge dates from 1843–50 and was once known as the Nicholas Bridge; the attractive iron railings were designed by A.P. Bryullov. Moving upstream, the river beyond is flanked on the left (N) by Universitetskaya Nab. (University Embankment) with the Classical Academy of Arts (nearest the bridge); the University, including the Menshikov Palace and the Twelve Colleges; the Academy of Sciences; and the Museum of Ethnography, with its tower. Nab. Krasnovo Flota and Admiralteyskaya Nab., on the right, contain an impressive row of 18C buildings and the ensemble around Pl. Dekabristov and the Bronze Horseman: the Senate and Synod, St. Isaac's Cathedral, and the Admiralty. Near Pl. Dekabristov and on the opposite bank can be seen the stone abutments of the former Isaakiyevskiy Most; this was a wooden pontoon bridge that was removed in the spring and autumn. It was the first bridge across the Neva, and was originally constructed in 1727; the final version was destroyed by fire in 1916.

The DVORTSOVYY MOST or Palace Bridge (Pl. 13; 2) is the most recent of the main Neva drawbridges. The pontoon bridge which had been placed in 1850 between the Winter Palace (State Hermitage) and the Strelka (Point) of Vasil'yevskiy Island was replaced in 1908–14 by the existing permanent structure. The finest and widest stretch of the river opens out beyond the Dvortsovyy Most. To the left are the Rostral Columns and the Naval Museum on the Strelka, and then the Malaya Neva and the Peter-Paul Fortress. The State Hermitage and a row of palaces and mansions extend along the opposite shore, on Dvortsovaya Nab.

The MALAYA NEVA (Pl. 12; 1) begins at the MOST STROITELEY and flows some 5km to the sea. To the left (W) is Vasil'yevskiy Island; the prominent domed building not far from the bridge is the Institute of Russian Literature. Opposite, on the Petrograd Side, are the warehouses of the Tuchkov Buyan, and then the Yubileynyy Sports Palace and the Cathedral of Prince Vladimir. The Lenin Stadium appears on the same side, beyond the TUCHKOV MOST.

Some 3.5km downstream the channel known as the Malaya Nevka River flows into the Malaya Neva from the right; the Coastal Victory Park with the Kirov Stadium lies to the N.

The broad part of the central Neva is spanned by the ten arches of the 582m KIROVSKIY MOST (Pl. 10; 3). For many decades, until the completion of the Most Aleksandra Nevskovo (1965), this was the longest bridge in Leningrad. The first pontoon bridge from the S shore to the Petersburg (Petrograd) Side was created in 1803, but the present version was built in 1897–1903 by the French Batignolles company (and inaugurated by President Félix Fauré). The Kirovskiy Most was given its present name in 1934; before the Revolution it was called the Troitskiy (Trinity) Bridge after Troitskaya Pl. and the Cathedral of the Trinity on the Petersburg Side. To the right of the bridge are Marsovo Pole and, further E, the Summer Gardens. The building containing the Cabin of Peter I is visible to the left, and some 500m farther along the embankment the Bolshaya Nevka River turns off to the N. The cruiser 'Avrora', a relic of the Revolution, is permanently moored by the junction of the two rivers; the modern Leningrad Hotel stands on the opposite bank.

The BOL'SHAYA NEVKA (Pl. 10; 2) separates the Petrograd Side from the

Vyborg Side and flows under the MOST SVOBODY and the GRENADERSKIY MOST.
Beyond the second bridge the narrow Karpovka River branches off the the left;
just to the N of the Karpovka are the Botanic Gardens. About 4km from the
Neva, Kamennyy Island divides this channel into two parts; the Malaya Nevka
flows to the S of the island, while the Bol'shaya Nevka continues around the N
side. The attractive Kamennoostrovskiy Palace is located at the E end of
Kamennyy Island, while a second palace, the Yelagin Palace, becomes visible
after the boats pass under the USHAKOVSKIY MOST and turn left into the
Srednyaya Nevka. Beyond is the 1-Y YELAGIN MOST which joins Yelagin Island
(and the Kirov Park) to Kamennyy Island. The Coastal Victory Park is situated
on Krestovskiy Island, which lies to the S of the Srednyaya Nevka.

The LITEYNYY MOST (Pl. 10; 4) joins Liteynyy Pr. to the Vyborg Side.
At the time of its construction, 1874–79, the Alexander Bridge (as it
was then called) represented a considerable engineering achievement. The section which can be lifted measures 57m, the longest in
Leningrad; there are five other spans, making a total length of 395m.
    The upper Neva, above the Liteynyy Most, is a partly industrial but
not without interest to the tourist. The square in front of the Finland
Station opens to the left; further along, amidst huge factory buildings, two former country mansions survive, the Durnovo and
Bezborodko dachas. The river turns sharply to the right (S) past the
domes of the Smolny Convent (right) and the apartment blocks on
Sverdlovskaya Nab. (left).
    The distance from the BOL'SHOY OKHTINSKIY MOST (1909–11),
with its twin steel arches and central drawbridge, to the 629m MOST
ALEKSANDRA NEVSKOVO is about 1.5km. The latter bridge is the
longest on the river. The Alexander Nevskiy Lavra is visible to the
right, just above the second bridge. The next road bridge is located
8km further S, the VOLODARSKIY MOST (Pl. 9; 5); this first post-
revolutionary bridge was opened in 1936 and was intended to serve
the proposed E–W avenue of the developing part of S Leningrad.
    The **Nevskiy Forest Park** (Nevskiy Lesopark) is situated on the
right (N) bank of the Neva, about 29km from the mouth of the river.
This popular resort occupies a site of some 600 ha and contains the
handsome _Zinov'yev Dacha_, a wooden Classical manor-house built
by the architect V.I. Beretti in the 1820s.

B.   The Fontanka River and the Moyka
       River

The trip by boat along the rivers and canals—in season—is one of the
best ways to see central Leningrad. The boats leave from several
piers, including one just upstream from (to the N of) the
Anichkovskiy Most (Pl. 10; 6) on Nevskiy Pr.; this is about 500m from
GOSTINYY DVOR METRO STATION. The boats follow the Fontanka
River W to the Kryukov Canal; the latter leads N to the Moyka River,
which returns E to the Fontanka. The roughly rectangular Rte
measures 9km and can also be followed on foot.
    The FONTANKA RIVER is nearly 7km long and until the mid-18C it
marked the S boundary of St. Petersburg. The name comes from the
fountains (fontany) of the Summer Gardens, which this river helped
to feed. The banks were sheathed in granite in the 1780s.
    Beyond the Anichkovskiy Most and the nearby buildings on
Nevskiy Pr.—notably the Anichkov Palace—the river bends gently to
the right. A number of houses for the aristocracy and Court officials

were built along here; the *House of Countess Karlova* at NAB. REKI FONTANKI, 46 (left), a four-storey structure with Baroque details, was begun in the early 18C. The impressive five-storey brick and stone façade at No. 54 belongs to a remarkable complex of flats built by the architect Lidval in 1910–12; three courtyards joined by arches stretch S to Ul. Rubinshteyna.

The MOST LOMONOSOVA (Pl. 10; 8), once the Chernyshev Most, is an attractive stone drawbridge with four squat rectangular towers. It dates from 1785–87, and is one of seven similar bridges built across the Fontanka by the French engineer J. Perronnet. Only one other, the Staro-Kalinkinskiy Most, survives. N of the bridge is PL. LOMONOSOVA, with a bronze *Statue of M.V. Lomonosov* (P.P. Zabello, 1892). From this square the beautiful Ul. Zodchevo Rossi leads back to Nevskiy Pr. Before the Revolution, the *Ministries of Education* and *Interior* had their offices here; the former occupied the W side of Ul. Zodchevo Rossi, while the latter was housed at Nab. Reki Fontanki, 57, on the W side of the square. Both buildings were designed by Rossi in the 1830s. The large modern building at No. 59 is where a number of newspapers are published, including 'Leningradskaya Pravda'.

The ballerina Olga Preobrazhenska (1870–1962) lived at Nab. Reki Fontanki, 68 (left). The former *Glavnoye Kaznacheystvo* next door (No. 70–72), a part of the Imperial Ministry of Finance, is of architectural interest as it was built in 1913–15 but designed to echo Rossi's buildings across the river. One of the architects was D.M. Iofan, who went on to design some of the Moscow skyscrapers.

The **Gorky Theatre**, also known as 'BDT' (Akademicheskiy Bol'shoy Dramaticheskiy Teatr im. M. Gor'kovo), stands on the Fontanka embankment at No. 65 (right).

The building dates from 1876–78 and originally housed the *Suvorin Theatre* (Malyy Teatr Suvorina). The present company was founded during the Civil War and a number of leading literary figures were associated with it, including M.F. Andreyeva, Lunacharsky, Blok, and Gorky; the first performance, Schiller's 'Don Carlos', took place in February 1919. After Gorky's return to Soviet Russia the theatre was given his name (1932) and began to perform his plays.

Ul. Dzerzhinskovo, intended in the 18C as one of the main streets of St. Petersburg, crosses the river about 300m downstream from the Gorky Theatre via the SEMYONOVSKIY MOST (1786) (Pl. 10; 7). It was planned in the 1760s to create squares around the various Fontanka bridges, but this was only carried through here. On the right two handsome Classical mansions flank Ul. Dzerzhinskovo as it opens into SEMYONOVSKAYA PL.: the *Kukanov House* (A.I. Mel'nikov, 1831–32) (Nab. Reki Fontanki, 79) and the *Yevment'yev House* (1780–90) (No. 81). One part of the semi-circular open space on the left side of the river is bounded by the former *Barracks of the Moscow Guards Regiment* (F.I. Volkov, 1789), at No. 90. Elements of this regiment took part in the Decembrist Uprising of 1825.

The OBUKHOVSKIY MOST carries Moskovskiy Pr. across the river. Just before the bridge (left) is the extensive territory of the former Obukhov Hospital (1782–90), now part of the *Kirov Military Medical Academy* (Nab. Reki Fontanki, 106); this has long been an important centre of Russian medicine. The **Yusupov Palace**, beyond the bridge (right), at No. 115, is one of the great houses built along the Fontanka in the 18C when it was still a suburb. The estate dates back to the 1720s, although the palace is the result of a reconstruction by

Quarenghi in the 1790s. An engineering institute was housed here in 1810, and the building still serves as the **Obrazstov Institute of Railway Engineers**. The public garden beyond extends to Sadovaya Ul.. The poet G.R. Derzhavin (1743–1816) lived in the large 'U'-shaped building on the opposite bank (No. 118).

The five great blue domes of the *Trinity Cathedral are visible beyond the IZMAYLOVSKIY MOST (left) (Pl. 13; 6).

According to some accounts, Peter I (whose first wife was still alive) married his mistress Catherine in a chapel here in 1707, with only Jacob Bruce as a witness. A wooden cathedral was erected on this site in the 1750s, in what was then the suburb of the Izmaylovskiy Guards Regiment. The present building dates from 1828–35 and is the work of V.P. Stasov. A bust of the architect was unveiled here in 1969 (M.T. Litovchenko). The handsome Classical cathedral takes the form of a Greek cross; at the end of each arm is a portico with six Corinthian columns. A sculptured frieze runs under the cornice and there are bas-reliefs on the drum of the main dome, above the colonnade. The interior is decorated with marble-faced columns. The semi-circular iconostasis with its colonnade is unusual.

The excursion boats turn right into the KRYUKOV CANAL (Pl. 13; 6) at this point. The canal was excavated between the Neva and the Moyka River in 1719 under the supervision of an officer named Semyon Kryukov; it was extended S to the Fontanka River in 1787.

The stretch of the Fontanka River downstream from the Kryukov Canal is not of particular interest. The attractive YEGIPETSKIY MOST was completed in 1955 on the site of an Egyptian-style bridge of 1826. Lermontovskiy Pr. crosses the river at this point; the 16-storey **Sovetskaya Hotel** rises to the left of the river at Lermontovskiy Pr., 43. Pushkin lived from 1817–20 at Nab. Reki Fontanki, 185 (right); the architect Carlo Rossi, the creator of some of the finest buildings in St. Petersburg, died here in poverty in 1849. Beyond are two bridges. The Malo-Kalinkinskiy Most spans the Griboyedov Canal as it enters the Fontanka from the right; the STARO-KALINKINSKIY MOST, across the Fontanka, has four towers and is to the same design as the Most Lomonosova; it was built in 1785–87 but much widened in the 1890s.

The 1100m Kryukov Canal follows a straight course from the Fontanka to the Moyka and beyond. The canal passes (left) the house where Generalissimo Suvorov died in 1800 (Nab. Kryukova Kanala, 23). Further on, Sadovaya Ul. and the Griboyedov Canal intersect the Kryukov Canal; to the right are the beautiful Cathedral of St. Nicholas with its detached bell tower and, after the next two bridges, the rear of the Kirov Theatre. After two more bridges the Kryukov Canal meets the Moyka River. To the left, N of the Moyka and W of the Kryukov Canal, is the 18C Novaya Gollandiya complex.

The MOYKA RIVER is some 5km long and originally flowed from a swamp in the vicinity of the present Marsovo Pole. The granite embankment dates from 1798–1810. Beyond the POTSELUYEV MOST (1808–16), which carries Ul. Glinki across the Moyka, is an angular Classical mansion (Nab. Reki Moyki, 94) (right). This is the **Yusupov Palace**, built to the plans of Vallin de la Mothe in the 1760s (this is not to be confused with the other Yusupov Palace, on the Fontanka). The building is most famous as the place where in December 1916 Rasputin was murdered by Prince Feliks Yusupov. It now serves as a *Palace of Culture for Teachers*. The French architect Montferrand lived from the 1820s to the 1850s at No. 86 (right). Montferrand's greatest creation, St. Isaac's Cathedral, is visible in the distance on the other side of the river.

The POCHTAMTSKIY MOST was one of the finest suspension footbridges in St. Petersburg (W. Traitteur, 1823–24). Beyond and to the left the Moyka embankment coincides with the W end of Ul.

Gertsena. The scientist Lomonosov died in 1765 on the site of what is now Ul. Gertsena, 61. The *Palace of Culture of Communications Workers*, between Ul. Gertsena (No. 58) and Nab. Reki Moyki, is the result of the fundamental reconstruction of what was once the Gothic *German Reformed Church* (G.A. Bosse, 1863–65).

The Moyka passes under Isaakiyevskaya Pl. through the SINIY MOST (1818) which, at 100m, is the widest in Leningrad. The name, 'Blue Bridge', comes from the colour which the original wooden bridge was painted. The Mariya Palace lies just to the S of the bridge (right), while St. Isaac's Cathedral may be seen to the N.

The next bridge over the Moyka, carrying Ul. Dzerzhinskovo, is the KRASNYY MOST or 'Red Bridge' (1808–14). One of four similar iron bridges built across the Moyka in the early 19C, it alone has kept its original appearance with four granite obelisks supporting the picturesque lamps. To the right, beyond the Krasnyy Most, several buildings of the large **Herzen Pedagogical Institute** line the embankment. The institute was founded in 1918 and is one of the largest centres of higher education in Leningrad. A number of its buildings are former foundling homes which had once been the mansions of the St. Petersburg aristocracy. The former *Nicholas Orphanage* at Nab. Reki Moyki, 52, was reconstructed in 1839–43. No. 50, much altered, was originally the work of B.F. Rastrelli (1750–53), while No. 48, now the main building of the Herzen Institute, was designed by Kokorinov and Vallin de la Mothe as the *Razumovsky Palace* (1762–66). K.G. Razumovsky, Hetman of the Ukraine, was one of the men behind the coup d'état of Catherine II.

Nevskiy Pr. (p 264) crosses the Moyka by the NARODNYY MOST (Pl. 10; 5). The Narodnyy (People's) Most was known before the Revolution as the Politseyskiy (Police) Most, after the nearby residence of an 18C Chief of Police. Although now much altered it dates from 1806–08 and was the first iron bridge in the city. To the right, before the bridge, is the Stroganov Palace.

Beyond the Nevskiy the river curves through one of the most historic districts of Leningrad. The rear of the Main Staff Building extends along the left as far as the PEVCHESKIY MOST (1839–40). The name of the bridge was sometimes used as a synonym for the Imperial Foreign Ministry, which was housed in that part of the Main Staff facing the Moyka. The bridge in turn took its name from the Pridvornaya Pevcheskaya Kapella or *Court Choir*, which was situated at its E end (Nab. Reki Moyki, 20). The choir was founded in the 18C, and Glinka, Rimsky-Korsakov, and Balakirev all taught here. The building, which dates from 1880, is now the home of the **Glinka Choir** (Gos. Akademicheskaya Khorovaya Kapella im. M.I. Glinki). The Bolshevik newspaper 'Pravda' was published in a building between Nevskiy Pr. and the Glinka Choir (Nab. Reki Moyki, 32/2) from early March 1917 until July, when it was banned. The **Lenin and Pravda Museum** (Muzey 'V.I. Lenin i Pravda') is now located here. To the left, beyond the Pevcheskiy Most, the beautiful little *ZIMNYAYA KANAVKA flows past the State Hermitage and under a line of picturesque bridges to the Neva.

The **Pushkin Museum** (Muzey-Kvartira A.S. Pushkina) was established at Nab. Reki Moyki, 12, in 1925.

The first stone house was built on this site in the 1730s, although it has been rebuilt several times; the six fluted Corinthian pilasters date from the 1770s. The poet A.S. Pushkin (1799–1837) lived in this building only briefly, from the autumn of 1836. He was brought home, mortally wounded, after his duel with d'Anthès and died here on 29 January 1837. Some of the rooms on the Ground

Floor have been restored to their appearance in Pushkin's time, and many of his
personal effects are on show. There is also an exhibition of documents and other
materials relating to the last years of the poet's life.

Inside the northern bend of the Moyka, beyond the BOL'SHOY
KONYUSHENNYY MOST (Pl. 10; 5), are the former **Court Stables**
(Pridvornyye Konyushni). These were originally built in the early
18C and then reconstructed by V.P. Stasov in 1817–23. The long
main façade looks S onto Konyushennaya Pl, but the row of squat
Doric columns on the W façade is visible from the river. Pushkin's
wake was held on 1 February 1837 in the church of the Court Stables
(located in the centre of the S façade). It was from here two days later
that the authorities spirited his coffin away to the Svyatigorsk
Monastery. The Baroque building on the S side of the square
formerly housed the Imperial Carriage Museum.

The left side of the river is occupied by the rear of the Pavlovskiy
Guards Regiment Barracks, and the former *Round Market* (Kruglyy
Rynok) designed by Quarenghi in 1790.

A remarkable set of bridges spans the junction of the Moyka and
the Griboyedov Canal (Pl. 10; 5); this complex iron structure was
created in 1829–31 to the design of Ye.A. Adam and W. Traitteur.
The TEATRAL'NYY MOST across the Moyka is set exactly in the axis of
the Griboyedov Canal; it is joined to the E and W banks of the canal
by the two parts of the MALO-KONYUSHENNYY MOST. Behind the
latter rise the onion domes of the Church of the Resurrection.

A straight part of the Moyka continues to the SADOVYY MOST (Pl.
10; 6), with open space on either side. To the left extends Marsovo
Pole, to the right the Mikhail Gardens (behind the Russian Museum).
An attractive Classical **Pavilion** by Carlo Rossi stands on the
embankment in the Mikhail Gardens; this elegantly proportioned
building dates from 1825. Beyond the Sadovyy Most (and Sadovaya
Ul.) and flanking the last part of the Moyka are the Engineers Castle
(right) and the Summer Gardens (left). The LEBYAZHIY (Swan)
CANAL, which separates Marsovo Pole from the Summer Gardens,
joins the Moyka here. The little canal is spanned by the stone
NIZHNE-LEBYAZHIY MOST (1835–37). From this point the excursion
boats pass under the 1-Y INZHENERNYY MOST (Pl. 10; 6) (1828–29)
and re-enter the Fontanka River. They then either turn right back to
the starting point near the Anichkovskiy Bridge, or left towards the
Neva.

The latter route begins with the MOST PESTEL'YA and is bounded on the left by
the Summer Gardens. The Summer Palace is visible here, just before the Neva.
To the right, between Ul. Pestel'ya and Gangutskaya Ul., is the site where the
'All-Russian Industrial Exhibition' of 1870 was held; this was the source of
Mussorgsky's piano suite, 'Pictures from an Exhibition'. Later Baron A.L.
Stieglitz sponsored the creation here of an art school (A.I. Krakau and R.A.
Gedike, 1879–81) and a museum (M.Ye. Mesmakher, 1885–95); the main
façades of both buildings look onto Solyanoy Per. Mesmakher borrowed many
of the museum's features from the St. Mark's Library in Venice. The *Mukhina
Higher Art Academy* is now housed here (no adm.). The long building with a
central dome set above a eight-columned portico, at Nab. Reki Fontanki, 6, was
one of the most exclusive schools in the Russian Empire, the Law School
(Uchilishche Pravovedeniya). Among those who studied here were
Tchaikovsky and the critic V.V. Stasov. In November 1917 an All-Russian
Congress of Peasants' Soviets was held in the Law School. The building dates
from the 1780s, but has been reconstructed several times, most notably by A.I.
Mel'nikov and V.P. Stasov in the 1830s and 1840s; the present domes were
added by P.Yu. Syuzor in 1909–10. The Fontanka ends with the treble arch of
the PRACHECHNYY MOST (Pl. 10; 4). Constructed in 1766–69, this is one of the

oldest stone bridges in the city. The name derives from the Court Laundry (Prachechnyye), which was located nearby.

The lower part of the Fontanka, to the S of its junction with the Moyka, also contains a number of interesting buildings. Nab. Reki Fontanki, 16 (left), was the headquarters of the Chief of the Gendarmes and of the Third Section of H.M. Own Chancellery, the political police of Nicholas I. The next two buildings (Nos 18 and 20), the *Pashkov* and *Golitsyn Houses* with their central porticoes, are typical of late-18C mansions of the aristocracy. On the right bank, downstream from the Engineers Castle, is the stone 2-y *Inzhenernyy Most* which once spanned the Voskresenskiy Canal, now covered over. Next comes the **Leningrad State Circus** (Leningrad Gos. Tsirk). The building dates from 1876 and formerly housed the Cinizelli Circus.

The MOST BELINSKOVO (Pl. 10; 6) was once called the Simeonovskiy Most. Lenin escaped death here on 1 January 1918, when shots were fired at a car containing him, his sister Mariya, and the Swiss socialist Fritz Platten. Beyond the bridge (left), at Nab. Reki Fontanki, 34, is the splendid Baroque **Sheremetev Palace**. The long yellow building with its numerous Corinthian pilasters was created by S.I. Chevakinsky in 1750–55 on the basis of an earlier mansion. The poetess Anna Akhmatova lived here in 1933–1941 and 1944–54. A fine wrought-iron fence was erected between the palace and the embankment in the 1840s. The former *Catherine Institute*, with its imposing eight-columned central portico was built next door (No. 36) to the designs of Quarenghi in 1804–07. It served as a school for the daughters of the nobility. The site is of particular interest, as Zemtsov built here a royal 'Italian Palace' for Catherine I; the palace fell into disrepair and was replaced by the new institute.

The former *Shuvalov Palace*, on the opposite bank at No. 21, is now the **House of Friendship** (Dom Druzhby i Mira s Narodami Zarubezhnykh Stran), where receptions are held for foreign visitors. The present Italian Renaissance appearance of the exterior dates from the reconstruction of an earlier building in 1844–46 by N.Ye. Yefimov. The Decembrist N.M. Murav'yov lived at No. 25. Here he wrote the Constitution of the 'Northern Society', one of the secret organisations which attempted to seize power in 1825. A later revolutionary, A.I. Zhelyabov, was arrested at No. 29. He was one of the leaders of the plot against Alexander II and his arrest came just two days before the assassination took place.

C. The Griboyedov Canal

The Griboyedov Canal flows at right angles to Nevskiy Pr., intersecting it near the Kazan Cathedral. This Rte affords a view of a picturesque part of central Leningrad, and the canal embankment has the additional advantage of being relatively free of traffic. The basic Rte, which ends near the Kirov Theatre, measures about 3km. The starting point is Konyushennaya Pl. (Pl. 10; 5) (p 332), 600m NE of the Nevskiy, and a tram terminal. One entrance to NEVSKIY PROSPEKT METRO STATION is situated at the point where Nevskiy Pr. crosses the canal.

The 4.5km long canal was laid out along the course of a small stream in the late

18C and by 1800 had been given a granite embankment. In the 1870s and later there was talk of draining the canal and replacing it with a new avenue or a railway line, but fortunately this came to nothing. For a long time it was known as the Catherine (Yekaterininskiy) Canal after the Empress in whose reign it was completed. The present name is that of the writer A.S. Griboyedov (1795–1829) who once lived by the canal (No. 104/25).

The canal begins at the Fontanka River. Nearby, the attractive Art Nouveau railings of the Mikhail Gardens face the dominant landmark of this district, the ***Church of the Resurrection of Christ** (Khram Voskreseniya Khristova), a picturesque multi-domed Pseudo-Russian building some 80m tall. It is clearly visible from the Nevskiy, on the right (E) bank of the canal, and marks the spot where Alexander II was assassinated.

On Sunday morning, 1 March 1881, the Emperor finished inspecting troops in the Mikhail Riding-School and began his short return trip to the Winter Palace. As his carriage, having passed the Mikhail Palace (now the Russian Museum), turned right onto the canal embankment a bomb went off underneath it. The Emperor was unharmed and got out to inspect the damage, as he did so he was hit by a second bomb, thrown by a terrorist named I.I. Grinevitsky from the 'People's Will' organisation. Both Tsar and assassin fell, mortally wounded.

That same year it was decided to build a church on the site of the attack, but work was prolonged. The final design, by I.V. Malyshev and A.A. Parland, was only approved in 1887 and the construction lasted until 1907. The Church of the Resurrection is perhaps the most striking example of the late-19C Pseudo-Russian style. The design with its numerous multi-coloured domes, four of them grouped around a tall tent-roof, is based loosely on that of St. Basil's Cathedral in Moscow; it is completely out of place in Classical and Baroque central Leningrad. An interesting feature of the design is the mosaic panels by V.M. Vasnetsov, which depict scenes from the Crucifixion and Resurrection of Christ. The interior, not at present accessible, contains many more mosaics. At one time the church contained a canopy over a section of the road surface that was stained with the Emperor's blood. It was also known as the Church of the Saviour 'On the Spilled Blood' (Khram Spasa na Krovi). (In the late 1930s there was a proposal to establish a 'People's Will' museum here.)

Along the left bank of the canal, NAB. KANALA GRIBOYEDOVA, extend the W sides of some of the buildings on Pl. Iskusstv (p 267), including the Russian Museum and the Maly Theatre. No. 8, known as the *House of the Jesuits*, was built to plans of Rusca in 1801. The richly-decorated former office of the *Joint Credit Society* (Obshchestvo Vzaimnovo Kredita), built around a central arch, stands on the right bank, at No. 13 (1888–90); the architect was P.Yu. Syuzor, who also designed the Singer building (Dom Knigi) on the corner of Nab. Kanala Griboyedova and Nevskiy Pr. An attractive footbridge, the ITAL'YANSKIY MOST (Italian Bridge), crosses the canal near the Joint Credit building. The next bridge is the KAZANSKIY MOST, which carries Nevskiy Pr.; on the far side of the avenue stands the Kazan Cathedral (p 266).

Beyond the Kazan Cathedral (right) and the arcade of Quarenghi's *Small Gostinyy Dvor* (1790s) (left), the canal bends to the right and passes under the ***Bankovskiy Most** (Pl. 10; 7), one of the most attractive in Leningrad (W. Traitteur, 1825–26). The cables of this suspension foot-bridge are supported by pairs of golden-winged griffons. To the left is the rear of the former Assignatsionnyy Bank, from which comes the name of the bridge.

After this point the canal, now tree-lined, becomes winding and more secluded. The humped granite KAMENNYY MOST (Stone Bridge) was built in 1776 and survives in its original form. UL. DZERZHINSKOVO passes over the canal here; to the right is visible the Admiralty, to the left the Theatre of Young Spectators. In the summer of 1880 'People's Will' planted dynamite under this bridge in the hope of blowing up the Emperor as he rode across it, but the plan failed. The former *Grabbe House* stands on the corner to the left of the bridge (Ul. Dzerzhinskovo, 26), a rare example of a Baroque mid-18C middle class (obyvatel'skiy) residence.

The canal then bends to the left; around the corner is the DEMIDOV MOST (Ye.A. Adam, 1834–35). Beyond, the canal approaches Pl. Mira and Sadovaya Ul. (p 289) and then turns right again. Several buildings in this district have connections with Dostoyevsky. The long straight section passes under PR. MAYOROVA, and then another of Traitteur's attractive suspension foot-bridges crosses the canal. The L'VINYY MOST or Lion Bridge was created at the same time as the Bankovskiy Most, and to a similar design. At either end are a pair of iron lions from whose mouths emerge the suspension cables. The canal bends sharply to the left, passes behind the Conservatory and Teatral'naya Pl. (Pl. 12; 6) (p 289), and continues S to near Sadovaya Ul. It is possible to take Trams Nos 3, 5, 13, or 14 E along Sadovaya Ul. to PLOSHCHAD MIRA METRO STATION or back to the Nevskiy.

The Griboyedov Canal continues W between Sadovaya Ul. and the Cathedral of St. Nicholas (p 289) and passes through the Kryukov Canal. The last stretch, after the PIKALOV MOST (1780s) on the W side of the Kryukov Canal, is not of great interest. The Griboyedov Canal ends at the MALO-KALINKINSKIY MOST with its four obelisks and attractive railing (1783); beyond is the Fontanka River (p 330).

33 Leningrad Outskirts

The immediate outskirts of Leningrad contain several places of extraordinary historical and cultural interest. The former Imperial palaces at PETRODVORETS (Peterhof), PUSHKIN (Tsarskoye Selo), and PAVLOVSK have been partially or wholly restored after being badly damaged during the Second World War. Also of note is the resort area NW of Leningrad with the museums at RAZLIV and REPINO.

At the time of writing, two major palaces lie *outside* the regions normally open to foreign tourists, and *may not be visited*. At LOMONOSOV (Oranienbaum), about 10km W of Petrodvorets on the coast, is a park with palaces built for Prince Menshikov and Peter III, as well as several pavilions; most notable is the Chinese Palace Rinaldi created for Catherine II. Oranienbaum was the only one of the suburban palaces to escape German occupation in 1941. A second royal estate is located 45km S of Leningrad, at GATCHINA; here are a palace, pavilions, and fine landscaped gardens. Gatchina was closely associated with Paul I.

Also *closed* to foreigners is the island town of KRONSTADT, a place with a famous naval and revolutionary history.

If there is any doubt as to whether a particular trip outside the city is permitted *tourists should check the arrangements with Intourist or other authorities.*

A. Petrodvorets

Petrodvorets (formerly Petergof or Peterhof) was the site of an Imperial palace; it lies 29km W of Leningrad (Pl. 1). Suburban trains travel between the Baltic Station and NOVYY PETERGOF RAILWAY STATION (40 minutes), and it is a short trip by Buses No. 278, 350, 351 and 352 to the Great Palace. An alternative route in summer is by hydrofoil from the piers at the Hermitage (Pl. 13; 2), Pl. Dekabristov (Pl. 13; 4), and Tuchkov Most (Pl. 13; 1). This provides a splendid trip up the Malaya Neva and across the Gulf, and it takes no longer than the train.

Peter the Great became interested in the site in the first years of the 18C when he was overseeing construction of a fortress on Kotlin Island; this is now known as Kronstadt and is clearly visible some 10km to the NW; the prominent dome at Kronstadt is the Naval Cathedral, completed in 1913. Peter built a small house on the nearby mainland so that he could reach Kotlin without a long and possibly dangerous voyage from St. Petersburg; the place was first referred to by the German name of Peterhof (strictly transliterated, Petergof) in 1705. After the successful battles of Poltava (1709) and Gangut (1714) against the Swedes, Peter decided to transform Peterhof into a major residence with elaborate parks, an expression of Russia's coming of age. A visit to Versailles in 1717 made Peter's ambition even greater. By the end of his reign the basis of the Peterhof ensemble had been created. The famous fountains began to work in 1721 and the Upper and Lower Parks were laid out; the Monplaisir Palace was built on the sea front, and the Great Palace had been started on a bluff to the S. The architect most closely associated with Peterhof's early development was A.J.-B. Le Blond (1679–1719) who before his death worked out the plans for the park and palaces.

Empress Elizabeth Petrovna (1741–61), the great patroness of the arts, took an interest in Peterhof and commissioned B.F. Rastrelli to expand the Great Palace. The future Catherine the Great was staying at Peterhof when, a few months after Elizabeth's death, she began her seizure of power. The town continued to be an important Imperial residence in the 19C; under Nicholas I (1825–55) Peterhof was further developed, with new parks laid out around the original one. The last Tsar, Nicholas II (1894–1917), was fond of Peterhof, and made several of his most important political decisions here.

The Germans captured Peterhof in September 1941 and occupied it for over two years. The front line between the invaders and the Soviet-held 'Oranienbaum Pocket' was just W of Peterhof; by the time the town was liberated in January 1944 most of its buildings, including the Great Palace, and its parks had been very badly damaged. Much successful restoration work has been carried out since that time. In 1944, when many 'German' names were changed, Peterhof was renamed Petrodvorets, or 'Peter's Palace'.

The long yellow *Great Palace (Bol'shoy Dvorets) was built on a hill overlooking the Gulf of Finland.

Le Blond's version, begun in 1714 and completed in 1721, was much altered in 1747–54 by B.F. Rastrelli. A third storey was added, as well as the steeply-pitched roof. The wings with their gilded Baroque cupolas were a further addition, but some of Le Blond's original conception survives in the central façade. The palace was looted, burned, and partly blown up by the Germans in 1942. Despite the terrible damage the basic reconstruction of the exterior was completed in 1958. Since then most of the interior has been restored; photographs in the various halls of their appearance in 1944 show how much has been achieved.

Interior. The State Rooms were on the 1st Floor of the palace. The first one open to inspection is on the S side, the *Study of Peter I;* some of its handsome oak panels are original, others are reproductions. Next (to the E) is the *Crown Room* (Koronnaya) with original Chinese silk wall hangings in an alcove. This white and gold room was the work of Velten, who re-designed many of Rastrelli's interiors in the

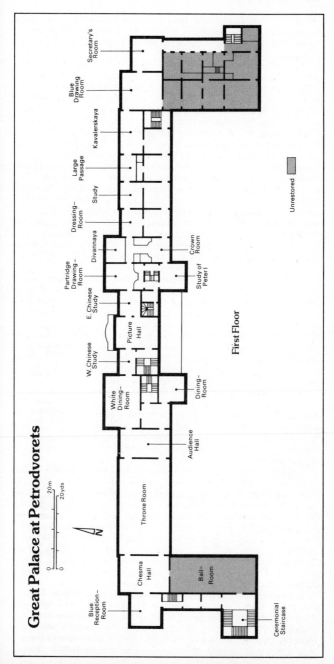

Great Palace at Petrodvorets

0 20m
0 20yds

N

First Floor

Unrestored

Secretary's Room

Blue Drawing Room

Kavalerskaya

Large Passage

Study

Dressing-Room

Divannaya

Crown Room

Partridge Drawing-Room

Study of Peter I

E. Chinese Study

Picture Hall

W. Chinese Study

White Dining-Room

Dining-Room

Audience Hall

Throne Room

Chesma Hall

Ball-Room

Blue Reception-Room

Ceremonial Staircase

1770s. The remaining four rooms on the S side have not been restored but contain examples of furniture, tapestries and paintings illustrating changing tastes from the time of Peter until the beginning of the 19C.

The next open room is on the N side, looking onto the sea: the *Kavalerskaya* (Room for Gentlemen-in-Waiting) has walls covered with raspberry-coloured silk, it was designed by Rastrelli and used for the reception of senior officers. To the E is the *Blue Drawing Room* (Golubaya Gostinaya) with a splendid chandelier and large royal portraits; beyond is the *Secretary's Room* (Sekretarskaya). From the Blue Drawing Room a splendid enfilade of rooms extends to the W. Each door is contained within the gold frame of the one preceding. The *Large Passage* (Bol'shaya Prokhodnaya), on the other side of the Kavalereskaya, was where the standards of the palace guard were once kept; royal portraits now hang on the walls. The *Study* is the first of the rooms in which the Imperial family actually lived; the walls are hung with white floral silk. The *Dressing-Room* (Tualetnaya) is decorated with beautiful green and white silk. The large room beyond is the *Divan Room* (Divannaya); prominent features are the Turkish divan and the Chinese silk wall covering, much of which is original. The *Partridge Drawing-Room* (Kuropatochnaya Gostinaya) takes its name from the birds depicted on the walls and curtains; it is largely Velten's work.

In the central part of the palace are two similar rooms, the *E Chinese Study* (Vostochnyy Kitayskiy Kabinet) and the *W Chinese Study*; the dominant feature of the decor is the black lacquered panels depicting Chinese scenes. These rooms were designed by Vallin de la Mothe in the 1760s when Chinoiserie was much in fashion, but what exists today is a post-war reconstruction, albeit very well executed. The *Picture Hall*, also called the 'Room of Fashions and Graces' (Kabinet Mod i Gratsiy), occupies the very centre of the palace, between the two Chinese rooms. There are 368 oil paintings on the walls by Pietro Rotari; the subjects were eight young women from the Court of Empress Elizabeth.

The *White Dining-Room*, beyond the W Chinese Study, was designed by Velten with bas-reliefs and elaborate moulding; the table has been set with a Wedgwood dinner service. The small room to the S contains paintings by Joseph Saunders and next to this, by the stairs, is the blue *Dining-Room* (Bufetnyy), which displays an 18C dinner service.

To the W is the magnificent *Audience Hall* (Audientszal), which is decorated in white and red with gilded baroque bas reliefs. The following room is one of the largest in the palace, the white *Throne Room*. With two tiers of windows on either side and mirrors set between the windows, the Throne Room is well lit; it was designed by Velten in 1779. Set between the upper windows are medallions of the Imperial family, and behind the throne hangs an equestrian portrait of Catherine II (V. Ericksen); she wears the uniform of the Semyonovskiy Guards Regiment, one of the units which supported her in the 1762 coup. At the opposite end of the hall are paintings of naval victories by Joseph Wright. There are similar huge canvases by P. Hackert in the adjacent *Chesma Hall*, which takes its name from the great victory of 1770 over the Turks. To the W is the blue *Reception-Room* (Priyomnaya), used by the Imperial secretary. The *Ball-Room* (Tantseval'nyy Zal) to the S is not yet open to the public. Here the Tsar conferred with the Grand Dukes and senior officials in July 1905 and agreed to permit the first consultative Russian parliament, the so-called 'Bulygin Duma'. The splendid *Ceremonial Staircase* nearby is decorated in white with gilded statues and baroque bas-reliefs.

The 102ha *Lower Park, between the palace and the sea, has a system of fountains that is among the world's finest. The *Great Cascade comprises 3 cascades, 64 fountains, and 37 statues; Shubin, Martos, and other noted sculptors took part in the work. The centrepiece, and the best known of the statues, is the gilded *Samson Fountain*; Samson defeats the lion, an analogy of the Russian victory over the Swedes at Poltava on St. Sampson's Day. The present Samson is a copy of M.I. Kozlovsky's 1802 version, which was destroyed during the war. From the foot of the Great Cascade the central *Sea Canal* flows into the gulf, emphasising the unique site of this Imperial palace. In accordance with the canons of the formal French park, cascades and fountains are arranged on either side of the Sea Canal. The *Adam* and *Eve* fountains are each the centre of an étoile. Further inland are the *Checkerboard* and *Golden Hill* cascades. Other fountains assume special shapes, such as the *Pyramid* (from the 1720s) and the *Sun* (from the 1770s). To trap the unwary there are even special trick fountains.

Flanking the Great Cascade are the *Voronikhin Colonnades*, built by the architect of that name in 1800. Three pavilions in the Lower Park are considerably older. **Marly**, set behind a pond at the W end, was built to the plans of J.F. Braunstein in 1721–23, and is still being restored. Braunstein also created the **Hermitage** (1721–26), to the E of Marly, with large windows looking onto the sea nearby. The little red and white building could be isolated behind its moat and used as a retreat; the airy dining-room on the 1st Floor has been preserved.

The little palace called *Monplaisir (Monplezir) was built on the shore to the E of the central canal in 1714–22 with the participation of Braunstein, Le Blond and Nicolo Michetti. Peter the Great spent much time here; N.N. Gay's painting 'Peter I Interrogating Tsarevich Aleksey' is set at Monplaisir, but it is questionable whether this is historically accurate.

Monplaisir was badly damaged during the Second World War but has been restored. Above the *Central Hall* with its tiled floor, wood panelling, and large windows, is an attractive plafond. Grouped around the hall are (to the E) the *Lacquered Study*, the *Kitchen*, and the *Pantry* as well as (to the W) the *Sea Study* (with its magnificent view of the gulf), the *Bedroom*, and the *Secretary's Room*. Galleries with paintings extend on either side of this central block.

The SW annexe of Monplaisir is the large **Catherine Building** (Yekaterininskiy Korpus) (Rastrelli, 1747–54, G. Quarenghi, 1785–86) which derives its name from the fact that during the short reign of her husband, Peter III, Catherine II lived in an adjacent pavilion called the 'Tea House' (Chaynyy Domik). She was staying here on the morning of 28 July 1762 when Aleksey Orlov arrived to begin the palace coup which overthrew the Emperor. The Catherine Building now comprises a Fore Hall, a Blue Drawing Room, a Yellow Hall, a Green Drawing Room, a Study, a Bedroom, a Heating Room, and a Corner Drawing Room.

The simpler and quieter **Upper Park**, behind the Great Palace, contains the *Neptune Fountain*, originally created for Nuremberg in the mid-17C and purchased for Peterhof by Paul I.

KRASNYY PR. marks the S boundary of the Upper Park. This avenue

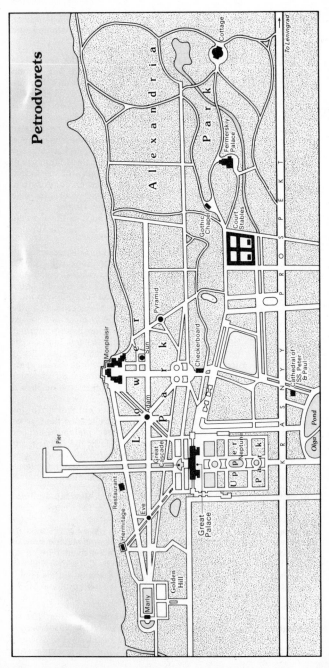

Petrodvorets

leads W to the former *H.M. Own Dacha* (Sobstvennaya Dacha) which was originally built in Petrine times for Prince Dolgoruky and was rebuilt for Grand Duke Alexander Nikolayevich (later Alexander II) by Stakenschneider. The Dacha was destroyed during the war, but restoration work finished in 1963. Beyond it is the former *Leuchtenberg Park* (Park Leykhtenbergskovo), bought by Mariya Nikolayevna (1819–76), the daughter of Nicholas I and wife of the Duke of Leuchtenberg. The *Palace*, built to the plans of Stakenschneider (1840–42), was restored in 1965.

Many buildings did not survive the war. The Kottedzh-Ferma in the former Oldenburg Park was destroyed, as was Quarenghi's splendid English Palace (1787–1805). The latter was set in the *English Park*, which was created by Catherine II as a reaction to the existing formal French gardens at Peterhof.

Krasnyy Pr. runs E from the Upper Park and passes (right) the *Cathedral of SS. Peter and Paul* (Sobor Petra i Pavla) (N.V. Sultanov, 1895–99), a brick Pseudo-Russian church; it is some 70m to the top of the main dome, which is surrounded by four smaller domes. Not far along the avenue passes (left) the *Post Office* created in the Gothic style popular in the mid-19C by N.L. Benois and A. Cavos. (Also by Benois is the *Novyy Petergof Station*, an interesting Gothic structure dating from 1857.) Another of the surprises of Petrodvorets is the former *Court Stables* (Pridvornyye Konyushni), a large complex next to the Post Office which now serves as the 'Petrodvorets' Rest Home. Benois, who built the Stables in 1847–54, was inspired by Cardinal Wolsey's palace at Hampton Court.

The royal *Alexandria Park* lay to the E of the Stables and extended N to the Gulf. This picturesque landscaped park was created by A. Menelaws (1826) and named after Alexandra Fyodorovna (1798–1860), the wife of Nicholas I. The main building of the park has been restored, the yellow **Cottage Palace** (Dvorets Kottedzh) (A. Menelaws, 1826–29), a relatively small, two-storey structure containing 20 rooms. Damaged in the war, it was restored to its original condition in 1978 and contains contemporary furniture and many attractive internal features. The Cottage Palace was built by Menelaws (1829) on a bluff on the E side of the park, and has excellent views of the gulf.

Several other interesting buildings survive in the woods nearby, albeit not fully restored. The *Gothic Chapel* (of St. Alexander Nevskiy) (K. Schinkel, 1835) with its four spires is located near the NE corner of the Stables; it was used by the Court. Alexander II frequented the *Fermerskiy* (lit., 'Farm') *Palace* just to the E (Menelaws, 1830–31).

Considerable historical interest was attached to the 'Lower Palace' (Nizhniy Dvorets), which once stood by the shore in the NE corner of Alexandria Park; regrettably all that remained after the war was a pile of rubble. The palace was built in 1885 by A.O. Tomishko and later expanded as the summer residence of Nicholas II. The Emperor could be easily guarded from his enemies at this isolated spot, and it was possible to travel from here to St. Petersburg by boat. In his study in the Lower Palace Nicholas signed the 'October Manifesto' of 1905, which granted a Duma (parliament) and civil liberties; two years later he signed here the decree of 3 June 1907 limiting the franchise for Duma elections. The order to mobilise the Russian armies in 1914, one of the decisions which plunged Europe into the First World War, was also signed at the Lower Palace.

Alexandria Park originally extended S of the main road. This section is now called *Proletarskiy Park*, and the pavilions here perished during the German occupation.

A number of parks and palaces survive between the coast and the road that leads E to Leningrad, but the buildings are not open to the public. The *Znamenskiy Park* is followed by the *Mikhaylovskiy Park*, formerly a Grand Ducal estate. Beyond, about 6km from Petrodvorets, is the *Konstantinovskiy Park* at STREL'NA. Here are located the *Konstantin Palace* and another palace originally built for Peter I in 1711.

A road leads S from the Upper Park at Petrodvorets past (left) the former *Kolonistskiy Park*, which was laid out by Stakenschneider during the reign of Nicholas I (the name came from the German colonists who had been settled here). Stakenschneider's *Tsaritsa Pavilion* (1842) and *Olga Pavilion* (1847) (named after the wife and daughter of the Emperor) were built on islands in the *Olga Pond*.

The *Lugovoy Park*, farther S, contains another Stakenschneider building, the *Belvedere* (1852–56), on the Babigonskiye Heights. Much of the ornamental sculpture was lost in the war and the building now serves as a rest home.

B. Pushkin

Pushkin, a town of Imperial palaces known formerly as Tsarskoye Selo, lies 25km S of Leningrad. It is most easily reached by suburban train from the Vitebsk Station to DETSKOYE SELO STATION (30 minutes). Buses No. 371 and 382 travel between the station and the palaces.

When St. Petersburg was first founded by the Russians this land belonged to Aleksandr Menshikov, but in 1710 it was granted to Catherine, the wife of Peter the Great. On old Swedish maps the place had been called Saaris Moisio or 'Island-Farmstead', which was Russianised to Sarskaya Myza or Sarskoye Selo. In 1716 Catherine was named Tsaritsa, and her estate soon became known as Tsarskoye Selo or 'Royal Village'. Although the first stone palace was constructed in 1717–23, the real founders of Tsarskoye Selo were the Empresses Elizabeth Petrovna (1741–61) and Catherine II (1762–96), who built the main palaces and laid out the parks.

Emperor Paul I (1796–1801) removed many of the fittings from the palaces of his hated mother for use elsewhere, but under Alexander I (1801–25) this damage was made good. Nicholas I (1825–55) and, most notably, Nicholas II (1894–1917) spent much of their time at Tsarskoye Selo. The town developed in the 19C as a summer resort for the aristocracy and the wealthy families of St. Petersburg. It was also said to be the first European town to be lit entirely by electricity.

After the February 1917 Revolution the Imperial family was held for some months under house arrest here. Some fighting took place around Tsarskoye Selo during the October Revolution, but there was little damage; by that time the most valuable objects had already been evacuated to Moscow. The town was occupied by the Whites in October 1919, but they only held it for a few days. After the Revolution the town was renamed Detskoye Selo ('Children's Village') and sanatoria for children were opened in several of the former great houses. The town received its third and present name in 1937, the centenary of the death of the poet Pushkin, who had studied at the Lycée here.

Regrettably, the eventful history of the town did not end with the Revolution. The German army captured Pushkin in September 1941, and by the time the Germans were finally driven out, in January 1944, the town and its palaces were in ruins. Since the war much effort has been devoted to repairing the damage, and many of the most important structures have been restored, externally at least, to their pre-revolutionary appearance.

Pushkin's outstanding building is the beautiful Baroque ***Catherine Palace** (Yekaterininskiy Dvorets).

It was built by Empress Elizabeth and named after her mother, the second wife of Peter the Great. The palace was developed on the site of the palace of Catherine I by Zemtsov, Kvasov, and Chevakinsky and was then completely rebuilt by B.F. Rastrelli in 1752–56. Rastrelli, perhaps the greatest architect working in Russia in the 18C, had already built the nearby Hermitage pavilion and would go on to design the Winter Palace in St. Petersburg. The palace served as an Imperial residence for a century and a half, although latterly it was used mainly for Court ceremonies. The Germans used it for a time after 1941 as a barracks, and it was later looted and blown up. Restoration work began in 1957, and the first few restored rooms were opened to the public two years later.

The 300m long E façade (on the park side) features a row of white columns and pilasters with dark gold Baroque mouldings set against a blue background. The elegant golden domes of the Church rise at the N end. The W façade (on the courtyard side) is enclosed by curved one-storey outbuildings which are joined by marvellous gilded **Gates** designed by Rastrelli.

The **Interior** was created in the Baroque style by Rastrelli but was soon much altered by the Scottish architect Charles Cameron (c 1740–1812) in the spirit of the Classical style preferred by Catherine II. The building was damaged by fire in 1820, but V.P. Stasov restored it.

The white Baroque *State Staircase* (Paradnaya Lestnitsa), the route to the State rooms on the 1st Floor, is actually a relatively recent addition; it was originally created by I.A. Monighetti in 1860. On the S side is the large *Kavalerskaya Dining-Room* (or Dining Room for the Gentlemen-in-Waiting). This room is essentially Rastrelli's work, and the decoration consists of gold moulding on white walls. Adjacent is the *Great Hall*, the largest room in the palace. Decorated with gilded bas reliefs and a ceiling painting, the feeling of spaciousness is enhanced by the windows and mirrors. The S wing, beyond, has not yet been restored; located here are three large Ante-Rooms, the Arabian, Lyons, and Chinese Halls, and private apartments which Cameron created for Catherine (in the SE corner).

In the N wing and on the park side, beyond the State Staircase, is a series of unrestored exhibition rooms tracing the history of the palace, its destruction, and its continuing restoration. The first restored room is the *Picture Hall* (Kartinnyy Sal), notable for its gilded mouldings, Dutch tiled stoves, and the 130 paintings that cover the walls. Most of the pictures are the 17C–18C originals which were evacuated in 1941 before the Germans arrived. The plafond—depicting Olympus—is a post-war copy.

The halls between the Picture Hall and the State Staircase on the courtyard (W) side begin with the famous *Amber Room* (Yantarnaya Komnata), which was decorated by Rastrelli with Persian amber and contained a collection of amber objects acquired by Peter the Great. The priceless contents were stolen by the Germans and disappeared in Königsberg in 1945; at the time of writing work is well advanced on creating a replica of the room. The adjacent *Portretnyy Hall* contains a portrait of Catherine I. Beyond are the *Green Pilaster Room* (Zelenaya Stolbovaya) and the *Raspberry Pilaster Room*. Next to the State Staircase is the white and gold *State Dining Room*.

The four rooms to the N of the Picture Hall (on the courtyard side) have not been restored, but contain 18C paintings and applied art. The third room (formerly the Bufetnyy or *Pantry*) leads right to the park side, to the brown *Arched Room* (Svodchataya Prokhodnaya

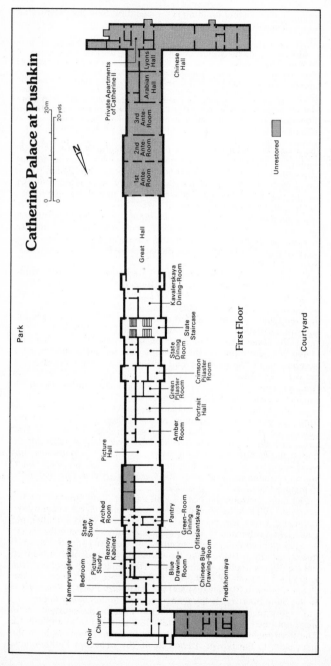

Catherine Palace at Pushkin

First Floor

Park

Courtyard

Unrestored

Private Apartments of Catherine II

Lyons Hall

Arabian Hall

Chinese Hall

3rd Ante-Room

2nd Ante-Room

1st Ante-Room

Great Hall

Kavalerskaya Dining-Room

State Staircase

State Dining Room

Crimson Pilaster Room

Green Pilaster Room

Portrait Hall

Amber Room

Picture Hall

Arched Room

State Study

Kameryungferskaya

Bedroom

Picture Study

Reznoy Kabinet

Pantry

Green-Room Dining

Ofitsiantskaya

Blue Drawing-Room

Chinese Blue Drawing-Room

Predkhornaya

Church

Choir

20m

20 yds

Komnata) and the pink *State Study* (Paradnyy Kabinet); the latter was created in the Classical style by V.P. Stasov for Alexander I in 1817.

The *Green Dining-Room*, the second room to the N beyond the former Pantry (on the courtyard side), was the work of Cameron. Stucco bas-reliefs by Martos are set on the green walls. Cameron was also the designer of the adjacent *Ofitsiantskaya* (or Service Room), but Stasov carried out alterations in the 1840s. The dominant features of the decoration are the angular brown pilasters; between these hang Romantic landscapes. The walls of Cameron's *Blue Drawing-Room* (Golubaya Gostinaya) are covered in silk with a blue floral pattern; the same design was used for the chairs and curtains. On the walls are royal portraits. The *Chinese Blue Drawing-Room* (Kitayskaya Golubaya Gostinaya) takes its name from the Chinese motifs painted on the silk wall covering; these were recreated on the basis of black and white photographs after the war. The plafond is a copy of Cameron's original, which perished in the fire of 1820. The final room on the courtyard side is the *Predkhornaya* (or Choir Ante-Room). Woven into the golden silk wall covering are pictures of pheasants and swans; the wall covering was found in storage after 1944.

From the Predkhornaya a door leads right to a suite of rooms on the park side. The simple *Kameryungferskaya* (Room for Ladies-in-Waiting) is decorated in green. Next door is the striking *Bedroom* (Opochival'nya) created by Cameron and associated with Elizabeth Alekseyevna, the wife of Alexander I. Thin fluted poles run from floor to ceiling and there are elegant moulded medallions on the pale green walls. From here the *Picture Study* (Zhivopisnyy Kabinet) and the *Reznoy Kabinet* (or Carved Study) lead back to the Blue Drawing-Room. Both studies are small but have fine carved and moulded decoration.

The Predkhornaya adjoins the *Choir* (Khory), which in turn overlooks the *Palace Church*; from the balcony of the Choir the Imperial family would watch religious services. Like the Church, it is painted deep blue and gold. Narrow stairs lead down into the Church which, although not yet completely restored, gives a good impression of Rastrelli's lavishly Baroque original conception. The *Predtserkovnyy Hall* (or Church Ante-Room) on the Ground Floor leads back to the entrance. This long white columned hall was built in 1843 to the plans of Stasov.

Cameron's **Agate Rooms** adjoin the Catherine Palace to the SE. These rooms were designed by Cameron as a bath house. The name derives from the stone facing used in the richly-decorated interior.

Beyond the small *Hanging Garden* stands the elegant *Cameron Gallery** (Kameronova Galereya) (1780–85), perhaps the finest work of the Scottish architect. The arcade affords a wonderful view of the lake and is lined with bronze busts of ancient philosophers and heroes. Flanking the E stairs are large bronze statues of Hercules and Flora, copies of Antique originals. The Cameron Gallery is used for exhibitions of applied art, costume, and carriages.

To the S of the palace, the Agate Rooms, and the Cameron Gallery is a *Ramp* by which the aging Catherine II could walk down to the park.

The **All-Union Pushkin Museum** (Vsesoyuznyy Muzey A.S. Pushkina), established in 1967, is in the Church (N) Wing of the Catherine Palace.

The museum has a rich collection of pictures, documents, first editions and

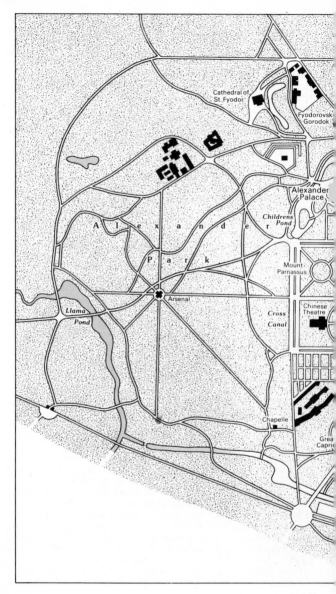

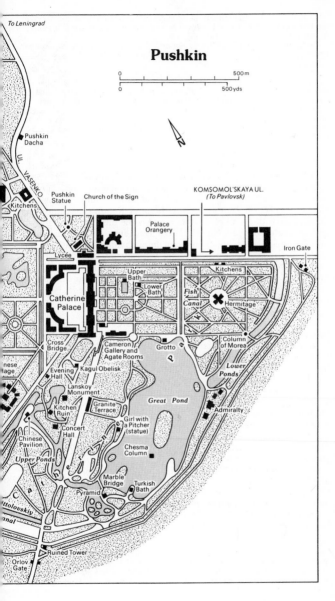

Pushkin

To Leningrad

UL. VASENKO

Pushkin Dacha

Kitchens

Pushkin Statue

Church of the Sign

KOMSOMOL'SKAYA UL. (To Pavlovsk)

Palace Orangery

Iron Gate

Lycée

Upper Bath

Lower Bath

Kitchens

Fish Canal

Hermitage

Catherine Palace

Cross Bridge

Cameron Gallery and Agate Rooms

Grotto

Column of Morea

nese lage

Evening Hall

Kagul Obelisk

Lanskoy Monument

Kitchen Ruin

Granite Terrace

Great Pond

Lower Ponds

Admiralty

Chinese Pavilion

Concert Hall

Girl with a Pitcher (statue)

Chesma Column

Upper Ponds

ittolovskiy anal

Marble Bridge

Pyramid

Turkish Bath

Ruined Tower

Orlov Gate

other materials related to the great Russian poet. Much attention is devoted to the Pushkin's friends and acquaintances, and the museum provides a general insight into life in Russia in the early 19C.

Across the road, just N of the Catherine Palace, stands the former Imperial **Lycée**, which has been open as a museum since 1949 (Memorial'nyy Muzey 'Litsey').

This was originally the 'new' wing of the Catherine Palace, built by I.V. Neyelov in 1789–91 for the children of Tsarevich Paul. The archway across the street from the palace allowed Catherine II to visit her grandchildren without having to climb stairs. The Lycée, intended for the families of the Court, was opened in 1811 (the school moved to St. Petersburg in 1843). Pushkin was a pupil here in 1811–17, and there has been an attempt to restore part of the interior—including the bedrooms and classrooms—to their appearance in Pushkin's time.

A walk around the *Catherine Park is to be highly recommended.

The terraces of the formal gardens (the so-called *Old Park*) extend to the E of the Catherine Palace. Here, amid geometric paths and marble statues, stand the *Upper Bath* and *Lower Bath* pavilions (I.V. Neyelov, 1777–79). The *Fish Canal* (Rybnyy Kanal) runs parallel to the main axis of the palace; at its S end is the blue domed Baroque *Grotto* created by Rastrelli (1753–57). The same architect designed the *Hermitage* (1744–56), a blue cruciform pavilion set nearby in the centre of an étoile. Thirty years later V.I. Neyelov built the Pseudo-Gothic *Kitchens* (1776) by the perimeter wall (on what is now Komsomol'skaya Ul.); these served the Hermitage. To the SE of these buildings lie three picturesque *Lower* or Cascade *Ponds*. Between two of them rises the marble *Column of the Morea* commemorating Russian victories in Greece in 1770.

The water in the ponds comes from the **Great Pond**, an artificial lake which forms the centre of the landscaped area of the Catherine Park (this was one of the first Romantic paysage parks in Russia). It is possible to hire a boat here in the summer months. On an island in the centre stands a pavilion by Quarenghi (1786) where musicians played in summer. Next to its rises Rinaldi's *Chesma Column* (1771–78), which was erected in memory of one of Russia's few great naval victories—in the Aegean in 1770. The 25m high rostral column is also known as the 'Orlov Column' after the nominal commander of the action, Count Aleksey Orlov (brother of Catherine's favourite).

A number of pleasant pavilions were built around the Great Pond. The red brick Pseudo-Gothic *Admiralty* (V.I. Neyelov, 1773–77) now serves as a small restaurant. The pink minareted *Turkish Bath* was built by Monighetti in 1852 as a memorial to the Russo-Turkish War of 1828–29. Behind it, on a little peninsula, is Cameron's *Pyramid* (1781) where Catherine buried three of her favourite dogs (including one called 'Sir Tom Anderson'). The lakeside path then crosses the attractive *Marble Bridge (1770–76); this is a copy of the Palladian bridge at Wilton in England (1737).

The *Vittolovskiy Canal* flows under the Marble Bridge and feeds the pond. To the S of this canal are situated the Romantic **Ruined Tower** (Velten, 1771) and the triumphal arch of the **Orlov Gate** (Rinaldi and Quarenghi, 1778–82); the arch celebrates the restoration of order in Moscow by Grigory Orlov (Catherine's lover) after the plague riots of 1771.

Beyond the Marble Bridge the path goes past a statue-cum-fountain called '*Girl with a Pitcher*' which was made by P.P. Sokolov in 1816 and inspired by a La Fontaine fable. From near here the *Granite Terrace* leads back to the Catherine Palace. To the left stand two monuments: the *Lanskoy Monument* commemorates one of Catherine's young 'protégés', who died suddenly of scarlet fever, and Rinaldi's *Kagul Obelisk* celebrates another victory over Turkey.

Several picturesque pavilions are set around the ponds W of the Granite Terrace. The island *Concert Hall*, a Classical structure by Quarenghi, was one of that noted architect's first works in Russia (1782–86). Quarenghi also designed here the circular artificial 'ruin' called the *Kitchen-Ruin*.

The path which runs to the SW from the Catherine Palace (N of the Upper Ponds) affords a view of several interesting park structures. To the right, not far from the palace, can be seen the *Cross Bridge* (Krestovyy Most), set at one corner of the square canal in the Alexander Park. The yellow Classical *Evening Hall* was designed by P.V. Neyelov as a ballroom-pavilion. One of the most unusual buildings is Velten's *Chinese Pavilion* (1778–86), a fine example of Chinoiserie. The remains of another example, Cameron's *Chinese Village* (1782–96), are to the right in the Alexander Park. Finally, there is the *Great Caprice* (Bol'shoy Kapriz), which straddles the path farther along and was created by V.I. Neyelov in the 1770s. A combination of bridge and folly, the Chinese roof is supported by Classical columns.

UL. VASENKO leads N from the Lycée and the N Wing of the Catherine Palace towards Pulkovskoye Shosse and eventually back to Leningrad. To the right, just by the Lycée, stands the **Church of the Sign** (Ts. Znameniya) (I.Ya. Blank, 1734–47); this little yellow church with its tall spire is one of the oldest stone buildings in Pushkin. A famous seated *Statue of Pushkin* (R.R. Bach, 1900) is set in a small garden next door; the sculptor depicted Pushkin wearing the uniform of the Lycée.

A little farther along this street (left) are the Classical *Kitchens* and behind them the *****Alexander Palace** which they served. The yellow and white palace was built to the plans of the Quarenghi (1792–96) and is regarded as one of his finest buildings.

Catherine II commissioned it for her grandson, the future Alexander I, hence the name. The Classical austerity of the Alexander Palace is in contrast with its Baroque neighbour. The main decorative feature is the double row of columns on the N façade. Alexander I preferred the Catherine Palace, but his brother Nicholas I spent much of his time at the newer palace. Although Alexander III lived here when he was the Tsarevich, the most notable inhabitant was his son, Nicholas II. The last Romanov family began staying here in 1895, and from 1904 made it their main residence. Nicholas and Alexandra lived on the Ground Floor of the E wing (nearest Ul. Vasenko); their children lived on the 1st Floor. For some time after the Revolution the Imperial apartments were preserved intact as a unique Soviet museum, but the palace was badly damaged in the war and has been closed since then.

The **Alexander Park** lies to the W of Ul. Vasenko and the NW of the Catherine Park. Before the Revolution it could only be visited with a special pass and in the absence of the Imperial family.

The regular area of the Alexander Park (the *New Gardens*) is contained in the square *Cross Canal* (just NW of the Catherine Palace). The square 'island' is reached via Cameron's *Chinese Bridge*. To the right of the central (SE–NW) *Treble Alley* are, first, a pond and then a hillock called *Mount Parnassus*. Opposite, to the left, are a geometrical parterre ('*The Mushroom*') and the *Chinese Theatre* (Cameron, 1777–79). At the turn of the century the little theatre was used for command performances, with sets by the 'World of Art' group.

Adam Menelaws laid out the paysage section of the Alexander Park to the W of the *Bridge of Dragons* in the early 19C. The continuation of the Treble Alley leads 500m NW to the Gothic *Arsenal* (Menelaws, 1830–35); 250m further on the path meets the *Llama Pond*. Rasputin was buried not far NW of here, near the village of Aleksandrovka, in December 1916; three months later his body was exhumed and moved to Pargolovo, N of Petrograd. A path leads S from the Arsenal to another Gothic folly, the *Chapelle* (Menelaws, 1827).

To the W of the Alexander Park lies the 300-ha *Babolovo Park*, once the late-18C estate of Prince Potyomkin. The Babolovo Palace was destroyed during the last war.

The N part of the Alexander Park, near the Alexander Palace, contains several structures associated with the last years of Tsardom. The Imperial family used the little island in the *Children's Pond* (W of the palace) as a private park. The **Cathedral of St. Fyodor** (Fyodorovskiy Sobor) stands 400m N of the palace. This was built in 1910–12 by V.A. Pokrovsky as the personal church of the Imperial family; Empress Alexandra Fyodorovna often attended services in the crypt. The remarkable **Fyodorovskiy Gorodok**, just to the E, beyond a small pond, was intended as a barracks for the Tsar's bodyguard. The architects, V.A. Pokrovsky and S.S. Krichinsky, used Early Russian forms to create a miniature kremlin. The poet Yesenin served at a hospital here during the First World War.

Menelaws built the *Palace Ferme* (Dvortsovaya Ferma) about 600m NW of the Alexander Palace in 1818–22. After the Revolution the Ferme became part of the *Leningrad Agricultural Institute*. The nearby Neo-Russian *Ratnaya Palata*, built as a barracks at the beginning of this century, now serves as a hostel for the institute's students.

The **Pushkin Dacha** (Dacha A.S. Pushkina) is located along Ul. Vasenko (right). Pushkin and his wife lived here with the widow Kitayeva in the summer of 1831. The house was opened as a branch of the All-Union Pushkin Museum in 1958. On the edge of the town, not far from the Pushkin Dacha, stands the sand-coloured *Egyptian Gate* (Menelaws, 1828). The road from Leningrad enters the town through here. A *Statue of Pushkin* by the sculptor L.A. Bernshtam was unveiled next to the Egyptian Gate in 1937.

The town of Pushkin retains the regular plan it was given in the early 19C, although there are many new buildings. One of the streets that has survived is KOMSOMOL'SKAYA UL. leading SE along the N edge of the Catherine Park. This is the road which Bus No. 280 follows to Pavlovsk. The writer and historian N.M. Karamzin (1766–1826) lived at No. 12, where the young Pushkin met him. Farther down the street, opposite the park, is the long building of the *Palace Orangery*, now part of the Leningrad Agricultural Institute. The former *Riding-School* and *Stables* lie beyond. Komsomol'skaya Ul. ends by the Lower Ponds of the Catherine Park; to the left, on the opposite sides of a stream, stand the *Lutheran Church* and the former *Zapasnyy Palace* (or Guest Palace); the latter, built by P.V. Neyelov in the early 19C, is now the Pioneers Palace. The massive *Iron Gate* on the park side was erected to the design of V.P. Stasov and commemorates the soldiers of 1812.

C. Pavlovsk

Pavlovsk is the third and last of the easily accessible former Imperial palaces near Leningrad, and is situated 27km S of the city. Suburban trains to PAVLOVSK RAILWAY STATION travel on the same line as those to Pushkin; the starting point is the Vitebsk Station, and the duration of the journey some 35 minutes. The distance from Pavlovsk Station to the Great Palace is about 1.5km. Pedestrians can walk to the S along UL. REVOLYUTSII or through Pavlovsk Park (an entrance to the park is opposite the railway station). There is a frequent if slightly roundabout service from the station to the palace on Buses No. 280, 283, 283a and 493 (10 minutes). Pavlovsk is only 3km S of Pushkin. Bus No. 280 travels from Komsomol'skaya Ul. (opposite Pushkin's Catherine Park) to Pavlovsk Railway Station (10 minutes).

Pavlovsk is the most recent of the suburban palace complexes near Leningrad. In 1777 Catherine the Great presented a tract of some 400ha on the Slavyanka River to her son Paul (Pavel, hence Pavlovsk). The heir apparent was then just 22 and was in his mother's favour; his wife had just given birth to a son and heir, Alexander (later Alexander I). The Empress selected Charles Cameron to design the palace and park, and the Great Palace was built in 1782–86. The young Grand Duke Paul spent some time at Pavlovsk, but then transferred his affection to Gatchina, further S. For the next 40 years the real mistress of Pavlovsk was Paul's wife (and widow) Mariya Fyodorovna (born Princess Sophie of Württemberg-Stuttgart in 1759; died 1828).

With the completion of the pioneering railway line from St. Petersburg, Pavlovsk and its parks became a popular resort. At the end of the 19C Pavlovsk ceased to be a residence of the Tsars; the last occupant was Grand Duke Konstantin Konstantinovich (1858–1915), a cousin of Alexander III. Because of this it was not well maintained in the first decades after the Revolution; far worse, Pavlovsk was occupied by the Germans in 1941–44 and both palace and park suffered very serious damage.

The *Great Palace* (Bol'shoy Dvorets) was built by Charles Cameron in 1782–86, a yellow rectangular Classical building surmounted by a low dome. The main façade (on the courtyard side) is decorated with four pairs of columns and flanked by curved service wings.

This basic plan survived a major alteration by Vincenzo Brenna (1745–1820) in the 1790s, a fire in 1803, and a second reconstruction by Voronikhin. The major external change was the addition of a second storey to the wings and their extension to form a near-circle around the courtyard. The interior was also considerably altered. In January 1944 the Great Palace burned down, but restoration work began after the war, and in 1970 it became the first suburban palace to be completely restored.

A *Statue of Grand Duke Paul*, stands in the centre of the courtyard. It is an 1872 copy of Vitali's statue at Gatchina.

   Interior. The first rooms on the N side of the **Ground Floor** are the *French Drawing-Room*, the *Dancing Room*, the *Old Drawing-Room*, and the *Billiard Room*; these are mostly the work of Cameron himself. The Old Drawing-Room is notable for its Gobelins. Cameron's *Large Dining-Room*, at the W end of the palace, is decorated with fluted pilasters and a moulded frieze. On display here is an early-19C dinner service. The *Corner Drawing-Room*, beyond, was one of the first major interiors designed by Carlo Rossi; he was 31 when the work was carried out in 1816. The birch furniture, the chandelier, and the curtains were all Rossi's designs. The room was altered in the 19C and only restored to the original conception of Rossi in 1970. Quarenghi created the adjacent *New Study*, with its mirrors set in marble frames; portraits are the main feature of the *General*

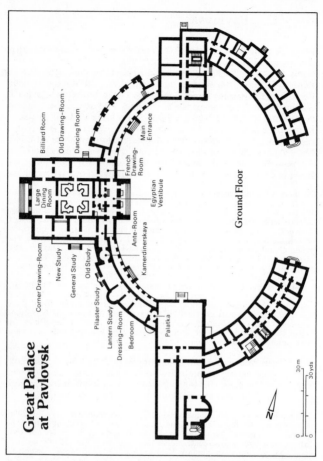

**Great Palace
at Pavlovsk**

Billiard Room

Old Drawing-Room

Dancing Room

Large
Dining
Room

French
Drawing-
Room

Main
Entrance

Egyptian
Vestibule

Ante-Room

Kamerdinerskaya

Corner Drawing-Room

New Study

General Study

Old Study

Pilaster Study

Lantern Study

Dressing-Room

Bedroom

Palatka

Ground Floor

30 m

30 yds

N

Study (Obshchiy Kabinet), which was designed by Brenna. Brenna
was also responsible for the *Old Study*, now hung with landscapes of
Gatchina; this room is also known as the Raspberry Study after the
colour of the walls. Paul himself used the Old Study. The adjacent
Ante-Room (Brenna) began the suite of private rooms and was used
by those waiting for an audience.

Beyond the round *Kamerdinerskaya* (or Room for Valets) begin the
main rooms of the S wing. Among the most striking is the long
Pilaster Study, in the design of which Quarenghi employed golden-
yellow Siena marble pilasters. Voronikhin, who created much of the
furniture in the Pilaster Study, was responsible for the delightful
Lantern Study (Kabinet 'Fonarik') next door; the 'Lantern' is the apse
containing the windows. The final rooms in this suite are the
Dressing-Room, by Quarenghi, and the *Bedroom* and the little
boudoir known as the *Palatka*, both by Voronikhin. The route to the
1st Floor is via the *Egyptian Vestibule*, in the centre of the building;

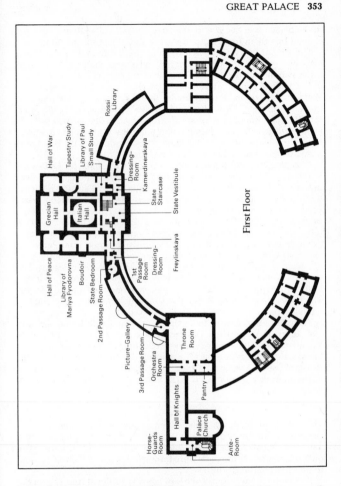

First Floor

Rossi Library

Hall of War
Tapestry Study
Library of Paul
Small Study

Grecian Hall
Italian Hall

Dressing-Room
Kamerdinerskaya
State Staircase
State Vestibule

Hall of Peace
Library of Mariya Fyodorovna
Boudoir
State Bedroom
2nd Passage Room

1st Passage Room
Dressing-Room
Freylinskaya

Picture-Gallery
3rd Passage Room
Orchestra Room

Throne Room

Hall of Knights
Pantry
Palace Church

Horse-Guards Room
Ante-Room

here are Egyptian figures representing the months of the year and, above them, the signs of the zodiac.

The finest rooms are on the **1st Floor** of the palace. At the top of Brenna's *State Staircase* and beyond the *State Vestibule* is the round central hall of the palace, the *Italian Hall*. It is situated directly under the lantern windows of the cupola, and was originally designed by Cameron. The walls are faced with imitation marble, and set in them are round niches with Antique Roman statues. To the N of the State Vestibule are another *Kamerdinerskaya* and *Dressing-Room*, by Brenna. These lead to the long *Rossi Library*, which Carlo Rossi built in the N wing in 1824; exhibitions are held here.

On the N side of the central part of the palace are the *Small Study*, and *Library of Paul*, the *Tapestry Study*, and the *Hall of War*. The Tapestry Study was created by Voronikhin, the other rooms by Brenna. This suite of rooms was intended for Paul, hence the martial themes in the decoration of the Hall of War. The most splendid room in the palace is at the W end, the *Grecian Hall* or Ball Room. Arrayed around this room by Brenna are green fluted Corinthian columns.

The *Hall of Peace* is the first room on the S side of the palace, in a suite of rooms belonging to Mariya Fyodorovna, Paul's wife. Following a similar idea used at the Versailles of Louis XIV, the decoration of the Hall of Peace is intended to contrast with that of the Hall of War. Instead of military symbols, there are musical instruments, flowers, fruit, etc. The *Library of Mariya Fyodorovna*, the *Boudoir*, the lavishly appointed *State Bedroom*, and the *Dressing-Room* (Tualetnaya) with its coffered ceiling, are the other major rooms in the suite. All are the work of Brenna. The decoration of the Boudoir is based on the Raphael Loggia in the Vatican.

After the Dressing-Room, the *Freylinskaya* (or Room for Ladies-in-Waiting) and two *Passage Rooms* lead to the curved *Picture-Gallery* in the S wing. In addition to paintings collected by Paul and his wife, there are a number of ornamental vases. The *Third Passage Room* connects the Picture-Gallery with the large *Throne Room*, which Brenna created for Paul in 1797 after his accession to the throne. This room was used in 1814, in the reign of Paul's son Alexander I, for a great reception of Guards officers recently returned from Paris. An elaborate dinner service is now on display here. The remainder of this wing is taken up mostly by the *Hall of Knights* (Kavalerskiy Zal) with its Roman sculpture. This was designed by Brenna for the Maltese Knights of St. John after Paul became their Grand Master. The final *Horse Guards Room* (Kavalergardskaya Komnata) contains an exhibition on the restoration of Pavlovsk.

The palace also houses two exhibitions. The **Exhibition of Russian 19C Interior Decoration** (Vystavka 'Russkiy Zhiloy Inter'yer XIX Veka') has on show an extensive collection of interiors from town houses and country estates. The second, the **Exhibition of 17C–19C Russian and Western China** (Vystavka 'Russkiy i Zapadnoyevropeyskiy Farfor XVII–XIX Vekov'), is contained in the N wing.

The **Park* at Pavlovsk now covers some 600ha. Cameron was responsible for the original layout, which was later transformed from a Grand-Ducal estate to an Imperial residence by Brenna. The outlying regions of the park were largely the work of Pietro Gonzaga in the first quarter of the 19C.

The *Treble Lime Alley* (Troynaya Lipovaya Alleya) runs E from the palace a distance of some 300m. To the right, between the alley and the main road, are Cameron's poetic *Aviary* (Vol'yer) (1781–83) and the *Rossi Pavilion*. The latter was built to Rossi's plans, but in 1914; it contains a statue of Empress Mariya Fyodorovna by V.A. Beklemishev. The parterre known as the *Great Circles* (Bol'shiye Krugi) lies to the left of the Treble Alley, with early-18C marble statues of *Peace* and *Justice* by P. Barratta.

About 300m N of the Treble Alley, beyond the Great Circles and on the S bank of the Slavyanka, stands the Classical **Temple of Friendship**. This round yellow pavilion with a colonnade was designed by Cameron in 1782 and is the oldest structure in the park. It is regarded as one of the finest park pavilions in Russia. The Temple of Friendship was intended to mark the friendship between Mariya Fyodorovna and her mother-in-law, Catherine the Great.

The Treble Alley ends with a common grave for Red soldiers killed during the defence of Pavlovsk in the Civil War.

To the NE lies the *Parade-Ground* (Paradnoye Pole) where Paul, a keen militarist, held frequent reviews of his troops; Pietro Gonzaga later developed this area as a park. Gonzaga also laid out the great expanse of parkland to the E, beyond the *Rose Pavilion Ponds*, which is called the **White Birch** (Belaya Beryoza). The site of the *Rose Pavilion* is just on the other side of the ponds. About 1000m along the straight *Rose Pavilion Alley* is the centre of an étoile.

A path leads N from the end of the Treble Alley, between the Parade Ground and the Slavyanka River. At the end lies an area known as the **Old Woods** (Staraya Sil'viya). Here, in an étoile, are bronze *Statues of the Muses* and their protector, Apollo. To the E are the *Old Woods Ponds*, the picturesque *Ruined Cascade*, and, on the opposite bank, a bronze *Statue of the Apollo Musagetète*.

The area of the park to the N, beyond the Old Woods Ponds and along the right bank of the Slavyanka, is called the **New Woods**. Located here is a little Classical temple with the inscription 'To the Spouse and Benefactor' (Suprugu Blagodatelyu) carved into the pediment. Thomas de Thomon created this *Mausoleum* for Mariya Fyodorovna in 1807–08 as a memorial to her husband Paul, who was murdered in a palace coup in 1801. Deep in the New Woods is a single column called *World's End*.

The *Visconti Bridge* crosses the Slavyanka to the NW of the Old Woods; the handsome bridge was designed by Voronikhin and built in 1802–03 under the supervision of P. Visconti. The main route now turns to the W, along the left (N) bank of the Slavyanka.

Downstream from the Visconti Bridge and the Old Woods Ponds, the Slavyanka flows through the **Beautiful Valley** (Krasnaya Dolina). Several park structures are located here, including a *Ruin* and the *Beautiful Valley Pavilion*.
To the W of the Visconti Bridge the *Green Woman Alley* leads beyond the *Vokzal'nyye Ponds* to the centre of the **Great Etoile** (700m). From here Gonzaga's **Valley of Ponds** may be followed for about 1.5km to the lower Slavyanka, near the Ruin.

Beyond the *Round Lake* with its *Great Cascade*, the Temple of Friendship is visible on the S bank. Further up the Slavyanka is the *Iron Gate*, near the *Humpbacked Bridge* (Gorbatyy Most) leading to the Palace. The next bridge upstream is called the *Bridge of Centaurs*; Cameron's domed *Cold Baths* (1799) are adjacent. Above the Bridge of Centaurs the Slavyanka forms a large pond. To the E above the pond is the façade of the Great Palace, with its eight-columned portico and low dome. To the W, between the pond and Ul. Revolyutsii, is one of the best park structures, Cameron's *Colonnade of Apollo* (1780–83). Here a statue of the Apollo Belvedere is surrounded by a broken double ring of Doric columns; originally a complete colonnade, it was damaged by a landslide in 1817 and left in its present form as a Romantic ruin.
Rossi's great *Iron Gate* to the NW forms one of the main entrances to the Pavlovsk Park from Ul. Revolyutsii. This street may then be followed back to the palace.

Just to the NE of the Iron Gate was once the terminus of the railway (the spur which once ran across the park has been removed, and Pavlovsk Station is now on the main line). Here, until the last war, stood the Kurzal (Kursaal) or Vokzal (Vauxhall), which Stakenschneider built in 1836 (and rebuilt in 1843–44). The Kurzal was famous for its popular summer concerts; Johann Strauss conducted the orchestra here on many occasions.

Next to the Great Palace, by Ul. Revolyutsii, is Cameron's *Pavilion of the Three Graces*. The 16 columns of the pavilion enclose a statue of the Three Graces by P. Triscornia. Cameron built the pavilion and

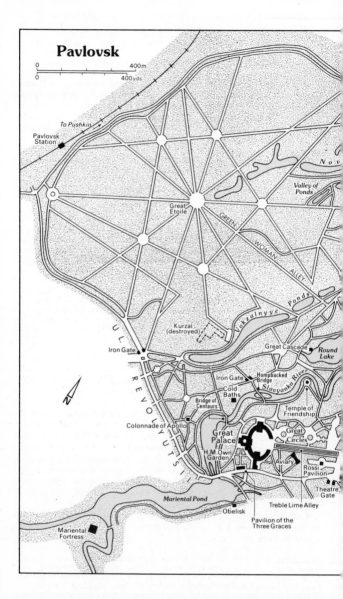

laid out the *H.M. Own Garden* (Sobstvennyy Sadik) in 1800–1801, some 20 years after his first work at Pavlovsk.

On the opposite side of Ul. Revolyutsii from the Great Palace is a large pond formed by the upper Slavyanka. This is the *Mariental Pond*, once called the

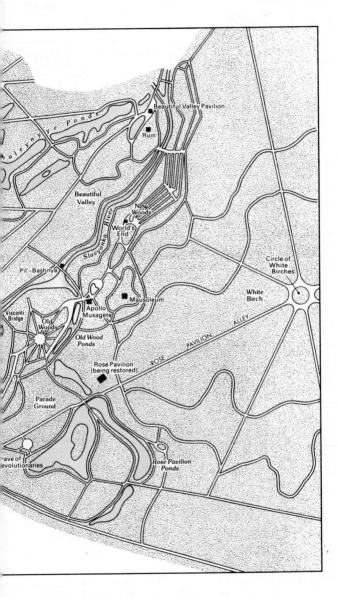

Russian Switzerland. Steps lead down from the road, and not far away an *Obelisk* commemorates the foundation of Pavlovsk. Hidden around a bend just upstream is a remarkable 'toy' *Mariental Fortress*, also known as 'Bip'. This large Gothic castle with twin towers was built for Paul by Brenna in 1795.

D.   Razliv

The Razliv area is associated with Lenin's activities in mid-1917, and contains two small museums.

The **Saray Museum** (Pamyatnik-Muzey V.I. Lenina 'Saray') (Pl. 1) is located off PRIMORSKOYE SHOSSE, beyond the town of LISIY NOS and about 30km NW of central Leningrad. The turn-off cannot be missed as it is marked by five pillars, each 20m high, which spell out 'LENIN'. The museum is about equidistant between LISIY NOS and SESTRORETSK RAILWAY STATIONS. The terminus in Leningrad is the Finland Station.

By the turn-off is a statue, *Lenin at Razliv*, by Pinchuk. The museum consists of a wooden barn (saray) where Lenin hid in 1917. It was made into a museum in 1925, and in the 1960s a huge glass case was built around it.

Armed demonstrators marched through the streets of Petrograd on 3 and 4 July 1917, calling for the overthrow of the Provisional Government. Although there was no evidence that the Bolshevik central organs had planned an uprising, the party had approved the demonstrations. This, coupled with unsubstantiated reports that the Bolsheviks were receiving German support, led the government to take action. Several Bolshevik leaders were arrested, and others went into hiding—among them Lenin. On 10 July Lenin arrived at Razliv, where he stayed in the barn (saray) of a veteran party member named N.A. Yemel'yanov, who worked in the nearby Sestroretsk Arms Factory. Yemel'yanov's house has been preserved, and in another outbuilding there is a small display on Lenin.

The **Shalash Museum** (Pamyatnik-Muzey V.I. Lenina 'Shalash') (Pl. 1) is about 4km away, along a road which follows the S shore of SESTRORETSKIY RAZLIV LAKE The centre of the museum is a hut made of hay (Shalash), a later hiding place of Lenin in July and August 1917. The museum was opened in 1928, with a replica of the famous hut (the materials are renewed from year to year); a granite *Monument*, by Gegello, was unveiled at the same time. In 1964 a new museum pavilion, with exhibits on Lenin's activities in 1917, was opened.

After Lenin had spent a few days in Yemel'yanov's barn, it was decided to find a safer place for him to stay. Yemel'yanov rowed Lenin in a little boat (now preserved in the museum) over to a hayfield on the other side of Sestroretskiy Razliv Lake. (Razliv means 'Flood'; the lake is an artificial one created in 1716 to supply water for the Sestroretsk Arms Factory.) Yemel'yanov quickly built the hut, and Lenin spent several weeks here in the guise of a Finnish seasonal labourer; in this pastoral setting he was able to continue his political writing. Finally, at the beginning of August, Lenin was moved to the greater safety and comfort of semi-autonomous Finland.

E.   Repino

The coast of the Gulf of Finland NW of Leningrad is an attractive resort area of sandy beaches and pine trees. Two popular places are SOLNECHNOYE (just N of Sestroretsk) and REPINO (Pl. 1). Both are on PRIMORSKOYE SHOSSE; the distance from Leningrad to Solnechnoye is about 36km and to Repino 47km. Suburban trains run between Leningrad's Finland Station and REPINO RAILWAY STATION.

Primorskoye Shosse is the main highway between Leningrad and

Finland. At Repino, which is some 187km from the Finnish border, there is a **Camping Site** (Kemping). The address is KLENOVAYA UL, 9.

The most notable feature of Repino is the **Penaty Museum** (Muzey-Usad'ba I.Ye. Repina 'Penaty'), the restored estate of the artist Il'ya Yefimovich Repin. This is a picturesque brown wooden house with numerous annexes and steeply-pitched glass roofs.

The village of Repino was formerly called Kuokkala, and Repin bought land here in 1899. The house was gradually extended to allow Repin to live at Kuokkala all year round; from 1907 it was his permanent home. The estate was called 'Penaty' after the Penates, the Roman household gods.

By the early 20C I.Ye. Repin (1844–1930) was one of the best known Russian artists. He had already painted The Volga Boatmen (1873), The Zaporozhets Cossacks (1891) and other well known works, including many portraits. At Penaty, Repin was host to the outstanding figures of the St. Petersburg cultural world, such as the singer Chaliapin, the writers Leonid Andreyev and Maxim Gorky, and most of the artists.

Kuokkala/Repino was a Finnish village; after 1917 it was outside Soviet Russia. (The border station, about 8km to the E, was Beloostrov.) Repin stayed on at Penaty, in 'emigration', until his death in 1930. He lies buried in the grounds behind the house. After the 'Winter War' of 1939–40 the Soviet Union took control of Kuokkala when it annexed the Karelian Isthmus.

Penaty was burned down during the Second World War, but restoration work began in 1958, and four years later the present building was opened to visitors. Penaty now contains exhibition rooms tracing Repin's career and also restorations of the main rooms as they were when the great artist lived here. Among the latter are the *Study*, the *Dining Room* (notable for its round table and rostrum), and, on the 1st Floor, the large *Winter Studio*. In the grounds of Penaty are a number of attractive wooden pavilions, including the *Temple of Osiris and Isis* and the *Tower of Scheherazade*.

Lenin also spent many months in this village, from February 1906 to December 1907—in the aftermath of the 1905 Revolution. Kuokkala/Repino had the advantage of being near St. Petersburg but outside the jurisdiction of the Russian police. The dacha where Lenin lived no longer exists; there is a monument on the site.

Changed Names of Streets, etc.

An unusual feature of Russian cities has been the widespread changes of place-names. Old names with religious or Imperial connections were replaced by new ones honouring revolutionary and military heroes and cultural figures. The following list indicates some of the most important changes; Soviet names are on the right. Although the late 1980s saw some historic names restored, the election of reformist town councils in 1990 may lead to the return of even more; Ul. Gor'kovo, the main street of Moscow, has been renamed Tverskaya Ul.

A. Moscow

St. Basmannaya Ul.	Ul. Karla Marksa
Bolotnaya Pl.	Pl. Repina
Bol. Dmitrovka Ul.	Pushkinskaya Ul.
Mal. Dmitrovka Ul.	Ul. Chekhova
Gorokhovaya Ul.	Ul. Kazakova
Il'inka Ul.	Ul. Kuybysheva
Kalanchovskaya Pl.	Komsomol'skaya Pl.
Kaluzhskaya Pl.	Oktyabr'skaya Pl.
Bol. Kaluzhskaya Ul.	Leninskiy Pr.
Kaluzhskoye Shosse	Leninskiy Pr.
Pl. Kaluzhskoy Zastavy	Pl. Gagarina
Krasnovorotskaya Pl.	Lermontovskaya Pl.
Kudrinskaya Pl.	Pl. Vosstaniya
Kudrinskaya Ul.	Barrikadnaya Ul.
Bol. Lubyanka Ul.	Ul. Dzerzhinskovo
Lubyanskaya Pl.	Pl. Dzerzhinskovo
Manezhnaya Pl.	Pl. 50-letiya Oktyabrya
Maroseyka Ul.	Ul. Bogdana Khmel'nitskovo
1-ya Meshchanskaya Ul.	Pr. Mira
Mokhovaya Ul.	Pr. Marksa
Myasnitskaya Ul.	Ul. Kirova
Bol. Nikitskaya Ul.	Ul. Gertsena
Mal. Nikitskaya Ul.	Ul. Kachalova
Nikitskiy Bul'v.	Suvorovskiy Bul'v.
Nikol'skaya Ul.	Ul. 25 Oktyabrya
Novinskiy Bul'v.	Ul. Chaykovskovo
Novoryazanskoye Shosse	Volgogradskiy Pr.
Okhotnyy Ryad	Pr. Marksa
Pokrovka Ul.	Ul. Chernyshevskovo
Povarskaya Ul.	Ul. Vorovskovo
Prechistenka Ul.	Kropotkinskaya Ul.
Prechistenskiy Bul'v.	Gogolevskiy Bul'v.
Bol. Presnenskaya Ul.	Krasnaya Presnya Ul.
Rogozhskaya Zastava	Pl. Il'icha
Serpukhovskaya Pl.	Dobryninskaya Pl.
Skobelevskaya Pl.	Sovetskaya Pl.
Spiridonovka Ul.	Ul. Alekseya Tolstovo
Strastnaya Pl.	Pushkinskaya Pl.
Bol. Sukharevskaya Pl.	Bol. Kolkhoznaya Pl.
Teatral'naya Pl.	Pl. Sverdlova
St. Triumfal'naya Pl.	Pl. Mayakovskovo

Pl. Tverskoy Zastavy	Pl. Belorusskovo Vokzala
Varvarka Ul.	Ul. Razina
Varvarskaya Pl.	Pl. Nogina
Vladimirskoye Shosse	Shosse Entuziastov
Vorob'yovskoe Shosse	Ul. Kosygina
Voskresenskaya Pl.	Pl. Revolyutsii
Vozdivhenka Ul.	Pr. Kalinina
Bol. Yakimanka Ul.	Ul. Dimitrova
Yekaterininskaya Pl.	Pl. Kommuny
Yelokhovskaya Ul.	Spartakovskaya Ul.
Zemlyanoy Val.	Ul. Chkalova
Znamenka Ul.	Ul. Frunze

B. Leningrad

Admiralteyskiy Kanal	Kanal Krushteyna
Aleksandrinskaya Pl.	Pl. Ostrovskovo
Aleksandrovskiy Most	Liteynyy Most
Angliyskaya Nab.	Nab. Krasnovo Flota
Basseynaya Ul.	Ul. Nekrasova
Birzhevaya Pl.	Pushkinskaya Pl.
Birzhevoy Most	Most Stroiteley
Blagoveshchenskaya Pl.	Pl. Truda
Furshtadtskaya Ul.	Ul. Petra Lavrova
Galernaya Ul.	Krasnaya Ul.
Gorokhovaya Ul.	Ul. Dzerzhinskovo
Bol. Ital'yanskaya Ul.	Ul. Rakova
Kamennoostrovskiy Pr.	Kirovskiy Pr.
Kirochnaya Ul.	Ul. Saltykova-Shchedrina
Konnogvardeyskiy Bul'v.	Bul'v. Profsoyuzov
Bol. Konyushennaya Ul.	Ul. Zhelyabova
Krasnaya Pl.	Pl. Aleksandra Nevskovo
Mikhaylovskaya Pl.	Pl. Iskusstv
Mikhaylovskaya Ul.	Ul. Brodskovo
Millionnaya Ul.	Ul. Khalturina
Bol. Morskaya Ul.	Ul. Gertsena
Mal. Morskaya Ul.	Ul. Gogolya
Nadezhdinskaya Ul.	Ul. Mayakovskovo
Narvskaya Pl.	Pl. Stachek
Narvskoye Shosse	Pr. Stachek
Nikolayevskaya Nab.	Nab. Leytenanta Shmidta
Nikolayevskaya Ul.	Ul. Marata
Nikolayevskiy Most	Most Leytenanta Shmidta
Nyustadtskaya Ul.	Lesnoy Pr.
Ofitserskaya Ul.	Ul. Dekabristov
Petergofskoye Shosse	Pr. Stachek
Pochtamtskaya Ul.	Ul. Soyuza Svyazi
Politseyskiy Most	Narodnyy Most
Polyustrovskaya Nab.	Sverdlovskaya Nab.
Porokhovskoye Shosse	Shosse Revolyutsii
Preobrazhenskaya Pl.	Pl. Radishcheva
Bol. Sampsoniyevskiy Pr.	Pr. Karla Marksa
Senatskaya Pl.	Pl. Dekabristov
Sennaya Pl.	Pl. Mira
Sergiyevskaya Ul.	Ul. Chaykovskovo
Shlissel'burgskiy Pr.	Pr. Obukhovskoy Oborony

Shpalernaya Ul.	Ul. Voinova
Teatral'naya Ul.	Ul. Zodchevo Rossi
Troitskaya Pl.	Pl. Revolyutsii
Troitskiy Most	Kirovskiy Most
Universitetskaya Liniya	Mendeleyevskaya Liniya
Voskresenskaya Nab.	Nab. Robesp'yera
Voznesenskiy Pr.	Pr. Mayorova
Yekaterininskiy Kanal	Kanal Griboyedova
Zabalkanskiy Pr.	Moskovskiy Pr.
Znamenskaya Pl.	Pl. Vosstaniya

INDEX

Topographical names are printed in **bold type** (modern names) or SMALL CAPS (obsolete names); names of persons are given in *italics*; other entries are in roman type. References to artists have been omitted when given in the context of the **Armoury Palace**, the **Pushkin Museum**, the **Tret'yakov Gallery**, the **Picture Gallery of the USSR**, the **Arkhangel'skoye Museum**, the **State Hermitage**, and the **Russian Museum**. Please note that this index contains large separate sections for Leningrad and Moscow, with numerous sub-headings.

370 INDEX

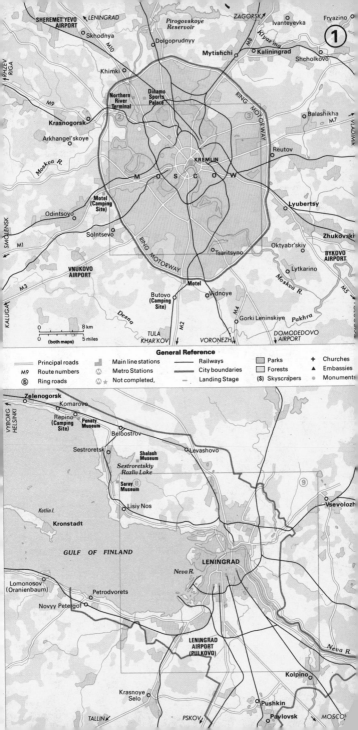

MOSCOW

SHEREMET'YEVO AIRPORT
LENINGRAD
Pirogovskoye Reservoir
ZAGORSK
Ivanteyevka
Fryazino
Skhodnya
M10
Dolgoprudnyy
Kalyaz'ma
Mytishchi
RING MOTORWAY
Kaliningrad
Shcholkovo
Khimki
RZHEV RIGA
Northern River Terminal
Dinamo Sports Palace
M9
Krasnogorsk
Balashikha
M7
Arkhangel'skoye
③
VLADIMIR
KREMLIN
Reutov
Moskva R.
M O S C O W
Motel (Camping Site)
②
Lyubertsy
Odintsovo
SMOLENSK
Zhukovski
Solntsevo
M1
BYKOVO AIRPORT
Tsaritsyno
Oktyabr'skiy
Lytkarino
VNUKOVO AIRPORT
M5
Moskva R.
Pakhra
M3
Motel
KALUGA
Butovo (Camping Site)
Vidnoye
Gorki Leninskiye
Desna
M4
DOMODEDOVO AIRPORT
0   8 km
0   5 miles
(both maps)
TULA KHAR'KOV
M2
VORONEZH

General Reference

— Principal roads	▭ Main line stations	— Railways	▨ Parks	+ Churches
M9 Route numbers	Ⓜ Metro Stations	— City boundaries	▭ Forests	▲ Embassies
⑥ Ring roads	Ⓜ★ Not completed,	‐‐ Landing Stage	($) Skyscrapers	● Monuments

LENINGRAD

Zelenogorsk
VYBORG HELSINKI
Komarovo
Repino (Camping Site)
Penaty Museum
Beloostrov
Sestroretsk
Shalash Museum
Levashovo
Sestroretskiy Razliv Lake
⑨
Saray Museum
⑧
Lisiy Nos
Vsevolozh
Kotlin I.
Kronstadt
GULF OF FINLAND
LENINGRAD
Neva R.
Lomonosov (Oranienbaum)
Petrodvorets
Novyy Petergof
LENINGRAD AIRPORT (PULKOVO)
Neva R.
Kolpino
Krasnoye Selo
Pushkin
TALLIN
PSKOV
Pavlovsk
MOSCOW

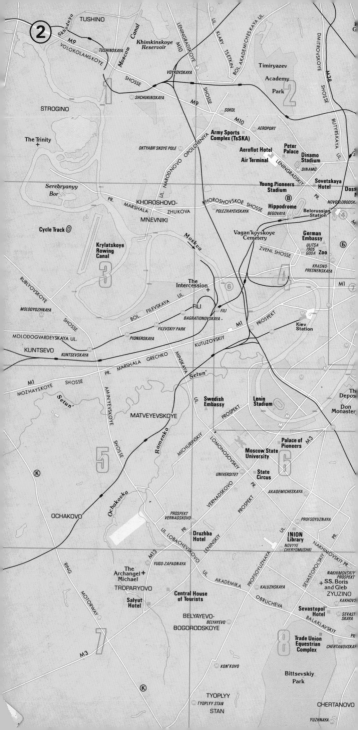

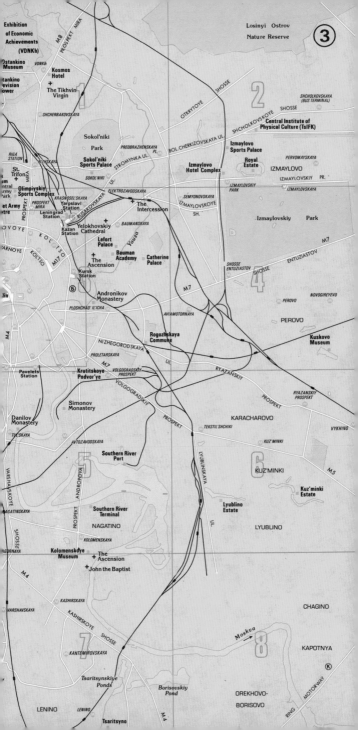

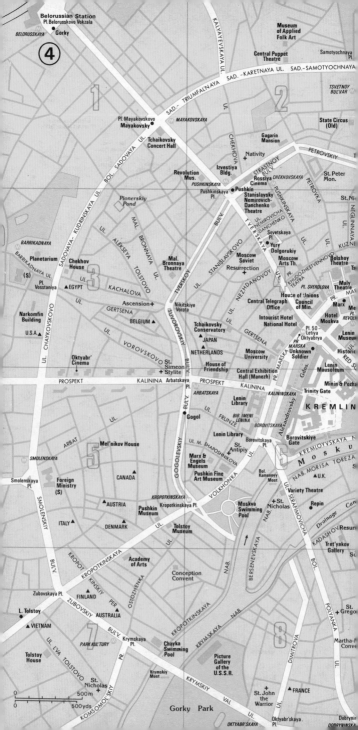

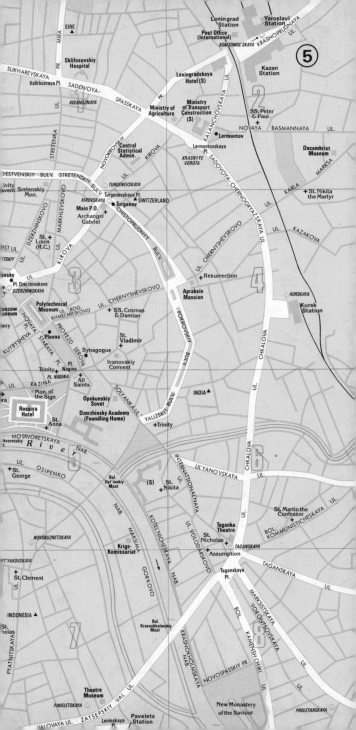

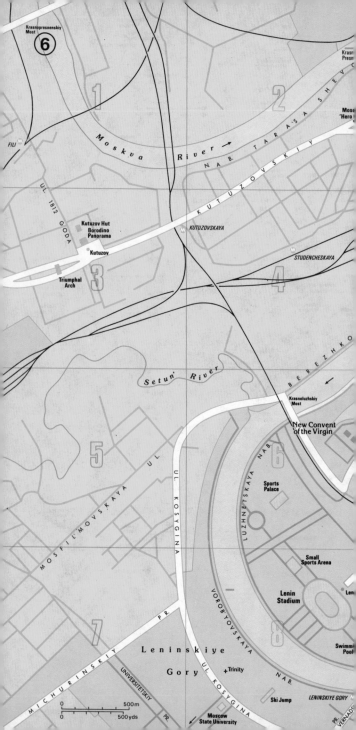

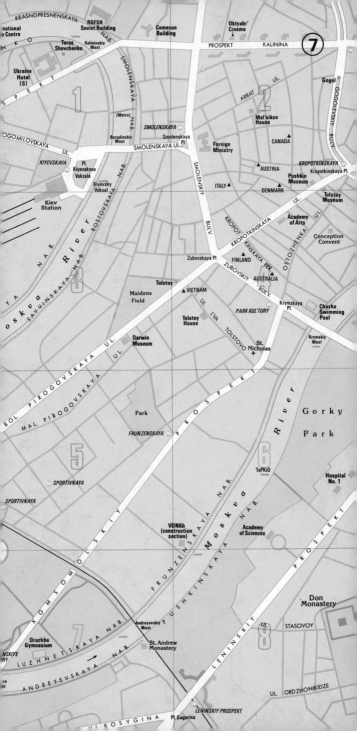

Kamenka

PARG

VYB

1

2

KOLOMYAGI

OL'GINO

UDEC NAB

LAKHTINSKIY

PIONERSKAYA

Chornaya

Serafimovskoye
Cemetery

BOGATYRSKIY
PR.

Pushkin
Obelisk

LAKHTINSKIY   PR.

Rechka

CHORNAYA
RECHKA

Me

PL. N.I. SMIR

PRIMORSKIY   Pk.

Kirov
Park

Yelagin I.

Yelagin
Palace

Bol.

Coastal
Victory Park
Kirov Stadium

Srednyaya

Nevka

3

MORSKOY   PR.

Krestovskiy I.

Aptekar·skiy I.

Lenin
Museum

Malaya   Nevka

BOL. ZELENINA

PETROGRADS

Petrovskiy I.

UL. KRASNAVO

PETROGRAD
SIDE

Malaya   Neva

4

13

Smolenka

PL. KIMA

NEVSKIY

Vasil'yevskiy   Island

Vitebsk
Station

5

Baltic
Station

Warsaw
Station

Sea   Canal

Narva
Triumphal
Arch

Kirovskaya
Pl.

Moscow
Triumphal
Arch

LIGO

MOSKOVSKIYE VOROTA

STACHEK

MOSKOVSKIY

KIROVSKIY ZAVOD

ELEKTROSILA

Komsomol'skaya Pl.

Mosc
Vict
Pe

KRASNOPUTILOVSKAYA

AVTOVO

PARK POBEDY

Krasnen'kaya

AVTOVO

UL. GASTELLO

Chesma
Palace

Dudergofka

ZHUKOVA

Southern
Coastal
Park

PETERGOFSKOYE

MARSHALA

LENINSKIY   PR.

Soviet House
MOSKOVSKAYA

STREL'NA

SHOSSE

UL'YANKA

DACHNOYE

Defenders of
Leningrad
Pulkovskaya
Hotel

SOSNOVAYA
POLYANA

Ivanovka

VETERANOV

PROSPEKT VETERANOV

PR.

PR.

K. NARODNOVO   OPOLCHENIYA

VOLODARSKIY

7

STAROPANOVO

Ligovskiy   Canal

PULKOVSKOI

VOLKHOVSKOYE   SHOSSE

LENINGRAD AIRPORT
(PULKOVO)

8

TALLINSKOYE   SHOSSE

GORELOVO

TORIKI

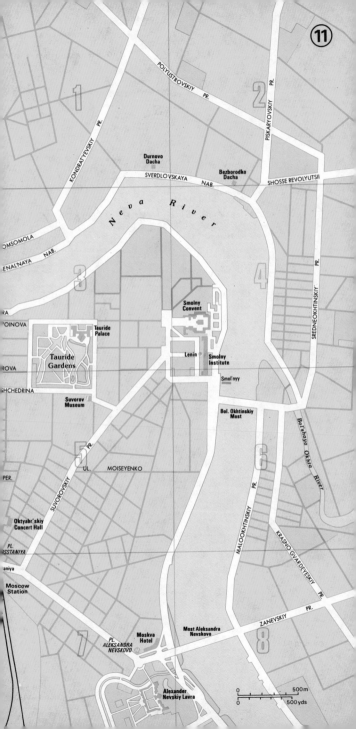

POLYUSTROVSKIY PR.

PISKARYOVSKIY PR.

1

2

KONDRAT'YEVSKIY PR.

Durnovo
Dacha

SVERDLOVSKAYA NAB.

Bezborodko
Dacha

SHOSSE REVOLYUTSII

N e v a   R i v e r

KOMSOMOLA

...ENAL'NAYA NAB.

3

4

SREDNEOKHTINSKIY PR.

...RA

POINOVA

Tauride
Palace

Smolny
Convent

Tauride
Gardens

Lenin

Smolny
Institute

...ROVA

Smol'nyy

...SHCHEDRINA

Suvorov
Museum

Bol. Okhtinskiy
Most

Bol'shaya Okhta River

5

SUVOROVSKIY PR.

UL. MOISEYENKO

6

MALOOKHTINSKIY PR.

...PER.

KRASNO GVARDEYSKIY PR.

Oktyabr'skiy
Concert Hall

PL.
...SSTANIYA

...aniya

Moscow
Station

7

PL.
ALEKSANDRA
NEVSKOVO

Moskva
Hotel

Most Aleksandra
Nevskovo

ZANEVSKIY PR.

8

Alexander
Nevskiy Lavra

0   500m

0   500yds

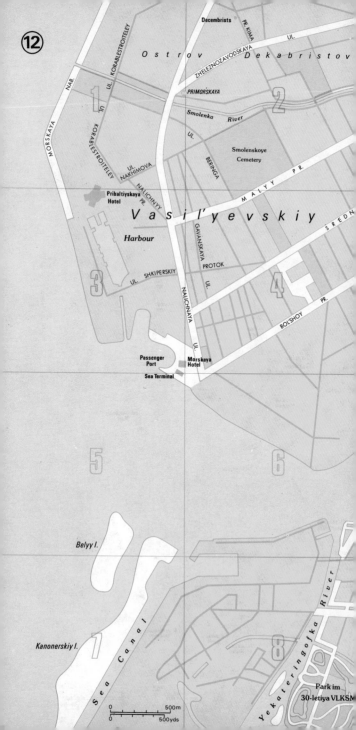

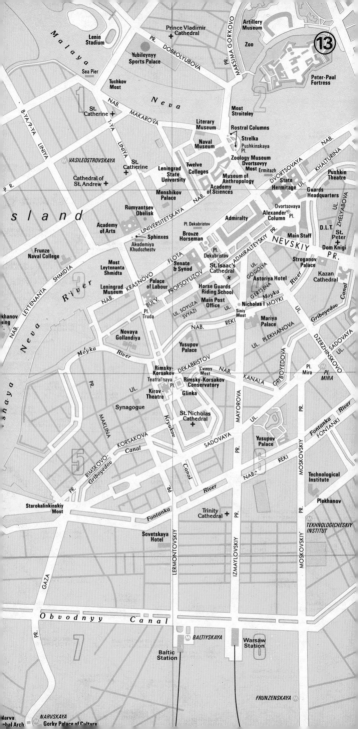

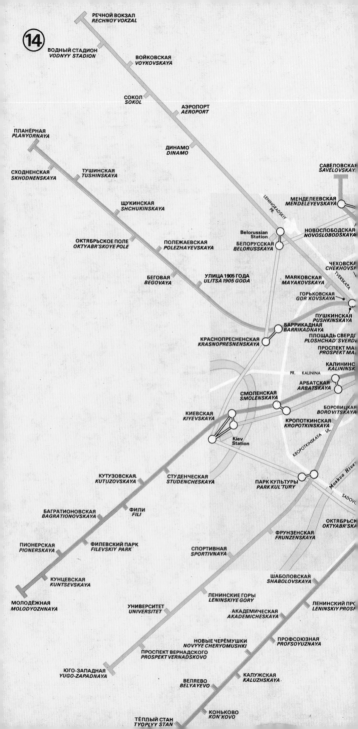

⑭

РЕЧНОЙ ВОКЗАЛ
RECHNOY VOKZAL

ВОДНЫЙ СТАДИОН
VODNYY STADION

ВОЙКОВСКАЯ
VOYKOVSKAYA

СОКОЛ
SOKOL

АЭРОПОРТ
AEROPORT

ПЛАНЁРНАЯ
PLANYORNAYA

ДИНАМО
DINAMO

САВЕЛОВСКАЯ
SAVELOVSKAY

СХОДНЕНСКАЯ
SKHODNENSKAYA

ТУШИНСКАЯ
TUSHINSKAYA

МЕНДЕЛЕЕВСКАЯ
MENDELEYEVSKAYA

ЩУКИНСКАЯ
SHCHUKINSKAYA

LENINGRADSKIY PR.

НОВОСЛОБОДСКАЯ
NOVOSLOBODSKAY

ОКТЯБРЬСКОЕ ПОЛЕ
OKTYABR'SKOYE POLE

ПОЛЕЖАЕВСКАЯ
POLEZHAYEVSKAYA

Belorussian
Station

БЕЛОРУССКАЯ
BELORUSSKAYA

ЧЕХОВСКА
CHEKHOVS

БЕГОВАЯ
BEGOVAYA

УЛИЦА 1905 ГОДА
ULITSA 1905 GODA

МАЯКОВСКАЯ
MAYAKOVSKAYA

TVERSKA

ГОРЬКОВСКАЯ
GOR'KOVSKAYA

ПУШКИНСКАЯ
PUSHKINSKAYA

БАРРИКАДНАЯ
BARRIKADNAYA

КРАСНОПРЕСНЕНСКАЯ
KRASNOPRESNENSKAYA

ПЛОЩАДЬ СВЕРДЛ
PLOSHCHAD'SVERDL

ПРОСПЕКТ МА
PROSPEKT MA

КАЛИНИНС
KALININSK

PR. KALININA

АРБАТСКАЯ
ARBATSKAYA

СМОЛЕНСКАЯ
SMOLENSKAYA

БОРОВИЦКАЯ
BOROVITSKAYA

КИЕВСКАЯ
KIYEVSKAYA

КРОПОТКИНСКАЯ
KROPOTKINSKAYA

Kiev
Station

KROPOTKINSKAYA UL.

Moskva River

КУТУЗОВСКАЯ
KUTUZOVSKAYA

СТУДЕНЧЕСКАЯ
STUDENCHESKAYA

ПАРК КУЛЬТУРЫ
PARK KUL'TURY

SADOVO

БАГРАТИОНОВСКАЯ
BAGRATIONOVSKAYA

ФИЛИ
FILI

ОКТЯБРЬСК
OKTYABR'SKA

ПИОНЕРСКАЯ
PIONERSKAYA

ФИЛЕВСКИЙ ПАРК
FILEVSKIY PARK

ФРУНЗЕНСКАЯ
FRUNZENSKAYA

СПОРТИВНАЯ
SPORTIVNAYA

КУНЦЕВСКАЯ
KUNTSEVSKAYA

ШАБОЛОВСКАЯ
SHABOLOVSKAYA

МОЛОДЁЖНАЯ
MOLODYOZHNAYA

ЛЕНИНСКИЕ ГОРЫ
LENINSKIYE GORY

ЛЕНИНСКИЙ ПРО
LENINSKIY PROSP

УНИВЕРСИТЕТ
UNIVERSITET

АКАДЕМИЧЕСКАЯ
AKADEMICHESKAYA

НОВЫЕ ЧЕРЁМУШКИ
NOVYYE CHERYOMUSHKI

ПРОФСОЮЗНАЯ
PROFSOYUZNAYA

ПРОСПЕКТ ВЕРНАДСКОГО
PROSPEKT VERNADSKOVO

ЮГО-ЗАПАДНАЯ
YUGO-ZAPADNAYA

БЕЛЯЕВО
BELYAYEVO

КАЛУЖСКАЯ
KALUZHSKAYA

ТЁПЛЫЙ СТАН
TYOPLYY STAN

КОНЬКОВО
KON'KOVO